THE
Biographical
Dictionary
OF
African
Americans

THE

Biographical Dictionary

OF

African Americans

RACHEL KRANZ AND
PHILIP J. KOSLOW

Facts On File, Inc.

Library of Congress Cataloging-in-Publication Data

Kranz, Rachel.
Biographical dictionary of African Americans / Rachel Kranz and Philip J. Koslow.
p.   cm.
Rev. ed. of: The biographical dictionary of Black Americans / Rachel C. Kranz. c1992.
Includes bibliographical references and index.
ISBN 0-8160-3903-8 (alk. paper)
1. Afro-Americans—Biography—Dictionaries, Juvenile. I. Koslow, Philip. II. Kranz, Rachel.
Biographical dictionary of Black Americans. III. Title.
E185.96.K73   1998
920′.009296073—dc21
[B] 98-12355

CONTENTS

INTRODUCTION

The Biographical Dictionary of African Americans includes more than 230 entries, covering black Americans from the earliest days of colonial America to the present. Prominent black figures in politics, religion, business, academia, science, sports, and the arts are profiled, as well as military heroes, leaders of slave revolts, journalists, inventors, and diarists.

Naturally, it has not been possible to include every African American worthy of note within the covers of a single volume. A word about our selection process, however, is in order.

First, we strove to be representative. We tried to include a wide variety of black Americans, choosing figures from every field of endeavor, from all historical periods, and from among both men and women. Black contributions to American life have been wide-ranging and diverse, from Jan Ernst Matzeliger's invention of a shoe-manufacturing machine (which served as the foundation for the New England shoe industry) to Jimi Hendrix's influential rock guitar style. Black Americans have achieved success in diverse fields as well, from John Johnson's publishing empire of *Ebony, Jet,* and a host of other publications to chemist, inventor, and entrepreneur Percy Julian.

Second, we wanted to include as many as possible of the black "firsts" in American life. Thus we have profiled Augustine Tolton, one of American's first black priests; Dean Dixon, our first black orchestra conductor; Edward Brooke, the first black senator from the Northeast; and Jackie Robinson, the first black man to play major-league

baseball. Firsts in academia, opera, theater, politics, and other fields are also included.

Likewise, we made sure to profile African Americans who are particularly well known to a wide range of people. Thus we have entries for Nobel Prize winners Ralph Bunche, Martin Luther King, Jr., and Toni Morrison; such well-known historical figures as Harriet Tubman, Sojourner Truth, and Frederick Douglass; and such famous artists as Duke Ellington, Bessie Smith, Tupac Shakur, and Wynton Marsalis.

In addition, we wanted to give a sense of the development of black American history. The reader who peruses these entries will find a sampling of key figures from each major movement of black America, from abolitionism and the anticolonialism of the 18th and early 19th centuries to Marcus Garvey's back to Africa movement; from the New Negro movement of the 1920s to the Black Power movement of the 1960s; from the civil rights movement to the Million Man March of the 1990s. Naturally, Booker T. Washington and W. E. B. DuBois are profiled, as are their rival views on black progress. Likewise, Ida B. Wells, Mary McLeod Bethune, Mary Church Terrell, as well other key black women leaders such as Carol Mosley-Braun have their entries.

Finally, we have tried to include figures that many readers will know—or will find particularly inspiring. Writers like Alice Walker, James Baldwin, and Richard Wright are frequently included in middle school and high school anthologies or are assigned to students in English classes. Figures like golfer Tiger Woods and TV star Oprah Winfrey will excite young readers with their impressive achievements. Whether readers are looking for someone familiar or someone to inspire interest, they will find a world of achievement in *The Biographical Dictionary of African Americans.*

No single book can provide all the answers to a researcher's questions. Thus, wherever possible, we have included notes on further sources of information about each figure, often both print and electronic. The book's general bibliography includes even more sources.

Finally, a word about the entries themselves. Each entry begins with a brief description of the figure's most significant accomplishments. If a person is known for a particular reason, such as being the inventor of a particular product, the founder of a movement, or the first to enter a particular field, that information is given in an entry's opening paragraph. Thus, readers can immedi-

ately identify the significance of a particular figure and will have a context in which to place that person.

The entries then proceed to a chronological review of a figure's life. In the interest of space, information is not always repeated within an entry.

Individuals on whom there are entries in this book are denoted in other entries by being set in SMALL CAPITAL LETTERS the first time their name is mentioned. These cross-references appear by surname. To find an entry, look under the last name of the person you are seeking.

The story of black people in America is rich and varied. It is sometimes tragic and always inspiring. *The Biographical Dictionary of African Americans* will introduce readers to the many dimensions of this history—and will inspire them to continue their study of the wide-ranging actions and accomplishments of African Americans.

A note on web sites

Internet sites tend to move around the Web a bit. We have tried to ensure that URLs are as up-to-date as possible, but if you have trouble finding a particular site, use an Internet browser to find a specific web site or type of information.

❖ AARON, HENRY LOUIS ("Hank")

(1934–   ), baseball player and executive

Baseball's all-time home run king, Hank Aaron slugged 755 home runs during his 23 seasons in the major leagues. In addition to his heroics on the field, Aaron has been a successful executive and a major voice for equal opportunity in baseball.

Born in Mobile, Alabama, on February 5, 1934, Aaron was the third of eight children. He developed an early love for baseball, playing first for a local sandlot team and then for Central High School. In 1952, when Aaron was 18, the Indianapolis Clowns of the Negro Leagues signed him to a $200-a-month contract. Later in the year, the Clowns made a tidy profit by selling Aaron's contract to the Milwaukee Braves of the National League for $10,000.

Aaron quickly worked his way up through Milwaukee's minor league system, and in 1954 he was promoted to the major league club as the starting right fielder. He performed well during his rookie season, batting .280 with 13 home runs and 69 RBI. The following year, Aaron did even better, raising his average to .314 and driving in 106 runs. He emerged as a star in 1956, winning the National League batting championship with a .326 average.

Aaron enjoyed his finest individual season in 1957, when he batted .322 with 44 home runs and 132 RBI

and won the National League pennant for the Braves with a dramatic late-inning home run against the St. Louis Cardinals. He continued to excel in the World Series, hitting three home runs as the Braves defeated the mighty New York Yankees in seven games. During the off-season, the nation's sportswriters selected Aaron as the National League's Most Valuable Player.

Throughout the 1960s, with the Braves relocated to Atlanta, Aaron's power totals mounted steadily. Fans and sportswriters soon realized that Aaron could even challenge Babe Ruth's lifetime mark of 714 home runs, once considered an untouchable record. Steadily closing in on Ruth, Aaron hit his 500th home run in 1968, his 600th in 1971, and his 700th in 1973. As he entered the 1974 season, his total stood at 713. Unfortunately, there were those who disliked the idea of an African American taking Ruth's crown, and Aaron received a large volume of hate mail and a number of death threats. Hurt and angry but undeterred, Aaron hit his 714th homer in the first game of the 1974 season, against the Los Angeles Dodgers at Atlanta's Fulton County Stadium. The following night, April 8, a nationwide TV audience watched as Aaron powered a fastball from pitcher Al Downing into the left field seats, touching off a wild celebration and putting himself in the history books.

Now an undisputed baseball legend, the 40-year-old Aaron completed the 1974 season with 20 home runs and was then traded to the Milwaukee Brewers of the American League. He played two seasons in Milwaukee, where he had remained a celebrity despite the Braves' departure, and retired with 755 lifetime home runs. In the ultimate gesture of respect, both the Braves and the Brewers retired Aaron's uniform number, 44.

Though Aaron's home run total claims the most attention from fans and baseball historians, his all-around production was truly remarkable. Eclipsing Ruth once again, he drove in a total of 2,297 runs, the most in major league history. In addition, Aaron ranks first on the all-time list in total bases (6,856), first in extra-base hits (1,477), third in hits (3,771), third in runs scored (2,147), and third in games played (3,298). It came as no surprise when Aaron was elected to the Baseball Hall of Fame in 1981, his first year of eligibility.

Upon his retirement as a player, Aaron joined the Atlanta Braves' front office as director of player development. In 1990, he became a vice president of the Turner Broadcasting Company and a special assistant to Braves president Ted Turner. As one of the few black executives in the game, Aaron has frequently criticized major league baseball for failing to create more opportunities for African Americans on the managerial level. He has also been active in a number of charities and devotes considerable time to the Hank Aaron Chasing a Dream Foundation, which raises funds to provide scholarships for young people.

Further Information: *I Had a Hammer: The Hank Aaron Story,* by Henry Aaron with Lonnie Wheeler, New York: HarperCollins, 1991; *Hank Aaron,* by Richard Scott Rennert, New York: Chelsea House, 1993; *Hank Aaron: Home Run King,* by Jacob Margolies, New York: Franklin Watts, 1992; Chasing the Dream Foundation web site, http://www.atlantabraves.com/web/hank.aaron/auto.html, includes information on obtaining Hank Aaron memorabilia in return for contributions.

—*P. K.*

❖ ABERNATHY, RALPH DAVID, SR.
(1926–1990), *minister, civil rights leader*

One of the major forces in the Civil Rights movement of the 1950s and 1960s, Ralph Abernathy was a leader in the Baptist Church and the principal aide of Rev. Martin Luther KING, Jr. A founder of the all-important Southern Christian Leadership Conference (SCLC), Abernathy risked his life countless times in the cause of freedom and justice.

Ralph Abernathy was born in Linden, Alabama, on March 11, 1926. Ralph's grandfather had been born into slavery, but in the years following the Civil War the Abernathys had prospered. By the time of Ralph's birth, the family owned a 500-acre farm. He was able to receive a first-rate education, earning a B.A. in mathematics from Alabama State College in 1950 and an M.A. in sociology from Atlanta University in 1951. After receiving his master's degree, Abernathy returned to Alabama State as dean of men and an instructor in sociology. At the same time, he became pastor of the First Baptist Church in Montgomery. (Abernathy had been ordained as a minister at the age of 18 and served as a pastor of the Demopolis Baptist Church while attending college.)

As a religious and academic leader, Abernathy was naturally drawn to the growing Civil Rights movement. He came to the forefront in 1955, when Montgomery seamstress Rosa PARKS was arrested for refusing to give up her seat to a white passenger on a bus. In response, Abernathy called a meeting that led to the 1955–56 Montgomery Bus Boycott and, eventually, the end of segregation on the city's buses. The historic campaign also brought Abernathy together with King (then pastor of the Dexter Avenue Baptist Church), who served as the main leader of the boycott. The following year, the two men helped organize the SCLC in Atlanta; King became the president of the organization, and Abernathy was elected secretary-treasurer. Some observers suggested that King had taken over the movement while pushing Abernathy aside, but Abernathy never saw it that way. "We started out together and I knew someone had to be the leader," he said. "We were never rivals."

Along with King, Abernathy became a prime target for violent racists, who firebombed both his house and his church. In addition, he was jailed 19 times for taking part in demonstrations aimed at ending segregation throughout the South. Deeply committed to nonviolent protest, Abernathy and King often shared a cell. As Abernathy later recalled, "We would spend the first 24 hours fasting to purify our souls in order that we would have no hatred in our hearts toward the jailer and a stronger determination to tear down the system responsible." By the 1960s, their efforts—and the courage of thousands who worked beside them—brought an end to segregation by law and began a new era for African Americans.

The two leaders stood together until the last. On April 4, 1968, when King was struck down by a sniper's bullet on the balcony of a motel in Memphis, Tennessee, Abernathy was at his side. Despite the danger of more shots being fired, Abernathy remained with King, cradling his friend's head during his final moments of life.

With King gone, Abernathy took over as head of the SCLC. The immediate focus of his efforts was the Poor

People's Campaign, a movement to create jobs for disadvantaged members of all races. In May 1968, Abernathy led a massive march on Washington, bringing thousands of unemployed people from all over the country to the nation's capital. For more than a month, the demonstrators lived in tents and other temporary shelters, while Abernathy urged the Congress and the public to address their needs.

Abernathy remained at the helm of the SCLC until 1976. After running unsuccessfully for Congress, he devoted himself full time to Atlanta's West Hunter Street Baptist Church, where he had been pastor since 1961. During the latter part of his life, he became more conservative politically, alienating some of his former allies in the Civil Rights movement. But when Abernathy died of a heart attack on April 17, 1990, it was clear to everyone that a great inspirational figure in American history had passed on.

Further Reading: *And the Walls Came Tumbling Down: An Autobiography,* by Ralph Abernathy, New York: Harper & Row, 1989; *Ralph David Abernathy,* by Catherine Reef, Parsippany, N.J.: Silver Burdett Press, 1995.

—*P. K.*

✤ AILEY, ALVIN, JR.
(1931–1989), *dancer, choreographer*

One of the great creative forces in modern dance, Alvin Ailey brought a unique artistic vision to the realm of the performing arts. The Alvin Ailey American Dance Theater (AAADT), which he founded in 1958, ranks among the world's most renowned repertory companies.

Ailey was born on January 5, 1931, in Rogers, Texas. An only child, he moved to Los Angeles with his mother at the age of 11, following his parents' divorce. As a student at Thomas Jefferson High School he played a number of sports and took dance lessons on the side. Graduating in 1948, Ailey enrolled at the University of California at Los Angeles, with the goal of becoming a teacher. At this time, he had no plans of becoming a professional dancer. The following year, however, a friend brought him to the studio of choreographer Lester Horton. Ailey became absorbed by Horton's ideas and began to study dance intensely while attending college. In 1952, Ailey transferred to San Francisco State College to study Romance languages, but the urge to perform won out. He was soon back in Los Angeles as a full-fledged member of the Lester Horton Dance Theatre.

Ailey's intense, athletic dance style inspired one critic to describe him as "a caged lion full of lashing power that he can contain or release at will." Like many exceptional dancers, he also had the desire to create works of his own. When Horton died at the end of 1953 and the dancers took over the direction of the company, Ailey was given the opportunity to work as a choreographer. The first public performance of an Ailey piece took place at the 1954 Jacob's Pillow Dance Festival in Los Angeles. During the next four years Ailey branched out, performing with a number of modern dance companies; he also appeared on Broadway in the musical *House of Flowers* and danced in the movie version of *Carmen Jones.* By 1958 he was ready to create his own company in New York City.

The AAADT's first performances took place at the 92nd Street YM-YWHA in New York City and drew raves from dance critics. In addition to creating excitement on the stage, Ailey achieved a new artistic perspective on the African-American experience. One of his first major works for the AAADT was *Blues Suite* (1958); set in a rundown honky-tonk, the piece depicted the hardscrabble world of poor blacks in the South. Two years later, he created his most famous work, *Revelations,* which became AAADT's signature dance. *Revelations* drew on Ailey's childhood experiences in the Baptist church. Set to a series of spirituals and gospel tunes, the work celebrated all the aspects of African-American religious life—in

Alvin Ailey, Jr. *(Library of Congress)*

music and movement, *Revelations* explored themes such as group prayer, baptism, private communion, and the bond between preacher and congregation.

Ailey stopped performing in 1965 in order to concentrate on choreography and the day-to-day tasks of running a major dance company. By this time, AAADT had gained a worldwide audience. Beginning with a tour of Asia and Australia in 1962, AAADT performed in Europe, Latin America, and Africa; in 1970, it became the first U.S. dance company to perform in the Soviet Union after World War II. In 1968, Ailey founded the Alvin Ailey American Dance Center School to increase knowledge of dance and inspire young dancers. Though Ailey had created AAADT to showcase the talents of African-American dancers, he welcomed members of all groups into the company. "We're trying to create a whole spectrum of experience for the dancer as well as the audience," he explained.

In addition to the many works he created for AAADT, Ailey choreographed Samuel Barber's opera *Antony and Cleopatra* (1966) and Leonard Bernstein's *Mass* (1971), as well as creating jazz dance sequences for the 1976 bicentennial celebration. In recognition of his work, Ailey received the NAACP's Spingarn Medal in 1976 and Kennedy Center Honors in 1988. Following Ailey's untimely death, Judith Jamison—who starred with AAADT from 1965 to 1980—succeeded him as artistic director of the company. It remains one of the world's great dance ensembles, a living monument to Ailey's vision and achievements.

Further Information: *Alvin Ailey: A Life in Dance,* by Jennifer Dunning, Reading, Mass.: Addison-Wesley, 1996; *Alvin Ailey,* by Andrea Davis Pinkney, New York: Hyperion, 1993; *Alvin Ailey American Dance Theater Home Page,* http://www.alvinailey.org (includes repertory, educational activities, and a video clip).

—P. K.

❖ ALDRIDGE, IRA FREDERICK
(1807?–1867), *actor*

Ira Frederick Aldridge is considered to be one of the greatest actors of his time. Acclaimed for his acting in the plays of William Shakespeare, he performed all over Europe and was most admired for his portrayal of *Othello.* Aldridge also played the lead in Thomas Southerne's *Oroonoko* and Thomas Morton's *The Slave.*

Aldridge was also renowned for reviving Shakespeare's play *Titus Andronicus,* which hadn't been staged for more than a century. In this production, Aldridge played Aaron the Moor. He also played roles that had previously been associated exclusively with white performers, such as Macbeth, Shylock, King Lear, and Richard III.

The major drama critics of the time were all white, and many did not believe that Aldridge could play the parts he undertook. Other critics praised him, however, as "the greatest actor that has ever been seen in Europe," and as "the great, one and only, the most beautiful male artist that one can imagine."

During his lifetime, he was honored with awards from rulers and arts societies in Haiti, Prussia, Switzerland, Hungary, Russia, and Austria. His fame endures: There is the Ira Aldridge Memorial Chair in the Shakespeare Memorial Theater at Stratford-upon-Avon in England and the Ira Aldridge Theater at Howard University in Washington, D.C.

There are different versions of Aldridge's early life. One story has it that he was born in Senegal to a royal family of the Fulah tribe. But it is more likely that he was born in New York City on July 24, 1807, the son of Daniel Aldridge, a lay preacher and a vendor of straw. His mother, a native of North Carolina, died when Aldridge was still quite young.

It is generally believed that Aldridge attended New York City's African Free School, which was founded for free black children. Aldridge's interest in theater began early, with a backstage job at the Chatham Theater in New York City and some acting experience in New York's African Theater. In 1824, he left for England, shipping out as a steward on the same boat as the actor James Wallack, and later becoming his personal attendant.

Documents show that a year later (on October 10, 1825), he opened at the Royal Coburg Theatre in London, in *The Revolt of Surinam, or A Slave's Revenge,* an adaptation of Southerne's *Oroonoko.* He also played in Morton's *The Ethiopian, or the Quadroon of the Mango Grove (The Slave)* and his *The Libertine Defeated, or African Ingratitude;* in H. H. Milner's *The Negro's Curse, or The Foulah Son,* which was originally written for him; and in J. H. Amherst's *The Death of Christophe, King of Hayti,* which was his first top billing in London.

Aldridge went on to play Othello and Oroonoko at the Theatre Royal in Brighton and toured the provinces in 1827. In 1831, Aldridge met Edmund Kean, one of the outstanding actors of his generation, who praised his work.

Aldridge first rose to national prominence in 1833, as Othello in his debut at the Theater Royal, Covent Garden, London. In 1852, he went on his first tour of Europe. He became a documented British citizen in 1863.

Aldridge was twice married: to Margaret Gill, an Englishwoman, who died at age 66 in 1864; and the following year, to Amanda Pauline von Brandt, of Sweden. One of his daughters became an opera singer and another became an actress.

On August 7, 1867, Aldridge died while on tour, in Lodz, Poland. Although he was planning an American tour, he never returned to the United States, where, for most of his lifetime, many black people were still slaves. Certainly it was not possible in the United States of that time for black actors to play the variety and quality of roles that Frederick had.

Further Reading: *Ira Aldridge, the Negro Tragedian,* by Herbert Marshall and Mildred Stock, Carbondale, Ill.: Southern Illinois Press, 1959.

—*R. K.*

❖ ALI, MUHAMMAD (Cassius Marcellus Clay)
(1942–), *boxer, activist*

Muhammad Ali's great reputation rests on two things: his determination to win and regain the world heavyweight championship and his well-publicized refusal on principle to serve in the armed forces, which temporarily cost him his boxing career. Ali's combination of sports prowess and outspokenness on political issues made him a symbol to many of black achievement and commitment.

Muhammad Ali was born Cassius Marcellus Clay, in the town of Louisville, Kentucky, on January 18, 1942. He soon won fame as an amateur fighter, taking the Golden Gloves and Amateur Athletic Union titles. He was a six-time Golden Gloves winner in Kentucky, and from 1959 to 1960, he held the National Golden Gloves title.

The young Cassius Clay became interested in black empowerment and African-American culture. In 1957, he became a Black Muslim, a version of the Moslem faith that focuses on black Americans' ties to Africa and respect for black history and culture.

In 1960, Clay won his last amateur championship, a Gold Medal for the light heavyweight title at the Olympic Games in Rome. Then he turned professional.

In 1964, Clay won his first professional heavyweight championship in a famous fight with Charles "Sonny" Liston. Liston was heavily favored to win. Clay knocked him out in seven rounds—and won their rematch even more decisively the following year.

Meanwhile, in 1964, Clay followed the example of the Black Muslims: He gave up his "slave name" and took one of African origin. His decision to call himself Muhammad Ali was controversial. This was because of Ali's prominence and influence as a sports champion and a role model for young people, along with the common perception that Black Muslims were antiwhite.

Ali was also well known for the good-naturedly boastful and witty pronouncements he would make before a bout, usually expressed in rhyme or as an epigram. "Float like a butterfly, sting like a bee" was a favorite—a self-description of the boxing artist at his graceful best.

As Ali became more political and outspoken, he seemed a greater threat to many white people. The 1960s were times of major political upheaval, particularly in black-white relations and in the growing opposition to the Vietnam War. Ali alienated many people in both conflicts, particularly after he was drafted in 1966.

Ali responded to the draft much as many antiwar activists were beginning to do. He claimed he was a conscientious objector—someone who refuses to fight in a war on grounds of conscience or religion. As a result, Ali was suspended from boxing and his championship status was taken away. Many felt that Ali was disciplined much more harshly than a white fighter would have been under the same circumstances. Others felt that precisely because Ali was black and suffered from prejudice, he was more aware of political issues than a white fighter might have been, and more willing to speak out.

Ali's suspension kept him out of the ring for four years of what should have been the peak of his career. Only after a four-year battle was he able to win a 1970 court decision revoking his suspension. Many people believed Ali had passed his prime, but he made an extraordinary comeback. In 1971, he fought Joe Frazier for the world heavyweight championship, and although he lost, he finally regained the title in 1974. At the time, Ali was 32, which in boxing is considered an advanced age. Nevertheless, he managed to knock out the powerful fighter George Foreman in eight rounds.

In 1976, Ali starred in a film biography of his life, *The Greatest,* named for Ali's frequent pronouncement: "I am the greatest!"

Ali once again lost the title—to Leon Spinks in 1978—and once again regained it—from Spinks in 1979. Finally, in his late 30s, the champion retired. Although Ali was no longer defending his title, he remained one of the black community's most beloved boxers and best-known fighters against racism.

In 1983 he was inducted into the Olympic Hall of Fame.

Although slowed by Parkinson's Disease, Ali lit the Olympic torch at the 1996 summer games, briefly resuming a place at the center of the world's stage. He was also the subject of the powerful, award-winning documentary *When We Were Kings,* released in 1997.

Further Reading: *The Greatest: My Own Story,* by Muhammad Ali, New York: Random House, 1975.

—*R. K.*

❖ ALLEN, RICHARD
(1760–1831), *religious leader, community organizer, anti-slavery activist*

Often called America's first civil rights leader, Richard Allen inspired African Americans to stand up for their rights. As the founder of the Free African Society and the African Methodist Episcopal (AME) Church, he played a pivotal role in the history of the United States.

Allen was born into slavery in Philadelphia, Pennsylvania, on February 14, 1760. Seven years later, the entire Allen family—mother, father, and four children—were sold to a plantation owner who lived near Dover, Delaware. In their new location, the Allens came into contact with Methodist preachers who were becoming active in the South and other areas; because they made no distinctions based on skin color and opposed slavery, the Methodists attracted many African Americans. As a young man, Richard joined the Methodist Society. He also taught himself to read and write and soon began preaching himself. Allen remained on the plantation until the age of 20, by which time he had saved enough money to purchase his freedom.

As a free man, Allen headed north to Philadelphia, working as a wagon driver, laborer, and shoemaker. He then served for several years as a full-time Methodist preacher, traveling on foot up and down the Atlantic coast from New York to North Carolina. In 1786, the Methodists recalled Allen to Philadelphia and assigned him to be the pastor of black Methodists at St. George's Church. But Allen was quickly disillusioned when he saw that white Methodists were softening their antislavery stand and were discriminating against black parish-

Richard Allen *(Library of Congress)*

ioners. Allen argued that African-American Methodists deserved to have their own congregation. The debate became heated, and finally the Methodist leaders expelled Allen and his followers from a Sunday prayer service. All the African-American members of St. George's left the church in protest, and a new movement was born. Allen's first step, with the assistance of Absalom Jones, was to found the Free African Society in 1787. The Free African Society operated as a beneficial and mutual-aid organization for African Americans and was the first of its kind in the United States.

One of the main goals of the Free African Society was the creation of an independent black church. Construction on a building began in 1792, and two years later Allen's Bethel African Methodist Episcopal Church—located on the corner of Sixth and Lombard Streets in Philadelphia—opened to parishioners. For the next 20 years, Allen battled the Methodist leadership, seeking independent status for his church. In 1815, the Pennsylvania Supreme Court ruled in Allen's favor. The AME Church was officially incorporated in 1816, with Allen as its first bishop.

Allen's activities were not limited to religious matters. In 1795, he organized a day school for 60 African-American students. He also worked diligently to bring about the abolition of slavery. In 1799, Allen and his followers petitioned the Pennsylvania state legislature to end slavery in the state, and in 1800 they made the same request of the U.S. Congress. Allen was committed to creating a just society in the United States, and he vigorously opposed plans for relocating free blacks to Africa. In an 1827 letter to the nation's first black newspaper, *Freedom's Journal,* Allen stated, "This land which we have watered with our tears and our blood, is now our mother country; and we are well satisfied to stay where wisdom abounds, and the gospel is free." In order to further the cause of equality, Allen joined with others in 1830 to create the American Society of Free Persons of Color. The society's aims included the purchase of land for African Americans and the establishment of free black communities in Canada.

Allen's legacy remains powerful today. The AME Church now has about 8,000 congregations and 3.5 million members in the United States, Canada, the Caribbean, and Africa. The church supports a number of historically black colleges, including Allen University in South Carolina and Wilberforce University in Ohio. Though a new building was erected in 1859, the Bethel AME Church still occupies its original site in Philadelphia. Allen and his wife, Sara, are interred in the basement, and the church also houses a museum commemorating Allen's achievements.

Further Reading: *Richard Allen: Apostle of Freedom,* by Charles H. Wesley, Washington, D.C.: Associated Publishers, 1969; *Segregated Sabbaths: Richard Allen and the Emergence of Independent Black Churches 1760–1840,* by Carol V. R. George, New York: Oxford University Press, 1973; *Richard Allen,* by Steve Klots, New York: Chelsea House, 1990.

—P. K.

❖ ALSTON, CHARLES H.
(1907–1977), *muralist, sculptor, illustrator*

Charles Alston won various national prizes and fellowships. His murals are on the walls of Harlem Hospital, the Abraham Lincoln High School in Brooklyn, the Harriet Tubman School in Manhattan, City College of the City University of New York, the Museum of Natural History in New York, and the Golden State Insurance Company in Los Angeles. His works are also in the collections of New York City's Metropolitan Museum of Art and Whitney Museum.

As an illustrator, Alston enjoyed wide recognition in such magazines as *Fortune, Redbook, Collier's, The New Yorker,* and *Mademoiselle.* In 1958, he was sent to the World's Fair in Brussels as one of three U.S. representatives from the Museum of Modern Art and the State Department.

Charles Alston was born in South Carolina in 1907 but soon moved to New York, where he received an M.A. degree from Columbia University in 1931. Alston went on to teach at the Harlem Art Center and the Harlem Art Workshop.

Alston's real rise to prominence, however, came during the depression. From 1937 to 1941, the federal government funded the Works Progress Administration (WPA), a program to provide jobs of all kinds to unemployed Americans. The WPA also sponsored positions in the arts for teachers, students, and amateurs, hiring professionals such as Charles Alston to paint and to instruct. As a teacher, he inspired many Harlem residents to paint, sculpt, and learn about art.

During this period, Alston won a number of fellowships and prizes, including the Rosenwald Fellowship in Painting and a first prize at the Atlanta University Annual Exhibit. Alston continued to win honors in the 1950s and 1960s, including a National Institute of Arts and Letters Grant in 1958 and the Joe and Emily Lowe

Award for achievement in the arts in 1960. Alston died in 1977.

Further Reading: *American Negro Art,* by Cedric Dover, Greenwich, Conn.: New York Graphic Society, 1960; *Negro Art: Past and Present,* by Alain Le Roy Locke, Washington, D.C.: Associates in Negro Folk Education, 1936.

—R. K.

❖ ANDERSON, MARIAN
(1902–1993), *concert and opera singer*

Marian Anderson's deep contralto voice was so magnificent that the great conductor Arturo Toscanini said such a singer was "heard only once in a hundred years." Anderson became one of the highest paid concert artists in America. She was the first black American to sing at

Marian Anderson (*Library of Congress*)

the Metropolitan Opera, and she toured throughout Europe and Asia.

One of the most famous incidents in Anderson's life came in 1939, when she was about to sing at Constitution Hall, in Washington, D.C. Because of her race, the Daughters of the American Revolution (D.A.R.) denied her the opportunity to sing there, causing a national scandal. Many musical leaders expressed their disapproval; Eleanor Roosevelt, the president's wife, resigned from the D.A.R. in protest. Four years later, on Easter morning in 1943, Mrs. Roosevelt invited Anderson to give a Washington, D.C., concert on the steps of the Lincoln Memorial—75,000 people came to listen.

Marian Anderson was born in 1902 in Philadelphia. She acquired her early musical background singing in church, but she soon obtained more professional training. Anderson's church raised the money for her to train for one year with a major music teacher, Giuseppe Boghetti. Boghetti was so impressed with her singing that he gave her an additional year of teaching for free.

In 1925, when Anderson was 23 years old, she made her professional debut with a concert at Town Hall, in New York City. The concert was a failure, and for a while, Anderson considered giving up her career. Then, in 1926, she sang at a banquet for the Spingarn Award, an honor bestowed each year by the National Association for the Advancement of Colored People for outstanding black achievement. The warm audience reaction she received at this dinner inspired Anderson to continue with her career.

The next year, she won a competition involving 300 singers. First prize was a contract for concert tours, which allowed her to appear with the New York Philharmonic Orchestra. Soon afterward, she won a Rosenwald Fellowship for Music, a grant that allowed her to continue with her studies in Germany.

Despite these successes, Anderson found that her American concern career was limited by her race. Few people wanted to book an African-American concert singer. In Europe, however, she found more opportunities. She went to Germany in 1929, and returned to Europe in 1933, where she spent two years marked by great honor and acclaim, giving concerts for the crowned heads of England, Denmark, Norway, and Sweden.

Eventually, Anderson's career was managed by Sol Hurok, the most important impresario in the United States at the time. Within three years of her second return from Europe, she became a leading concert artist. Her live concerts usually sold out, and Columbia Records enjoyed commercial success with her best-selling recordings. By 1941, she was at the top of her profession, one of the highest paid concert artists in the United States.

In 1939, Anderson herself received the Spingarn Award for artistic achievement. In the same year, she was the recipient of the Bok Award, given to distinguished Philadelphians. In 1942, she established the Marian Anderson Award for young singers.

In 1955, Anderson became the first black singer to perform at the Metropolitan Opera in a leading role. As Ulrica in Giuseppe Verdi's *Un Ballo in Maschera,* she became a symbol of black achievement in new fields.

Perhaps as a result, in 1957, the Department of State sent Anderson to tour India and the Far East as a representative of the United States. The following year, President Dwight D. Eisenhower appointed her to be a delegate to the 13th General Assembly of the United Nations.

In later years, Anderson won many other awards and honors. Her achievements were long considered to be symbols of African-American accomplishment in what was once an all-white field. Anderson died in 1993.

Further Reading: *My Lord, What a Morning: An Autobiography,* by Marian Anderson, New York: Viking Press, 1956; *Marian Anderson: A Portrait,* by Kosti Vehanen, Westport, Conn.: Greenwood Press, 1970 revision of 1941 ed.

—*R. K.*

❖ ANGELOU, MAYA (Marguerite Johnson)
(1928–), *writer*

Maya Angelou has had a long, rich career as a performer, writer, and director. She is best known for the first volume of her autobiography, *I Know Why the Caged Bird Sings* (New York: Random House), which was nominated for a National Book Award in 1970. In 1972, she received a Pulitzer Prize nomination for her collection of poetry, *Just Give Me a Cool Drink of Water 'fore I Diiie* (New York: Random House). In 1973, she won a Tony Award nomination for her performance in *Look Away,* a play in which she made her Broadway debut.

Maya Angelou was born Marguerite Johnson in St. Louis, Missouri. Her father, Bailey Johnson, was a naval dietician. Her mother, Vivian (Baxter) Johnson, left her father when the young Marguerite was only three years old. Marguerite and her brother Bailey were put on a train by themselves and sent from Long Beach, California, to Stamps, Arkansas, a segregated southern town with a strong Ku Klux Klan presence.

In Stamps, she was raised by her father's mother, Annie Henderson. There were times, too, that she spent with her mother in San Francisco.

As Angelou describes her childhood, it was one of both great richness and great bitterness. She describes her early love of black culture—and of Shakespeare, whom she says she believed was black because of the richness of his speech. She also describes being raped by her mother's boyfriend at the age of eight, and the experience of having a child whose father she barely knew at the age of 16.

As recounted in her book, Angelou's story is ultimately one of triumph. She decides to raise her son, and she becomes the first black attendant on the San Francisco streetcars.

Later volumes of Angelou's autobiography are *Gather Together in My Name* (New York: Random House, 1974); *Singin' and Swingin' and Gettin' Merry Like Christmas* (New York: Random House, 1976); *The Heart of a Woman* (New York: Random House, 1981); and *All God's Children Need Traveling Shoes* (New York: Vintage Books, 1986). In these books, Angelou describes her early work experience as cook, waitress, dancer, and madam, as well as her first attempts to become a performer.

In 1954 and 1955, Angelou went on a round-the-world tour with the black opera *Porgy and Bess.* When she returned to the United States, she appeared in various plays, including the 1960 Off-Broadway production of Jean Genet's *The Blacks.* With famed black comedian Godfrey Cambridge, she produced and performed in *Cabaret for Freedom* in 1960.

In 1961, Angelou went to Egypt, where she was the associate editor of the *Arab Observer,* an English-language news weekly in Cairo. She worked there for two years.

From 1963 to 1966, Angelou lived in Ghana, which had just gained its independence from Britain. There she worked at the University of Ghana's School of Music and Drama, and acted in the university's production of *Mother Courage.* From 1964 to 1966, Angelou was also a feature editor of *African Review.*

When Angelou returned to the United States, she began to teach at the University of California at Los Angeles (UCLA), and in 1966, she appeared on stage in Hollywood, in the Greek tragedy *Medea.*

Angelou's other writings include four more volumes of poetry, *Oh Pray My Wings Are Gonna Fit Me Well* (New York: Random House, 1975); *And Still I Rise* (New York: Random House, 1978); *Shaker, Why Don't You Sing?* (New York: Random House, 1983), and *I Shall Not Be Moved* (New York: Random House, 1990).

Angelou has also written several television plays, screenplays, and theatrical plays, which were produced during the 1960s and 1970s. Her screenplay, *Georgia, Georgia* (1972), was the first original screenplay by a black woman to be made into a film. She directed her own screenplay, *All Day Long,* in 1974, and she directed her own play, *And Still I Rise,* in 1976.

Angelou continues to write, direct, teach, and perform. Her message in all media is the need for self-awareness and self-acceptance, which are won through a connection to one's people, one's family, one's heritage, and the experiences of one's past.

In January 1993, Angelou became the first woman and the first African American to read her works at a presidential inauguration. Her poem "On the Pulse of Morning" celebrates the diversity of the American and world communities, and urges them to work together to create a better future.

Further Reading: *On the Pulse of Morning,* by Maya Angelou, New York: Random House, 1993; *The Complete Collected Poems of Maya Angelou,* New York: Random House, 1994.

—*R. K.*

❖ ANTOINE, CAESAR CARPETIER
(1836–1921), *army officer, politician, businessperson, editor*

Caesar Carpetier Antoine was born during the time of slavery, but he lived most of his adult life during and after Reconstruction, the period following the Civil War when new opportunities for black people were made available. Antoine made the most of these opportunities. He became one of three black people to be elected lieutenant governor of Louisiana, and he founded several businesses. He also worked with the civil rights organization known as the Comité des Citoyens, which sponsored the test case for the Supreme Court's famous *Plessy vs. Ferguson* decision in 1896. Homer Plessy had sued a Louisiana railroad company that had refused to let him sit in a car reserved for whites. Plessy contended that segregation violated the Fourteenth Amendment, providing equal protection. The Supreme Court ruled against Plessy, upholding segregation as long as "equal" accommodations were provided to all races.

Antoine was born in New Orleans in 1836. His mother was West Indian, daughter of an enslaved African chief. Antoine's father was a veteran of the War of 1812 who had fought the British at the Battle of New Orleans. His father's mother, Rose Antoine, was apparently a remarkable woman whose work as a midwife enabled her to purchase her own freedom and acquire a small fortune.

Antoine himself was educated at private schools in New Orleans and was fluent in both French and English. But when he graduated, he found himself restricted to one of the few occupations open to black people in the pre-war South—barbering. However, he did not remain a barber for long. When federal troops captured Baton Rouge in 1862, Antoine organized Company I, 7th Louisiana Colored Regiment (Corps d'Afrique), of which he was captain. After the war, he moved to Shreveport, where he opened a family grocery, and soon afterward he began a career in politics.

Reconstruction offered black people a new opportunity to hold electoral office, and Antoine held a number of important state positions from 1867 to 1877.

Meanwhile, Antoine also put his financial abilities to use, investing in railroad and lottery stocks, raising racehorses and founding various businesses. With former Lieutenant Governor P. B. S. Pinchback, he was partner in a cotton sales business and, from 1870 to 1872, in the *New Orleans Louisianian* newspaper. In 1880, he became president of the Cosmopolitan Life Insurance Company. By the time of his death in 1921, he had purchased a plantation, several city lots, and a home worth $1,300, a considerable sum of money at the time.

In his later years, Antoine was vice president of the New Orleans Comité des Citoyens, a civil rights organization formed in 1890 by free people of color. In addition to *Plessy vs. Ferguson*, the Comité also tried to have the Supreme Court declare unconstitutional a law against miscegenation (intermarriage between races), but it was unsuccessful.

Further Reading: *Men of Mark, Eminent, Progressive, and Rising* by William J. Simmons, New York: Arno Press, 1968 reprint of 1887 ed.; *Black New Orleans 1860–1880*, by John W. Blassingame, Chicago, Ill.: University of Chicago Press, 1973; on the Comité des Citoyens, *Our People and Our History*, by Sister Dorothea Olga McCants, Baton Rouge, La.: Louisiana State University Press, 1973.

—R. K.

❖ ARMISTEAD, JAMES LAFAYETTE
(1760–1832), *Revolutionary War spy*

James Armistead was one of many successful black spies used by the Americans during the Revolutionary War.

The British were often careless around black people, with the result that supposedly "ignorant" slaves and free black people were able to obtain secret information.

Armistead was perhaps the greatest of all these spies. America's French ally, the marquis de Lafayette, sent him to infiltrate the camp of British general Charles Cornwallis. Armistead was so good at avoiding suspicion that Cornwallis asked him to spy on Lafayette. So Armistead became a double agent, giving Lafayette true information while feeding Cornwallis false reports.

We know little about Armistead's early life. What we do know dates from the time that he began to serve in the American army during the Revolutionary War.

Because the Americans so desperately needed people to fight on their side during the Revolution, slaves were sometimes allowed to enlist in the army as soldiers. Armistead's owner, of New Kent County, Virginia, gave him permission to serve with General Lafayette in March 1781.

At that time, Cornwallis controlled most of Virginia. The nearby American force was only half as large as the British army. Naturally, the Americans wanted to keep close track of British activities.

Lafayette tried to send several spies into Cornwallis's camp, but no one was able to return reliable reports— until James Armistead began to do so, in July 1781. Armistead's intelligence reports were famous for their detail and accuracy. Posing as a servant to Cornwallis, he sent back key information as to the number of guns, horses, and ships the British had, and how the army was positioned. As a result of his work, American and French leaders decided to put a French fleet in Chesapeake Bay, which forced Cornwallis's surrender. One can imagine the general's surprise when he met his former servant in the French camp.

Lafayette later wrote that Armistead had "done essential services to me." Despite the praise, it took the Virginia legislature some time to grant Armistead his freedom. Although a special act of 1783 had offered freedom to slaves who served as soldiers, Armistead didn't qualify, since he had served as a spy. Finally, in 1786, Armistead was freed.

The former spy settled on a farm near New Kent County in 1816 and raised a family. His services were further recognized by the Virginia legislature in 1819, when they awarded him a pension of $40 a year (a much more significant sum of money in those days, of course, than it is today). His greatest honor after the war was bestowed in 1824, when General Lafayette, during his return to the United States, greeted him personally.

Further Reading: *The Letters of Lafayette to Washington 1777–1779,* ed. by Louis Gottschalk, Philadelphia, Pa.: American Philosophical Society, 1976; *Virginia Negro Soldiers and Seamen in the Revolutionary War,* by Luther Porter Jackson, Norfolk, Va.: VA Guide Quality Press, 1944.

—*R. K.*

❖ ARMSTRONG, LOUIS ("Satchmo")
(1900–1971), *jazz musician*

Louis Armstrong, also known as "Satchmo," was often called "the jazz ambassador." Besides having a successful jazz career in the United States, Armstrong played in several command performances before the king and queen of England, toured Europe often, and appeared in a number of motion pictures. His recording career goes back to the 1920s, and collectors value many of his rare recordings to this day.

Armstrong came from a poor family. When he was 13 years old and living in New Orleans, he was sent to the Waif's Home for Boys for having fired a pistol in the streets. At that time, Armstrong could play only a home-made guitar, but the bandmaster of the Waif's Home soon taught him to read music and to play the cornet and the bugle. Clearly, Armstrong had a strong musical bent—by the time he was released from the home, 18 months later, he was leading the band.

In 1915, the teenaged Armstrong was probably ready to perform publicly as a musician, but he was too young for any band to hire him, so he supported himself by selling newspapers and working in a dairy. He also began to hang around the places where he could hear his idol, the musician Joe "King" Oliver, who was one of the pioneers of the "Dixieland" sound—the roots of a new type of music called jazz.

King Oliver, a member of Kid Ory's band, took the young Armstrong under his wing and taught him the trumpet. When King Oliver went on to Chicago in 1917, he made sure that Louis Armstrong took his place with Kid Ory.

Armstrong played and toured with that band for the next five years. Then, in 1922, he joined King Oliver in Chicago. For two years, Armstrong played second cornet in Oliver's Original Creole Jazz Band.

In 1924, Armstrong worked with Fletcher Henderson's orchestra, which played at the famous Roseland Ballroom in New York. Armstrong had moved from the cornet to the trumpet and was also singing. The combination of his singing and trumpet playing would eventually become Armstrong's trademark.

In 1925, Armstrong returned to Chicago, where he began to establish a reputation for improvisation and newly invented rhythms. In 1926, he worked with famed jazz musicians Erskine Tate and Earl "Fatha" Hines.

Armstrong was such a success that his name was up in lights as the "World's Greatest Trumpeter." This inspired him to form his own band, Louis Armstrong and His Hot Five. Later, he had a group known as the Hot Seven. This was the beginning of his maturity as a musician, the "four golden years" of recordings he made with these two bands.

In 1930, after a headlining role in a Broadway revue, Armstrong moved from leading small bands to leading big ones. Instead of the old Dixieland sound, he began to use popular songs as his basic material, which distressed many jazz purists. Jazz lovers continued to worry about their beloved music as white musicians copied Armstrong's innovation, forming "big bands" and "swing bands" whose work was closely tied to popular and commercial tunes, rather than being based on the freer improvisation that had once shaped jazz.

In addition to his musical ability, Armstrong was a dynamic performer. He had a distinctive, rasping, half-growl of a voice and a flamboyant sense of theater, often telling jokes and performing as a comedian to accompany his musical work.

Armstrong's performing style was also effective on the stage. When he returned to New York in 1929, he starred in the musical *Hot Chocolates,* one of several popular revues that featured black people dancing, singing, and playing jazz. In 1939, he appeared on Broadway in a show called *Swingin' the Dream,* an adaptation for African Americans of Shakespeare's *A Midsummer Night's Dream,* in which Armstrong played the comic character Bottom.

Armstrong's open, friendly, energetic quality made him a favorite with audiences around the world. In 1932, he toured Europe, and in 1934, he appeared in his first command performance before Britain's King George V. After World War II, Armstrong continued to travel, frequently as a goodwill ambassador from the United States.

In 1936, Armstrong began his movie career with *Pennies from Heaven,* followed by *Every Day's a Holiday, Going Places, Cabin in the Sky,* and *The Glenn Miller Story.*

By 1947, when Armstrong had gone from big bands back to small ones, his fame as a performer overshadowed his musical talents. The focus of his appearances was more on Armstrong himself than on his band as a whole.

In the 1950s, Armstrong was featured in the film *High Society,* where he played and sang with Bing Crosby. As late as 1969, he appeared in the film *Hello, Dolly,* with Barbra Streisand and Walter Matthau. He also appeared frequently on television.

Further Reading: *Louis Armstrong: A Cultural Legacy,* edited by Marc H. Miller, Seattle: University of Washington, 1994; *Louis Armstrong: An Extravagant Life,* by Laurence Bergreen, New York: Broadway Books, 1997; *Satchmo, My Life in New Orleans,* by Louis Armstrong, New York: Da Capo Press, 1986 reprint of 1954 ed.; *Satchmo,* by Gary Giddins, New York: Doubleday, 1988.

—*R. K.*

❖ ASHE, ARTHUR ROBERT, JR.
(1943–1993), *tennis champion, author, and humanitarian*

Arthur Ashe made history in 1968 when he won the men's singles title at the U.S. Open, becoming the first African-American man to win a Grand Slam tennis event. In the years that followed, Ashe continued to distinguish himself both as an athlete and a human being, exemplifying the qualities of sportsmanship and social responsibility.

Born in Richmond, Virginia, on July 10, 1943, Ashe began to play tennis on the public courts at Brookfield Park. At the age of 10, he caught the eye of Ronald Charity, a part-time coach. Charity saw the slender youngster's potential and brought him to the attention of Dr. Walter Johnson. Johnson had recently coached Althea Gibson, who was soon to become the first African-American tennis champion, and he now devoted himself to developing Ashe's talents as well. At this time, the United States Tennis Association (USTA), the sport's governing body, was opening its tournaments to African-American players, ending decades of discrimination. Ashe started playing in USTA events at the age of 16, and it took him only a year to reach the top. He won the Junior Indoor Singles title in 1960 and successfully defended his crown in 1961.

In 1962, Ashe entered the University of California at Los Angeles on a tennis scholarship. During his sophomore year, he became the first African-American man named to the U.S. Davis Cup team, and in 1965 he won the NCAA men's singles title. After graduating with a degree in business administration, Ashe devoted himself single-mindedly to tennis. His hard work paid off handsomely in 1968, when he won the U.S. Open at Forest Hills, New York, defeating Tom Okker of the Netherlands. Ashe won his second Grand Slam event, the Australian Open, in 1970, and captured a third Grand Slam title at Wimbledon in 1975. Tennis fans admired Ashe not only for his athletic skill but also for his character; at a time when some male tennis stars were taunting opponents and abusing referees, Ashe conducted himself like a true champion in everything he did.

Having experienced segregation and prejudice during his early years, Ashe was determined to provide opportunities for others. With this goal in mind, he helped found the USTA National Junior Tennis League, a program that concentrated on developing young players from the inner city. Ashe played a hands-on role in this endeavor, supervising numerous tennis clinics throughout the country. He was also deeply concerned with human rights around the world. Beginning in 1970, Ashe steadfastly condemned the antiblack policies of the South African government and worked to have South Africa barred from international sports competitions.

In 1979, two years after his marriage to photographer Jean Moutoussamy, Ashe suffered a severe heart attack while conducting a tennis clinic. He underwent heart surgery later in the year and retired from competitive athletics, having won 818 matches and 51 tournaments. Ashe remained active in tennis as the captain of the U.S. Davis Cup team; he also worked as a consultant, began a number of writing projects, and continued to fight for human rights. The 1980s held many bright moments for Ashe—among the highlights were his 1985 induction into the International Tennis Hall of Fame and the birth of a daughter, Camera, in 1986.

In April 1992, Ashe learned that he had contracted AIDS through a blood transfusion administered several years earlier, during a second heart operation. Despite this cruel twist of fate, Ashe was never heard to complain or feel sorry for himself. He became an effective advocate for increased AIDS research and established the Arthur Ashe Foundation to assist in combating the disease.

On February 6, 1993, Arthur Ashe died of AIDS-related pneumonia at the age of 49. In 1997, when a new stadium to house the U.S. Open was completed in Flushing Meadows, New York, the USTA named the facility Arthur Ashe Stadium. At the dedication ceremony, USTA president Harry Marmion hailed Ashe as "the finest human being the sport of tennis has ever known."

Further Reading: *Days of Grace: A Memoir,* by Arthur Ashe and Arnold Rampersad, New York: Knopf, 1993; *A Hard*

Road to Glory: A History of the African-American Athlete, by Arthur Ashe, 3 volumes, New York: Amistad, 1993; *Arthur Ashe on Tennis,* by Arthur Ashe and Alexander McNab, New York: Knopf, 1995.

—*P. K.*

❖ ATTUCKS, CRISPUS
(1723?–1770), *early American patriot*

Crispus Attucks is known as the first American to die for independence. Attucks died in the Boston Massacre on March 5, 1770. This action is generally agreed to have been vital in the American decision to declare war and, subsequently, independence.

Scholars place the birth of Attucks in Framingham, Massachusetts, and note that he was a slave of Deacon William Brown. He is said to have been a tall, striking man, of a mixed African, European, and Natick Indian heritage.

At age 27, Attucks apparently escaped from slavery and went to work on the whaling ships docked along the east coast of Massachusetts. By all accounts, he was a rebel, a drifter, and a man who prized his own freedom. Evidently, he was also a natural leader, one who could inspire large numbers of people to action.

This leadership ability led to Attucks's role in the Boston Massacre. According to witnesses of the time, a crowd of both black and white Americans gathered around the soldiers' barracks in Boston's center. The Americans began to insult and argue with the British soldiers. Attucks was one of the American crowd, urging the others forward. The soldiers ordered people to disperse, but Attucks encouraged them to stand firm; and they did.

Led by Attucks, a crowd of Americans forced the soldiers back into the barracks. Then the soldiers regained their strength and drove the Americans back.

Into the midst of the fight ran a man who claimed that he had been hit with a musket by a British sentry. The crowd was furious, and they moved to the customshouse, where the sentry was standing. With Attucks in the lead, the crowd went forward and began to throw snow and ice at the soldiers.

According to one witness, Attucks was the boldest of the crowd, and he actually hit one of the armed British soldiers. Another story has it that someone else in the crowd threw a stick at the soldier. Whatever the provocation, the soldier fired, and instantly killed Attucks. Four other civilians were killed, as well.

Crispus Attucks (*Library of Congress*)

In the trial of the British soldiers afterward, both sides focused on Attucks. The side accusing the soldiers stressed how Attucks had been killed first, and "with malice aforethought." The defense said that Attucks had actually grabbed the soldier's bayonet and knocked him down, provoking the shooting.

Crispus Attucks's fame lasted long after his death. African-American military companies before the Civil War took the name of the "Attucks Guards." From 1858 to 1870, black Americans living in Boston held a Crispus Attucks Day. In 1888, the Boston black community had a Crispus Attucks memorial built on the Boston Common, honoring Attucks and the four others killed during the Massacre.

Further Reading: *The Negro in the American Revolution,* by Benjamin Quarles, Chapel Hill, N.C.: University of North Carolina Press, 1961; *The Boston Massacre,* by Miller B. Zobel, New York: W.W. Norton, 1970; *The African-American Soldier: From Crispus Attucks to Colin Powell,* edited by Michael Lee Lanning, New York: Birch Lane Press, 1997; *Memorial of Crispus Attucks, Samuel Maverick, James Caldwell, Samuel Gray and Colin Powell, from the City of Boston (Black Heritage Library Collection),* by Boston City Council Staff, Boston: Ayer Co. Pub., 1989.

—*R. K.*

❖ BALDWIN, JAMES ARTHUR
(1924–1987), *writer*

James Baldwin wrote numerous novels, essays, and plays. He came of age as legal segregation in the United States was ending, and his writings reflected the rise of the Civil Rights movement. Baldwin's writings are known for their honest, perceptive, and often painful descriptions of the effects of racism on both black and white Americans.

Baldwin won many fellowships and awards during his lifetime, including an American Book Award nomination for the novel *Just Above My Head* (New York: Dial Press, 1979) and appointment to the rank of commander in the French Legion of Honor, a distinction given to those credited with outstanding achievements in their fields. Critic Juan Williams of the *Washington Post* once wrote that "black people reading Baldwin knew he wrote the truth. White people reading Baldwin sensed his truth about the lives of black people and the sins of a racist nation."

James Baldwin was born in Harlem on August 2, 1924, the son of David and Berdis (Jones) Baldwin. He was one of a large family later headed by his stepfather, an evangelical preacher.

When Baldwin was 14 years old, he experienced a profound religious conversion, and he too became an evangelical preacher. Later, Baldwin speculated that this decision was a response to the troubled atmosphere of drugs and crime that he had encountered growing up.

When Baldwin graduated from high school in 1942, he was the sole supporter of his family, since his stepfather had become mentally unstable. He went to work in a defense-industry plant in New Jersey, which brought him face to face with brutal discrimination. After Baldwin's stepfather died, the young man left the factory and began his apprenticeship as a writer in Greenwich Village, taking any odd job he could get to support himself.

Baldwin struggled with his writing, receiving help from such authors as Richard Wright and selling his articles and stories to prestigious magazines. In 1948, he moved to Paris, which he felt freed him to do his creative work. He once said in a *New York Times* interview that the move helped him see more clearly who he was and where he had come from, while freeing him from the more immediate impact of American racism. "I am the grandson of a slave, and I am a writer," Baldwin said in the interview. "I must deal with both."

Gradually, Baldwin came to terms with his heritage, and also with his bisexuality. His novel *Go Tell It on the Mountain* (New York: Knopf, 1953) and his play *The Amen Corner* (New York: Dell Publishing Company, 1990 reprint of 1968 ed.) are striking examples of Baldwin's search for his African-American past.

During the 1960s, many black writers criticized him for writing about homosexual experiences and for directing his work to white readers as well as black ones. Baldwin refused to accept these criticisms. He insisted that he was an "American writer" rather than a "black writer," and that he was part of a multiracial society.

Some of Baldwin's best-known novels include *Notes of a Native Son* (Boston: Beacon Press, 1955), *Go Tell It on the Mountain* (New York: Dial Press, 1953), *Tell Me How Long the Train's Been Gone* (New York: Dial Press, 1968), and *If Beale Street Could Talk* (New York: Dial Press, 1974). His book *Little Man, Big Man: A Story of Childhood* (New York: Dial Press, 1976) was written for children.

Baldwin's essay collections include *Nobody Knows My Name: More Notes of a Native Son* (New York: Dial Press, 1961); *The Fire Next Time* (New York: Dial Press, 1963); and *A Dialogue,* a transcript of a conversation with poet Nikki GIOVANNI about male and female issues, among others.

Baldwin died of stomach cancer on November 30, 1987, at his home in St.-Paul-de-Vence, France. He remained a social activist as well as a writer to the end. He was a member of the Congress of Racial Equality's national advisory board, and of the National Committee for a Sane Nuclear Policy.

Further Reading: *James Baldwin: A Biography,* by David Leeming, New York: Knopf, 1994; *James Baldwin: Collected Essays,* by James Baldwin, New York: Library of America, 1998; *James Baldwin: Early Novels and Stories* (Library of America), by James Baldwin, New York: Library of America, 1998; *Conversations with James Baldwin,* ed. by Fred L. Standley, H. Pratt Louis; Jackson, Miss.: University Press of Mississippi, 1989; *Baldwin, Three Interviews,* by Malcolm King, Middletown, Conn.: Wesleyan University Press, 1985; *James Baldwin,* by Carolyn Wedin Sylvander, New York: Ungar, 1980; *James Baldwin,* by Louis Hill Pratt, Boston: Twayne Publishers, 1978.

—R. K.

❖ BAMBARA, TONI CADE
(1939–1995), *author*

Toni Cade Bambara won numerous awards for her writing and film work, including the 1981 American Book Award for her novel *The Salt Eaters* (New York: Random House, 1980). Bambara's work has been widely anthologized and her short stories are often found in textbooks. In addition to her writing, Bambara taught English and African studies, and was a noted civil rights activist. This concern with literature, her African heritage, and social justice is a central theme in her work.

Bambara was born Toni Cade in 1939, the daughter of Helen Brent Anderson Cade. She changed her name legally in 1970. After her 1959 graduation from Queens College in New York City, she went on to study theater in Florence, Italy, and Paris, France, before returning for more study and a master's degree from City College of the City University of New York.

Bambara held a variety of jobs, including social investigator for the welfare department of New York State, director of recreation for the psychiatry department of New York City's Metropolitan Hospital, and program director of a New York community center. In 1965, she began teaching English, which remained her profession for many years.

Bambara's first book was *Gorilla, My Love* (New York: Random House), a collection of short stories published in 1972. This book centered on stories about young girls, either recounting their lives or giving their perspective on events involving adults.

In 1977, Bambara published a second short-story collection, *The Sea Birds Are Still Alive* (New York: Random House). These stories concerned adults, particularly those involved with political causes or coming to political awareness.

Three years later, Bambara published *The Salt Eaters,* her first novel. It tells the story of two women who barely know each other until they are brought together by one's suicide attempt. The book is known for its use of myths and dreams in its exploration of black culture and politics.

In 1987, Bambara published *If Blessing Comes* (New York: Random House), her second novel. She also wrote several screenplays, including adaptations of her own work, and won awards for her contributions to various film documentaries.

Further Reading: *Deep Sightings and Rescue Missions: Fiction, Essays, and Conversations,* by Toni Cade Bambara, ed. by Erroll McDonald, New York: Pantheon, 1996; *Sturdy Black Bridges: Visions of Black Women in Literature,* by Bell Parker and Beverly Guy-Sheftall, Garden City, N.Y.: Anchor Press/Doubleday, 1979; *Women Writers of the Contemporary South,* ed. by Peggy Whitman Prenshaw, Jackson, Miss.: University Press of Mississippi, 1984; *Black Women Writers at Work,* ed. by Claudia Tate, New York: Continuum, 1983.

—R. K.

❖ BANNEKER, BENJAMIN
(1731–1806), *mathematician and astronomer*

Benjamin Banneker is best known for the almanacs in which he calculated the ephemerides. Ephemerides are

Benjamin Banneker (*Library of Congress*)

tables that give the positions of the planets and stars for each day of the year. Banneker's almanacs were published from 1792 through 1797, and were widely distributed in the United States. One almanac went to President Thomas Jefferson (in manuscript form), along with a note from Banneker saying that slavery should be abolished. Jefferson's praise of Banneker's almanac became part of an antislavery campaign.

Banneker is also known for helping to survey the territory that became the nation's capital, Washington, D.C., determining the boundaries, area, and elevations of land, by means of measuring angles and distances. At that time, surveying an area involved making charts of the positions of the stars from different parts of the area. Comparing the different angles of the stars helped surveyors know how far apart two different points were.

In 1791, although almost 60 years old and often sick, Banneker assisted chief surveyor Major Andrew

Ellicott with the capital territory project. Banneker worked in the observatory tent, where he made and recorded astronomical observations, maintained the field astronomical clock, and compiled other data. It was this experience that led him to calculate the ephemerides and publish his almanac.

The self-taught astronomer and mathematician was born on November 9, 1731, near the Patapsco River in Baltimore County, Maryland. Banneker's father was a freed slave named Robert (we don't know his last name); his mother, Mary Bannka, was the daughter of a freed slave and an indentured Englishwoman. (At this time, people who wanted to earn money to go to America often indentured themselves to someone who had the money; that is, they promised to work for the person for several years in exchange for room, board, and the price of their transatlantic ticket.) This woman, Molly Welsh, had established a farm, bought two slaves, freed them, and married one of them. The man she married was named Bannka, which became the source of the name "Banneker."

Banneker spent his life on the tobacco farm that his father established. He had little formal education beyond a few seasons at the country school. However, he was naturally gifted in mathematics, teaching himself after hours spent working in the fields.

At 21, the talented young Banneker built a clock with wood-carved gears, using as a guide a pocket watch that he had once examined. This complicated clock continued to strike every hour for 40 years.

In 1759, Banneker's father died. Banneker remained on the farm even after the marriage of his three sisters and the death of his mother. Except for frequent visits from his sisters, he lived in relative isolation from the community. Slavery was still active in Maryland, and Banneker was probably afraid of persecution because of his color.

In 1771, Banneker's life took an eventful turn. The Ellicott brothers, a Pennsylvania Quaker family, purchased a large tract of land next to Banneker's farm. They developed this land into a major mill center, where grain was milled into flour. Banneker made friends with George Ellicott, the son of one of the founding brothers. Ellicott gave Banneker several books about astronomy, as well as instruments for observing the stars. Without any further help, Banneker taught himself astronomy and calculated an ephemeris (the position of the celestial bodies) for the year 1791. Although several publishers rejected this effort, Banneker continued to study.

In 1791, George Ellicott's cousin, Major Andrew Ellicott, received his commission to survey the "Federal

Territory"—now known as the District of Columbia. From his cousin, Major Ellicott learned of Banneker and hired him as his scientific assistant.

After helping Ellicott, Banneker calculated the ephemeris for 1792. With the Ellicott family's assistance, he reached the Pennsylvania and Maryland abolition societies. They sponsored publication of his work—the same work that President Jefferson praised. Then they cited Banneker's work as proof that, as Senator James McHenry put it, "the powers of the mind are disconnected with the colours of the skin."

Banneker was encouraged by his success and retired from tobacco farming to devote himself full time to work on these almanacs that bore his name. The books he produced through 1797 went into several editions and were widely distributed.

After 1797, times became more difficult for Banneker. The nation became less interested in abolition, so there was less interest in books by black people. Banneker still continued to calculate ephemerides until 1804, but he was no longer able to publish his work.

During Banneker's final years, he lived alone in his log house, reading and writing. He visited the Ellicotts' mill and store frequently, and was often visited by two of his sisters. He died on October 9, 1806.

After his death, Banneker was memorialized in various ways and referred to as "the first Negro American man of science." Silvio Bedini's 1972 review of his work suggests that without the limitations of opportunity caused by racism and his isolated location, Banneker would certainly have become a more important figure in early American science.

Further Reading: *The Life of Benjamin Banneker,* by Silvio Bedini, Baltimore, Md.: Maryland Historical Society, 1998.

—*R. K.*

❖ BANNISTER, EDWARD MITCHELL
(1828–1901), *painter*

Edward Bannister was a major American landscape painter of the late 19th century. In 1876, his painting *Under the Oaks* won the gold medal at the Philadelphia Centennial Exhibition. His works today hang in the collections of the Providence Art Club, the Rhode Island School of Design, the Howard University Art Gallery, and the John Hope Collection at Atlanta University.

In addition to his artistic achievements, Bannister is noted for being the only black founding member of the Providence Art Club. This is America's oldest art club, founded in 1873, and it still exists today. Moreover, the club gave birth to the Rhode Island School of Design, now one of the most respected art schools in the country.

Edward Bannister was born in 1828 in Nova Scotia to Edward Bannister, a black native of Barbados, and Hannah (Alexander) Bannister, a white Canadian. Bannister's father died when the child was six, and his mother also died when he was young. Nevertheless, Bannister received a grammar school education in his home—an unusual accomplishment for a black child born during the years of slavery.

After his parents died, Bannister went to live with a lawyer by the name of Harris Hatch. From a very early age, Bannister liked drawing and painting, and he began copying family portraits and the engravings in the family Bible. Because Bannister had no drawing paper, he drew on barn doors, fences, and any other surface he could find.

Bannister continued to paint as he grew up, but he also had to work at a number of jobs to support himself. At various times he was the cook on a ship, the janitor at a Boston barbershop, and a handyman in the Boston area. Bannister's shipboard experience undoubtedly inspired his lifelong love of the sea, which was later to be a major subject of his work.

By 1850, Bannister had settled in Boston, where he learned to make solar prints. He developed this skill into a successful business, so there was finally time to sketch and paint. He then began to get commissions. His first commissioned painting, done in 1854, was called *The Ship Outward Bound.*

Bannister managed to study privately with Dr. William Rimmer, who taught at the Art Academy in Boston. He also studied at the Lowell Institute in Boston, where he found himself ignored and ostracized by the white artists.

In 1855 or 1856, Bannister married Christiana Cartreaux, a Narraganset Indian working in Boston as a wigmaker and hairdresser. Cartreaux had many ties with the abolitionist movement and was active in black politics in Boston. An energetic, spirited person, she was a great inspiration to her husband.

Bannister, it is reported, was further inspired by an article in the *New York Herald Tribune* in 1867, which said that "the Negro seems to have an appreciation of Art while being manifestly unable to produce it." This angered Bannister so much that he set out to disprove the statement. His dedication to a career in art increased.

In 1871, Bannister moved to Providence, Rhode Island, where he could sail on Narragansett Bay and in Newport Harbor. There he continued to sketch and paint, and was an active member of the Providence Art Club.

A turning point in Bannister's career came when he won the gold medal in the Philadelphia Centennial Exhibition in 1876 for *Under the Oaks,* a huge landscape painting. But the triumph was not easily won. When Bannister came to pick up the prize, guards at the Philadelphia gallery asked what he was doing there. They couldn't believe that a black man had won the award. When Bannister identified himself, the judges wanted to give the award to somebody else.

However, the other artists would not agree to this. They said that if Bannister was denied the award on account of his race, they would withdraw from the contest and announce their protest to the world. The judges backed down and gave the award to Bannister.

After that victory, there were more honors, more medals. Bannister received so many commissions that he was finally able to stop doing odd jobs and concentrate on his painting.

Bannister's work is characterized by a gentle, poetic quality. Critic John Nelson Arnold wrote: "He looked at nature with a poet's feeling. Skies, rocks, fields were all absorbed and distilled through his soul and projected upon the canvas with a virile force and a poetic beauty."

On January 9, 1901, Bannister died of a sudden heart attack while attending church.

Further Reading: *Edward Mitchell Bannister, 1828–1901,* by Juanita Marie Holland and Corrine Jennings, New York: Harry N. Abrams, 1993; *Negro American Art,* by Cedric Dover, Greenwich, Conn.: New York Graphic Society, 1960; *The Negro in Art,* by Alain Locke, Washington, D.C.: Associates in Negro Folk Education, 1940.

—*R. K.*

❖ BARAKA, IMAMU AMIRI (LeRoi Jones)
(1934–), *playwright, poet, political activist*

Imamu Amiri Baraka was born LeRoi Jones in Newark, New Jersey. He won fame as an Obie Award–winning playwright for avant-garde theater. (The Obies are awards given each year for the best off-Broadway—"O.B."—theater, that is, theater that is not as commercial as "Broadway" theater.) Baraka's best-known early plays are *Dutchman, The Toilet,* and *The Slave* (*Dutchman and the*

Amiri Baraka (L) and Cecil Taylor *(Chris Felver/Archive Photos)*

Slave, Two Plays, New York: Morrow, 1964; *The Toilet,* New York: Sterling Lord Agency, 1964).

Baraka wrote more than 20 plays, as well as 13 volumes of poetry and essays on black culture, music, and history. He founded the Black Arts Repertory Theater in Harlem, which became a major resource for the development of black culture. He also received a Guggenheim Fellowship, among others, for his writing.

Baraka's reputation rests both on his literary output and on his political importance. He began as an avant-garde Beat poet and went on to become a radical black nationalist and Marxist-Leninist. His views affected many others, particularly the young black writers Nikki GIOVANNI and Don L. Lee (later known as Hai R. Madhubuti). His plays have been produced in the United States as well as in Paris, Berlin, and Dakar, Senegal.

Some of Baraka's more recent plays include *The Motion of History, Boy and Tarzan Appear in a Clearing, Money,* and *What Was the Relationship of the Lone Ranger to the Means of Production?* (New York: Anti-Imperialist Cultural Union, 1978). His poetry collections, *Black Magic: Sabotage, Target Study* and *Black Art* are included in *Collected Poetry, 1961–1967.* More recent poetry can be found in *Afrikan Revolution: A Poem* (Newark, N.J.: Jihad Publishers, 1973); and *Reggae or Not!* (New York: Contact II Publishers, 1981). His essays are collected in *Blues People: Negro Music in White America* (New York: Morrow, 1963); *Black Music* (with Amina Baraka; New York: Morrow, 1968; and Greenwood Press, 1980); *The Music: Reflections on Jazz and Blues* (New York: Morrow, 1987), and *Daggers and Javelins: Essays, 1974–1979* (New York: Morrow, 1984).

The young LeRoi Jones attended Rutgers University in Newark; earned his B.A. from Howard University in Washington, D.C.; and later did graduate work at Columbia University and the New School for Social Research in New York City. He became a leading poet of the "Beat Generation," a literary movement based in New York and San Francisco that included such writers as Jack Kerouac and Allen Ginsberg.

In 1960, Jones visited Cuba, which had recently become a socialist nation under the leadership of Fidel Castro. This trip had a profound influence on him, and he reconsidered his lack of interest in politics. Although his political ideas were to change often, from then on he retained a strong commitment to the necessity for political change.

Throughout the early 1960s, Jones wrote and published plays and poetry. In 1964, his reputation soared with the publication of *Dutchman,* which won the Obie Award for best play produced off-Broadway. This play is the story of a middle-class black man who must fight for his identity against a white woman, Lula, who symbolizes the world of the whites.

Many feminists have criticized Jones for using a woman to symbolize evil in the white world. Writer Norman Mailer, on the other hand, called it "the best play in America." In any case, *Dutchman* was important in black theater, moving it away from strict realism to a more experimental form.

Jones gradually became disillusioned with the white people he had been working with. He began to voice this frustration in his work, and also to experiment with the literary use of African rhythms. *Blues People: Negro Music in White America* (New York: Morrow), his major study of black music in America, was published in 1963.

In 1965, the black leader Malcolm X was assassinated. This was a profound turning point in Baraka's life, and he left Greenwich Village for Harlem. Like many other black people of the time, he became a Muslim. And he, too, saw Islam as an African religion, with which to oppose European Christianity. It was now that Baraka took his African name. He later dropped the name "Imamu," which means "spiritual leader," but he kept the name "Amiri"—"blessed"—and "Baraka"—"prince."

Baraka became a black nationalist—that is, someone who believes the primary division throughout history has been between black and white people, and that white people must be seen as the enemy and black people must work as separately as possible. During this period, Baraka founded the Black Arts Repertory Theater, which became a center of black culture.

There were other Baraka works: many volumes of poetry, more plays, and essays on black music, history, and culture. Then, in the 1970s, his politics were again altered. He became a Marxist-Leninist, believing that economic divisions are more important than racial ones, and that white and black working people could find common ground and should work together for social justice.

Baraka himself described this change to the *New York Times.* He said, "It is a narrow nationalism that says the white man is the enemy." More recently Baraka's political leanings have been described as left-of-center liberal. He is a professor of African studies, at the State University of New York at Stony Brook.

Critics see Baraka in many different ways. His strong politics often make it difficult to evaluate him, since the strength of his ideas must be dealt with, along with the quality of his writing. However, most critics agree that, like it or not, Baraka has had an enormous influence on black writing of the late 20th century. In terms of literary influence, Arnold Rampersad ranks him with Phillis WHEATLEY, Frederick DOUGLASS, Paul Laurence DUNBAR, Langston HUGHES, Zora Neale HURSTON, Richard WRIGHT and Ralph ELLISON.

Further Reading: *Motion of History and Other Plays,* by Amiri Baraka, New York: Morrow, 1978; *The Autobiography of LeRoi Jones/Amiri Baraka,* by Amiri Baraka, New York: Lawrence Hill & Co., 1997; *Conversations With Amiri Baraka,* by Amiri Baraka, ed. by Charlie Reilly, Jackson, Miss.: University Press of Mississippi, 1994; *Transbluesency: The Selected Poems of Amiri Baraka/Leroi Jones (1961–1995),* by Amiri Baraka/Leroi Jones, ed. by Paul Vangelisti, New York: Marsilio Pub., 1995; *Baraka: The Renegade and the Mask,* ed. by Kimberly W. Benston, New Haven, Conn.: Yale University Press, 1976; *Imamu Amiri Baraka (Le Roi Jones): A Collection of Critical Essays,* by Kimberly W.

Benston, Englewood Cliffs, N.J.: Prentice Hall, 1978; *Amiri Baraka,* by Lloyd Brown, Boston: Twayne Publishers, 1980; *Five Black Writers: Essays on Wright, Ellison, Baldwin, Hughes, LeRoi Jones,* by Donald B. Gibson, New York: New York University Press, 1970; *Amiri Baraka: The Kaleidoscopic Torch,* ed. by James B. Gwynne, 1985; *The Poetry and Poetics of Amiri Baraka: The Jazz Aesthetic,* by William J. Harris, Columbia, Mo.: University of Missouri Press, 1985; *From LeRoi Jones to Amiri Baraka: The Literary Works,* by Theodore Hudson, 1973; *To Raise, Destroy, and Create: The Poetry, Drama, and Fiction of Imamu Amiri Baraka (LeRoi Jones),* Troy, N.Y.: Whitson Publishers, 1981.

—R. K.

❖ BARNETT, CLAUDE ALBERT
(1889–1967), *founder of the Associated Negro Press*

Claude Barnett had a startling new idea: a press service that supplied news of black people, nationally and internationally. Barnett founded the Associated Negro Press, or ANP, in 1919, in response to requests from black-owned newspapers for more news. At its height, the ANP sent news items to nearly 200 papers—95 percent of the Negro press. When the ANP went out of business in 1967, it was still serving 112 newspapers.

There were many honors in the course of Barnett's career. From 1930 to 1953, he was a consultant to the Department of Agriculture, advising the secretary on help for the black farmers in the South (until the department decided to dispense with such consultants). In 1951, Barnett was made a chevalier (knight) in Haiti's Order of Honor and Merit, and in 1952, he was named a Commander in Liberia's Star of Africa.

In addition, he served on many boards of directors, including Chicago's Supreme Liberty Life Insurance Company, Chicago's Provident Hospital (where he was chairman of the board), and the American Red Cross. At that time, there was much controversy over whether blood taken from whites and blacks should be maintained separately, so that "Negro blood" would not be given to white soldiers in the army. Barnett fought against this blatant example of segregation. He also worked with other black publishers in getting the army to unbend and allow black reporters overseas assignments, where they could cover the racial situation in the military.

Claude Barnett was born in Sandford, Florida, to William Barnett and Celena (Anderson) Barnett, but when he was only a year old, he went to live with his mother's parents in Matton, Illinois. He traveled a good deal as a child, living with relatives, attending various schools in the North and South, and graduating from college at Tuskegee Institute in Alabama, in 1906.

Barnett's first job after college was as a postal clerk in Chicago. In the post office, he came across so many interesting magazines about publishing that he decided to make it his career. He started a mail order business in 1913 for the distribution of portraits of and by black people. Then he became the advertising manager for a cosmetics company that he had helped to found.

As he traveled around the country trying to sell ads to black newspapers, he discovered that editors were concerned about their lack of access to news of black people. Thus was born Barnett's idea for the Associated Negro Press, which was originally funded by his cosmetics company. At first, the ANP gave publishers national news releases in exchange for free advertising space, but eventually, newspapers began to pay for the ANP's news.

The ANP staff of seven sent out packets of original stories two or three times a week. Its material was gathered from "stringers," or free-lance reporters, working around the United States and, eventually, in Africa and the Caribbean. Since papers in these areas also subscribed to the ANP, the service began to print African news in French as well as in English.

Barnett and his wife, actress Etta Moten, traveled frequently to Europe, the West Indies, and Africa, and they did a great deal to promote African culture in the United States. Despite his many activities, Barnett continued to run the ANP until his death of a cerebral hemorrhage in 1967.

Further Reading: *The African American Press: A History of News Coverage During National Crises, With Special Reference to Four Black Newspapers, 1827–1965,* by Charles A. Simmons, York, Pa.: McFarland & Co., 1998; *Who Was Who in America, IV, 1961–1968; The Negro Vanguard,* by Richard Bardolph, New York: Rinehart, 1961.

—R. K.

❖ BARTHÉ, RICHMOND
(1901–1989), *sculptor*

Richmond Barthé's sculpture may be found in collections of New York's Whitney Museum of American Art, the Metropolitan Museum of Art, and the Schomburg Collection of the New York Public Library. In 1946, Barthé received the first commission ever given to a black person to produce a bust for New York University's Hall of

Fame. Barthé won numerous awards for his work, including a Rosenwald Fellowship, a Guggenheim Fellowship, and membership in the National Academy of Arts and Letters. All honors were given in recognition of his outstanding artistic achievement.

Richmond Barthé was born in Bay St. Louis, a small town in Mississippi, on January 28, 1901, of African-American, French, and Indian ancestry. He first tried enrolling in art school in New Orleans, but was refused because of his color. He then succeeded in entering the Art Institute of Chicago, where he studied from 1924 to 1928.

Barthé originally chose painting, but soon found himself drawn to sculpture. In 1927, he began to attract the attention of teachers and other art experts, and soon there were commissions for his work, including a bust of the famous Haitian revolutionary, Toussaint Louverture. He was exhibited in a one-person show in Chicago, and then won a Rosenwald Fellowship for further art studies in New York.

In 1929, Barthé displayed his work in New York at the Harmon Foundation (established to support black artists), where he also exhibited in 1931 and 1933. He also participated in a show at the Whitney in 1933, and in 1939 at the World's Fair. In 1931, Barthé studied at the Art Students League in New York.

He received a Guggenheim Fellowship for 1940 to 1941. In 1947, he was one of 15 artists chosen to modernize the sculpture in U.S. Catholic churches.

Although his chief medium remained sculpture, Barthé also continued to paint in oils. His work, both powerful and moving, drew its inspiration from African art. His style is realistic; his subjects are largely taken from black history.

Some of his major works are *Shoe Shine Boy, The Boxer, Lot's Wife,* and *Booker T. Washington.* He also sculpted busts of such celebrities as Gypsy Rose Lee and John Gielgud. His bas-relief sculptures can be seen at Harlem River Houses in New York. The sculpture of the American eagle standing in front of the Social Security Building in Washington, D.C., is by Barthé.

In addition to sculpture, Barthé designed coins, including several that are still in circulation in Haiti.

Richmond Barthé eventually went to live in Pasadena, California. He died there, at home, in 1989, at the age of 88.

Further Reading: *Modern Negro Art,* by James A. Porter, New York: Arno Press, 1969 reprint of 1943 ed.; *The Negro Vanguard,* by Richard Bardolph, New York: Rinehart, 1961.

—*R. K.*

❖ BASSETT, EBENEZER DON CARLOS
(1833–1908), *America's first black diplomat*

When Ebenezer Bassett was appointed minister to Haiti and the Dominican Republic by President Ulyssess S. Grant in 1869, he became the first black diplomat in U.S. history. Bassett served in Haiti for the eight years of Grant's two terms. During that time, he was highly regarded for his tact and skill. Frederick DOUGLASS, ex-slave and fierce abolitionist, wrote that Secretary of State Hamilton Fish said "he wished one-half of his ministers abroad performed their duties as well as Mr. Bassett."

After acting as U.S. representative to Haiti, Bassett went on to serve as Haitian representative to the U.S. From 1879 to 1888, Bassett was the Haitian consul general in New York. When Frederick Douglass was appointed minister to Haiti and the Dominican Republic in 1889, Bassett accompanied him as secretary and interpreter.

In the 1900s, Bassett again worked in the Haitian consul general's office in New York, and during this period, he wrote *A Handbook on Haiti* for the Pan American Union. This publication brought him membership in the American Geographical Society.

Bassett was born in Litchfield, Connecticut, to Tobias Bassett, a man of mixed race, and Susan Gregory, a Pequot Indian. He was unusually well educated for a black child in the days of slavery, graduating with honors from the Connecticut State Normal School before going on to Yale University.

Bassett's studies at Yale are all the more impressive in that he attended while serving as principal of a high school in Pennsylvania. From 1857 to 1869, he headed a Quaker school, the Institute for Colored Youth in Philadelphia. His, then, was an extraordinary commute between New Haven, Connecticut, and Philadelphia.

The institute was designed to prepare black youth as teachers. Referring to Bassett's leadership, the mayor of Philadelphia said the school was "widely known and unquestionably the foremost institution of its kind in the country."

Before going to the institute, Bassett had married Eliza Park, with whom he had five children.

Bassett was held in such high regard by his Yale professors and other prominent citizens that they wrote to President Grant, urging his appointment to the ministerial position in Haiti.

This was a time when the Haitian post was a difficult one, requiring great diplomatic skill. The United States was trying to annex the Dominican Republic, a strategy opposed by the Haitian government. They were extremely uneasy about possible American plans to annex Haiti—fears that were fed by U.S. interest in obtaining a coaling station (to fuel part of its naval fleet) at the Haitian port of Môle St.-Nicolas.

Bassett handled this delicate situation with success, for the United States made no overt annexation attempts while he was minister, and the Haitians so appreciated him that he was appointed their consul when he returned to New York. Thus Bassett spent most of the years from 1869 through the early 1900s in various diplomatic assignments involving Haiti.

The last years of Bassett's life were spent in ill health, involving symptoms that had only appeared after his departure from Haiti in 1879. He evidently suffered from the tropical diseases of dengue or malaria, or both. In 1894, Bassett wrote to his old friend Frederick Douglass, complaining of a heart condition and problems with his eyes.

Bassett was replying to a rather unpleasant letter from Douglass. Bassett was asked to repay a loan, and to reply to a rumor that he had accepted a bribe to influence decisions made by Douglass as minister. This letter paints a sad picture of Bassett's last years, which were spent in poverty and obscurity with his family in Philadelphia.

Further Reading: "America's First Black Diplomat," by Nancy Gordon Heinl, *Foreign Service Journal,* August, 1973, pp. 20–22; "Diplomats to Haiti and Their Diplomacy," by James A. Padgett, *Journal of Negro History,* XXV, July, 1940, pp. 265–330; *The Diplomatic Relations of the United States with Haiti, 1776–1891,* by Rayford W. Logan, Chapel Hill, N.C.: University of North Carolina Press, 1941.

—*R. K.*

✦ BEARDEN, FRED ROMARE HOWARD
(1914–1988), *artist*

A leading innovator in 20th-century American art, Romare Bearden was renowned for collages and paintings that brought new vision to the African-American experience. In addition to the work he created, he also exerted a powerful influence on American culture by studying and promoting the work of other artists.

Romare Bearden was born in Charlotte, North Carolina, on September 2, 1914. He grew up in a comfortable home established by three generations of hardworking ancestors. Despite their achievements, however, the Beardens were still subjected to the harsh discrimina-

tion that prevailed in the South during the early 1900s. When Bearden was nine years old, his parents decided they had had enough; they packed their belongings and headed north. After living in Canada for a time, they moved to New York and settled in Harlem. This was the era of the Harlem Renaissance, when African-American writers, artists, and musicians were coming into their own, and the Beardens were right in the middle of it. Their apartment on West 131st Street welcomed a steady stream of illustrious visitors, ranging from Duke ELLING-TON to Paul ROBESON. This dazzling atmosphere, and the intellectual influence of his mother, Bessye, had a powerful influence on Bearden's development.

An outstanding baseball player and a talented student, Bearden attended Lincoln and Boston Universities before returning home to finish his studies at New York University. He had once thought of becoming a doctor, but by the time he graduated with a degree in mathematics in 1935, he was totally committed to being an artist. His first move was to join both the Harlem Artists Guild and a more informal group known as 306 (after 306 West 141st Street, their gathering place). Providing one another with stimulation and moral support, Bearden and his comrades tackled the realities of African-American life, facing a world where the glitter of the Harlem Renaissance had given way to the gloom of the Great Depression.

In order to support himself, Bearden took a job as a caseworker with the New York City Department of Welfare. He found a studio on 125th Street and began to paint; in some canvases he depicted the life he saw around him, while in others he drew on his memories of North Carolina. By 1940, Bearden's work had gained solid recognition, meriting a solo exhibition at 306 and a prominent place in a group show at the Downtown Gallery.

After serving in the U.S. Army during World War II, Bearden returned to his studio. He began moving away from the realism of his early works and experimented with vibrant colors and abstract forms. But he had difficulty finding a style that suited him, and eventually he began to doubt his own ability. The low point came in 1953, when Bearden suffered a nervous breakdown and had to be hospitalized. Bearden's personal and artistic revival began in 1954, when he married Nanette Rohan. Rohan believed in Bearden's talent and gave him the confidence to move forward.

In the years following his marriage, Bearden began creating collages, using images clipped from magazines and newspapers to construct dramatic and colorful scenes. He then photographed his collages and enlarged them to monumental size, producing a powerful effect on the viewer. One of Bearden's greatest works was *Projections* (1964), a series of immense collages that depicted the realities of life in an African-American neighborhood. By the late 1960s, Bearden was selling enough work to quit his civil-service job and become a full-time artist. During the next several years he produced notable works—such as *The Block* (1970), the *Odysseus* series (1977), and the *Jazz* series (1980)—that made him world famous. He began to receive numerous awards and honors, including a Guggenheim Fellowship, a solo exhibition at the Museum of Modern Art, and election to the National Institute of Arts and Letters.

Bearden used his prestige and contacts to help numerous other artists. In 1969, for example, he teamed up with Ernest Crichlow and Norman Lewis to create the Cinque Gallery, a nonprofit organization that fosters the work of African-American painters and sculptors. Despite his tremendous creative energy, Bearden's health began to decline in the late 1980s—in March 1988, only a few months after receiving the National Medal of Arts at the White House, Bearden died of cancer.

Further Reading: *Romare Bearden: His Life and Art,* by Myron Schwartzman, New York: Abrams, 1990; *The Art of Romare Bearden,* by M. Bunch Washington, New York: Abrams, 1973; *A History of African-American Artists: From 1792 to the Present,* by Romare Bearden and Harry Henderson, New York: Pantheon, 1993.

—*P. K.*

❖ BECKWOURTH, JAMES PIERSON
(Beckwirth)
(1798–1866), *explorer, trader, scout, trapper*

James Beckwourth scouted for years for fur companies and, notably, for the exploratory expedition of General John Charles Frémont, leading to his discovery of an important pass in the Sierra Nevada mountain range of California. Beckwourth Pass was later used by many pioneers heading west.

Beckwourth also lived as a "mountain man," and made friends with the Indian nation of the Crow. His own story relates that he became a chief of the Crow and served as a mediator between them and the U.S. government in 1866. His life has been called "unbelievable in many respects, but true." Like another mountain man, Kit Carson, and other famous explorers, he became a part of American mythology as well as the history of American exploration of the West.

James Beckwourth *(Marquette University Archives)*

The major source of information on Beckwourth is his autobiography. Although many of the stories about him are conflicting, the following account is believed to be valid:

James Beckwourth was born in Fredericksburg, Virginia, on April 16, 1798, the son of a white Revolutionary War veteran and an African-American woman, perhaps a slave. As a child, he was given some schooling and then apprenticed to a blacksmith, but he ran away to New Orleans. There he faced racial discrimination, which he refused to accept, so he signed up as a scout for the 1823 and 1824 expeditions of General William Henry Ashley's Rocky Mountain Fur Company.

For the next 13 years, Beckwourth was a mountain man. During this time, he was accepted by and taken into the Blackfoot and Crow Indian nations.

In 1837, Beckwourth left life among the Native Americans and went to St. Louis. But he soon quit the city again for the Second Seminole War, which ended in 1842. Then he remained in the wilds, building and operating several trading posts in places that included the headwaters of the Arkansas and South Platte Rivers, St. Fernandez (today's city of Taos, New Mexico), and Pueblo de Angeles (today's city of Los Angeles).

Beckwourth continued soldiering, both in the 1846 California uprising against Mexico and the 1846–48

Mexican War. In that war, he acted as guide and dispatch carrier for General Stephen Kearny. It was after the war ended in 1848 that he made his important discovery in the Sierra Nevada of what would later be called the Beckwourth Pass, between California's Feather and Truckee Rivers.

The facts of his death are somewhat obscure. We know that he was living with the Crow in 1866, trying to help carry out the policies of the U.S. government there. An account has it that the Crow insisted Beckwourth stay with them, and when he refused, they poisoned him. The Crow side of the story, however, is not available.

Regardless of how James Beckwourth died, his life remains a fascinating and significant episode in American history.

Further Reading: *Mountain Man, Indian Chief,* by J. P. Beckwourth, New York: Harcourt, Brace, 1968 ed.; *The Life and Adventures of James P. Beckwourth,* by J. P. Beckwourth, New York: Arno Press, 1969 ed.; *Jim Beckwourth: Black Mountain Man and War Chief of the Crows,* by Elinor Wilson, Norman, Okla.: University of Oklahoma Press, 1972.

—*R. K.*

✤ BELAFONTE, HAROLD GEORGE, JR.
("Harry")
(1927–   ), *singer, actor, humanitarian*

One of the most successful American performers of the 1950s and 1960s, Harry Belafonte created new opportunities for other African-American artists. In addition to his achievements as an entertainer, he has been a lifelong champion of equal rights and has devoted enormous amounts time and money to humanitarian causes around the world.

Belafonte was born in New York City on March 1, 1927. His father, Harold, Sr., was a native of Martinique, and his mother, Melvine, had been born in Jamaica. In 1935, when rioting broke out in Harlem, the Belafontes moved to Jamaica and remained there for five years. After attending high school in New York, Belafonte dropped out in 1944 and joined the U.S. Navy for a two-year hitch. He then took advantage of the educational benefits offered by the G.I. Bill of Rights and began to study acting. In 1948, Belafonte joined the American Negro Theater (ANT), an influential group formed in Harlem in 1940. Though he performed in several ANT productions, Belafonte decided that racial stereotyping would limit the roles available to him in the theater. He branched out into singing, making his first appearance at a nightclub called the Royal Roost in 1949.

After singing popular songs on the nightclub circuit for a year, Belafonte became a successful folk singer, playing the Village Vanguard and other top-rank clubs. His growing popularity opened new opportunities. Belafonte appeared on Broadway in *John Murray Anderson's Almanac* in 1953, winning a Tony Award, and the following year he toured with Marge and Gower Champion in *Three for Tonight.* In 1954, when Belafonte starred with Dorothy Dandridge in *Carmen Jones,* moviegoers were captivated by his charm and good looks, and he became the nation's first black matinee idol. Other notable Belafonte films include *Island in the Sun* (1957); *The World, the Flesh, and the Devil* (1959); *Buck and the Preacher* (1971); and *Uptown Saturday Night* (1974).

Belafonte achieved his greatest acclaim as a singer in the mid-1950s, when he began performing the West Indian calypso songs he learned as a youngster. His renditions of songs such as "Matilda," "Jamaica Farewell," "Brown Skin Girl," and "Banana Boat Song" were collected in the 1956 album *Calypso,* which created a calypso craze in the United States and became the first solo album in history to sell more than a million copies. During the following decade, Belafonte recorded 11 more albums and gave numerous concerts. In 1960, he became the first African American to star in a TV special, earning an Emmy Award for his efforts. He also formed his own production company, Harbel, which undertook a variety of television and movie projects.

From the 1950s on, the Civil Rights movement played a major role in Belafonte's life. He became a close friend and ally of Rev. Martin Luther King, Jr., who stayed in Belafonte's huge Upper West Side apartment whenever he was in New York. Belafonte's activities included fundraising for civil rights campaigns, taking part in strategy sessions, and using his prestige and contacts to educate government officials. He refused to perform in the South until segregation was abolished, and he was instrumental in creating the Southern Free Theater in Jackson, Mississippi.

During the 1980s and 1990s, Belafonte turned his attention to human rights causes throughout the world. He devoted a great deal of effort to aiding victims of famine in Africa. (It was Belafonte who inspired Michael Jackson and Lionel Richie to record "We Are the World" and donate the proceeds to needy Africans.) In recognition of his efforts, Belafonte was appointed goodwill ambassador for the United Nations Children's Fund (UNICEF) in 1986. In 1990, when the South African freedom fighter Nelson Mandela visited the United States, Belafonte served as chairperson of the welcoming committee. He continued to perform throughout these years, often appearing with African musicians.

Belafonte's contributions to the arts and society have earned him numerous awards, including an honorary doctorate from Spelman College in 1990 and the National Medal of Arts in 1994. He has also had the satisfaction of seeing his daughter Shari enjoy a successful career as a model and actress.

Further Reading: "Belafonte's Balancing Act," in *Thirteen Ways of Looking at a Black Man,* by Henry Louis Gates, Jr., New York: Random House, 1997; *Belafonte: An Unauthorized Biography,* by Arnold Shaw, Philadelphia: Chilton, 1960.

—P. K.

❖ BETHUNE, MARY JANE McLEOD

(1875–1955), *educator, civil-rights leader, adviser to presidents, government official*

Mary McLeod Bethune began as a teacher, then went on to create the Daytona Normal and Industrial School, now Bethune-Cookman College, in Daytona, Florida. It took her 20 years to build this school, during which time she won national attention. She became a vice president of the National Urban League in 1920, served as president of the National Association of Colored Women from 1924 to 1928, and established the National Council of Negro Women in 1935.

The New Deal administration of Franklin D. Roosevelt welcomed Bethune's participation as director of the Division of Minority Affairs under the National Youth Administration from 1936 to 1943. In 1945, she was a special representative of the State Department at the founding conference of the United Nations. In the same year, she served as special assistant to the Secretary of War for the selection of candidates for the Women's Army Corps.

Mary McLeod was born on July 10, 1875, into a small farm family that, although poor by material standards, became a symbol of stability in the black community of Mayesville, South Carolina. Her parents, former slaves, gathered together their surviving 14 children from the plantations to which they had been sold and focused their energies on seeing that Mary, their 15th child, would be educated.

The young Mary studied at Concord, North Carolina's Scotia Seminary, and at the Institute for Home and Foreign Missions of evangelist Dwight Moody in

Mary McLeod Bethune (*Library of Congress*)

Chicago. It was while she was teaching at Haines Institute in Augusta, Georgia, and only 20 years old, that she decided her life's goal would be the education of black people.

In 1897, she married Albertus Bethune. When their son was only six months old, she accepted another teaching position—in Palatka, Florida, where she became interested in the problems of the African-American railroad workers, particularly the absence of schooling for their children. In 1904, she and her son joined them in Daytona Beach. With only $1.50, but armed with determination, she founded the Daytona Normal and Industrial School for Negro Girls.

Bethune succeeded in building this school and other community institutions as well: a hospital for local black residents (after her students were refused service at the white hospital) and a series of mission schools in the logging camps around Daytona where turpentine was manufactured. She also formed a singing group that visited jails and local hotels. In 1920, Bethune organized a campaign in the local black community to vote for municipal services, despite the active opposition of the Ku Klux Klan.

Because there was always the need for money to fund the school and her other projects, Bethune traveled widely and recruited support from other black leaders, such as Booker T. WASHINGTON and Mary Church TER-

RELL of the National Association of Colored Women. Her growing prominence led to an appointment to the National Child Welfare Commission during the Coolidge and Hoover administrations, and to her work in Washington under the Roosevelt administration.

Bethune had a reputation for refusing to answer to "Auntie" or any other demeaning terms for black women. When she was at Johns Hopkins Hospital in 1940 for a sinus operation, she demanded that black doctors be allowed to observe the operation—a first for that hospital.

In her final years, she continued to travel and to publish in newspapers and in anthologies.

Further Reading: *Mary McLeod Bethune/Educator,* by Bernice Anderson Poole, Los Angeles, Calif.: Holloway House Pub. Co., 1994; *Mary McLeod Bethune,* by Catherine Owens Peare, New York: Vanguard Press, 1951; *Mary McLeod Bethune, a Biography,* by Rackham Holt, Garden City, N.Y.: Doubleday, 1964; *Mary McLeod Bethune,* by Emma Gelders Sterne, New York: Knopf, 1957.

—R. K.

❖ BINGA, JESSE
(1865–1950), *banker, realtor, financier*

By the turn of the century, Jesse Binga had built a financial empire on the South Side of Chicago, amassing a fortune through the buying, selling, and renting of real estate to black people. With the profits, he opened the Binga State Bank in 1908, which at its height held nearly $1.5 million in deposits. But like many others during the Depression, the bank was closed in 1932 for lack of funds, and Binga went to prison for financial mismanagement. Later, however, there would be a presidential pardon.

Jesse Binga was the youngest of 10 children, born in Detroit to a Canadian barber, William Binga, and an American mother, Adelphia (Lewis) Binga. In 1912, Binga married Eudora Johnson. Eudora's uncle left his niece nearly a quarter of a million dollars, which Binga used as the basis of his business.

However, even before his marriage, Binga had already become one of the most successful black realtors in Chicago. By 1926, he owned more property fronting on Chicago's famed State Street below 12th Street than any other person, black or white.

To expand the black real estate market, Binga pushed for opening white neighborhoods to black people, although he faced strong white protest. He eventu-ally became known as the financial wizard of the South Side. His private bank, opened in 1908, became the Binga State Bank in 1921. The Chicago black community patronized his bank, bringing deposits up in three years from $300,000 to $1,153,000.

Binga clearly enjoyed making money but also saw himself as providing a service. At that time, the large white banks of Chicago frequently discriminated against black customers. Black people could only borrow money from loan sharks, small-time criminals who lent money at huge interest rates. Now they had an alternative—Binga's bank.

But after the stock market crash of October 1929, which brought on the Great Depression, Binga ran into the same financial difficulties as many other small bankers. In addition to the general economic problems, Binga had made some unwise decisions and possibly had practiced some illegal activities, such as not keeping adequate reserves of money on hand. Finally, he was convicted of embezzling $22,000.

Some African Americans resented Binga, feeling that he had stolen from the community. Others thought he had been punished unfairly and successfully petitioned for Binga's release in 1938.

The former realtor worked as a handyman at St. Anselm's Catholic Church until his death on June 14, 1950. He died penniless.

Further Reading: *The Negro as Capitalist,* by Abram L. Harris, Philadelphia, Pa.: American Academy of Political and Social Science, 1936; "The Rise and Fall of Jesse Binga, Black Banker," by Carl R. Osthaus, *Journal of Negro History,* January 1973, pp. 39–60.

—R. K.

❖ BLAKE, JAMES HUBERT ("Eubie")
(1883–1983), *composer, songwriter*

Eubie Blake, born in Baltimore, Maryland, on February 7, 1883, was one of the most enduring figures in American musical theater. He was the composer of such songs as "I'm Just Wild about Harry" and "Love Will Find a Way," songs that are still classic jazz and pop standards. In the 1920s, he wrote the scores of several long-running Broadway hits. His 1976 score, *Bubbling Brown Sugar,* was also a hit.

Blake won numerous awards and honors from a wide range of musical, theater, and civic groups. He received honorary doctorates from Brooklyn College in New York, Dartmouth College in New Hampshire, Rutgers University in New Jersey, and the New England Conservatory of Music in Massachusetts. In 1972, at 89, he started his own record company. In 1978, Broadway saw yet another hit—*Eubie*—a revue based on Blake's music.

The young James Hubert Blake began playing his family's pump organ before he was six years old. At six, there were piano lessons, and his musical study continued for the rest of his life.

In 1898, when he was only 15, Blake began his professional musical career. Like most black musicians of the time, he played in honky-tonks, bars, and brothels, developing the "ragtime" style of the 1890s. Much of American music sprang from this form, both jazz and popular song styles. Throughout this early part of his career, Blake met the major musicians of the time.

In 1915, Blake met his songwriting partner, Noble Sissle, and they formed a vaudeville act. (Vaudeville was a popular entertainment of the time. Like today's variety shows, it featured a series of performers singing, playing music, dancing, or telling jokes.) Blake and Sissle wrote songs and performed. Their first song, "It's All Your Fault," performed by white singer Sophie Tucker, was an instant success.

By 1920, Blake and Sissle decided they were ready for another kind of performance. They teamed up with another vaudeville pair and produced the Broadway musical *Shuffle Along*.

Because *Shuffle Along* was so successful, it started a trend of Broadway shows featuring African-American performers. In 1921, there were three companies of the show touring the country simultaneously. *Shuffle Along* also featured great artists, many of whom later became famous: Josephine Baker, Florence Mills, and Paul ROBESON, to name a few.

Blake continued to write hit Broadway shows, including *The Chocolate Dandies,* 1924; *Blackbirds of 1930; Shuffle Along of 1933; Swing It,* 1937; and *Shuffle Along of 1952.* Blake and Sissle also wrote and performed in Britain.

After World War II, Blake retired temporarily. But in the 1950s, ragtime became popular once more. Now Blake had a new career. He played ragtime piano and lectured about that music, touring worldwide and appearing frequently on radio and television.

Blake recorded his music throughout his life. In 1969, he made an album called *The Eighty-Six Years of Eubie Blake.* When he formed his own company in 1972, he issued recordings of himself and others. In 1981, he was awarded the Presidential Medal of Freedom.

Further Reading: *Eubie Blake: Keys of Memory,* by Lawrence Carter, Detroit: Balamp Publishers, 1979; *Reminiscing*

with Sissle and Blake, by Robert Kimball and William Bolcom, New York: Viking, 1972; *Eubie Blake,* by Al Rose, New York: Schirmer Books, 1979.

—*R. K.*

❖ BLAND, JAMES
(1854–1911), *composer, minstrel performer*

James Bland was a member of the first all-black group of minstrel performers, the Georgia Minstrels. He performed in various minstrel shows throughout the United States and in Europe. In England he became known as "The Idol of the Music Halls" and gave command performances for Queen Victoria and the Prince of Wales.

Bland also wrote songs for his performances, including the well-known "Carry Me Back to Old Virginny," which in 1940 became Virginia's official state song. Bland was supposedly one of only three American composers known in Germany, along with Stephen Foster and John Philip Sousa. Many of Bland's songs are extremely well known, including "Oh, Dem Golden Slippers," "In the Evening by the Moonlight," and "The Missouri Hound Dog." What is less well known is that their composer was a black person.

Bland's music has also been used more than most people are aware. The opening bars of "In the Evening . . ." are note-for-note identical with the opening chorus of "There's a Long, Long Trail a-Winding," the popular World War I song, suggesting that the composer of "Long, Long Trail" was imitating Bland, to say the least. Other Bland tunes have been used as background music in film, radio, and television, as well as for campaign songs.

James Bland was born in 1854 in the borough of Queens, New York City. Although this was a time of slavery, both his parents were free-born. His father, Allen Bland, was particularly ambitious. He had studied with Daniel Alexander Payne, who became bishop of the African Methodist Episcopal Church and later founded Wilberforce University in Ohio. Allen Bland went on to study at Ohio's Oberlin College, and then graduated from Wilberforce, after which he worked as the first black examiner in the U.S. Patent Office. He accomplished all this while working for a law degree from Howard University in Washington, D.C. Thus, James grew up in the nation's capital as his father studied there.

Allen wished his son to follow in his footsteps at Howard, and James did study briefly there, but had little interest in the law. His time at Howard actually inspired him to seek a musical career. While at the university, he heard and was drawn to the folk songs and spirituals sung by the ex-slaves working on campus. He taught himself to play the banjo and began to play in houses and private clubs, as well as to compose. About this time, he met John Philip Sousa, who was later to become a famous band conductor and composer and who would arrange some of Bland's songs for his U.S. Marine Band.

In the late 1870s, Bland performed as a black minstrel. Until the post–Civil War era, minstrel shows had been an all-white entertainment. In 1843, during the period of slave ownership when such shows were first presented, white people made themselves up in blackface with enormous red lips and white makeup around their eyes, in crude caricatures of what they imagined "Negroes" to look like. Then they sang and told jokes in "Negro" dialect.

When black people began portraying themselves in minstrel shows, around the time of slavery's abolition in America, they too followed this pattern. They put on black makeup and painted their lips in exaggeration. They also used dialect, slapstick, comic songs, and stylized dances. However, they also developed distinctive American dance styles, including stop-time, the buck and wing, and the jig.

The Georgia Minstrels, founded in 1865, was the first successful all-black minstrel troupe. Bland joined the troupe in 1878, the same year that he published "Carry Me Back to Old Virginny." Bland wrote that song while visiting the parents of Mamie Friend, whom he later married.

The Georgia Minstrels soon became a major production that toured the United States and Europe, and met with spectacular success. Meanwhile, Bland had written "Oh, Dem Golden Slippers" for the show, a song which by 1880 had sold 100,000 copies.

Bland's stay in Britain was from 1881 to 1901, although he made a few visits to the United States. Finally, however, he came home, only to find that the minstrel craze had died out. It had been replaced by vaudeville. Instead of a line of men in blackface, all sitting on stage together, telling jokes, singing songs, and dancing, vaudeville now had both black and white performers who came out on stage one at a time to perform their acts.

When Bland returned to Washington, D.C., in 1910, he was penniless. Although 30 years earlier he had had many prominent friends there, now he knew almost no one. Two of his sisters were still alive, but he had lost touch with them during the years of his success. Bland did meet up again with a childhood friend, William

Silence, who let him use a desk in his law office. There, Bland wrote a musical, *The Sporting Girl,* which he sold for $250, marking the end of his composing career.

In 1911, Bland tried joining a troupe in Philadelphia, but he was tired and discouraged. Alone, without friends, he died of tuberculosis there on May 5, 1911. His songs are still popular, and in 1946, a memorial tombstone was erected honoring the composer of "Carry Me Back to Old Virginny."

Further Reading: *Famous Men of Flushing,* by Charles Haywood, Flushing, N.Y.: Flushing Historical Society, 1944; *The James A. Bland Album of Outstanding Songs: A Collection for Voice and Piano,* compiled, edited, and arranged by Charles Haywood, New York: Edward B. Marks Music Corp., 1946; *A Song in His Heart,* by John J. Daly, Philadelphia, Pa.: Winston, 1951; *The Music of Black Americans: A History,* by Eileen Southern, New York: W.W. Norton, 1971.

—R. K.

❖ BONTEMPS, ARNA
(1902–1973), *writer*

Arna Bontemps was one of the most prolific black writers of the 20th century. There are more than 25 books to his credit, including fiction, drama, poetry, criticism, history, and biography. He wrote many books for young people, focusing on black history, culture, and folklore.

Bontemps was one of the key figures of the Harlem Renaissance, that period in the 1920s when black culture flourished. Bontemps worked with such major writers as Langston HUGHES, Claude MCKAY, and Countée CULLEN. As the last survivor of that group, his memoirs and reminiscences of the Harlem Renaissance have been invaluable to historians. His anthologies and introductions to the works of other black authors have helped define the study of black American literature.

Arna Bontemps was born on October 13, 1902, in Alexandria, Louisiana, the son of Paul Bismark Bontemps, a brick mason, and Maria Caroline (Pembrooke) Bontemps, a schoolteacher. He got his B.A. in 1923 at Pacific Union College in California and began work himself as a teacher. In the 1920s, he taught school in New York. He also taught in Huntsville, Alabama, and Chicago. His career as a public school teacher lasted until 1938.

In 1926, Bontemps married Alberta Johnson, with whom he had six children. Also in 1926, he won the poetry prize from *Crisis* magazine, the publication edited

Arna Bontemps (*Library of Congress*)

Bontemps also wrote many histories and biographies of key black figures, with young reading audiences in mind.

In 1943, the Harlem Renaissance was well over, and Bontemps went to the University of Chicago to receive his M.A. He then became a librarian at Fisk University in Tennessee, where he worked until 1965. The following year, he went to the University of Illinois, where he taught until 1969.

Bontemps spent a year at Yale, curating the James Weldon JOHNSON collection. James Weldon Johnson was a major African-American writer of the early 20th century. Then he returned to Fisk, where he worked as a writer in residence until his death on June 4, 1973.

Throughout his life, Bontemps never stopped writing and editing. His 1972 book, *The Harlem Renaissance Remembered: Essays* (New York: Dodd, Mead), is a colorful portrait of New York in the 1920s. His fiction appears in many anthologies, as well as in collections of his own works.

Further Reading: *Black Literature in America,* by Houston A. Baker, Jr., 1971; *The Negro Novel in America,* by Robert A. Bone, New York: McGraw-Hill; *Arna Bontemps-Langston Hughes Letters, 1925–1967,* ed. by Charles H. Nichols, New York: Dodd, Mead, 1980.

—R. K.

✤ BROOKE, EDWARD WILLIAM
(1919–), U.S. Senator

When Edward Brooke was elected to the U.S. Senate in 1966, he became the first black U.S. Senator since the Reconstruction Era of the 1860s and the first elected by popular vote.

Before he became a senator, Brooke had a distinguished career in Massachusetts politics. He served two terms as state attorney general, although he was a Republican at a time when Republicans were losing elections both in Massachusetts and across the nation.

Brooke has won a number of awards, including the Charles Evans Hughes Gold Medal Award given by the National Conference of Christians and Jews for humanitarian leadership, and the NAACP's Spingarn Medal for black achievement, which he received in 1967.

Edward Brooke was born on October 26, 1919, in Washington, D.C., the son of Edward W. Brooke, a lawyer for the Veterans Administration, and Helen (Seldon) Brooke. When Brooke grew up in the 1920s and 1930s, Washington, D.C., was still rigidly segre-

by W. E. B. DUBOIS for the National Association for the Advancement of Colored People (NAACP). In 1926 and 1927, he won the Alexander Pushkin poetry prize as well, which established him as a successful poet.

Throughout the next 30 years, Bontemps continued to write. His novel, *God Sends Sunday* (New York: AMS Press, 1972 reprint of 1931 ed.), was first published in 1931, and was reprinted in 1972. He and poet Countée Cullen later turned the book into a successful Broadway play, *St. Louis Woman,* which opened in 1946.

Bontemps's first anthology appeared in 1941. *Golden Slippers: An Anthology of Negro Poetry for Young Readers* (New York: Harper & Row) was a milestone book, proving that poetry by African Americans was worth reading and teaching to young people.

Bontemps later edited several more anthologies of poetry primarily for adults, sometimes collaborating with such authors of distinction as Langston Hughes. These were volumes that helped make poetry by African Americans available to a wider public. They also demonstrated that black writers were working within a tradition that came out of their own culture, rather than as isolated authors trying to "break into" the white literary world.

gated. Brooke attended Washington's all-black Dunbar High School, a school noted for the many students it graduated who went on to professional fields.

Brooke took up pre-med studies at Howard University in Washington, D.C., and when he graduated from Howard in 1941, Brooke was drafted by the U.S. Army as a second lieutenant and assigned to an all-black regiment at Fort Devens, Massachusetts. According to custom, Brooke and other young officers were given the duty of defending enlisted men accused of various crimes. This early experience was important later in Brooke's decision to become a lawyer.

Meanwhile, however, World War II continued, and Brooke was sent into combat duty in Italy. There he distinguished himself with his knowledge of Italian and his ability to work with Italian partisan guerrillas behind the lines. After the war in Europe was over, Brooke took a brief Italian vacation and met Remigia Ferrari-Scacco, the daughter of a paper merchant.

Brooke decided to go into law and in 1946, he enrolled in Boston University Law School. Until that time, Brooke had lived, worked, and gone to school almost exclusively with African Americans.

Edward Brooke (*Library of Congress*)

Now, however, he was one of the few black students at B.U., and was living in an Italian-American neighborhood. Brooke accommodated himself to this new situation, which was to continue for much of the rest of his life.

Brooke had kept up a correspondence with Ferrari-Scacco, and when he proposed to her by mail, she accepted. In 1947, the two were married and went to live in Roxbury, Boston's predominately African-American neighborhood. The couple later had two children and moved to Newton, a wealthy white neighborhood.

Brooke was an excellent student at B.U., becoming an editor of the *Law Review* and earning his master's in law by 1950.

At this time, Brooke was fairly apolitical. At age 30, he had never voted. But in 1950, he filed for both Democratic and Republican primaries to run for state representative from Roxbury.

Brooke won the Republican nomination and remained in that party. Although one might think that a black candidate would be successful in a black district, he lost the election—and lost again in 1952. Some observers believed that his marriage to a white woman hurt him with people of both races.

In 1960, however, Brooke was urged to run for Massachusetts secretary of the commonwealth. Although he lost that election, too, it was by such a small margin that he continued to pursue his political ambitions. In 1962, he ran for state attorney general—and won.

Brooke served two terms as attorney general, from 1962 through 1966, then ran for the Senate in 1966; he won 62 percent of the nearly 2 million votes cast. He had probably been helped by the earlier publication of his book, *The Challenge of Change* (Boston: Little, Brown, 1966), in which he called on the Republican Party to become more responsive to social change.

Brooke served two terms as U.S. Senator. He was defeated in 1978 and went into private practice.

—R. K.

❖ BROOKS, GWENDOLYN
(1917–2000), *poet*

Gwendolyn Brooks was the first African-American recipient of a Pulitzer Prize, which she won in 1950 for her second book of poetry, *Annie Allen* (Westport, Conn.: Greenwood Press). She has received much recognition for her work, including membership in the National Academy of Arts and Letters and selection as the first

African-American woman poetry consultant to the Library of Congress.

Brooks became Carl Sandburg's successor as poet laureate of Illinois. Although she is best known for her 15 books of poetry, she has also written a distinguished novel, *Maud Martha.*

Gwendolyn Brooks was born on June 7, 1917, in Topeka, Kansas. She was the daughter of David Anderson Brooks and Keziah Corinne (Wims) Brooks. As a young woman, she worked as publicity director for the National Association for the Advancement of Colored People (NAACP) Youth Council in Chicago after graduating from Wilson Junior College. In 1939, Brooks married Henry Lowington Blakely, with whom she had two children.

Brooks published her first book of poetry, *A Street in Bronzeville* (New York: Harper & Bros.), in 1945. In the same year, *Mademoiselle* magazine named her one of 10 "Women of the Year." Her writing brought several grants and fellowships, which enabled her to publish *Annie Allen* in 1949.

The poems in these first two books centered on poor black people living in cities. Karen Kennerly, executive director of PEN, the prestigious writers group, has called Brooks "a classic writer of African-American poetry, and one of our best poets. She is one of the first American poets to use black speech in an artful way, and she has remained a master."

Brooks's next book was a novel, *Maud Martha* (New York: AMS Press, 1974), a portrait of a ghetto woman who in the book's beginning believes that she is ugly but eventually manages to stand up for herself and protect her dignity.

After her novel, Brooks published two more books of poetry, *The Bean Eaters* (New York: Harper, 1960) and *In the Time of Detachment, In the Time of Cold* (Springfield, Ill.: The Civil War Centennial Commission of Illinois, 1965).

Brooks's earlier books relate to race primarily by her portrayal of black subjects, but her later books embrace the topic in a more political way. Brooks says that this change in her writing was partly caused by a 1967 conference she attended at Fisk University in Tennessee. As Brooks described the experience, "The poets among them felt that blacks should write as blacks, about blacks, and address themselves *to* blacks." The first book Brooks wrote from this new perspective, *In the Mecca* (New York: Harper & Row), was published in 1968.

As Brooks became more interested in young black writers, she decided to leave the major publishing house,

Harper & Row, that had published many of her books. Instead, she published her poetry with Broadside Press, headed by black editor and writer Dudley Randall. Brooks also gave Broadside the first volume of her autobiography, *Report from Part One* (Detroit: Broadside Press), which came out in 1972.

Brooks later published with Third World Press, which was run by Haki R. Madhubuti (formerly Don L. Lee), another young black poet. She now publishes with The David Company, a small black press.

To some extent, Brooks's reputation suffered from her dedication to black presses, since works published by them were less widely reviewed and distributed. In any case, reviewers often criticized the political content of Brooks's poems, and a critic once accused her of "celebrating violence."

Brooks always emphasized that her writing might be "*to* Blacks," but that it was "*for* anyone who wants to open the book." Many critics praised Brooks's generous, objective work, which gives space to all people.

Throughout her career, Brooks taught poetry at numerous colleges and universities, including Chicago Teacher's College and the University of Wisconsin at Madison. In 1971, she was a Distinguished Professor of the Arts at City College of the City University of New York.

Brooks's dedication to young poets was such a high priority for her that over recent decades, she contributed $2,000 to sponsor a competition and award prizes to 10 high-school poets and 10 grade-school poets. In 1994 Brooks was honored by the National Book Foundation for distinguished contributions to American letters. Brooks died at the age of 83 on December 3, 2000.

Brooks's work has been collected in *Selected Poems* (New York: Harper & Row), published in 1963; *The World of Gwendolyn Brooks* (New York: Harper & Row, 1971); and *Blacks* (1987). For young people she wrote two writing manuals: *Young Poet's Primer* (Chicago: Brook's Press) and *Very Young Poets* (Chicago: Brook's Press).

Further Reading: *On Gwendolyn Brooks: Reliant Contemplation (Under Discussion),* ed. by Stephen Caldwell Wright, Ann Arbor, Mich.: University of Michigan Press, 1996; *Report from Part Two,* by Gwendolyn Brooks, Chicago: Third World Press, 1996; *Say That the River Turns: The Impact of Gwendolyn Brooks,* by Haki R. Madhubuti, Chicago: Third World Press, 1991; *To Gwen with Love: An Anthology Dedicated to Gwendolyn Brooks,* ed. by Patricia L. Brown, Don L. Lee and Francis Ward,

Chicago: Johnson Publishing Company, 1971; *A Life of Gwendolyn Brooks,* by George Kent, Louisville, Ky.: University of Kentucky Press, 1988; *Gwendolyn Brooks,* by Harry F. Shaw, Boston: Twayne Publishers, 1980; *Black Women Writers (1950–1980),* ed. by Mari Evans, New York: Doubleday/Anchor, 1984; *Black Women Writers at Work,* by Claudia Tate, New York: Doubleday/Anchor, 1983.

—R. K.

❖ BUNCHE, RALPH JOHNSON
(1904–1971), diplomat, U.N. mediator, winner of Nobel Peace Prize

Ralph Bunche was the first black person to win the Nobel Peace Prize, which was awarded to him in 1950 for his successful mediation of the Arab-Israeli conflict at the time of the founding of Israel. Subsequently, Bunche became the Undersecretary of the United Nations, a post he held from 1955 until his retirement in 1971. He was the highest-ranking American in that international organization.

Bunche personally did not consider his work with the Arabs and Israelis to be his greatest accomplishment. He also managed peacekeeping troops in the Congo (now Democratic Republic of Congo), Yemen, Cyprus, India, and Pakistan. He rated his work in the Suez area of Egypt as his greatest accomplishment. From 1956 to 1967, Bunche organized and directed 6,000 U.N. troops to keep the peace in that volatile area.

Bunche was one of many "black heroes" who rose to prominence in the 1950s and 1960s, gaining a new kind of recognition for black achievement. *Newsweek* called him "the foremost Negro of his generation—the distinguished symbol of how far a black man could rise in the Establishment." Although later activists considered this kind of praise to be "tokenism," he was admired far and wide.

Ralph Bunche was born in Detroit on August 7, 1904. His father, Fred Bunche, was a barber; his mother, Olive Agnes (Johnson) Bunche, was a musician.

His parents died when he was 13, and he moved to California, where he attended the University of California at Los Angeles (UCLA), from which he graduated summa cum laude in 1927. In 1928, he received his M.A. in government from Harvard University in Cambridge, Massachusetts, and went on to teach political science at Howard University in Washington, D.C.

Ralph J. Bunche *(Library of Congress)*

In 1930, Bunche married Ruth Ethel Harris with whom he had three children. He returned to Harvard for his doctorate, which he completed in 1934.

Bunche continued to study political science at Northwestern University in Evanston, Illinois, the London School of Economics in England, and Capetown University, South Africa. His focus was anthropology—the study of native peoples—and the effects of European nations' colonial policies in Africa. In 1937, he published a book, *A World View of Race* (Port Washington, N.Y.: Kennikat Press). In that year he was also made chair of Howard University's department of political science.

In 1938, Bunche began working with the famous Swedish sociologist Gunnar Myrdal, who wrote a groundbreaking book on racial prejudice, *An American Dilemma* (New York: Harper & Bros., 1944). Bunche helped Myrdal study the conditions of black people in the South, where they came close to being lynched by segregationists.

During World War II, Bunche was asked to serve as a specialist in African and Far Eastern Affairs for the Office of Strategic Services, the predecessor of the Central Intelligence Agency (CIA). Bunche went on to work in the State Department as associate chief of its Division of Dependent Area Affairs (a "dependent area" was a region, usually in Africa or Asia, that had been governed by a European power). He was the first black person to hold a high-ranking job in the State Department.

Bunche had been interested in the United Nations since its first, founding conference, held in San Francisco in 1945. He had attended that conference along with several other prominent black Americans, including Mary McLeod BETHUNE, W. E. B. DUBOIS, and Walter WHITE.

Bunche had also become known as an expert on colonial affairs, as well as trusteeship, the process of setting up transitional governments for countries moving toward independence. In 1947, he was the logical choice to direct the Trusteeship Division at the United Nations.

At that time, the formation of the independent state of Israel was just beginning. Although Jews had been living in the region for several years alongside native Palestinians, the territory had been controlled as a colony by the British. Israeli independence was a complicated process, involving conflicting wishes of Jewish and Arab residents.

In 1948, Ralph Bunche was appointed head of the U.N.'s Palestine Commission. This was a difficult and dangerous job—the previous head of the commission had been assassinated. It was Bunche's task to mediate between the two sides and to set up a peaceful ceasefire.

Bunche conducted 81 days of negotiations and finally worked out the "Four Armistice Agreements." The two sides stopped fighting, and for a while peace was ensured. Bunche won worldwide admiration for his role in these delicate negotiations, which, according to *Time* magazine, required "painstaking, brilliant diplomacy." Bunche was credited by other observers with "seemingly boundless energy" and an extraordinary sense of timing and strategy. In 1950, he was awarded the Nobel Peace Prize for his work.

Bunche continued other peacekeeping efforts at the United Nations, where in 1955 he was made undersecretary. He served at the United Nations until a series of painful illnesses led to his retirement and death on December 9, 1971.

Further Reading: *Ralph Bunche: An American Life,* by Brian Urquhart, New York: W.W. Norton & Co., 1993; *Ralph J. Bunche: Selected Speeches and Writings,* by Ralph J. Bunche, ed. by Charles P. Henry, Ann Arbor, Mich.: University of Michigan Press, 1995; *Ralph J. Bunche: Fighter for Peace,* by Alvin J. Kugelmass, New York: Julian Messner, 1962; *Ralph Bunche, U.N. Peacemaker,* by Peggy Mann, New York: Coward, McCann & Geoghegan, 1975.

—*R. K.*

❖ CARDOZO, WILLIAM WARRICK

(1905–1962), *doctor, research scientist, pioneer investigator of sickle-cell anemia*

W. Warrick Cardozo, as he was known, is famous for his ground-breaking research on sickle-cell anemia, an inherited blood disease especially common among black people.

The term "sickle cell" refers to the shape of some of the blood cells, which contributes to anemia, a shortage of red blood cells. Cardozo discovered that this disease is, in fact, inherited, and is almost exclusively found among people of African descent. He also found that not all people with a "sickle cell" had anemia, and that, although no successful treatment had been found, not everyone who had this disease necessarily died from it.

Although a great deal of research has been done on sickle-cell anemia in the past 40 years, Cardozo's research is still valid. He also worked for several years studying gastrointestinal disorders in children, while publishing articles on Hodgkin's disease and on the early development of black infants.

W. Warrick Cardozo was born in Washington, D.C., on April 16, 1905. His grandfather, Francis Cardozo, was a politician and educator, and his father, Francis Cardozo, Jr., a school principal. Cardozo adhered to his family's traditional respect for education. He received his medical degree from Ohio State University, then interned at Cleveland's City Hospital. He did his residency at Provident Hospital in Chicago, after which he was awarded a fellowship in pediatrics at two hospitals, Provident and Children's Memorial.

While training in medicine, Cardozo pursued his research. He received a grant from Alpha Phi Alpha fraternity to study sickle-cell anemia, and in 1937, he published his pioneering study of the disease in the *Archives of Internal Medicine*.

In that year, he returned to Washington, where he set up his private practice and became a part-time teacher in pediatrics at Howard University College of Medicine and Freedmen's Hospital.

Cardozo married and had a daughter. He went on to receive much professional recognition. In 1942, he was certified by the American Board of Pediatrics; in 1948, he was made a fellow of the American Academy of Pediatrics.

He continued in his private practice and teaching, while working for 24 years as a school medical inspector for the District of Columbia Board of Health.

Cardozo died suddenly of a heart attack on August 11, 1962.

—*R. K.*

❖ CARNEY, WILLIAM H.

(1840–1908), *Civil War veteran, winner of the Congressional Medal of Honor*

Carney was a sergeant in the 54th Massachusetts Infantry, the first Northern regiment of troops that fought in the Civil War. For his actions in the 1863 assault on Fort Wagner, near Charleston Harbor, he was cited for bravery, and 37 years later, he received a Congressional Medal of Honor for his heroism.

William Carney was born in 1840 to Ann and William Carney in Norfolk, Virginia. At the time of his birth, his mother was a slave. Thus, it was illegal for him to learn to read and write. However, he attended a secret school run by a local minister.

When he was 14, his owner died, leaving instructions to set Carney and his mother free. The next year, he joined his father in the coasting trade. The following year, 1856, Carney's father took his family to New Bedford, Massachusetts, where he thought he would find more freedom and opportunity.

The young Carney was a very religious person. While considering the ministry, he worked at a number of odd jobs to help his family. Then the Civil War broke out. Although the Union Army was at first reluctant to arm black men and train them to be soldiers, it soon became evident that their help would be an important addition to the war effort. Black men began to be recruited.

In February 1863, Carney joined the 54th Massachusetts Infantry, and was soon promoted to sergeant. By July, he was fighting in South Carolina, in the famous attack on Fort Wagner. His company faced heavy losses, but Carney did not falter. When he saw the soldier holding the Union colors start to fall, he grabbed the flag and carried it forward. He managed to cross the ditch that surrounded the fort, where the guns were, and to reach the parapet of the fort.

Although a bullet hit Carney in the thigh, he held onto the flag, even when fallen to his knees. In this manner, Carney stood his ground, despite the flying musket balls and grapeshot (a type of small bullet), holding the flag aloft in the hail of ammunition for more than an hour.

When the Union troops could take no more of the heavy fire, they began a retreat, and Carney followed. He had to crawl on one knee and was shot two more times. When the other soldiers saw him carrying the flag, they began to cheer. Carney was exhausted from loss of blood, but as they carried him into the hospital, he reportedly said, "Boys, the old flag never touched the ground."

Carney's wounds left him disabled, and he was discharged from the army in 1864. There followed a short stay in California, then 32 years as a mail carrier in New Bedford, Massachusetts. He married the first African-American woman to graduate from New Bedford High

School and become one of the first African-American women schoolteachers in Massachusetts.

In 1900, Carney received his highest recognition: the Congressional Medal of Honor, awarded for his heroism at Fort Wagner. The flag that he had held and guarded was preserved in the Massachusetts State House (the state capitol), and Carney often told children the story of his famous deed. He frequently spoke at Memorial Day rallies.

Carney retired from his job as a mail carrier in 1901 and moved to Boston to work as a messenger in the State House. In 1908, he was injured in a fatal elevator accident. When he died, the governor of Massachusetts had the flag flown at half-mast, and the chaplain of the state senate spoke at his funeral.

Further Reading: *Deeds of Valor,* ed. by W. F. Beyer and O. F. Keydel, Detroit: Perrien-Keydel Company, 1906.

—*R. K.*

❖ CARVER, GEORGE WASHINGTON
(1861?–1943), *agricultural scientist, researcher*

George Washington Carver is known in popular history as the man who discovered many new uses for the

George Washington Carver (*Library of Congress*)

peanut, and this was indeed one of his accomplishments. It is more accurate, however, to say that he is the man who saved southern agriculture, which had become far too dependent on cotton. When boll weevils and exhausted soil threatened the entire cotton crop, southern agriculture had nowhere to turn—until Carver found new ways to restore the soil, diversify the crops, and develop new agricultural techniques.

Among Carver's major accomplishments were the invention and promotion of a new organic fertilizing method; the introduction of crop rotation as a method for restoring the soil; and the development of the peanut and the sweet potato as southern agricultural staples.

Carver developed more than 300 different products from the peanut, including wood stains, shampoo, face powder, printer's ink, vinegar, soap, coffee, butter, milk, and cheese. He also pioneered the new science of chemurgy—that is, finding new industrial uses for agricultural products. For example, Carver found ways of making many industrial materials from sweet potatoes, including rubber. He also produced paint pigment and talcum powder from southern clay, and many dyes from southern plants.

Carver's reputation was so great that he assisted scientists from Australia, Africa, India, and the Soviet Union. He was elected a fellow of Great Britain's Royal Society of Arts and was appointed to work on an important survey for the U.S. Department of Agriculture. He received the National Association for the Advancement of Colored People's Spingarn Medal for achievement by a black American in 1916, and an honorary doctorate from the University of Chicago in 1941. Carver was also invited to work on the staff of the great inventor Thomas A. Edison but chose to continue his work in the South, instead.

There are two stories told relating to Carver's early childhood. One is his family's story—that he was born around 1861 to slave parents on the plantation of Moses and Susan Carver, near the town of Diamond, Missouri. During the last years of the Civil War, the baby George and his mother were kidnapped and carried into Arkansas. Later, their owner paid the ransom of a racehorse to get the baby back.

Moses Carver's own story is that he sent his slaves into Arkansas to keep them from being kidnapped, and he personally went to look for them after the Civil War, but was only able to find the baby.

In either case, even after slavery, Carver and his brother James stayed on with their former owners, working in exchange for room and board. When Carver was

rescued, he was very sick with whooping cough and was to suffer from poor health for many years. Fortunately, this meant that he was spared most physical work and was able to spend time in the woods, learning about plants and flowers. He earned his keep by cooking, cleaning, sewing, and doing laundry; and he also found time to teach himself to read.

As a teenager, Carver finally attended school—one for black children, in Neosho, Kansas. He spent the next 10 years traveling through the Midwest, finding whatever work he could while studying whenever the opportunity arose. He finally finished high school in his late twenties, and was accepted at a church-supported college. At registration, however, he was turned away. After time spent working as a farmer, he tried again, and was able to attend Simpson College in Iowa from 1890 to 1891, when he was close to 30 years old. With the help of a teacher, he went on to study botany and agriculture at Iowa State College.

Carver received a good education in Iowa. He stayed at the top of his class and also won awards for his still-life paintings of plants. He studied with several professors who would go on to become U.S. secretaries of agriculture. One of them was Henry C. Wallace, whose son, Henry A. Wallace, would also serve in that position under President Franklin D. Roosevelt. Henry A. Wallace, like his father, had been influenced by Carver, and gave him credit for teaching him about plant fertilization.

In 1894, Carver became the first African-American graduate of Iowa State. He then worked as an assistant in the college's experimental station—the college-owned farm where agricultural experiments were carried out and where local farmers were eventually given the benefit of the latest agricultural research. In 1896, he received his master's degree from Iowa State, while building a growing reputation as an authority on mycology (the study of fungi and parasites) and horticulture (the growing of plants).

In 1896, Carver was invited to work at Booker T. WASHINGTON's Tuskegee Institute in Alabama. When Carver accepted, he was given the task of building an agriculture department at Tuskegee, and had only 13 students and some laboratory odds and ends to start with. By 1897, however, the U.S. Department of Agriculture funded a small experimental station at Tuskegee, with Carver at its head. It was then that he began to analyze the problems of southern agriculture, and to develop new solutions.

By the turn of the century, most of the South had been planted in either cotton or tobacco for years. This had exhausted the soil, removing from it many nutrients and chemicals that plants needed to grow. As a result, crops became smaller, and small farmers, both black and white, grew poorer.

Carver's plan was to teach farmers better soil care, either by restoring it with organic fertilizer or by planting other crops that would give back some of the chemicals that the cotton or tobacco had taken away. Carver's lab would analyze a particular type of soil, and then recommend the chemicals it needed, and the fertilizers that could supply them. Carver traveled all around the region, teaching local farmers better techniques, and he also published a newsletter with practical suggestions. Eventually, he developed the idea of a "Movable School," which was adopted in India, China, Albania, and Zimbabwe (then called Rhodesia) as a way of teaching rural people better farming methods.

Another problem of southern agriculture was the boll weevil, an insect that ate cotton "bolls" or puffs. Boll weevils invaded the South between 1890 and 1910, threatening the cotton crop. At Carver's suggestion, many farmers switched to the peanut. Then there were too many peanuts—so Carver developed new products that could make use of the surplus crop. In 1921, he testified about his discoveries to the U.S. House Ways and Means Committee.

Carver created some 118 products from the sweet potato, as well as more than 500 dyes from various southern plants. Other products resulting from his pioneering research were synthetic marble made from sawdust; woven rugs from okra stalks; and wallboard from pine cones, peanut shells, and banana stems.

An added accomplishment of Carver's was his use of peanut oil and massages to treat people crippled with polio. He worked with hundreds of patients and helped other scientists develop new methods of therapy.

Carver was known for being a religious man as well as a loner. He never married. He was not terribly interested in money, and many of his salary checks were said to have never been cashed. When he was nearing the end of his life, in 1940, he donated his life savings to set up the George Washington Carver Research Foundation at Tuskegee Institute to study agriculture and industry. This organization eventually had a budget of 5 million dollars, devoted to research, training, and outreach.

Carver died of anemia at Tuskegee Institute on January 5, 1943, and was buried next to Booker T. Washington. In 1948, he was honored with a commemorative stamp. In 1953, Congress set up a George Washington Carver National Monument near his birthplace in Missouri—the first federal monument dedicated to an African American.

Further Reading: *George Washington Carver: Scientist and Symbol,* by Linda O. McMurray, New York: Oxford University Press, 1981; *George Washington Carver: The Man Who Overcame,* by Lawrence Elliott, Englewood Cliffs, N.J.: Prentice-Hall, 1971; *George Washington Carver: An American Biography,* by Rackham Holt, Garden City, N.Y.: Doubleday, Doran & Co., Inc., 1943.
                                                                —R. K.

❖ CHAMBERLAIN, WILTON NORMAN ("Wilt")
(1936–), basketball player

Perhaps the most unstoppable offensive player in the history of basketball, Wilt Chamberlain burst upon the NBA in 1959 as a seven-foot-one-inch scoring machine. The only player ever to score 100 points in a single NBA game, the man known as Wilt the Stilt and the Big Dipper was named the NBA's Player of the Decade for 1957–66 and won four Most Valuable Player Awards.

Born on August 21, 1936, in Philadelphia, Pennsylvania, Chamberlain was one of nine children. No one in his family was especially tall—his father, William, a shipyard welder, stood only five feet nine—so it came as a surprise when Chamberlain began to tower over his classmates during his grade school years. By the time he reached Philadelphia's Overbrook High School he was an unstoppable force on the basketball court, once scoring 90 points in a 36-minute game.

Avidly recruited by numerous colleges, Chamberlain entered the University of Kansas in 1955 and soon made the Jayhawks a power in collegiate basketball. He was an all-American in 1957 and 1958 and led his team to the 1958 NCAA finals. Chamberlain also excelled in track and field at Kansas, performing impressive feats of all-around athleticism in the decathlon. His impact on college basketball was enormous. College officials changed the rules of the game in order to keep Chamberlain from standing under the basket and dominating the action—among other things, they widened the foul lane and outlawed offensive goaltending.

Eventually, Chamberlain grew weary of all the measures taken to bottle him up. At the end of his junior year, he left Kansas and briefly toured with the Harlem Globetrotters. The Philadelphia Warriors of the NBA had already drafted Chamberlain, but league rules prevented him from joining the team until 1959, when his college class graduated. He was worth waiting for. In his first season with the Warriors (1959–60), he averaged 37.6 points and 27 rebounds per game and became the first player ever to be chosen both Rookie of the Year and MVP. Chamberlain put up his most spectacular numbers in 1961–62, when he averaged an astonishing 50.4 points per game and broke the 4,000-point barrier for the season, a feat accomplished by no other player before or since. His greatest single moment came on March 2, 1962, in Hershey, Pennsylvania, when he scored 100 points in a 169-147 victory over the New York Knicks.

Over the course of his 14 seasons, Chamberlain led the NBA in scoring 7 times and won 11 rebounding titles. He won two league championships, the first with Philadelphia in 1967, the second with the Los Angeles Lakers in 1972. When he retired after the 1973 season, he had scored 31,419 points and snared 23,924 rebounds. In addition, he had scored 50 or more points in a game 118 times.

After leaving the NBA, Chamberlain satisfied his need for competition by playing volleyball, and his involvement helped to popularize the sport throughout the country. He also flirted with the idea of boxing professionally, became an author, built a spectacular house outside of Los Angeles, and devoted himself to a number of business interests, which included restaurants, night clubs, and sports medicine clinics. Throughout the years, Chamberlain has retained close ties to the Los Angeles Lakers franchise. Named one of the NBA's 50 all-time greats in 1996, he frequently offers his candid opinions on the state of the game.

Further Information: *Wilt: Just Like Any Other 7-Foot Black Millionaire Who Lives Next Door,* by Wilt Chamberlain with David Shaw, New York: Macmillan, 1973; *A View from Above,* by Wilt Chamberlain, New York: Villard, 1991; Official Wilt's World web site, http://www.wiltsworld.com, includes a biography, photographs, video and audio clips, feature stories, and excerpts from Chamberlain's books.
—*P. K.*

❖ CHESNUTT, CHARLES WADDELL
(1858–1932), *author*

Charles Chesnutt is considered to be the first African-American professional writer of fiction. Although there had been African-American writers before him, he was the first to achieve real standing as a novelist and writer of short stories. His many stories and three novels were famous for their sympathetic portrayal of southern black people—a subculture that had not been previously portrayed by one of its own.

In 1899, Chesnutt published his first two volumes of short stories, *The Conjure Woman* (New York: Houghton Mifflin) and *The Wife of His Youth* (New York: Houghton Mifflin), along with a biography of Frederick DOUGLASS. His first novel, *The House Behind the Cedars,* came out in 1900, and it went into four printings almost immediately. *The Marrow of Tradition* was published in 1901, to much controversy. *The Colonel's Dream* (New York: Doubleday, Page & Co.), published in 1905, was not a commercial success at the time, although today it is prized for its exploration of the political and moral dilemmas of the South after the Civil War.

Charles Chesnutt was born on June 20, 1858, to Andrew Jackson and Ann Maria (Sampson) Chesnutt. Although Chesnutt was born during the time of slavery, his parents were free and had traveled north to get away from the difficulties that faced free black people in North Carolina. Chesnutt was born in Cleveland, Ohio, but returned to North Carolina in 1866 to join his father, who had served there in the Union Army.

Chesnutt was an ambitious, determined man. Although he was saddened by the death of his mother in 1871, he didn't allow personal sorrow to interfere with his rigorous program of study—which included French, German, Latin, math, and law. He also studied legal stenography, which would prove for him to be a useful way of earning a living.

In 1878, just before he turned 20, Chesnutt married Susan Perry. At that time, he was a teacher and administrator in Fayetteville, North Carolina. He planned to move north and work as a legal stenographer, but, unable to find such a position in Washington, D.C., he returned to Fayetteville, and at 22, became principal of the State Normal (high) School for Negroes instead. He continued with his studies and self-improvement.

In 1883, Chesnutt found work as a stenographer and journalist in New York City. He then went on to Cleveland, where he became a lawyer, graduating in 1887 at the top of his class. At the same time, he was publishing short fiction in national newspapers and magazines, including the prestigious *Atlantic Monthly* in 1887 and 1888.

In 1889, Chesnutt wrote his first novel, *Rena Walden,* which was eventually published in 1900, in revised form, as *The House Behind the Cedars.* In this book, Chesnutt dealt with the controversial topic of interracial marriage. The heroine of the book is light enough to "pass" for white, as Chesnutt himself was. Modern critics admire this book's effort to deal with major themes of black life, but feel that its story is somewhat contrived.

Between the time that Chesnutt first wrote his novel and the year in which it saw print, he published two volumes of short stories. *The Conjure Woman* is narrated by a northern white man who has come to live in the South. The stories told by his black servant provide insight into the relations between white masters and black slaves or servants. *The Wife of His Youth* is a collection of unrelated stories, often featuring people of mixed heritage and their problems with both races.

After Chesnutt had published his first three books and his novel was accepted, he thought success as a professional author would be his, and closed his legal office. Two of his daughters had been sent to college, and there were two others to support. Earnings from his writing proved to be insufficient. His books did well, but not well enough to sustain him and his family at the level that they wished.

Chesnutt's books also met with the difficulty of appealing to a white audience that did not especially want to read about "the Negro problem," particularly not with the critical views that Chesnutt had of the treatment of blacks by whites.

This critical spirit is to be found in *The Marrow of Tradition* (New York: AMS Press, 1972 reprint of 1901 ed.). This novel concerns a fictional town, Wellington, and the admirable black doctor, Dr. Miller, who represents the educated and "elevated" black person. The book conveys the pessimistic admission that there is no real solution for such people—for no matter how well educated or cultured they become, they remain subject to the same prejudice and violence as all black people.

Chesnutt eventually went back to his law practice and his business, but still managed to write *The Colonel's Dream,* which Doubleday brought out in 1905. The book concerns the plans of a white southern colonel to reform his town. The man fails, because of the prevailing superstition and ignorance that surround him.

In 1910, Chesnutt collapsed into unconsciousness for several days and spent months recovering his health. In 1920, he was permanently injured by attacks of appendicitis and then peritonitis. Although he wrote one more novel, *The Quarry,* he was unable to get it published. By this time, all of his books had gone out of print, although *The Conjure Woman* was reissued in 1929.

On November 15, 1932, Chesnutt died at home. He had received the National Association for the Advancement of Colored People's Spingarn Medal for black achievement in 1928, and was later honored by critics and scholars for his pioneering fiction about southern life.

Further Reading: *An American Crusade: The Life of Charles Waddell Chesnutt,* by Frances R. Keller, Provo, Utah: Brigham Young University Press, 1977; *Charles Waddell Chesnutt: Pioneer of the Color Line,* by Helen M. Chesnutt, Chapel Hill, N.C.: University of North Carolina Press, 1952.

—*R. K.*

❖ CHILDRESS, ALICE
(1920–1994), *playwright, novelist, actress, director*

Alice Childress has won numerous awards for her plays and children's books, including an Obie Award for best off-Broadway play in 1956 (for *Trouble in Mind*); a Rockefeller grant for writing; and "Outstanding Books of the Year" awards by the *New York Times Book Review* for *A Hero Ain't Nothin' but a Sandwich* (New York: Coward, McCann & Geoheghan, 1973) and *Rainbow Jordan* (New York: Coward, McCann & Geoheghan, 1981). She has adapted many of her own works for film and television.

Childress's 1952 play, *Gold Through the Trees,* was the first professionally produced play by an African-American woman. As a result of Childress's successful productions of the 1950s, she was able to ensure that Harlem's first off-Broadway contracts were given only to union members of the Actors Equity Association and the Harlem Stage Hand Local.

Alice Childress was born on October 12, 1920, in Charleston, South Carolina. In 1940, she began her life in the theater as an actress, the start of an 11-year association with the American Negro Theater of New York. She wrote, directed, and acted in *Florence,* a play produced in 1949. Her acting credits included Broadway and television.

Near the beginning of her career, Childress married and had a daughter. Later, she divorced and, in 1957, married the musician Nathan Woodard.

Meanwhile, Childress was moving from acting to directing, and then to writing. She adapted a play based on Langston HUGHES's "Simple" stories, *Just a Little Simple,* produced in New York in 1950. Two years later, *Gold Through the Trees* was produced. In 1955, her Obie Award–winning *Trouble in Mind* opened off-Broadway. This groundbreaking work is the story of a black actress troubled by the stereotypes she is asked to portray.

From 1956 to 1958, Childress wrote a column called "Here's Mildred" in the *Baltimore Afro-American,* featuring the first-person stories of a fictional character who worked as a housekeeper. These columns were based on a book called *Like One of the Family: Conversations From a Domestic's Life* (Boston: Beacon Press), which was published in 1956 and reissued in 1986.

The year 1966 marked the Michigan production of one of Childress's most famous plays, *Wedding Band: A Love/Hate Story in Black and White* (New York: French, 1973). The plot concerns an interracial marriage, a controversial topic at the time. In 1972, it was produced off-Broadway at the New York Shakespeare Festival Theatre, directed by Childress and Joseph Papp.

In 1969, Childress's other major play, *Wine in the Wilderness: A Comedy-Drama,* was produced in Boston by the city's public television station. Both *Wine* and *Wedding Band* continue to be performed and read.

Childress kept at her writing and work in the theater throughout the 1970s and 1980s, while teaching and lecturing at various schools. Her children's books include *A Hero Ain't Nothin' but a Sandwich,* the story of a teenager's heroin addiction, published in 1973. Her screen adaptation of the book in 1977 won a Virgin Islands film festival award, as well as the first Paul ROBESON Award for outstanding contributions to the performing arts from the Black Filmmakers Hall of Fame.

Childress's 1979 novel *A Short Walk* (New York: Coward, McCann & Geoheghan) relates the story of a black woman born in the early 1900s and living through many social upheavals throughout the middle of the century. Her novel *Rainbow Jordan,* published in 1981, was named one of the year's best books by *School Library Journal* and the Children's Book Council, as well as by the *New York Times Book Review.*

In 1987, Childress published *Many Closets.* That year also saw the off-Broadway production of her play about comedienne "Moms" Mabley, *Moms: A Praise Play for a Black Comedienne.*

Further Reading: *Alice Childress* (Twayne's United States Authors Series, No. 652), by LA Vinia Delois Jennings, New York: Twayne Publishers, 1995.

—*R. K.*

❖ CHUCK D (Carlton Ridenhour)
(1960–), *musician*

As the founder and leader of Public Enemy—regarded by many as rap's most influential group—Chuck D has been noted for the sharp political and social bite of his lyrics. He has also taken an active role in trying to correct the social problems he addresses in his songs.

Born Carlton Ridenhour on August 1, 1960, in Roosevelt, Long Island, Chuck D attended Adelphi University, where he studied graphic arts. While working as a deejay at the college radio station, WBAU, he formed a close friendship with two other students, Hank Shocklee and Bill Stepheny. The three men began working on shared musical projects, and at one point Chuck D rapped over one of Shocklee's songs, "Public Enemy No. 1." The tape of the song reached Rick Rubin of Def Jam Records, who approached Chuck D about creating a group. Though he was reluctant at first, feeling that he was too old to start out from scratch as a performer, Chuck D eventually agreed to test the waters. With Shocklee acting as producer and Stepheny signing on to do publicity, Chuck D enlisted DJ Terminator X (Norman Lee Rogers) and Professor Griff (Richard Griffin). Finally, he asked an old friend, William Drayton, to join him in performing raps. Drayton adopted a flamboyant comic persona, known as Flavor Flav, as a counterpoint to Chuck D's deep-voiced, serious rapping, and Public Enemy was born.

Def Jam released Public Enemy's first album, *Yo! Bum Rush the Show,* in 1987. Rap fans and critics were enthusiastic, but the group got little notice from the general public. Public Enemy forged ahead, and the group's second album, *It Takes a Nation of Millions to Hold Us Back* (1988), was a huge success, reaching the top spot on the R&B charts and selling 1 million copies. It was hailed for the innovative music created by Shocklee and his production crew (known as the Bomb Squad), for Flavor Flav's flights of fancy, and for Chuck D's politically focused messages. The group's stature was further boosted in 1989, when Public Enemy provided the theme song, "Fight the Power," for Spike LEE's hard-hitting film *Do the Right Thing.* Nevertheless, Chuck D was criticized for some of his lyrics and offstage remarks, especially when he hailed Louis Farrakhan, the controversial leader of the Nation of Islam, as a prophet. Public Enemy came under intense fire when Professor Griff made anti-Jewish remarks in a newspaper interview; as a result, Chuck D dismissed him from the group.

Public Enemy's third album, *Fear of a Black Planet,* was released in 1990 and reached the Top 10 on the pop charts. The following year, *Apocalypse 91 . . . The Enemy Strikes Black* was equally well received—the album was notable for Chuck D's condemnation of fathers who abandoned their children, drug dealers, and black-on-black crime. Public Enemy began to lose momentum in 1992, however, and the group's next two albums—*Greatest Misses* (1992) and *Muse Sick-N-Hour Message* (1994)—did poorly. In 1995, Chuck D decided to stop touring and ended his association with Def Jam. He created his own record label and publishing company and released a solo album, *Autobiography of Mista Chuck,* in 1996. The new album marked a new direction for Chuck D's music, showing a greater influence of soul, funk, and R&B elements.

Throughout his career, Chuck D has followed the political ideas set forth in his lyrics, working to promote solidarity and achievement among African Americans. In 1992, he became a major financial supporter of the Black United Fund, an organization dedicated to funding affordable housing in New York City. Chuck D has also joined with other musicians in a nationwide campaign to combat drug use. He has lectured at numerous colleges and universities, talking to students about black pride and self-improvement. His efforts have won him a number of honors, including the Black History Maker of the Year Award from *Urban Profile* magazine and the Chairman Award at the Black Music and Media Awards.

Further Information: *Fight the Power: Rap, Race, and Reality,* by Chuck D with Yusaf Jah, New York: Delacorte, 1997; Official Public Enemy web site, http://www.public-enemy.com, see also http://www.defjam.com/artists/pe/enemy.html

—*P. K.*

❖ CINQUE, JOSEPH
(1811–1879), *leader of the revolt aboard the slave ship* Amistad

Joseph Cinque is famous for having led a successful revolt while a captive on a slave ship. Ultimately, he and the other Africans on the ship managed to win their passage back to Africa, their native land.

Cinque's African name was "Sing-gbe," given when he was born into the Mende people, in the African region that is now the country of Sierra Leone. As a young husband and father in his early twenties, he was captured by slave traders and sold to the Spanish owners of a "slave factory" on the island of Lomboko. This was a place where Spanish slave traders brought Africans who had been bought or captured. From the "factory," slaves could be sold to plantation owners in the Americas.

From Lomboko, Cinque was sent to Havana, Cuba. The voyages on the slave ships were notorious for cruelty and horrible living conditions. Half of the Africans on Cinque's voyage died—but Cinque survived.

For many years, traders had brought Africans into Cuba as slaves, but in 1815, importing slaves had been declared illegal. Ironically, slavery itself was legal in Cuba until 1886—it was simply the *importing* of slaves that had been outlawed. So Cinque and the other slaves were given Spanish names, to appear as if they were slaves born in Cuba, rather than illegally imported. Sing-gbe became Joseph (or José) Cinque.

Along with 48 other African men, Cinque was sold to a Cuban planter named Ruiz, who loaded the men onto the slave ship *Amistad* at night, to avoid discovery of his illegal trade. The African people were shackled together in the hold—the bottom of the ship, below decks—and chained to the ship's wall in iron collars. When they asked the cook for more food, they were told in sign language that food was not only scarce but they would probably be killed and eaten by the Spaniards.

Somehow, Cinque got hold of a nail and used it to free himself and the men. They found cane-knives and killed most of the crew except two slave owners, whom they chained in the hold, and two sailors, who managed to escape in a lifeboat. These sailors managed to reach Havana, where they reported the revolt.

Meanwhile, the Africans had trouble navigating the waters in this unfamiliar part of the world. One of the

Joseph Cinque and others rebel aboard *Amistad*. (*Library of Congress*)

slave owners offered to navigate, but tricked them by sailing west instead of east. The ship finally landed on Long Island, New York, where it was captured by the U.S. Coast Guard, who had been alerted by Cuban authorities.

At this time, the fight against slavery, known as abolitionism, was at a fever pitch in the United States. The Cubans and Spanish requested that the Africans be returned to Havana—where they certainly would have been burned at the stake. But U.S. abolitionists claimed the guilty parties were not the Africans but the Spanish Cubans who had kidnapped them. The abolitionists insisted that the case be tried in the U.S. courts.

The case moved from higher to higher court. One man who agreed with the abolitionists was former president John Quincy Adams. By then, Adams was in his seventies, serving in Congress. When the case reached the Supreme Court in February 1841, Adams agreed to defend Cinque and the others.

The Court was persuaded. Cinque and his fellow captives were set free. In early 1842, Cinque returned to his native land, where he lived out the rest of his days.

The uprising led by Cinque received worldwide exposure in 1997 with the release of the Steven Spielberg movie *Amistad.*

Cinque's story is significant for two reasons. First, his court case helped to reinforce the illegality of the slave trade and, by implication, the fact that Africans were human beings with legal and moral rights, rather than mere property. Second, Cinque and his fellow rebels served as an important symbol of African-American resistance to slavery and oppression.

Further Reading: *Amistad: A Long Road to Freedom,* by Walter Dean Myers, N.Y.: Dutton Books, 1998; *Black Mutiny: The Revolt on the Schooner Amistad,* by William A. Owens, N.Y.: Plume, 1997.

—*R. K.*

❖ CLAY, CASSIUS MARCELLUS
see ALI, MUHAMMAD

❖ COLEMAN, BESSIE
(1892–1926), *pioneering aviator*

The first African American to obtain a pilot's license, Bessie Coleman astonished crowds with her daring feats at air shows during the 1920s. Conscious of her role as a trailblazer, she refused to be discouraged by racism and discrimination.

Born in Atlanta, Texas, on January 26, 1892, Coleman was one of 13 children. When she was nine years old, her family split up—George Coleman took his nine sons to live in Oklahoma, and Susan Coleman remained in Texas with her four daughters. Bessie, the oldest daughter, helped look after the younger girls. All the children worked in the cotton fields and helped their mother take in laundry. Despite the pressures of earning a living, Susan Coleman made sure her girls went to school, and she always got books for them from the traveling library wagon. Bessie was an especially quick learner and often read to her sisters; she was able to finish high school, a considerable accomplishment for a poor African-American girl in those days. She then enrolled in Langston Industrial College in Oklahoma, but she ran out of money after the first semester and had to drop out.

After working in Texas for several years, Coleman moved to Chicago in 1915, where she stayed with one of her brothers and worked as a manicurist in a barber shop. World War I was raging in Europe, and the feats of daring aviators were front-page news. Coleman grew fascinated with the art of flying and dreamed of becoming a pilot. When the war ended in 1918 and surplus airplanes became available, Coleman tried to find a flying instructor. However, because she was a woman and an African American, no one was willing to accept her as a pupil. Coleman refused to give up, and her quest brought her into contact with Robert S. Abbott. Abbott published the *Chicago Defender,* the most influential black newspaper in the city. He advised Coleman to go to France, where she would encounter less prejudice.

Coleman began to study French and diligently saved the money that she was earning as a restaurant manager. Aided by loans from Abbott and other friends, she left for France in November 1920. After seven months of intensive training at France's number-one flight school, Coleman earned her pilot's license from the Fédération Aéronautique Internationale and returned home in triumph.

Coleman's dream was to open her own flying school, where she would pass on her skills to other African-American women. In order to raise the money for this undertaking, she resolved to go barnstorming. This was a popular activity during the 1920s, when groups of aviators would fly into a town, rent a field, and put on a flying show for the local population. Coleman took part in her first air show—billed as "the first public flight of a black woman in this country"—in September 1992 at Curtiss Field, outside New York City.

A dashing, crowd-pleasing performer, Coleman turned up at her shows dressed in a stylish military uniform. Soaring above the ground in her Curtiss JN-4 "Jenny" biplane, she performed spectacular feats, including loops, spirals, and heart-stopping dives. At some shows, Coleman would have an assistant pilot her plane while she performed a daring parachute jump. Everyone was aware of the risks she was taking. During one show in California, Coleman suffered broken ribs and a broken leg when she had to crash-land after mechanical difficulties. Her injuries kept her out of action for nearly two years, but she returned to make a highly successful tour of Texas and the South. The tour brought in a substantial sum of money, and Coleman felt she would be ready to open her school after doing a final tour of Florida. On April 30, 1926, Coleman and a mechanic were making a test flight in Jacksonville when the plane went into a sudden dive and crashed, killing both occupants.

Coleman was buried in Chicago, where 5,000 admirers attended her funeral. In the years since her tragic death, Coleman's legacy has inspired numerous African-American women to realize their ambitions.

Further Information: *Queen Bess: Daredevil Aviator,* by Doris L. Rich, Washington, D.C.: Smithsonian Institution Press, 1993; *Up in the Air: The Story of Bessie Coleman,* by Philip S. Hart, Minneapolis: Carolrhoda, 1996; International Women's Air & Space Museum web site, http://www.infinet.com/~iwasm; *Women Aviators,* by Lisa Yount, New York: Facts On File, 1995.

—P. K.

Bill Cosby *(Frank Capri/Saga/Archive Photos)*

❖ COSBY, WILLIAM HENRY, JR. ("Bill")
(1937–), *actor, comedian, philanthropist*

One of America's best-loved entertainers, Bill Cosby broke new ground in 1965 as the first African American to star in a television drama series (*I Spy*). Throughout the 1980s, his portrayal of Dr. Heathcliff Huxtable on *The Cosby Show* delighted 60 million viewers a week and set the standard for an entire industry.

Born on July 12, 1937, in the Germantown section of Philadelphia, Pennsylvania, Cosby was the eldest of three brothers and grew up in an all-black housing project. Though he qualified for Germantown's High School for Gifted Students, he was more interested in sports and comedy than studying. When Cosby learned that then he would have to repeat the 10th grade, he dropped out of school and took a series of odd jobs. In 1956, he enlisted in the U.S. Navy and served four years as a physical therapist. Realizing that he could not go anywhere without an education, Cosby also completed his high school equivalency. Upon leaving the service he returned to Philadelphia to enroll at Temple University, where he starred in track and football.

Cosby got his first taste of performing during his sophomore year, when he took a part-time job as a bartender/comedian at a campus tavern. Bitten by the show business bug, he dropped out of college and began a career as a stand-up comic. After working in clubs and night spots all over the country, Cosby got his big break in 1965 when he appeared on *The Tonight Show with Johnny Carson.* His performance impressed the TV producer Sheldon Leonard, and Cosby was cast to play the secret agent Alexander Scott on the action-adventure series *I Spy.* The show ran for three seasons (1965–68), earning Cosby two successive Emmy Awards as the Outstanding Lead Actor in a Drama Series. As portrayed by Cosby, Scott was a unique character in television annals—a black man serving his country in an important job, maintaining a confident African-American identity while enjoying success in the white world.

Now established as a star, Cosby plunged into a host of new projects. His first TV sitcom, *The Bill Cosby Show,* aired from 1969 to 1971. He also hosted and produced the cartoon series *Fat Albert and the Cosby Kids* and appeared regularly on *Sesame Street* and *The Electric Company.* At the same time, Cosby recorded a string of Grammy Award–winning comedy albums and appeared in movies such as *Hickey and Boggs* (1971) and *Uptown Saturday Night* (1974). During these years Cosby also resumed his education, earning a B.A. from Temple in 1976. He then went on to obtain a master's degree and a doctorate in education from the University of Massachusetts at Amherst.

Cosby's career reached new heights with the advent of *The Cosby Show* in 1984. This sitcom featured Cosby as a gentle, humorous physician pursuing the American dream. Like Cosby and his real-life wife, Camille, the Huxtables had five children—four girls and a boy—and shared a home full of laughter, love, music, and art. *The Cosby Show* appealed to viewers of all ethnic groups and presented a rich, positive portrait of African-American family life. It remained on the air through 1991, ranking as television's number-one show and making NBC the nation's leading network.

The spectacular success of *The Cosby Show,* added to Cosby's earnings from concerts, movies, record albums, commercials, and several best-selling books (*Fatherhood, Childhood, Love and Marriage,* and others), have made him one of the wealthiest individuals in show business. Over the years, Bill and Camille Cosby have made major donations to a variety of African-American institutions, most notably a record $20 million gift to Spelman College in Atlanta in 1987.

In 1996, Cosby launched a new series, *Cosby,* on CBS. The success of the new show was marred by tragedy in January 1997, when Cosby's son, Ennis, was shot to death during an attempted holdup in Los Angeles. Despite his grief, Cosby continued working, and a second new series, *Kids Say the Darndest Things,* premiered on CBS in 1998.

Further Reading: *Bill Cosby: Actor and Comedian,* by Michael Schuman, Springfield, N.J.: Enslow, 1995; *Cosby: The Life of a Comedy Legend,* by Ronald L. Smith, Amherst, N.Y.: Prometheus, 1997.

—P. K.

✤ COUVENT, JUSTINE (Madame Couvent)
(1757?–1837), pre–Civil War philanthropist

Madame Couvent's fame rests on her envisioning and funding a school for the orphans of free black people in New Orleans—the first of its kind in the United States. Setting aside the money and property left by her husband, she made arrangements for the school in her will. This was a radical and daring move in times of slavery, as was her stipulation that all the school's teachers be black. Madame Couvent's school, founded in 1852, continues to operate today.

From the few facts available, it would seem Justine Couvent was born in Africa and brought to New Orleans as a slave. She was given the name Justine Fervin; but this changed with her marriage to Gabriel Bernard Couvent. Her husband may well have purchased her freedom, although it could well have been her master's gift.

The people of New Orleans thought highly of Madame Couvent, noting particularly her common sense and compassion. Couvent was especially concerned for young people of color, who suffered under slavery or found it difficult as free people to find work. Couvent wanted a school for the orphans of these free black people. Many of the children had white fathers who were still alive but from whom they could expect little or no help.

Couvent's husband was a prosperous carpenter, and they were both devout Catholics. When Gabriel Bernard Couvent died in 1829, at age 71, he left Justine Couvent his fortune. Couvent's priest apparently influenced her in using her inheritance to found a school that would be run by the Catholic Church.

Although Couvent died in 1837, her school did not come into being until 1847. Organizing this institution was a delicate matter, since even with the church's protection, the city leaders of New Orleans might well have frowned on a school for black children. Finally, however, it became a reality, established by the Catholic Church.

The Couvent school was open to both boys and girls, who were taught in separate classes. Any black child, regardless of religion, could attend without charge. If a child's parents or guardians could afford it, however, they were encouraged to make a monthly donation. The children's education was demanding and included the classics in English, French, and Spanish.

After Slavery was abolished, black children in New Orleans were able to attend public schools along with the white children. The Couvent School might have been closed as attendance fell off, but black leaders worked to keep it open. The school still functions, under the name of the Holy Redeemer School.

—R. K.

❖ CROMWELL, OLIVER

(1752–1853), *Revolutionary War soldier*

Oliver Cromwell crossed the Delaware with George Washington. According to his personal account, he fought in the battles of Princeton, Brandywine, Monmouth, and Yorktown, where he believed he saw the last man killed in the Revolutionary War. Although his version may not be entirely reliable, his honorable discharge as a private was signed by General George Washington himself. The discharge papers note that Cromwell was "honored with the Badge of Merit for Six Years faithful service" in the American Revolutionary Army.

Scholars have ascertained that Cromwell was, apparently, born free in Columbus, New Jersey.

When the Revolutionary War broke out, Cromwell, by then a New Jersey farmer, joined the 2nd New Jersey Regiment, and fought in many battles. After the war, he was granted a federal pension of $96 a year in recognition of his services.

Cromwell married, raised six children, and, by his own account, lived to be 100 years old. When he died in January 1853, his survivors included many grandchildren and great-grandchildren.

Further Reading: *The Negro in the American Revolution,* by Benjamin Quarles, Chapel Hill, N.C.: University of North Carolina Press, 1961; *The Black Presence in the Era of the American Revolution 1770–1800,* by Sidney Kaplan, Greenwich, Conn.: New York Graphic Society, 1973.

—*R. K.*

❖ CRUMMELL, ALEXANDER

(1819–1898), *minister, writer*

Alexander Crummell, an Episcopal priest, became one of the leading black abolitionists of his time. He was also a missionary in Liberia—the nation founded by African Americans who had gone back to Africa.

Crummell helped to found and was first president of the American Negro Academy, organized to promote such literature, art, and science as would counteract racist propaganda directed against black people. And his was the idea of the "Talented Tenth," later picked up by W. E. B. DUBOIS—the proposition that a "talented tenth" of well educated black Americans prominent in the professions could enable the rest of African Americans to advance as well.

Although slavery still existed at the time of his birth in 1819, Crummell was born free in New York City, the child of an African, Boston Crummell (from the area later known as Sierra Leone), and a woman who came from generations of free black Americans. Crummell's community believed in self-improvement for black people, particularly as achieved through education. The young Crummell went to the African Free School, an institution for free black Americans. His classmates included future prominent black people, such as Henry Highland GARNET and Ira Frederick ALDRIDGE.

Crummell and Garnet also attended Noyes Academy in New Hampshire, but were forced to leave when local farmers destroyed the school buildings out of anger at the many students at this school who attended abolition meetings.

Crummell did graduate in 1839 from Oneida Institute, a school in Whitesboro, New York, staffed by black and white abolitionists. He aspired to a ministry in the Episcopal Church, which at the time was an almost completely white institution. It followed that church attitudes were not exactly welcoming. Crummell was rejected from New York's General Theological Seminary in 1839 because of his color, but he studied privately with leading ministers and was finally ordained in 1844—although not allowed to enter the diocese of Pennsylvania as an equal. Crummell finally organized an Episcopal congregation of poor black people in New York while remaining active in the abolition movement.

Crummell eventually went to England, raising money for his church, lecturing and studying there from 1848 to 1853. Then, deciding that more opportunity awaited in Africa, he journeyed to Liberia, the nation founded by free African-Americans. Crummell focused on religious work, but he was also an important spokesperson for African nationalism and the idea that black people were able to build for themselves a new nation.

He became known for his educational activities in Liberia—working in high schools and colleges, and seeking to establish his own school. But before he could begin with the construction of the new school building, he had to leave Liberia. The country was torn between two groups: "mulattos," or people of mixed race, largely from America; and "pure" blacks, or African natives. The Americans had become the ruling group. Since Crummell believed that native Africans should have full equality, the ruling mulattos threatened his life, and he returned to the U.S. in 1872.

In 1873, Crummell went to live in Washington, D.C., where he later was to found St. Luke's Church. He became a prominent speaker to black audiences, preaching the need for educated black people to help "improve the race." His first wife died in the 1870s, and in 1880, he was remarried, to Jennie M. Simpson.

Crummell retired from the ministry in 1894, but taught at Howard University in Washington, D.C., from 1895 to 1897. In that time, he helped to organize the American Negro Academy to foster black scholarship.

Crummell's views paralled Booker T. WASHINGTON's, advocating manual labor and trade skills for most black people, yet he believed in the higher education of a talented minority—a leadership group who would show the way to advancement for all. In stressing intellectual achievement, he was closer to DuBois.

Crummell died of heart disease on September 10, 1898. His funeral was held in the same church in New York City where he had been baptized as an infant.

Further Reading: *We the Children of Africa in This Land: Alexander Crummell,* by Otey M. Scruggs, Washington, D.C.: Howard University Dept. of History, 1972 ed.; *Alexander Crummell: An Apostle of Negro Culture,* by William Henry Ferris, New York: Arno Press, 1969.

—*R. K.*

❖ CUFFE, PAUL
(1759–1817), *Colonial merchant*

Paul Cuffe was unusual for his time: a wealthy black owner of a shipping business who fought for black equality and civil rights. As a young man, Cuffe and his brother refused to pay their taxes, and joined with other black people to petition for the right not to pay taxes, since they were not permitted to vote. Finally, in 1783, they won the right to vote.

Cuffe is also well known for his efforts to colonize Sierra Leone, an African nation. He had two goals: to convert the Sierra Leone natives to Christianity and to help black Americans resettle in Africa. Although most black Americans never supported "colonization"—the movement to resettle black Americans in Africa—Cuffe was rich enough to furnish passage to Africa for 38 black people, purchased with $4,000.

Cuffe was the seventh of 10 children born to Cuffe Slocum, a former slave, and Ruth Moses, a Wampanoag Indian. Cuffe was born on the Massachusetts island of Cuttyhunk. This led to an early interest in the sea, as well as to contact with the Quakers, a religious group which opposed war and slavery, and which worked for abolition and equality.

As a young man, Cuffe arranged to have his family's name changed from Slocum to Cuffe, because Slocum had been the name of his father's master. In 1783, Cuffe married Alice Pequit, an Indian from his mother's tribe. Meanwhile, the young man was establishing a thriving shipping business in whaling, coastal fishing, and Caribbean and European trade. With black crews, Cuffe sailed to Sweden, Russia, and France, building up a fortune and expanding his fleet.

Cuffe used part of his wealth to further religious causes, helping to build a new Friends (Quaker) Meeting House in Westport, Massachusetts. He also bought a farm in Cuttyhunk—and spent his own money in setting up a school there for free black children—youngsters who had no other place for study in the New Bedford area.

Cuffe became interested in Sierra Leone as a place to convert native Africans to Christianity, and as a new place of resettlement for black Americans. In 1810, he embarked on a two-year trip to explore Sierra Leone, and there, in 1811, founded the Friendly Society to foster black American emigration.

The War of 1812 between the United States and Britain interrupted Cuffe's plans, since he had been working closely with people in both countries. But in December 1815, Cuffe sailed once again to Sierra Leone, accompanied by 18 adults and 20 children.

This voyage strengthened his belief that African re-emigration was a better solution than attempting to reform the United States. This view of colonization looked especially attractive during times when the work to abolish slavery was not going well. Many prominent black Americans, such as James FORTEN and Richard ALLEN, supported this idea.

However, the majority of black Americans never favored emigration, even when it was most difficult for them to succeed in the United States, and many black leaders continued to oppose this plan.

Nevertheless, Cuffe continued to believe in colonization. Other trips to Africa were planned, but he was unable to continue because of poor health. He died in 1817, leaving behind a business that lasted for another generation and a dream that endured.

Further Reading: *Captain Paul Cuffe's Logs and Letters, 1808–1817: A Black Quaker's Voice from Within the Veil,* by Rosalind Cobb Wiggins et al., Washington, D.C.: Howard University Press, 1996; *Paul Cuffe: Black America and the African Return,* by Sheldon Harris, New York: Simon & Schuster, 1972; *Paul Cuffe, the Black Yankee, 1759–1817,* by George Salvador, New Bedford, Mass.: Reynolds-DeWalt, 1969.

—*R. K.*

❖ CULLEN, COUNTÉE (Countée Porter)
(1903–1946), *poet*

Countée Cullen was a major writer of the Harlem Renaissance, which was a flourishing movement in the 1920s of young black novelists, poets, and painters who depicted the lives of black Americans in completely new ways. Cullen's book of poetry, *Color* (New York: Arno Press), published in 1925 when he was only 21, pioneered new approaches in writing about matters of race and black culture.

Cullen was also the author of four other collections of poetry, some books for children, and a novel. With Arna BONTEMPS, he adapted Bontemps's novel into a play, and then into a successful Broadway musical, *St. Louis Woman.*

Countée Cullen (*Library of Congress*)

Cullen was known for writing about Africa and its meaning to black Americans, a subject that was quite radical for its time. One of his most famous poem asks, "What Is Africa to Me," as the poet tries to imagine the rich land of his ancestors. Another, "Yet Do I Marvel," was the opening poem in *Color.* Here, the poet lists all the the mysteries that only God can explain. Then he writes, "Yet do I marvel at this curious thing:/To make a poet black, and bid him sing!"

Cullen was born in New York City on May 30, 1903, as Countée Porter. He is thought to have lived with his maternal grandmother until her death in 1918. He was then adopted by the Reverend and Mrs. Frederick A. Cullen, and was given the name he used thereafter. Reverend Cullen was the minister at one of the largest and most influential churches in Harlem, and was able to send his new son to DeWitt Clinton High School, one of the best public schools in the city, although few black people attended it at the time.

Cullen did very well in school, receiving academic honors and winning various poetry contests. His scholastic record at New York University was outstanding—he was one of 11 students in his class to be elected to the Phi Beta Kappa Honor Society. He also continued to win prizes for his poetry, gaining national recognition by the time he graduated.

For the 21-year-old Cullen, 1925 was a year of amazing accomplishment. That year, he took second prize in the *Opportunity* poetry contest (*Opportunity* was a magazine devoted to black literature and journalism); he won the John Reed Memorial Prize in a contest sponsored by *Poetry,* a national poetry magazine; and he published *Color,* his first book of poetry.

Cullen obtained his M.A. at Harvard in 1926, and from 1926 to 1928, he was assistant editor of *Opportunity.* Meanwhile, in 1927, he recevied an award from the Harmon Foundation for black artistic achievement, as well as a Guggenheim Fellowship to study abroad, in recognition of his outstanding poetry. He also published *Copper Sun* (New York: Harper & Bros., 1927), his second volume of poems.

In 1928, Cullen married Yolande DuBois, daughter of W. E. B. DUBOIS, the black scholar and critic, just before leaving for Paris on his Guggenheim Fellowship. As W. E. B. DuBois and Cullen were both famous, the wedding received a lot of publicity, but the marriage lasted little more than a year, ending in a divorce in 1930.

After 1934, he became a schoolteacher in Harlem, where he continued to work until his death. In 1940,

Cullen remarried, to Ida Mae Roberson. This was apparently a happy marriage.

Cullen died at the relatively young age of 42, on January 10, 1946. The funeral was officiated by his father at their church in Harlem.

Although Cullen was praised for his racial themes and portraits of black life, he insisted that he was a poet, not a "Negro poet." That was a contradictory theme in his own thinking, for he felt that his poetry ended up treating racial themes "of itself," as though it had a life of its own that he could not control.

In a similar contradiction, Cullen wrote poetry that contrasted the difficulties of racist America with the beauties of his lost land of Africa. Yet he also wrote, in 1927, that as long as black people spoke English, their poetry would be more influenced by English and American literature than by any "yearnings toward an African inheritance."

There were also "nonracial" subjects, themes of religious faith, death, love, and nature. Some critics believe that even in these poems, there is evidence of Cullen's self-perceived identity as a black poet in a white-dominated country. At any rate, he seemed to turn away from obviously racial themes in his poetry after 1929.

Cullen's other books of poetry include *The Black Christ, and Other Poems* (New York: Harper & Bros., 1929); *The Ballad of the Brown Girl: An Old Ballad Retold* (New York: Harper & Bros., 1927); and *The Medea, and Some Poems* (New York: Harper & Bros., 1937). The last was a new version of the Greek play *Medea,* but also included some new poems. The best anthology of Cullen's work is probably *On These I Stand: An Anthology of the Best Poems of Countée Cullen* (New York: Harper & Bros.), a collection that he prepared himself, although it was not published until 1947.

Cullen's only novel, *One Way to Heaven* (New York: AMS Press), was published in 1932. It contrasts the churchgoing black people of Harlem and the new, better-educated Harlem intellectuals.

Further Reading: *My Soul's High Song: The Collected Writings of Countée Cullen, Voice of the Harlem Renaissance,* by Countée Cullen, ed. by Gerald Early, Garden City, N.Y.: Doubleday, 1991; *A Bio-Bibliography of Countée P. Cullen 1903–1946,* by Margaret Perry, Westport, Conn.: Greenwood Publishers, 1971; *Countée Cullen and the Negro Renaissance,* by Blanche E. Ferguson, New York: Dodd, Mead, 1966; *Roots of Negro Racial Consciousness, the 1920's: The Harlem Renaissance Authors,* by Stephen H. Bronz, New York: Libra Books, 1964; *Black Poets of the United States,* by Jean Wagner, Urbana, Ill.: University of Illinois Press, 1973.

—R. K.

✤ DAILEY, ULYSSES GRANT
(1885–1961), *surgeon*

Ulysses Grant Dailey was a prominent surgeon who founded his own hospital in Chicago. He served as president of the nation's major association of black physicians, the National Medical Association. In addition, he was the author of more than 40 articles for the association's *Journal* and a fellow of the American Medical Association. Over the course of his long career, he worked with health officials in Haiti, established a chapter of the International College of Surgeons in Karachi, Pakistan, and toured Africa and Asia for the State Department.

Dailey was honored by Howard University in Washington, D.C., with an honorary doctor of science degree in 1947, and by Chicago's Northwestern University with a similar degree in 1955. Haiti made him an honorary consul in Chicago, and an officer of their National Order of Honor and Merit.

Ulysses Grant Dailey was born in 1882 to S. Toney Hanna and Missouri (Johnson) Dailey in Donaldsonville, Louisiana. He went to high school in Fort Worth, Texas, but returned to Louisiana for his college studies, attending Straight University (now called Dillard) in New Orleans. Dailey was fifth in his class at Northwestern University Medical School in 1906. At age 21, he was also the youngest to graduate. For two years, he was assistant demonstrator of anatomy at his alma mater, then went on

to work as an ambulance surgeon, gynecologist, and surgeon. After postgraduate work in Paris and Berlin, he returned to teach and practice surgery in Chicago.

Dailey broadened the scope of his surgical practice with study in Europe. During this time, in 1916, he married Eleanor Jane Curtis. Then, in 1926, he founded the Dailey Hospital and Sanitarium in Chicago, while establishing a permanent place for himself at Chicago's Provident Hospital. From 1926 to 1932, Dailey was Provident's surgeon in chief, and from 1932 to 1961, senior attending surgeon and senior attending surgeon emeritus.

Ulysses Dailey's prominence was noted in the 1950 edition of *Who's Who in Colored America* (Yonkers-on-Hudson, N.Y.: C. E. Burckel, 1950); and numerous eulogies were delivered by his colleagues at his death in 1961. Dailey, as a respected medical authority, demonstrated the potential for achievement by black people. Beyond his life as an exemplary model, he left as his legacy a hospital and sanitarium, serving the people of Chicago.

—*R. K.*

✤ DAVIS, ANGELA YVONNE
(1944–), *educator, activist*

Angela Davis, a member of the National Committee of the Communist Party of the United States (CPUSA) and

Angela Davis (*Archive Photos*)

a nationally known theorist, activist, and political leader, ran twice for vice president on the Communist Party ticket, in 1980 and 1984. As a leader and cofounder of the National Alliance Against Racist and Political Repression, Angela Davis works to free people believed to have been jailed for racial or political motives.

Davis is also the author of several works on women, the family, and black culture. Her essays are collected in *Women, Race and Class* (New York: Random House), published in 1981, and the 1990 *Women, Culture and Politics* (New York: Vintage Books).

Angela Davis was born on January 26, 1944, the daughter of B. Frank Davis, a teacher and businessperson, and Sallye E. Davis, a teacher. She grew up in the Dynamite Hill area of Birmingham, Alabama. During her childhood, segregation was in full force, and black residents were constantly on guard against violence. In the famous 1963 Ku Klux Klan bombing of the

Sixteenth Street Baptist Church, four of Davis's friends, who had been attending Sunday school, died.

Davis's family had communist friends, so she had an early exposure to radical politics. While she was attending a Quaker high school on scholarship in New York City, she participated in civil rights marches, helped form interracial study groups, and joined a communist youth group.

In 1965, Davis earned a B.A., magna cum laude, from Brandeis University in Massachusetts. Her M.A. was granted in 1968 by the University of California at San Diego—where she studied with Herbert Marcuse, a leftwing political philosopher. Although Marcuse's politics were quite different from Davis's, she was considered by him to be the best student he had ever taught.

She continued her political activism at San Diego, helping to found the Black Student Council and participating in the San Diego Black Conference and the Student Nonviolent Coordinating Committee (SNCC), a major civil rights organization of the time.

At 24, Davis joined the Communist Party and continued her organizing work. In her autobiography, she explains the attraction of communism and her belief that it best explained why people were oppressed. She was also drawn to the idea of creating a society run entirely by working people, which seemed the best way for black people and other minorities to win freedom and equality.

Meanwhile, in 1969, Davis had begun her teaching career as an assistant professor of philosophy at the University of California, Los Angeles (UCLA). However, because of her political views, the State Board of Regents dismissed her. Although a court order reinstated her, Davis's contract was not renewed the next year.

This decision was protested by the American Association of University Professors, the major professional organization for college teachers. The AAUP pointed out that Davis's rating had been "excellent" and that no one had claimed that she was biased. However, she was never rehired.

In 1970, Davis became involved with George Jackson, a black activist jailed in Soledad Prison. He and others attempted to escape from a California courthouse, in an incident that erupted into a shootout. Davis was accused of planning the escape and of supplying a gun that killed four people. She was jailed for 16 months, but was finally acquitted and freed in 1972.

She continued working on behalf of other political prisoners, and traveled around the country and the world, speaking on political topics. In the late 1970s, Davis began teaching at San Francisco State University, which she continued until 1991. In 1991, she joined the staff of the University of Santa Cruz, where she is currently professor of history of consciousness, teaching about feminism, African-American studies, and other subjects. She holds the Presidential Chair in African-American and feminist studies. She is also on the board of directors of the National Political Congress of Black Women and of the National Black Women's Health Project.

Further Reading: *The Angela Y. Davis Reader* (Blackwell Readers), by Angela Y. Davis, ed. by Joy James, New York: Blackwell Publishers, 1998; *Angela Davis: An Autobiography,* by Angela Y. Davis, New York: International Publishers, 1989; *Angela Davis: With My Mind on Freedom, An Autobiography,* by Angela Davis, New York: Random House, 1974; *If They Come in the Morning: Voices of Resistance,* by Angela Davis, Ruchell Magee, the Soledad Brothers and others, New York: Third World Press, 1971; *The People vs. Angela Davis,* by Charles R. Ashman, New York: Pinnacle Books, 1972.

—*R. K.*

❖ DAVIS, BENJAMIN OLIVER, JR.
(1912–   ), *war hero, aviator*

The long military career of Benjamin Davis, Jr., has been one of rare distinction. He was the fourth black student ever to graduate from the U.S. Military Academy at West Point, became the first black general in the Air Force and was appointed assistant secretary in charge of civil aviation security at the U.S. Department of Transportation.

Benjamin Davis came from a military family: His father, Benjamin Oliver DAVIS, SR., was the first black general in the U.S. Army. The junior Davis was born in 1912, in Washington, D.C. He was a West Point cadet and graduated in 1936. While Davis, Sr., was pursuing his notable career in the army, his son decided his own future lay with the Air Force. He transferred and, in 1942, received his wings. He soon became the commander of the 99th Fighter Squadron, which fought in northern Italy, Sicily, and North Africa. Later, he led the 332nd Fighter Group.

His World War II decorations were many, and included the Silver Star and the Distinguished Flying Cross. He also distinguished himself in the Korean War, where he commanded the 51st Fighter-Interceptor Wing, and was director of operations and training of the Far East Air Forces.

Perhaps his greatest honor came in 1954, when he was made the first black brigadier general in the Air Force. Eleven years later, he was promoted to lieutenant general, a rank he held until his 1970 retirement.

Davis remained active after leaving the military, serving a year as director of public safety in Cleveland, Ohio, before his federal appointment to the post in the Transportation Department.

Further Reading: *Benjamin O. Davis, American: An Autobiography,* Washington, D.C.: Smithsonian Institution Press, 1991; *Black Wings: The American Black in Aviation,* by Von Hardesty, Washington, D.C.: Air and Space Museum, 1983.

—*R. K.*

❖ DAVIS, BENJAMIN OLIVER, SR.
(1877–1970), *army officer, educator, government official*

Benjamin Oliver Davis, Sr., was the first black general in the U.S. Army. His extensive career included military service and intervals spent as a professor of military science at Wilberforce University in Ohio and Tuskegee Institute in Alabama. He was the father of Benjamin Oliver DAVIS, JR., the first black general in the U.S. Air Force.

Davis, Sr., was born in 1877, in Washington, D.C., where he also attended Howard University. Unlike his son, who began his military career with a West Point commission, Davis, Sr., enlisted as an army private. In 1898, he served a year in the infantry as a volunteer in the Spanish-American War, then went on to enlist in the regular army in 1899. Davis was then assigned to the Philippines, a territory the United States had taken from Spain in the recently concluded war.

In 1901, Davis received an unusual honor for an African-American soldier. He was given a commission—the entitlement to serve as an officer—and was made a second lieutenant in the cavalry (at that time, still soldiers on horseback). Davis was stationed at various posts within the United States for many years before assignment to Monrovia, Liberia, where he served as military attaché until 1912.

Throughout these and other years of his career, he taught military science at Wilberforce and Tuskegee and continued to rise through the ranks. In World War I, he was promoted to major; in 1930, he became a full colonel. In 1940, he achieved the rank of brigadier general.

Davis retired from military service the following year, but was later recalled to active duty during World War II. He was made special adviser to the commander of the European Theater of Operations, and later served

Benjamin Oliver Davis, Sr. *(Library of Congress)*

as assistant to the inspector general in Washington, D.C. In 1948, he fully retired from the armed forces. Until his death in 1970, he had the satisfaction of seeing his son continue on the same path of military achievement.

—R. K.

❖ DAVIS, OSSIE
(1917–), *actor, director, writer*

Ossie Davis has acted, written and directed for the stage, movies, and television. With his wife, actress Ruby Dee, he was one of the post–World War II actors who tried to present a more accurate image of black people—as complex and intelligent men and women concerned with genuine problems—far from the stereotyped Hollywood portrayal of happy slaves or comic servants.

One of his most notable triumphs was the 1961 Broadway play *Purlie Victorious,* a satirical comedy, which he wrote and starred in. In 1963, the play became a movie, *Gone Are the Days;* a Broadway musical, *Purlie;* and a television special.

Davis was nominated for an Emmy for his work in "Teacher, Teacher," a 1969 television special in which he played the teacher of a young, retarded white child.

Ossie Davis was born on December 18, 1917, in Cogdell, Georgia, the son of Kince Charles Davis, a railway construction worker, and Laura (Cooper) Davis. His parents wanted to name him "Rayford Chapman," or "R. C." Davis, after his grandfather, but the clerk misheard the name as "Ossie." In those days, it was a considerable risk for a black southerner to disagree with a white official, so "R. C. Davis" was forever after known as "Ossie."

Davis attended Howard University in Washington, D.C., and Columbia University in New York, during the years before World War II (in 1973, Howard University honored him with a doctorate). He studied acting in 1941 with Harlem's Rose McClendon Players. During World War II, he spent nearly three years in the army, where he wrote and produced shows for the troops.

After the war, in 1946, Davis returned to acting. He played the title role in the Broadway show *Jeb Turner.* Although the play ran for only nine performances, it had great personal significance for Davis. There he met fellow cast member Ruby DEE, and they married two years later, after they finished touring in *Anna Lucasta.* Eventually, the couple had three children.

The 1950s were lean times for black actors who resented playing servants or stereotypical roles. Davis once said that it was peculiar having to compete with others "to fight to say words you were ashamed of." In fact, Davis appeared in such Broadway shows as *Green Pastures,* a comedy-fantasy about an all-black heaven, which contained many racist images.

Davis found more rewarding work in Lorraine Hansberry's *A Raisin in the Sun,* but generally, it was difficult for him to find roles he could be proud of. Davis also would have preferred to be a writer, but felt he could make a better living as an actor.

In the 1960s, Davis appeared often in television shows, as well as in movies, such as *The Cardinal,* in 1963; *Shock Treatment,* in 1964; *The Hill,* in 1965; *A Man Called Adam,* in 1966; and *The Scalphunters,* in 1968.

Although Davis's play about McCarthyism, *Alice in Wonder,* was poorly received, his writing was critically acclaimed with the appearance of *Purlie Victorious* in 1961. Davis later adapted this play into the movie *Gone Are the Days,* which starred himself and Ruby Dee. In 1970, *Purlie* became a Broadway musical, praised by the *New York Times* as "by far the most successful and richest of all black musicals."

Davis's directing and producing brought him further success in 1970, with the film *Cotton Comes to Harlem.* He continued to act throughout the 1970s and 1980s, in films and television, and directed movies as well. In 1971, he directed and produced *Kongi's Harvest,* from the play by African writer Wole Soyinka; and in 1972, he directed and produced *Black Girl,* from the play by black woman writer J. E. Franklin.

Davis always brought a political perspective and an underlying message to his work, no matter which format. The comedy he directed and in which he starred, *Cotton Comes to Harlem,* made important statements about racism, as did the 1973 action film *Gordon's War* under his direction. The 1976 movie *Countdown at Kusini,* directed by Davis and in which he starred, related the story of an African nation's struggle for liberation.

Davis's writing credits also include political material. He cowrote "For Us the Living," a dramatic work on the life of civil rights leader Medgar EVERS.

Davis and Ruby Dee began a nightclub career in 1964, when they performed at the famous Village Vanguard. They continued as a team in such productions as a dramatic reading of Langston HUGHES's poetry. In the 1970s, they had a radio program, and in the 1980s they cohosted a television series on PBS, *With Ossie and Ruby.*

Political work has absorbed Davis throughout his career, and he has lent his name and energy to numerous causes, particularly those involving civil rights. He testified at a 1962 Congressional investigation into racial discrimination in the entertainment industry. He represented black Americans at meetings of the World Festival of Black and African Arts and Culture in 1975. Davis has also been a strong supporter of Local 1199, of New York City's Union of Hospital and Health Care Employees. In 1970, he and Ruby Dee received the Frederick Douglass Award from the New York Urban League for distinguished leadership in the field of civil rights.

Filmmaker Spike LEE has paid tribute to Ossie Davis in five of his films, with a featured cameo as the coach in *School Daze* (1988); the "Da Mayor" role in *Do the Right Thing* (1989); the part of the retired preacher in *Jungle Fever* (1991); a cameo as himself in *Malcolm X* (1992), and the role of Jeremiah in *Get on the Bus.*

Other film and television work of Davis's includes parts in the TV movies *12 Angry Men* (1997) and *Miss Evers' Boys* (1997); a role in the series *Evening Shade* (1990); and parts in the films *I'm Not Rappaport* (1996), *The Client* (1994), and *Grumpy Old Men* (1993).

Further Reading: *Purlie Victorious: A Commemoration,* by Ossie Davis, New York: Emmalyn Enterprises, 1993.

—*R. K.*

❖ DEE, RUBY
(1923–), *actress, director, writer*

Ruby Dee is perhaps best known for her praiseworthy performance in the film version of *A Raisin in the Sun.*

There have been numerous films, plays, and television shows. With her husband, actor Ossie DAVIS, she cohosted a PBS series, *With Ossie and Ruby.*

Dee's honors include an Emmy nomination from the Academy of Television Arts and Sciences for *Express Stop from Lenox Avenue,* a 1964 television special; an Obie Award for best off-Broadway performance in the 1971 production of Athol Fugard's play *Boesman and Lena;* a 1972 Martin Luther King Award from Operation PUSH; and a 1974 Drama Desk Award. In 1970, with Ossie Davis, she received the Frederick Douglass Award of the New York Urban League, in recognition of her leading role in the civil rights movement.

Dee has also been active in women's issues. She has written poetry and dramatic monologues; developed an evening's dramatic reading of Langston HUGHES's poetry, along with Davis, who appeared with her; and performed in numerous benefits and lunchtime specials for Local 1199, the union of New York City's hospital and health-care workers.

Dee was born in 1923 in Cleveland, Ohio, as Ruby Ann Wallace—the daughter of Marshall Edward Wallace, a railroad porter, and Emma (Benson) Wallace, a teacher. She attended New York City's Hunter College, graduating in 1945. While in college, she changed her last name and also began studies at the American Negro Theater, from 1941 to 1944. Her classmates included Ossie Davis and Sidney POITIER.

In 1943, Ruby Dee made her first stage appearance. Other small Broadway roles followed, including a bit part in the 1946 *Jeb Turner,* where she met her future husband, Ossie Davis. (Later, they would have three children.)

In the 1950s, Dee managed to work in films, although there were few roles for black women and even fewer for those who refused to play servants or other stereotypical roles. Instead, Dee was frequently cast as a supportive wife.

Her first movie role was as Jackie Robinson's wife in *The Jackie Robinson Story,* in 1950, and she had a key part in the 1957 film *Edge of the City,* which costarred Sidney Poitier and white filmmaker-actor John Cassavetes.

Dee starred on Broadway as Ruth Younger in the now-classic *A Raisin in the Sun,* which was the first play written by a black woman to be produced on Broadway. In 1961, Dee played the same character in the movie version, costarring with Sidney Poitier and Claudia McNeil. In 1961, she also starred in Ossie Davis's musical *Purlie Victorious.* In the 1963 film *The Balcony,* she played an unusual role for her—a prostitute.

In 1965, Dee broke theatrical ground at the American Shakespeare Festival in Stratford, Connecticut, as the first black actress to play major classical roles. She continued to play a variety of roles in both classical and contemporary drama.

Her movies continued into the 1990s, and she was featured in two of Spike LEE's films, *Do the Right Thing* (1989) and *Jungle Fever* (1991). She has made numerous television appearances, starring in both series and specials, including the 1979 *Roots: The Next Generation* and the 1982 black version of Eugene O'Neill's *Long Day's Journey Into Night.*

Dee is also a writer. She collaborated with Jules Dassin and Julian Mayfield on the screenplay for *Up Tight,* a 1968 film about a black man who betrays his friends after a robbery and murder. She also wrote *Take It from the Top,* a stage musical she directed and starred in as well, as an angel who returns to Earth and recruits good people to battle an evil capitalist.

Ruby Dee's prose and poetry include *Glowchild and Other Poems* (New York: Third World Press, 1972); *My One Good Nerve: Rhythms, Rhymes, Reasons* (a collection of stories, poems and essays) (Chicago, Ill.: Third World Press, 1986); and *Two Ways to Count to Ten* (New York: Henry Holt, 1989). She was once a columnist for New York's major black newspaper, the *New York Amsterdam News,* and has been an associate editor of the black journal *Freedomways.*

In 1998 her one-woman show, *My One Good Nerve,* based on her book of the same title, premiered in New York.

—*R. K.*

❖ DELANY, MARTIN ROBISON
(1812–1885), *ethnologist, abolitionist, black nationalist*

Martin Delany had a long and varied career as an editor, doctor, writer, and political activist. His work was constant in its theme of greater rights for African Americans. There were times when he agitated against slavery: He founded the first black newspaper west of the Allegheny Mountains, worked with abolitionist John Brown, and recruited black troops for the Union during the Civil War. There were also times when his emphasis was more on urging black people to leave the United States and set up their own colony in Latin America or Africa.

But whatever the approach, Delany did much to disseminate the history of the African people, particularly through his book, *Principia of Ethnology: The Origin of*

Races and Color. Written in 1879, *Principia* argued that black people produced by black cultures had made key contributions to world civilization—a view quite unheard-of then, but which today has gained much acceptance.

Martin Delany was born on May 6, 1812, in Charles Town, Virginia (today, West Virginia), to the slave Samuel Delany and the free woman Pati (Peace) Delany. As a child, he heard from his grandmother, Graci Peace, the stories of his African grandparents, who had been enslaved and brought to the United States.

It was illegal then in southern states for slaves to learn reading and writing, but a Yankee peddler violated the law and taught the five Delany children. When the family's white neighbors learned of it, Delany's mother was threatened with jail. To make sure her children would be educated, she brought them to the northern state of Pennsylvania, where black literacy was legal. In 1823, Delany's father bought his own freedom and joined his family.

At 19, Martin Delany left home. He walked across the Allegheny Mountains to Pittsburgh, where he found a tutor and a night school. A white doctor taught him some medical techniques of the time.

Delany soon became an officer of the Pittsburgh Anti-Slavery Society and an activist in the Underground Railroad—the clandestine system for smuggling escaped slaves to freedom. At this time, in 1843, Delany married Catherine Richards, the daughter of the wealthiest black man in Pittsburgh. Over the next 24 years, they had seven surviving children.

In 1843, he also began to publish *The Mystery*, the area's first black paper, covering the anti-slavery movement. In 1847, however, lack of funds forced Delany to work on Frederick DOUGLASS's paper, the *North Star*.

He decided in 1848 to study medicine, which at that time was a far less costly undertaking than today. In 1850, however, his acceptance at Harvard University in Massachusetts was protested by students, who did not wish to have a black man in their classes. The medical faculty, led by Oliver Wendell Holmes, Sr., gave in to their demand and expelled Delany the next semester. Fortunately for him, since doctors were not then required to finish school, Delany was able to practice medicine anyway, and call himself "doctor."

The year 1850 was a time of strong sentiment against the Fugitive Slave Act, the law that made it illegal to help a runaway slave. Abolitionists of all races protested this law, with Delany helping to organize such activity in Pittsburgh. Meanwhile, he continued his medical work and served as principal of a black school.

In light of his Harvard experience, the Fugitive Slave Act cautioned Delany even more as to the prospects for black people in the United States. There was at this time a great debate about "colonization"—whether black people should work for equal rights in the United States or emigrate to a colony that they could control. Delany became a colonizationist, recommending emigration to Latin America or, should that not be possible, to Africa. He expressed his views in 1852 in *The Condition, Elevation, Emigration and Destiny of the Colored People of the United States, Politically Considered* (New York: Arno Press, 1968 reprint of 1852 ed.).

Delany himself emigrated to Canada. But he stayed in touch with U.S. activists, particularly John Brown, who was ultimately to organize the ill-fated antislavery raid on Harper's Ferry, Virginia.

Delany traveled throughout Europe and North America, to attract more followers and raise funds for his movement. He wore an elaborate embroidered African robe at his lectures, which he felt demonstrated a high level of African culture.

Meanwhile, the Civil War had begun. In 1863, President Lincoln signed the Emancipation Proclamation, which freed all slaves in areas at war with the Union and made them eligible to fight in the Union Army. Delany became a recruiter, and came up with a plan to arm slaves in the South. To this end, he met with Lincoln, was made the first black major in the army, and enlisted two regiments of ex-slaves in Charleston, South Carolina.

During the Reconstruction period following the war, Delany worked at the South Carolina Freedmen's Bureau, facilitating the transition of slaves to life as free citizens. In 1874, he was appointed to be a trial justice. In various capacities, he worked for civil rights under Reconstruction, that period when blacks began increasingly to participate on an equal footing in the economic and political life of the South. However, many whites were trying to put blacks "back in their place." Contrary to many younger black activists of the time, Delany believed that it was important to compromise with these reactionary forces; otherwise, he believed, Reconstruction had little chance in succeeding.

Thus, Delany ran for lieutenant governor with conservative support. Although he lost this election, two years later, he still supported the Democrats (at the time, the more conservative party, as opposed to the Radical Republicans who backed broad social changes in the South).

Delany continued to make compromise overtures to white Democrats. In 1876, he was almost killed by a group of black people who were furious over his support of the Democratic candidate for governor. When the governor won, Delany was rewarded by being appointed as a trial justice once again.

Then in 1877, the Democrats and the Republicans made a deal. To settle a close election for president, the parties agreed that Rutherford B. Hayes, the Republican candidate, could win if he would agree to withdraw federal troops from the South.

As soon as this happened, white segregationists and former slave owners quickly rolled back almost all earlier gains by blacks. Lynchings and terrorizing of blacks increased, and thousands of black farmers lost the land that they had been previously granted. Many left for Kansas. These difficulties led some black people to consider emigration to Africa as a more attractive opportunity.

Delany continued to work under the white administration, but supported emigration as well. In 1878, he assisted the Liberian Exodus Joint Stock Exchange Company, which bought a steamship to carry black people to the African-American colony of Liberia in Africa.

Delany planned to move to Africa himself, after his children were grown. Meanwhile, he returned to Washington in 1880, but he failed to get a government appointment. In the end, he joined his family in Wilberforce, Ohio, where he died on January 24, 1885.

Delany, the black nationalist, took great pride in his African background, his people, and himself. Frederick Douglass said of him, "I thank God for making me a man simply, but Delany always thanks him for making him a black man."

Further Reading: *Martin R. Delany, The Beginnings of Black Nationalism,* by Victor Ullman, Boston: Beacon Press, 1971; *The Making of an Afro-American: Martin Robinson Delany,* by Dorothy Sterling, Garden City, N.Y.: Doubleday, 1971.

—R. K.

❖ DIXON, DEAN CHARLES
(1915–1976), *conductor*

Dean Dixon was the first black American to achieve international recognition as the conductor of a symphony orchestra. Although there had been other black conductors working in Europe, Dixon was the first to tour worldwide, and also the first to hold positions of considerable duration with major orchestras. His American con-

ducting included concerts with the New York Philharmonic and the Boston Symphony.

He won many honors for his musical work, including a Rosenwald Fellowship in music and the Alice M. Ditson Award for outstanding American conductor of 1947–48.

Dean Dixon was born in Harlem (in New York City) of West Indian parents on January 10, 1915, when there were few black people active in classical music. Yet he began to study the violin before the age of four, and through diligence and talent, he was able to attend New York' Juilliard School of Music—which was the preeminent musical school of the time.

At age 17, Dixon began to organize his own musical groups. These interracial groups were able to survive because of the support of the Harlem community. In 1944, Dixon formed the American Youth Orchestra.

Dixon also served as guest conductor for a number of orchestras—such as the NBC Symphony and the New York Philharmonic. Although his brilliance was obvious to the musically knowledgeable, prejudice barred him from a regular position with an American orchestra. When the French National Radio Orchestra invited him to Paris in 1949, he went to Europe and stayed there for 21 years.

Dixon's career included conductorship of Sweden's Göteborg Symphony, 1953–60, and Frankfurt's Hesse Radio Symphony Orchestra, 1961–74. In 1964, he also conducted Australia's Sydney Symphony Orchestra. He spoke several languages besides the international one of music.

Dixon did return to the United States in 1970 to conduct a summer series of concerts with the New York Philharmonic, and the following year he toured with that orchestra. He continued to conduct until his retirement due to illness in 1974. Then he settled in Switzerland, where he died on November 4, 1976.

—R. K.

❖ DOUGLASS, FREDERICK
(1817–1895), *abolitionist, diplomat, publisher, statesman*

Frederick Douglass has often been called the "father of the Civil Rights movement." His book *Narrative of the Life of Frederick Douglass* became a best-selling account of life under slavery and his escape to freedom. Published in 1845, his story was a major contribution to the antislavery movement.

Douglass was active in antislavery causes, women's rights and, after the Civil War, the movement for black worker who seals the cracks in wooden ships). In 1838, he managed to escape by posing as a sailor.

Douglass fled to New York, where he was assisted by the black-run New York Vigilance Committee, a group that helped runaway slaves. There he married Anna Murray, a free black woman whom he had met in Baltimore. The couple traveled to New Bedford, Massachusetts, where Douglass changed his slave name "Bailey" to "Douglass."

Although Douglass was a skilled caulker, racial prejudice kept him from being employed in the New Bedford shipyard. However, he became an active abolitionist, and it was soon apparent that he had a talent for public speaking. The Massachusetts Anti-Slavery Society asked him to become an agent—one who traveled and spoke for the abolitionist cause.

Ironically, his very skill as a speaker was a handicap in some people's eyes. He was sometimes told that he spoke "too well," and that no one would believe he had ever been a slave. Sometimes he was asked simply to relate his experiences of slavery, and to leave out his own analysis of the problem and the solution.

Nevertheless, Douglass continued to speak in his own way. In 1845, he also published his famous autobiography, *Narrative of the Life of Frederick Douglass.* Unlike many slave narratives of the time, this was completely written by a black person, not ghost-written by a white person. Douglass and his colleagues believed that the book would help convince white people that black people were truly and wholly human and, therefore, their equals.

Because Douglass's book was so specific about the details of his life, it exposed him to the danger of being found by his master. So, later that year, he sailed for England, where he was celebrated for his abolitionist work. After his British friends had helped to buy his freedom, he returned to the United States.

Soon after, in 1847, Douglass and his family moved to Rochester, New York, where he began to publish the *North Star,* an abolitionist newspaper. For a while, he and Martin DELANY shared the editorship of the paper. Together they used their journal to advocate a sense of racial pride. This paper was later called *Frederick Douglass' Paper,* and then *Douglass' Monthly.*

Douglass's emphasis was on job training for black people. Along with encouraging blacks to fight discrimination, he also urged them to improve themselves—to become thrifty, honest, and hard-working.

In 1848, Douglass took part in another important national movement: He attended the original Seneca Falls

Frederick Douglass (*Library of Congress*)

equality and self-improvement. He became an important figure in the postwar Republican Party, and was given a number of government appointments.

Frederick Douglass was born Frederick Bailey, a slave in Tuckahoe, Maryland, the son of Harriet Bailey and an unidentified father. Douglass personally thought his father was his white master, Aaron Anthony. He took February 14, 1817, as his birthdate.

His mother worked as a field slave on a rural plantation some 12 miles away from her son, and she died when he was about eight or nine years old. In 1825, he was sent to Baltimore to be a houseboy. Here, his mistress wished to teach him the alphabet, but the master would not allow it. "Learning would spoil the best nigger in the world," he said. The boy somehow learned to read in secret.

In 1832, Douglass was returned to the rural plantation, and there he forged passes for himself and four others and tried to escape. The attempt failed, but rather than being punished, Douglass was sent again to Baltimore, where he worked as a caulker (a shipyard conference at which Susan B. Anthony and Elizabeth Cady Stanton began the women's rights movement.

Throughout the 1850s, Douglass continued to write, speak, and organize against slavery and for equal rights. For a while, Douglass became discouraged and began to explore the possibility of black Americans emigrating to Haiti. Then the Civil War broke out, and Douglass could perceive the possibility of ending slavery once and for all.

Douglass called upon Lincoln to enlist black people in the Union Army. He suggested that if Lincoln freed the slaves, they too could be recruited to fight for the Union. After the Emancipation Proclamation of 1863, which abolished slavery in the Confederate states, Douglass became a recruiting agent for the army.

After the Civil War, Douglass's focus turned to black voting rights. This was a controversial issue, even after slavery had been ended. Finally, in 1870, the Fifteenth Amendment was ratified, guaranteeing equal access to the ballot despite race, color, or former status as a slave.

In 1870, Douglass began to edit the *New National Era,* which he published until 1874. This newspaper was directed to the newly freed slaves. Douglass was also active in the Republican Party, which he saw as the party most devoted to the interests of black people.

In 1877, the federal government, under the leadership of the Republican Party, backed away from its commitment to Reconstruction—the political and economic integration of African-Americans in the conquered South. Some historians believe that Douglass lost touch with the vast majority of black people during this period. He continued to emphasize self-help and self-improvement, which many viewed as a compromise with white segregationists.

Douglass's wife died in 1882. Then, in 1884, he entered into a second, controversial marriage with a white woman, Helen Pitts. Douglass was criticized for this marriage, but he said it proved that black and white people could live together in harmony and equality.

Douglass received government appointments from the administrations of both President Rutherford B. Hayes and President James A. Garfield. As marshal and then recorder of deeds for the District of Columbia, he was the first black person to hold such positions. In 1888, Douglass worked hard for the election of Republican President Benjamin Harrison, who later appointed him minister resident and consul general to Haiti. He served there until his resignation in 1891.

Historians who believe that Douglass lost touch with his people also recognize that he once again became an active leader during his last five years. He continued to write and to call for active struggle against discrimination and inequality, but retained his broad perspective on social change. On February 20, 1895, he spoke to a meeting of the National Council of Women, then suffered a fatal heart attack that night.

Douglass was greatly honored after his death. His home was later purchased by the federal government as a national shrine; a bridge in Washington, D.C., was named for him; and in 1967, a postage stamp bearing his likeness was issued in his honor. Douglass was also the subject of a PBS documentary, "When the Lion Wrote History."

Further Reading: *Life and Times of Frederick Douglass,* by Frederick Douglass, New York: Pathway Press, 1941 reprint of 1892 ed.; *Frederick Douglass,* by Benjamin Quarles, New York: Atheneum, 1948; *Frederick Douglass,* by Philip Foner, Secaucus, N.J.: Citadel Press, 1964; *Frederick Douglass, A Sample of His Writings,* Philip Foner, ed., New York: International Publishers, 1964; *Frederick Douglass and the Fight for Freedom,* by Douglas T. Miller, New York: Facts On File, 1988; *Frederick Douglass,* by William S. McFeely, New York: W. W. Norton, 1991.

—*R. K.*

❖ DREW, CHARLES RICHARD
(1904–1950), *surgeon, scientist, teacher*

Charles Drew is widely known as a pioneer in the development and preservation of blood plasma, the substance used in transfusions to save lives. He was also known for his effective teaching methods at Howard University Medical School in Washington, D.C., where he trained many black students and surgeons. Drew's work as a teacher was so highly respected that in 1949, he was one of four American doctors asked to tour hospitals in occupied Europe (after the defeat of the Nazis) in order to improve the quality of medical care and instruction there.

Drew's achievements as surgeon, scientist, and teacher were well recognized during his lifetime. He was named diplomate of surgery by the American Board of Surgery at Johns Hopkins University, in Baltimore, in recognition of his outstanding medical work. He received honorary degrees from Virginia State College and Amherst College in Massachusetts. In 1944, he was awarded the NAACP's Spingarn Medal for black achievement, and in 1946, he was made a fellow of the International College of Surgery.

Charles Drew (*National Archives*)

Charles Drew was born in 1904, the oldest child of Richard Drew, a carpenter, and Nora (Burrell) Drew. In 1926, Drew graduated from Amherst College, one of the few "white" colleges at the time to welcome sizable numbers of black students. However, even at Amherst, Drew faced discrimination. He was a talented athlete and was awarded the trophy for Most Valuable Player on the school football team—but, while white players so awarded were customarily elected captain, Drew was not. Two years before, two other black athletes had met with similar opposition, so this further example of prejudice aroused campus protest. The protest was quieted when Drew, also the highest scorer in track and field, was elected captain of the track team instead. When he graduated, Drew was awarded another trophy, for being Amherst's most valuable athlete.

Drew earned the money to continue his studies by coaching athletics. Still, he could not have afforded medical school without loans offered him by his old Amherst classmates.

Drew received his medical degree from McGill University in Canada. He had been waiting on tables there to help pay his tuition, but in 1930, a scholarship enabled him to concentrate exclusively on his schoolwork and improve his grades.

After serving his internship and residency in Canada, Drew became a teacher of pathology at Howard University and a resident at Freedmen's Hospital in Washington, D.C. He then taught and worked in New York at Columbia-Presbyterian Hospital.

In 1939, Drew married (Minnie) Lenore Robbins, with whom he later had four children.

While in New York, in 1940, Drew received the Med.D.Sc. (Doctor of Medical Science) degree from Columbia University, where he wrote a dissertation on the condition of blood stored in blood banks. Drew's research focused on transfusions of plasma—clear, sterilized blood fluid, with the red and white cells removed—rather than whole blood. He discovered that plasma could be preserved and stored longer than whole blood.

He also supervised the blood-plasma division of New York City's Blood Transfusion Association, which was involved in collecting blood for the British Army. In 1940, the war in Europe had begun, and collecting blood was important for the soldiers in combat. Drew's work is credited with saving many lives, for his New York experiments led to new and more effective ways of storing and shipping blood and preventing its contamination.

Drew continued his involvement with stored blood plasma. Although he briefly returned to Howard University, by February 1941, he was back in New York as director of the blood bank of the American Red Cross. He also assisted the director of the National Research Council, which collected blood for the army and navy.

This important work with blood was not without controversy. In those years, the Red Cross segregated white people's blood from that of black people—a policy that eventually led Drew to resign his post. He returned to Washington, where in 1942 he became head of Howard University's department of surgery and chief surgeon at Freedmen's Hospital. In 1944, he was elevated to hospital chief of staff and medical director, a position he held until 1948.

Drew was killed in an automobile accident on April 1, 1950.

In 1976, the National Institutes of Health paid tribute to Charles Drew and unveiled a painting of him in a special ceremony.

Further Reading: *Charles Richard Drew, Pioneer in Blood Research,* by Richard Hardwick, New York: Scribner, 1967.

—*R. K.*

❖ DuBOIS, WILLIAM EDWARD BURGHARDT
(1868–1963), *social scientist, activist, writer*

W. E. B. DuBois (pronounced "Do Boys") was a writer and scholar who helped to found the National Association for the Advancement of Colored People (NAACP), which was for many years the major civil rights organization in the United States. A spokesperson for the NAACP later said that DuBois's ideas had "transformed the Negro world as well as a large portion of the liberal white world, so that the whole problem of the relation of black and white races has ever since had a completely new orientation." DuBois himself said, "My stinging hammer blows made Negroes aware of themselves, confident of their possibilities [for] determined self-assertion."

DuBois's contributions were many, and he has come to be considered an authentic African-American radical and prophet of social protest. He is perhaps best remembered for his concept of a black intelligentsia—of scholars, writers, and theorists—who could best combat discrimination and elevate the general well-being of all black people by gaining the power to work on equal terms with white leaders. DuBois was also a powerful

W. E. B. DuBois *(Library of Congress)*

essayist, and is well remembered for his groundbreaking book of 1903, *The Souls of Black Folk,* in which he forged a new image of racial pride.

W. E. B. DuBois was born on February 23, 1868, in Great Barrington, Massachusetts, to Alfred and Mary Silvina (Burghardt) DuBois. His family was poor, and his father left when DuBois was still young, but the young DuBois encountered little racial prejudice and was acclaimed as an exceptional student and athlete.

His mother died in 1884, soon after he had graduated from Great Barrington High School. DuBois then enrolled at Fisk University in Nashville, Tennessee, where he graduated in 1888.

From Fisk, DuBois returned to Massachusetts to study at Harvard University. Since Harvard considered its standards superior to those of Fisk, DuBois entered Harvard as a junior, despite his having already received his B.A. In 1890, he received a B.A. cum laude from Harvard and was one of five students chosen to speak at the commencement ceremony. After acquiring a master's degree from Harvard in 1891, he then worked for his doctorate, studying for two years in Europe as well. His primary field of interest was always black history and culture and the social situation of his people.

In 1895, DuBois became the first African American to get a Ph.D. from Harvard, and then taught languages and literature at Wilberforce University in Ohio until 1897. From 1897 to 1910, he taught economics and history at Atlanta University in Georgia.

During those years, he wrote many key works, including *The Souls of Black Folk* and a study of black people living in Philadelphia. He also became interested in Pan-Africanism, the movement to unite black people worldwide, linking Africa with all the black people of the Americas and even Asia.

In 1896, DuBois married Nina Gomer, with whom he had one surviving child.

For most of the 1890s, DuBois maintained a good relationship with Booker T. WASHINGTON, the major black leader of the time. Washington advocated self-help and industrial education for black people, with emphasis on their need to learn work skills. But by 1905, DuBois was deeply critical of Washington. He believed him to be accommodating and lacking firmness in his stand against racism and prejudice, and felt strongly that black people needed access to the higher education that would allow them to develop their own thinkers and leaders.

Thus, in 1905, DuBois founded the Niagara Movement, a group of black leaders who met at Niagara Falls to develop new, more militant approaches to politics. At its second meeting, in 1906, at Harper's Ferry, West Virginia, he said, "We will not be satisfied to take one jot or tittle less than our full manhood rights. We claim for ourselves every single right that belongs to a free-born American, political, civil and social; and until we get these rights we will never cease to protest and assail the ears of America." The Niagara Movement was in some ways a precursor of the NAACP, which was founded by both black and white leaders in 1909.

In 1910, DuBois resigned from academia to become the NAACP's only black officer, serving as director of publicity and research, a member of the board of directors, and editor of its journal, the *Crisis.* DuBois edited the *Crisis* until 1934, turning it into a central and essential publication for black intellectuals and artists. It was there that he was able to expound on his idea of a black intelligentsia whose leadership would elevate the social position of black people as a whole.

By 1934, DuBois's views had become more militant than those of the NAACP, and he resigned from the *Crisis* to chair Atlanta University's department of sociology. He continued to write and to remain politically active. In 1944, he returned to the NAACP as director of special research, a position he held until 1948.

DuBois participated in the organization of the United Nations, and remained active in the Pan-African movement and left-wing American politics. After his first wife's death in 1950, DuBois married Shirley Graham, in 1951.

The 1950s were a time when many activists were harassed by the federal government on the grounds that they were involved with communism or the Soviet Union. In 1948, DuBois had been fired by the NAACP, largely for his outspoken views on foreign policy. The government indicted him in 1951 for being an agent of the Soviet Union. These charges were groundless and he was found innocent, but he continued to suffer from right-wing persecution.

Nevertheless, DuBois remained supportive of the Soviet Union, which he saw as being a staunch advocate of the cause of African independence. And he continued with his work as a Pan-Africanist. In 1945, he attended the Fifth Pan-African Congress in Manchester, England, where he was elected the congress's permanent chair and president. From 1948 to 1956, he was the co-chair of the Council on African Affairs, a private group that published information on Africa.

In 1961, he made the decision to join the Communist Party of the United States. In his letter of application for membership, he wrote, "Capitalism can-not reform itself," and "Communism—the effort to give all men what they need and to ask of each the best they can contribute—this is the only way of human life."

Later in 1961, DuBois was invited by the left-wing president of Ghana, Kwame Nkrumah, to live in Ghana. He became a citizen of that country, where he died on August 27, 1963—on the eve of the historic civil rights march on Washington.

For several years, the federal government prevented DuBois's widow from returning to the U.S. But in 1968, the 100th anniversary of his birth was honored by the American Historical Association. And in 1976, in a reversal of the federal government's long-term attitude toward DuBois, his birthplace was designated a historical landmark.

Further Reading: *An A B C of Color,* by W. E. B. DuBois, New York: International Publishers, 1963; *His Day is Marching On, A Memoir of W. E. B. DuBois,* by Shirley Graham DuBois, Philadelphia, Pa.: Lippincott, 1971; *W. E. B. DuBois: A Profile,* edited by Rayford W. Logan, New York: Hill & Wang, 1971.

—R. K.

✦ DUNBAR, PAUL LAURENCE
(1872–1906), poet

Paul Laurence Dunbar is best known for his poems in black dialect, which portray the lives of black people in the rural South. He also wrote verse in standard English and produced several novels, short stories, plays, and essays.

Dunbar's books of poetry include *Oak and Ivy, Majors and Minors, Lyrics of Lowly Life, Lyrics of Love and Laughter* and *Lyrics of Sunshine and Shadow.* All of these books were extremely popular and achieved both critical and financial success. At one point, Dunbar was so popular that one publisher gave him a fee just for the right to the first look at his next manuscript, whatever it might be.

Paul Laurence Dunbar was born on June 27, 1872, in Dayton, Ohio, to Joshua Dunbar, a slave who had escaped to Canada and then returned to fight in the Union Army and to Matilda (Murphy) Dunbar, a former slave and laundry worker. She was a widow with two children from a previous marriage when she and Joshua Dunbar married.

Although Joshua Dunbar died when Paul was only 12, Matilda Dunbar continued to play an important role in her son's life. Despite her former slave status, she had somehow learned to read and write and she supported her

Paul Dunbar (*Library of Congress*)

son's efforts to become a poet. She and her husband related stories to Dunbar about life in the South—a social context that was to become the foundation of his writing.

Dunbar went to Central High School in Dayton, where he was elected president of the high school literary society and editor of the school paper, although he was the only black person in his class. Lacking money for college, he began to work as an elevator operator in 1891.

For almost a year, Dunbar sent his poems to newspapers, trying to establish a writing career. Some of his poems were published; many were not. In 1892, he tried to collect the poems that had been published into a book, *Oak and Ivy.* He planned to print the book himself but could not afford it. Then in 1893, he borrowed the $125 that he needed from a white friend. He was able to recover the money by selling copies of his book to those who rode his elevator.

Dunbar continued to work at various jobs and to pursue his writing. Then in 1895, a group of white people helped him to publish his next book of poetry, *Majors and Minors.*

Here began an ongoing conflict in Dunbar's appraisal of his work. He considered his poems in black dialect "minor"; his poems in standard English seemed "major." But the critics and his readers did not agree; to them the dialect poems were the more interesting.

Meanwhile, Dunbar's career received a new boost. His work was reviewed in a major literary magazine, *Harper's Weekly,* by William Dean Howells, one of the country's leading critics. The favorable review made Dunbar famous, while emphasizing his dialect over his standard verse.

Dunbar may not have been happy with such an assessment, but he was pleased with the success it brought. He went on a major reading tour, hired a manager, and in 1896, published *Lyrics of Lowly Life,* which also became a great success.

Although Dunbar worked for a short time at the Library of Congress, he did not neglect his writing career. Magazines and publishers were all pressing him for work, and he began to write prose sketches. In 1898, he published *The Uncalled,* his first novel. The book was the story of a young minister searching for his identity in the midst of his frustration with the lack of Christianity in so-called Christian churches.

The year 1898 was significant for Dunbar in other ways. He also published *Folks from Dixie,* a short-story collection. As with most of Dunbar's work, these stories presented a happy picture of life in the South, with cheerful, carefree black folks peacefully serving whites. Dunbar was aware that these were the images that the white-owned magazines of the time would buy, and he wanted to sell his work.

In 1898, Dunbar married Alice Ruth Moore, a fellow poet and a schoolteacher. The couple went to live in Washington, D.C.

From 1898 until his early death in 1906, Dunbar maintained an impressive writing schedule that may have weakened his health. And, although he drank heavily, he never stopped writing. He published three more novels, several more books of verse, and additional prose sketches and articles. He also wrote two unpublished plays. He gave reading tours and helped to raise money for black institutions, such as Hampton Institute in Virginia and Tuskegee Institute in Alabama.

Dunbar's novel *Love of Landry,* published in 1900, is primarily a sentimental love story about white people. His next novel, *The Fanatics,* came out the following year. It describes an Ohio town torn between a pro-Confederate and a pro-Union family. Although there are some minor black characters, the book by and large avoids racial issues.

The Sport of the Gods, published in 1902, is Dunbar's only novel to feature black characters. It describes a pointless injustice done to a respectable southern black family, forcing them to move north. Interestingly, the book suggests that however unjust the South may be, the loose morals of New York are more hazardous for black people.

In 1902, Dunbar and his wife separated. He then moved to Chicago, and finally back to Dayton, where he died on February 6, 1906, at his mother's home.

Today Paul Laurence Dunbar is primarily remembered for his poetry. Like Robert Burns, who wrote in Scottish dialect, he seemed to give voice to a people and a culture that had not yet been faithfully represented in literature.

Further Reading: *The Complete Poems of Paul Laurence Dunbar,* New York: Dodd, Mead, 1988; *A Singer in the Dawn: Reinterpretations of Paul Laurence Dunbar,* edited by Jay Martin, New York: Dodd, Mead, 1975; *The Paul Laurence Dunbar Reader,* edited by Jay Martin and Gossie H. Hudson, New York: Dodd, Mead, 1975.

—*R. K.*

❖ DUNHAM, KATHERINE
(1919–   ), dancer, choreographer, anthropologist, writer, activist

Katherine Dunham revolutionized American dance when she infused it with African and Caribbean rhythms and movements—the expressions of a black cultural heritage that she had explored as an anthropologist. As well, she holds the distinction of having been the first African-American choreographer to work at the Metropolitan Opera House in New York City, where in 1963 she created dances for the Verdi opera *Aida.*

Katherine Dunham was born in Glen Ellyn, Illinois, and grew up in the predominately white community of Joliet, Illinois, where her father operated a dry-cleaning establishment. Although she showed promise as a dancer from childhood, it was not her intention as a young woman to dance professionally. Her abiding interest in dance, however, led to her forming a dance group, called alternately the Ballet Negre or the Negro Dance Group, while a student of anthropology at the University of Chicago. Following the group's first public performances at the Chicago World's Fair in 1934 and later with the Chicago Civic Opera Company, Dunham received a fellowship from the Julius Rosenwald Fund to study anthropology and dance in the West Indies, in pursuit of a master's degree. Dunham's fieldwork allowed her to observe sacred rituals and dances, elements of which she would incorporate in her own work.

Once again in the United States, Dunham joined the Federal Theatre Project of the Works Progress Administration, a government agency formed to stimulate employment in all fields, including the arts. She created a ballet, *L'Ag 'Ya,* and went to New York to coach the dancers in the Labor Stage's production of *Pins and Needles.* In New York, she appeared on Broadway as Georgia Brown in *Cabin in the Sky* (1940), which she also choreographed, and formed the Katherine Dunham Dance Company. Until it was dissolved, the company toured the United States and more than 60 other countries with a program of dances choreographed, produced, and directed by Dunham, such as *Tropics* (choreographed 1937) and *Le Jazz Hot* (1938), and later *Tropical Revue* (1943), *Carib Song* (1945), *Bal Negre* (1946), *New Tropical Revue* (1948), and *Bamboche* (1962). The company helped to popularize the "Dunham technique" and became a major influence in the careers of many performing artists.

Dunham's work was not restricted to the stage, however. From 1940 she appeared in and/or choreographed several Hollywood films, including *Carnival of Rhythm* (1942); *Star Spangled Rhythm,* whose jitterbug featuring Dunham may be the first inherently African-American dance sequence on film (1942); *Pardon My Sarong* (choreography, 1942); *Cabin in the Sky,* which she co-choreographed with George Balanchine (1943); *Stormy Weather* (1943); *Casbah* (1947); *Mambo* (1955); and *Green Mansions* (1959).

Dunham disbanded her company in 1965, when she became an adviser to the Ministry of Culture of Senegal. She returned to the United States in 1967 to accept an academic appointment as artist in residence and then professor at Southern Illinois University in East St. Louis, forming the Performing Arts Training Center and the Katherine Dunham Museum and Children's Workshop to help community youth. She was also a technical adviser to the Kennedy Center for the Performing Arts and directed Scott JOPLIN's ragtime opera *Treemonisha* at the celebrated Wolf Trap Farm for the Performing Arts in Virginia in 1972.

Continuing her lifelong struggle for justice, Dunham went on a hunger strike in 1992 to protest the treatment of Haitian refugees refused asylum in the United States and in support of democratic rule in Haiti. In honor of her commitment to humanitarian causes, as well as her pioneering work in the celebration of black heritage through dance, Dunham has been the recipient of numerous awards, including the Kennedy Center Honors Award (1983), the Dance Magazine Award, the Albert Schweitzer Music Award, and induction into the Black Filmmakers Hall of Fame.

Further Reading: *Journey to Accompong,* by Katherine Dunham, Westport, Conn.: Negro Universities Press, 1946; *Dances of Haiti,* by Katherine Dunham, Los Angeles, Calif.: Center for Afro-American Studies, UCLA, 1949; *Touch of Innocence,* by Katherine Dunham, New York: Harcourt Brace, 1959; *African Rhythm— American Dance: A Biography of Katherine Dunham,* by Terry Harnan, New York: Knopf, 1974.

—*R. K.*

❖ DU SABLE, JEAN-BAPTISTE POINTE
(1745?–1818), pioneer, entrepreneur, founder of Chicago

Jean-Baptiste Pointe Du Sable was the first settler in the area of what is now Chicago, Illinois. He had a complicated and adventurous career that included spying for the British during the Revolutionary War; serving as a liaison officer between whites and Indians; and owning a prosperous trading post, from which the future city of Chicago evolved. What is known about his life suggests it was one of exploration and adventure, great risk, and good luck.

His birthplace has been given variously as the St.-Domingue (Haiti), or French Canada; his ancestry may have been both French and African. An account has it that he was the son of a French merchant who went to live in the French colony that became Haiti, where he married a freed slave from the Congo.

According to this version, Du Sable's French father sent him to France to be educated. There, he made a lifelong friend, Jacques Clemorgan, a white man from the West Indian island of Martinique.

In 1765, he was sent to New Orleans to develop new business for the family company—New Orleans at that time still being under the dominion of the French. But upon their arrival, Du Sable and his friend Clemorgan found that the Spanish had taken over.

Du Sable pressed on, traveling up the Mississippi River to St. Louis, another French-controlled city, where he traded with the Indians. However, it was the British this time who soon wrested the city from the French. So, in this year of 1767, Du Sable moved on again—stopping at a place that is currently the city of Peoria, Illinois.

He settled there with the Peoria and Potawatomi Indians, married an Indian woman named Chikiwata, and remained in the area for two years.

Then in 1769, Du Sable journeyed to Canada, trapping and trading along the Illinois River and Lake Michigan. By 1772, he had decided to settle at a place that the Indians called Eschikagou—a marshy, unpleasant location halfway between Canada and the southern ports where Du Sable had been trading. He settled in this new spot, built a cabin there, and in 1774, brought his family and some other Indians to settle there with him. Eschikagou would one day be known as Chicago, Chikiwata would become Catherine and their daughter Suzanne would take her place in history as Chicago's first child.

Du Sable's original plot was fairly large—30 acres. The cabin he built was a house of several rooms, and it is likely he lived fairly well. He and his wife had several more children, and his fur-trading business flourished.

When the Revolutionary War broke out, Du Sable spied for the British for a short time. Eventually, however, he was put in jail, because they thought his sympathies favored the French, who at that time were supporting the Americans. The British may also have feared that Du Sable's influence with the French and the Indians made him too powerful a figure in the area. Whatever their reasons, he was released from jail after a few months, but his career as a spy was finished.

His relations with the Indian peoples of the Midwest were very close, to the extent that in 1780, the Indians of the Port Huron area asked territorial governor Patrick Sinclair to appoint Du Sable as the liaison officer between Indians and whites. The Indians apparently thought that he would negotiate on their behalf with the white officials in the territory, and help protect their interests. Du Sable took the post for a short while, but he returned to Chicago in 1782.

From 1782 to 1800, Du Sable did very well in Chicago. He trapped furs and owned his own trading post; and his holdings eventually included a flour mill, a bakehouse, a dairy, a smokehouse, a poultry house, and a stable. To his original property, he added another 400 acres, on which he built two barns. As his property expanded, he purchased more cattle and other types of livestock. Du Sable's large house became well-known for its elegant furnishings, and for having the latest modern conveniences of the time.

Then in 1800, Du Sable left Chicago, apparently because he was unhappy with the U.S. government's policies for disposing of land in the Northwest Territory. He sold his Chicago holdings for $1,200 (a considerable amount of money at the time), to one Jean Lalime—another trader, John Kinzie, witnessing the sale. Ironically, Kinzie was later considered to be the founder of Chicago, although he didn't live there until 1804, four years after Du Sable had left.

Du Sable and his wife returned to Peoria. When his wife died in 1809, he moved to St. Charles, Missouri, where he bought a house from another black man, Pierre Rodin. Eventually, Missouri's first governor, Alexander McNair, would live in the same house.

Although he was free himself, Du Sable was always sympathetic to slaves and interested in their problems. He bought several slaves simply to grant them their freedom.

He died in 1818, completely penniless, and was buried in an obscure grave. In 1968, however, a granite memorial marker was affixed to the site. The state of Illinois and the city of Chicago had finally acknowledged Jean-Baptiste Pointe Du Sable to be the city's founder.

Further Reading: *Checagou: From Indian Wigwam to Modern City,* by Milo Milton Quaife, Chicago, Ill.: University of Chicago Press, 1933; *Chicago and the Old Northwest, 1673–1835,* by Milo Milton Quaife, Chicago, Ill.: University of Chicago Press, 1913.

—R. K.

❖ EDELMAN, MARIAN WRIGHT
(1939–   ), civil rights leader, children's advocate

The foremost advocate of children's rights in the United States, Marian Wright Edelman has been president of the Children's Defense Fund (CDF) since 1973. She has lived her life according to a simple credo: "If you don't like the way the world is, you change it. You have an obligation to change it. You just do it, one step at a time."

Born in Bennettsville, South Carolina, on June 6, 1939, Edelman grew up in the segregated environment of the Deep South. Her father, Arthur Jerome Wright, was a Baptist minister with a keen sense of social justice. Responding to laws that prohibited African Americans from using public parks and other facilities, he opened a recreation center for blacks behind his church. He and his wife, Maggie Leola Wright, had also founded a nursing home for elderly black citizens. Marian, the youngest of five children, was inspired by her parents' example of activism as she grew up. An outstanding student and a talented musician, she entered Atlanta's Spelman College in 1956. During her college years, fellowships allowed her to spend a year studying in France and a summer in Moscow.

Edelman was planning to join the U.S. foreign service when she graduated, but during her senior year she got caught up in the Civil Rights movement. Because legal issues were so crucial in the fight for equality,

Edelman realized that a law degree would enable her to make a greater contribution. She was admitted to Yale Law School and received her LL.B. in 1963. After undergoing a year of training with the National Association for the Advancement of Colored People (NAACP) in New York, Edelman traveled to Mississippi and began work as a civil rights lawyer.

Edelman remained in Mississippi for four years, living with the constant threat of violence from segregationists. Much of her time was taken up with efforts to secure voting rights for African Americans, but Edelman also turned her attention to economic issues. She was especially concerned about the situation of black children, many of whom were living in desperate poverty. Edelman understood that political rights for African Americans would have little meaning if their children could not have adequate food, health care, and education. As she worked to secure federal funding for programs that would offer a fair chance to those in need, Edelman realized that there was no effective voice in Washington to further this important cause. She resolved to fill that void.

In 1968, Edelman got married and moved to Washington, D.C., with her husband, a fellow lawyer. (Marian and Peter Edelman now have three sons.) She began to work with the Washington Research Project, seeking to influence the Congress to provide more funding for children's services. In 1973, Edelman created the

Marian Wright Edelman (*CNP/Archive Photos*)

Children's Defense Fund. Based in Washington, the CDF is financed by private foundation grants. It conducts research, seeks to educate the public on issues affecting children, monitors the performance of federal agencies, helps in drafting legislation, and provides information to Congress.

As the president of the CDF, Edelman works tirelessly to keep the needs of children—of all races—a major item on the national agenda. In speeches, interviews, press conferences, testimony before Congress, magazine articles, and books, she argues that the United States cannot remain a great nation without providing care and opportunities for its children. In her best-selling book *The Measure of Our Success,* she states the case clearly and simply: "The question is not whether we can afford to invest in every child; it is whether we can afford not to."

In recognition of her valuable work, Edelman has received numerous awards during the course of her career. They include the Albert Schweitzer Humanitarian Prize, the Rockefeller Public Service Award, and a MacArthur Foundation Fellowship.

Further Information: *Families in Peril: An Agenda for Social Change,* by Marian Wright Edelman, Cambridge: Harvard University Press, 1987; *The Measure of Our Success: A Letter to My Children and Yours,* by Marian Wright Edelman, Boston: Beacon, 1992; *Marian Wright Edelman: The Making of a Crusader,* by Beatrice Siegel, New York: Simon & Schuster, 1995; Children's Defense Fund web site, http://www.childrensdefense.org/index. html.

—P. K.

❖ **ELDERS, MINNIE JOYCELYN**
(1933–   ), *physician, U.S. surgeon general*

The second woman and the first African American to serve as surgeon general of the United States, Joycelyn Elders rose from an Arkansas shack to the highest levels of public service. An outspoken advocate of sex education and abortion rights, Elders made her presence felt in Washington during the early 1990s and refused to back down under political pressure.

Born in Schall, Arkansas, on August 13, 1933, Elders grew up in a three-room cabin that had no electricity or indoor plumbing. The oldest of eight children, she worked in the cotton fields with the rest of her family and still managed to excel at her studies. At the age of 15, Elders was awarded a scholarship by the United Methodist Church, and the award enabled her to attend Philander Smith College, a small Methodist school in Little Rock. Despite the family's poverty, four of Elder's siblings also managed to obtain a college education.

Elders received her B.A. from Philander Smith in 1952 and then joined the U.S. Army, where she attained the rank of first lieutenant while training to be a physical therapist. Upon finishing her military service in 1956, Elders took advantage of the educational benefits in the

Dr. Joycelyn Elders (CNP/Archive Photos)

G.I. Bill of Rights and enrolled in the University of Arkansas Medical School. She obtained her M.D. degree in 1960, the same year she married Oliver Elders, a high school basketball coach. Elders then completed her internship in Minneapolis and took up a residency in pediatrics at the University of Arkansas Medical Center in Little Rock. Elders demonstrated exceptional ability in her specialty, becoming chief pediatric resident in 1964 and professor of pediatrics in 1967. During this time, she also obtained an M.S. degree in biochemistry and qualified for a subspecialty in pediatric endocrinology.

Elders held her professorship for 20 years, publishing more than 200 articles and papers in the field of pediatrics. In 1987, Governor Bill Clinton appointed her director of the Arkansas State Department of Health. Supervising 2,600 employees, Elders concentrated on improving the health of Arkansans. She boosted the rate of childhood innoculations from 34 percent to 60 percent and stepped up programs for prenatal care, HIV prevention and treatment, home care, and breast cancer screening. Attacking the problem of teenage pregnancy in the state, she vigorously advocated improved sex education, contraception, and abortion rights, despite opposition to such measures by a number of influential groups. Her achievements earned her a variety of honors, including the National Governors' Association Distinguished Service Award and the American Medical Association's Dr. Nathan Davis Award.

When Bill Clinton was elected president of the United States in 1992, he picked Elders to be the nation's surgeon general. The nomination was unpopular with a number of conservatives in Congress, and Elders was not confirmed by the Senate until September 1993. It was a bruising process, and Elders did not enjoy the treatment she received from her opponents. "I came to Washington as prime steak," she remarked, "and after being here a little while I feel like low-grade hamburger."

As surgeon general, Elders supervised the 6,000 uniformed officers of the U.S. Public Health Service and oversaw the President's Council on Physical Fitness and Sports. She undertook the job of providing the American people with up-to-date information about major health problems and their prevention, and in doing so, she refused to pull her punches. Elders spoke out forcefully against the use of tobacco and alcohol and continued to express her belief in the need for widespread sex education. Toward the end of 1994, Elders made a series of statements on contraception that made the headlines and aroused a furor among conservatives. Politically embarrassed by the controversy, the White House asked for Elders's resignation. She complied and returned to the University of Arkansas as professor of pediatrics, having fought unswervingly for the things she believed in.

Further Reading: *Joycelyn Elders, M.D.,* by Joycelyn Elders and David Chanoff, New York: Morrow, 1996; *Dancing with the Bear and Other Facts of Life: The Story of Dr. M. Joycelyn Elders, By Her Brother,* by Chester R. Jones, Pine Bluff, Ark.: Delta, 1995.

—P. K.

❖ ELLINGTON, EDWARD KENNEDY ("Duke")
(1899–1974), *jazz pianist, composer*

Duke Ellington was one of the greatest of all jazz composers. His sophisticated musical ideas and innovations opened the way for a wider range of musical styles to influence jazz. Before his time, jazz was largely a folk music developed by musicians working out of the blues, ragtime, and black-spiritual traditions. Ellington was the first authentic jazz "composer." He not only played but wrote down his music—in the composition of relatively long and abstract pieces that made stringent demands on the skills of jazz musicians and broadened the range of possibilities for other jazz composers.

Ellington's key musical inventions include utilizing the wordless human voice as an instrument; providing jazz groups with the sound of an orchestra; adding Cuban and Latin elements as well as a "jungle" sound to jazz; and using echo chambers to create new sound effects. Ellington also wrote jazz compositions based on classical music, such as his version of Tchaikovsky's *Nutcracker Suite.* He initiated a jazz concert series at Carnegie Hall in New York, and was the first to perform a jazz concert (of a "jazz mass") in a church.

His list of honors includes a Grammy Award for achievement in the music industry; 16 honorary doctorates from such schools as Columbia, Yale, and Brown; presidential medals from Johnson and Nixon; membership in the French Legion of Honor; and the NAACP's Spingarn Medal for achievement by black Americans. He also established a Duke Ellington fellowship program at Yale University, where the Ellington Collection of his papers and music is held.

Although his name was Edward Kennedy, he was nicknamed "Duke" because of his elegant way of dressing. (He was always "duked out" in stylish clothes.) His family was musically talented; both parents played the piano, although neither could read music.

Ellington was born on April 29, 1899, in Washington, D.C., where he started piano lessons at the age of six and continued to study music in the public schools. He later studied with noted classical musician Will Marion Cook.

Ellington wrote his first song, "The Soda Fountain Rag," at age 17. By the time he was in high school, he was playing piano at local events, and soon began to perform professionally with local groups. He formed his first group in 1919, and in 1923, he took a group to New York. He returned for a time to Washington, but later that year, he was back in New York again.

From 1924 to 1927, Ellington played at the Cotton Club, a whites-only nightclub in Harlem featuring black performers. Ellington's prestige was such that he reportedly was given a private table at which his own black guests could sit.

Ellington played at other clubs and theaters, toured the country, and wrote hundreds of songs. He had sold his first music to Broadway publishers in 1923 and recorded his first songs in 1924. Later, in 1929, his band played in a Broadway musical. In 1930, they appeared in a film, and in 1933 and 1939, they toured throughout Europe.

Ellington was famous for wielding his orchestra like an instrument, in which the group worked together to create a single unified sound. In this way, he helped to initiate the era of the "Big Bands" and their "swing" music, although white band leaders like Benny Goodman were better known.

When William "Billy" Strayhorn joined the Ellington band in 1939, it was a major addition of talent. Ellington and Strayhorn were to collaborate closely over the next 28 years of great music-making.

Many of Ellington's songs are classics: "Mood Indigo," "Caravan," "It Don't Mean a Thing If It Ain't Got That Swing," "Take the 'A' Train," "In a Sentimental Mood," "I Got It Bad and That Ain't Good," and "Sophisticated Lady." His jazz suites are also famous, particularly *Black, Brown and Beige.*

Ellington composed revues, musicals, an opera, film scores, and television productions. He wrote and performed until his death in 1974. His son, Mercer Ellington, took over the Duke Ellington Band until his death in 1996.

Further Reading: *Music Is My Mistress,* by Duke Ellington, New York: Doubleday, 1973; *Duke Ellington,* by James Collier, New York: Oxford University Press, 1987.

—R. K.

Duke Ellington (*Library of Congress*)

❖ ELLISON, RALPH WALDO
(1914–1994), writer

Ralph Ellison is best known for *Invisible Man* (New York: Vintage Books, 1989 ed.), a 1952 novel that won him a National Book Award. In a 1965 literary poll, the book was deemed "the most distinguished single work" published in the United States since 1945.

Ralph Ellison was born on March 1, 1914, in Oklahoma City, the son of Lewis Alfred Ellison, a construction worker, and Ida (Millsap) Ellison. He later observed that growing up in Oklahoma spurred him to explore the black experience and identity in a new and complex way, since the state had no tradition of slavery and therefore had more "fluid" relations between races than could be found in the Old South.

From 1933 to 1936, Ellison attended Tuskegee Institute in Alabama. Although he enrolled as a music major, he soon became more interested in writing.

At Tuskegee, Ellison took a sociology course that was to change his life. He felt that the course presented such a humiliating portrait of black Americans that he felt a new sense of urgency to discover the truth about black culture for himself. When Ellison ran out of college funds, he went to New York.

Ellison's New York years helped to shape him as a writer. He met the poet Langston HUGHES, who suggested that he read the Marxist writer André Malraux. Ellison later met novelist Richard WRIGHT, who urged him to read other key white writers. Although Ellison and Wright became friends, Ellison rejected Wright's portrait of Bigger Thomas in *Native Son,* believing that Wright had portrayed black people as helpless victims, rather than as people with intelligence and imagination.

From 1938 to 1942, Ellison worked with the Federal Writers' Project. The project was a federally funded program designed to combat unemployment while supporting the arts. Ellison also published short stories and essays in left-wing journals. Critics have mixed feelings about these works: Some praise them more than his later work; others view them as only a preparation for the important work that was to come. Ellison's two best-known stories from this period are "Flying Home" and "King of the Bingo Game."

In 1942, Ellison briefly edited the magazine *Negro Quarterly.* When his mother died, he left for her home in Dayton, Ohio. He lived there with his brother for a while, barely getting by.

During World War II, Ellison served in the U.S. Merchant Marine. After the war, he received a grant from the Julius Rosenwald Fund that afforded him the time and financial security to continue writing. He began *Invisible Man,* which took him seven years to complete.

Invisible Man is the story of a black man's journey from innocence to knowledge, and makes use of jazz imagery, historical and cultural myths, and the philosophical interests and stylistic innovations of modern European and American writers. The Invisible Man is continually fooled by people who make promises to him and hold out various illusions about how to achieve happiness. Again and again, he is forced to give up his illusions and accept the painful truth—that he, too, is responsible for the failure of the American dream.

Ellison's book won many awards and much acclaim. It led to lecture tours in Europe and many posts teaching literature and writing at American colleges and universities, including such schools as Yale University and the University of Chicago.

Further Reading: *Shadow and Act,* by Ralph Ellison, New York: Random House, 1964; *Ralph Ellison: Modern Critical Views,* edited by Harold Bloom, New York: Chelsea House, 1986; *Ralph Ellison: The Genius of an Artist,* by Rudolph F. Dietze, Nuremberg, Germany: H. Carl, 1982; *Five Black Writers: Essays on Wright, Ellison, Baldwin, Hughes, and Le Roi Jones,* compiled by Donald B. Gibson, Nuremberg, Germany: H. Carl, 1970; *Ralph Ellison: A Collection of Critical Essays,* edited by John Hersey, Englewood Cliffs, N.J.: Prentice-Hall, 1974; *Interviews with Black Writers,* by John O'Brien, New York: Liveright, 1973; *Writers at Work: The Paris Review Interviews,* second series, edited by George Plimpton, London: Secker and Warburg, 1963; *A Casebook on Ralph Ellison's Invisible Man,* edited by Joseph F. Trimmer, New York: T. Y. Crowell, 1972.

—R. K.

❖ EVANS, MARI
(1923–), writer

Mari Evans's poetry has been widely published, and has been collected into several books. She has written many stories and poems for young people, and is the author of several plays and musicals. In 1970, Evans won the Indiana University Writers' Conference award and the Black Academy of Arts and Letters award for her collection *I Am a Black Woman.*

She has been further honored with the Black Liberation award from the Kuumba Theater Workshop, the Black Arts Celebration Poetry award, and fellowships in recognition of her literary achievement from the

MacDowell Colony, Yaddo Writers Colony, Amherst College, and the National Endowment for the Arts.

Mari Evans was born on July 16, 1923, in Toledo, Ohio, and brought up in a family that was warmly supportive of her work. She was also nourished and sustained by Langston HUGHES's book of poetry, *Weary Blues.* She believed that two key influences—Hughes and her father—enabled her to withstand the racism and the rejection of her work that she encountered at the beginning of her career.

For a time, Evans attended the University of Toledo. She later worked as an editor for an industrial company, where she had to deal with prejudice in a variety of ways.

In 1968, Evans began to write, direct, and produce a television program, *The Black Experience,* which was broadcast in Indianapolis, Indiana. Many critics praised the show. In the same year, Evans's first book was published. *Where Is All the Music* (London: P. Bremen, 1968) did not receive good reviews; however, today's critics are more positive in their response.

In 1969, Evans began teaching at Purdue University in Indiana. The following year, she went to Indiana University, where she remained until 1978.

Evans's second book, *I Am a Black Woman* (New York: Morrow, 1970), came out during this period of her life. It was more political, more controversial, than her first. Here, Evans celebrates her black identity. The last poem asks rhetorically, "Who can be born black and not exult!"

Nightstar: 1973–1978 (Los Angeles: Center for Afro-American Studies), Evans's third collection of poetry, was published in 1981. Critics found this book to be more political, and more polished in its poetic technique. One reviewer described the book as being full of "humane grace." Another wrote: "Mari Evans is a powerful poet . . . We need to hear this authentic voice again and again, for there is strength in exquisitely revealing expressions of ghetto dynamics."

In the 1980s Evans taught while working on *The Black Experience* and gave poetry readings around the country. Since 1985, she has been an associate professor at the State University of New York at Albany.

The writings of Mari Evans include *Eyes,* a musical adapted from Zora Neale HURSTON's novel *Their Eyes Were Watching God.* The play was produced in New York in 1979 and then at Cleveland's famous Karamu Theater in 1982. Her *Black Women Writers (1950–1980): A Critical Evaluation* (New York: Doubleday Press/Anchor), published in 1984, is a major work of literary criticism.

Evans's books for young people include *J.D.* (New York: Avon, 1975); *I Look at Me* (Chicago, Ill.: Third World Press, 1974); *Rap Stories* (New York: Third World Press, 1974); *Singing Black: Alternative Nursery Rhymes for Children* (Indianapolis: Reed Ursuals, 1976); *Jim Flying High* (Garden City, N.Y.: Doubleday, 1979); and *A Dark and Splendid Mass* (New York: Writers & Readers, 1992).

—R. K.

❖ EVANTI, MADAME LILLIAN (Lillian Evans)
(1890–1967), *opera singer*

Lillian Evanti was the first African-American woman to sing in opera with an organized company anywhere in the world. She was celebrated first as a coloratura soprano and later as a lyric soprano. From 1925, she sang in France, Italy, England, Germany, the United States, Brazil, Argentina, Cuba, Haiti, the Dominican Republic, Liberia, and Nigeria. In 1940, she traveled as goodwill ambassador with Arturo Toscanini and the NBC Symphony Orchestra to Argentina and Brazil. In 1962, she went to Ghana to act as toastmistress at the inauguration of President Nnamdi Azikiwe. She was hailed as the equal to the famed and revered singer Amelita Galli-Curci and was recognized worldwide as a great and talented singer.

Evanti was born in 1890 to W. Bruce Evans, M.D., a physician and prominent educator, and Anne (Brooks) Evans, a music teacher. Her unusual voice was discovered early: At age four, she was the featured soloist at a concert in Friendship Gardens in Washington, D.C. Evanti studied piano throughout her youth, later attending a technical high school and teacher's college before earning a bachelor of music degree in 1917 from Howard University in Washington, D.C.

In 1918, she married Roy W. Tibbs, her music professor, and created the name *Evanti* from *Evans* plus *Tibbs.* She was much in demand for Washington-area concerts for many years. Eventually, she sang with the Paris Opera, debuting in 1925.

Evanti's Paris success was hailed by black papers in Washington. The *Washington Daily American* reported, however, that the white newspapers printed her picture but failed to mention her race. Had she been a criminal, they conjectured, her race would have been highlighted.

She gave recitals in New York City, as well as in several European cities. She sang a command performance at the White House for Franklin and Eleanor Roosevelt in 1934 and toured U.S. cities throughout the 1930s, while maintaining her European career. She also enjoyed considerable acclaim in Latin America.

Her Latin American tours inspired Evanti to compose the "Himno Panamericano" in 1941. The U.S. Office of Education later selected the piece for a Latin American exhibition. Evanti also composed other pieces, dedicated to Ghana, to U.S. soldiers and their sweethearts, and to the United Nations.

During World War II, Evanti was cited by Generals Dwight Eisenhower and Mark Clark, and by Admiral Chester Nimitz, for her army and navy concerts. She also sang at the White House for Presidents Eisenhower and Truman.

Evanti was a founder of the National Negro Opera Company, in Washington, D.C. She sang in and spoke five languages fluently, and had a repertoire of 24 operas—an unusually large number for a singer—including *La Traviata, Rigoletto, The Barber of Seville, Manon Lescaut, Roméo et Juliette, La Bohème, Thaïs, Carmen, The Magic Flute, Der Rosenkavalier,* and *Turandot.* She spent her final years singing, coaching, and teaching voice. Madame Evanti died on December 6, 1967, after a long illness.

—*R. K.*

✤ EVERS, MEDGAR WILEY
(1925–1963), *civil rights leader*

Although Medgar Evers was assassinated before he reached the age of 40, he was already a symbol of the determination of African Americans to win full equality in America. As Mississippi field secretary of the National Association for the Advancement of Colored People (NAACP), Evers coordinated the effort to desegregate public facilities in Jackson, Mississippi. This mass action led President John F. Kennedy to advocate a new, comprehensive civil rights program. It also made Evers the target of a killer—in an assassination that led Kennedy to seek further civil rights legislation.

Medgar Evers was born in 1925 in Decatur, Mississippi, to James Evers, a farmer who also worked in a sawmill, and Jessie Evers, a domestic of mixed white, black, and Indian parentage. In the 1920s and 1930s, education was not easily available to southern black people, and at one point, Evers had to walk 12 miles each way to attend school.

He spent a year in the segregated army during World War II, participating in the Normandy invasion, then returned to Mississippi, where he faced the severe racial restrictions of that period. In 1946, he and his brother Charles tried to vote in their home town—causing their entire family to be threatened with violence.

Evers attended Alcorn A & M College in Mississippi from 1946 to 1952. At that time, in 1951, he married Myrlie Beasley, with whom he later had three children.

After graduation in 1952, he joined the NAACP, a major civil rights organization. In 1954, he was selected as Mississippi field secretary for the group.

The year 1954 was highly significant in the history of civil rights. The Supreme Court decided that "separate but equal" facilities were not constitutional. It was now no longer legal to segregate black and white public schoolchildren. Mississippi, however, was deeply committed to segregation, and the efforts of Evers to enforce the landmark *Brown* decision brought him into grave danger. He risked further danger by encouraging black voter registration and supporting boycotts of local white businesses that discriminated against black people.

Civil rights activity continued throughout the 1950s, sparked by the Montgomery, Alabama, bus boycott led by Martin Luther KING, JR., in 1955. King was a member of the Southern Christian Leadership Conference (SCLC), a group of ministers active in civil rights, which Evers supported after the boycott.

By 1963, civil rights activity had escalated, involving not only southern black people but also many northerners, both black and white, who traveled to Mississippi, Alabama, and other southern states to participate in nonviolent mass actions. At this time, protest marches were initiated, and there were "sit-ins"—group protests, in which hundreds or thousands of blacks would actually sit down in front of a segregated lunch counter or other public place, refusing to move until the facility was integrated.

Although the demonstrators avoided violence, the police did not. They frequently used vicious dogs, high-pressure water hoses, electric cattle prods, and nightsticks to break up the peaceful but disruptive protests.

The year 1963 also marked the 100-year anniversary of the Emancipation Proclamation, which had abolished slavery in the Confederate states. Civil rights activity for equal employment, voting rights, and desegregation reached a new level of agitation. So did the opposition of powerful southern officials. Mississippi governor Ross Barnett and Alabama governor George Wallace refused to obey federal court orders that required African Americans to be admitted to all-white state universities.

President Kennedy sent federal marshals to enforce the new rulings. On June 11, 1963, he delivered a nationally televised address calling for new civil rights legislation—the first time an American president had publicly said that segregation was morally wrong.

Meanwhile, Evers continued to lead demonstrations to integrate public facilities in Jackson, Mississippi. Evers knew that his actions were perilous. He told one colleague that he expected to be shot, and said to another that he was being followed.

Early in the morning of June 13, 1963, upon returning home after dropping off another civil rights worker, Evers was shot in the back as he walked up the driveway to his house.

The angry reaction to Evers's death, as well as to the increasing police brutality, prompted Kennedy to take a strong stand. On June 19, 1963, the day of the funeral, Kennedy sent Congress a civil rights bill that gave the attorney general power to file lawsuits forcing state and local governments to comply with the Fourteenth and Fifteenth Amendments, which guarantee equal protection under the law, regardless of race, color, or creed. Kennedy's bill also called for guaranteed equal access to public places, such as restaurants, stores, and government buildings.

Evers was later honored with a military burial in Arlington National Cemetery, in May of 1964.

"Ghosts of Mississippi," a movie about the trial of his assassin, was released in 1997.

Byron De La Beckwith was arrested for Evers's murder and tried twice in 1964. Both times the all-white juries deadlocked. After years of urging from Evers's widow, Myrlie Evers-Williams (who in 1995 became the national chairperson of the National Association for the Advancement of Colored People [NAACP]), De La Beckwith was again brought to trial in 1994. This time a jury of eight blacks and four whites convicted him.

Further Reading: *For Us the Living,* by Myrlie Evers, Garden City, N.Y.: Doubleday, 1967; *Of Long Memory: Mississippi and the Murder of Medgar Evers,* by Adam Nossiter, Reading, Mass.: Addison Wesley Longman, Inc., 1994; *Medgar Evers: Civil Rights Activist,* by Jennie Brown, Los Angeles: Halloway House, 1994.

—R. K.

❖ FAUSET, JESSIE REDMON
(c. 1882–1961), *novelist of the Harlem Renaissance*

Jessie Fauset was an important novelist of the Harlem Renaissance, that period in the 1920s when black culture flourished and became more visible. With Zora Neale HURSTON and Nella LARSEN, Fauset wrote about black women of her time and was much acclaimed for her portraits of middle- and upper-class black families, as well as for her stories of ambitious women artists. Fauset was among the most prolific novelist of the Harlem Renaissance, having written four books between 1924 and 1933.

She was also an important literary influence. For seven years, she was literary editor of the *Crisis,* the magazine of the National Association for the Advancement of Colored People (NAACP), working with editor W. E. B. DUBOIS. In this position, she encouraged Langston HUGHES and provided support to him and many other young authors.

Jessie Fauset was the child of Reverend Redmon, an African Methodist Episcopal minister, and Anna (Lehman) Fauset, an old Philadelphia family. Her membership of this elite black society furnished her with the major themes of her later writing.

Fauset graduated in 1905 from Cornell University, where she was elected to Phi Beta Kappa, a major academic honor society. She later earned a master's degree in

French from the University of Pennsylvania and studied at the Sorbonne in Paris.

From 1906 to 1919, Fauset taught Latin and French in the Washington, D.C., public high schools. Then, at the beginning of the Harlem Renaissance, she went to New York to work at the *Crisis* as literary editor, a post she held from 1919 to 1926.

Those were busy years for Fauset. She also worked with *The Brownies' Book,* a children's monthly magazine, from 1919 to 1923, as literary and then managing editor. And in 1924, she wrote *There Is Confusion* (Boston: Northeastern University Press, 1989 reprint of 1924 ed.), her first novel.

In 1926, Fauset became a contributing editor to the *Crisis,* a less demanding job, which left her time for her own fiction. She returned to teaching, first in a Harlem junior high school, then at the prestigious DeWitt Clinton High School. In 1929, she wrote *Plum Bun* (Boston: Beacon Press, 1989 reprint of 1929 ed.). This was followed in 1931 by *The Chinaberry Tree* (New York: AMS Press, 1969 reprint of 1931 ed.), and, in 1933, *Comedy: American Style* (College Park, Md.: McGrath Publishing Company, 1969 reprint of 1933 ed.).

Fauset's work concerned ambitious, well-educated black people who eventually became successful in business or the arts. Her depiction of a black upper class was praised in its time, particularly by black critics who wished to show the rest of society that black people were

Jessie Redmon Fauset *(Library of Congress)*

not all poor and ignorant. Fashions change, however, and in the 1960s, Fauset's work was criticized for not dealing with the broader black community and for its optimistic assumption that white society might ultimately welcome successful black people. Critics today admire Fauset's portraits of black women, and her influence as a literary figure.

Fauset later married New York businessman Herbert Harris. She died on April 30, 1961, in Philadelphia.

—R. K.

❖ FLORA, WILLIAM
(?–1818?), *Revolutionary War soldier, businessperson*

William Flora was a soldier in the American Revolution who fought in the Battle of the Great Bridge during the winter of 1775–76.

After the Revolution, Flora became one of the first black property owners in Portsmouth, Virginia, where he prospered and expanded his wagon and freight business.

Flora was born free, most likely in Portsmouth. In 1775, Virginia governor Lord Dunmore declared that any black slaves who would fight for the British would be set free. These soldiers were organized into a company called the Ethiopian Regiment.

As a free black man, Flora was not interested in Dunmore's offer. He fought with the Americans. When the Ethiopian Regiment drove back the Americans in Colonel William Woodford's 2nd Virginia Regiment, Flora was among those who opposed them.

After the Revolution, Flora's Portsmouth business did so well that he was able to buy the freedom of his wife and children. He bought land, horses, wagons, carriages, and set up a business of hauling freight and hiring out horses and carriages.

Shortly before his death in 1818, Flora applied as a Revolutionary War veteran for a land grant from the state of Virginia. He was recognized as a documented veteran and given 100 acres.

Further Reading: *The Black Presence in the Era of the American Revolution 1770–1800,* Amherst, Mass.: University of Massachusetts Press, 1989 reprint of 1973 ed.

—R. K.

❖ FORTEN, CHARLOTTE L.
(Charlotte Grimké)
(1837–1914), *poet, educator, diarist*

Charlotte Forten wrote poetry and was a teacher for many years. She was an active abolitionist before the Civil War, and worked to help freed slaves in South Carolina after the war. Her real fame, however, derives from her detailed diary, which offers intimate insights into the conditions of black people before and during the Civil War.

Charlotte Forten was the granddaughter of James FORTEN, noted Philadelphia abolitionist. The second generation of Fortens, also active in the movement, included Forten's parents, Mary Wood and Robert Bridges Forten, and several aunts and uncles. Charlotte's parents, highly critical of segregation, would not allow their daughter to attend Philadelphia's segregated public schools; the young Charlotte was educated at home by tutors.

In 1854, the teenaged Charlotte Forten went to live with family friends in Salem—Sarah and Charles Lenox Remond, who were sister and brother. At their home she met prominent abolitionists, including William Lloyd Garrison and the poet John Greenleaf Whittier.

She graduated from Salem Normal School (a "normal" school was a teacher's college), and began teaching at a Salem grammar school in 1856.

Her time in Salem was a rich experience for Forten. She was active in the Female Anti-Slavery Society, and attended antislavery lectures by such prominent men as Ralph Waldo Emerson. She also continued with her writing, completing an essay and more poems.

Forten's health was fragile—she suffered from "lung disease"—and in 1858, she returned to Philadelphia to recuperate. She continued to teach for brief periods of time as she struggled with her health. In 1862, Forten sailed for Port Royal, St. Helena Island, off the coast of South Carolina, to take part in a new social experiment.

The Union forces had captured the area in 1861, and the federal government had set up a colony of freed slaves. Land, teachers, and other resources were given them to prove that they could attain the educational and cultural level of white people with the same advantages. Forten went to the colony as a teacher, and remained there until 1864.

She enjoyed teaching at Port Royal, although it was demanding. And she continued keeping the journal she had begun in Salem in 1854, and in which she made entries until 1892.

But Forten's health problems had not disappeared, and in 1864, she left Port Royal and returned to Philadelphia, where she stayed for seven years. Then she went to Washington, D.C., where she first assisted a principal at a local school, then worked as a clerk in the Treasury Department. When Forten was 41, she married the pastor of her church, Francis James Grimké, who was 13 years her junior.

They had one child, who died in infancy. For most of the rest of Forten's life, she and her husband lived in Washington, D.C. In 1913, she was stricken with a cerebral embolism and was confined to bed for more than a year, until her death in 1914.

Further Reading: *The Journal of Charlotte Forten,* edited by Ray Allen Billington, New York: Dryden Press, 1953; *A Tribute to Charlotte Forten, 1837–1914,* by Roberta H. Wright, Southfield, Mich.: Charro Book Co., 1993; *The Journals of Charlotte L. Forten Grimké,* ed. Brenda Stevenson, New York: Oxford University Press, 1988.

—*R. K.*

❖ FORTEN, JAMES, SR.
(1766–1842), *abolitionist, businessperson*

James Forten was one of the most prominent abolitionists of his time. He fought for equal rights for black people, for women suffrage, and for peace.

Forten amassed a fortune of $100,000 by 1832, from his sailmaking business. Although it was highly unusual at the time, he employed white as well as black workers. He used his fortune to support William Lloyd Garrison's famous abolitionist newspaper, *The Liberator.*

In 1833, the American Anti-Slavery Society was organized by Garrison, Forten and others, in Forten's Philadelphia home. He served on its board of managers and supplied it with much of its funds. Throughout his life, he was an active organizer in social causes. His granddaughter, Charlotte FORTEN, carried on his tradition, working as a teacher in a South Carolina colony for freed slaves.

James Forten was born in 1776 to free parents, and it is thought that his great-grandfather was a slave brought over from Africa, but later freed. Although Forten's parents may have been free, they were not wealthy. When his father died, Forten worked in a grocery store to support his mother.

During the American Revolution, the young Forten, at age 15, served as a powder boy on a naval ship out of Philadelphia (powder boys handled the gunpowder used to fire the weapons). When a British ship captured his vessel, Forten spent seven months as a prisoner. Then he spent a year in England, where he met prominent abolitionists.

When Forten returned to the United States, he began to work in a sailmaking business owned by Robert Bridges, a free black man. He eventually became supervisor and was able to buy the business in 1798, when Bridges retired. Over the next 34 years, Forten amassed a fortune.

Although he ran a successful business, he found time for black community affairs. Philadelphia at this time was a major center of black activism—both for the abolition of slavery and the opposition to segregation.

Forten also worked on a state level. In 1813, he wrote a pamphlet protesting the Pennsylvania Senate's proposal to prevent black people of other states from moving to Pennsylvania. If the law had passed, citizens receiving black visitors would have had to report them.

A major debate was whether black people should create a colony of their own in Africa or remain in the United States and fight for their freedom. Forten eventually came out against colonization.

In addition to his work with the American Anti-Slavery Society, Forten served as president of the American Moral Reform Society, a group of black men who worked for temperance and civil rights. He organized mass meetings, petition drives, and other political actions. After his death in 1842, many men and women, black and white, attended a huge memorial service in his honor.

Further Reading: *Forten the Sailmaker, Pioneer, Champion of Negro Rights,* by Esther M. Doughty, Chicago, Ill.: Rand McNally, 1968; *The Journal of Charlotte Forten,* edited by Ray Allen Billington, New York: Dryden Press, 1953.

—R. K.

❖ FORTUNE, TIMOTHY THOMAS
(1856–1928), *journalist, civil rights leader*

T. Thomas Fortune was editor and founder of the *New York Age,* the most influential black newspaper of its time. He was a political leader who urged black people to break away from the Republican Party and seek political independence. He also helped to establish the National Afro-American League in 1890, and the National Afro-American Council in 1898—forerunners of modern civil rights organizations.

T. Thomas Fortune was born on October 3, 1856, the child of Sarah Jane and Emanuel Fortune, who were slaves in Jackson County, Florida. He came of white, black, and Indian ancestry, and was the grandson of the Irish Thomas Fortune, his father's father.

After the Civil War, many black people had their first opportunity to run for political office in the South. One such politician was Emanuel Fortune, Thomas's father, who in 1868 was elected to the Florida constitutional convention and then to the lower house of the state legislature. However, Reconstruction was also a time when many white groups like the Ku Klux Klan were organized to thwart black people's drive for equality. Klan threats forced the Fortunes to leave their small town of Marianna and move to Jacksonville.

Education for black people was not easily available, and Fortune was able to attend only three terms of a school sponsored by the Freedmen's Bureau—an agency set up to help newly freed slaves. Fortune then became a printer. He studied at Howard University in Washington, D.C., for a while, but had to leave for lack of funds.

When he was in Washington, however, two events helped to shape his future life. He worked on an African-American newspaper, the *People's Advocate.* And he married Carrie C. Smiley, a Jacksonville woman with whom he later had two surviving children.

In 1879, Fortune left Florida for New York City, where he quickly rose to prominence in the newspaper world. Starting as a printer, he went on to be part owner of a weekly paper known as *Rumor.* In 1881, he became editor of this journal, renamed the *Globe.* Although the *Globe* went out of business in 1884, Fortune began to publish a new periodical, the *New York Age.* He stayed with this journal until 1907, and the *Age* itself survived until 1960.

Fortune also wrote a book, *Black and White: Land and Politics in the South* (New York: Arno Press, 1968 reprint). Both his book and his newspapers strongly favored full equality and opposed any form of discrimination.

During the 1890s, Fortune continued to publish the *Age* as well as to write for the *New York Sun* and the *Boston Transcript.*

In 1903, the U.S. Treasury Department sent Fortune to Hawaii and the Philippines to study race and labor conditions there. Fortune claimed that Filipinos showed no racial prejudice against black people, and he encouraged black people to migrate to their country. The Philippines had recently become an American colony, and Fortune advocated the appointment of a black American as governor, but his proposal was ignored.

In 1906, Fortune and his wife separated. He had become an alcoholic, and in 1907, he suffered a mental breakdown, which forced him to sell his newspaper and plunged him into poverty and isolation.

Later, in 1916, Fortune regained his health and began to write again.

From 1919 on, Fortune wrote for the *Norfolk Journal and Guide.* In 1923, he became editor of *Negro World,* which was published by Marcus GARVEY's Universal Negro Improvement Association. Garvey advocated black emigration to Africa, where he wanted black Americans to found their own country. Although Fortune did not agree with this kind of self-segregation, he did admire Garvey's leadership.

When Fortune suffered a collapse in 1928, he was cared for by his son, a surgeon practicing in Philadelphia. He died soon after.

Further Reading: *T. Thomas Fortune, Militant Journalist,* by Emma Lou Thornbrough, Chicago, Ill.: University of Chicago Press, 1970.

—R. K.

❖ FRANKLIN, JOHN HOPE
(1915–), *historian, educator*

Franklin is generally recognized as the preeminent black historian of our time. His work *From Slavery to Freedom* is a standard college text on African-American history. He is the author and editor of several books on black history and a contributor to many key textbooks and collections of historical writings. He has been active in many professional, educational, and governmental organizations. He is a past president of the American Studies

Association (1967), the Southern Historical Association (1970), the United Chapters of Phi Beta Kappa (1973–76), the Organization of American Historians (1975), and the American Historical Association (1979). He has been a member of the Board of Trustees of Fisk University, the Chicago Public Library, and the Chicago Symphony Orchestra Association.

John Hope Franklin was born January 2, 1915, in Rentiesville, Oklahoma. His father, Buck Colbert Franklin, was a lawyer who became the first black judge to sit in chancery (where wills are determined) in Oklahoma district court. His mother was Mollie (Parker) Franklin.

Like so many black students of his time, Franklin went to Fisk University in Tennessee, where he graduated in 1935. The following year, he entered Harvard. While teaching at various southern schools, he continued his studies, receiving his Ph.D. from Harvard in 1941.

Franklin taught at Howard University in Washington, D.C., from 1947 to 1956, then went on to chair the history department at Brooklyn College in New York. In 1964, he joined the history department of the University of Chicago, where he remained until 1982.

In addition to his academic duties, Franklin was busy writing his pioneering books on black history. Although courses had not been offered in this field, Franklin knew that he wanted to write about the past of his people. He was one of the scholars who helped to establish that such a field as "black history" did exist and that it deserved to be studied in high schools and colleges.

In 1943, Franklin published *The Free Negro in North Carolina, 1790–1860* (New York: Russell & Russell, 1969 reprint of 1943 ed.). In 1947, he published *From Slavery to Freedom* (New York: Knopf, 1967 reprint of 1947 ed.), which has gone through several editions. Franklin continued to write about the pre–Civil War South and the period of Reconstruction in *The Militant South, 1800–1860* (Cambridge, Mass.: Belknap Press of Harvard University Press, 1970 revision of 1956 ed.); *Reconstruction After the Civil War* (Chicago, Ill.: University of Chicago, 1961); and *The Emancipation Proclamation* (Garden City, N.Y.: Doubleday, 1963).

After almost 20 years at Chicago, Franklin moved to Duke University in North Carolina, where he taught from 1982 until his retirement in 1985. In that year, after writing and editing numerous books, Franklin published *George Washington Williams: A Biography* (Chicago, Ill.: University of Chicago Press, 1985), the biography of a major 19th-century black historian. This figure was of lifelong importance to Franklin. As he himself had tried imagining what a comprehensive history of black Americans might be like, Franklin was inspired by the thought that an earlier scholar had actually attempted to write such a history.

In 1993 Franklin published *The Color Line: Legacy of the Twenty-first Century.* His most recent book is an autobiography of his father, which he edited.

In 1995, Franklin was honored with the foundation of the John Hope Franklin Research Center at Duke University, a repository for documents on African and African-American studies. In 1997, the 50th anniversary of *From Slavery to Freedom* was commemorated in a special symposium at Duke University. Currently he serves on the advisory board of President Clinton's One America: The President's Initiative on Race.

John Hope Franklin has received numerous honors and awards. He was named by *Who's Who in America* as one of eight Americans who has made significant contributions to society in 1978. Also in that year, he was elected to the Oklahoma Hall of Fame. He received the Jefferson Medal, awarded by the Council for the Advancement and Support of Education, in 1984. In 1989, he was the first recipient of the Cleanth Brooks Medal of the Fellowship of Southern Writers, and in 1990 received the Encyclopedia Britannica Gold Medal for the Dissemination of Knowledge. In 1993, Dr. Franklin received the Charles Frankel Prize for contributions to the humanities, and in 1994, the Cosmos Club Award and the Trumpet Award from Turner Broadcasting Corporation. In 1995, he received the first W. E. B. DuBois Award from the Fisk University Alumni Association, the Organization of American Historians Award for Outstanding Achievement, the Alpha Phi Alpha Award of Merit, the NAACP's Spingarn Medal, and the Presidential Medal of Freedom. In 1996, Franklin was elected to the Oklahoma Historians Hall of Fame and in 1997 he received the Peggy V. Helmerich Distinguished Author Award. In addition, Dr. Franklin has received honorary degrees from more than 100 colleges and universities.

Further Reading: *The Negro Handbook,* compiled by the editors of *Ebony,* Chicago, Ill.: Johnson Publishing Company, 1963.

—*R. K.*

❖ FREEMAN, MORGAN
(1937–), actor, director

One of the most successful and recognizable American actors of the late 20th century, Morgan Freeman has compiled a long list of achievements on the stage and the screen. Best known for his work in films such as *Driving Miss Daisy, Glory, The Shawshank Redemption,* and

Morgan Freeman *(Victor Malafronte/Archive Photos)*

Amistad, he has been honored with three separate Academy Award nominations.

Freeman was born in Memphis, Tennessee, on June 1, 1937. His parents moved several times during his early years, but he finally settled in Chicago with his mother and sister when he was nine. Growing up in a rough neighborhood on the South Side, he joined a street gang for the sake of survival while studying hard and acting in school plays. When Freeman was 11, the family moved to Greenwood, Mississippi, where he won a statewide prize for a seventh-grade dramatic performance. After graduating from high school he joined the U.S. Air Force; discharged in 1959, he headed for Hollywood, hoping to break into the movies.

Freeman found it hard to get work in Hollywood, and he eventually moved to New York, where he worked at a variety of jobs in and out of show business. His luck began to change in 1966 when he was playing a bit part with a touring theater company and was called on to fill in for an ailing cast member who had a leading role.

Freeman's performance impressed audiences and critics alike, and he soon found himself working steadily on the off-Broadway and Broadway stages, playing varied roles in both classical and contemporary works. From 1971 through 1976, Freeman also appeared on television in *The Electric Company,* an innovative daytime show designed to develop children's reading skills.

Freeman's stage work earned him a number of honors, including a 1978 Drama Desk Award for *The Mighty Gents,* and Obie Awards for *Coriolanus* (1979), *Mother Courage* (1980), and *The Gospel at Colonus* (1983). In 1987, Freeman starred opposite Dana Ivey in *Driving Miss Daisy,* which had a successful run at the Playwrights Horizon in New York and earned him another Obie Award.

Freeman began working in films in the early 1980s, drawing compliments from film critics even though he was cast in secondary roles. His breakthrough came in 1987, when he played a violent pimp in the film *Street Smart* and prompted one leading critic to call him the finest actor in America. The performance won him several awards from major film critics' societies as well as his first Oscar nomination. Freeman now began making films in rapid succession, adding class and interest even to second-rate vehicles. He gained his first starring role in 1989 when he played a no-nonsense high school principal in *Lean on Me.* Freeman then returned to the role of the aging chauffeur Hoke Colburn in the film version of *Driving Miss Daisy,* earning a Golden Globe Award and his second Academy Award nomination. Of all his film roles, his favorite was that of Sergeant John Rawlins in *Glory,* the saga of the all-black 54th Massachusetts Regiment in the Civil War. Involvement with this film meant a great deal to Freeman, as it explored a major historical contribution made by African Americans. "This is a moment in history that has been excised, forgotten about," he told an interviewer. "To bring that back where it belongs, close to the heart, is a wonderful undertaking."

Following *Glory,* Freeman's major film credits have included *The Bonfire of the Vanities* (1990); *Unforgiven* (1992); the *Shawshank Redemption* (1994), for which he earned a third Oscar nomination; *Outbreak* (1995); *Moll Flanders* (1996); *Amistad* (1997); *Kiss the Girls* (1997) and its sequel *Along Came a Spider* (1999); and *Deep Impact* (1998).

Further Reading: "Morgan Freeman," in *Current Biography Yearbook 1991,* New York: H. W. Wilson, 1992; "Morgan Freeman," by Robert Abele, *Us,* May 1997; "Morgan Freeman Takes Off," by Ross Wetzteon, *New York,* March 14, 1988.

—P. K.

✤ GARNET, HENRY HIGHLAND
(1815–1882), minister, abolitionist, diplomat

Garnet was born a slave, but would achieve national recognition as an abolitionist and a diplomat. In 1843, he spoke at the first National Negro Convention, in Buffalo, New York—a convention that drew African Americans together from across the United States to develop common strategies for ending slavery. Garnet gave a speech, "Call to Rebellion," in which he urged both free and enslaved black people to take a "motto of resistance" to slavery, including armed rebellion, if necessary.

The speech had a profound impact on the thinking of black people across the country. Heretofore, black people had resisted slavery in many ways, but this was the first time a black American had publicly called for widespread revolt.

With slavery legally abolished in 1865, Garnet was the first black person to deliver a sermon before the U.S. House of Representatives. In 1882, he was appointed minister to Liberia, the African nation that had been founded by African-Americans.

Henry Highland Garnet was born in 1815 on a slave plantation in New Market, Maryland. His grandfather was reportedly a ruler of the Mandingo people in Africa. When Henry was nine, he and his father escaped to New York with the help of Quaker abolitionists. His father went to work as a shoemaker, and Henry entered the African Free School No. 1.

In 1834, Garnet studied at Noyes Academy, in New Hampshire, along with future writer and minister Alexander CRUMMELL. But in 1835, white residents of the area were so enraged at the idea of education for black students that they destroyed the school.

Garnet then studied at a theological institute near Utica, New York, and in 1842, at Troy, he became the minister of New York's only black Presbyterian church. In that year he also married Julia Williams.

As a minister, Garnet was furnished a base from which to present his abolitionist and social activist views. He was concerned with racial equality, but also sought the end of economic and political exploitation and was an activist for peace and women's rights. Although his famous "Call to Rebellion" in 1843 shocked most conservative black leaders, it missed approval by only one vote—and in 1847, another National Negro Convention unanimously passed a similar Garnet resolution.

In 1850, Garnet was a delegate to the World Peace Congress in Frankfurt, Germany. On that European trip, he also addressed many antislavery societies. The Scottish United Presbyterian Church was so impressed with Garnet that they asked him to be pastor of their church in Jamaica.

Garnet supported colonization even before he went to Jamaica. He also believed that a strong Africa was important to black Americans.

Henry Highland Garnet (*Library of Congress*)

During the Civil War, Garnet was one of the first to demand that President Lincoln allow black men to be recruited as soldiers, despite the popular fear at the time of arming black people. In 1864, he became pastor of the fashionable 15th Street Presbyterian Church in Washington, D.C., and gave his famous sermon before the House of Representatives in 1865.

Eventually, Garnet returned to New York and directed the energies of his entire career toward civil rights. He later became discouraged by the federal government's failure to carry forward the goals of full black equality under Reconstruction.

In 1879, Garnet married Sarah Thompson, the sister of Susan Maria Smith Thompson, one of the first women doctors in the United States. Then, in January 1882, Garnet became a diplomat with his appointment as minister to Liberia. He died there, soon afterward, on February 13, 1882, and was honored with a state funeral.

Further Reading: *Let Your Motto Be Resistance,* by Earl Ofari, Boston, Mass.: Beacon Press, 1972; *Black Abolitionists,* Benjamin Quarles, New York: Oxford University Press, 1969; *They Who Would Be Free, Blacks' Search for Freedom 1830–1861,* by Jane H. Pease and William H. Pease, New York: Atheneum, 1974.

—*R. K.*

❖ GARVEY, MARCUS MOSIAH
(1887–1940), *orator, black nationalist*

Marcus Garvey led the largest mass movement of black people ever witnessed in America. In his efforts to organize black Americans for emigration to Africa, he involved up to a million people and reached millions more.

Although Garvey was criticized by many other black leaders, and although many of his projects failed, his ability to attract large numbers of people to his cause remains impressive. Even leaders who did not agree with Garvey's ideas appreciated his efforts to build black pride and political independence.

Marcus Garvey was born to a poor family in Jamaica on August 17, 1887, the youngest of Marcus and Sarah Garvey's 11 children. In later years, Garvey was to recount his pride in the unmixed African heritage of his parents. Garvey's father, a stonemason, was supposedly descended from the Maroons, escaped African slaves who defended their freedom against both Spanish and British invaders.

Garvey had little schooling and was required to become a printer's apprentice at age 14, in order to help his family. In 1904, he went to the Jamaican city of Kingston to work. There he began speaking at street meetings, where he displayed a talent for public oratory.

In 1907, he was involved in a printers' strike, but the effort failed. This experience caused him to doubt the value of trade unions for black workers. He worked on a banana plantation and then on newspapers in various Central American countries. When he complained to British authorities about the mistreatment of Jamaicans, there was little response, which left him quite skeptical about any hope of justice from white people.

In 1912, Garvey studied in London, where he first met Africans. He wrote for African publications and became an avid supporter of African independence. He also read Booker T. WASHINGTON's *Up From Slavery* and responded warmly to its thesis of black self-help.

Soon afterward, Garvey returned to Jamaica. There, in 1914, he founded the Universal Negro Improvement and Conservation Association and African Communities League (U.N.I.A.), the group that would work for black emigration to Africa. The U.N.I.A. also helped to promote racial pride, education, and black business activity.

Garvey tried to establish a Jamaican trade school similar to Booker T. Washington's Tuskegee Institute, but it failed. In 1916, he went to New York and tried to organize American branches of the U.N.I.A. At first, his main support came from West Indians, but black Americans soon joined.

In 1918, Garvey founded *Negro World,* a leading black weekly, which soon had 50,000 readers in the United States, Latin America, the West Indies, and Africa. The British and French eventually banned Garvey's newspaper from their African colonies.

By 1920, Garvey's followers numbered in the thousands, and the U.N.I.A. had become a major organization. Garvey built many organizations, including the Universal Black Cross Nurses, the Universal African Motor Corps, the Black Flying Eagles, and the African League. His major business effort, however, began in 1919: the Black Star Line, a shipping company for purchasing the boats that would return black people to Africa, their homeland.

This stock was sold to black people only, at the fairly low price of $5.00 per share. In the first year, he raised over $600,000 and bought three ships. However, these ships were overpriced and badly in need of repair. The Black Star Line could not possibly operate successfully—a situation not yet apparent to Garvey and his followers.

In 1919, Garvey established the Negro Factories Corporation to promote black economic independence by providing money and labor to black businessowners. Again, stock was offered only to black people, at $5.00 per share. Grocery stores, a restaurant, a laundry, a tailor shop, and a publishing house were among the businesses that were established by the organization.

It was in 1919 that Garvey married his secretary, Amy Ashwood. The couple divorced in 1922, and Garvey then married Amy Jacques. She, too, had worked as his secretary.

Meanwhile, 1920 was the year of the first international convention of the U.N.I.A., which was represented by several thousand delegates from the United States and representatives from other countries as well.

At this convention, Garvey was elected the provisional president of the Republic of Africa. Historians later noted the impossibility of a West Indian being elected in the United States as "president" of Africa. After all, the African people had not chosen Garvey for themselves. In addition, Africa was not a unified country that could elect a single president—it included many nations, languages, and people, most of whom were not even aware of Garvey. At the time, however, the move served to reinforce his influence.

Garvey tried to support construction loans in Liberia, the African nation founded by Americans. However, the Liberian loans, the Black Star Line, and Garvey's other ventures all suffered from insufficient funds. The Black Star Line in particular was a financial disaster. In 1922, Garvey and his colleagues were arrested and charged with fraudulent use of the mail to sell Black Star stock. This action was initiated by some of Garvey's black critics, including W. E. B. DUBOIS.

In 1923, Garvey was convicted, fined, and sentenced to jail. For a while, it looked as though the U.N.I.A. could still continue its work. It raised $25,000 for his bail, and he began his appeal. New stockholders bought shares of its new steamship line, and Garvey continued to negotiate with Liberia to build U.N.I.A. settlements there.

But the British and the French pressured Liberia to cancel its agreement. And in 1925, the U.S. Supreme Court refused to hear Garvey's appeal. In February of that year, he went to jail.

The combination of his imprisonment and the U.N.I.A.'s financial problems proved to be too much for the organization, which began to decline. When Garvey was released in 1927, he was deported to Jamaica, and that effectively ended any possibility of his founding another U.S. organization. However, he tried to establish a Jamaican Peoples Party, which advocated home rule and reform.

Marcus Garvey (*Library of Congress*)

During the 1930s, support for Garvey declined, as black people in both the United States and the West Indies looked for more immediate economic solutions. In 1935, Garvey went to London, where he published a magazine and taught. Although the U.N.I.A. still existed, its conventions dwindled in frequency and attendance.

Garvey's health was declining. He had pneumonia twice in the 1930s, he suffered from asthma, and in 1940 he was felled by two strokes. He died on June 10, 1940, in London, penniless and obscure.

Further Reading: *Black Power and the Garvey Movement,* by Theodore G. Vincent, Berkeley, Calif.: Ramparts Press, 1971; *Garvey: The Story of a Pioneer Black Nationalist,* by Elton C. Fax, New York: Dodd, Mead, 1972.

—*R. K.*

❖ GASTON, ARTHUR GEORGE
(1892–1996), *entrepreneur, millionaire*

Arthur G. Gaston controlled a financial empire worth more than $140 million. He was head of A. G. Gaston Enterprises, based in Birmingham, Alabama, where he was a major stockholder in the Citizen's Federal Savings Bank. He also owned the Booker T. Washington Insurance Company, Booker T. Washington Business School, Vulcan Realty, two radio stations, and portions of a major Birmingham racetrack.

Gaston was a major philanthropist. He donated scholarships throughout the Alabama college system and supported Boys' Clubs and other organizations for children. Gaston was one of two black people honored in the University of Alabama's Business Hall of Fame; the other is George Washington CARVER.

Arthur Gaston was born on July 4, 1892, into a poor family in Demopolis, Alabama. Gaston's father died when he was still a child, so his mother went to work in Birmingham as a maid and housekeeper. The young Arthur then lived with his grandmother.

Even as a child, however, Gaston demonstrated his flair for business. He charged the neighborhood children a button or a pin to use the swing in his grandmother's backyard—then sold the pins and buttons to local women who needed them.

Gaston spent some time in the army, then worked in Westfield, Alabama, for the Tennessee Coal, Iron and Steel Company, earning $3.10 per day. For extra money, he sold peanuts and made loans to his coworkers.

In 1921, Gaston had the chance to use his motto: "Find a need and fulfill it." He noticed that black people

were unable to get decent burials because of segregated funeral parlors. So he started a burial society—which soon prospered.

He launched a new enterprise in 1923. The fact that many banks would not consider home mortgages for African Americans inspired Gaston to start the Citizens Federal Savings and Loan.

In 1939, he married Minnie Gardner, who began to work with him as well. Gaston had noticed the lack of trained black office workers for his bank, so he and his wife established the Booker T. Washington Business School, which is still operating today.

Gaston used his accumulated wealth and power to make an important contribution to the Civil Rights movement of the late 1950s and 1960s. He frequently gave Martin Luther KING, JR., and others, bail money when they had been jailed for peaceful protests. When King's group, the Southern Christian Leadership Conference (SCLC), needed a meeting place, he allowed them to use his motel as their headquarters.

Gaston and his wife were married for more than 48 years. Although their only child died, they had five grandchildren, one of whom worked in Gaston's real estate firm.

Further Reading: *Green Power: The Successful Way of A. G. Gaston,* Birmingham, Ala.: Southern University Press, 1968.

—*R. K.*

❖ GATES, HENRY LOUIS, JR.
(1950–), *educator, literary scholar, writer*

One of the leading African-American intellectuals of his generation, Henry Louis Gates, Jr., has made major contributions to American culture. As a professor at Yale, Cornell, Duke, and Harvard Universities, Gates has been a powerful force in furthering the study and appreciation of African-American life and literature.

Born in Keyser, West Virginia, on September 16, 1950, Gates grew up in nearby Piedmont, where his father worked in the local paper mill. An outstanding student throughout grade school and high school, Gates was admitted to Yale University in 1969. He had originally intended to become a doctor, and during his undergraduate years he received a fellowship to work in a hospital in East Africa. But by the time Gates received his B.A. degree (summa cum laude) in 1973, he had a different goal in mind. He had realized in the course of his studies that the works of black writers and artists were

Henry Louis Gates, Jr. (R) with Wole Soyinka (L) and Cornell Lake (C) *(Reuters/Bryan Snyder/Archive Photos)*

largely ignored, both by scholars and the public. Following the example of W. E. B. DUBOIS and other pioneers of African-American scholarship, Gates dedicated himself to correcting this situation.

Having received a fellowship for graduate study in history, Gates enrolled in England's prestigious Cambridge University, where he earned an M.A. in 1974 and began to study for a doctorate. While at Cambridge, he came into contact with the Nigerian playwright and novelist Wole Soyinka (winner of the Nobel Prize in 1986), who encouraged Gates to study literature rather than history. In 1979, having written a dissertation on racial attitudes in the literature of the Enlightenment, Gates became the first African American to receive a Ph.D. from Cambridge.

Gates then returned to Yale as assistant professor of English and director of the graduate program in African-American studies. In addition to teaching and writing literary criticism, Gates began combing libraries and archives in search of forgotten or neglected works by African-American writers. Over the next decade, he uncovered more than 70,000 individual pieces—short stories, poems, and reviews—from the 19th and 20th centuries. His greatest discovery was the 1859 novel *Our Nig, or Sketches from the Life of a Free Black,* written by Harriet E. Wilson. Scholars had previously believed that the book was really the work of a male white author, but Gates established Wilson's identity, and *Our Nig* took its rightful place as the first African-American novel. Gates's tireless research has resulted in three important collections: *The*

Classic Slave Narratives, The Schomburg Library of Nineteenth-Century Black Women Writers, and the *Norton Anthology of African-American Literature* (coedited with Nellie McKay).

In his role as a literary critic, Gates has produced a number of important books. They include *Black Literature and Literary Theory* (1984); *Figures in Black: Words, Signs, and the "Racial" Self* (1987); and *The Signifying Monkey: A Theory of African-American Literary Criticism* (1988). The work on these and other writings was aided in part by funds from the MacArthur Foundation, which chose Gates to receive a coveted "genius award" in 1981.

By the mid-1980s, Gates had become an academic superstar. In 1985, he left Yale for a post at Cornell University, where he taught for five years before moving on to Duke University as the John Spencer Basset professor of English. In 1990, Gates accepted a position at Harvard, where he became the W. E. B. DuBois Professor of the Humanities, director of the W. E. B. DuBois Institute of Afro-American Research, and chairman of the Department of Afro-American Studies. In his new post, Gates set out to create the number-one African-American studies department in the nation. In pursuit of this goal, he successfully recruited a number of leading black scholars from other universities, drawing Cornel WEST from Princeton University and William Julius WILSON from the University of Chicago, among others.

Gates's wide-ranging interest in modern culture, combined with his intellectual brilliance and personal charm, have spread his influence far beyond the academic world. Through countless interviews, book reviews, magazine articles, and television appearances, he has informed and excited his fellow Americans about the importance of the African-American experience.

Further Information: *Colored People: A Memoir,* by Henry Louis Gates, Jr., New York: Random House, 1994; *Thirteen Ways of Looking at a Black Man,* New York: Random House, 1997; W. E. B. DuBois Institute web site, http://web-dubois.fas.harvard.edu

—*P. K.*

❖ GIBSON, ALTHEA

(1927–), *tennis champion*

The first African American to win a Grand Slam tennis tournament, Gibson broke through the sport's color barrier in 1950. After winning the 1956 French Open, she went on to win five more Grand Slam titles, setting the

Althea Gibson *(Library of Congress)*

standard for all the women players of her era. In 1971, she became the first African American elected to the International Tennis Hall of Fame.

Gibson was born in Silver, South Carolina, on August 25, 1927, but her family moved to New York when she was a small child. Along with three sisters and a brother, Gibson grew up in a crowded apartment on West 143rd Street in Harlem. She was an insecure and restless teenager who dropped out of school at the age of 14, but she always felt sure of herself playing sports. When Buddy Walker, a musician and part-time city recreation worker, saw Gibson playing paddle ball at a local schoolyard, he encouraged her to try tennis. Gibson developed her game on the public courts and won a Parks Department tournament. Harlem's prestigious Cosmopolitan Tennis Club then offered her a junior membership and free lessons. The lessons paid off when she won a statewide tournament in 1942.

At this time, the United States Lawn Tennis Association (USLTA) did not allow black players to compete in its tournaments. In response, African Americans had formed their own organization, the American Tennis Association (ATA), which sponsored a full complement of tournaments. Gibson won the ATA girls' singles title in both 1944 and 1945 and, having turned 18, became eligible for the women's championship the following year. Though she finished second in the 1946 tournament, Gibson attracted the attention of two prominent ATA members, Herbert Eaton and Robert W. Johnson. Both men were successful doctors, and they offered to help Gibson succeed in tennis and in life. During the winter, Gibson lived in the home of Dr. Eaton in Wilmington, North Carolina, and attended high school; in the summer, she received coaching from Dr. Johnson in Lynchburg, Virginia, and traveled with him to ATA tournaments.

In 1947, Gibson won the first of her 10 consecutive ATA women's singles titles. After getting her high school diploma in 1949 at the age of 22, she continued her education at Florida A&M, where she starred in tennis and basketball and played saxophone in the school's marching band.

During her first year of college, Gibson competed against white players on the indoor circuit, but she was still barred from the USLTA's showcase events. Finally in 1950, after former champion Alice Marble publicly blasted the USLTA for its discriminatory policies, Gibson received an invitation to play in the national amateur championships at Forest Hills, New York. She was eliminated in the second round, but the door had at last been opened to African-American tennis players.

During the early 1950s, Gibson's tennis career developed slowly. She graduated from Florida A&M with a degree in physical education, took a teaching job at Lincoln University in Missouri, and even contemplated joining the U.S. Army. When she returned to competition her game began to blossom, enabling her to win 16 of 18 tournaments in Europe and Latin America. On May 26, 1956, Gibson made history by winning the women's singles title at the French Open, defeating Angela Mortimer in straight sets.

Gibson was now at the height of her game, possessing a combination of skill and power that no other female player could match. She dominated the circuit in 1957 and 1958, capturing two singles titles at Forest Hills and two more at Wimbledon. In addition, she paired with Darlene Hard to win the Wimbledon doubles title in 1957. Gibson appeared capable of staying on top for years to come, but at the end of the 1958 season she suddenly announced her retirement. In those days there was little money to be made from tennis, and Gibson wanted to explore other opportunities.

Pursuing her lifelong passion for music, Gibson performed as a professional singer and cut a number of records. She gave tennis lessons, played exhibition matches, acted in a film, and promoted various products. During the 1960s, Gibson became a professional golfer and played on the women's tour for several years. Gibson ultimately got married and settled down in East Orange, New Jersey. Since 1988, she has been a special consultant to the New Jersey Council on Physical Fitness and Sports.

Further Reading: *I Always Wanted to Be Somebody,* by Althea Gibson, New York: Harper, 1968; *So Much to Live For,* by Althea Gibson, New York: Putnam, 1968; *Althea Gibson: Tennis Champion,* by Tom Biracree, Los Angeles, Calif.: Holloway House Publishing Company, 1990.

—*P. K.*

❖ GILPIN, CHARLES SIDNEY
(1878–1930), *singer, actor*

Charles Gilpin won renown on Broadway, playing the lead in Eugene O'Neill's *The Emperor Jones.* He was probably the first black actor to play a major role in an American tragedy. The play won the Pulitzer Prize in 1921, which some scholars attribute, in part, to Gilpin's stellar performance.

After the play's success in February 1921, the Drama League voted him one of 10 people who had contributed most to the American theater.

Charles Gilpin was born in 1878, in Richmond, Virginia, to Peter Gilpin, a steelworker, and Caroline (White) Gilpin, a nurse. He was the youngest of their 14 children.

At a time when many African-American children received little or no education, Gilpin attended a Catholic school for black children until he was 12 years old. While learning the printing trade at the *Richmond Planet,* he also acted in theaters and restaurants.

The recognition he received for his appearances inspired the teen-aged Gilpin to leave home in 1896 to join the minstrel show called Brown's Big Spectacular Log Cabin Company. (A minstrel show featured a group of black people onstage, made up in stereotypical blackface, singing, dancing, and telling jokes, with slapstick and exaggerated dialect.

When the company was stranded for lack of funds after touring only two towns, Gilpin joined another minstrel group. A few months later, that company, too, ran out of money. Gilpin then settled in Philadelphia, where he worked as a printer, a barber, and a prizefighter trainer.

From 1903 until 1905, Gilpin toured with the Carey and Carter Canadian Jubilee Singers. He sang with various companies, spending one year with Bert WILLIAMS and George WALKER, the famous entertainment team.

Finally, in 1907, Gilpin became a member of Chicago's Pekin Stock Company, the first "legitimate" black theater ("legitimate" meaning drama or comedy, rather than musicals or vaudeville). At last, Gilpin had become a dramatic actor, and he soon had leading roles in both plays and operas. Gilpin was highly praised for his work in *The Mayor of Dixie*—later revived as a musical under the title of *Shuffle Along,* featuring compositions by Eubie BLAKE.

From 1907 to 1915, Gilpin was onstage with various companies in Chicago and New York and performed in vaudeville. By 1915, he had returned to dramatic acting with the Anita Bush Players, a troupe that soon merged with Lester Walton's Lafayette Theater Company, the first black dramatic theater in New York.

Gilpin starred in this expanded company. There were many opportunities for him to work; the company staged a new play each week. In January 1916, the group produced Dion Boucicault's *The Octoroon,* a play about slavery, in which he played a white character, in whiteface.

Gilpin eventually became so famous that a March 1916 play was advertised as starring Gilpin "supported by the Lafayette Stock Company." The next month, he resigned from the group over a salary disagreement.

In 1919, Gilpin made his Broadway debut, in John Drinkwater's *Abraham Lincoln,* playing a black preacher. His success in that role, however, cannot be compared to the ovations and acclaim he received for *The Emperor Jones,* which opened in November 1920 at a small theater in Greenwich Village. By 1921, the play had moved to a large Broadway house, where it had a long run and then left New York for a two-year national tour.

When Gilpin was honored by the Drama League, some white people objected to inviting him to the awards banquet. However, the Drama League did not give in, and Gilpin attended the banquet with the others.

He was never again to achieve the fame he had enjoyed while in *The Emperor Jones,* but he continued to work in the theater and supported black dramatic work. While on tour with *Jones* in Cleveland, he donated 50 dollars to the Karamu Players, a black dramatic group that had a major influence on black theater in Cleveland. In 1924, he starred in the all-black play *Roseanne,* depicting African-American life in the South.

In 1929, Gilpin suffered a breakdown while appearing in a New Jersey show. He died the following year,

leaving his second wife, Alma (Benjamin) Gilpin, and a 27-year-old son. He remains an important historical figure in the development of black theater. James Weldon JOHNSON wrote that Gilpin "reached the highest point of achievement on the legitimate stage that had yet been attained by a Negro in America." Margaret Just Butcher considered Gilpin "the first modern American Negro to establish himself as a serious actor of first quality."

Further Reading: *The Negro In the American Theater,* by Edith J. R. Isaacs, College Park, Md.: McGrath Publishing Company, 1947; *Black Drama: The Story of the American Negro in the Theater,* by Loften Mitchell, New York: Hawthorn Books, 1975.

—*R. K.*

❖ GIOVANNI, NIKKI
(Yolande Cornelia Giovanni, Jr.)
(1943–   ), *poet*

Critics have dubbed Nikki Giovanni the "princess of black poetry" for her well-attended poetry readings. She first won acclaim in the 1960s with the rise of the black literary renaissance, when she began to write poetry that dramatized the development of a young black woman into a militant activist.

She has received a profusion of awards, including the *Ladies Home Journal* citation for Woman of the Year in 1972; a National Book Award nomination for her collection, *Gemini;* and election to the Ohio Women's Hall of Fame. Her *Spin a Soft Black Song* was selected by the United States Information Agency for inclusion in an exhibition to the Soviet Union, and was cited as a classic by *The Quarterly Black Review* in April 1995.

Nikki Giovanni was born on June 7, 1943, in Knoxville, Tennessee, as Yolande Cornelia Giovanni, Jr. Her father, Jones Giovanni, was a probation officer; her mother, Yolande Cornelia (Watson) Giovanni, was a teacher. The family moved to Cincinnati, Ohio, when Giovanni was very young, but she remained very close to her mother's mother, Louvenia Terrell Watson. Her grandmother was undoubtedly very important in helping Giovanni develop a sense of responsibility to her people.

At the time of her entrance to Fisk University in Tennessee in 1960, her politics were quite conservative. She believed in the supremacy of the individual and supported right-wing Republican Barry Goldwater. She also clashed frequently with Fisk's dean of women and was expelled from the school.

Several years later, Giovanni returned to Fisk as a dedicated student as well as a civil rights activist. She helped to organize a demonstration to restore the Fisk chapter of the Student Nonviolent Coordinating Committee (SNCC), a major civil rights group. She graduated with honors in 1967 and later did graduate work at the University of Pennsylvania and Columbia University in New York City.

Giovanni gradually dropped her conservative politics and instead became identified with the Black Power movement. A prolific writer, she published three books of her poetry between 1968 and 1970: *Black Feeling, Black Talk* (New York: Morrow, 1968), *Black Judgement* (Detroit: Broadside Press, 1968), and *Re: Creation* (Detroit: Broadside Press, 1970). These books focused on her commitment to black activism and also portrayed her family, her childhood, and her lovers. Critic Alex Batman wrote that Giovanni was "not so much urging violence for itself as she is demanding black assertiveness, although . . . she may be willing to accept violence, even if she is not enthusiastic about it." Some critics considered Giovanni's early work somewhat simplistic as compared to the sophistication of her later poetry.

Despite these criticisms, Giovanni's early poetry was enormously popular. *Black Judgement* sold 6,000 copies in three months, five to six times more copies than the average book of poetry, and she became "one of the three leading figures of the new black poetry between 1968 and 1971," according to critic Mozella G. Mitchell.

In 1969, Giovanni began teaching at Rutgers University in New Jersey. In the same year, she gave birth to her son, Thomas.

She extended her literary output with poetry for children, as well as two more books of adult verse, *My House* (New York: Morrow Quill paperbacks, 1981 reprint of 1972 ed.) and *The Women and the Men* (New York: Morrow, 1975). The main focus of this work is on the family—the family of her origin as well as the family she was creating.

Giovanni founded her own publishing company, Niktom, in 1970. A year later, she personally recorded the best-selling *Truth Is on Its Way*. She continued to make such recordings, as well as videotapes dramatizing her work.

Cotton Candy on a Rainy Day (New York: Morrow) was Giovanni's next book of poetry, published in 1978. Many critics described this as a book of mourning for the lost ideals of the 1960s; and although Giovanni views the future dimly, she still expresses some hope.

In 1983, Giovanni published *Those Who Ride the Night Winds* (New York: Morrow). As with her earlier books, it centered on political activism, as well as black history. According to critics, this book represents a departure in her writing style. Mitchell, for one, says the book shows "a steady progression toward excellence in craftsmanship."

In 1985, Giovanni became professor of creative writing at the college of Mount St. Joseph in Ohio. In 1989 she accepted the position of professor of English at Virginia Polytechnic Institute and State University. She continues to write, to lecture, to appear on television, and to give poetry readings nationwide and abroad. In 1986, a television film, "Spirit to Spirit: The Poetry of Nikki Giovanni," was aired on public television.

Further Reading: *The Selected Poems of Nikki Giovanni,* by Nikki Giovanni, New York: William Morrow & Co., 1996; *Love Poems,* by Nikki Giovanni, New York: William Morrow & Co., 1997; *Shimmy Shimmy Shimmy Like My Sister Kate: Looking at the Harlem Renaissance Through Poems,* ed. by Nikki Giovanni, New York: Henry Holt & Co., Inc., 1996; *A Dialogue: James Baldwin and Nikki Giovanni,* New York: Lippincott, 1973; *Black Women Writers, 1950–1980: A Critical Evaluation,* ed. by Mari Evans, New York: Doubleday/Anchor Press, 1984; *Gemini: An Extended Autobiographical Statement on My First Twenty-five Years of Being a Black Poet,* by Nikki Giovanni, Indianapolis, Ind.: Bobbs, Merrill, 1972; *Black Women Writers at Work,* by Claudia Tate, New York: Continuum, 1983.

—R. K.

❖ GOLDBERG, WHOOPI (Caryn Johnson)
(1949–), *comedian, actor*

One of America's most beloved entertainers, Whoopi Goldberg has achieved stardom in film, television, and theater. The first woman in history to host the annual Academy Awards presentation, she has developed a winning style by blending oddball comedy with a keen sense of life's harsh realities.

Goldberg was born Caryn Johnson in New York City on November 13, 1949. Her father left home shortly after she was born, and she and her brother were brought up by their mother, Emma Johnson, in a racially mixed housing project on the Lower West Side of Manhattan. From early childhood, the outgoing Johnson was determined to become a performer, but her road to that goal was far from easy. Taking part in the

Whoopi Goldberg (N. Rica Schiff/Saga/Archive Photos)

freewheeling youth culture of the late 1960s, she developed a drug problem and checked into a treatment center. She soon became romantically involved with her drug counselor, married him, and gave birth to a daughter, Alexandrea, when she was 18. Only a year later, however, Johnson divorced her husband and moved back in with her mother.

There seemed little chance of a performing career for Johnson at this point, but she was determined to realize her ambition. In 1974, when she learned that a friend was driving out to California, Johnson packed up her daughter and headed west. Settling in San Diego, she worked at a number of odd jobs and began performing with the San Diego Repertory Company. It was at this time that she adopted the stage name Whoopi Goldberg, combining suggestions made by her fellow actors and her mother. Whatever she called herself, however, acting was not paying Goldberg's bills, and she was finally forced to go on welfare in order to care for her daughter.

Goldberg's fortunes finally improved in 1980, when she moved to Berkeley and joined a dramatic troupe called the Blake Street Hawkeyes. At this time she began to develop a routine called "The Spook Show," in which she portrayed a variety of offbeat characters. Audiences loved it, and Goldberg gradually built a following over the next three years as she toured the country with the Blake Street company. Finally, when the troupe was performing in New York, producer Mike Nichols caught

Goldberg's act and signed her to do a one-woman show on Broadway.

Whoopi Goldberg: Direct from Broadway, opened at the Lyceum Theatre in 1984. It was a smash hit at the box office, and the recorded version won a Grammy Award for Best Comedy Album. Goldberg's new-found celebrity led to a major role in Steven Spielberg's acclaimed film *The Color Purple,* for which she won a Golden Globe Award and an Academy Award nomination.

Now a major star, Goldberg followed up with numerous TV appearances and a succession of films, including *Jumpin' Jack Flash* (1986), *Clara's Heart* (1988), *Ghost* (1990), *Sister Act* (1992), *Made in America* (1993), and *Corrina, Corrina* (1994). Her work won consistent praise from critics, and her performance as Oda Mae Brown in *Ghost* earned her an Academy Award in 1991 for Best Supporting Actress. Though she had always felt destined for success, the experience of winning an Oscar overwhelmed her. "I was so floored," she recalled, "there was nothing I could do except sort of gasp, 'Thank you.'"

Goldberg was back at the Oscars in 1994 as the first woman host in the history of the awards ceremonies. Living up to her reputation as a sometimes outrageous stand-up comedian, she made several biting remarks that definitely spiced up the evening. Praised by the *New York Times* as a "poised and funny host," she made an equally memorable return engagement in 1996.

Having experienced hard times on her way to the top, Goldberg has always used her stardom to promote humanitarian causes. She is a member of the Creative Coalition, an organization of socially concerned performers, and she has taken part in many benefits to raise funds for disaster relief, AIDS research, and other causes. Perhaps her best-known public service effort has been *Comic Relief,* a long-running series of cable TV specials with fellow comedians Billy Crystal and Robin Williams that has raised millions of dollars to aid homeless people in the United States.

Further Reading: *Book,* by Whoopi Goldberg, New York: Weisbach, 1997; *Whoopi Goldberg,* by Rose Blue and Corinne J. Naden, New York: Chelsea House, 1995; "The Whoopi Goldberg Nobody Knows," by Laura B. Randolph, *Ebony,* March 1991.

—*P. K.*

❖ GORDY, BERRY, JR.
(1929–), *songwriter, producer, entrepreneur*

As the founder and creative force behind Detroit's legendary Motown Records, Berry Gordy played a pivotal role in the development of popular music in the United States. He has also been a pioneer in African-American business achievement, making Motown the first black-owned company to venture into television and motion picture production.

Born in Detroit, Michigan, on November 28, 1929, Gordy derived his work ethic from his parents—his father was a plastering contractor, his mother an insurance agent. However, Gordy did not take a straight road to success in business. As a teenager, he was mainly interested in music and boxing. Dropping out of high school after his junior year, he entered the ring as a featherweight. Gordy was fairly successful, winning 12 bouts and losing 3, but his boxing career was cut short when he was drafted into the U.S. Army in 1951. Discharged two years later, Gordy opened a record store in Detroit. He specialized in jazz but found that most of his customers were interested in rhythm and blues (also known as R&B), an increasingly popular music style being pioneered by African-American artists such as Chuck Berry and Fats Domino.

Gordy's store soon went bankrupt, but he had learned some valuable lessons about the new directions in popular music. While working with his father as a plasterer and pulling a shift on the Ford assembly line, he began writing songs in his spare time. After developing some valuable contacts on the Detroit music scene, he began working with the up-and-coming R&B singer Jackie Wilson to record a number of his songs: Released by Decca, Wilson's recordings of three Gordy songs—"Reet Petite," "Lonely Teardrops," and "That's Why"—became solid hits. In 1959, Gordy borrowed $800 from his parents and started his own record company in a modest frame house at 2648 West Grand Boulevard. Working with talented songwriters and producers—notably the writing team of Eddie and Brian Holland and Lamont Dozier—Gordy created the "Motown sound," which was basically a combination of classic R&B with elements derived from gospel music, propelled by an irresistible beat. He also recruited a roster of talented performers that eventually included the Marvelettes, the Supremes, the Four Tops, Smokey Robinson and the Miracles, Martha Reeves and the Vandellas, Marvin Gaye, Mary Wells, Al Green, the Temptations, Stevie Wonder, the Jackson 5 (see Michael JACKSON), and others.

Gordy ran Motown with phenomenal efficiency and thoroughness. In addition to supervising every aspect of the recording process, he created a company to recruit new talent and a special department to school Motown's performers in matters of personal style. His attention to

detail—and above all, his flair for creating hits and discovering potential stars—paid off handsomely. During the decade of the 1960s, Motown produced 79 Top-10 singles, a feat matched by no other record company. Motown's top performers appealed to members of all ethnic groups, and the company played a central role in bringing African-American music styles to the forefront of American popular culture.

By 1974, Motown was the most successful black-owned company in the United States, with annual sales of more than $50 million. At this point, Gordy moved his headquarters to Los Angeles, where he delved into television and movie production. No other African-American company had ever ventured into these fields, and Gordy made sure Motown would be successful. Among his major achievements in this area were three films starring Diana Ross—*Lady Sings the Blues*, *Mahogany*, and *The Wiz*—and Motown's memorable 25th anniversary TV special.

By the late 1980s, the costs involved in producing and marketing records had skyrocketed, and Gordy realized that an individual entrepreneur could no longer compete. He sold Motown Records to the giant MCA corporation for $61 million in 1988, retaining control over Jobete, the publishing company holding the rights to all the classic Motown songs, as well as Motown's TV and film subsidiaries. During the 1990s, Gordy branched out into several new areas, including sports management and horse racing. In addition to his business interests, he has devoted a great deal of time to the creation of the Motown Museum, housed in the original Motown offices on Grand Boulevard. Gordy was inducted into the Rock and Roll Hall of Fame in 1988.

Further Information: *To Be Loved: The Music, the Magic, the Memories of Motown: An Autobiography,* by Berry Gordy, New York: Warner, 1994; *The Story of Motown,* by Peter Benjaminson, New York: Grove, 1970; Official Motown web site, http://www.motown.com

—*P. K.*

❖ GRIMKÉ, ARCHIBALD HENRY
(1849–1930), *lawyer, writer, civil rights leader*

Although Archibald Grimké was born during a time of slavery, by the time he reached adulthood, it had ended. He was thus able to take advantage of the new opportunities for blacks opened up by Reconstruction, but later suffered from the political and social setbacks following that turbulent era.

Grimké's achievements were many: He established the first black newspaper in the New England area; published numerous articles and books about civil rights; served as consul at Santo Domingo, in the Dominican Republic; and worked with the National Association for the Advancement of Colored People (NAACP) against discrimination in the federal government. He worked with W. E. B. DUBOIS, the founder of the NAACP, and was influential in black organizational politics in the first few decades of the new century.

Archibald Grimké was born on August 17, 1849, the child of a slave, Nancy Weston, and a white lawyer, Henry Grimké. Henry was the brother of two famous abolitionists, Sarah and Angelina Grimké, and in an unusual move for the time, he acknowledged paternity of Archibald, Francis (who later married Charlotte FORTEN), and John. The boys were born on "Caneacres," the plantation near South Carolina where their mother was enslaved.

When Henry Grimké died in 1852, he left instructions for his white son to free his three black children. Francis was temporarily enslaved, but eventually all three boys moved to Charleston, where they attended a private school for free black children run by liberal white men. Later, they entered a high school operated by an abolitionist woman, who sent Archibald and Francis to Lincoln University in Pennsylvania, where they each received two degrees. Archibald earned his B.A. in 1870, graduating second in his class, and he received his M.A. in 1872.

Archibald Grimké worked as the only black librarian in Lincoln. He helped organize a local church and was known for his deep religious beliefs. With the help of his aunts, he went to Harvard Law School, and in 1874, became its second African-American graduate to receive the LL.B. degree.

For a while, Grimké practiced in Boston, but times were difficult. There was prejudice against black lawyers; even black clients believed that white lawyers would have more influence with the white judges and all-white juries of the time. Nevertheless, Grimké continued his efforts. And, meanwhile, in 1879, he married Sarah Stanley, the daughter of a white family who favored racial equality but opposed interracial marriage. In 1880, they had their only child, Angelina Weld Grimké, who became a noted writer. The family eventually lived with the white Grimké sisters.

While he waited for his law practice to become more lucrative, Grimké turned to journalism. In 1883, he set up the *Hub,* New England's first black newspaper, which

he operated for three years as a voice of protest. The Republican Party was one source of his funding (at the time, "Abraham Lincoln's party" was more pro-equality than the Democrats).

At first, Grimké was a staunch Republican, and even attended the 1884 Party Convention as an alternate delegate. But in 1883, the "Republican" Supreme Court had ruled against the 1875 civil rights bill. By 1886, Grimké was still calling himself a Republican, but he also wrote, "The Republican party is no longer devoted to the colored man."

Meanwhile, Grimké's law practice had begun to improve. He fought cases of racial discrimination and joined an attempt to integrate a Boston skating rink. Although this case was lost on appeal, it helped the passage of an 1885 civil rights bill. Grimké had become president of the Massachusetts Suffrage League and a leader among Boston's "radicals"—well-educated black African Americans who fought discrimination.

He received several political appointments, including the office of consul in Santo Domingo (capital of the Dominican Republic), where he served from 1894 to 1898.

In 1898, Grimké returned to the United States at a crucial point in the debate over civil rights. On the one hand, Booker T. WASHINGTON stressed gradual progress and racial "accommodation," or compromise. But leaders such as W. E. B. DuBois advocated confrontation against all forms of discrimination.

Grimké was evidently closer to the DuBois position and participated in writing an open letter to President McKinley protesting discrimination. However, he would not break with Booker T. Washington. In fact, in 1904, he was treasurer of the Committee of Twelve, which had been formed to promote cooperation among rival black organizations. But in 1905, he was supporting DuBois's Niagara Movement, which was founded to oppose Washington's conservative policies and called for the ending of all distinctions of race.

Finally, in 1906, a significant incident persuaded Grimké to side completely with DuBois and to break with Washington. Black soldiers raided Brownsville, Texas, in revenge for "racial insults." One white man was killed, and two were wounded. President Theodore Roosevelt dismissed the soldiers—an act that Washington supported but Grimké found unfair.

Grimké eventually moved with his daughter to Washington, D.C., where he lived with his brother Francis and became a full-time civil rights activist. In 1909, he joined the Committee of Forty—one of the precursors of the National Association for the Advancement of Colored People (NAACP), an organization headed by DuBois. He then became president of the Washington branch of the NAACP, and, as such, fought against discrimination in the government of President Woodrow Wilson.

In 1914, Grimké testified before the House Committee on Reform in the Civil Service. His testimony was apparently effective, for none of the pro-segregation bills introduced under Wilson ever passed Congress. Grimké also protested laws against interracial marriage.

Grimké remained active in civil rights work until he was 75 and in poor health. He died on February 25, 1930, at his home in Washington, D.C.

Further Reading: *A History of the National Association for the Advancement of Colored People,* Vol. 1, *1909–1920,* by Charles Flint Kellogg, Baltimore, Md.: Johns Hopkins University Press, 1967; *The Betrayal of the Negro from Rutherford B. Hayes to Woodrow Wilson,* by Rayford W. Logan, New York: Collier Books, 1965; *Negro Thought in America, 1880–1915,* by August Meier, Ann Arbor, Mich.: University of Michigan Press, 1963.

—*R. K.*

❖ GRIMKÉ, CHARLOTTE
see FORTEN, CHARLOTTE

❖ HALE, CLARA McBRIDE ("Mother")
(1905–1992), *social activist*

The founder of Hale House, a pioneering facility that cares for infants born to drug-addicted mothers, Clara "Mother" Hale set a unique example for all Americans in community service. "I love children and I love caring for them," she once said about her life's work. "That is what the Lord meant me to do."

Hale was born on April 1, 1905, in Philadelphia, Pennsylvania. Her father died when she was very young, and her mother's ability to keep the family together provided a model of determination that Hale never forgot. Her own adult life proved far from easy. She married Thomas Hale right after leaving high school and moved to New York, where her husband set up a floor-waxing business. But Thomas Hale died of cancer in 1932, leaving his widow to raise three children. Hale worked as a domestic for a time, but she disliked being away from her children throughout the day. As an alternative, she began looking after other people's children during the day in her five-room apartment on West 146th Street; the children enjoyed being with Hale so much that some became full-time boarders during the week and only lived with their parents on the weekends.

Eventually, Hale began taking in abandoned and orphaned children who had been in public institutions, receiving two dollars a week per child from New York City. On average, she cared for seven or eight foster children at a time, raising more than 40 children over a 27-year period. "My daughter says she was almost sixteen before she realized all these other kids weren't her real brothers and sisters," Hale told an interviewer years later.

By the late 1960s, Hale felt that she had worked long enough and was thinking about retirement. One day in 1969, however, Hale's daughter, Lorraine, came upon a heroin addict nodding off in a park with a two-month-old baby in her arms. Lorraine Hale sent the woman to her mother for help; word got around, and before long Mother Hale had 22 infants in her apartment. For the next year and a half, Lorraine Hale and her brothers, Nathan and Kenneth, provided funds to maintain the children. Finally, the City of New York offered an annual grant to support the project, and several individual donors also contributed money. With an additional grant from the federal government, Hale renovated a five-story brownstone at 154 West 122nd Street and opened Hale House in 1975.

Over the next two decades, Hale House took in more than 500 infants born to drug-addicted mothers, caring for the children until the mothers completed drug rehabilitation and were able to resume parenting. Lorraine Hale, who earned a Ph.D. in child development, served as executive director, and much of the day-to-day work was done by Mother Hale herself. She worked tirelessly, feeding and cleaning the children and comforting them as they went through the harrowing process of withdrawal from the drug dependencies that they had developed in the womb. Hale House was the only agency in the city providing complete care for these children, and Hale's work gradually won recognition throughout the country.

In February 1985, Hale was invited to Washington, D.C., to attend President Ronald Reagan's State of the Union Message. In his speech, the president praised Hale as "an American hero," at which point she received a standing ovation from all the dignitaries present in the chamber of the U.S. House of Representatives. On the following day, Hale visited the White House and received more tributes from the president and other government officials. As a result of this public recognition, many people learned about Hale House for the first time; upon returning to New York, Hale was gratified to find that new offers of financial support were pouring in.

As Hale grew older, she and her daughter took steps to ensure that the dedicated Hale House staff would be fully capable of running the facility. When Hale died of a stroke on December 18, 1992, the continuation of her life's work was assured. Her funeral, conducted at Riverside Church in Manhattan, attracted thousands of friends and admirers. Hale's achievements are now celebrated each year at a benefit dinner where worthy individuals receive Mother Hale Awards for Caring; the proceeds from the event help to sustain Hale House and its valuable work.

Further Information: "Clara Hale," in *Current Biography Yearbook 1985,* New York: H. W. Wilson, 1986; *I Dream a World: Portraits of Black Women Who Changed America,* by Brian Lanker, New York: Stewart, Tabori & Chang, 1989.

—*P. K.*

❖ HALEY, ALEX PALMER
(1921–1992), *author*

Alex Haley was best known for his pioneering work *Roots: The Saga of an American Family* (Garden City, N.Y.: Doubleday, 1976), a bestselling book that traces the story of his family from its roots in Africa through slave times until emancipation. Some 85 percent of the national television audience watched the TV version of *Roots,* which aired in 1977; almost 2 million people saw the eight-part series.

"Roots" was significant because it was the first program that portrayed slavery from the viewpoint of the slave in a popular media production. It also broke new ground in linking the African with the African-American experience. Vernon JORDAN, then executive director of

the National Urban League, called the television version of *Roots* "the single most spectacular educational experience in race relations in America."

Roots won special citations from the National Book Award Committee and the Pulitzer Prize Committee in 1977, which was also the year Haley won the NAACP's Spingarn Medal for outstanding achievement by a black American. In the early 1970s, he received honorary degrees from Simpson College in Iowa, Howard University in Washington, D.C., Williams College in Massachusetts, and Capitol University in Ohio.

Haley also assisted in the writing of *The Autobiography of Malcolm X* (New York: Grove Press, 1965), a highly influential book in black political history.

Alex Haley was born on August 11, 1921, in Ithaca, New York, the son of Simon Alexander Haley, a professor, and Bertha George (Palmer) Haley, a teacher. He attended Elizabeth City Teachers College from 1937 to 1939, then served in the U.S. Coast Guard for 20 years. In 1941, Haley married Nannie Branch.

In 1959, he left the Coast Guard to become a freelance writer. Times were often difficult, and his financial situation was frequently unstable. In addition, his marriage ended in 1964. He married Juliette Collins in the same year, but that marriage, too, ended in divorce.

Haley wrote numerous articles during his freelance career, but only two books: *The Autobiography of Malcolm X* (with Malcolm X), in 1965, and *Roots: The Saga of an American Family,* in 1976. He then went on to act as consultant for the television production of *Roots,* and its sequel, "Roots: The Next Generation."

He received so much attention because of *Roots* that his time was completely taken up with promoting and speaking about the book. He later wrote *My Search for Roots,* about the research involved in writing his best-seller.

Many critics wondered about the accuracy of the book, which is presented as though it were the actual history of Haley's family. Haley referred to the book as "faction," a mixture of fact and fiction. The events in the story have their basis in real history; the characters' thoughts, dialogue, and reactions are Haley's own creation.

—*R. K.*

❖ HANDY, WILLIAM CHRISTOPHER
(1873–1958), *composer, band leader*

Handy is justly famous for his blues compositions, and for the traditional songs he collected and published. These collections preserve an important part of the southern black heritage. He gathered the songs while traveling throughout the South, writing down the

W. C. Handy (*Library of Congress*)

notes of music improvised by black people. Handy saw his contribution as helping to sustain and preserve an American musical tradition—a national legacy bequeathed by black culture.

Many of the songs that Handy wrote himself have remained popular, including "A Good Man Is Hard to Find," "St. Louis Blues," "Careless Love," "Beale Street Blues," and "Make Me a Pallet on the Floor."

W. C. Handy was born in 1873, in a log cabin in Florence, Alabama. His grandparents were slaves; his mother, Elizabeth (Brewer) Handy, a freed slave. His father, Charles Bernard, was a Methodist minister.

When Handy attended the Florence District School, he had an opportunity to study music with a Fisk University graduate. Fisk was renowned for its music department, and The Fisk Jubilee Singers were recognized musicians throughout the U.S. and Europe. As a young man, Handy organized a quartet that sang at the

Chicago Columbian Exposition. Later, he toured the South, playing the cornet in minstrel shows.

Handy later led his own band in a minstrel troupe, traveling with the group throughout the United States, Cuba, and Mexico. But he began to use Memphis, Tennessee, as a home base. This southern city was a rich, creative center of black music.

In 1898, Handy married Elizabeth Price, his childhood sweetheart. They had six children during their life together.

Meanwhile, Handy was beginning to discover the blues. Black working people had created two types of music—spirituals, about their hopes for heaven; and the blues, about their lives on this earth. Because of extreme segregation, few white people were aware of blues music. Other trained musicians had heard the blues, but considered the music rude, crude, or too sexual.

Handy, however, recognized the value of this music and by performing and publishing it, he made it available to the larger society, thereby making an important contribution to the black cultural heritage as well as to the American musical tradition as a whole.

He continued to direct his own bands, and brought one to New York in 1918. Later, he recorded. Working with Harry Pace, who was based in Memphis, Handy started a New York–Memphis publishing operation. During the craze for "race records" (of black music) in the 1920s, Handy and his partner Pace became financially successful.

In spite of his professional success, Handy faced personal tragedies. He had lost much of his sight after World War I, although he regained it for a time. In 1937, his wife died. In 1943, he fell from a subway platform and became blind. But he continued to be active. He published his autobiography, *Father of the Blues,* in 1941, and married Irma Louise (Logan) Handy in 1954, at the age of 80. He died of pneumonia four years later, on March 28, 1958.

Further Reading: *Father of the Blues,* by W. C. Handy, edited by Arna Bontemps, New York: Da Capo Press, 1985 reprint of 1941 ed.; *The Music of Black Musicians, A History,* by Eileen Southern, New York: Norton, 1971.

—*R. K.*

✤ HANSBERRY, LORRAINE VIVIAN
(1930–1965), *playwright*

Hansberry is best known for her award-winning story of black American life, *A Raisin in the Sun* (New York: Random House, 1959), the first play written by an

African-American woman to be produced on Broadway. *Raisin* opened on Broadway in 1959. In 1964, Hansberry had a second play on Broadway, *The Sign in Sidney Brustein's Window,* which was still running when she died of cancer in 1965.

Hansberry, born in Chicago, on May 19, 1930, was the daughter of a well-to-do businessman who founded one of Chicago's first black banks. When Lorraine was eight years old, her father tried to move his family into an all-white neighborhood, a move that was blocked by Illinois state law. Mr. Hansberry took the case all the way to the U.S. Supreme Court, where he won *Hansberry vs. Lee* in 1940, while his wife guarded their home against white violence. Hansberry wrote about a similar situation in *Raisin in the Sun.* Her father suffered enormously from his action. Five years later, he died of a cerebral hemorrhage in Mexico.

Hansberry attended college for two years at the University of Wisconsin, then moved to New York and worked at a variety of jobs. She met and married Robert Nemiroff, and began to write short stories, poems, and plays, culminating in a full year devoted to writing *Raisin.* The play won instantaneous success, and it was eventually made into a movie.

Hansberry continued to write, despite her now frequent bouts with cancer. After her death in 1965, Nemiroff compiled and edited her autobiographical writings in *To Be Young, Gifted, and Black* (Englewood Cliffs, N.J.: Prentice-Hall, 1969), which itself became a play. Hansberry's last play, *Les Blancs* (published in *Les Blancs: The Last Plays of Lorraine Hansberry,* New York: Random House, 1972), opened at the Longacre Theater in 1970 to a short run.

Hansberry's work was the subject of much criticism during the Black Nationalist period of the 1960s and 1970s. Many called her work "assimilationist" and accused her of being old-fashioned. Later critics, however, praised her contributions to the American realist tradition, noting her commitment to the African heritage of black Americans, and acknowledged the depth of her inspiration to later authors. Only 34 years old, and at the beginning of her career, Hansberry died on January 12, 1965.

Further Reading: "The Talk of the Town," *The New Yorker,* May 9, 1959; Introduction, by Robert Nemiroff and Julius Lester, to *Les Blancs: The Last Plays of Lorraine Hansberry,* New York: Random House, 1972; "Me Tink Me Hear Sounds in the Night," by Lorraine Hansberry, *Theater Arts,* Oct. 1960; "Sweet Lorraine," by James Baldwin, *Esquire,* Nov. 1969.

—*R. K.*

❖ HAYES, ROLAND
(1887–1976), *concert singer*

Roland Hayes was one of the leading concert tenors of the world from the 1920s through the 1940s. At a time when black concert singers had a hard time being accepted in the United States, Hayes had a brilliant musical career in Europe. This was the springboard to his finally winning recognition in the United States as well.

Hayes became the first African American to sing with a major U.S. orchestra when he performed with the Boston Symphony in 1923. That concert also won him the distinction of being the first black person to sing in Boston's Symphony Hall. In 1950, he gained further recognition with his appointment to the music faculty of Boston University.

Hayes was admired by his colleagues in the music world. When he was given the first Amistad Award for contributing to improved human relations, noted composer Virgil Thomson said, "You do the human race honor to exist."

Roland Hayes, born in a small rural Georgia town in 1887, was the son of former slaves. When he was 13, his family moved to Chattanooga, Tennessee. There the young singer began his musical studies and developed his voice by singing in a church choir.

Roland Hayes (*Library of Congress*)

As a young man, Hayes had an important experience: His teacher played him some records of the great tenor Enrico Caruso. When he heard them, Hayes knew he wanted to be a professional concert singer, even though at the time such a career was unheard-of for a black person.

From 1905 to 1910, Hayes studied music at Fisk University in Tennessee, where he sang with the famous Fisk Jubilee Singers. Then he went to Louisville, Kentucky, supporting himself with various jobs, including one that called for him to sing backstage, accompanying silent movies.

In 1911, after traveling north on tour with the Jubilee Singers, he decided to settle in Boston. He felt that better training for his voice would be available to him there.

Hayes gave his first American concert in 1916. He sang both Negro spirituals and classical *Lieder* (German for "song"—musical dramatizations of poems, especially by Schubert, Schumann, and Brahms.) He began to tour the United States, singing at Carnegie Hall as well as at other concert halls in large cities. He also toured black churches and colleges.

Although Hayes managed to sing in Boston recital halls, he felt that his race was restricting him to certain types of concerts. By 1920, he had saved the necessary funds to sail for Europe, where he found a better reception. His first concert, at London's Aeolian Hall, was a great success, and he eventually sang in all the major capitals of Europe.

This European success led Hayes to a triumphal return to the United States in 1923. From then on, he toured both the United States and Europe, secure in his position as a leading classical singer.

Hayes wanted his music to be available to all people. He insisted on low-cost admissions so that poor people of all races could come to his concerts. By singing spirituals along with classical selections, he continued to acknowledge his cultural heritage. He was also extremely helpful to concert singer Marian ANDERSON, and sang recitals with her to help her launch her own splendid career. He gave lessons and, at times, financial support to many young black singers, encouraging them to enter the profession that he had helped to make available to them.

Hayes continued to sing until his 75th birthday, in 1962, when he gave a farewell concert at Carnegie Hall for the benefit of black colleges.

He died in 1976. His daughter, Afrika, also became a professional singer.

Further Reading: *Distinguished Negro Georgians,* by Cornelius V. Troup, Dallas, Tex.: Royal Publishing Company, 1962; *Angel Mo' and Her Son Roland Hayes,* by McKinley Helm, New York: Greenwood Press, 1969.

—R. K.

✦ HEALY, JAMES AUGUSTINE
(1830–1900), *first African-American Catholic bishop*

James Healy was the first African-American Catholic priest in the United States, and also the country's first African-American bishop. He was an influential religious leader, who proposed major church legislation and helped to establish the Catholic University of America in Washington, D.C. He was a personal friend of Pope Pius IX and of Pope Leo XIII, who made him an assistant at the papal throne, at a rank just below that of cardinal.

Healy was born on April 16, 1830, a slave on a plantation near Macon, Georgia. He was the child of an Irish father, Michael Morris Healy, and a mixed race slave mother, Mary Eliza Smith. James Healy was the oldest of ten children from this relationship, which under Georgia law made him a slave whose freedom could only be granted by the state legislature.

But Michael Healy, James's father, wanted his son to be free. He took James north to Long Island, where he enrolled him in a Quaker school in 1837. Seven years later, James Healy entered the Jesuit College of the Holy Cross in Worcester, Massachusetts, where he received a B.A. in 1849 and an M.A. in 1851. (Two of his brothers and one sister were also sent to the Long Island school; and, later, the brothers also attended Holy Cross.)

Healy's days at the Catholic school had turned him toward the priesthood. He went first to a Canadian seminary, then to a French one in Paris, where he was ordained in 1854 at the Cathedral of Notre Dame.

When Healy returned to the United States, he worked as secretary and chancellor to the bishop of Boston. He became pastor of the Cathedral of the Holy Cross during the Civil War. In 1866, he began nine years of service at St. James Cathedral, the largest church in Boston.

Healy's congregation was largely Irish, and at first, there was an uneasiness about his being a black priest. Healy benefited, however, from the political changes of Reconstruction. After the Civil War, African Americans were granted the vote and other political rights that had once been denied them. This sparked many other reforms, and more black people were able to enter the arts, the professions, and the business world.

Most of these gains were lost again when Reconstruction ended, and African Americans would not make similar dramatic advances until the 1960s. Meanwhile, however, there were those like Healy who were able to take long-term advantage of the new opportunities. Overcoming any previous racial prejudice, Healy won the support of his congregation.

Healy became the bishop's deputy for social action, helping to develop several children's homes. He also helped to organize Boston's first Catholic Union, a militant group that fought for immigrants' rights. Healy became known as a priest who fought for the rights of juvenile delinquents, farmers, and poor people in hospitals and other institutions that denied them access to Catholic services. Healy also argued for the right of the church to be free from taxation.

In 1875, Pope Pius IX appointed Healy to become the bishop of Portland, Maine, with a diocese that included Maine and New Hampshire. Healy ran the diocese for 25 years and became known as "the children's bishop" because of his work to establish children's homes. He also fought against child labor and helped to pay the taxes and doctor bills of the poor and the bereaved.

Healy's oratorical skills served him well as the most prominent Catholic speaker in New England, while his diplomatic talents made him an influential member of the church hierarchy. Nonetheless, when he visited southern cities, he was often the victim of racial slurs and discrimination. In New England, however, he was honored and respected as an outstanding church figure by the white priests who served under him. His old college in Massachusetts named a building after him, as did other schools in Maine and as far away as St. Louis.

Healy's brother, Patrick Francis Healy, also became a Jesuit priest and later was president of Georgetown University in Washington, D.C.

James Healy died of a heart attack on August 5, 1900, in Portland, Maine.

Further Reading: *Bishop Healy: Beloved Outcast,* in *The American Negro: His History and His Literature,* by Albert S. Foley, New York: Farrar, Straus & Young, 1969; *God's Men of Color,* by Albert S. Foley, New York: Farrar, Straus & Young, 1955.

—R. K.

❖ HEMINGS, SALLY
(1773–1835), *alleged slave mistress of Thomas Jefferson*

Sally Hemings was said to have been the mistress of Thomas Jefferson, as well as his slave. New evidence of this relationship was revealed in November 1998 by DNA tests; most historians now believe it existed. Many writers see it as symbolic of the contradictions within the mind of Jefferson—the man who opposed slavery but owned slaves.

Sally Hemings's father was the white slaveholder John Wayles, which made her a half-sister of Jefferson's wife. Her mother, Elizabeth Hemings, was descended from an African slave and a British sea captain. When Wayles died, his daughter, Martha Jefferson, inherited all of his slaves, who moved to the Jefferson estate in Monticello in 1775.

Hemings was sent to Paris with Jefferson's second daughter, Mary, who went to join her father there in the 1780s. While there, Hemings was paid a small salary and was tutored in French. She lived with her brother James, who worked as Jefferson's valet.

Historians examining Jefferson's journals and letters believe that he fell in love with Hemings in 1788. That was the year in which Jefferson's intimate friend, Maria Cosway, returned to London. When Jefferson was about to return to the United States, he planned to take Hemings with him. However, under French law, she was free, and she refused to go back with Jefferson unless he promised to free all her children when they reached the age of 21. Hemings was apparently pregnant at the time, and gave birth soon after their return, late in 1789.

There were many rumors about Jefferson's "scandalous" liaison with Hemings. Despite the scandal, Jefferson won the 1804 election to the presidency. About this time, their oldest son, Tom, left Monticello. Although he was apparently allowed to leave freely, the story given by the family was that he "ran away" so that Jefferson would not appear to be freeing a slave.

According to a memoir by one of Hemings's sons, Jefferson was kind to all the people on the plantation, but showed no special fatherly treatment to his black children. While they were growing up, the children lived in the plantation's main house and did comparatively light work. At age 14, they were taught trades, with the welcome understanding that at 21, they would be free. Some were light-skinned enough to "pass" for white, and married wealthy white people.

Jefferson began his political career as an opponent of slavery, but by the end of his life, he was discouraged and apathetic about the issue. Although many people in Virginia had similar interracial relationships, the state's laws made the acknowledgment of these liaisons subject to severe penalty. In addition, if Jefferson had set Hemings free, she would have had to leave the state—unless he could petition the state legislature to let her remain. Thus, when Jefferson died in 1826, he did not free Hemings, but left that matter to his daughter, Martha Randolph.

Hemings was still on the slave inventory in 1827, with an official worth given as $50. The next year, she was freed and went to live in a small home near Monticello with her son. Although he was listed in the census as white, he identified with the black community and married women of mixed ancestry. Ironically, in one census, Hemings herself is described as white.

Hemings died in 1835, at the age of 62. Her descendants fought in the Civil War and achieved varied prominence in western states: Frederick Madison Roberts was the first African American in the California state assembly; John Wayles Jefferson became a banker and cotton broker; Beverly Jefferson was a hotel owner.

Further Reading: *Thomas Jefferson, an Intimate History,* by Fawn M. Brodie, New York: W. W. Norton, 1974; *Jefferson the President, First Term, 1801–1805,* by Dumas Malone, Boston, Mass.: Little, Brown, 1970 (in Appendix II, "The Miscegenation Legend," Malone argues against the idea that Hemings was Jefferson's mistress).

—*R. K.*

❖ HENDRIX, JIMI
(1942–1970), *musician*

One of the all-time rock and roll legends, Jimi Hendrix was a masterful guitar player and an unforgettable performer. Though his career lasted only a handful of years, he created a legacy that has influenced many rock musicians who followed him.

Hendrix was born in Seattle, Washington, on November 27, 1942. His parents divorced when he was very young, and he was raised in Seattle by his father, Al. A sensitive, somewhat lonely youngster, Hendrix showed an early fascination with music. He played his first notes on a one-string ukelele and immersed himself in the recordings of blues guitarists such as Muddy Waters and B. B. King. When Hendrix was 16, his father bought him his first actual guitar, a secondhand acoustic model. Hendrix began to practice almost nonstop, and a year later, he got his first electric guitar, a Supro Ozark 1560S. He then joined a local band called the Rocking Kings. Playing at clubs and parties throughout the Seattle area, he began to develop the flamboyant style that later became his trademark.

After graduating from high school in 1961, Hendrix joined the U.S. Army and trained to be a paratrooper at

Jimi Hendrix (*Archive Photos*)

Fort Campbell, Kentucky. He had his guitar sent to him at the base and spent most of his spare time practicing. In 1962, Hendrix and a fellow soldier, Billy Cox, formed a band called the King Casuals, playing at local clubs whenever they could. Later in the year, Hendrix injured himself while making a jump and was discharged from the army on medical grounds.

In 1964, Hendrix moved to New York City and began working on the club circuit, using the name Jimmy James. The following year he formed his own band, Jimmy James and the Blue Flames. One night, when the band was performing in a Greenwich Village coffeehouse, the audience included Chas Chandler, a member of the Animals, one of the top British bands of the 1960s. Chandler was amazed by Hendrix's guitar playing, and he convinced Hendrix that he could make it big in England.

When Hendrix arrived in London in 1966, Chandler got to work on his behalf, recruiting bassist Noel Redding and drummer Mitch Mitchell. The new band, called the Jimi Hendrix Experience, released two hit singles—"Hey Joe" and "Purple Haze"—in early 1967 and followed up with a debut album, *Are You Experienced?*, later in the year. As Chandler predicted, Hendrix took the London pop scene by storm. Whenever he played, British rock stars such as Paul McCartney, Keith Richards, and Eric Clapton flocked to see him, awed by his guitar technique and his musical inventiveness.

Hendrix remained unknown in the United States until 1967, when he appeared at the Monterey Pop Festival in California. His show-stopping performance at the festival, which included setting his Fender Stratocaster on fire at the end of "Wild Thing," made Hendrix a star. He and his bandmates undertook two successful U.S. tours, and in 1968, the Experience released two consecutive hit albums: *Axis: Bold as Love* and *Electric Ladyland*.

By the end of 1968, disputes over management and musical direction caused the breakup of the Experience. Hendrix began performing with new musicians, making a memorable appearance at the Woodstock Festival in 1969, where he performed his unique and moving version of the "Star-Spangled Banner." He then formed a new group called Band of Gypsies and issued two more albums, *Band of Gypsies* and *Cry of Love*. By this point, Hendrix's many innovations—including the use of feedback as a musical element—were influencing the world of rock music.

In 1970, Hendrix returned to England to play at the Isle of Wight Festival and then went on to London. Early on the morning of September 18, he returned to his apartment after a night of partying, took a potent sleeping pill, and went to bed. He never regained consciousness. Though rumors of suicide soon became part of the growing Hendrix legend, most people believe that his death was accidental, resulting from the combination of barbiturates and alcohol. Hendrix was inducted into the Rock and Roll Hall of Fame in 1992.

Further Information: *Cherokee Mist: The Lost Writings,* by Jimi Hendrix, edited by Bill Nitopi, New York: HarperCollins, 1993; *Are You Experienced?: The Inside Story of the Jimi Hendrix Experience,* by Noel Redding, London: Picador, 1990; *'Scuse Me While I Kiss the Sky: The Life of Jimi Hendrix,* by David Henderson, revised edition, New York: Bantam, 1983; Experience Hendrix Interactive, http://www.jimi-hendrix.com—includes video and audio clips.

—*P. K.*

❖ HENSON, MATTHEW ALEXANDER ("Matt")
(1866–1955), *codiscoverer of the North Pole*

Matthew Henson accompanied Lt. Robert Peary on all of his Arctic treks except the first one, and was with him on the final dash to the North Pole in 1909. Yet, undoubtedly due to his race, Henson was for years denied recognition of his role in this discovery. His friendship with Peary ended with the last expedition, and Peary had Henson promise not to lecture about the trip himself. Henson kept this promise until financial need led him to break it 12 years later.

Eventually, Henson did win the recognition he deserved: In 1944, Congress awarded him one of the joint medals that honored him along with the five whites of the expedition. And in 1948, he was given the Gold Medal of the Geographical Society of Chicago. Henson was honored by Presidents Truman and Eisenhower, and was awarded a commemorative plaque by the state of Maryland six years after his death.

Henson, the son of freeborn parents, was born in 1866, in Charles County, Maryland. Accounts of his life differ, but scholars generally agree that he was orphaned at an early age and lived with an uncle in Washington, D.C. There, he worked in a restaurant and went to school.

In 1879, Henson shipped out of Baltimore as a cabin boy on a merchant vessel. He became an able-bodied seaman, serving on the same ship until he was 18. Then he worked in Boston as a stevedore (a loader and unloader of ships), in Providence as a bellhop, in Buffalo as a laborer and in New York as a coach attendant. Then, at 19, he returned to Washington.

In 1887, he met Lt. Robert Peary. The chance meeting took place in a store, whose owner recommended that Peary take Henson as his valet on a trip to survey a canal route through Nicaragua. Peary soon discovered that Henson could chart a path through the jungle, and that he was an experienced sailor. Henson was clearly more valuable as a colleague than as a valet, and was invited to accompany Peary on his Arctic explorations.

On April 6, 1909, the team of Peary, Henson, and four Eskimos reached the North Pole, although other white men had been with the expedition earlier. Commander Donald B. MacMillan was one of those who were sent back before that final journey. In 1934, he said that Henson went with Peary "because he was a better man than any of his white assistants." Peary lauded Henson, who in turn later called Peary "a great man."

Matthew Henson *(Library of Congress)*

Nevertheless, for years, the only explorer to receive credit for reaching the Pole was Robert Peary.

Henson died of a cerebral hemorrhage in March 1955. In 1998, the TV movie "Glory & Honor" commemorated Henson's life and work.

Further Reading: *North Pole Legacy,* by Robert Counter, Amherst, Mass.: University of Massachusetts Press, 1991; *How Peary Reached the North Pole,* by Comdr. Donald B. MacMillan, Boston: Houghton, Mifflin, 1934; *Washington Post,* article by Joel Dreyfus, April 10, 1976, p. 3; *New York Times,* obituary, March 10, 1955, p. 27.

—*R. K.*

❖ HOLIDAY, BILLIE
(1915–1959), *vocalist*

Regarded by many as the greatest jazz singer of all time, Billie Holiday combined a haunting voice, refined technique, and emotional power to create a unique singing style. Known to her fans as Lady Day, she made incomparable recordings of songs such as "Am I Blue," "I'll Get By," and "God Bless the Child."

Born in Baltimore, Maryland, on April 7, 1915, Holiday endured enormous hardship during her early years. Her father, a traveling musician, left home when she was very young. Her mother soon went north to work as a maid, leaving Holiday in the care of a cousin, who often mistreated her. Holiday began working at the age of six. When she was 10, a man tried to rape her; claiming it was for her own protection, a judge sent her to a reform school, where she endured two horrible years of confinement. Finally, at the age of 12, Holiday was able to rejoin her mother in New York.

Life up north was just as hard, and when the Great Depression began in 1929, Holiday and her mother were destitute. Finally, when they were on the verge of being evicted from their Harlem apartment, Holiday scoured the streets in search of a job. Entering a local club called Pop and Jerry's, she asked for work as a dancer. The owner quickly saw that she had no experience and told her to leave. However, the club's pianist felt sorry for Holiday and asked if she could sing. Holiday agreed to try a popular song of the day, "Trav'lin Alone." By the time she finished, the club's patrons—many with tears in their eyes—began to throw money at her feet. Her career as a singer was launched.

Performing in clubs and theaters around Harlem, Holiday developed her unique singing style by listening to jazz musicians—she learned to do with her voice what they did with their instruments. In 1933, she began to make her first recordings. Before long, Holiday had bought a restaurant for her mother, and the two women were settled in a comfortable apartment upstairs.

Holiday's reputation among jazz enthusiasts was cemented by her recordings on the Commodore label, which she began to make in 1936—in the words of one music historian, these sides "constitute one of the major bodies of work in jazz." Holiday widened her appeal even more in 1938, when she began appearing at Café Society, an integrated nightclub in Greenwich Village. People from all walks of life filled the club every night, amazed at Holiday's ability to make even the most familiar songs sound brand new. When she performed "Strange Fruit," a haunting protest against the lynching of African Americans in the South, Holiday became an influential public figure as well as a star entertainer.

By the 1940s, Holiday was a living legend. She performed at all the fashionable clubs that lined New York's West 52nd Street, sometimes earning as much as $1,000 a week, a small fortune at that time. But Holiday had never really recovered from the ordeals of her childhood, and she continued to struggle with personal demons. She married a man who was addicted to opium and soon began to share his habit; when the marriage fell apart, Holiday turned to heroin. To make matters worse, Holiday's mother died in 1945, depriving her of the one person she could look to for advice and encouragement.

Holiday hit rock bottom in 1947 when she was arrested on a drug charge and served nine and a half months in a federal prison in West Virginia. She appeared to bounce back quickly after her release, performing brilliantly at Carnegie Hall before a cheering, standing-room-only audience. Because of her prison record, however, Holiday could no longer get a permit to sing in New York clubs, and this severely hampered her ability to make a living. Though she continued to record and made a successful tour of Europe in 1954, she was constantly battling her craving for drugs and alcohol. "All dope can do for you is kill you—and kill you the long slow hard way," she wrote in her autobiography. By the late 1950s, Holiday's health declined rapidly, and she died on July 17, 1959, at the age of 44.

Further Reading: *Lady Sings the Blues,* by Billie Holiday with William Dufty, New York: Penguin, 1984 (reprint of 1956 edition); *Lady Day: The Life and Times of Billie Holiday,* by Robert G. O'Meally, New York: Arcade, 1991; *The Billie Holiday Companion: Seven Decades of Commentary,* edited by Leslie Gourse, New York: Schirmer, 1997.

—*P. K.*

Billie Holiday (*Library of Congress*)

❖ HORNE, LENA MARY CALHOUN
(1917–), singer, actress

Lena Horne created a new image for black women in films. She was the first African-American actress to be presented in Hollywood films as a glamorous adult woman, rather than as a maid or a child, and she was the first black actress to receive a full publicity buildup from her studio. She was also the first African-American artist of either sex to be given a long-term contract at the major Hollywood studio Metro-Goldwyn-Mayer.

Her notable Hollywood career took place largely in the 1940s, but in later years she made frequent television appearances and sang jazz and popular melodies in clubs and concert appearances. She has headlined at all of the major nightclubs in the United States and continues to entertain on stage and in television. She remains a symbol of glamour.

Horne's awards include a New York Drama Critics Poll Award as Best Female Musical Lead for her 1958 work on Broadway in *Jamaica;* a New York Drama Critics Circle Award and a special Tony Award for her 1981 Broadway show *Lena Horne: The Lady and Her Music;* a 1983 Spingarn Award given by the NAACP for achievement; and awards from Actors Equity and the American Association of Composers, Authors and Publishers (ASCAP). In 1984 she was a Kennedy Center honoree. She has also been honored with two Grammy Awards.

Lena Horne was born in 1917 in Brooklyn, New York, to middle-class parents who divorced when she was three. Her grandmother, Cora Calhoun Horne, was an activist for black and women's rights from the 1890s to the 1930s, and Horne always admired her.

Horne's singing career began at the Cotton Club, a Harlem nightclub that featured black performers but was restricted to all-white audiences. Horne performed as a chorus girl there at age 16, when she had not yet finished high school. In 1934, she made her Broadway debut, as the "Quadroon Girl" in *Dance With Your Gods* (a "quadroon" is a person with one-quarter black ancestry).

At 18, Horne left the Cotton Club to sing with the jazz orchestras of Noble Sissle and Charlie Barnet. She returned to Broadway to star in Lew Leslie's *Blackbirds of 1939,* one of the many revues of the 1930s featuring black song and dance. However, the show closed after only nine performances.

Horne later sang at Cafe Society Downtown, a club that she helped revive. During some of these New York years, she was known as "Helena Horne."

In 1937, Horne had married Louis J. Jones, but the couple was divorced in 1938. They had one surviving child, Gail Jones, who became an actress.

Horne left for California in the 1940s, where she sang in nightclubs. She was spotted by a talent scout from MGM, and was eventually offered a Hollywood contract.

For a while, Horne's work in Hollywood was viewed with optimism by civil rights leaders. Until then, black women in Hollywood films had been seen almost exclusively as maids, a role for which the glamorous Horne was clearly not suited. However, she was also denied stardom. She was restricted primarily to musical numbers. In a scene that was more or less unrelated to the rest of the movie, Horne would appear, look beautiful, and sing beautifully. The movie would then continue.

The scenes in which Horne appeared were often cut when her movies played in the South. Studio heads were afraid that southern audiences might be offended by the image of a glamorous, self-assured black woman. Other black actresses, like jazz pianist and performer Hazel Scott, received similar treatment during the 1940s, as did the less glamorous Hattie MCDANIEL, because of the assertive tone she took in her portrayal of servants.

However, when Hollywood made all-black musicals, Horne was able to play a leading role. In 1943, she starred in *Cabin in the Sky* and *Stormy Weather.* Her striking beauty was considered acceptable because it conformed to prevailing standards.

Later, reviewing her Hollywood work, Horne said that she had never felt entirely comfortable, and that those years had been difficult. Her studio sent out glossy publicity photos, which GIs of World War II pinned up in their lockers. But Horne's "sex-symbol" image never brought her the starring movie roles of such other "pin-up girls" as Betty Grable or Rita Hayworth. And she refused to be cast as a Latin American or any other racial or cultural stereotype.

In the late 1940s, Horne faced new dilemmas. She was married in 1947 to Lennie Hayton, a white arranger and composer. Interracial marriages were frequently condemned, especially by white people. Thus, she kept the relationship secret for three years. When it became public, she met with much hostility.

And then she had to deal with the blacklist. Although studios never admitted this practice, many people believed there existed a blacklist of "undesirable" actors whose current or former radical views kept them from being employed. The late 1940s saw the beginning of the cold war—a time of growing paranoia about the Soviet Union and the Communist Party. Hollywood was often targeted as a hotbed of subversion, and magazines sprang up listing the names of supposed "communists" and "communist sympathizers," who then ended up on the alleged blacklist. One such magazine, *Red Channels,* considered Horne politically dangerous, and she felt this cost her much television work.

Racial prejudice would also mark her career, sometimes in an ironic way. In 1957, she lost the role of Julie—the woman of mixed race in the film *Showboat*—to Ava Gardner. Although Horne was actually black, like Julie, and Gardner was white, Hollywood was unwilling to use her in the part, since the character, while passing for white, marries a white man.

Nevertheless, Horne continued with her nightclub career in both the United States and Europe. In 1957, she played on Broadway in *Jamaica.* Her movie career, which had been stalled since 1956, resumed in 1969 with a dramatic role in *Death of a Gunfighter,* with Richard Widmark. Almost 10 years later, she played in *The Wiz,* an all-black version of *The Wizard of Oz.*

Throughout the 1960s, Horne was active in the Civil Rights movement. She continues to speak out on social issues and against discrimination.

Horne's most recent triumph was in 1981, when she starred on Broadway in *Lena Horne: The Lady and Her Music,* which played on public television and was taped in 1984 for cable.

In 1971, Horne's husband died. However, her own business continued to be called "Horne-Hayton Enterprises."

Horne's films include one made outside Hollywood, called *The Duke Is Tops* or *Bronze Venus.* Her Hollywood work includes *Panama Hattie,* 1942; *I Dood It,* 1943; *Thousands Cheer,* 1943; *Broadway Rhythm,* 1944; *Two Girls and A Sailor,* 1944; *Ziegfeld Follies,* 1946; *Till the Clouds Roll By,* 1946; *Words and Music,* 1948; *Duchess of Idaho,* 1950; *Meet Me in Las Vegas,* 1956; *That's Entertainment!,* 1976, and *That's Entertainment! III,* 1994. Her television work includes appearances on *The Ed Sullivan Show, The Perry Como Show, The Flip Wilson Show,* and *Sanford and Son,* as well as specials of her own. In 1997, the PBS series American Masters focused on Lena Horne in a documentary called *Lena Horne: In Her Own Voice.*

Further Reading: *Lena: A Biography of Lena Horne,* by James Haskins, Lanham, Md.: Scarborough House, 1991; *The Hornes: An American Family,* by Gail Lumet Buckley, New York: Knopf, 1986; *Lena,* by Lena Horne and Richard Schickel, Garden City, N.Y.: Doubleday, 1965.

—R. K.

❖ HOUSTON, CHARLES HAMILTON
(1895–1950), *lawyer, educator*

One of the major architects of the legal campaign that abolished segregation in the United States, Charles Houston played a leading role in bringing justice to American society. As a longtime professor at Howard University's School of Law, he also helped train an entire generation of African-American attorneys and legal scholars.

Born in Washington, D.C., on September 3, 1895, Houston was the only child of William Houston, a lawyer, and Mary Houston, who was trained as a teacher but worked mainly as a hairdresser and dressmaker. A brilliant student, Houston graduated from high school at 15 and entered Amherst College in Massachusetts. After graduating with Phi Beta Kappa honors, he spent two years teaching at Howard University. When the United States entered World War I in 1917, Houston enlisted in the U.S. Army. Commissioned as a lieutenant, he saw action in France with the 351st Field Artillery.

After leaving the army in 1919, Houston entered Harvard Law School, where he continued to excel. During his third year he became the first African American chosen to be an editor of the prestigious *Harvard Law Review,* and he graduated in 1922 in the top 5 percent of his class. After studying in Madrid, Spain, on a fellowship, Houston was admitted to the District of Columbia bar and began to practice law with his father and William Hastie.

Though Houston was to remain with his father's firm for the next 25 years, his activities ranged far beyond the everyday practice of law. In 1927, he received a foundation grant to produce a report on African Americans and the law, and in 1929 he was appointed a dean at the Howard Law School. In the years that followed, Houston played a leading role in upgrading the curriculum of the law school and making it into a top-flight institution.

Houston's greatest contribution to law and society took form in 1934, when he began to work with a committee created by the National Association for the Advancement of Colored People (NAACP) and the American Fund for Public Service. The committee's immediate plan was to wage a legal battle against racial discrimination in public education and public transportation—the long-term goal was to wipe out segregation in the United States. Houston was to be the driving force in this historic campaign, preparing lawsuits that would be argued in state and federal courts.

In 1935, Houston personally argued the case of *Hollins v. Oklahoma* before the U.S. Supreme Court. He won a reversal of the death sentence for a black man convicted of rape, after showing that African Americans had been purposely excluded from the jury. Another of Houston's major cases was *Missouri ex rel. Gaines v. Canada* (1938), in which the Supreme Court ordered the admission of an African American to the University of Missouri Law School. In *Steele v. Louisville & Nashville Railroad* (1944), Houston convinced the Supreme Court to order an all-white labor union to represent African-American railroad workers. By this time, Houston had become the full-time legal counsel to the NAACP, working closely with his former student Thurgood MARSHALL. He also served as general counsel for the Association of Colored Railway Trainmen and Locomotive Firemen.

Step by step, Houston's legal victories prepared the way for the landmark 1954 Supreme Court decision in *Brown v. Board of Education of Topeka,* which outlawed segregation in all public schools. Unfortunately, Houston was not able to see the crowning achievement of his life's work. He began to suffer from heart disease during the mid-1940s, and this ailment claimed his life in 1950.

Because Houston did so much of his work behind the scenes, he has not received as much public acclaim as others who were more visible in the fight for equal rights. However, no one involved in that great struggle failed to appreciate Houston's monumental achievements. Shortly after his death, the NAACP awarded Houston its prestigious Spingarn Medal. In the ensuing years, a major building at Howard University and a number of public schools have been named in Houston's honor. Perhaps the greatest tribute of all came from Thurgood Marshall, who referred to his teacher and colleague as the First Mr. Civil Rights.

Further Reading: *Groundwork: Charles Hamilton Houston and the Struggle for Civil Rights,* by Genna Rae McNeil, Philadelphia: University of Pennsylvania Press, 1983; *Charles Hamilton Houston,* by G. S. Prentzas, Broomall, Pa.: Chelsea House, forthcoming.

—*P. K.*

❖ HUGHES, JAMES LANGSTON
(1902–1967), *writer*

Langston Hughes was one of the most prolific American writers of this century. He wrote poetry, songs, novels, plays, biographies, histories, and essays. His work was published in newspapers and books, performed in theaters, and collected in anthologies. He received numerous awards, including one from the American Academy of Arts and Letters.

Books of poetry by Hughes include *Weary Blues* (New York: Knopf, 1926) and *Ask Your Mama* (New York: Knopf, 1961 ed.). His novels are *Not Without Laughter* (New York: Knopf, 1930) and *Tambourines to Glory* (New York: J. Day Company, 1958). His short stories are collected in *The Ways of White Folks* (New York: Knopf, 1934); *Laughing to Keep from Crying* (Franklin Center, Pa.: Franklin Library, 1981); and *Something in Common and Other Stories* New York: Hill & Wang, 1963). He also wrote many books for adults and young people about black history and black music, as well as a two-volume autobiography: *The Big Sea* (New York: Hill & Wang, 1963) and *I Wonder as I Wander* (New York: Rhinehart, 1956).

Hughes was one of the first writers of the Harlem Renaissance, the black cultural movement of the 1920s that initiated a new black literature—more realistic, and more involved with native black American culture. His poetry was known for its identity with the blues and its use of folk material. In later years, his poetry included more social protest, particularly regarding race relations. His fiction was praised for its humorous, generous view of both black and white characters.

Langston Hughes was born on February 1, 1902, in Joplin, Missouri, the son of James Nathaniel Hughes and Carrie Mercer (Langston) Hughes. He lived in a number of places while growing up, including Buffalo, New York; Cleveland, Ohio; Lawrence, Kansas; and Mexico City. In 1914, his parents separated, and Hughes went to live with his mother and stepfather in Lincoln, Illinois, where he finished grammar school and was class poet.

In 1916, Hughes moved to Cleveland, where he attended high school. Although he was one of the few black students there, he was elected editor of the yearbook in his senior year.

Hughes went to Mexico in 1921, where he taught English and began to publish his prose and poetry. His first poem, "The Negro Speaks of Rivers" was published in *The Crisis,* the magazine of the National Association for the Advancement of Colored People (NAACP), edited by W. E. B. DUBOIS. In 1921, Hughes also entered Columbia University in New York City, but was not happy there and soon left.

In 1922, his education took a different form. Working as a mess steward on a ship, he sailed to the Azores, the Canary Islands, and Africa. In 1923, he continued his travels, working his way on a freighter and ending up in Paris and Italy.

Hughes returned to the U.S. in 1924 and lived with his mother in Washington, D.C. There, the poet Vachel Lindsay discovered him, working as a bus boy. In 1925,

Langston Hughes (*Library of Congress*)

Hughes won several writing contests and began to establish his reputation as a poet. He entered Lincoln University in Pennsylvania in 1926—the same year his first book of poems was published.

Hughes had worked at a variety of jobs, but wished passionately to make a living as a writer. In 1931 and 1932, he toured the South and West, reading poetry and trying to sell his books. He also had the opportunity of visiting the Soviet Union and Haiti. In 1937, he reported on the Spanish Civil War for a black newspaper.

Hughes was back in the United States by 1938, and by 1940 had founded three black theater groups: in Harlem, Los Angeles, and Chicago. He kept writing and publishing poetry, fiction and plays, and gave readings whenever and wherever possible.

A important year for Hughes was 1943, when he began his famous "Simple" column in the Chicago *Defender,* a black newspaper. "Simple" was a black character who met the column's "author" in a bar and philosophized about life, love, and race relations. The "Simple" columns were eventually collected into several books, including *Simple Speaks His Mind, Simple Takes a Wife, Simple Stakes a Claim, Simple's Uncle Sam* (New York: Hill & Wang, 1965) and *Best of Simple* (New York: Hill & Wang, 1961).

In 1947 and 1948, Hughes taught writing at Atlanta University; in 1949 and 1950 he was poet-in-residence at the University of Chicago. Throughout the 1930s and 1940s, he had been politically active, so in the 1950s, he faced some difficulties with the McCarthy witch hunts. Senator Joseph McCarthy's war against "communism" and "communist subversives" brought him into conflict with many political artists and writers. However, it was only a brief, irritating encounter with Hughes, and McCarthy did not destroy his career, as he had so many others'.

In 1953, Hughes won the Anisfeld-Wolfe Award for the year's best book on race relations. In 1960, he won the NAACP's Spingarn Award for achievement by a black American. And in 1961, he was elected to the National Institute of Arts and Letters.

Hughes continued to write and publish throughout the 1950s and 1960s. In 1965, he lectured in Europe, representing the U.S. Information Agency. Hughes died of heart failure on May 22, 1967 in New York City.

Langston Hughes's work helped to change the face of both African-American and American literature. As part of the Harlem Renaissance, he was one of a generation of writers who for the first time turned to the ordinary experiences of black working people for their subject matter. As a poet, he helped to bring the rhythms and styles of jazz, and the sound of black speech, into the realm of poetry. And as a writer, he created some of the best-loved, most critically acclaimed and widely anthologized works in American literature.

Further Reading: *Langston Hughes, Before and Beyond Harlem,* by Faith Berry, Westport, Conn.: L. Hill, 1983; *The Life of Langston Hughes,* by Arnold Rampersad, New York: Oxford University Press, 1986–1988.

—*R. K.*

❖ HUNT, RICHARD HOWARD
(1935–), *sculptor*

Richard Howard Hunt is a major avant-garde sculptor of our time. His huge works, sculpted mainly in metal, led the art critic Hilton Kramer to assess Hunt as "one of the most gifted and assured artists working in the direct open form medium . . . and I mean not only in his own country, but anywhere in the world."

Hunt's work has been exhibited worldwide, at such prestigious institutions as the Carnegie International at Pittsburgh, the Museum of Modern Art and the Whitney Museum in New York, and the Art Institute of Chicago. He has won numerous prizes, including a Ford Foundation Fellowship in recognition of artistic achievement. He has taught art at many schools, including Yale University in Connecticut, Purdue University in Indiana, and Northwestern University in Illinois.

Richard Howard Hunt was born on September 12, 1935, in Chicago, the son of Howard Hunt, a barber, and Inez Hunt, a librarian. In 1948, when only 13 years of age, he began to study at Chicago's Art Institute. At age 15, he began taking sculpture with Nelli Bar, who recognized his early promise. After graduating from high school in 1953, he entered the Art Institute on a scholarship.

His first major award, at age 21, was the Mr. and Mrs. Frank G. Logan Prize for artistic achievement. The following year, he graduated from the Art Institute and studied in Europe on a fellowship. While in rome in 1957, he married Betty Scott, with whom he settled in Chicago in 1958. The couple had one child and later divorced.

Hunt's art career was interrupted by army service, but after his discharge, in 1960, he returned to Chicago and began to teach at the Art Institute. Once again, he received the Mr. and Mrs. Frank G. Logan Prize for outstanding work. Nurturing the academic side of his dual career, he taught at the University of Illinois and various other schools and continued to receive more awards and recognition for his art.

In 1966, Hunt's work was included in a show called *Ten Negro Artists from the United States*, which was exhibited at the first World Festival of Negro Arts in Senegal.

Since 1966, Hunt has taught at various major universities and has been exhibited throughout the United States. His work is in permanent museum collections in Chicago, New York, Cleveland, Milwaukee, and Israel.

Further Reading: *Sculpture of Richard Hunt,* New York: Museum of Modern Art, 1971.

—*R. K.*

❖ HUNTER-GAULT, CHARLAYNE
(1942–), *journalist*

The first African-American woman to attend the University of Georgia, Charlayne Hunter-Gault went on to become one of the leading journalists of her generation. In a career that has included all the major media, she has reported incisively on political and social issues in the United States and abroad.

Born on February 27, 1942, in Due West, South Carolina, Hunter-Gault was the oldest of three children. At the age of 12, shortly after her family moved to Atlanta, Georgia, she decided that she wanted to be a journalist. At Henry McNeal Turner High School, Hunter-Gault edited the school newspaper in preparation for her future career. Though everyone urged her to become a teacher instead—a far more traditional path for an African-American woman in those days—she refused to give up her dream.

When Hunter-Gault graduated from high school in 1959, she was determined to attend the University of Georgia, the only school in the state with a journalism program. Challenging the university's whites-only policy, Hunter-Gault enlisted the support of civil rights groups and took her case to federal court. As lawyers argued back and forth over the ensuing months, Hunter-Gault studied at Wayne State University in Detroit. Finally, in January 1961, the courts ordered the University of Georgia to admit Hunter-Gault and another African-American student, Hamilton Holmes. Their arrival on campus sparked a riot by white students, but nothing could turn back the tide of integration.

Hunter-Gault received her B.A. from Georgia in 1963 and went to work for the *New Yorker* magazine, where she rose to the position of staff writer. In 1967 she accepted a Russell Sage Fellowship for graduate study in social science at Washington University in St. Louis. At the same time, she worked as a correspondent for *TransAction* magazine,

which focuses on human rights issues in Africa and the Americas, and also appeared as a news reporter on WRC-TV in Washington, D.C. In 1968, Hunter-Gault became a metropolitan reporter for the *New York Times,* specializing in coverage of the urban black community. Her work at the *Times* earned her several awards, including a Publishers Award for her reporting on the death of a 12-year-old heroin addict.

Hunter-Gault remained at the *Times* until 1978, when she joined the Public Broadcasting System's *MacNeil/Lehrer Report* as a correspondent and part-time anchor. In 1983, when the nightly program expanded its format and became the *MacNeil/Lehrer NewsHour,* Hunter-Gault was named national political correspondent. In this role, she took on a wide variety of assignments and was noted for her ability to uncover the human dramas at the heart of political issues. This emphasis was a conscious choice, and it stemmed from Hunter-Gault's wrenching experiences at the University of Georgia. "It seems to me," she later told an interviewer, "that if there were a basic understanding on each side about the humanity of people, none of us would have been in the situation we were in."

During the U.S. invasion of Grenada in 1983, Hunter-Gault provided on-site coverage that focused on the lives of the Grenadian people, and her work earned her an Emmy Award for news reporting. In 1986, her five-part series on apartheid in South Africa was recognized with a Peabody Award and the Journalist of the Year Award from the National Association of Black Journalists. Other memorable on-air reports by Hunter-Gault included examinations of health care in the black community and the high rate of infant mortality among children born to poor black teenagers.

During her years as a television reporter, Hunter-Gault continued to work as a print journalist. She contributed pieces to the *New York Times Magazine, Saturday Review, The New York Times Book Review, Essence, Vogue,* and other publications. Her book *In My Place,* recounting her experiences at the University of Georgia, appeared in 1992. In 1997, after nearly two decades on public television, Hunter-Gault was ready for new challenges. Moving to Johannesburg, South Africa, she became chief of National Public Radio's African Bureau.

Further Reading: *In My Place,* by Charlayne Hunter-Gault, New York: Farrar, Straus & Giroux, 1992; "A Talk with Charlayne Hunter-Gault," by Claudia Dreyfus, *Dial,* February 1987.

—*P. K.*

❖ HURSTON, ZORA NEALE
(1891–1960), *writer, anthropologist*

Zora Neale Hurston was a major literary figure from the Harlem Renaissance of the 1920s through the 1950s. Her creative output inspired many writers today, particularly Alice WALKER, who helped to "rediscover" Hurston after her death. Hurston is best known for her novel *Their Eyes Were Watching God* (New York: Negro Universities Press, 1969 reprint of 1937 ed.), a sensuous and dramatic portrait of a young southern black woman's coming of age and of her search for love.

In addition to her many novels, plays, short stories, and articles, Hurston also produced scholarly publications. She was a trained anthropologist who worked in the United States, the Carribean, and Central America, and published two major works on the folklore of peoples there.

Zora Neale Hurston was born on January 7, 1891 (though she claimed to have been born 10 years later), in the all-black town of Eatonville, Florida, the first of its kind incorporated in the United States. This unusual town gave Hurston an early impression of her people as being very capable and powerful. Since her father, John Hurston, was the town mayor (as well as a minister and carpenter), Hurston grew up with a unique appreciation of black people's abilities undeterred by racism.

When her mother, Lucy Ann Hurston, died, her father remarried. Hurston was sent to live with various relatives, until at age 14 she became a maid and wardrobe assistant for a theatrical company. She left the troupe in Baltimore, where she completed her high school education at Morgan Academy in 1918. She then studied at Howard University in Washington, D.C., until 1924.

While still a student, Hurston began to publish her short stories. This work reflected her Eatonville background. "Drenched in Light," for example, concerns a mischievous, secure, daring young girl, much like Hurston herself. The story also suggests an all-black world, much like the one she experienced as a child.

When Hurston received an award for her 1925 story "Spunk," she moved to New York City. There, she found herself in the exciting climate of the Harlem Renaissance, in which many black writers and artists were publishing new views of black culture and life.

While studying anthropology on a scholarship at Barnard College in New York from 1925 to 1927, she continued to write. She and her friends Langston HUGHES and Wallace Thurman saw themselves as young rebels. Hurston especially had a vision of black people freed from racial pressure, a theme that continued to illuminate her work.

In 1927, Hurston's personal life took a stormy turn. After a six-year relationship, she married Herbert Sheen—but the marriage lasted only four months. And, in the late 1920s, her creative life faced a challenge shared by many of her colleagues: money. She and Langston Hughes shared a rich white patron, Mrs. Rufus Osgood Mason, who supported Hurston financially but insisted on her total devotion, in addition to ownership of her material.

Hughes and Hurston were close friends, but in 1931, they had a serious quarrel. They had been collaborating on a play, *Mule Bone,* when Hughes claimed that Hurston was trying to take full credit for the work. The issue was never completely resolved to their satisfaction.

In 1934, Hurston found a new source of funds: a Rosenwald fellowship; and in 1935 and 1936, she received two Guggenheim fellowships. These enabled her to write *Mules and Men* (New York: Negro Universities Press, 1969), a study of African Americans in Louisiana, and the first study of voodoo among black Americans. In

Zora Neale Hurston (*Library of Congress*)

1938, she published *Tell My Horse* (Philadelphia, Pa.: J. B. Lippincott, 1938), a study of Jamaica and Haiti. In both works, Hurston showed that she herself had become a participant in the culture she studied, rather than remaining an outside observer.

Meanwhile, Hurston continued to write fiction, publishing, in 1934, her first novel, *Jonah's Gourd Vine* (Philadelphia, Pa.: Lippincott, 1971 reprint of 1934 ed.). The book's rich folklore won it praise; however, many critics of the time objected to the book's not focusing on racism and prejudice.

In 1937, Hurston published her novel *Their Eyes Were Watching God.* The book, considered her best work of fiction, is a kind of love story, and Hurston wrote it in eight weeks while dealing with a love affair of her own.

Two years later, Hurston brought out *Moses, Man of the Mountain* (Urbana, Ill.: University of Illinois Press, 1984), in which the biblical story of Moses is told as though it were happening to contemporary southern black characters.

In 1939, Hurston married again, to a man several years younger than she, Albert Price III. They filed for divorce after eight months, although the split was not final until late in 1943. Hurston seems generally to have felt that the men she knew expected her to give up her creative work to focus on being a wife.

In 1942, Hurston published *Dust Tracks on the Road* (New York: HarperCollins, 1996), which was her autobiography and the book that brought her the greatest commercial success. Modern scholars note that the book is not an accurate portrait of Hurston's life but rather the creation of her own myth.

She continued to struggle for funds throughout the 1940s. Her study of black communities in Central America was put off until 1947. While there, she wrote *Seraph on the Suwanee* (New York: AMS Press, 1974 ed.), her last published novel, this time about white people.

When Hurston returned from the Caribbean, she was not able to fund her research, and had trouble publishing her work. Hurston was no longer considered avant-garde. She could not understand her fall from popularity, and she was hurt by the false accusations against her. She left New York to live in the South, where she worked at various jobs. For a while, she taught drama and wrote film scripts.

Hurston became even more controversial in the 1950s, due to her unconventional political stance. In 1954, she opposed the Supreme Court decision to integrate schools, because she felt that black people were not really hurt by "separate but equal" treatment. This view was understandably fostered by her unique experience in Eatonville, where the segregation of black people had represented security.

When Hurston died in 1960, she was poor and isolated. Her early brilliant career had suffered a steep decline. Yet her work remains today an important record of black pride and the black female experience. Her studies of black folk culture retain their importance, and her novels continue to be read and appreciated.

Further Reading: *Zora Neale Hurston, A Literary Biography,* by Robert Hemenway, Urbana, Ill.: University of Illinois Press, 1977; *I Love Myself When I Am Laughing and Then Again When I Am Looking Mean and Impressive,* a collection of Hurston's writing edited by Alice Walker, with an introduction by Mary Helen Washington, Old Westbury, N.Y.: Feminist Press, 1979; *Novels and Stories: Jonah's Gourd Vine; Their Eyes Were Watching God; Moses, Man of the Mountain, Seraph on the Suwanee; Selected Stories (The Library),* by Zora Neale Hurston, ed. by Cheryl A. Wall, New York: Library of America, 1995; *Every Tub Must Sit on Its Own Bottom: The Philosophy and Politics of Zora Neale Hurston,* by Deborah G. Plant, Champaign, Ill.: University of Illinois Press, 1995; *Social Rituals and the Verbal Art of Zora Neale Hurston,* by Lynda Marion Hill, Washington, D.C.: Howard University Press, 1996; *Zora Neale Hurston: Critical Perspectives Past and Present (Amistad Library),* ed. by Henry Louis Gates, Jr., and K. A. Appiah, New York: Amistad Press, 1993.

—R. K.

❖ JACKSON, JESSE LOUIS

(1941–), *minister, civil rights leader, political figure*

The most prominent African-American leader in the United States since the death of Martin Luther KING, JR., Jackson has provided hope and inspiration for countless Americans, both black and white. His dramatic and wide-ranging career has taken him from the barricades of the Civil Rights movement to center stage at the Democratic National Convention.

Born in Greenville, South Carolina, on October 8, 1941, Jackson was an excellent student and a brilliant athlete at Sterling High School. Upon graduation he was offered a professional baseball contract, but he was determined to attend college. Jackson accepted a football scholarship from the University of Illinois, but when he learned that African Americans were barred from playing quarterback at the school, he enrolled at North Carolina A&T instead. In 1960, Jackson joined in sit-in campaigns to integrate lunch counters in Greensboro, where A&T was located. He made a wholehearted commitment to the Civil Rights movement, and by his senior year he was director of southeastern operations for the Congress of Racial Equality (CORE).

After graduating in 1964 with a degree in sociology, Jackson attended the Chicago Theological Seminary and was ordained as a Baptist minister. He then joined the Southern Christian Leadership Conference (SCLC), the influential civil rights organization led by Dr. King. In 1967, Jackson became head of the SCLC's Operation Breadbasket, a nationwide campaign directed at influencing businesses to hire a fair proportion of black workers.

After the assassination of Dr. King in 1968, Jackson gradually drifted away from the SCLC. In 1971, he founded his own organization, People United to Save Humanity (PUSH). In addition to promoting black economic progress and political participation, PUSH was dedicated to fighting drugs, teenage pregnancy, and violence in the black community. An inspiring speaker with a powerful physical presence, Jackson soon gained national media attention and a widespread following. His ideals became even more important after 1980, when the Reagan administration took measures threatening social programs and civil rights. Jackson emerged as the nation's most eloquent spokesperson for all those Americans adversely affected by the "Reagan Revolution." In 1983, he announced his intention to run for president on the Democratic ticket.

Though Jackson made a good showing in the primaries and delivered an impressive speech at the Democratic convention, it was a forgone conclusion that former vice president Walter Mondale would get the nomination. Jackson tried again in 1988, and this time his growing stature and added political experience made him a serious contender. Jackson's multiracial organization, the Rainbow Coalition, won nine state primaries

Rev. Jesse Jackson (*Jim Wells/Archive Photos*)

nered 7 million votes out of the 23 million cast. At the Democratic convention, Jackson made a passionate speech that electrified the assembled delegates and a nationwide television audience. "I was born in the slum," he proclaimed, "but the slum was not born in me. And it wasn't born in you, and you can make it. Wherever you are tonight, you can make it. Hold your head high, stick your chest out. You can make it. It gets dark sometimes, but the morning comes. Don't you surrender."

Though Jackson once again fell short of the nomination, he had become a major force in the nation's political life. In addition to highlighting vital issues, he had inspired many people to consider the possibility of a black president for the first time. He had also become an important player on the world scene. Even those hostile to the United States respected Jackson as a man of principle, and in several instances he was able to negotiate the release of hostages and political prisoners in foreign nations.

Jackson's son Jesse, Jr. followed his father into politics and was elected to Congress in 1995. As a representative from Illinois, he ran virtually unopposed in his 1996 reelection bid and was reelected again in fall 1998.

During the 1990s, Jesse Jackson, Sr. turned away from presidential politics and focused anew on civil rights, social justice, and economic development. Among his major efforts were a campaign to gain statehood for the predominantly black District of Columbia and a program to monitor the hiring practices of major U.S. corporations.

Further Reading: *Straight from the Heart/Jesse L. Jackson,* edited by Roger D. Hatch and Frank E. Watkins, Philadelphia: Fortress, 1987; *Jesse Jackson: The Man, the Movement, the Myth,* by Barbara A. Reynolds, Washington, D.C.: JFJ Associates, 1985; *I Am Somebody!: A Biography of Jesse Jackson,* by James Haskins, Hillside, N.J.: Enslow, 1992.

—P. K.

❖ JACKSON, MICHAEL JOSEPH
(1958–), *singer, songwriter, performer*

A major figure on the entertainment scene since childhood, Michael Jackson reigned as the King of Pop during the 1980s. His 1983 record *Thriller* has sold more copies than any album in history, and his early music videos played a major role in launching the MTV era.

Born on August 29, 1958, in Gary, Indiana, Jackson was the fifth of nine children and grew up in a home that was filled with music. At the age of six, he began performing with his four older brothers—Jackie, Tito, Jermaine, and Marlon—as the Jackson 5. Quickly progressing from local talent contests to professional gigs, the Jacksons came to the attention of Motown Records president Berry GORDY after playing the famed Apollo Theater in Harlem. Gordy signed the Jacksons in late 1968 and promoted them vigorously. Once they were given nationwide exposure, the group was an instant hit with young people of all races and turned out four number-one singles in 1970 alone. As the lead singer and sparkplug of the group, Michael was hailed as the most appealing child star since the advent of Shirley Temple during the 1930s.

Motown capitalized on Michael's immense popularity by having him record solo singles and albums throughout the early 1970s. As he approached adulthood, Jackson began to function more and more apart from his brothers. In 1978 he appeared as the Scarecrow in the film *The Wiz,* and during the filming he met Quincy Jones, the multifaceted jazz star, entrepreneur, and music producer. Jones agreed to become Jackson's producer and guided him in developing a musical style that combined soul and rock. *Off the Wall* (1979), Jackson's first album with Jones, sold more than 10 million copies and established Jackson's identity as a solo performer.

Jackson and Jones followed up in 1982 with a second album, *Thriller,* which contained six Top-10 singles and sold a record total of 40 million copies. *Thriller's* impact was magnified by the emergence of the music video and MTV. Jackson's dramatic flair and brilliant dancing made him a natural for this new entertainment form—his videos for the singles "Billie Jean," "Beat It," and "Thriller" helped develop the medium and also shattered the whites-only formula that had governed the MTV format. In 1984, Jackson reached the pinnacle of international superstardom when he unveiled his dazzling Moonwalk dance step on the *25 Years of Motown* TV special and joined his brothers for a worldwide Victory Tour. The following year, Jackson further enhanced his reputation when he teamed up with Lionel Richie to write and perform "We Are the World," the theme song for a highly effective campaign to aid famine victims in Africa.

Though he was fabulously wealthy and adored by fans throughout the world, Jackson had set daunting standards for himself. His next two albums, *Bad* (1987) and *Dangerous* (1991), sold millions of copies, but they could not approach the success of *Thriller.* In addition, many people objected to the violent images at the end of his 1992 video for "Black and White." Observers began to note changes in Jackson's facial features and skin tone, and it was alleged that he was trying to shed his African-American identity through plastic surgery and chemical treatments. The low point came in 1993, when Jackson was accused of molesting a young boy who had been his guest at Neverland, the lavish estate (complete with a zoo and ferris wheel) that Jackson had built in California.

Following an out-of-court settlement of the abuse charges, Jackson worked hard to repair his image and counter unflattering rumors about his private life. In 1994, he married Lisa Marie Presley, the daughter of another pop music legend, and the following year he released a new album, *HIStory,* which reprised many of his old hits. Jackson and Presley were divorced after 18 months; Jackson then married Deborah Rowe in 1996. Later in the year, Rowe gave birth to a son, Prince Michael Jackson, Jr. All these events received intensive coverage in the media, proving that Jackson still had a powerful hold on the attention of the public.

Further Reading: *The Michael Jackson Story,* by Nelson George, New York: Dell, 1984; *Trapped: Michael Jackson and the Crossover Dream,* by Dave Marsh, New York: Bantam, 1985; *Moonwalker,* by Michael Jackson, New York: Doubleday, 1988; *Michael Jackson: Entertainer,* by Lois P. Nicholson, New York: Chelsea House, 1994.

—*P. K.*

❖ JACKSON, REGINALD MARTINEZ ("Reggie")
(1946–), *baseball legend*

Known as Mr. October because of his heroics in postseason play, Reggie Jackson was a powerful slugger with a unique flair for the dramatic. In 21 seasons with the Oakland A's, New York Yankees, and California Angels, he clouted 563 home runs and created excitement every time he stepped on the field.

Jackson was born in Wyncote, Pennsylvania, on May 18, 1946. His parents divorced when he was very young. Three of the couple's six children went to live with their mother in Baltimore; Jackson was among the three who remained with their father, resettling in Cheltenham, a suburb of Philadelphia. A star athlete at Cheltenham High School, Jackson received an athletic scholarship to Arizona State University, where he excelled in both baseball and football. At the end of his sophomore year in 1966, Jackson signed a contract with the Kansas City A's, receiving a $95,000 bonus.

After a year and a half in the minor leagues, Jackson was called up to the majors at the end of the 1967 season. Playing his first full season for the A's in 1968—the team was now in Oakland—he hit 29 home runs and added 74 RBI. In 1969 Jackson's home run total soared to 47, establishing him as one of baseball's premier sluggers. As the A's built a powerhouse team during the early 1970s, Jackson was their most dangerous weapon. A leg injury kept him out of the 1972 World Series, but he made up for it the following year, driving in six runs against the New York Mets and winning the Most Valuable Player Award for the series.

Despite his contributions on the field, Jackson's salary demands angered Oakland's tight-fisted owner, Charles O. Finley, who traded Jackson to the Baltimore Orioles after the 1975 season. Jackson became a free agent a year later, and Yankees owner George Steinbrenner brought him to New York with a lucrative five-year contract.

Playing in Yankee Stadium, Jackson finally had the showcase he had always craved. After hitting 32 home runs and driving in 110 runs during the 1977 regular season, he dominated the World Series against the Los Angeles Dodgers, batting .450 and hitting five home runs. Jackson became a baseball legend during the sixth game, when he smashed three consecutive home runs—no other player in World Series history has ever matched that feat.

Throughout his five years with the Yankees, Jackson was always at center stage. When he hit a home run, he stood in the batter's box and watched the ball sail into the seats, seemingly awed by his own power. He even struck out with a flourish, swinging from the heels and yelling at himself as he went back to the dugout. When he heard boos from the stands, he would take it as a compliment. "Fans don't boo nobodies," he observed. Intelligent, witty, and outspoken, Jackson had an endless supply of juicy quotes for the reporters who flocked around him.

Jackson's exploits with the Yankees made him one of the world's most famous athletes, but there was a price to pay. Some of his teammates resented the attention that he received from the media. He feuded constantly with the fiery Billy Martin, who managed the Yankees during much of Jackson's tenure, and finally fell out of favor with the equally temperamental Steinbrenner. When Jackson's contract expired at the end of the 1981 season, the Yankees decided not to re-sign the 35-year-old slugger.

Deeply hurt by the Yankees' rejection, Jackson signed with the California Angels and showed the baseball world that he was far from through. He led the league in home runs in 1982 and went on to play five more seasons. Idolized by the younger Angels players, Jackson became a leader on and off the field, sharing his baseball knowledge and offering guidance on coping with the day-to-day pressures of big-time sports.

When Jackson retired from baseball following the 1987 season, he ranked sixth on the all-time home run list and had the highest slugging average (.755) in World Series history. During his career, his teams won 11 division titles, six pennants, and five World Series. When he was inducted into the National Baseball Hall of Fame in 1993, Jackson's status as one of baseball's immortals was fully confirmed.

Further Reading: *Reggie: The Autobiography,* by Reggie Jackson with Mike Lupica, New York: Villard, 1984; *Mr. October: The Reggie Jackson Story,* by Maury Allen, New York: Times, 1981; *Reggie Jackson,* by Norman L. Macht, Broomall, Pa.: Chelsea House Publishers, 1994.

—*P. K.*

❖ JEFFERSON, LEMON ("Blind Lemon")
(1897–1929?), *blues singer*

Blind Lemon Jefferson was one of the greatest of all blues musicians. He helped to develop that form, and influenced such singers as Sonny Terry, Muddy Waters, Joe Turner, T-Bone Walker, Sam "Lightnin'" Hopkins, Huddie LEDBETTER ("Leadbelly"), and Josh White. Their blues renditions, in turn, shaped the styles of such modern artists as Bob Dylan, Paul McCartney, and other rock singers.

The blues style of singing and playing was first developed in the early 1900s. It had its roots in African rhythms, Negro spirituals, and slave work songs, which combined European and African melodies and song styles. The music was created by men who wandered through the South, earning their keep by singing in bars, honky-tonks, and brothels.

Of the many early blues singers who laid the foundations of jazz, Blind Lemon Jefferson was probably the best known. Certainly he was the one who was most extensively recorded.

Lemon Jefferson was born in 1897 in rural Texas, the youngest of seven children. Although he was born blind, he taught himself to play the guitar and began singing and playing at local dances and other events. Before he was 15, he was earning money from these performances and by the time he was 20, he had left home to sing professionally in Dallas, Texas.

In Dallas, Jefferson met Huddie Ledbetter, better known as Leadbelly. The two bluesmakers teamed up to play and travel together. Later, Jefferson toured with Lightnin' Hopkins and Josh White, when the latter two were still young.

Like ragtime, blues had its start in all-black clubs, but its popularity soon reached the white world. In the 1920s, white record companies began recording this music. In 1925, Jefferson went to Chicago, where he made his first recordings, released in 1926. His music caught on promptly and he continued to make recordings until his death in 1929. His presence also helped to create the famous "Chicago-style" blues.

Accounts of Jefferson's death vary. The more credible ones suggest that his life ended in difficulty, and that he was found frozen to death on a Chicago street one February morning in 1929.

Jefferson left a legacy of more than 80 records to future generations, along with a tremendous influence on the music of his time. However, he profited very little from his recordings, which were owned outright by the companies who made them.

Further Reading: *Blind Lemon Jefferson,* edited by Bob Groom, Knutsford, Cheshire, U.K.: Blues World, 1970; *Blues World Booklet,* includes three page essay and discography.

—*R. K.*

❖ JEMISON, MAE CAROL

(1956–), *physician, scientist, astronaut, educator*

Gifted with a seemingly unlimited range of talents, Mae C. Jemison had accomplished more by the age of 35 than most people do in a lifetime. Her most famous achievement took place in 1992, when she blasted off in the space shuttle *Endeavour,* becoming the first African-American woman in outer space.

Jemison was born in October 17, 1956, in Decatur, Alabama, but her family moved to Chicago when she was three years old. Her parents, Charles and Dorothy, believed deeply in the value of education. They often took their three children—Mae, Charles, Jr., and Ada—to Chicago's great museums, such as the Museum of Science and Industry and the Field Museum of Natural History. By the time Jemison began school, she was already determined to become a scientist. Many teachers felt that this was not a realistic goal for an African-American girl, but Jemison refused to give up her dream. By the time she reached Morgan Park High School, she was an honor student who excelled in chemistry, biology, and physics.

Jemison graduated from high school at the age of 16 and entered Stanford University on a National Achievement Scholarship. Pursuing a double major, she earned a B.S. in chemistry and a B.A. in Afro-American studies, while also taking an active part in plays and dance performances. Jemison then enrolled in New York's Cornell Medical College. During the course of her medical studies, she received grants that enabled her to spend time in Africa and Asia, where she did research on local health problems. With a grant from the International Travelers Institute, Jamison traveled to Kenya in 1979, where she studied the public health condition of the Kenyan nation. In 1980 Jemison went to Thailand, where she volunteered, along with other Cornell medical students, at a Cambodian refugee camp. There she treated refugees suffering from malnutrition, dysentery, tuberculosis, and other health problems. Jemison earned her M.D. degree in 1981, completed an internship, and spent two years as a general practitioner in Los Angeles. She then joined the Peace Corps and served as a medical officer in West Africa for two years. Spending most of her time in Liberia and Sierra Leone, she helped design public health programs and conducted research on hepatitis and parasitic diseases.

In 1985, Jemison returned to private practice in Los Angeles, but she was still eager for new challenges. The field of spaceflight appealed to her more and more, and in 1987 she joined the astronaut program of the National Aeronautics and Space Administration (NASA). For nearly five years, Jemison performed a variety of scientific duties on the ground, monitoring the various mechanical and electronic systems involved in spaceflight. Finally, NASA chose Jemison to serve as a mission specialist on the 50th space shuttle flight, which was lauched on September 12, 1992. While orbiting the Earth on *Endeavour,* Jemison and her colleagues studied the effects of weightlessness, the use of intravenous fluids in space, and other essential issues involved in human spaceflight. Jemison, in particular, was in charge of an experiment that examined the fertilization process of frogs' eggs and the subsequent process of tadpole development under weightless conditions. More than 400 tadpoles were born during her orbit, proving that amphibian reproduction can occur without gravity. Jemison also participated in an experiment that allowed her, via satellite radio, to communicate with schoolchildren around the world.

When *Endeavour* returned to Earth after eight days in space, Jemison was widely honored for her historic achievement. The most lavish celebrations were held in Chicago, where Jemison visited her old high school and encouraged students to pursue their dreams as she had. "People don't see women—particularly black women—in science and technology fields," she has observed. "My participation in the space shuttle mission helps to say that all peoples of the world have astronomers, physicists and explorers."

In 1993 Jemison made a guest appearance on the TV program *Star Trek: The Next Generation;* she has stated that Nichelle Nichols ("Lieutenant Uhura" in the original series) was her main inspiration to become an astronaut. Ever eager to explore new fields, Jemison retired from NASA in 1993 and founded the Jemison Group, Inc., a technology development organization based in Houston, Texas. Projects sponsored by the Jemison Group include a satellite-based telecommunications system for delivery of health care services in West Africa. Another of Jemison's endeavors is The Earth We Share, a yearly science camp attended by teenagers from countries around the world. Jemison divides her time between Houston and Hanover, New Hampshire, where she is a professor of environmental studies at Dartmouth College and director of Dartmouth's Jemison Institute for

Mae Jemison (*NASA*)

Advancing Technology in Developing Countries. In addition to all these activities, Jemison also serves on the boards of several scientific organizations, including the World Sickle Cell Foundation, the American Medical Association, and the American Association for the Advancement of Science.

Further Reading: *Mae Jemison: Space Scientist,* by Gail Sakurai, Danbury, Conn.: Children's Press, 1995; *Mae Jemison,* by Della A. Yannuzzi, Springfield, N.J.: Enslow, 1998; *Black Explorers,* by Catherine Reef, New York: Facts On File, 1996.

—*P. K.*

❖ JOHNSON, CHARLES SPURGEON

(1893–1956), social scientist, educator, first black president of Fisk University

Charles S. Johnson was the virtual founder of black sociology. He wrote numerous books analyzing the condition of black people in the United States, including such groundbreaking works as *The Negro in Chicago* (New York: Arno Press, 1968 reprint of 1922 ed.), *The Negro in American Civilization* (New York: Henry Holt & Co., 1930), *Negro Housing* (Washington, D.C.: President's Conference on Home Building and Home Ownership, 1932), *Economic Status of the Negro* (Nashville, Tenn.: Fisk University Press, 1933), *Shadow of the Plantation* (1934), *Collapse of Cotton Tenancy* (Chapel Hill, N.C.: University of North Carolina Press, 1935), *Growing up in the Black Belt* (Washington, D.C.: American Council on Education, 1941), and *Into the Mainstream* (Chapel Hill, N.C.: University of North Carolina Press, 1947).

In 1946, Charles Johnson became the first black president of Fisk University in Tennessee. Although Fisk was founded in 1865 to educate African Americans, it had never before been run by one. Johnson's prominence as a scholar brought him invitation to many White House youth conferences and appointments to many international commissions on education.

Charles Johnson was born in 1893, in Bristol, Virginia, the son of Baptist minister Charles Henry Johnson, who taught him literature, theology and history. His mother, Winifred (Branch) Johnson, often took him to a local soda fountain at the town drugstore. One day, the owner refused to serve them at the counter, and this early experience of racial prejudice made a deep impression on the young Johnson.

When Johnson was 14, he went to Richmond, Virginia's Wayland Academy and Virginia Union University, from which he graduated after three years, in 1916. Only two years later, in 1918, he had a doctorate from the University of Chicago. From 1917 to 1919, Johnson worked as research director of the Chicago Urban League, under Urban League president Robert Park, who was also a sociologist.

After a brief stint in the army during World War I, he returned to Chicago. After World War I, there was a period of race riots in the United States. Black soldiers who had fought in the war were unwilling to accept prejudice at home, whereas many white people expressed anxiety about rising black militancy. The race riots in Chicago lasted 19 days and led to Johnson's being named the associate executive director at the Chicago Commission on Race Relations. This group produced a classic study on race relations.

In 1920, Johnson married Marie Antoinette Burgette, with whom he eventually had four children.

He continued to work for the Urban League when he moved to New York in 1921. In 1923, he became the editor of *Opportunity,* the Urban League's magazine, which was one of the era's two major black literary and political publications (the NAACP's *Crisis,* edited by W. E. B. DUBOIS, was the other). Johnson edited such major writers as Langston HUGHES, Countée CULLEN, and Claude MCKAY.

In 1928, he became chairman of Fisk's Social Science Department, where he began to do more of his own writing on sociology. For the next 18 years, until he became president of Fisk in 1946, Johnson authored or coauthored 17 books and also wrote articles for diverse publications.

Johnson's work focused on the condition of black people in various sectors of American life. He wrote on black college graduates, rural black people, and the class structure within the black community.

He also held various government appointments under Presidents Hoover, Roosevelt, Truman, and Eisenhower. He advised foundations such as the Carnegie and Ford Foundations, and in 1946, he counseled Japan on the reorganization of its school system.

When Johnson became president of Fisk University, he strengthened the social science department's focus on race relations, as well as the scholarly integrity of the department in general. Under his supervision, the university also increased its budget, adding many major buildings and expanding its programs.

While still president of Fisk, and en route to a trustees meeting in New York City, Charles Johnson died of a heart attack, on October 27, 1956, in a Louisville, Kentucky, railroad station.

Further Reading: "Charles S. Johnson: A Scholar and a Gentleman," in *Thirteen Against the Odds,* by Edwin R. Embree, New York: Viking Press, 1944.

—R. K.

❖ JOHNSON, EARVIN, JR. ("Magic")
(1959–), *basketball player, businessperson, foundation president*

One of the greatest basketball players of all time, Earvin "Magic" Johnson sparked the Los Angeles Lakers to five NBA championships during the 1980s. Following his retirement from the game, Johnson has continued to make a difference, creating successful business ventures in the inner city and educating young people about the dangers of AIDS.

Johnson was born in Lansing, Michigan, on August 8, 1959, the sixth of ten children. His father, Earvin, Sr., worked two jobs to support his family, but he always made time to talk basketball with Earvin, Jr., who grew

"Magic" Johnson *(Sporting News/Archive Photos)*

up with a passion for the game. By the time he reached Everett High School, Earvin, Jr. had already earned the nickname Magic for his wizardry on the court. He was all-state for four years in a row, and in his senior year he led Everett to the state championship.

In 1977, Johnson enrolled in Michigan State University and led the Spartans to the Big Ten title during his freshman year. The following year, Johnson claimed the national spotlight when Michigan State won the national championship and he was named outstanding player of the NCAA Final Four series. Though only a sophomore, Johnson was now the most sought-after college player in the country. When he decided to enter the NBA draft, the Los Angeles Lakers chose him with the first pick overall.

Johnson provided an instant boost for the struggling Lakers franchise. At six feet nine, he was the tallest guard in NBA history, and the most devastating—opposing guards were too small to defend against him, and the bigger men could not keep up with him. Along with this advantage, Johnson possessed a dazzling array of skills. He could shoot from outside, drive to the hoop, lead the fast break, pass the ball with uncanny accuracy, and fight for rebounds under the basket. If that were not enough, his vibrant personality and obvious love for the game completely captivated fans, teammates, opposing players, and the media. It was Johnson's flair and style, as well as the Lakers' rise to the top of the NBA, that drew the Hollywood stars to courtside seats at the L.A. Forum.

Throughout the 1980s, Johnson teamed up with center Kareem Abdul-Jabbar and forward James Worthy to power a supercharged Lakers offense known as Showtime. The Lakers were perennial champions of the NBA's Western Conference, and nearly every year they squared off with Larry Bird's Boston Celtics to battle for the NBA crown. Johnson and Bird had first matched up in 1979, when Michigan State beat Indiana State for the NCAA title, and the two superstars' annual battle for supremacy was basketball's greatest attraction. In their first NBA season, 1979–80, Bird edged Johnson for the Rookie of the Year Award—but Johnson was named playoff MVP as the Lakers beat the Celtics in the NBA finals. While the Lakers went on to four more titles—in 1982, 1985, 1987, and 1988—Johnson was named league MVP three times.

As the 1991–92 season got under way, Johnson was still playing at the highest level and enjoying all the fruits of his success. He had recently married, and he and his wife, Cookie, were expecting a child. But on November 9, he made the shocking announcement that he had tested positive for HIV and was retiring from basketball on the advice of his doctors. In typical fashion, Johnson decided to make something positive out of the situation. He spoke candidly about the careless behavior that exposed him to HIV and urged young people to protect themselves against sexually transmitted diseases. He also created the Magic Johnson Foundation, which raises funds for HIV and AIDS education, prevention, and care.

After leaving basketball, Johnson has also been active as a businessperson. His most notable venture has been Magic Johnson Theaters, which operates multiplex cinemas in black neighborhoods in Los Angeles, Atlanta, and Houston. In addition to providing jobs for local residents, the successful theaters encourage other businesses to invest in the inner city.

When the NBA celebrated its 50th anniversary in 1996, Johnson was chosen as one of the league's 50 all-time best players. In 906 regular-season games, he averaged 19.5 points, 11.2 assists, and 7.2 rebounds.

Further Information: *My Life,* by Earvin "Magic" Johnson with William Novak, New York: Random House, 1992; *Magic, More than a Legend,* by Bill Gutman, New York: HarperCollins, 1992; Magic Johnson Foundation web site, http://www.magicjohnson.org

—*P. K.*

❖ JOHNSON, JAMES WELDON
(James William Johnson)
(1871–1938), *poet, novelist, songwriter, leader of the NAACP*

James Weldon Johnson was a prolific writer, as well as an activist and a diplomat. He is best known for two works: *Autobiography of an Ex-Colored Man* (New York: Penguin Books, 1990 reprint), a novel about passing for white, and "Lift Every Voice and Sing," a song which became a kind of black national anthem in the 1940s. His poem "God's Trombones" is still read, studied, and performed as a dramatic reading.

Johnson was also the first African-American secretary of the National Association for the Advancement of Colored People (NAACP). He served as U.S. consul to Nicaragua and Venezuela.

James Weldon Johnson was born in 1871 to James and Helen Louise (Dillet) Johnson in Jacksonville, Florida. Johnson's father, a headwaiter, was born free, of mixed ancestry; his mother, a teacher, was born in the West Indies, of French and black Haitian ancestry.

Johnson was originally named James William Johnson, but in 1913, he changed his middle name.

Jacksonville was one of the most liberal southern towns in which a black man could spend his youth. Thus, Johnson's memories of his early years are generally warm and positive. He was particularly influenced by the black folk culture he absorbed in church, through songs and sermons, although he himself was not religious.

Since all the high schools in Jacksonville were for whites only, Johnson received his high school and college education at Atlanta University. During summer vacations, he worked as a teacher in rural Georgia, where he experienced the severe problems and difficulties faced by most black people. He began to write poetry—partly in dialect, partly in standard English—on racial issues. By the time Johnson graduated in 1894, he had decided that black people must take responsibility for educating themselves in order to ensure their equality.

From 1894 to 1901, he was a principal in a Jacksonville school. Although it was an elementary school when Johnson began there, he eventually expanded it into a high school, so that secondary education would finally be available to black people of the area.

James Weldon Johnson (*Library of Congress*)

In 1895, Johnson founded the *Daily American*. Although the paper lasted but one year, Johnson, as an editorial writer, had the opportunity to reflect on racial issues. Like most other thinkers then, he found it difficult to come up with consistent policies, especially with regard to black separatism. Separateness could be the way for black people to develop their own culture and their own leaders; but it could also lead to segregation and opportunities inferior to those of white people.

Johnson continued his education and in 1898, became the first African American to pass the bar in his county. He practiced law with a friend who had once passed for white—which became the basis for his later novel.

Johnson was slowly beginning to develop his voice as a writer. In 1900, he wrote the lyrics to "Lift Every Voice and Sing," for which his brother wrote the music. The two brothers had been successful, writing songs with Robert Cole, including one called "Under the Bamboo Tree." This song was included in a major musical comedy and sold more than 400,000 copies, enabling Johnson and his brother to leave Jacksonville for New York.

This team of three songwriters continued to enjoy success, writing for major singers and shows. Meanwhile, Johnson was also studying literature at Columbia University in New York. He was active in Republican politics, and wrote two campaign songs for Theodore Roosevelt in 1904.

At the time, there were two major factions in black politics. One was led by Booker T. WASHINGTON, who believed that African Americans should become skilled industrial workers who progressed gradually and were careful not to threaten white people. The other view was articulated by W. E. B. DUBOIS, who favored higher education and ongoing agitation to win political power. In 1905, DuBois organized a group—the Niagara Movement, so named because it met in Niagara, New York—to oppose Washington's more conservative policies.

Johnson had worked with Washington and his associates, thereby avoiding contact with DuBois. Washington had close ties with Theodore Roosevelt and helped to arrange Johnson's appointment as diplomatic consul to Venezuela, in 1906; and to Nicaragua, in 1908.

While assigned to Nicaragua, Johnson briefly returned to New York City and married Grace Nail, the daughter of a prosperous real estate broker. He continued to serve in Nicaragua until 1913. It was during these years that the United States gained control of Nicaragua, despite rebellions and protests. Johnson played a key role in this process, preventing rebels from taking over, while waiting for U.S. troops to enter the country.

He might have stayed on as consul, but when the Democrat Woodrow Wilson was elected president, Johnson perceived that neither black people nor Republicans would be given much opportunity to serve in diplomatic posts. He resigned and returned to New York.

In 1912, while he was in Nicaragua, Johnson published his major novel, *The Autobiography of an Ex-Colored Man*. The book sold poorly until the 1920s, when there was a flowering of black culture known as the Harlem Renaissance.

However, Johnson was unable to make a living as a writer, and in 1914, began to edit the newspaper *New York Age*. He managed to stay clear of the DuBois-Washington controversy, while emphasizing racial pride and the importance of the black press. However, he had many conservative views, as evidenced in his support for some segregated facilities for black people and his opposition to such "modern" ideas as an eight-hour work day or the League of Nations (a forerunner of today's United Nations).

Although Johnson had not publicized DuBois in his paper, DuBois had been cultivating his support. But Washington had kept Johnson close to him. And, after his death in 1915, Johnson still maintained his ties with Washington's Tuskegee Institute. Gradually, though, he began to realize that DuBois's NAACP organization was the group that was going to effect the changes that he wanted. In 1917, he became a field organizer for the NAACP, adding 13 branches and 738 new members to the growing organization.

Johnson was then appointed to national office. He played another important role in the Civil Rights movement when he chose Walter WHITE to become his assistant. (White would later become an important leader in the NAACP.)

During World War I, conditions seemed to improve for black Americans, but after the war, there was a strong backlash. With DuBois, Johnson led the NAACP in its response to the many postwar problems. He also went to Haiti in 1920, to report on the United States' brutal occupation of that country.

In 1920, Johnson became the secretary of the NAACP, a post that he held through the end of 1930. He was an effective leader on many key issues. He became an active supporter of the labor movement, and particularly of A. Philip RANDOLPH's efforts to organize the Brotherhood of Sleeping Car Porters. He frequently suffered from exhaustion, but after each leave of absence, returned to another rigorous work schedule.

Part of Johnson's physical problems stemmed from his strenuous writing schedule while leading the NAACP.

He wrote two books of black spirituals as well as a book of poetry called *God's Trombones, Seven Negro Sermons in Verse* (New York: Viking Press, 1927). In 1930, he wrote *Black Manhattan* (New York: Arno Press, 1968 reprint of 1930 ed.), a major history of black life in New York City, from its earliest days through 1930.

In 1930, Johnson began teaching at Fisk University in Nashville, Tennessee. While there, he wrote his autobiography, *Along This Way* (New York: Da Capo Press, 1973 reprint of 1933 ed.). He again suffered from overwork and had to take a leave of absence in 1934 while he underwent surgery. Later in 1934, he started a series of lectures at New York University. He and his wife began to spend summers in Maine, where he was able to relax.

Although he was no longer secretary, Johnson stayed active in NAACP affairs. In 1934, he wrote a book called *Negro Americans, What Now?* (New York: Viking Press; CAMS Press, 1971 reprint of 1934 ed.), in which he spoke out in favor of integration, although DuBois at that time argued that integration was not possible.

Johnson was killed on June 26, 1938, in Maine, in a tragic auto accident. Over 2,000 people came to his funeral in New York, including many important African-American writers and activists.

Further Reading: *James Weldon Johnson: Black Leader, Black Voice,* by Eugene Levy, Chicago: University of Chicago Press, 1973; *James Weldon Johnson,* by Jane Tolbert-Rouchaleau, New York: Chelsea House, 1988, *James Weldon Johnson,* by Robert E. Fleming, Los Angeles: Holloway House, 1997.

—R. K.

❖ JOHNSON, JOHN HAROLD
(1918–), *publisher*

John H. Johnson founded *Negro Digest* (later *Black World*), *Ebony,* and *Jet,* as well as *Tan Confessions* (later *Black Stars*). In the course of his career, he built a $200-million-per-year publishing business. His magazines were each the first of their kind: publications modeled after similar white efforts but with a special focus on black people.

Johnson was born on January 18, 1918, in Arkansas City, Arkansas, to Gertrude (Jenkins) and Leroy Johnson. His father, a laborer in the local sawmill and an itinerant worker along the Mississippi River, was killed when Johnson was eight. His mother was a woman of strong character whom Johnson credits with instilling in him the values and drive that enabled him to succeed. She was influential in local community organizations and in her church. She was later remarried, to James Williams, a bakery delivery man.

Black-white relations in Arkansas City were generally peaceful, although Johnson recalls hearing "horror stories" about lynchings from across the river in Mississippi. However, there was no high school for black students in Johnson's town. When he finished the eighth grade, his mother planned on moving to Chicago, where he could complete his education. When she found herself unable to afford the move, she insisted that Johnson repeat the year at school, to prevent his becoming a delinquent.

In 1933, Johnson's mother temporarily left her husband and went with her son to Chicago, where Johnson attended school. Chicago was rigidly segregated at that time, and Johnson graduated from the city's all-black Jean Baptiste Pointe Du Sable High School in 1936. His classmates there included Redd Foxx and Nat King Cole.

His high school years were difficult. Some time after his stepfather joined the family, both adults lost their jobs and had to go on relief (the term for "welfare" at the time). Johnson also felt isolated from his classmates, and began reading the self-help books of Dale Carnegie, who preached that a positive attitude would win success. Johnson believed in Carnegie's message and went on to become junior- and senior-class president, editor of the high school paper, and an honors graduate.

When he was 18, Johnson went to work for the company magazine of the Supreme Liberty Life Insurance Company, a black-owned company that greatly impressed him with its vision of black business success. He also studied at the University of Chicago from 1936 to 1938, and at Northwestern University's School of Commerce from 1938 to 1940. During this time, he became assistant editor, then editor, of *Supreme* magazine. In 1941, Johnson married Eunice Walker, with whom he later had two children.

While working at *Supreme,* he became involved in local politics. He also had the idea of founding *Negro Digest,* a magazine with reprints of articles that had appeared around the country in black newspapers. Most white newspapers did not cover black events, and black Americans had to rely on their own press. Johnson wanted his magazine to compile stories on black issues from around the country, so that black readers could get a broad picture of their condition in the United States.

Johnson was also influenced by the success of *Reader's Digest,* which reprinted excerpts from many different publications. However, *Negro Digest* tended to publish entire articles, rather than exerpts. It was also far more critical of social problems, and much more involved with social issues than *Reader's Digest,* which preferred a generally satisfied and upbeat image of the United States.

Johnson was unable to get financing for his venture, but managed to procure a $500 commercial loan, using his mother's furniture as collateral. This money went for postage to pre-sell subscriptions to his magazine. The idea worked and, in 1942, *Negro Digest* hit the newsstands. It soon had a circulation of 50,000, which doubled in 1943, when Eleanor Roosevelt wrote an article especially for the publication.

In 1945, Johnson founded *Ebony,* a picture magazine based on *Life* and *Look,* but with a black focus. The magazine was an immediate success, selling out its first 25,000 copies immediately and reprinting a run of 25,000 more. Although many criticized *Ebony* for its lack of attention to politics, it later became a major photographic record of the Civil Rights movement.

In 1951, Johnson founded *Jet,* a weekly news magazine in pocket-size form, again focusing on black issues. Within six months, it was selling 300,000 copies per week, making it the largest black news magazine in the world.

Later he added the magazine that is now called *Black Stars,* as well as *Ebony Jr!* The company includes a book division, a book club, and a travel service and produces Ebony Fashion Fair and Supreme Beauty Products.

An influential figure in publishing and in politics, Johnson became chairman of the board of the Supreme Liberty Life Insurance Co. and served on the boards of directors of several banks, as well as the Twentieth Century-Fox Film Corporation. He eventually bought Chicago radio station WGRT.

Further Reading: *Succeeding Against the Odds,* by John H. Johnson, with Lerone Bennett, Jr., New York: Amistad Press, 1993; *John Harold Johnson, the Man Who Wouldn't Take No for an Answer (Business Whizzes),* by Bertram T. Knight, New York: Crestwood House, 1998; *John Johnson: Media Magnate (Made in America),* by Bill Greenberg, New York: The Rourke Book Co., Inc., 1993.

—*R. K.*

❖ JONES, JAMES EARL
(1931–), actor

James Earl Jones first rose to national prominence in the Broadway role of Jack Jefferson, the heavyweight champion in the 1968 play *The Great White Hope.* Jones won

James Earl Jones *(Joyce George/Saga/Archive Photos)*

a Tony Award and a Drama Desk Award for the part, which effectively gave him star status. In 1970, he was nominated for a Best Actor Oscar, for his performance in the film version of *The Great White Hope.*

Jones continued to act on stage and television, and in the movies. One of his most famous roles was in George Lucas's Star Wars trilogy: *Star Wars,* 1977; *The Empire Strikes Back,* 1980; and *The Return of the Jedi,* 1983. Jones did not physically appear in those films, but he provided the powerful voice for the arch-villain Darth Vader. Jones won subsequent critical praise for his Broadway appearance in August Wilson's play *Fences.*

James Earl Jones was born in Tate County, Mississippi, in 1931. His father, Robert Earl Jones, was also an actor on stage, screen, and television.

Jones was raised by his grandparents on a farm in Michigan. In 1953, he graduated from the University of Michigan, after which he went into the army. Two years later, in 1955, he made his first stage appearance; in 1957, he made his Broadway debut. He went on to play a variety of roles in New York.

His work came at a time when some black actors were beginning to be cast in traditionally "white" plays. His Shakespearean roles included both traditional black parts, such as Othello, a Moorish general, and less traditional roles—Oberon, in *A Midsummer Night's Dream,* and Caliban, in *The Tempest.* He also played in Jean Genet's *The Blacks,* in 1961; Athol Fugard's *Blood Knot* (about South Africa), in 1964; and Chekhov's *The Cherry Orchard,* in 1968. In 1962, he was awarded the Obie for off-Broadway excellence, as well as the Theater World Award.

In the 1960s, Jones also acted on television. In 1967, he played Dr. Jerry Turner in *The Guiding Light,* becoming one of the first black regulars on a soap opera. He also guest-starred in many dramatic series.

Although Jones's acknowledged film success came in the 1970s, he did have a small part in the 1964 film *Dr. Strangelove or How I Learned to Stop Worrying and Love the Bomb,* directed by Stanley Kubrick. And he appeared in the 1967 film *The Comedians,* starring Richard Burton and Elizabeth Taylor.

After his film success in *The Great White Hope,* Jones starred in more movies, including *The Man,* in 1972; *Claudine,* in 1974; *The River Niger,* in 1976; and *The Bingo Long Traveling All-Stars and Motor Kings,* also in 1976. Key television work included narrating a special on Malcolm X in 1972; a part in *Roots: The Next Generation* in 1979; and two series, *Paris,* in 1979 and 1980, and *Gabriel's Fire,* in 1990 and 1991. He later appeared in the films *Matewan,* 1987, and *Field of Dreams,* 1989.

Jones once remarked that the only place a black actor could really count on being needed was in doing commercials, since advertisers depended on black actors to reach black consumers. But he continues to find steady work and rewarding roles in all three dramatic media.

Further Reading: *James Earl Jones: Voices and Silences,* by James Earl Jones with Penelope Niven, New York: Touchstone Books, 1994.

—*R. K.*

❖ JONES, LEROI
see BARAKA, IMAMU AMIRI

❖ JOPLIN, SCOTT
(1868?–1917), *composer*

Scott Joplin is best known as the "King of Ragtime." Developed in saloons and brothels, ragtime was an early jazz form that, naturally, was not heard by most "respectable" black people—and most white people. Joplin's achievement was to write many beautiful, well-crafted "rags" that were published and promoted to a wider audience, helping to develop and publicize this unique American musical form.

One of Joplin's biggest hits was the "Maple Leaf Rag," which sold over a million copies in sheet music. This piece is said to have started the "ragtime madness," which made this musical form overwhelmingly popular in both the United States and Europe.

Joplin also wrote waltzes, marches, and ragtime opera. Most famous of such works is the extraordinary *Treemonisha,* which was a failure in his time but a success later. Possibly, audiences of his time were not ready to accept a grand opera written by a black composer. Today, Joplin is recognized as a great composer and in 1976, he was awarded a posthumous Pulitzer Prize. In 1983 he was honored with a commemorative stamp.

Scott Joplin was born in Texarkana, Texas, the son of Giles Joplin, a former slave who had played the fiddle at his owner's parties, and Florence (Givens) Joplin, a free-born black woman who sang and played banjo. Joplin, two sisters, and three brothers all grew up in this musical household, where Joplin soon developed a reputation as a child prodigy on the piano.

When Giles Joplin left his wife and six children, Florence went to work as a cleaning woman. She took her son Scott with her and managed to get permission for him to practice piano at the houses where she worked. White citizens of Texarkana were soon very impressed with the young Scott, and one legendary German music teacher reportedly volunteered to teach him the European style and method. This may or may not be true, but we know that many people did offer to teach him basic music theory as well as piano-playing, and that Joplin's music reflected a strong classical European background in harmony and composition.

As a teenager, Joplin played at churches, bars, and brothels—the only places that a black musician was allowed to play in late 19th-century America. Finally he left home and traveled throughout the South, playing in bars and bordellos, absorbing the ragtime music, both black and white, that was being played at the time.

Joplin eventually settled in Sedalia, Missouri, where he played at the Maple Leaf Club and attended George R. Smith College to study music. He performed in honky-tonks (dance halls that often accommodated prostitution) and saloons (which featured gambling and prostitution), but he was also warmly received in more conventional venues, and he eventually turned to vaudeville (a type of entertainment similar to our variety shows, which featured singing, dancing, music, and joke-telling). He also began to compose music.

Joplin's first compositions were sentimental songs, but later he created the ragtime melodies for which he is known today. In 1899, he published *Original Rags,* marking a turning point in his work. Also in that year, the "Maple Leaf Rag" was published and became the rage. With the money he made from "Maple Leaf Rag," Joplin stopped working in saloons and concentrated on composing. This was made possible because Joplin had an unusual financial arrangement—his white publisher agreed to pay him a percentage of the money derived from the sale of his music. It was much more common for black composers to sell their work outright. They would receive a fixed amount, and the white publishers would get everything else, no matter how many copies were sold, nor how many times the music was publicly performed.

Joplin's new prosperity may have led to his marriage, in 1900, to Belle Hayden, with whom he went to live in St. Louis. Joplin settled down there to teach, study, and compose music.

In 1905, when the marriage ended, he left St. Louis and apparently disappeared for two years, until his arrival in New York in 1907. No one knows where he was during that time, but some believe that he was working on *Treemonisha,* his second opera. (His first, *A Guest of Honor,* was performed in 1903 in St. Louis, but the music itself seems to have vanished. Perhaps Joplin felt it wasn't good enough and destroyed all copies.)

Joplin spent years trying to get *Treemonisha* accepted by a publisher or an opera company, but even his popularity and commercial success were not enough to guarantee success in the world of opera. Finally, in 1911, he tried publishing it himself, which was a very discouraging task. Joplin continued to face one failure after another.

In 1909, Joplin married Lottie Stokes, who supported him through all of his efforts with *Treemonisha.* She watched him try to stage the opera personally, only to fail each time. Joplin was also losing his mental capacities to syphilis. In 1916, Joplin's wife realized that the disease was too far advanced and she finally had him committed to Manhattan State Hospital. He died there on April 1, 1917.

At that time, ragtime was about to give way to newer forms of jazz. But in the 1970s, Joplin's music enjoyed a rebirth, with a new popularity and appreciation, especially as the basis for the movie soundtrack of *The Sting.* Eventually, in 1972, even *Treemonisha* was performed, to critical acclaim.

In 1976, Joplin was awarded a posthumous Pulitzer Prize for his compositions.

Further Reading: *King of Ragtime: Scott Joplin and His Era,* by Edward A. Berlin, New York: Oxford University Press, 1994; *Dancing to a Black Man's Tune: A Life of Scott Joplin (Missouri Biography Series),* by Susan Curtis, Columbia, Mo.: University of Missouri Press, 1994; *Scott Joplin & the Age of Ragtime (Life, Times and Music Series),* by Timothy Frew, New York: Michael Friedman/Fairfax Publishing, 1996; *The Art of Ragtime,* by William J. Shafer and Johannes Riedel, New York: Da Capo Press, 1973; *They All Played Ragtime,* by Rudi Blesh and Harriet Janis, New York: Oak Publications, 1971; *The Collected Works of Scott Joplin,* ed. by Vera Brodsky Lawrence, New York: New York Public Library, 1971.

—R. K.

❖ JORDAN, BARBARA
(1936–1996), *congressional representative*

Barbara Jordan was the first African American since 1883 to be elected to the Texas State Senate, and the first woman ever to hold such a position. When Jordan was elected by her colleagues to serve as senate president *pro tempore,* she became the first black woman in the United States to preside over a legislative body. When she was elected to the House of Representatives from Texas, she became the first black woman from a southern state to serve in Congress. And, in 1976, Jordan became the first black keynote speaker at a Democratic national convention.

Barbara Jordan was born on February 21, 1936, in Houston, the youngest child of Baptist minister Benjamin Jordan and Arlyne (Patton) Jordan. Jordan's father could not support his three children on his minister's salary, so he worked in a warehouse as well.

Jordan made her choice of a law career in the tenth grade at Phillis Wheatley High School. Before that, she recalled, she had no idea that a woman *could* be a lawyer. She came to that realization when attorney Edith Sampson (later a judge) came to speak at Jordan's school.

In 1956, Jordan graduated magna cum laude from Texas State University, having been a star on the debating team. In 1959, she graduated from Boston University Law School, the only woman in a class of 128. She opened up a law practice out of her family's living room while working as an assistant to a local county judge.

In 1960, Jordan entered politics as a volunteer. She set up Houston's first one-person-per-block precinct organization to campaign for President John F. Kennedy

Barbara Jordan (*Library of Congress*)

and his vice president, a Texan, Lyndon B. Johnson. During this campaign, Jordan became known for her remarkable speaking abilities.

This experience convinced Jordan to get on her own ticket, and in 1962, she ran for a seat in the Texas House of Representatives. She lost that race and again in 1964—but in 1966, she won a contest for the state senate by a margin of two to one.

While in the state senate, Jordan worked for voting rights and against job discrimination. She also worked to set a minimum wage for domestics and farm workers, who had not been covered by previous legislation.

Jordan soon gained the support of the press. She also made the most of her ties with Lyndon Johnson, who was now president. In 1968, as a delegate to the Democratic national convention, she succeeded in getting the Texas delegation to support Johnson's waging of the Vietnam War. Many observers criticized this stand, particularly since she personally opposed the war—but to Jordan, the political advantage of Johnson's support was crucial.

In 1971, Jordan was once again accused of making politically advantageous moves at the cost of her principles. She was vice chair of a Texas committee to create new congressional districts that carved out a Houston district that was 42 percent black, a logical place from which she could run for Congress. When she announced her candidacy for national office, another African-American candidate, Curtis Graves, accused Jordan of agreeing to trade the new congressional district for later redistricting that would eliminate her black state senate district. In fact, with the new state senate districts, there were no increase in black state senators in Texas.

Nevertheless, Jordan denied that she had done anything improper. She also denied Graves's charges that she was too close to the white establishment and the state's oil interests.

The voters apparently supported Jordan, for she won 80 percent of the primary vote against Graves in 1972, and won the congressional election by a margin of more than four to one. After her victory, Jordan's old friend Lyndon Johnson used his influence to get her on the Judiciary Committee, even though he had already retired. She soon earned a reputation for being hardworking, aloof, and somewhat intimidating.

While Jordan was in Congress, the Watergate hearings were held, and later, the 1974 impeachment proceedings for President Nixon. In addition, the appointments of two vice presidents were confirmed.

Jordan became a national figure, with much television exposure of her activity on the Judiciary Committee during the hearings on Watergate. She was active in insisting that Nixon be impeached, arguing that he had committed the "high crimes and misdemeanors" that the Constitution said warranted impeachment.

When Gerald Ford was proposed for vice president, Jordan voted against him, voting for Nelson Rockefeller instead. However, once Ford became president, he appointed her to his first congressional mission to China.

Jordan left the House in 1979 and became a professor at the Lyndon B. Johnson School of Public Affairs at the University of Texas. She continued to be in demand as a lecturer and Democratic Party fundraiser. She held 29 honorary doctorates, was a member of many corporate boards, and was on the Board of Directors of the Public Broadcasting System. She was a founder and board member of People for the American Way, a liberal group that fights censorship and government corruption.

Further Reading: *Barbara Jordan: The Biography,* by Austin Teutsch, Dallas, Tex.: Golden Touch Press, 1997; *Barbara*

Jordan: A Self-Portrait, by Barbara Jordan and Shelby Hearon, Garden City, N.Y.: Doubleday, 1979; *The Great Society: A Twenty-Year Critique,* edited by Barbara Jordan with Elspeth Rostow, Austin, Tex.: Lyndon B. Johnson Library, Lyndon B. Johnson School of Public Affairs, 1986.

—*R. K.*

❖ JORDAN, MICHAEL
(1963–   ), *basketball player*

Hailed by many as the greatest basketball player of all time, Michael Jordan dominated the NBA between his arrival in 1984 and his retirement in 1999. With his dazzling play and magnetic personality, he almost singlehandedly made professional basketball a global entertainment phenomenon; in the process, Jordan transcended the world of sports to become an international celebrity.

Jordan was born on February 17, 1963, in Wilmington, North Carolina. Growing up with two brothers and two sisters, he was given solid moral values and a strong work ethic by his parents, James and Delores, both of whom held important supervisory jobs. Michael enjoyed sports as a youngster, but he did not seem in any way destined to be a superstar. In fact, he was cut from the varsity basketball team at Wilmington's Laney High School during his sophomore year. Over the following months, however, Jordan grew from five feet eleven to six feet three. He made the team easily in his junior year and soon became its best player.

Standing six feet six when he graduated from Laney in 1981, Jordan accepted a basketball scholarship to the University of North Carolina at Chapel Hill, where he majored in geography. Playing under the legendary coach Dean Smith, Jordan had an inconsistent freshman year at the small forward position, but he made up for it at the end. In the final game of the NCAA tournament, he won the national championship for North Carolina by sinking a last-second jump shot against Georgetown. The following year he vastly improved his all-around game, especially on defense; in addition to being named an all-American, he was chosen by the *Sporting News* as the college basketball player of the year. Jordan earned both honors again in 1984 and also won a gold medal at the Los Angeles Olympics as a member of the U.S. national team.

Jordan's acrobatic feats on the court had made him one of the most exciting players in the game, and the Chicago Bulls of the NBA believed that he could turn their struggling franchise around. They chose Jordan with the third pick in the 1984 draft; he decided to leave North Carolina after his junior year and signed a lucrative five-year contract with the Bulls.

Jordan was not quite tall enough to be a forward in the NBA, and some experts wondered if he could make the adjustment to playing in the backcourt. He soon put all doubts to rest, electrifying fans with his soaring dunks and leading the league in scoring for 1984–85 with a 28.2 average. Jordan became an instant celebrity, snapping up awards and signing lucrative deals to endorse Nike sneakers and other products. Being an intense competitor, however, Jordan wanted a league championship more than anything. He finally achieved his goal in 1991, leading the Bulls to the NBA crown while averaging 31 points throughout the playoffs. For the next two seasons (1991–92 and 1992–93) the Bulls and Jordan repeated as champions, becoming the first team in more than 30 years to win three straight titles.

Jordan appeared to be on top of the world in 1993, but he was not immune to personal tragedy. During the summer, his father was murdered during a robbery, and a grieving Jordan announced his retirement from basketball, saying that he had nothing more to prove. In 1994 he played baseball in the Chicago White Sox minor league system, partly as a tribute to his father, who had been a passionate baseball fan. In the spring of 1995 Jordan began to miss basketball nearly as much as it missed him, and he returned to the Bulls in time for the playoffs. The following season (1995–96) he played with a new sense of dedication, leading the Bulls to the best regular-season record in history and a fourth NBA championship. After the final playoff victory, Jordan wept openly and dedicated the title to his father.

Jordan and the Bulls won both the 1996–97 and 1997–98 championships. A labor dispute delayed the start of the 1998–99 season. When the dispute ended, Jordan announced his retirement from basketball—January 13, 1999.

In addition to his on-court heroics and his many business interests, Jordan has consistently worked to benefit the community. Following his retirement, Jordan continued his involvement with basketball when he became the president of basketball operations for the Washington Wizards in January 2000. In 2001 he came out of retirement again to play for the Wizards.

Further Information: *Rare Air: Michael on Michael,* text by Michael Jordan, photographs by Walter Iooss, Jr., San Francisco: HarperSanFrancisco, 1993; *Michael Jordan,* by Sean Dolan, New York: Chelsea House, 1994; SportsLine Michael Jordan web site, http://jordan.sportsline.com, provides information on Jordan's career, complete statis-

Michael Jordan (*Library of Congress*)

tics, photos, audio and video clips, a chat room, and a selection of feature articles.

—*P. K.*

❖ JORDAN, VERNON EULION, JR.
(1935–), *lawyer, civil rights leader*

A mainstay of the Civil Rights movement for more than two decades, Vernon Jordan has held important posts in the NAACP, the United Negro College Fund, and the National Urban League. As a prominent Washington attorney since 1981, he has been an influential figure in corporate boardrooms and in the highest councils of the U.S. government.

Born in Atlanta, Georgia, on August 15, 1935, Jordan was the second of three sons. His father, Vernon, Sr., worked as a postal clerk, and his mother, Mary, ran a successful catering business. During his youth, Jordan often helped out in his mother's business, gaining valuable insight into many different social worlds. He especially enjoyed catering the monthly meetings of the Lawyers Club of Atlanta; on these occasions he would carefully observe how the city's leading attorneys handled themselves.

After graduating with honors from David T. Howard High School in 1953, Jordan attended DePauw University in Greencastle, Indiana, where he majored in political science. He excelled at public speaking, winning several awards in this area during his college career. In 1957 Jordan moved on to Howard University's School of Law. After earning his law degree three years later, he returned to Georgia and immersed himself in the Civil Rights movement. Jordan became a law clerk for the prominent black attorney Donald L. Hollowell, who was leading the fight to end segregation in Georgia's colleges. In May 1961, when a federal court ordered the University of Georgia to admit two African-American students, Jordan personally escorted Charlayne HUNTER-GAULT onto the campus, defying a mob of angry whites.

Later in 1961, Jordan became field director for the Georgia branch of the NAACP. He remained in that post for two years and helped to coordinate a variety of civil rights campaigns. Among his achievements was a successful boycott campaign that forced a number of businesses to hire black employees. In 1964, Jordan moved to Pine Bluff, Arkansas, where he headed the Voter Education Project of the Southern Regional Council. During his four years in this post, 2 million additional

Vernon Jordan (*Reuters/Larry Downing/Archive Photos*)

black voters were entered on the rolls, and the number of black elected officials in the South rose dramatically.

Jordan emerged on the national scene in 1970, when he became executive director of the United Negro College Fund. He had an immediate impact on the organization, raising more than $10 million for African-American education within a single year. After only a year in his new job, Jordan was chosen to replace Whitney Young as director of the National Urban League, following Young's accidental death. As head of this long-established organization, Jordan emphasized issues such as full employment, voter registration, and national health coverage. Tirelessly traveling around the country, he raised money and support for the Urban League, expanding its staff and operations. Jordan also forged important links between the Urban League and leading corporations; after joining the boards of Xerox, Bankers Trust, Dow Jones, RJR Nabisco, and several other firms, he pressed them to create more opportunities for women and minorities.

In May 1980, Jordan was hit in the back by a sniper's bullet in the parking lot of an Indiana hotel. He spent more than three months recuperating, returning to his desk in September with renewed determination. A year later, Jordan resigned his Urban League post and entered private law practice, working for a variety of corporate clients. He continued to voice his support for economic justice and equal rights, though he had little influence in the conservative Reagan and Bush administrations. The election of Bill Clinton to the presidency in 1992 brought Jordan back into public life. He and Clinton had been close friends for 20 years, and Jordan played a pivotal role in choosing the members of the new administration. Though he was rumored to be a candidate for attorney general, he returned to his law practice after Clinton's inauguration, remaining one of the president's most trusted advisers.

Further Reading: "Vernon Jordan," *Current Biography Yearbook 1993,* New York: H. W. Wilson, 1994.

—P. K.

❖ JOYNER-KERSEE, JACKIE
(1962–), *champion athlete*

Often called the greatest female athlete of all time, Jackie Joyner-Kersee was a major force in track and field for more than 15 years. She dominated the women's heptathlon event in two successive Olympics, winning six Olympic medals overall and setting a standard of excellence that may never be surpassed.

Jackie Joyner was born in East St. Louis, Illinois, on March 3, 1962. She was one of four children. Her parents, Alfred and Mary Joyner, worked hard to make ends meet. They were not particularly happy when their daughter took up track and field at the age of nine, but when she showed unmistakable talent they began to encourage her. By the time Joyner was 12, she was long-jumping more than 17 feet. She was also working hard in the classroom and earning excellent grades.

Joyner began competing in the seven-event heptathlon—the ultimate test of athleticism in women's track and field—while still in junior high school. She won the first of four National Junior Pentathlon Championships at the age of 14. While attending Lincoln High School, Joyner was often hailed as the finest athlete in Illinois; in addition to her heptathlon achievements, she set a state record in the long jump and starred in basketball and volleyball.

After graduating in the top 10 percent of her class in 1980, Joyner attended UCLA on a basketball scholarship. In addition to starting on the basketball team all four years, she also won the NCAA heptathlon championship in 1982 and 1983. Despite a hamstring injury, Joyner managed to win a silver medal in the heptathlon at the 1984 Olympics in Los Angeles. She had the satisfaction of seeing her brother, Al Joyner, Jr., win the gold medal in the triple jump.

On January 1986, the budding track star married Bob Kersee, who had been coaching her since her freshman year at UCLA. Following her marriage, Joyner-Kersee began training with renewed enthusiasm, and her work soon paid off. At the Goodwill Games in Moscow that summer, Joyner-Kersee became the first woman in history to surpass the 7,000-point mark in the heptathlon. Her achievement earned her the Jesse Owens Award for excellence in track and field and the Sullivan Award as top amateur athlete of the year.

Joyner-Kersee continued to dominate in 1987, winning the heptathlon and the long jump at the World Track and Field Championships in Rome—she was the first woman in history to win both a multisport event and an individual event at a major meet. Joyner-Kersee swept on to take the gold medal in the heptathlon at the 1988 Olympics, setting a world record for total points with 7,291. She repeated as Olympic heptathlon champion at Barcelona in 1992, also capturing a bronze medal in the long jump.

Now one of the most celebrated athletes in the world, Joyner-Kersee uses her celebrity to work for numerous charitable causes. Remembering the hard times her family had faced in East St. Louis, she created the Jackie Joyner-Kersee Community Foundation to provide assistance and encouragement to young people in her hometown.

Joyner-Kersee competed in her fourth Olympics at Atlanta in 1996, hoping for a third straight gold medal in the heptathlon. This dream would remain unfulfilled. On July 27, an injured right hamstring muscle forced Joyner-Kersee to drop out after only one event. To the amazement of sports fans, she bounced back on August 2, placing third in the long jump and winning her sixth Olympic medal overall.

Following the Olympics, Joyner-Kersee announced her retirement from competition, amid an outpouring of tributes from fellow athletes and fans. Wasting no time, she immediately plunged into a new field of endeavor—sports management. After forming a company known as Elite Sports Marketing, Joyner-Kersee announced plans to position her company as a leading agent for National Football League players.

Further Reading: *A Kind of Grace: The Autobiography of the World's Greatest Female Athlete,* by Jackie Joyner-Kersee

Jackie Joyner-Kersee (*Reuters/Charles Platiau/Archive Photos*)

with Sonja Steptoe, New York: Warner, 1997; *Jackie Joyner-Kersee, Superwoman,* by Margaret J. Goldstein and Jennifer Larson, Minneapolis: Lerner, 1994.

—*P. K.*

❖ JULIAN, PERCY LAVON
(1899–1975), *chemist*

Percy Julian made a number of contributions to the field of chemistry, registering 105 patents during his lifetime. Julian's successful innovations in chemistry included new processes for manufacturing paints; a method of extracting sterols from soybean oil in order to synthesize the drug cortisone (used, among other things, in the treatment of inflammatory arthritis); and a method for mass-producing sex hormones, leading to the development of birth-control pills. In recognition of his achievements, Julian has been named to the Inventors Hall of Fame.

In addition to his scientific endeavors, Julian was also an entrepreneur. He founded Julian Laboratories, Inc., which operated in three countries: the United States (Chicago), Mexico, and Guatemala. He also established the Julian Research Institute. His contributions to the field of chemistry were accompanied by a great number of related research papers, which he published in scholarly journals. In 1947, Julian was awarded the Spingarn Medal by the NAACP for outstanding achievement by a black American. In 1993, a commemorative stamp was issued in his honor.

Percy Julian was born in 1899, in Montgomery, Alabama, at a time when many black Americans were but a few decades removed from slavery. Nevertheless, Julian was one of the few black students from his high school class to attend college. In 1920, he earned his B.A. degree from DePauw University in Indiana. In 1922, his fellowship to Harvard led to his M.A.

Julian taught while continuing to study. From 1920 to 1925, he was an instructor of chemistry at Fisk University, in Nashville, Tennessee. Later, he taught chemistry at West Virginia State College. In 1927, he was an associate professor of chemistry at Howard University in Washington, D.C. He also helped to develop the chemistry department and a new chemistry building at Howard.

Julian continued his advanced education and, in 1931, received his Ph.D. from the University of Vienna, Austria. He returned to DePauw, where from 1932 to 1936, he worked as a research fellow in organic chemistry.

As a research fellow, Julian was granted funds to do research but not teach. Although he had already made several important discoveries in chemistry, the DePauw administration was reluctant to appoint him to the actual faculty because he was black. In the face of this discrimination, Julian left the academic world and turned to business instead.

Julian's first corporate position was in research for the Institute of Paper Chemistry in Wisconsin. From there, he became director of research in soy products for the Glidden Company of Chicago, where he worked from 1936 to 1953.

After almost 20 years at Glidden, Julian became his own boss. He established the Julian Laboratories, which he maintained from 1954 to 1961. Then he sold his labs. The Guatemala plant was bought by the Upjohn Company, a major pharmaceutical corporation. Smith Kline & French purchased the Chicago branch and kept Julian on as president of the laboratory.

Even in his mid-60s, Julian remained active in his field. In 1964, he founded Julian Research Institute, where he continued to study and experiment until his death in 1975.

Further Reading: *The Negro Vanguard,* by Richard Bardolph, New York: Rinehart, 1961.

—*R. K.*

❖ JUST, ERNEST EVERETT
(1883–1941), *biologist*

Ernest Just's major scientific contributions were his pioneering investigations into the fertilization of the egg by the sperm, and the structure of the cell. His background was in marine biology—the study of animals that live in the sea—and his early work was in embryology—the study of the embryo in its preliminary stage, when it is still gestating inside its mother.

Just made many significant contributions in all of these fields. He also taught biology at Howard University in Washington, D.C., for many years and conducted research during the summers. His work was recognized in 1930, when he was elected vice president of the American Society of Zoologists, and again in 1936, when he was elected to the Washington Academy of Sciences. He also served on the boards of many prestigious scientific magazines in the United States and abroad.

Ernest Just came from a family of wharf builders who had constructed docks in Charleston, South Carolina, where Just was born in 1883. His father, Charles, died when Just was only four years old, so his mother, Mary (Matthews) Just, became a schoolteacher to support her family. She also founded a cooperative farm and industrial settlement that was later named Maryville in her honor.

Just attended the academy of South Carolina State College from 1894 to 1900, then worked his way north on a steamship, and eventually studied at Dartmouth College in New Hampshire. When he graduated in 1907, Just had received top honors in both history and biology.

He taught English at Howard University in 1907. In 1912, he married a fellow teacher, Ethel Highwarden, with whom he later had three children.

Although Just began teaching English, the president of Howard University persuaded him to turn to biology. In 1908, he started his graduate work in biology. These studies paralleled his teaching career through 1916, when he received his doctorate from the University of Chicago. He spent some 20 summers studying at the Marine Biology Laboratory at Woods Hole, Massachusetts.

When Just got his advanced degree, he had been publishing research papers for four years—an unusual accomplishment for a scientist. And, in 1915, he received the NAACP's Spingarn Medal for achievement by an African American.

He continued to teach at Howard, where he headed the Medical School's department of physiology from 1912 to 1920. Rather than focusing on current practical medical techniques, Just was a pioneer in introducing the results of new research into Howard's medical curriculum.

Although Just's position at Howard was secure, his race denied him acceptance at the more venerable and better funded white universities—and their superior research facilities. Eventually, philanthropist Julius Rosenwald and the National Research Council came to his rescue, financially, enabling Just to devote six months of each year to research, rather than teaching full time.

Some of Just's research was useful in the treatment of edema (an accumulation of fluid that results in swelling of the tissues) and nephritis (a disease of the kidneys).

Eventually, however, he became less interested in specific research issues and more interested in developing a general theory of the nature of biological life. Just called his new theories "a revolution in our biological thinking."

But Just's responsibilities at Howard interfered at times with his research goals. He continued to receive grant money—but Howard president Mordecai Johnson wanted to divert these funds to train other black scientists, not simply to support Just. The president also wanted him to continue teaching, whereas Just wanted to spend his time more exclusively on research.

Just's dissatisfaction with Howard, combined with his discouragement by American racism, led to his decision to work in European laboratories. There, he thought, people were more likely to be "color blind."

Just worked in Berlin in the 1930s, until the racial policies of Adolph Hitler made Germany unsafe for him as well. He went on to Naples, Italy, and to Paris, where he continued to develop his theory of a holistic (all-inclusive) biology. Beyond the study of simple biological mechanisms, Just wanted to show how many different aspects of the physical world interacted with one another. And he drew on philosophy and physics as well as biology.

His work was quite controversial. In 1939, he summarized his ideas in a major book, *The Biology of the Cell Surface* (New York: Garland Publishers, 1988 reprint of 1939 ed.), which created much discussion in the scientific community. Just continued to be criticized for what he felt were the restrictions that others placed on him. In 1936, he wrote, "As I am black, I am supposed to keep within a certain sphere of activity. Now . . . I do not want to be told over and over again that my place is with my people; that only within the circumscribed arena of the black world must I work."

In 1939, he married German biologist Hedwig Schnetzler. The couple soon faced severe difficulties: When Germany and France went to war in September 1939, the French authorities forbade Just to return to the laboratories where he had been working. The racist policies of Hitler were following Just to France, and in 1940, he and his wife returned to Howard University.

He continued to receive scientific honors. In 1941, for example, he was elected to the New York Academy of Sciences. But later that year, he died of cancer.

Further Reading: *Black Apollo of Science,* by Kenneth P. Manning, New York: Oxford University Press, 1983; *Black Pioneers of Science and Invention,* by Louis Haber, San Diego, Calif.: Harcourt Brace Jovanovich, 1991; *Black Scientists,* by Lisa Yount, New York: Facts On File, 1991.

—*R. K.*

❖ KING, MARTIN LUTHER, JR.
(1929–1968), civil rights leader

Martin Luther King, Jr. is widely recognized as being the most important and charismatic U.S. civil rights leader of the 20th century. He led many of the major civil rights actions of the 1950s and 1960s, including the 1955 Montgomery bus boycott, the 1963 desegregation actions in Birmingham, and the 1963 March on Washington.

In 1964, King was awarded the Nobel Peace Prize; he was the youngest man ever to receive a Nobel Prize. He received many other honors and awards throughout his lifetime. Today, his birthday is recognized as a federal holiday that is observed by most states.

As a result of the Civil Rights movement, legal segregation was ended and the economic position of black Americans was markedly improved. Much of the effective leadership of that movement is credited to Martin Luther King.

Martin Luther King, Jr., was born on January 15, 1929, in Atlanta, the son of Reverend Martin Luther KING, SR., who was pastor of the influential Ebenezer Baptist Church. King, Jr., attended Booker T. Washington High School, the first black public high school in Atlanta. He skipped the ninth and twelfth grades, and was only 15 when he entered Morehouse College in Atlanta.

King was ordained as a minister in 1947 and graduated from Morehouse with a B.A. in sociology in 1948. He went on to earn a B.D. (bachelor of divinity) degree in 1951 from Crozer Theological Seminary in Pennsylvania, where he was elected senior class president and awarded a prize for "most outstanding student." King chose Boston University for his Ph.D. work, and while there, he met Coretta Scott, who was studying voice at the New England Conservatory of Music. They were soon married.

He left B.U. in 1954, and went to preach at the Dexter Avenue Baptist Church in Montgomery, Alabama. This church already had a tradition of civil rights leadership under former pastor Vernon Johns. In 1955, King finished his thesis and received his doctoral degree.

King had attended a sermon preached by Howard University president Mordecai Johnson on the subject of pacifist-activist Mohandas Gandhi, and this had inspired him to study Gandhi's words and actions. By this time, he had also read the works of a number of philosophers and theologians, such as Reinhold Niebuhr and Martin Buber, which were leading him to formulate his own personal philosophy of nonviolence.

The opportunity to put both his ideas and his leadership to the test came in late 1955. In December of that year, Rosa PARKS refused to give up her seat on a Montgomery bus to a white person. She was arrested and taken to jail. Parks, King, and other leaders decided that

Martin Luther King, Jr. (*Library of Congress*)

this might be the occasion to end the segregation on Montgomery buses. They called a boycott that lasted for a year, and which finally resulted in ending the "white-only" sections of Montgomery buses—and ultimately all public transportation in the country.

This nonviolent political action brought King national recognition and made him one of the most powerful and effective leaders of the Civil Rights movement, while he was still only in his mid-twenties. It also brought danger: In January 1956, his home was bombed.

King's next move was to organize the Southern Christian Leadership Conference (SCLC), a church-based civil rights group. He continued to speak at civil rights demonstrations and to organize activities. He also faced continued violence, stabbings, beatings, and arrests.

In 1959, King left Montgomery to work with his father at Ebenezer Baptist Church in Atlanta. By 1960, his ideas on nonviolence were a major influence in the Civil Rights movement.

In December 1961, King was invited to Albany, Georgia, to head a campaign against segregation. King was in the forefront of five mass marches on city hall, which resulted in the arrests of over 700 demonstrators. The Albany movement continued into 1962, and in late July, King himself was jailed there. By August, almost a thousand people had been arrested in Albany.

But the Albany movement did not end segregation there, and finally King withdrew. He had learned from the experience, though, and improved his strategy by the time he began the next campaign in Birmingham, Alabama, in 1963. King and his colleagues reasoned that if they could end segregation in a big city like Birmingham, the rest of the South would have to follow.

Day after day, demonstrators pressed on with their sit-ins and protests, only to be met with the fire hoses and police dogs of Sheriff Eugene "Bull" Connor, a militant segregationist. It looked as if the situation would be a standoff, with Connor ultimately wearing down the demonstrators. Then King decided to send in the schoolchildren and high school students of Birmingham. These young people joined the front lines of the demonstrators—only to meet the same violent treatment from police.

The nation was outraged, and President Kennedy sent a representative to aid in the negotiations. Finally, Birmingham political leaders and the leaders of the protest agreed to a desegregation plan.

This success attracted other leaders to help King in organizing the extraordinary 1963 March on Washington, the largest demonstration of its time. Some 250,000 people—60,000 of them white—marched to Washington to push for civil rights legislation. It was at the end of this march, in front of the Lincoln Memorial, that King made his famous "I Have a Dream" speech.

In 1964, President Johnson signed the Civil Rights Act, which provided for integrated public accommodations and forbade employment discrimination. Soon afterward, the focus of civil rights activity moved north, with riots breaking out in black areas of many major cities. King traveled to all the "trouble spots," although he was not always welcome.

In 1965, King helped to lead a march that contributed to the passage of the 1965 Voting Rights Act, a key step in guaranteeing southern African Americans access to political participation. King went north, then returned to the South in 1966, when the shooting of black leader James Meredith disrupted a voter-registration march between Memphis, Tennessee, and Jackson, Mississippi. King helped to start the march again, which lasted a total of three weeks and ended with a rally of 30,000 people in Jackson.

During this march, leader Stokely Carmichael developed the phrase "black power." Although King would not accept it until 1968, this phrase and concept had an enormous influence on African Americans throughout the 1960s and 1970s.

In 1966, King voiced his opposition to the Vietnam War. It was a major step: Black leaders had intentionally avoided criticism of U.S. foreign policy, dwelling instead on civil rights. King made efforts to unite the antiwar and Civil Rights movements, and strongly suggested that money spent on the military could be used better to fight poverty at home. He also linked the injustice of racism with the causes of war.

King was seeking a coalition of black and white people in 1968, when he called for a Poor People's March on Washington. This was his attempt to broaden the Civil Rights movement to include the goals of bringing about economic justice and ending the Vietnam War. While organizing this march, however, he made a ill-fated stop in Memphis to help local striking sanitation workers. There, on the 4th of April, at age 39, he was assassinated by a man later identified as James Earl Ray.

King's death resulted in riots and disorder in more than 120 U.S. cities. Eventually it inspired and helped to bring about the development of social programs and other progressive moves to honor the leader and further his civil rights work. Many years after his death, the FBI admitted to a full-fledged, six-year campaign to harass and discredit King.

Further Reading: *Stride Toward Freedom, the Montgomery Story,* by Martin Luther King, Jr., New York: Harper, 1968; *Why We Can't Wait,* by Martin Luther King, Jr., New York: Harper, 1969; *Bearing the Cross: Martin Luther King, Jr. and the Southern Christian Leadership Conference,* Norwalk, Conn.: Easton Press, 1989; *King: A Biography,* by David Levering Lewis, Urbana, Ill.: University of Illinois Press, 1978, 2nd ed.; *My Life with Martin Luther King, Jr.,* by Coretta Scott King, New York: Puffin, 1994; *Crown of Thorns: Political Martyrdom in America from Abraham Lincoln to Martin Luther King, Jr.,* by Eyal J. Naveh, New York: New York University Press, 1992; *The Last Crusade: Martin Luther King, Jr., the FBI, and the Poor People's Campaign,* by Gerald D. McKnight, Boulder, Co.: Westview Press, 1998; *Let the Trumpet Sound: A Life of Martin Luther King, Jr.,* by Stephen B. Oates, New York: Harper Perennial Library, 1994; *Martin Luther King, Jr.,* by Adam Fairclough, Athens, Ga.: University of

Georgia Press, 1995; *Martin Luther King: The Inconvenient Hero,* by Vincent Harding, Maryknoll, N.Y.: Orbis Books, 1996; *Martin Luther King, Jr., Companion: Quotations from the Speeches, Essays, and Books of Martin Luther King, Jr.,* by Martin Luther King and Coretta Scott King, New York: St. Martin's Press, 1995; *The Preacher King: Martin Luther King, Jr., and the Word that Moved America,* by Richard Lischer, New York: Oxford University Press, 1997; *Martin Luther King, Jr., and the Freedom Movement (Makers of America),* by Lillie Patterson, New York: Facts On File, 1993.

—*R. K.*

❖ KING, MARTIN LUTHER, SR.
(1899–1984), *minister, civil rights activist*

Martin Luther King, Sr. is best known for being the father of Martin Luther KING, JR., the great civil rights leader. However, King, Sr. was an important civil rights leader in his own right. In the 1930s, he built up the small membership of Atlanta's Ebenezer Baptist Church to a congregation of several thousand. This gave King a base in the African-American community from which he could preach about civil rights and advocate progressive social action.

In 1936, King, Sr., led the first black voting-rights march in the history of Atlanta. In 1960, he played a key role in mobilizing black support to elect John F. Kennedy. King also offered crucial support to his son at many times in his career.

Martin Luther King, Sr., was born on December 19, 1899, in rural Georgia, to a family of poor sharecroppers. He was the second of 10 children. Growing up in the early part of the century, he saw firsthand the brutality of southern racism. In his early teens, he was beaten by a white mill owner. He also saw a black man hanged by a white mob.

Yet his family continued to advocate nonviolence. When his mother was dying, King cursed white people, but his mother disagreed. "Hatred makes nothin' but more hatred . . . Don't you do it," she told him.

When King was 16, he left rural Georgia for the capital city of Atlanta, to complete his education. He worked on the railroads and went to school at night, graduating from high school in 1925. He was able to convince the president of Atlanta's Morehouse College that he should be admitted to the School of Theology, in spite of not fully meeting the school's educational requirements.

In 1926, King married Alberta Hunter, whose father was pastor at the leading black church called Ebenezer Baptist. As King continued his education, he also took over some of the duties at the church. When his father-in-law died in 1931, King became pastor. He increased the church's membership and preached his message of social action and nonviolence.

In the 1930s, King joined the National Association for the Advancement of Colored People (NAACP), the Atlanta Negro Voters League, and the Interracial Council of Atlanta. In addition to leading the voting-rights march, he worked at integrating the Ford Motor Company and ending segregation of the elevators in the Atlanta courthouse.

From 1956 to 1968, King's son was one of the major national leaders of the Civil Rights movement. King was with his son when he was killed in Memphis, Tennessee. Other tragedies soon followed: His younger son was drowned in a mysterious swimming pool accident in 1969, and his wife was shot while playing the organ in church in 1974. (The assassin later admitted that King had been his target.)

King continued to preach at Ebenezer Baptist and to work for civil rights. In 1976, when presidential candidate Jimmy Carter made a remark about "ethnic purity," many believed that would lose him the southern black vote. King played an instrumental role in preventing that, saying, "It is wrong to jump on a man for a slip of the tongue that everyone knows does not represent his thinking." When King hugged Carter on a public platform, it symbolized Carter's acceptance by black civil rights leaders, and Carter went on to win 90 percent of the black vote.

Martin Luther King, Sr., died of heart failure on November 11, 1984. Nearly 3,000 people attended the service.

Further Reading: *Not Only Dreamers: The Story of Martin Luther King, Sr. and Martin Luther King, Jr.,* by David R. Collins, 1986; *Daddy King: An Autobiography,* by Martin Luther King, Sr. and Clayton Riley, Boston, Mass.: G. K. Hall, 1981.

—*R. K.*

❖ LAFON, THOMY
(1810–1893), *philanthropist*

Thomy Lafon was one of the major black philanthropists of the 19th century. He supported the American Anti-Slavery Society, the Underground Railroad, and other groups working for black freedom and equality. He also supported the school for orphans founded by Madame Justine COUVENT in New Orleans. After his death, Lafon left money to many other charitable groups and schools.

Thomy Lafon was born in 1810 in New Orleans. Although he was born during the time of slavery, his parents were free. It is thought that his father, Pierre Laralde, was either French or of mixed French and African ancestry; his mother, Modest Foucher, is believed to have been Haitian.

Although Lafon's early years were poor—it appears that his father had deserted the family—he did get an education and taught for a while. In 1850, he opened a store and began to lend money at profitable interest rates. He then used the profits to invest in real estate.

Lafon had a talent for business, and in the years after the Civil War he became one of the wealthiest black people in New Orleans. At the time of his death in 1893, he controlled almost half a million dollars in cash, property, and other holdings—an impressive sum at the time.

He was apparently a frugal man, and also a devout Catholic who believed deeply in charity and philan-thropy. He was well educated, and spoke French and Spanish as well as English.

During the Civil War years, Lafon worked with other black activists in demanding political equality for his race. His contributions to charities were highly regarded and widely acknowledged. A few years after he died, the state legislature voted to install a bust of his likeness—marking the first time a state government had chosen to honor an African American in such a public manner. A New Orleans public school bears his name.

—R. K.

❖ LARSEN, NELLA
(1893–1963), *writer*

Nella Larsen was the first African-American woman to win a Guggenheim Foundation award for creative writing. Her two novels, *Quicksand* (New York: Knopf, 1928) and *Passing* (New York: Collier Books, 1971 ed.; both novels available in one volume, New Brunswick, N.J.: Rutgers University Press, 1986 ed.), are bitter, incisive portraits of middle-class black women and their search for authentic identities in a world of conflicting values.

Larsen was born in 1893, in Chicago, Illinois, of mixed African-American and Danish ancestry. Her father was a Danish sailor, her mother a black American. The conflicts surrounding this dual identity provided Larsen with much of the material for her novels.

She attended Fisk University in Nashville, Tennessee, but graduated from New York's Lincoln Hospital Training School for Nurses in 1915. She was superintendent of nurses at Tuskegee Institute in Alabama. Her experiences at Fisk and Tuskegee provided her with a model for Naxos, the southern school for blacks in her novel *Quicksand*. Larsen paints a bitter picture of the school, which she suggests was trying to teach black students "white" values, rather than educating them about their authentic black identities and the black cultural heritage.

Eventually, Larsen left Tuskegee for New York, returning to Lincoln Hospital Training School to become supervisor of nurses. From 1918 to 1921, she held the position of district nurse for New York City's health department.

Larsen changed jobs in 1921 to become a children's librarian for the New York Public Library. In 1929, she became general assistant librarian.

In the 1920s Larsen took part in the Harlem Renaissance movement—describing it in both of her novels—but she was also quite critical of it. Although she and the women about whom she writes were intellectually inclined, Larsen chastises the black intellectuals of her time for being too remote from the black masses and too enthralled with white culture and manners.

In 1928, Larsen published *Quicksand*, the story of a young Danish-African-American woman's search for a culture and a way of life to which she can truly belong. In 1929, she published *Passing*, the story of a wealthy doctor's wife and her conflicts concerning a woman whom she believes is passing for white.

In 1930, Larsen received the Guggenheim award, a grant honoring her work that allowed her the financial freedom to continue her writing. Controversial claims of plagiarism in that same year over a short story published in *Forum* tarnished her reputation. Although these claims were never proven, Larsen would publish no more. Little is known of her life in later years. She died in 1963.

Further Reading: *Nella Larsen, Novelist of the Harlem Renaissance: A Woman's Life Unveiled*, by Thadious M. Davis, Baton Rouge: Louisiana State University Press, 1994; *The Politics of Color in the Fiction of Jessie Fauset and Nella Larsen*, by Jacquelyn Y. McLendon, Charlottesville: University Press of Virginia, 1995; *Invisible Darkness: Jean Toomer & Nella Larsen*, Iowa City: University of Iowa Press, 1993.

—*R. K.*

❖ LATIMER, LEWIS HOWARD
(1848–1928), *inventor*

Lewis Latimer had a long, varied career with many accomplishments. He was the only black member of the "Edison Pioneers," a group of inventors who had responded to inventor Thomas A. Edison's call for colleagues. In addition, he published a book of poetry and a book about electric lighting.

Latimer was born on September 4, 1848, in Chelsea, Massachusetts, the son of a slave who had escaped to the Boston area. Such prominent abolitionists as Frederick DOUGLASS and William Lloyd Garrison raised money to buy his father's freedom. When Latimer was only 10 years old, his father disappeared.

Latimer's mother could not support her four children. So Lewis and his brother William were sent to a farm school for boys. It was a difficult place where young men were virtually forced to do heavy farm labor in exchange for room and board. But the brothers escaped, returned to Boston, and began earning money for their family. Lewis sold copies of the abolitionist paper *The Liberator,* edited by William Lloyd Garrison. When the Civil War broke out, he joined the Union Navy.

After the war, in 1865, Latimer had difficulty finding work, but he was eventually employed as an office boy in a patent solicitor's firm.

Latimer enjoyed being around the plans for new inventions. He bought books on engineering and on drafting (drawing plans) and when he asked his employers if he could use his new skills, they agreed and raised his pay.

His office was not far from the school where Alexander Graham Bell was working on his new invention, the telephone. Latimer and Bell soon became friends, and it is believed by some that Latimer collaborated to some extent on Bell's drawings and diagrams of the parts used in the new telephone.

In 1873, Latimer married Mary Wilson, with whom he later had two daughters. He was remembered by his friends as being a devoted husband and father.

In 1880, he went to work at an electric light company, where he invented carbon filaments for electric lamps. (A filament is the material within a light bulb that actually glows.) Latimer obtained a patent for his invention in 1881, and railroad stations in North America soon began using the convenient new invention. Latimer also invented a new and inexpensive way to make light-bulb filaments.

In 1883, Latimer went to work for the Board of Patent Control. His job was to gather and analyze information concerning stolen patents and to testify about it in court. In this work, Latimer met Thomas Edison, who was involved in many patent disputes.

In 1890, Latimer published *Electric Lighting: A Practical Description of the Edison System.* This was a pioneer work explaining how electric lights actually worked.

Latimer had a continuing interest in civil rights and equal protection under law. He always stressed that for black people, it was patriotic to protest against any type of discrimination. Latimer's interest in equality was not restricted to African Americans: In 1906, he taught mechanical drawing to immigrants at a settlement house (social service agency) in New York City.

Latimer was a cultivated man who enjoyed reading literature and poetry. In 1925, for a 77th birthday gift, his friends gave him a bound copy of *Poems of Love and Life,* a book of his own poetry that they had privately published.

Latimer died on December 11, 1928, in Flushing, New York. The "Edison Pioneers" issued a statement praising his work and a Brooklyn public school was later named in his honor.

Further Reading: *Eight Black American Inventors,* by Robert C. Hayden, Reading, Mass.: Addison-Wesley, 1972; *Black Pioneer of Science and Invention,* by Louis Haber, New York: Harcourt, Brace and World, 1970; *The Hidden Contributors: Black Scientists and Inventors in America,* by Aaron E. Klein, Garden City, N.Y.: Doubleday, 1971; *Lewis Howard Latimer,* by Glennette Tilley, Englewood Cliffs, N.J.: Silver Burdette Press, 1990; *Black Inventors,* by Nathan Aaseng, New York: Facts On File, 1997.

—R. K.

✤ LAWLESS, THEODORE K.
(1892–1971), *dermatologist, philanthropist*

Dr. Theodore K. Lawless was one of the world's leading skin specialists and made important contributions in the treatment of syphilis and leprosy. He eventually became director of his own dermatological clinic in the heart of a black Chicago neighborhood.

Lawless is also known for his philanthropic contributions. He made substantial donations to Dillard University, a black institution in New Orleans, and the chapel there is named for him. Other traditionally African-American schools also received grants from Dr. Lawless. So did the state of Israel, where the dermatology clinic at the Beilinson Hospital Center bears his name.

Lawless was honored in 1954 with the Spingarn Medal for outstanding achievement by a black American.

Theodore Lawless was born in 1892, in the rural town of Thibodeaux, Louisiana. Before becoming a doctor, he attended Talladega College in Alabama, the University of Kansas, Columbia University in New York, and Harvard University in Massachusetts. He received his M.D. from Northwestern University in Chicago.

Like many scientists of the time, Lawless had also studied in Europe. His research in syphilis and diseases of the skin took him to Freiburg (Germany), Paris, and Vienna, as well as to Boston, where he was a fellow of dermatology and syphilology at Massachusetts General Hospital.

From 1924 to 1941, Lawless taught medicine at Northwestern University, while consulting in dermatology at Geneva Community Hospital in Wisconsin. His work was recognized with various honors—he was made associate examiner in dermatology for the National Board of Medical Examiners and consultant to the U.S. Chemical Warfare Board.

Eventually, Lawless opened his own clinic, where he was well known for seeing—and listening to—patients from all social classes, economic levels, and ethnic backgrounds. In 1963, the mayor of Chicago and the governor of Illinois attended a dinner in his honor, celebrating his achievements in medicine and his contributions to the community.

—R. K.

✤ LAWRENCE, JACOB ARMSTEAD
(1917–2000), *artist*

One of the major American artists of the 20th century, Lawrence has chronicled the African-American experience in a uniquely expressive style. He is most famous for his narrative paintings depicting the Great Migration, the Haitian struggle for independence, the antislavery movement, and the civil rights campaigns of the 20th century.

Lawrence was born on September 7, 1917, in Atlantic City, New Jersey, the oldest of three children. Lawrence's father, a railroad cook, deserted his family in 1924. The children and their mother, Rosalee, first moved to Pennsylvania and finally settled in Harlem, a section of New York City. In addition to attending school, Lawrence spent his afternoons at the Utopia Children's Center, where his mother had enrolled him to keep him off the streets. There were many opportunities to learn arts and crafts at the center, and Lawrence took up drawing. His work caught the eye of Charles ALSTON (1907–72), a leading African-American artist who was teaching at Utopia. Alston began to encourage Lawrence, beginning a long and fruitful friendship.

Lawrence dropped out of high school at the age of 16 and went to work so that he could help his mother make ends meet. But he continued to study with Alston at the Harlem Art Workshop. When he visited Alston's studio he met a dazzling array of African-American writers and artists, including Aaron Douglas, Langston HUGHES, and Claude MCKAY. These contacts were a powerful inspiration for the young painter.

In 1936, Lawrence began producing his first major works, which depicted Harlem street scenes. He had already developed a distinctive style, which involved geometric shapes, simplified forms, flattened perspective, and bold primary colors. The following year he won a two-year scholarship to the American Arts School and had his first exhibition, at the Harlem Artists Guild. Further recognition came in 1938, when Lawrence had a one-man show at the Harlem YMCA. By this time, he was already working on his first important series of panels, *Toussaint L'Ouverture.* Consisting of 41 separate paintings, the series dramatized the plight of enslaved Africans in the Caribbean and chronicled the Haitian struggle for independence. Having discovered the narrative form that he needed to express his ideas, Lawrence quickly followed up with the *Frederick Douglass* series (32 paintings) and the *Harriet Tubman* series (31 paintings).

In 1940, Lawrence received a foundation grant, which enabled him to open his own studio. There he began work on his best-known series, *The Migration of the Negro.* This monumental 60-painting epic chronicled the mass movement of African Americans that had begun about 25 years earlier, bringing hundreds of thousands of people from the rural South to the cities of the North. In creating the paintings, Lawrence dug deeply into his own family's experiences and the lives of his Harlem neighbors. Exhibited at the Downtown Gallery in Manhattan in late 1941, *The Migration of the Negro* was a monumental success. Parts of the series were reprinted in magazines and exhibited at prestigious museums, confirming Lawrence's arrival as a major American artist. His marriage to fellow artist Gwendolyn Clarine Knight made 1941 a milestone year in his personal life as well.

After serving in the Coast Guard during World War II, Lawrence returned to work, creating a number of new series. His subjects included the life of the abolitionist John Brown; his wartime experiences; life in the postwar South; and episodes from American history. During the 1950s, Lawrence began teaching at a variety of institutions, including the Art Students League and Brandeis University. At this point the Civil Rights movement became the main focus of his work, inspiring paintings such as *The Ordeal of Alice,* which evokes the anguish of a young black tormented by segregationists.

In 1970, Lawrence relocated to Seattle, where he was appointed to a professorship at the University of Washington. Major retrospectives of his work were mounted by the Whitney Museum of American Art in 1974 and the Seattle Art Museum in 1986. Lawrence was elected to the American Academy of Arts and Letters in 1984, and the following year the Washington State Senate recognized his contributions with a special citation. He died June 9, 2000.

Further Reading: *Jacob Lawrence,* by Richard Powell, New York: Rizzoli, 1992; *Jacob Lawrence: American Painter,* by Ellen Harkins Wheat, Seattle: University of Washington Press, 1990; *The Great Migration: An American Story,* by Jacob Lawrence (illustrator), New York: HarperCollins, 1993; *Toussaint L'Ouverture,* by Walter Dean Myers, illustrated by Jacob Lawrence, New York: Simon & Schuster, 1996.

—P. K.

❖ LEDBETTER, HUDDIE ("Leadbelly")
(1885–1949), *singer, composer*

Huddie Ledbetter was best known as "Leadbelly," a play on his name and a reference to his powerful bass voice. His songs, popular during his lifetime, continue to be sung today. "Rock Island Line," "Midnight Special," and "Good Night, Irene" all became popular American standards, widely and frequently performed throughout the 1950s and 1960s.

Leadbelly was also a symbolic figure who represented the black blues tradition as well as the difficulties of southern blacks. His prison record and his time spent on a chain gang were incorporated into the legend of the black singer-songwriter.

Huddie Ledbetter was born in 1885, of mixed black and Cherokee ancestry, to Wess and Sallie (Pugh) Ledbetter, a farming couple in rural Mooringsport, Louisiana. His mother led the church choir and gave him music lessons; his father's brothers taught him the accordion.

The young Ledbetter got into trouble at an early age. In 1900, his childhood sweetheart had a daughter, and although Ledbetter was the father, he refused to marry her. Then he dropped out of school to work on the family farm.

At 16, Ledbetter was already known as the best singer and guitarist in Louisiana. He married another woman, Lethe, with whom he worked on Texas farms during the summers. In the winters, however, he played in the red-light district of Dallas, where his reputation as a singer grew. He picked up several songs from the famous blues player Blind Lemon JEFFERSON.

Although Ledbetter—now known as Leadbelly—was married, he continued to associate with many women, and once even attacked a woman who resisted his advances. This led to a sentence of a year on the chain gang, from which Ledbetter escaped. He was later caught and convicted again, this time for murder and assault to murder another woman. He escaped a second time, was again re-sentenced to a term on a prison farm, escaped a third time, and once again was recaptured. In 1920, he was put to work on the chain gang of the Central State Farm, near Houston. He was known as the strongest, fastest worker of all the prisoners.

Leadbelly continued to sing, drawing the attention of visitors to the prison. Both the publicity and a song Leadbelly wrote, asking for mercy, influenced Governor Pat M. Neff to pardon him in 1925.

From 1926 to 1930, Leadbelly kept singing and working on his music. He also worked at an oil refinery. But in 1930, he was sentenced to another 10-year prison term, convicted of assaulting five men with intent to kill.

Once again, Leadbelly was lead man on the chain gang. And again, he won a pardon, in 1934.

His efforts had been helped by Alan Lomax, a folk singer and scholar, who recorded his song, "Good Night, Irene," while Leadbelly was still in prison. They traveled together after that, visiting prisons, where Leadbelly would sing, and then encourage prisoners to sing their own songs, so that Lomax could collect them and perhaps publish them. Leadbelly also sang in local bars along the way.

Eventually, Leadbelly returned with Lomax to New York, where he became well known in fashionable circles. Ironically, his manner and way of speaking were so different from those of the New York audiences whom he entertained that many literally could not understand his words. Yet they were moved by his music—and Leadbelly learned to explain what his songs were saying to this new audience.

In 1935, Lomax arranged for Leadbelly's companion, Martha Promise, to come north for their wedding. Although Leadbelly never stopped his womanizing, the couple stayed together. Leadbelly tried to survive financially as a folk singer in New York and Hollywood. His performances went well, but music studios were reluctant to make recordings, since they felt his music lacked commercial value.

Leadbelly died in 1949 of Lou Gehrig's disease, or amytrophic lateral sclerosis. His life was the subject of much controversy. There were those who looked on him as a heroic figure and others who regarded him as a common criminal. Whatever they thought of his personal life, however, critics agreed that his music was powerful and influential, affecting such later singers as Pete Seeger, Bob Dylan, and Paul McCartney.

Further Reading: *The Leadbelly Legend: A Collection of World Famous Songs,* by John and Alan Lomax, New York: Folkways Music, 1965; *The Blues Revival,* by Bob Groom, London: Studio Vista, 1971; *Midnight Special,* by Richard Garvin, New York: B. Geis Associates, 1971.

—R. K.

❖ LEE, CANADA
(Lionel Cornelius Canegata)
(1907–1952), *actor*

Canada Lee was a leading black theater and film actor of the 1940s and 1950s, whose career was ended by the Hollywood blacklist. His films included Alfred Hitchcock's *Lifeboat* and Robert Rossen's *Body and Soul.* He was known for his dignified presence, a rare image for black screen actors in mainstream films of that time.

The blacklist—a policy initiated by the Hollywood movie studios in the early 1950s to refuse employment to anyone who had ever participated in left-wing political activity—ended Lee's career and probably led to his death. With the exception of Paul ROBESON, no other black American actor was so openly and adversely affected by the blacklist.

Canada Lee was born on May 3, 1907, in Harlem. He was the son of James Cornelius Lee and Lydia (Whaley) Canegata Lee. He grew up as a boyhood friend of future congressman Adam Clayton POWELL, JR. Lee studied violin as a child, and played in a major student concert at age 14, but then he ran away from home, leaving behind his musical studies.

He became a jockey at the racetrack in Saratoga, New York. After two years in that profession, and two years as a horse trainer, he returned home. He had become too tall and heavy to ride horses, and he had run out of money.

Lee then took up prize-fighting, and, as a professional, he became a leading contender for the welterweight championship and lost only 25 fights out of more than 200. However, in 1933, a blow to the head resulted in a detached retina, and Lee left boxing.

For a time, Lee returned to music. In 1934, he had his own band, but it wasn't doing well financially. In that year, the Works Progress Administration (WPA), a federal program that supported theatrical projects to generate employment, was producing a show at the Harlem YMCA. Lee tried out, got a part, and decided to become an actor.

He was 28. Unable to make a living in the theater, he became a stevedore, or dockworker, but he kept acting. In 1936, he appeared in the Federal Theater's all-black production of *Macbeth,* known as *Voodoo Macbeth,* which was produced by John Houseman and Orson Welles. He also appeared in *Haiti,* starring prominent black actor Rex Ingram, and in *Stevedore,* a play about dockworkers. In 1939, he appeared in *Mamba's Daughters,* which starred Ethel WATERS.

Lee's breakthrough came in 1941, when he played Bigger Thomas in John Houseman's and Orson Welles's Broadway adaptation of Richard WRIGHT's *Native Son.* The *New York Times* called his work "the most vital piece of acting on the current stage."

He appeared as a sailor in *South Pacific* in 1943, in *Anna Lucasta* in 1944, and in Shakespeare's *The Tempest* in 1945, playing the "primitive" character of Caliban. In 1946, he played in *The Duchess of Malfi,* a John Webster's classic, in whiteface.

Lee was also being cast in films, most notably, Hitchcock's *Lifeboat* (1944), Rossen's *Body and Soul* (1947), and Alfred L. Werker's *Lost Boundaries* (1949). Critics were intrigued by Lee's aloofness and by his portrayal of an outsider bravely meeting difficult circumstances with dignity.

Lee met with difficult circumstances of his own when the Hollywood blacklist began to keep so-called radicals out of work. The blacklisters were mainly concerned with preventing those who had been associated with the Communist Party from working. Many people considered it against their principles to publicly answer questions about their political affiliations, believing such questions were an invasion of privacy and in contradiction to American principles of political freedom. Lee tried to maintain such a stand, but finally, he announced at a 1949 press conference that "I am not a Communist or a joiner of any kind."

Nevertheless, he was still considered "controversial," and was turned down for many parts. Lee had married Juanita Waller, with whom he had two children, but he was unable to support himself or his family. One writer believes that Lee had been kept out of almost 40 productions by 1952. In desperation, he attacked leading black actor Paul Robeson, who was also being accused of Communist ties. Even this attack did not convince conservative industry heads that Lee was "safe."

Finally, in 1952, Lee got work in *Cry, the Beloved Country,* a film criticizing apartheid in South Africa. He costarred with Sidney POITIER. After this film, however, Lee found no more work—and his health was declining, largely as a result of the pressure he was experiencing.

Sidney Poitier recalls that in the last weeks of his life, Lee insisted on going to White Plains, New York, to support some black people who had suffered an injustice. Since his pockets were empty, Lee walked the 15 miles from New York City to the suburb of White Plains. Poitier was later asked to sign a statement attacking Robeson and Lee, but declined because he had too much admiration and respect for the two men.

On May 9, 1952, Lee died of a heart attack. His son, Carl Vincent Lee, also became an actor.

Further Reading: *Blacks in American Films and Television,* by Donald Bogle, New York: Simon & Schuster, 1989 ed.; *Naming Names,* by Victor Navasky, New York: Viking Press, 1980.

—R. K.

❖ LEE, SHELTON JACKSON ("Spike")
(1957–), *filmmaker*

One of the major talents in modern American cinema, Spike Lee has been described as brilliant, original, provocative, outspoken, and controversial. In films such as *Do the Right Thing, Jungle Fever,* and *Malcolm X,* Lee has explored the meaning of the African-American experience and has confronted the poisonous effects of racism on American society.

Lee was born on March 20, 1957, in Atlanta, Georgia, but his family moved to the Fort Greene section of Brooklyn when he was a small child. As the son of a jazz musician and a schoolteacher, Lee (along with his five younger siblings) grew up in a vibrant, cultured atmosphere. After attending John Dewey High School, he enrolled in Atlanta's prestigious Morehouse College in 1975, majoring in mass communications. Lee made his first film, a 45-minute student documentary entitled *Last Hustle in Brooklyn,* in 1977. Upon graduating from Morehouse in 1979, Lee entered New York University's (NYU) Graduate Film School, where he became a teach-

Spike Lee (*Bob Grant/Fotos International/Archive Photos*)

ing assistant as well as a student. Lee's senior project at NYU, *Joe's Bed-Stuy Barbershop: We Cut Heads* (1982), was showcased at New York's Lincoln Center and won a Student Academy Award from the Academy of Motion Picture Arts and Sciences.

Despite his obvious talent, Lee could not obtain a contract from any of the major movie studios, who were clearly not ready to deal with a young, outspoken black filmmaker. Lee decided to make films on his own. After scraping together $125,000 from a variety of sources, Lee completed *She's Gotta Have It*, a comedy about a Brooklyn woman with three boyfriends. (In addition to directing, Lee wrote the screenplay and played the role of Mars Blackmon.) Released by Island Films in 1986, *She's Gotta Have It* won a prize at France's prestigious Cannes Film Festival and became a major hit in U.S. movie theaters.

Lee was now able to get funding from the major studios, and in 1988 he released *School Daze*, a humorous look at African-American college life (complete with musical numbers composed by his father, Bill). He then

established himself as a major American filmmaker with *Do the Right Thing* (1989), a powerful drama about explosive racial tensions in a Brooklyn neighborhood. Lee followed up with *Jungle Fever* (1991), the story of an ill-fated interracial romance, and then turned his attention to an epic film biography of the political leader Malcolm X. Shot in Harlem, upstate New York, and the Middle East, *Malcolm X* was a massive undertaking; at one point, the studio was about to cut off Lee's funding, but he managed to complete the film with contributions from leading African-American celebrities such as Bill Cosby and Oprah Winfrey.

Though *Malcolm X* ranks as the high point of his career, Lee was not prepared to rest on his laurels. His later projects have included *Crooklyn* (1994), a nostalgic look at his Brooklyn childhood; *Clockers* (1995), a hard-hitting drama about the urban drug scene; and *4 Little Girls* (1997), a documentary about the 1963 bombing of a black church in Birmingham, Alabama; *Get on the Bus* (1997), the fictional story of a group of men taking a bus to the Million Man March; and *He Got Game* (1998), a movie about basketball. Among his long-term projects is a film biography of baseball great Jackie ROBINSON.

Lee's wide-ranging career has also included numerous television commercials (notably a series of Nike spots featuring Michael Jordan) and music videos with artists such as Tracy Chapman and Stevie Wonder. Throughout all these various projects, Lee has maintained his solidarity with the black community. His production company, Forty Acres and a Mule, is based in the Fort Greene section of Brooklyn, where he still lives, and he has always worked to provide jobs and training for residents of the neighborhood. He is also a lifelong fan of the New York Knickerbockers—nearly every home game at Madison Square Garden finds Lee in his courtside seat, cheering on his team and razzing the opposition.

Further Reading: *Spike Lee,* by James Earl Hardy, New York: Chelsea House, 1996; *Toms, Coons, Mulattoes, Mammies, and Bucks: An Interpretive History of Blacks in American Film,* by Donald Bogle, New York: Continuum, 1989 (revised edition); *Best Seat in the House: A Basketball Memoir,* by Spike Lee, with Ralph Wiley, New York: Crown, 1997.

—*P. K.*

❖ LEIDESDORFF, WILLIAM ALEXANDER
(1810–1848), *California pioneer, entrepreneur*

William Leidesdorff acquired thousands of acres of California land during the time when Mexico still owned that territory. He settled in San Francisco as that city was being founded, becoming town treasurer and a member of the City Council and the school board. Named in his honor is Leidesdorff Street in today's downtown San Francisco.

Leidesdorff was born in 1810, in the Danish West Indies, to a Danish planter father and a mother of mixed ancestry. When quite young, his father sent him and his two brothers to the United States, where they worked in his cotton business. Leidesdorff preferred shipping, and in 1841, he landed in California as skipper of a large schooner.

From 1841 to 1845, Leidesdorff did business in San Francisco, and traveled back and forth to the West Indies. He acquired a 35,000-acre ranch near Sutter's Mill in 1844. In that same year, he became a Mexican citizen—a strategic move, since Mexico still controlled the California territory.

Nonetheless, the next year, the American consul named Leidesdorff as his vice consul, although theoretically, only another American citizen should have held that post.

Leidesdorff continued to amass land in San Francisco. In 1846, Captain John Montgomery brought 70 U.S. Marines to San Francisco, claiming the land for the United States. Legend has it that Leidesdorff translated Montgomery's announcement of U.S. ownership into Spanish so that the Mexican residents could understand they were under the rule of a new country.

United States rule didn't stop Leidesdorff from prospering. On the contrary, in 1846 he opened a hotel and the following year bought a house where he lived out his days. Leidesdorff maintained his association with shipping, and, reportedly, launched the first steamship to sail in San Francisco Bay.

While Leidesdorff was on the school planning committee, San Francisco opened its first public school in 1848. Leidesdorff probably also staged the first formal horse race in California. He was known to be flamboyant, jealous, and quick-tempered, but a fair and honest businessperson.

On May 18, 1848, 38-year-old Leidesdorff died from typhus—just two months after the gold rush had begun. By the time his will was settled, his property had risen in value to more than a million dollars.

Further Reading: *The Negro Trail Blazers of California,* by Delilah L. Beasley, New York: Negro Universities Press, 1969.

—R. K.

❖ LESTER, JULIUS BERNARD
(1939–   ), writer, musician, folklorist, historian

Julius Lester has had a varied career, focusing his work on the creation and understanding of black culture. At first a professional musician, then a scholar and critic, Lester is known for his collections of black folktales and his writings on black history. His books have been nominated for the National Book Award; and the Newbery Award for best children's book of the year. As a teacher, he has won several awards and "professor of the year" citations.

Julius Lester was born on January 27, 1939, in St. Louis, Missouri, the son of Julia (Smith) Lester and W. D. Lester, a minister—which gave him early contact with the organized black church.

His first work as a professional musician was recorded by Vanguard Records. From 1966 through 1968, he was director of the prestigious Newport Folk Festival (in Rhode Island).

In 1968, Lester gained a certain notoriety for his controversial book *Look Out Whitey! Black Power's Gon' Get Your Mama!* (New York: Dial Press, 1968), an analysis of the Black Power movement of that decade, and of white people's fear of it.

Lester married Joan Steinau, a researcher, in 1962. The couple had two children, Jody Simone and Malcolm Coltrane, but were divorced in 1970. In 1979, Lester married Alida Carolyn Fechner, with whom he had a son, David Julius.

Lester then began to establish a new career as a professor of Afro-American Studies and of Near Eastern and Judaic Studies at Amherst College in Amherst, Massachusetts. Lester also began to work as a folklorist and historian, writing such books as *Black Folktales* (New York: Grove Press, 1969); and *Search for the New Land: History as Subjective Experience* (New York: Grove Press, 1968). *Black Folktales* was considered particularly important at the time for including African legends as well as American slave tales.

Lester's books for young people include *To Be a Slave* (New York: Dial Press, 1968); *Young and Black In America* (New York: Random House, 1970), an anthology he collected with Rae Pace Alexander; and *The Long Journey Home: Stories from Black History* (New York: Dial Press, 1993). He has gathered and presented many other black folktales, including the tales of Uncle Remus. Originally, these tales were collected by the white writer Joel Chandler Harris; Lester wanted to recapture the stories' original black perspective.

Lester's contribution in both history and folklore is directed toward creating what he calls a "usable past." That is, he wants black people of all ages to understand their history and culture, so they can use it as a basis for action in the future. Historian Eric Foner and critic Naomi Foner once wrote a review of Lester for *The New York Review of Books,* in which they commented that his work gives young readers "a sense of history which will help shape their lives and politics."

Lester's books have been translated into seven languages. They have been praised by numerous authors, black and white. The Foners note in particular that "Lester does not feel it is necessary to make every black man and woman a superhero." Yet Lester's view of what he calls "history from the bottom up" shows the real heroism of ordinary people in difficult circumstances.

Further Reading: *From Slave Ship to Freedom Road,* by Julius Lester, New York: Dial Books for Young Readers, 1998; *And All Our Wounds Forgiven,* by Julius Lester, San Diego, Calif.: Harvest Books, 1996; *You and Me,* by Seymour Krim, New York: Holt, Rinehart & Winston, 1974; *All is Well: An Autobiography,* by Julius Lester, New York: William Morrow, 1976; *Lovesong: Becoming a Jew,* New York: Bulfinch Press, 1995.

—*R. K.*

❖ LEWIS, MARY EDMONIA (Wildfire)
(c. 1845–c. 1890), *sculptor*

Edmonia Lewis achieved renown as an accomplished sculptor during a period when very few women or African Americans of either sex were working in that medium. She created both full-length figures and busts. Critics of her time admired her *Death of Cleopatra,* writing that it "could only have been produced by a sculptor of very genuine endowments."

Many wealthy businesspeople in Europe and America bought Lewis's work. Her sculpture was commissioned by the prestigious Union League Club and may be seen today at the Harvard College Library in Boston, the Moorland-Spingarn Research Center of Howard University in Washington, D.C., and the Carver Museum of Tuskegee Institute in Alabama.

Edmonia Lewis is believed to have been born in 1845, in Greenwich, New York, the daughter of a Chippewa Indian mother and an African-American father. Her given name was Wildfire.

Her mother died when Wildfire was about three; the following year, her father left her to be raised with two Indian aunts. As the little girl grew up, she created and sold beaded moccasins and baskets in upstate New York.

Wildfire's brother Sunrise was a successful gold miner in California, and his financial aid enabled her to attend school, first in Albany, New York, then at Oberlin College in Ohio. There she changed her name to Mary Edmonia Lewis.

Oberlin was known for being receptive to black and minority students, yet prejudice continued to be a problem there. Lewis was accused of poisoning two white classmates in 1862. She was exonerated of the charges due to insufficient evidence but, nevertheless, she left Oberlin and went to live in Boston.

Through the abolitionist William Lloyd Garrison, Lewis met Edmund Brackett, a local sculptor who became her teacher. By 1864, she was selling small medallions of abolitionist leaders and war heroes. Then she did a bust of the leader of the Union Army's first black regiment, Colonel Robert Gould Shaw. Garrison helped Lewis to sell her work, and with help from other friends, she was able to study in Rome.

Lewis worked well in Rome. One of her best-known early marbles was the 1867 *Forever Free,* depicting a black couple hearing the news of the end of slavery. At present, that work is at Howard University.

Lewis exhibited her work in Chicago in 1870, Rome in 1871, and Philadelphia in 1876. She was interested in female figures believed in the 19th century to have been black, as evidenced by *Hagar in Her Despair in the Wilderness* (1868) and *Death of Cleopatra* (1876). Her works sold well, some for several thousand dollars each.

Rome in those years had a lively social circle of American artists and their famous visitors, and Lewis soon became part of this group. She began to receive commissions for her work. In 1870, for example, she was commissioned to do a lifesize statue of John Brown for New York's Union League Club. In general, she was able to sell most of her work.

In this Roman "artist colony," many of the women, Lewis included, wore male clothing. This created a scandal, but the women claimed that it gave them more freedom. It left their arms and legs more room to move, they said, and liberated them from women's customary, tightly laced corsets, which impeded breathing and led to fatigue.

Sculpting is physically demanding work. Lewis was known for her ability to work directly from marble, rather than making models first. This is extremely difficult work and requires great technical precision as well as physical strength.

Lewis worked in the neoclassical style, similar to that developed by the ancient Greeks and Romans. This style of work had been out of favor for many years, but when Lewis began sculpting, its popularity was revived.

Lewis received her last major commission in 1883 from a Baltimore church. (She had converted to Catholicism in Rome in 1868.) After 1885, little is known of her life, and although she is mentioned in the 1911 *American Catholic Who's Who* (which has her living in Italy), it is likely that she died in 1890.

Further Reading: *American Negro Art,* by Cedric Dover, Greenwich, Conn.: New York Graphic Society, 1960; *The Negro in Art,* by Alain Locke, New York: Hacker Books, 1971 revision of 1940 ed.

—R. K.

❖ LOCKE, ALAIN LEROY
(1886–1954), *philosopher, educator*

Alain Locke was the first black Rhodes scholar, recipient of an award that represents both a high level of student academic achievement and outstanding performance in extracurricular activities, such as athletics. After Locke, no black person was thus honored until the 1960s, when civil rights protests helped to once again make this opportunity available to black students.

Locke achieved prominence as a teacher, philosopher, and writer. He was the first black president of the National Council of Adult Education. His book, *The New Negro* (New York: A. & C. Boni, 1925; Arno Press, 1968 reprint), a collection of new black writing published in 1925, was an influential work of the Harlem Renaissance—the movement of black writers and artists in the 1920s that helped to create a new definition of black culture. Locke's writings on black history, music, and art helped to promote and influence the development of black culture in America.

Alain LeRoy Locke was born on September 13, 1885, in Philadelphia, into a genteel and well-educated family, the son of Pliny Ishmael Locke and Mary (Hawkins) Locke. When Locke was six years old, his father died and his mother supported the family by teaching. Locke was sent to an Ethical Culture school. These institutions provided an alternate, experimental form of education that pioneered many modern ideas about teaching—particularly in the exposure of students to ethical philosophy, and humanistic values. At that time, such educational experiments were quite rare.

As a child, Locke became seriously ill with rheumatic fever, which permanently damaged his heart. He dealt with his restricted physical condition by turning to books and music.

He attended Central High School in Philadelphia, then entered Harvard University in Cambridge, completing its curriculum in a remarkable three years instead of four. He won the school's most prestigious award, the Bowdoin Prize for an essay in English, and was elected to Phi Beta Kappa, the national honor society. He also graduated magna cum laude. In 1993, Henry Louis GATES, JR., chair of the Department of Afro-American Studies at Harvard University, established the Alain Locke Prize in Locke's honor.

Locke graduated from Harvard in 1907, only three years after Cecil Rhodes had established his famous scholarship. Thus, he became one of the first Rhodes Scholars, a distinction that was cited throughout his life as evidence of black academic achievement. Locke's accomplishment was even more significant in light of the many "scientific" efforts to prove that black people were intellectually inferior. Locke became an exemplary proponent of the view that black students with opportunities would perform well.

With his Rhodes scholarship, Locke now had the funds to attend Oxford University in England. The scholarship did not guarantee acceptance into the university, which was organized into many separate colleges, each of which made its own admissions decisions. Because of his race, Locke was turned away by five colleges at Oxford before he found one that would accept him. From 1907 to 1910, he studied at Oxford's Hertford College, where he became founder and secretary of the African Union Society. This was the basis for Locke's later ties with Africa and the Caribbean.

From 1910 to 1911, he studied at the University of Berlin. His European experience heightened his interest in modern art, music, and writing.

In 1912, Locke began to teach at Howard University in Washington, D.C., which had become a center for black intellectual life. He had his own ideas about education, however, and in 1915, he petitioned for a groundbreaking course on the subject of race. The university saw itself as nonracial, and refused, so Locke taught the course through the auspices of the National Association for the Advancement of Colored People (NAACP). In his course, he argued that racial inequalities are caused by economic and social factors.

Locke went to study and teach at Harvard University, receiving a doctorate from there in 1918. He also taught at Howard University from 1912 to 1924, during which time he went to Egypt to conduct archaeological studies.

At the same time, J. Stanley Durkee, Howard's white president, was in conflict with students and teachers on several issues. Students alleged that Durkee acted arbitrarily, while faculty protested the way salaries and academic rank were awarded. In 1925, Locke and many other professors were fired. Although the university claimed that the firings were simply a part of the efficient reorganization of the school, others believed that the school was losing some of its best scholars—and possibly treating them unfairly.

He continued to write articles for both newspapers and research journals, and in 1925, he published his collection, *The New Negro*. This book made Locke the spokesperson of "The New Negro Movement," the effort to win full integration of black people into all areas of American life.

Since Locke was no longer employed, he needed a patron—someone who would offer financial support for his intellectual work. Locke began to receive funds from Charlotte Mason, a wealthy white woman. She helped to pay for Locke's trips to Europe and for his collection of African art. He, in turn, was Mason's guide in her talent hunt for other artists to support—such as Langston HUGHES, Zora Neale HURSTON, and Richmond BARTHÉ—and assisted her in eliciting the kind of work from these artists that was in conformity with her tastes.

Clearly, Mason did not give her aid without restrictions. In Locke's case, she influenced his thinking about race. Mason was intrigued by what she saw as the "exotic" nature of African culture, and under her influence, Locke began to talk about an "African temperament" that seemed to be racially inherited, rather than a result of historical and economic conditions, as he had emphasized earlier.

Hurston and Hughes found Mason's influence oppressive and eventually broke with her. Locke remained loyal until her death, but by the mid-1930s, he had rejected her mystical ideas about racial temperament and returned to his own more scientific way of thinking.

Locke himself had become disillusioned with the New Negro movement that he had helped to start. In 1939, he wrote that the movement had become egotistical and false, a cover for people who used the idea of race either to gain fame or to hide their own inferiority. He now believed that "racial" art was in fact "universal" art, so that young artists did not need to choose between writing about their own racial experiences and creating "universal" works.

Alain Locke (*National Archives*)

By 1928, Locke had returned to Howard University, under its first black president, Mordecai Johnson. He continued to promote the study of race relations and Africa, although Howard University did not adopt an African studies program until 1954. Nevertheless, he worked on establishing and improving Howard's social science division, which pioneered many important studies of race. Locke also assisted in the reform of the university's general curriculum.

In the 1930s, Locke helped to initiate a series of "Bronze Booklets" by leading black scholars, for making information about black history and culture more readily available to the average reader. Locke himself wrote *The Negro and His Music* (Port Washington, N.Y.: Kennikat, 1968), *Negro Art: Past and Present* (Washington, D.C.: Associates in Negro Folk Education, 1936), and *The Negro in Art: A Pictorial Record of the Negro Artist and the Negro Theme in Art* (New York: Hacker Art Books, 1971).

Throughout the 1930s and 1940s, Locke continued to study philosophy, anthropology, and culture. In 1942, he coedited *When Peoples Meet: A Study in Race and Culture Contacts* (New York: Hinds, Hayden & Eldridge, 1946 ed.). By the end of World War II, Locke was one of America's best-known black scholars.

After the war, Locke taught at the University of Wisconsin, the New School for Social Research, and City College of New York. He also worked on *The Negro in American Culture* (New York: Knopf, 1957), a book that was completed by another editor after his death.

In 1953, Locke moved to New York. There, on June 9, 1954, he died—victim, finally, of his recurring heart condition. In 1994, the Alain Leroy Locke Society was founded in Boston as part of the American Philosophical Association, to promote Locke's work.

Further Reading: *Alain Locke and Philosophy: A Quest for Cultural Pluralism,* by Johnny Washington, Westport, Conn.: Greenwood Publishing Group, 1968; *Philosophy of Alain Locke: Harlem Renaissance and Beyond,* ed. by Leonard Harris, Philadelphia: Temple University Press, 1991; *Alain Locke: Reflections on a Modern Renaissance Man,* by Russell J. Linnemann, Baton Rouge: Louisiana State University, 1982; *From the Dark Tower: Afro-American Writers 1900–1960,* by Arthur P. Davis, Washington, D.C.: Howard University Press, 1974 (see pp. 51–60, 240–244).

—*R. K.*

❖ LOUIS, JOE (Joseph Louis Barrow)
(1914–1981), *boxing champion*

Rated by many experts as the greatest heavyweight champion of all time, Louis dominated the world of boxing from 1937 to 1949. Over that span of time, the man known as the Brown Bomber defended his title against all comers, bringing a new sense of pride and accomplishment to African Americans.

Born Joseph Louis Barrow in Lafayette, Alabama, on May 13, 1914, Louis was the youngest of eight children. (He shortened his name when he began his boxing career.) While Louis was still very young, his father deserted the family. Louis's mother, Lilly, took her children north to Detroit, where the family lived in dire poverty. Under these circumstances, Louis had little chance to gain an education; he dropped out of school after the fifth grade and began to work. In his spare time, he began sparring in a local recreation center. At the age of 18, while working on the assembly line at an automobile plant, Louis decided to take up boxing seriously.

The powerful young fighter made an immediate impact in the ring. During his two years as an amateur, he knocked out 43 of 54 opponents and won the national amateur light-heavyweight championship. After signing a contract with promoter Mike Jacobs, Louis quit his job and turned professional in 1934. Winning his first 27 fights (23 by knockout), he earned more than $350,000. His only defeat came on June 19, 1936, when he was beaten by the German heavyweight Max Schmeling, who had detected a flaw in Louis's technique. Louis bounced back quickly from this setback, winning seven more bouts in a row. Finally, on June 22, 1937, Louis got a shot at the title. He made the most of it, knocking out heavyweight champion James J. Braddock in the eighth round.

Louis was a remarkably active champion, successfully defending his title 25 times over a span of 12 years while African Americans cheered his every move. His greatest moment came in 1938, when he engaged in a rematch with Schmeling. Germany's Nazi rulers had been jubilant over Schmeling's previous victory, boasting that an "inferior" black man could never beat a member of the "master race." When Louis stepped into the ring to face Schmeling on June 22 in New York's Yankee Stadium, he was fighting not only for the honor of African Americans but for everyone who detested the Nazis and their ideas. This time Louis had trained intensely, and he pounced on Schmeling as soon as the bell rang. Caught in a devastating barrage of punches, the German went to the canvas four times before the referee stopped the bout, after only two minutes and four seconds. Louis was now a national hero, and his name became synonymous with strength and toughness.

When the United States went to war with Germany and Japan in 1941, Louis joined the U.S. Army. He could have been an officer, but with his customary modesty he chose to be an ordinary enlisted man. Working with fellow soldier Jackie ROBINSON, he set up integrated athletic programs for the troops, helped raise money for military benefit programs, and put on boxing exhibitions for soldiers and sailors. When the war ended in 1945, Louis was discharged by the army with a special commendation for meritorious service.

Louis returned to the ring on June 9, 1946, knocking out challenger Billy Conn in the eighth round, but it was clear to fans that he had lost something during his four-year layoff. After three more title defenses, Louis retired as the undefeated champion in 1949. He attempted a comeback in 1950 but lost a decision to the new champion, Ezzard Charles; following a knockout by future champion Rocky Marciano in 1951, Louis retired for good. During his unparalleled career, he compiled a record of 68 wins and 3 losses, with 54 knockouts.

Further Reading: *Joe Louis: My Life,* by Joe Louis with Edna and Art Rust, Jr., Hopewell, N.J.: Ecco Press, 1996; *Champion: Joe Louis, Black Hero in White America,* by Chris Mead, New York: Scribner, 1985; *Joe Louis: Heavyweight Champion,* by Robert Jakoubek, New York: Chelsea House Publishers, 1989; *Joe Louis,* by Jim Campbell, San Diego, Calif.: Lucent Books, 1997.

—*P. K.*

✤ McCOY, ELIJAH
(1843–1929), *inventor*

Elijah McCoy, a well-known inventor, is believed by many to be the person behind the famous phrase "the real McCoy," meaning the real thing. McCoy acquired more than 57 patents. His inventions were primarily the lubricating parts of a steam engine. His lubrication system was so popular that customers would ask if they were buying "the real McCoy."

Elijah McCoy was born in 1843, in Colchester, Ontario, Canada. His parents were fugitive slaves who had fled Kentucky for Canada. His father, George McCoy, served in the Canadian army. His mother, Mildred (Goins) McCoy, raised 12 children, including Elijah.

Elijah McCoy first went to school in Canada, then in Edinburgh, Scotland. He apprenticed himself to a mechanical engineer there, then went to Detroit to learn more about engineering.

In Detroit, he ran into severe discrimination and was unable to find employment as an engineer. Instead, he began as a fireman (the person who maintains the engine) on the Michigan Central Railroad.

This proved to be fateful, since one of his duties was to oil the engine. The long, demanding job had to be done by hand—until McCoy began to develop a means for the engine to lubricate itself. After two years of experimenting, he came up with his first automatic lubricator in 1872.

From then on, McCoy developed many other inventions. He continued to develop other types of lubricators, but as he could not afford to refine these ideas himself, he had the patents assigned to others who would fund him. This gave McCoy the opportunity to work—but it meant that others would make huge profits from his creations.

McCoy developed a folding ironing board and invented traction-increasing tread—in the form of corrugated ridges—for tires. He also invented a lawn sprinkler, a device to support the top of a buggy, and a basic support for scaffolding.

By the time of his death, McCoy had been granted 42 patents—yet he had very little in the way of material reward to show for his genius. By 1926, his health began to fail. Tired and discouraged, McCoy went to live in the Eloise Infirmary, a nursing home in Michigan, where he died in 1929.

Further Reading: *African-American Inventors: Lonnie Johnson, Frederick McKinley Jones, Marjorie Stewart Joyner, Elijah McCoy, Garrett Augustus Morgan,* by Fred M. B. Amram and Jetty Kahn, Minneapolis, Minn.: Capstone Press, 1996; *Eight Black American Inventors,* by Robert Hayden, Reading, Mass.: Addison-Wesley, 1972; *The Negro Vanguard,* by Richard Bardolph, New York: Rinehart, 1961.

—R. K.

❖ McCULLOUGH, GERALDINE HAMILTON
(1922–   ), sculptor

Geraldine McCullough's sculpture has won numerous awards, including a gold medal from the 159th annual exhibit at the Pennsylvania Academy of Fine Arts, a first place in an exhibit of alumni from Chicago's Art Institute School, and first place in an Atlanta Life Insurance competition. Her work—huge welded metallic structures weighing hundreds of pounds—is known for its depiction of strength and power. Her art is also known for its implicit but unmistakable commitment to social change. She says that her sculpture portrays "the universal struggle of people, their wrestling with adversity, their eventual triumph and the perfection that resulted from their struggle."

Geraldine McCullough was born on December 1, 1922, in the little town of Kingston, Arkansas, although she lived in Chicago from the age of three. By 1948, she had earned a degree in art education from Chicago's Art Institute and in 1955, a master's degree as well.

She received many honors while at the Art Institute, including two scholarships and a citation for her painting. She then taught for 14 years at Wendell Phillips High School in Chicago, while continuing with her artistic endeavors. Her husband, Lester McCullough, a professional welder, taught her how to weld and to work with the heavy metal objects she created. In 1963, McCullough debuted as a sculptor at the Century of Negro Progress Exposition in Chicago.

Only one year later, in 1964, she won the gold medal at the Pennsylvania Academy of Fine Arts competition in Philadelphia. This was a special triumph because the exhibition was by invitation only. McCullough entered it without an invitation—and won.

This honor brought McCullough quick acknowledgment, and there were pieces written about her in *Time, Ebony,* and *Chicago* magazines. She made guest appearances on television shows, and in 1966, she was officially invited to visit the Soviet Union.

McCullough continued to create and exhibit her sculpture. She also taught at Rosary College in River Forest, Illinois, where she eventually headed the art department.

McCullough's work is marked by its social awareness. One piece, *War Dance,* suggests the dehumanizing effect of war. *Phoenix,* McCullough's prize-winning sculpture, is based on the mythical bird that continually rises from the ashes to live again. McCullough said this symbol suggested to her "The Negro, crushed so long under the weight of oppression . . . now reborn and soaring toward complete freedom . . ."

—*R. K.*

❖ McDANIEL, HATTIE
(1895–1952), actress

Hattie McDaniel was the first African American to win an Academy Award. She was Best Supporting Actress for her role as Mammy in the 1939 movie *Gone With the Wind.*

Hattie McDaniel was born in 1895 in Wichita, Kansas. Her parents were Henry McDaniel, a Baptist minister, and Susan (Holbert) McDaniel, a church singer. Hattie was the family's 13th child.

The family moved to Denver before McDaniel started school. She soon found her way to the stage, performing at age 16 as a singer in tent shows—traveling performances—in small towns. She went on to sing on the radio with Professor George Morrison's Negro Orchestra. It is thought that she was the first black woman to sing for a radio audience.

In 1924, McDaniel sang as a headliner in vaudeville. In 1931, she went to Los Angeles and worked in radio on a variety show where her title was "Hi-Hat Hattie." Later, her radio career included work on *The Amos 'n' Andy Show* and *The Eddie Cantor Show.*

However, her goal was the movies, and her film career began in 1932, with a Twentieth Century-Fox picture, *The Golden West.* From then on, she took whatever roles were available, even very small ones or those for which she would not receive screen credit.

McDaniel married four times. She was widowed once, then, 16 years later, she married and divorced Nym Langford, James Lloyd Crawford, and Larry Williams, respectively. Other members of her family, her sister Etta and her brother Sam, also worked in Hollywood films, but were not nearly as successful as she was. Her nephew Elzey Emanuel also became a film actor.

McDaniel became famous for her portrayal of the mammy figure—the proud, domineering woman who knows everything and always has a clever putdown for overbearing white people. However, her mammy figure always gave total support to her white employers, despite her grumbling—a feature that helped to make McDaniel acceptable to the white audiences of her day.

McDaniel found work in more than 70 films, including some of Hollywood's best-known movies. She also worked with some of the most prominent stars of the time, including Marlene Dietrich, Katharine Hepburn, and Jean Harlow.

One striking feature of her acting was her refusal to back down or take a servile position with a white employer on screen. Instead, she looked them straight in the eye and spoke her mind fearlessly.

When McDaniel won the Academy Award, Hollywood gossip columnist Louella Parsons wrote, "We are beginning to realize that art has no boundaries and that creed, race, or color must not interfere where credit is due." Yet when McDaniel went to the Academy Awards dinner where she was to be honored, she and her escort had to sit at a special table at the back of the room.

In the 1940s, McDaniel was criticized by the National Association for the Advancement of Colored People for her portrayals of servile black characters. McDaniel defended her characters, however, saying, "I portray the type of Negro woman who has worked honestly and proudly to give our nation the Marian ANDERSONs, Roland HAYESes and Ralph BUNCHes." McDaniel also continued to support other black people, donating her Oscar to Howard University, a major black school in Washington, D.C. She cofounded the Fair Play Committee, which sought to make gradual changes in the film industry.

Servant roles began to disappear, affecting the employment of many black actors. McDaniel continued to work, however, returning to radio in the series *Beulah*—another story of a black maid in a white family. McDaniel took over the role in 1947 and she continued to play it until she became ill in 1951. If she had lived longer, she would have played the role on television, having signed the contract just before she died of cancer in 1952.

Further Reading: *Toms, Coons, Mulattoes, Mammies and Bucks: An Interpretive History of Blacks in American Film,* by Donald Bogle, New York: Viking Press, 1973; *Blacks in American Films and Television: An Illustrated Encyclopedia,* by Donald Bogle, New York: Simon & Schuster, 1989; *The Negro in Films: Literature of the Cinema,* by Peter Nobel, New York; Arno Press, 1970.

—*R. K.*

❖ McKAY, CLAUDE
(1890–1948), *poet, fiction writer*

Claude McKay was one of the major black writers of the 1920s the time of the so-called Harlem Renaissance, a movement of black writers and artists that helped to develop a new type of black culture in the United States. His poem "If We Must Die," is a call to courage that Winston Churchill often quoted during World War II. His most popular novel was *Home to Harlem* (Boston, Mass.: Northeastern University Press, 1987 ed.), although *Banana Bottom* (New York: Harcourt, Brace,

Jovanovich, 1974 reprint of 1933 ed.) is considered his best work of fiction.

Claude McKay was born in 1890, in Clarendon Hills, a community in central Jamaica, then part of the British West Indies. His parents were prosperous peasants. At age six, he moved into the home of his brother, a schoolteacher who taught McKay about socialism and free-thinking (a school of thought that challenged conventional religion by questioning traditional morality and the existence of God).

When he was 16, McKay moved to Kingston, the Jamaican capital city. He briefly apprenticed to a trade, then he joined the police force. In Kingston, McKay met one of the many white people who were to influence his life—Edward Jekyll, a British visitor, who taught McKay much about literature and encouraged him to write poetry in the local dialect. In 1912, McKay published two books of poetry, *Songs of Jamaica* (Miami, Fla.: Mnemosyne Publishers, 1969 reprint of 1912 ed.) and *Constab Ballads* (1912).

Later that year, McKay went to Tuskegee Institute in Alabama, planning to study agriculture. But Booker T. WASHINGTON's curriculum and outlook were too limited for McKay, and the young poet spent the next two years at Kansas State College.

McKay finally gave up studying agriculture and went to New York City, where he aspired to a writing career. He supported himself there by working at odd jobs.

In his autobiography, he mentions a brief marriage, but gives no details—not so much as his wife's name. He does describe meeting two men who helped him with his writing: Frank Harris, who published McKay's poems in *Pearson's Magazine,* and Max Eastman, editor of the left-wing *Liberator* magazine, who later hired him as assistant editor.

McKay pursued his interest in politics on a 1919 trip to England. There he met Sylvia Pankhurst, the most radical and working-class-oriented of the suffragist leaders seeking equal rights for women. McKay assisted Pankhurst on her publication *Workers Dreadnaught.* And while in London, he published another book of poetry, *Spring in New Hampshire* (London: Grant Richard, 1920).

When McKay returned to New York, he brought out the book of poetry that helped to spark the Harlem Renaissance: *Harlem Shadows* (New York: Harcourt Brace & Co.), published in 1922.

McKay was absent from the United States from 1922 to 1934—a period of cultural flowering in the black community. Yet during this interim, he wrote works that were a vital part of the renaissance of African-American literature:

the novels *Home to Harlem* (1928), *Banjo* (New York: Harcourt, Brace, Jovanovich, 1970 reprint of 1929 ed.), and *Banana Bottom* (1933), and the short-story collection *Gingertown* (1932). McKay's travels took him to the Soviet Union, where he met many Communist leaders; he also lived in France, Spain, and Morocco.

McKay continued with his commitment to labor and left-wing politics after his return to the United States. He wrote about the Harlem labor movement for *American Mercury* and the *Nation*. In 1937, he published *A Long Way From Home* (New York: L. Furman, Inc.), which was his autobiography. In 1940, he published *Harlem: Negro Metropolis* (New York: E. P. Dutton).

In the winter of 1941, McKay became ill, and in 1943, he had a stroke that further weakened him. In 1944, McKay converted to Catholicism. Formerly a radical and a freethinker, he became a religious conservative and attacked many of the causes he had once defended. On May 23, 1948, Claude McKay died in a Chicago hospital.

—R. K.

❖ MARSALIS, WYNTON
(1961–), *musician*

A virtuoso trumpeter who excels at both jazz and classical music, Wynton Marsalis is one of the most dynamic figures in the world of the arts. As a band leader, composer, author, and educator, Marsalis has enriched the world's treasury of music and has confirmed the importance of jazz as an essential American art form.

Born in New Orleans, Louisiana, on October 18, 1961, Marsalis was the second of six sons in a distinguished musical family. Both his parents, Ellis and Dolores Marsalis, were gifted jazz musicians, and Wynton began to show his ability on the trumpet when he was only six years old. However, he did not really get serious about the instrument until he was 12. He then began taking formal lessons and practicing nonstop, with spectacular results. Marsalis performed with the New Orleans Philharmonic Orchestra at the age of 14, playing Haydn's Trumpet Concerto; he also played with local jazz bands and formed a rock band with his brother Branton and a few high school friends. Whenever he performed, Marsalis amazed experienced musicians and critics with his ability to play both jazz and classical music with refined technique and a genuine feel for the music.

In 1979, Marsalis won a scholarship to attend New York's famed Juilliard School of Music. During his first year, however, he was increasingly annoyed by the dismissive attitude both students and faculty took toward jazz. He spent his summer vacation touring with drummer Art Blakey and his Jazz Messengers, gaining valuable experience. Though Marsalis returned to Juilliard in the fall, he left at the end of his second year, without a degree, and joined Herbie Hancock's V.S.O.P. Quartet for an extended tour and a number of recording sessions.

Marsalis was now attracting a following among music lovers. In 1981 Columbia Records offered the 20-year-old artist a contract to record both jazz and classical music, and his debut album, *Wynton Marsalis,* appeared later in the year. The album sold 125,000 copies, a large amount for a jazz recording, and Marsalis was named Musician of the Year in the 1982 *Down Beat* magazine poll. He then formed his own quintet, which included his brother Branford on saxophone; the group released its first album, *Think of One,* in 1983, the same year Marsalis recorded his first classical album, *Trumpet Concertos.*

Marsalis was now a musical superstar, and he branched out into many new directions. Expanding his group into a septet, he began to nurture the careers of many young musicians, including the pianist Marcus Roberts and the trumpeter Roy Hargrove. He also used his popularity and prestige to organize jazz concerts and special tributes to long-established performers. In 1987, Marsalis cofounded Jazz at Lincoln Center, a regular series of concerts that brought together the biggest names in jazz and attracted widespread enthusiasm from the public.

Deeply committed to music in all its forms, Marsalis believed it was important to communicate his knowledge to young people. He began to give a series of master classes for promising musicians and also hosted regular Saturday concerts at Lincoln Center, illustrating the fundamentals of music for young audiences. These innovative sessions, recorded on videotape, were broadcast on WNET-TV in 1995 under the title *Marsalis on Music.* The following year, National Public Radio aired a 26-part series hosted by Marsalis, *Making the Music.*

Marsalis disbanded his septet at the end of 1994 and devoted himself to leading the Lincoln Center Jazz Orchestra, with which he has toured extensively. He also intensified his wide-ranging activities as a composer. Marsalis has written a number of ballet scores for major companies, including *Griot New York, Jazz: Six Syncopated Movements,* and *Jump Start.* His major jazz compositions include *Blue Interlude; In This House, On This Morning;* and *Blood on the Fields,* the first jazz composition to win the Pulitzer Prize for Music (1997). Marsalis has also composed a string quartet, "Octoroon's

Wynton Marsalis (*Deborah Feingold/Archive Photos*)

Ball," which had its world premiere in 1995, and he has written numerous scores for films and television shows. His achievements have earned him honorary music degrees and a variety of other awards, including several Grammys. In 1998 he released a new album *The Midnight Blues—Standard Time,* featuring Marsalis performing with a 31-piece string orchestra.

Further Information: *Marsalis on Music,* by Wynton Marsalis, New York: Norton, 1995; *Sweet Swing Blues on the Road: A Year with Wynton Marsalis and His Sextet,* by Wynton Marsalis and Frank Stewart, New York: Norton, 1994; Marsalis on Music web site, http://www.wnet.org/archive/mom/

—*P. K.*

❖ MARSHALL, THURGOOD

(1908–1993), *civil rights lawyer, Supreme Court justice*

Thurgood Marshall is the first African American to have served on the Supreme Court of the United States. Before

his appointment to the Supreme Court, he was U.S. solicitor general, the legal representative for the U.S. government in Supreme Court cases—the third-highest position in the Justice Department. Marshall is the first African American to have held that position as well.

Before his federal appointments, Marshall was a distinguished civil rights lawyer for the National Association for the Advancement of Colored People (NAACP). It was Marshall who successfully argued the 1954 *Brown vs. Board of Education* case, in which the Supreme Court finally ruled that "separate but equal" school facilities, segregated by race, could not be considered equal, and were therefore unconstitutional.

Arguing this and other cases, Marshall helped to lead the great shift in civil rights activity in the 1950s and 1960s from an effort to win "separate but equal" facilities for black people to the struggle for full-fledged integration.

The son of William Canfield and Norma (Arica) Marshall, Thurgood Marshall was named after his great-grandfather, Thoroughgood, a slave whose rebellious nature secured his eventual freedom, but he explains that

Thurgood Marshall (*Library of Congress*)

as a child, he grew tired of spelling out the long name and shortened it. He was born on July 2, 1908, in Baltimore, Maryland, which at the time was a highly segregated city. Although the Marshalls were middle-class homeowners and taxpayers they could not shop at Baltimore's department stores or use its public bathrooms.

Marshall was a good student in high school, finishing his studies half a year early. However, at Lincoln University, "The black Princeton" in Pennsylvania, he was expelled for hazing—indulging in the pranks that upper-level students sometimes pull on underclassmen. However, Marshall was soon back in the school's good graces, after marrying Vivian Burey, a student at the University of Pennsylvania, and became a star on the debating team.

Although Marshall applied to the University of Maryland's law school, he was rejected on racial grounds. He then entered Howard University in Washington, D.C., instead, where he studied under the great teacher Charles HOUSTON.

In 1933, he graduated at the head of his class, and soon built up the largest law practice in the city of Baltimore. However, he often defended poor people, and had to struggle to make ends meet during the depression.

In 1935, Marshall challenged the state-funded University of Maryland in court when the school denied entry to Donald Murray, a qualified African-American student whom Marshall had encouraged to apply. The court ruled in Murray's favor, giving Marshall his first landmark civil rights victory.

In 1935, Houston went to New York to become chief counsel for the NAACP, and he brought Marshall with him. When Houston went into private practice in 1938, Marshall became director counsel of the NAACP's Legal Defense and Education Fund. In this position, Marshall would win many of the 20th century's major civil rights cases.

In 1950, Marshall triumphed in a case allowing African-American student Herman Sweatt to enter the University of Texas Law School. Although the law school tried to set up a separate facility for black students to preserve segregation, over 200 white law students set up their own NAACP chapter to raise money to fight against their school's policies. Soon afterward, Marshall broke the color bar at Oklahoma State University as well. In the following year, more than a thousand black students entered southern university graduate schools.

Marshall flew to Korea in 1951, in order to investigate charges of discrimination against black soldiers in the armed forces. He substantially assisted some 22 servicemen who had received harsh punishments under court-martial.

For some time, Marshall had wanted to attack the "separate but equal" doctrine that permitted segregation in the public schools. He came up with a unique strategy: He would use testimony from black psychologist Kenneth Clark to demonstrate that segregation implied that black children were inferior. Thus, separate facilities could not be equal.

His strategy was successful in the Supreme Court's landmark *Brown vs. Board of Education of Topeka* decision of 1954. Now the Civil Rights movement had a new task—actually integrating the schools, which the Court had only said should be done "with all deliberate speed." When Arkansas Governor Orval Faubus refused to allow integration of Arkansas schools, President Eisenhower sent federal troops to Little Rock to protect the black schoolchildren trying to enter formerly white schools.

Marshall was facing a personal tragedy at this time: His wife was suffering from cancer and would die in 1954. Later, Marshall married Cecilia Suyat, an NAACP secretary, with whom he had two children.

Many private law firms offered Marshall huge salaries to leave the NAACP, but he remained with the organization. He won 29 of 32 Supreme Court cases and became known as the country's leading constitutional lawyer.

In 1961, President John F. Kennedy appointed Marshall to be a judge of the U.S. Circuit Court of Appeals. Segregationists in the Senate delayed Marshall's confirmation for a year, but he was finally accepted. In 1965, President Lyndon Johnson offered Marshall the post of solicitor general. This time, although opposition continued, he was quickly confirmed.

In 1967, he received his final "promotion." President Johnson appointed him to be a justice of the Supreme Court. He served in that capacity for 24 years, before retiring in 1991 at the age of 82.

Marshall played a key role on the Supreme Court. On being appointed, he replaced a justice who had often voted with the conservative majority, and this had led to many conservative court decisions. Marshall, on the other hand, came down most often on the liberal side, favoring civil rights, women's rights, and civil liberties issues. For a while, Marshall helped to create a liberal majority on the court. Later, as justices appointed by President Nixon took office, the balance tipped again, and Marshall found himself in the minority.

One of his main concerns on the court was sustained support of the so-called *Miranda* decision, which holds that police must inform the alleged lawbreaker as to his or her rights, and must be sure that those who are arrested have access to a lawyer if they so wish. He took a strong stand on other such citizens' rights—limiting the ability of the police to engage in preventive detention (holding someone whom they believe *might* commit a crime, rather than someone whom they can prove *has* committed a crime), illegal searches and surveillance (searching private effects without a warrant, and engaging in undercover observation of suspected criminals), and improper methods of interrogation (questioning people under arrest in a violent, threatening, or abusive way). Marshall consistently said that it is more important to protect the rights of the innocent than to expand the powers of the police.

Marshall also strongly opposed capital punishment. He wrote opinions in favor of a woman's right to safe, legal, and affordable abortion and he upheld people's rights to read whatever they choose, including so-called obscene material. Thurgood Marshall stood for the rights of individuals to the maximum amount of liberty and privacy possible and against the infringement upon those rights by the government or the police.

Thurgood Marshall died in 1993. In 1996 he was honored with a memorial statue on State House Square in Annapolis, Maryland. The statue shows the young Marshall, backed by pillars inscribed, "Equal Justice Under Law," and faced by two benches. On one bench sits Donald Gaines Murray, whose entrance into the Law School of the University of Maryland was Marshall's first important victory in the battle for school integration. On the other bench are figures of two children representing those who were allowed to attend integrated schools as a result of Marshall's victory in *Brown vs. Board of Education of Topeka.*

Further Reading: *Making Civil Rights Law: Thurgood Marshall and the Supreme Court, 1936–1961,* by Mark V. Tushnet, New York: Oxford University Press, 1996; *Dream Makers, Dream Breakers: The World of Justice Thurgood Marshall,* by Carl T. Rowan, Boston: Little Brown & Co., 1994; *The Importance of Thurgood Marshall,* by Deborah Hitzeroth and Sharon Leon, San Diego, Calif.: Lucent Books, 1997; *Private Pressure on Public Law: The Legal Career of Justice Thurgood Marshall, 1934–1991,* by Randall W. Bland, Lanham, Md.: University Press of America, 1993; *Thurgood Marshall,* by Lisa Aldred, New York: Chelsea House, 1990; *Thurgood Marshall, Fighter for Justice,* by Lewis H. Fenderson, New York: McGraw-Hill, 1969; *Racial Equality: Criminal Proceedings and the Courts,* by Thurgood Marshall, Santa Barbara, Calif.: Center for the Study of Democratic Institutions.

—*R. K.*

❖ MATZELIGER, JAN EARNST
(1852–1889), *inventor*

Jan Earnst Matzeliger did what for many years seemed impossible. He invented a machine that could complete the manufacture of a shoe. His invention was further developed by the United Shoe Machinery Company of Boston, which made millions of dollars from it, although Matzeliger himself saw little financial benefit.

Matzeliger also invented several other machines that were useful to manufacturers. These machines distributed tacks and nails and hammered nails into shoes or other items.

Jan Earnst Matzeliger was born on September 15, 1852, to a black woman of Paramaribo, Suriname, and a Dutch engineer who was living in South America at the time. Around the age of three, Matzeliger was sent to live with his paternal aunt. When he was 10, he began to

Jan Matzeliger (*Washington Post, DC Public Library*)

work in his father's shop, where he learned a great deal about machinery.

Despite this early interest, Matzeliger did not immediately become an engineer or inventor. Instead, in 1871, he left Suriname and became a sailor. Several years later, he quit the ship in Philadelphia. After working various odd jobs in that area, he went farther north, and settled in Lynn, Massachusetts.

The town of Lynn was completely dependent on the shoe industry. Shoes were originally handmade—which was a slow process, requiring highly skilled workers. The shoe companies were looking for a faster process that did not require such highly skilled—and highly paid—employees. They began to develop machines that could complete some of the steps used in making shoes.

Some inventors introduced machines that did such things as cutting the shoe leather and shaping the sole. However, the shaping of the leather "upper"—the top part of the shoe—could not be done by machine. This process, known as "lasting," had to be done by highly paid lasters, each of whom could produce only 40 to 50 pairs of shoes a day.

Many had tried to invent a mechanical laster, but all had failed. Matzeliger learned of this problem while working in a shoe factory, where he operated a sole-sewing machine, a heel-burnisher, and a buttonholer.

After working all day in the factory, Matzeliger went to night school to improve his limited knowledge of English. He then began to read and educate himself—largely in scientific study, but in oil-painting as well.

In 1880, Matzeliger began his first lasting machine. With only crude materials at his disposal—wire, wood, and cigar boxes—he worked for more than four years. The final product was evidence of Matzeliger's limited resources: It was made of castings and iron parts, and assembled in a corner of the factory where he worked.

Since money is necessary to develop and patent an invention, Matzeliger sought investors. Two town citizens, C. H. Delnow and M. S. Nichols, finally provided some funds—but only in exchange for two-thirds ownership of his invention.

In 1883, Matzeliger applied for his patent. The drawings he sent in explanation were so complicated that the Washington, D.C., Patent Office had to send a representative to Lynn to look at the machine. In 1885, the machine was operated publicly for the first time—and lasted 75 pairs of shoes.

A new company was formed to manufacture the lasting machine, which soon turned out from 150 to 700 pairs of shoes per day. This was the Consolidated Lasting Machine Company, formed by Matzeliger's two "partners," who brought two more investors into the business. Eventually, this company bought the rights to other patents and became a multimillion-dollar success that dominated the shoe-machinery industry.

Matzeliger continued to tinker with various inventions and patented them. But in 1886, he contracted tuberculosis, from which he never really recovered. Although confined to bed, he managed to continue painting and working on inventions; but he died on August 24, 1889, not quite 37.

Matzeliger's invention had revolutionized the shoe industry. It also changed life in Lynn by making the town the shoe capital of the world. In 1901, years after his death, this extraordinary inventor was awarded the Pan-American Exposition's Gold Medal and Diploma.

Further Reading: *Shoes for Everyone: A Story about Jan Matzeliger,* by Barbara Mitchell, Minneapolis, Minn.: Carolrhoda Books, 1986; *Black Inventors,* by Nathan Aaseng, New York: Facts On File, 1997.

—R. K.

❖ MAYS, BENJAMIN ELIJAH
(1895–1984), educator, college president

Benjamin Mays was one of the outstanding educators of his time. Martin Luther KING, JR., called Mays "my spiritual mentor." He was the first African-American vice president of the Federal Council of Churches of Christ and the first black president of Atlanta's school board. For many years, he served as president of Atlanta's Morehouse College, one of the major black colleges in the United States.

Benjamin Mays was born on August 1, 1895, in Epworth, South Carolina, the youngest of seven children. He came from a family of slaves and poor farmers but was soon recognized as a brilliant child, particularly in mathematics and oratory.

Mays started to attend college at Virginia Union University but soon transferred to Bates College in Maine, where he was elected a Phi Beta Kappa. After graduating from Bates in 1920, he earned an M.A. at the University of Chicago in 1925. In 1935, he received his doctorate from the same university.

Mays had been teaching at Morehouse from 1921 to 1924, and at South Carolina State College from 1925 to 1926. After holding various civic positions in South Carolina, he returned to teach at South Carolina State until 1934, when he became dean of the school of religion at Howard University in Washington, D.C.

Throughout the 1920s, Mays held various positions in major organizations. He was an official of the Urban League from 1926 to 1928, the national student secretary of the Young Men's Christian Association (YMCA) from 1928 to 1930, and director of the first scientific study of black American churches from 1930 to 1932.

He continued to write on religious topics, and in 1933, he published *Negro's Church.* He later published a book called *Negro's God.*

In 1940, he moved from Howard to Morehouse, where he served as president until 1967. During this time, he wrote a column called "My View" that appeared in black newspapers nationwide. He also wrote many articles and wrote or contributed to many books.

While Mays was president of Morehouse, it became known as the "black Oxford of the South." "Morehouse men," as its graduates were called, included many prominent black leaders, such as Martin Luther King, Jr., who remembered Mays with affection.

In 1942, Mays filed a suit that eventually helped to desegregate railroad dining cars. In 1944, with his inclusion on the Schomburg Honor Roll of Race Relations, he was honored as one of 12 African Americans responsible for outstanding work in that area of endeavor. He was known as a conciliator in the Civil Rights movement and as one who opposed extremists.

After retiring from Morehouse, Mays became a member of the Atlanta Board of Education, where he served until 1981. Mays died in Atlanta on March 28, 1984.

Further Reading: *Born to Rebel,* by Benjamin Mays, Athens, Ga.: University of Georgia Press, 1987.

—*R. K.*

❖ MICHEAUX, OSCAR
(1884–1951), *African-American independent film producer*

Oscar Micheaux was an independent African-American film producer who offered a black alternative to Hollywood movies. Between 1919 and 1948, he produced almost 30 films and was one of the few black filmmakers to work in both sound and silent eras. His films were shown throughout the country—although some southern theaters refused to show the more controversial ones.

While there are many technical and artistic shortcomings in his work, his movies offer a fascinating commentary on the black middle class and African-American life of the time. Micheaux attempted to present an "alternate" world in which black people on screen were as rich, well-educated, and cultured as white movie characters appeared to be.

Oscar Micheaux, born in 1884, grew up on a farm near Cairo, Illinois, one of 13 children. His parents were former slaves. Micheaux disliked farm life and left home at 17 to work at a variety of jobs, including one as a Pullman porter.

In 1904, he purchased a South Dakota homestead and farmed for some years. He admired Booker T. WASHINGTON and his doctrine of self-improvement and self-help—to the extent of feeling superior to black urban dwellers who would not take advantage of western agricultural opportunities.

Micheaux experienced a difficult romance and an unhappy marriage, which inspired him to write fiction loosely based on his own life. In 1913, he published at his own expense *The Conquest: The Story of a Negro Pioneer* (Lincoln, Neb.: Woodruff Press). This book, which listed no author, appears to be quite autobiographical, with one "Oscar Devereaux" as its main character. Devereaux falls in love with a Scottish girl but doesn't marry her—partly because of a personal principle against interracial marriage, partly because of laws

opposing such marriages in South Dakota. Instead, he weds a minister's daughter, but the hypocritical pastor breaks up the marriage.

Micheaux went on to publish other novels, which he aggressively promoted throughout black communities in the South. *The Forged Note: A Romance of the Darker Races* came out in 1915 and was concerned with his experiences promoting *The Conquest. The Homesteader,* written in 1917, repeats the finale of *The Conquest* in a more melodramatic vein. Today's critics find all of Micheaux's books of poor literary quality, but he marketed them effectively and they sold well.

In 1918, he found a new opportunity. The film company that produced the racist classic *The Birth of a Nation* asked him for the rights to *The Homesteader.* Micheaux wanted to direct the film himself. When the film company refused, Micheaux raised money among the Oklahoma farmers who had bought his book and founded his own film company in New York. In 1919, he produced his first film, *The Homesteader.*

He had very little money with which to make his films, and as a result, they are all of a very low technical standard. And, too, the acting is often inferior and appears to have been improvised at the last minute. Micheaux could not re-shoot scenes, so if an actor forgot some lines, he or she might have to cover for it on camera and continue. Some scenes were done in a single shot, following an actor nonstop, throughout the take. In this way, Micheaux was able to film his pictures in six weeks.

One of his ideas was an alternative star structure, using black instead of white stars. His lead actors tended to be light-skinned and Caucasian-looking—promoted by him as the "black Valentino," the "sepia Mae West," the "colored Cagney" and the "negro Harlow."

Some of Micheaux's films stand up today as fascinating studies of race relations. The 1920 film, *Within Our Gates,* is a story of black southern life, and includes a controversial lynching scene that almost caused the film to be censored. *Birthright,* made in 1924, is the story of a young black Harvard graduate who hopes to start a black school in his southern home town. The film portrays both white segregationists and black "Uncle Toms" who oppose the effort.

Some of his other films make interesting racial statements by repeating conventional Hollywood plots with all-black casts. *Underworld* was a black gangster film; *Daughter of the Congo,* a black explorers-in-Africa film. Micheaux's work was an interesting combination of popular entertainment and racial commentary.

It is also noteworthy that Micheaux was responsible for providing actor Paul ROBESON with his first movie role, in the 1924 film *Body and Soul.*

In 1925, he married actress Alice B. Russell, and the two lived together for the rest of Micheaux's life.

Because Micheaux was so gifted at publicity and promotion, his work was successful. Although he went bankrupt in 1928, he had arranged his finances in a such a way that he could continue to produce movies. Finally, in 1937, he suspended his activities due to left-wing protests concerning *God's Stepchildren,* a film about black people passing for white.

In the 1940s, Micheaux resumed publishing books, but in 1948 he produced *The Betrayal.* This film reworked, once again, the love story from *The Homesteader* and his earlier books (a story that he had related yet a fourth time in a later book). The three-hour film retold the story of a black South Dakota farmer. It failed thoroughly—not only due to its melodramatic and confusing plot, but because audiences were no longer willing to accept the lower technical quality of such independent filmmaking. Now that more acceptable black characters had made their way into Hollywood films, Micheaux's melodramas had become much less attractive.

Micheaux died on April 1, 1951, while on a promotional tour in Charlotte, North Carolina.

Further Reading: *Toms, Coons, Mulattoes, Mammies and Bucks: An Interpretive History of Blacks in American Films,* by Donald Bogle, New York: Viking Press, 1973; *From Sambo to Superspade: The Black Experience in Motion Pictures,* by Daniel J. Leab, Boston, Mass.: Houghton, Mifflin, 1975.

—*R. K.*

❖ MORGAN, GARRETT A.
(1875–1963), *inventor, editor*

Several of Garrett Morgan's inventions are in wide use today, most notably the gas mask and the three-way traffic signal (one that includes a "caution" signal, like today's flashing yellow light, as well as "go" and "stop" signals).

Morgan received several awards for his inventions, including the National Safety Device Company's First Grand Prize Golden Medal; honorary membership in the International Association of Fire Engineers; and a U.S. government citation for the invention of the traffic signal.

Garrett Morgan, born in 1875 on a farm near Paris, Kentucky, was the child of Sidney Morgan and Elizabeth (Reed) Morgan, a former slave who had been freed by the Emancipation Proclamation. Morgan was the seventh of 11 children in his family.

As with many black people of the time, Morgan had very little education. At 14, he went to work as a handyman in Cincinnati, and hired a tutor to help him with his grammar.

In 1895, he moved to Cleveland to work as a sewing machine adjuster in a clothing firm. This factory work sparked Morgan's lifelong interest in mechanical equipment, and he made Cleveland his permanent home. In 1908, he married Mary Anne Hassek, with whom he had several children, and with whom he lived until his death some 55 years later.

In 1907, Morgan had gone into business for himself, repairing and selling sewing machines. This venture was so successful that, by 1909, he was able to start a second business, a tailor shop, where he employed 32 workers. In 1913, Morgan launched a third enterprise, the marketing of a hair-straightening process—his original discovery.

Morgan continued to manufacture hair products and to fabricate new inventions. From 1912 through 1914, Morgan worked on a device that he called a "safety hood," which we know as a gas mask. Morgan's mask could be put on quickly and carried easily, and enabled the user to endure smoke or dangerous gases for up to 20 minutes. It was extremely useful to firefighters, to workers trying to rescue others from dangerous places, and to U.S. soldiers in the trenches of World War I, where poison chlorine gas was frequently used.

In 1916, this mask was used with great success in an industrial accident, which led many fire departments to adopt his invention. However, despite such an important device to his credit, Morgan ran up against racial prejudice. When he traveled to southern states to demonstrate his invention, he often had to hire a white person to meet the public, while he went in the guise of an Indian. Even so, when it was learned that Morgan was black, many people stopped using his mask.

Morgan's second important invention was the three-way traffic signal. At the time, traffic signals were not self-changing. Officers had to physically turn them from "stop" to "go," and vice versa. When no traffic officer was present, motorists simply ignored the signs—with consequent danger for those on the road.

In Morgan's version, however, the "stop" and "go" signs could be left at half-mast—the equivalent of today's flashing yellow light. This third kind of signal meant that cars should slow down and proceed with caution. The device protected many pedestrians and schoolchildren and was also used at railroad crossings. General Electric bought the rights to the signal for $40,000.

Morgan was quite active in his community. He founded the newspaper the *Cleveland Call,* which he published from 1920 through 1923. He worked with a precursor of the National Association for the Advancement of Colored People (NAACP) and then with the NAACP itself. In 1931, he ran unsuccessfully for city council.

In 1943, Morgan developed the eye disease glaucoma, which gradually took his vision away. He died in 1963, in Cleveland. Some 13 years later, a Harlem public school was named in his honor.

Further Reading: *African-American Inventors: Lonnie Johnson, Frederick McKinley Jones, Marjorie Stewart Joyner, Elijah McCoy, Garrett Augustus Morgan,* by Fred M. B. Amram and Jetty Kahn, Minneapolis, Minn.: Capstone Press, 1996; *Eight Black American Inventors,* by Robert C. Hayden, Reading, Mass.: Addison-Wesley, 1972; *Stop & Go: Garrett Morgan, Inventor,* by Doris J. Sims, Los Angeles, Calif.: Childrens Cultu-Lit, 1980.

—R. K.

❖ MORRISON, TONI
(Chloe Anthony Wofford)
(1931–), Pulitzer Prize–winning writer

Toni Morrison, recipient in 1993 of the Nobel Prize for Literature, has won many awards for her novels. In 1975, she received a National Book Award nomination and the Ohioana Book Award (for recognition of best fiction by an Ohio writer) for *Sula* (New York: Knopf, 1974). In 1977, she won a National Book Critics Circle Award and American Academy and Institute of Arts and Letters award for *Song of Solomon* (New York: Knopf, 1977). In 1987 and 1988, her novel *Beloved* (New York: Knopf, 1987) won nominations for the National Book Award and the National Book Critics Circle Award, given for literary achievement; it garnered her the Pulitzer Prize.

Toni Morrison was born Chloe Anthony Wofford in the small Lake Erie town of Lorain, Ohio, on February 18, 1931. She believes that her youth taught her the importance of community spirit and gave her a feeling for the supernatural.

Morrison's first novel was not written until she was in her thirties. She attended Howard University in Washington, D.C., receiving her B.A. in 1953 and an M.A. from Cornell in 1955. In 1958 she married Harold

Toni Morrison *(Helen Marcus/Archive Photos)*

Morrison, with whom she had two children. The couple were divorced in 1964.

Morrison taught English at Texas Southern University and Howard University from 1955 to 1964. She then moved to New York, where she became a senior editor at Random House. She also taught English literature at universities within the New York state system, as well as at Princeton, Yale, and New York's Bard College.

Morrison's first novel, *The Bluest Eye* (New York: Holt, Rinehart & Winston, 1969), was published in 1969. This work is set in her home town of Lorain and depicts a year in the life of Pecola Breedlove, a young black girl growing up in the 1940s. The book conveys the difficulties for African-Americans in finding a positive identity in a world where blue eyes and white people's looks are most valued and where the white and blue-eyed thereby inherit most of the power.

Sula, published in 1973, is the story of a profound friendship between two black women growing up in the 1920s and 1930s. The two women belong to a strong black community yet they also find that community repressive and restrictive. Their relations with men are also unsatisfying, while their friendship with each other is a source of liberation and excitement.

In 1977, Morrison published *Song of Solomon,* in which she continues her exploration of black heritage and history. The young man, Milkman Dead, searches for his roots through fairy tales, children's rhymes and a trip back to his family's former home in the South. The man must come to terms with his family's response to slavery and to white violence, as well as with the positive aspects of his history.

The 1981 *Tar Baby* was Morrison's exploration of the relations between black and white cultures in both the United States and the Caribbean. The book was a U.S. best-seller for four months. As with her earlier books, *Tar Baby* explores the difficulties of coming to terms with one's heritage. She examines this theme through the relationship of a well-educated black model with a wandering young man who resents white culture.

In *Beloved,* her prize-winning 1987 novel, Morrison examines in more detail the black response to slavery. The book was inspired by Morrison's work on *The Black Book,* an anthology of black history that she edited for Random House. While working on this project, Morrison read about a runaway slave who killed her child in order to save it from slavery. That incident led her to write *Beloved,* which examines the interior life of slavery.

Morrison's work is marked by a sense of the supernatural throughout. "Ancestors," or the dead, make their presence felt in the community. Mysterious events—such as the marigolds refusing to grow in *The Bluest Eye*—signal that something is wrong. Strength can often be drawn from connecting with these mysterious forces.

She has expounded on the need to develop a large body of black work. As a writer and editor, she is interested in work "where black people are talking to black people," rather than writing for whites about how awful their own lives are.

Many writers object to being labeled "black" or "female," but Morrison welcomes that description. In a *New York Times* interview, she said, "I really think the range of emotions and perceptions I have had access to as a black person and a female person are greater than those of people who are neither . . . My world did not shrink because I was a black female writer. It just got bigger."

When Morrison gave her Nobel Prize speech, she expanded on that theme: ". . . what is most wonderful for me, personally, is to know that the prize at last has been awarded to an African American. Winning as an American is very special—but winning as a black American is a knockout."

In 1986, her first play, *Dreaming Emmet,* was produced, and her critically acclaimed novel *Jazz* (New York: Knopf) was published in 1992.

Further Reading: *The Nobel Lecture in Literature, 1993,* by Toni Morrison, New York: Random House (audio), 1994; *Playing in the Dark: Whiteness and the Literary Imagination,* Cambridge, Mass.: Harvard University Press, 1992; *Birth of a Nation 'Hood: Gaze, Script, and Spectacle in the O. J. Simpson Case,* ed. by Toni Morrison and Claudia Brodsky Lacour, New York: Pantheon, 1997; *Toni Morrison: Contemporary Critical Essays,* ed. by Linden Peach, New York: St. Martins Press, 1998; *Circles of Sorrow, Lines of Struggle: The Novels of Toni Morrison,* Baton Rouge: Louisiana State University Press, 1998; *The Dancing Mind: Speech upon Acceptance of the National Book Foundation Medal for Distinguished Contribution to American Letters,* New York: Pantheon, 1997; *Dangerous Freedom: Fusion and Fragmentation in Toni Morrison's Novels,* by Philip Page, Jackson, Miss.: University Press of Mississippi, 1996; *Black Women Writers at Work,* edited by Claudia Tate, New York: Continuum, 1986; *Black Women Writers (1950–1980): A Critical Evaluation,* edited by Mari Evans, New York: Doubleday Press/Anchor, 1984; *Sturdy Black Bridges: Visions of Black Women in Literature,* edited by Roseann P. Bell, Garden City, N.Y.: Anchor Press/Doubleday, 1979; *Black Women Novelists: The Development of a Tradition, 1892–1976,* by Barbara Christian, Westport, Conn.: Greenwood Press, 1980.

—*R. K.*

❖ MOSELEY-BRAUN, CAROL ELIZABETH
(1947–), *political leader*

The first African-American woman ever elected to the U.S. Senate, Carol Moseley-Braun has devoted her political career to furthering the rights of women, minorities, and working people.

Born on August 16, 1947, in Chicago, Illinois, Moseley was the oldest of four children. The daughter of a Chicago police officer and a medical technician, she enjoyed a comfortable childhood, but she also grew up with a desire to improve the lives of those who were less fortunate. Moseley became a civil rights activist while

Carol Moseley-Braun (*Reuters/Jim Bourg/Archive Photos*)

still in high school. On one occasion she staged a personal sit-in at a restaurant that refused to serve African Americans, and she also took part in Rev. Martin Luther KING's campaign to end racial discrimination in the city. After graduating from high school, Moseley attended the University of Chicago, where she majored in political science. She received her B.A. degree in 1968 and then earned a law degree from the University of Chicago Law School. While in law school, she married Michael Braun—the couple later had a son, Matthew, and divorced in 1986.

From 1973 to 1978, Moseley-Braun served as an assistant U.S. attorney in Illinois, earning a Special Achievement Award from the Justice Department for her work. She entered the political arena in 1978, running successfully for a seat in the Illinois House of Representatives. As a state legislator, Moseley-Braun fought for better schools, universal health care, welfare reform, gun control, and other causes. A skillful debater and a hard worker, she rose to the position of assistant majority leader, becoming the first woman and the first African American to fill that post. Moseley-Braun remained in the legislature until 1987, when she was elected recorder of deeds for Cook County, with authority over a staff of 300 employees. Within four years, Moseley-Braun modernized the office's procedures, installed a new code of ethics, and upgraded staff salaries.

By 1992, Moseley-Braun was ready to move on, and she decided to challenge incumbent U.S. senator Alan J. Dixon in the Democratic primary. Friends and advisers felt this was a rash move that would wreck her political career, but Moseley-Braun was convinced that the all-white, all-male U.S. Senate needed some new blood. The voters clearly agreed—Moseley-Braun won a three-way primary race and then defeated a conservative male Republican in the November election, gaining 95 percent of the black vote and 58 percent of the women's vote.

As the first African-American woman in the Senate and only the second African since the end of Reconstruction in 1877, Moseley-Braun made her presence felt in Washington. "I am—by definition—a different kind of senator," she declared. "I cannot escape the fact that I come to the Senate as a symbol of hope and change." In order to fulfill this role, Moseley-Braun focused on three main areas: education, employment, and retirement security. During her first term, Moseley-Braun served on the Finance Committee; the Banking, Housing, and Urban Affairs Committee; and the Special Committee on Aging. She introduced numerous pieces of legislation, including the Gender Equity in Education Act and the Violence Against Women Act. Moseley-Braun also contributed key provisions to other important laws that dealt with child support, crime, education, and fair employment practices. She saw half her proposed measures enacted into law, a remarkable success rate for a freshman senator and a sign that Moseley-Braun was emerging as a major force in American politics. Moseley-Braun held this Senate seat until she lost the election in November 1998.

Further Information: Senator Carol Moseley-Braun web site, http://www.senate.gov/~moseley-braun (includes all the bills introduced by Senator Moseley-Braun, information about her committee assignments, and texts of all the press releases she has issued); *Carol Moseley-Braun: Breaking Barriers*, by Mellonee Carrigan, Chicago: Children's Press, 1994 (Picture Story Biography).

—*P. K.*

❖ MOTLEY, CONSTANCE BAKER
(1921–   ), *lawyer, government official, judge*

Constance Baker Motley worked for many years as a civil rights lawyer. She argued James Meredith's famous suit in 1962, in which a black person was finally admitted to the University of Mississippi. Motley served in many key government posts in New York. In 1966, she became the first black woman to be appointed to a federal judgeship and in 1982, was named chief judge.

Constance Baker Motley was born September 14, 1921, one of eight children born to the West Indian couple Willoughby and Rachel (Baker) Motley. She grew up in New Haven, Connecticut, where her father was a chef for a Yale University fraternity.

Although the Bakers could not afford to send their daughter to college, the young Constance so impressed a local contractor that he offered to pay her way.

Motley graduated from New York University in 1943. She went on to study law at Columbia University in New York, where she met Thurgood MARSHALL, the future Supreme Court justice.

At the time, Marshall was chief counsel for the National Association for the Advancement of Colored People's (NAACP's) Legal Defense Fund. Motley began to work at the Fund as a clerk and, after graduating from law school in 1946, she stayed on the legal staff. Also in 1946, she married Joel Motley, Jr., a real estate broker, with whom she later had a son.

The late 1940s and 1950s were an exciting time to be working for the NAACP, which was engaged in fighting school segregation. Motley participated in major cases of this kind, winning much acclaim in her efforts to have James Meredith, a black student, admitted to the previously all-white University of Mississippi. She won similar admissions for other African Americans, to universities in Alabama, Georgia, and Florida.

In addition, she fought cases involving segregation in housing, recreation, transportation, and other public sites and facilities. She also argued in defense of students arrested at sit-ins and other protests. From 1961 to 1964, she argued 10 cases before the U.S. Supreme Court—and won nine.

In 1964, Motley left the legal world to enter politics, running for New York State Senate. The local Democratic Party refused to nominate her, however, believing that, as a middle-class woman, she would not attract the black working-class vote. Nevertheless, she won, becoming New York's first woman state senator.

She held that seat until 1965, when she was appointed to fill a vacancy as Manhattan borough president. When elections for the office were held, Motley ran with the endorsements of three political parties—Democratic, Republican, and Liberal. She won the election, and served until 1966, when President Lyndon B. Johnson appointed her U.S. district judge for New York's Second District.

In 1982, Constance Baker Motley rose to become chief judge. She held that position until 1986, when she retired from the bench.

Further Reading: *Equal Justice Under Law: An Autobiography*, by Constance Baker Motley, New York: Farrar Straus & Giroux, 1998; *Perspectives on Justice*, by

Constance Baker Motley, Evanston, Ill.: Northwestern University Press, 1975.

—R. K.

❖ MUHAMMAD, ELIJAH (Elijah Poole)
(1897–1975), religious and political leader

One of the major figures in the history of black nationalism, Elijah Muhammad led the Nation of Islam for more than 30 years. Building the organization into a major force in the black community, he changed the lives of many African Americans and gave new life to the historic ideal of black self-determination.

Elijah Muhammad was born Elijah Poole in Sandersville, Georgia, on October 10, 1897, one of 13 children in the family of a sharecropper who also preached in the Baptist church. Throughout his youth, Poole worked in the fields alongside his brothers and sisters, and he was able to attend school only through the third grade. In 1919, he married a local woman, Clara Evans, and the couple moved to Macon, where Poole was employed as a railroad worker and brickyard laborer. In 1923, Poole and his wife left the South and moved north to Detroit, where he got a job in an auto plant. He and his wife lived uneventfully for several years, raising a family that ultimately grew to include eight children. But when the Great Depression hit in 1929, Poole found himself out of work along with millions of other Americans.

In 1931, Poole came into contact with Wallace Fard (also known as Wali Farrad), the founder of the Nation of Islam, which had an estimated 8,000 members at that time. Poole adopted the religion of Islam, shedding his "slave" name in favor of an Arabic name (Elijah Muhammad), and soon emerged as Fard's chief aide. When Fard disappeared in 1934, the Nation of Islam split into competing factions. Muhammad and his followers relocated to Chicago, where he established a temple and developed his own doctrine. Muhammad maintained that Christianity had been forced upon African Americans by whites, whom he called "blue-eyed devils." As a remedy for the white racism that oppressed black Americans, he preached a doctrine of black pride, solidarity, and self-help. "Accept your place in the sun as it was originally before the creation of the world," he later wrote in *Message to the Black Man in America*. "The black man is the first and last, maker and owner of the universe."

Muhammad's ideas had a powerful appeal in the black community, bringing new hope to many people, including a large number of prison inmates and former prisoners. Members of the Nation of Islam were expected to follow a strict code of personal conduct that included avoidance of pork, drugs, tobacco, and alcohol. In order to further his ideas, Muhammad opened more than 100 temples, created a separate school system (the Clara Muhammad Schools), and a newspaper, *Muhammad Speaks*. As the Nation of Islam gained followers, the organization opened numerous small businesses in African-American neighborhoods; it also acquired major assets, including a bank, farmland in several states, a trucking company, and a printing plant.

When the United States entered World War II in 1941, Muhammad urged African Americans to avoid serving in the armed forces; as a result, he spent four years in federal prison. Despite this temporary setback, the Nation of Islam (also known as the Black Muslims) continued to grow. By the late 1950s, the organization had more than 500,000 members and controlled an estimated $80 million in assets. As the Civil Rights movement grew during the 1950s and 1960s, the Nation of Islam gained new prominence because of its opposition to racial integration, which in Muhammad's words amounted to "self-destruction, death, and nothing else." This message, expressed in the fiery rhetoric of Muhammad's principal aide, Malcolm X, made the Nation of Islam a controversial and influential force on the national scene.

In the early 1960s, the Nation of Islam was shaken by a growing rift between Muhammad and Malcolm X. Following a pilgrimage to the holy city of Mecca, Malcolm softened his attitude toward working with whites, and he also charged Muhammad with breaking the Nation of Islam's rules on personal morality. Malcolm was expelled from the organization in 1964, and a year later he was assassinated. Three members of the Nation of Islam were convicted of the murder. Muhammad himself was never personally implicated in Malcolm's death, and he died peacefully in Chicago on February 25, 1975.

Further Information: *Message to the Black Man in America*, by Elijah Muhammad, Chicago: Muhammad Mosque of Islam No. 2, 1965; *The Black Muslims in America*, by C. Eric Lincoln, revised edition, Westport, Conn.: Greenwood, 1973; Nation of Islam Online, http://www.noi.org

—P. K.

❖ MYERS, ISAAC
(1835–1891), labor leader

Isaac Myers helped to found the first union of black caulkers (seam sealers in shipbuilding). He led the union, whose first action was to buy a shipyard—which the workers owned as a group—in order that black workers could be employed. Myers also helped to found the (Colored) National Labor Union, a national black labor organization. He was the first president of the (C)NLU, which reached out to white workers as well. Myers was an important pioneer in the black union movement, and in the effort to untie black and white workers for the benefit of all.

Isaac Myers was born on January 13, 1835 to free, but poor, parents in Baltimore, Maryland—which at that time was a slave state. Maryland offered no public education for black children, and Myers had to be schooled privately. At 16, he went to work with a ship's caulker (sealing the cracks in aging wooden ships), and he soon became a skilled worker.

Although there were many black caulkers in Baltimore, some white people were uncomfortable with that situation, wanting to restrict the trade to whites only. In October 1865, white caulkers and ships' carpenters went on strike against black workers in the caulking trade. The workers held a meeting, and Myers proposed a radical idea. He suggested they form a union of black caulkers and that the union buy its own shipyard and work cooperatively—the workers owning the shipyard as a group.

The caulkers agreed with this idea, and sold shares of stock to raise funds for the project. They borrowed other funds, bought a shipyard and a railway, and went into business early in 1866.

The company soon became a profitable business, employing 300 black workers at fair wages. Then it began to hire white workers as well. Later, historian W. E. B. DUBOIS wrote that the action of the Baltimore caulkers had prevented other white workers from trying to drive black people from their trades.

After the Civil War, labor unions of all kinds were being formed by African-American workers as well as white. With Myers as president of the black union, the black and white caulkers' unions began to work together.

This experience taught Myers the importance of unity, both within the black labor movement and between blacks and whites. Meanwhile, white unions joined to form America's first national labor organization, the National Labor Union. At the end of 1868, the NLU invited everyone, regardless of color or sex, to attend its annual convention.

Myers went to the 1869 convention, to which he made a passionate call for unity. He said that regardless of the past, his members would be happy to work with anyone in good faith. He also announced that black unions would be holding their own national convention, to which white workers were cordially invited.

When the (Colored) National Labor Union met, it elected Myers as its president. Through early 1870, he traveled around the country, speaking to both black and racially mixed audiences, raising support for the new organization. He continued to stress the need for blacks to unite among themselves, and for blacks and whites to unite together.

However, the 1870 convention of the National Labor Union revealed a deep split within the labor movement. The white delegates wanted an independent labor party. The black delegates—of whom there were only five—were deeply committed to the Republican Party, which they saw as the party of emancipation. After that convention, black delegates no longer worked with the NLU.

The (C)NLU soon fell on hard times, and managed to hold only three conventions, the last in 1871. For the next seven years, Myers worked as a post office detective. In 1879, he opened a coal yard in Baltimore, but left that in 1882 to become a United States gauger (revenue officer, or customs agent), holding that job until 1887.

Myers continued to organize various groups to promote black business. In the course of his life, he married twice—the second time, to Sarah Deaver. Their son, George Myers, became a leading Ohio politician. Isaac Myers died on January 26, 1891, in his Baltimore home.

Further Reading: *History of the Labor Movement in the United States, Volume I,* by Philip S. Foner, New York: International Publishers, 1947; *Organized Labor and the Black Workers, 1619–1973,* by Philip S. Foner, New York: Praeger, 1974; *The Black Worker: A Documentary History from Colonial Times to the Present,* edited by Philip S. Foner and Ronald L. Lewis, New York: Temple University Press, 1978.

—R. K.

❖ NEWTON, HUEY PERCY

(1942–1989), *political activist*

One of the most dynamic political figures of the turbulent 1960s, Huey Newton personified the revolutionary Black Power movement. As a founder and leader of the Black Panther Party, he gave voice to the hopes and frustrations of a new generation of African Americans unwilling to compromise in their quest for freedom and justice.

Born in Monroe, Louisiana, on February 17, 1942, Newton was the seventh and youngest child of a tenant farmer who worked three jobs to provide a living for his family. Though Newton got little encouragement from his teachers, he was determined to educate himself. In his teens he moved to Oakland, California, to live with relatives. After attending Oakland Technical High School, he enrolled in Merritt College, where he obtained an associate arts degree after two years of study. Newton then began taking courses at San Francisco Law School. At the same time, he delved into community politics in Oakland's black ghetto, where political disputes were often settled with violence. Newton began to carry a gun, and after an incident in 1964 he was convicted of assault with a deadly weapon and sentenced to three years in prison. However, he was granted probation after serving six months and returned to Oakland.

During his time at law school, Newton had become friendly with a fellow student named Bobby Seale, who also lived in Oakland. Newton resumed contact with Seale, and the two men planned a new political initiative. At this time, the Civil Rights movement had scored major victories against segregation in the South. However, many African Americans, especially the younger generation, felt that these victories were hollow, having no real effect on the day-to-day problems caused by racism, poverty, and police brutality. They believed that African Americans had to take direct action rather than waiting for concessions from the white power structure.

This new political approach—known as the Black Power movement—had its roots in the Lowndes County Freedom Organization (LCFO) of Alabama, which emerged in 1965 as an all-black political party that used a black panther as its emblem. The success of the LCFO, which organized numerous black voters without any help from white civil rights workers, inspired Newton and Seale to form the Black Panther Party in October 1966. Cornerstones of the Black Panther program included community control of key institutions, armed self-defense, and exemption of African Americans from military service. The Panthers' first order of business was to organize patrols that monitored police activity, seeking to make sure that inner-city residents were not victims of police brutality.

The Panthers' bold attitude and their calls for armed revolution brought them many new recruits from the inner city of Oakland and several other cities, including

Huey Newton *(Camera Press Ltd./Archive Photos)*

action. He also resumed his education, attending the University of California, Santa Cruz, where he earned a B.A. degree and a Ph.D. Despite his new attitude, Newton had several more scrapes with the law, and at one point he spent three years in Cuba in order to avoid arrest. Finally, on August 22, 1989, Newton was found dead on an Oakland street, the victim of a shooting. No motive for the crime was ever established, and no one was arrested. In 1993, his widow, Fredrika Newton, and David Hillard founded the Dr. Huey P. Newton Foundation, which is dedicated to studying the documents Newton left behind and furthering his ideals of community development.

Further Information: *To Die for the People: The Writings of Huey P. Newton,* New York: Random House, 1972; *Shadow of the Panther: Huey Newton and the Price of Black Power in America,* by Hugh Pearson, Reading, Mass.: Addison-Wesley, 1994; Black Panther Party web site, http://www.blackpanther.org

—P. K.

❖ NORTON, ELEANOR HOLMES

(1937–   ), *civil rights lawyer, Congressional representative*

Eleanor Holmes Norton was the first woman to chair the Equal Employment Opportunity Commission, a position she held under President Jimmy Carter from 1977 to 1981. Before holding that national post, she was a prominent civil rights and civil-liberties lawyer, and served as head of the New York City Human Rights Commission. Since 1990, she has been a congresswoman representing the District of Columbia.

Norton has written extensively on civil rights, women's rights, and civil liberties. She has been awarded more than 50 honorary degrees, and was once selected by the *Ladies Home Journal* as one of America's "100 Most Important Women." She is currently a professor of law at Georgetown University in Washington, D.C.

Eleanor Holmes Norton grew up in Washington, D.C., where she was born on June 13, 1937. After graduating from Dunbar High School as a member of its last segregated class, she went to Antioch College in Ohio for her B.A., in 1960. She earned both her law degree and an M.A. in American studies from Yale University.

At Yale, Norton decided to use the law as a way of creating social change. As soon as she passed the bar exam in 1964, she became one of three lawyers who worked for the Mississippi Freedom Democratic Party. This was the group that protested the all-white official Mississippi

New York and Chicago. They were instantly identifiable in their black berets and black leather jackets, and their revolutionary slogan—Power to the People—became a rallying cry for all the various groups protesting racism and the Vietnam War during the late 1960s. But the Panthers also attracted the attention of the Nixon administration and the FBI, who determined to destroy them. Police and federal agents raided Black Panther headquarters around the country, and several party members were killed in shootouts. Newton himself was arrested in 1967 and charged with killing a police officer during an Oakland gun battle. Sentenced to 15 years in prison, he was granted a new trial two years later, and the charges were dropped after two separate juries failed to agree on the question of his guilt.

By the time of Newton's release, the Black Panther Party had been severely damaged, and he sought to rebuild its strength by advocating nonviolent political delegation to the 1964 Democratic Convention. The racially mixed group of Freedom Democrats tried to seat itself as a rival delegation. Although the effort failed, it did draw attention to the deep discrimination within the Mississippi Democratic Party.

Later, Norton worked with activists such as Stokely Carmichael; then she served as a law clerk to the federal judge A. Leon Higginbotham, Jr.

In 1965, she married Edward W. Norton, an attorney in private practice. The couple later had two children.

Another important aspect of Norton's work was civil liberties—the effort to defend Americans' constitutional rights to free speech, free press, and unorthodox or unpopular political activities. Norton went to work with the American Civil Liberties Union (ACLU) as a specialist in the First Amendment—which guarantees free speech, freedom of the press and of assembly.

While with the ACLU, Norton defended both left-wing and right-wing clients. She worked with Muhammad ALI and Adam Clayton POWELL, Jr.—but she also worked with conservative Alabama governor George Wallace and his National States Rights Party, which was deeply opposed to integration. Norton believed in political freedom for people of all different types of beliefs.

In 1970, Norton went to work with the administration of New York City mayor John Lindsay. She later served as his Human Rights Commission chairper-son—a position she also held during Mayor Abraham Beame's term.

From New York, Norton went to Washington, to head President Carter's Equal Employment Opportunity Commission. After Carter's defeat, Norton worked with the Urban Institute, then taught at Georgetown University Law School.

In 1988, Norton returned to the political arena, as presidential candidate Jesse JACKSON's platform representative at the Democratic national convention.

As congresswoman, she won senatorial courtesy from President Bill Clinton, allowing her to recommend federal District Court judges and a U.S. Attorney, and she continues to fight for full voting privileges for representatives of the District of Columbia. Although the District is third per capita in the payment of federal income tax, this largely African-American area has long been denied full voting rights in Congress.

Norton has always been a strong supporter of women's rights. She is currently on the National Women's Political Caucus Advisory Board. She has written and spoken extensively on feminism and women's rights.

Further Reading: *A Conversation with Commissioner Eleanor Holmes Norton,* by Eleanor Holmes Norton, Washington, D.C.: The American Enterprise Institute for Public Policy Research, 1980.

—*R. K.*

ODETTA (Odetta Gordon; Odetta Felious Gordon; Odetta Holmes)
(1930–   ), *folksinger*

Odetta rose to prominence during the folk movement of the 1960s and continues to be a major figure in black culture and folk music. She has won numerous awards from the music industry. In 1965, at the height of the Civil Rights movement, she was given the key to the city of Birmingham, Alabama.

Odetta was born on December 30, 1930, in Birmingham as Odetta Holmes. When she was seven, her family moved to Los Angeles. There she studied music, first in the public schools and later at Los Angeles City College.

In 1949, when still a teenager, Odetta had her first professional music job—as a member of the chorus in a local production of the musical *Finian's Rainbow.* Odetta decided that she was more interested in folk music than in popular music, and taught herself to play guitar.

Soon, the young singer was performing in nightclubs in Los Angeles and San Francisco. The international star Harry BELAFONTE appreciated her music and supported her career.

As the folk movement grew in popularity, so did Odetta. She toured the world, appeared on television, and continued to sing throughout the United States at folk festivals, college campuses, concert halls, and night-clubs. Her film appearances include *Cinerama Holiday* (1955) and *Sanctuary* (1960).

Odetta began to record her music in 1956. It includes folk songs, spirituals, blues, and children's songs.

In 1974, Odetta toured the Soviet Union and Eastern Europe. There she attracted wide attention as a woman performer who worked completely alone—just Odetta and her guitar. She has continued to perform, and has gained wide recognition for her distinctive music. Her 1987 album *Movin' It On* is a live recording of a concert she gave in 1986 marking 40 years of performances.

—*R. K.*

OVERTON, ANTHONY
(1864–1946), *banker, manufacturer*

Anthony Overton was a successful entrepreneur who operated several companies over his lifetime, including the Overton Hygienic Products Company, the Douglass National Bank, the Victory Life Insurance Company, and the *Chicago Bee,* a black newspaper. In 1928, he received the National Association for the Advancement of Colored People's Spingarn Medal, given to the person who contributed most distinctively to the progress of black people in the previous year.

Anthony Overton was born on June 24, 1864, into an enslaved family on James Masterson's plantation in

Monroe, Louisiana. After the Civil War, the freed Overtons were given 60 acres of land by their former owner and remained in Louisiana, where young Anthony studied with a black woman neighbor. When he was seven, a one-room school for African Americans was established in the neighborhood, and Overton was sent there. However, no black high school existed within 100 miles.

In 1877, Overton's father became part of the "Exodus"—a great movement of black people out of Louisiana and other southern states into Kansas. These "Exodusters" believed that antiblack violence and prejudice in the South would increase when federal troops, who had been stationed there to protect black people after the Civil War, finally pulled out.

The Overtons' move to Topeka, Kansas, enabled Anthony Overton to attend high school, which was an unusually high level of education at the time, especially for an African American. While he was still a student, Overton worked at a local grocer's, and demonstrated such a flair for business that the store soon showed a handsome profit for the first time in its existence.

In 1881, Overton graduated from South Side High School and went into the wholesale fruit business. He pioneered several aggressive business methods, such as going directly to the growers to get the best selection of the crop.

In 1883 his mother died, and his father moved the family back to Louisiana. Anthony Overton remained in Kansas, sending money to his family for many years to come.

When he was 23, he fell in love with a woman named Anna Tone but was unable to marry her because she had tuberculosis. Tone died in 1887. Her death deeply affected Overton, who sold his business and left Kansas for a long trip to California, New York, and Florida. Upon his return to Topeka, he enrolled in the University of Kansas law school.

Overton did well in law school, which at this time was integrated. Legend has it that during a class, a white classmate claimed that "niggers have no rights." Overton reportedly looked back at the student and said, "Son, we had better all have rights, or the day will come when none of us will have them."

He graduated in 1890 and soon passed the bar exam. He was able to develop a thriving practice with both black and white clients. He was active in Republican politics and became a municipal court judge in 1892. In 1901, he married Edith Dunbar, with whom he later had a son.

Overton was well respected as a judge, but he missed the world of business. In 1907, on a trip to Oklahoma City, he bought a small wholesale hardware business, which he managed until 1909.

In 1909, Overton's friend John Forbes visited him and suggested a partnership in manufacturing kitchen products and cosmetics for the growing women's market. Overton returned with Forbes to Topeka and founded the Overton Hygienic Products Company, which, by 1910, he was running as sole owner. In 1911, he moved the business to Chicago, where it prospered for many years.

Overton was known as a generous employer who paid high wages and maintained good labor relations. He was also known as someone who never discriminated on the basis of race and hired both black and white workers. By 1920, his business was bringing in more than $1 million a year.

In 1922, he decided to open a bank to counteract the discrimination that most black people encountered in applying for loans with the white banks of the time. The Douglass National Bank was located in the Overton Building. He also founded the Victory Life Insurance Company.

Douglass Bank did well during the 1920s, as did most U.S. banks. And similarly, it had great financial difficulties after the 1929 stock market crash. In 1932, the bank was forced to close, and, like many others, could not return all the funds that had been deposited. This was because most of the borrowers were bankrupt and unable to pay back their loans. However, Overton's bank paid 38 cents on the dollar—the highest pay-back rate of any bank forced to close.

Overton eventually went back to the business world. In 1940, he bought the *Chicago Bee,* a black newspaper, and its circulation soon doubled under his management. Overton continued to run the paper until he died of a heart attack on September 16, 1946, after a career that had lasted more than 60 years. His friends and family would not forget Overton's personal motto: "Make each day count for more than the previous day."

Further Reading: *The Negro Vanguard,* by Richard Bardolph, New York: Rinehart, 1961.

—R. K.

❖ OWENS, JESSE (James Cleveland Owens)
(1913–1980), *Olympic gold medalist*

At first, Jesse Owens was famous for having set three world's records in one afternoon while still in college in 1935. Then, while at the Olympic Games in Berlin in 1936, he broke 10 Olympic records and matched two,

Jesse Owens (National Archives)

winning four gold medals and helping the U.S. team win 12 of 23 men's track-and-field events. Owens also set a world record at the Olympics in the broad jump.

His victories at the Olympics had a special significance, for the games that year were held in Adolf Hitler's Nazi Germany. Hitler had preached the overall superiority of the "Aryan race," or more specifically northern white Europeans, and the athletic successes of Owens did much to counter this racist propaganda.

Owens received no official recognition for his feat in his own country until 40 years after the fact, when he was awarded a 1976 Presidential Medal of Freedom, in recognition of his lifetime achievement.

Jesse Owens was born on September 12, 1913, the seventh of 11 children, in the rural hamlet of Oakville, Alabama. His parents were sharecroppers—farmers who rented their land in exchange for giving up a share of the crop. Originally Jesse was called "James Cleveland

Owens," but when his family later moved north to Ohio, the "J. C." for James Cleveland was interpreted as "Jesse," and the name stuck.

As a child, Owens was thin and frail, and he came near death while suffering from recurring pneumonia. But his mother nursed him back to health—as she would do time and again.

Owens was still young when, largely out of concern for his having better health care, his family moved north to Cleveland, Ohio. Times were hard for the future star athlete, since Henry Owens, his father, was past 40 and not trained for work other than farming; he could neither read nor write. Emma Owens, his mother, worked as a domestic, and the Owens brothers all got jobs. Jesse worked for a grocery and a greenhouse.

Owen's athletic coach was concerned about his poor health, the result of his four bouts with pneumonia. The coach encouraged Owens to run, in order to strengthen his lungs for the cold northern winters. However, Owens couldn't come out for track, as he had to work after school. The coach encouraged him to come to school an hour early for a morning workout and would bring Owens a large breakfast each day as further practical support. The sickly Owens soon became a champion athlete.

He was popular at Cleveland's East Technical High School, and, despite being one of the few black students there, he was elected student council president. His family was still poor, so Owens shined shoes while attending high school. Even then, he was an outstanding athlete, winning a broad-jump championship.

His athletic feats brought him many scholarship offers from colleges and universities. Initially, however, he turned them down. Even though he had already married at the age of 16 and needed to support his wife, he told his coach that he couldn't bear the thought of living well while the rest of his family went hungry.

Once again his supportive coach took action. He arranged for the coach at Ohio State University to get Owens's father a permanent state job. Then Owens enrolled in the school—but stuck to his plan to do without a scholarship. Instead, he held several jobs at the school—waiting on tables, working in the library, and operating an elevator—and paid his own way.

At Ohio State, Owens continued to excel as an athlete. When he was a sophomore, Owens had one particularly spectacular day—on May 25, 1935, at a Big Ten track-and-field meet in Ann Arbor, Michigan. Although Owens was still complaining of a sore back from a fight he had recently been in, he broke three track-and-field records, in the broad jump, the 220-yard dash, and the 220-yard low hurdles, while matching the world record for the 100-yard dash. He accomplished all of this in 75 minutes of one afternoon.

When Owens went to the Olympics, he was closely watched by both black and white Americans, all of whom had heard of Hitler's theories about black "inferiority." Perhaps because of the symbolic quality of his victories, there was a rumor that Hitler had snubbed Owens at the Olympics and had refused to shake his hand. However, Owens himself denied that it had happened, as did a sportswriter who attended the games.

His victories helped to contribute to the integration of American sports. After the 1936 Olympics, a writer asked Horace Stoneham, president of baseball's New York Giants, how long it would be before blacks were playing with whites on professional baseball teams. "Within 10 years," Stoneham answered, anticipating Jackie ROBINSON's 1947 debut with the formerly all-white Brooklyn Dodgers.

After his Olympic victory, Owens won the Associated Press's Athlete of the Year citation. But this time, he and his wife had had a child and were expecting a second (they eventually had three daughters). He couldn't afford to finish school, and he was only able to find a job as a $30-a-week Cleveland playground instructor. He eventually earned his tuition by racing against a horse—a degrading but profitable feat.

Later, his name was used to promote a chain of cleaning stores, and he was made full partner in the operation, returning him enough income to buy a new house. But the business suddenly went bankrupt and his partners deserted him, leaving him with a $55,000 debt. He managed to pay off this and his other debts by recruiting black workers for the Ford Motor Company during World War II.

Owens eventually settled in Chicago. By this time he had become a charismatic public speaker and he traveled extensively, speaking about sports, civil rights, and his own life. In 1955, President Eisenhower named him "Ambassador of Sports," and he toured the world for the State Department. Later, he started a jazz radio program and developed a public relations agency, finally achieving financial security.

He spoke out critically of some black activists in his 1970 book *Blackthink* (New York: William Morrow). However, in 1972, Owens rethought his position and published his new views in a book called *I Have Changed* (New York: William Morrow).

In 1971, as a result of health problems, Owens retired and moved to Phoenix. He died of lung cancer on March 31, 1980. In 1983 he was inducted into the Olympic Hall of Fame.

Further Reading: *Jesse Owens: The Man Who Outran Hitler*, by Ralph Neimark, New York: G.P. Putnam & Sons, 1978; *Jesse Owens,* by Mervyn Kaufman, New York: Crowell, 1973; *Jesse Owens,* by William Baker, New York: Free Press, Collier, Macmillan, 1986; *Jesse Owens, Olympic Hero,* by Francene Sabin, Mahwah, N.J.: Troll Associates, 1986.

—*R. K.*

❖ PAIGE, LEROY ROBERT ("Satchel")
(1906–1982), baseball player

Satchel Paige was one of the greatest baseball players who ever lived. Although prejudice kept him from playing in the white-only major leagues for most of his life, he had an outstanding reputation in the Negro leagues. When he was finally allowed into the major leagues, following Jackie ROBINSON's pioneer entry, he was already in his mid-forties. Yet he led the American League's Cleveland Indians to win the 1948 pennant. And in 1952, playing with the St. Louis Browns, he was elected to be one of the American League All Stars.

Leroy Paige was born in Mobile, Alabama, on July 7, 1906. From a very early age, he worked at various jobs to earn money. When he was 12, he was sent to a local reform school for stealing toy rings from a store. It was during the five years he spent in reform school that Paige discovered his innate talent for pitching a baseball.

Paige was soon nicknamed "Satchel," although no one agrees on just how he got that name. Some say it was because of his huge, "satchel-sized" feet. Others say it had something to do with "Satchmo," the nickname of the great trumpet player Louis ARMSTRONG. Still others say it derived from a job he had held as a seven-year-old, carrying satchels (small suitcases) from the local train station.

Although he first worked as an ice carrier and a porter, Paige later pitched for the Mobile Tigers in 1924 and 1925, and for the Chattanooga Black Lookouts in 1926. He continued to play for various semi-pro black teams, pitching for the Birmingham Black Barons in 1928 and the Nashville Elite Giants in 1931.

Throughout the 1920s and 1930s, Paige built up a phenomenal record that made him legendary in the sports world. In 1933, he won 31 games and lost four. In 1934, while he was pitching for a white club in Bismarck, North Dakota, his team won 104 of 105 games. Paige himself was said to have started 29 games within a single month.

Although professional baseball was segregated, Paige's reputation was so great that white ballplayers sometimes arranged to play against him. In 1933, he pitched a game against Dizzy Dean—and won, 1–0. In 1937, he pitched to Joe DiMaggio, who called him "the best pitcher I ever faced."

Paige seemed to be able to remain an active athlete, holding himself to the highest standards, at an age when many others were too old to play. In 1942, he was over 35 years old, yet he led the Kansas City Monarchs to victory in the Negro World Series. Even more surprisingly, he helped his team take the pennant four years later, racking up some new records: pitching 64 straight innings with no score; and allowing only two runs in 93 innings.

Paige continued to play until he was 65, traveling on the exhibition circuit with the Harlem Globetrotters and similar teams of athletic showmen. In 1969, the Atlanta Braves hired him as a coach for a year. In 1972, Paige was elected to the Baseball Hall of Fame. He died at the age of 76, in 1982, after a long struggle with heart problems and emphysema.

Further Reading: *Maybe I'll Pitch Forever,* by Satchel Paige, as told to David Lipman, Garden City, N.Y.: Doubleday, 1964; *Only the Ball Was White,* by Robert W. Peterson, New York: McGraw-Hill, 1984 ed.; *Invisible Men: Life in Baseball's Negro Leagues,* by Donn Rogosin, New York: Atheneum, 1983; *The Kansas City Monarchs: Champions of Black Baseball,* by Janet Bruce, Lawrence, Kan.: University Press of Kansas, 1985.

—R. K.

❖ PARKER, CHARLES, JR.
(1920–1955), *jazz musician*

Perhaps the single most influential figure in modern jazz, Charlie Parker transformed the art of playing the saxophone during the early 1940s. Known throughout the jazz world as Bird, this legendary figure helped to create the revolutionary jazz style known as bebop.

Born on August 29, 1920, in Kansas City, Kansas, Parker was an only child. His father left home when he was very young, and he grew up under the influence of his devoted mother, Adele. Adele Parker wanted her son to be a doctor and urged him to work hard in school. However, when Charlie reached high school he discovered the alto saxophone, and from then on his burning desire was to be a great musician. He organized a band called the Deans of Swing and devoted so much time to practicing that his grades suffered. Upon learning that he was going to be left back, Parker quit school. Before he even turned 16, he married his high school sweetheart, Rebecca Ruffin, and moved her into his mother's house.

Though Parker was full of confidence in his ability, he soon found that the music world was not waiting for him with open arms. In 1936, shortly after his marriage, he took part in a jam session at Kansas City's Reno Club, where many of the leading jazz musicians congregated. He tried to impress the veterans by taking a solo, but he fumbled badly and was hooted off the stage. Angry and humiliated, Parker went home and began to practice with redoubled·passion. With the aid of a friend, he spent months studying music theory and experimenting with new techniques on his horn. He later explained

what took place during these intensive sessions: "I realized by using the high notes of the chords as a melodic line, and by the right harmonic progression, I could play what I heard inside me. That's when I was born."

Parker first emerged onto the jazz scene as a member of the Jay McShann Orchestra, which he joined in 1939. According to legend, the other members of the band began calling him Yardbird—later shortened to Bird—because he was so fond of chicken. They were also deeply impressed by Parker's playing. Audiences, on the other hand, were not yet ready for Parker's solos—compared to the lush sound of the swing music that ruled jazz during the 1930s, Parker's dazzling innovations sounded rough and unmusical.

Determined to achieve recognition, Parker moved to New York in 1942. He played in large bands for two years and then gravitated toward the clubs on West 52nd Street, where he could play in smaller combos and have more scope for creativity. In 1944, Parker teamed up with four other jazz greats—trumpeter Dizzy Gillespie, bassist Ray Brown, pianist Bud Powell, and drummer Max Roach. Together, these five pioneers created bebop, a fast-paced, free-ranging style that changed the face of jazz forever.

When Gillespie left the group in 1945, Parker formed his own combo and became the rage of 52nd Street. He also began to make recordings, some of which—"Ko Ko," "Billie's Bounce," and "Now's the Time," to name a few—rank among the all-time classic jazz discs. Parker then took his group out to Los Angeles, introducing bebop to West Coast audiences. He was now realizing all his musical ambitions, but his personal life was in complete disarray. Parker had been using heroin since the age of 17, and the drug was taking a devastating toll. Parker had already been through two failed marriages, and he was notorious for missing engagements and failing to pay the musicians who worked for him. At the end of 1946, he suffered a nervous breakdown and was committed to a state hospital.

Thanks to expert treatment, Parker made a complete recovery and emerged from the hospital in 1947. He went back to New York, enjoying huge success and a degree of personal tranquility. By 1951, however, Parker had gone back to heroin and was drinking heavily. Because of his association with drug dealers, he could not get a permit to play in night clubs, and his income declined dramatically. By 1955, he was living like a vagabond; while recovering from an illness in a friend's apartment, he suffered a fatal heart attack. Though his career was tragically cut short at the age of 35, Parker created a legacy that has inspired new generations of musicians.

Further Reading: *Celebrating Bird: The Triumph of Charlie Parker,* by Gary Giddins, New York: Morrow, 1986; *Charlie Parker,* by Brian Priestly, New York: Hippocrene, 1984; *Charlie Parker,* by Ron Frankl, New York: Chelsea House, 1993.

—P. K.

❖ PARKS, GORDON ROGER

(1912–), *photographer, cinematographer, film director, novelist, writer, poet*

Gordon Parks began his professional life as a photographer, but went on to become a cinematographer, film director, and writer. He brought these talents together in his film *The Learning Tree,* which he directed and which is based on his novel (New York: Fawcett Books, 1992).

Parks was born in 1912 on a small farm in Fort Scott, Kansas. When he was a teenager, he went to St. Paul, Minnesota. As a young man, he had many different jobs—waiter, lumberjack, piano player, band leader, and semi-professional basketball player.

In 1937, the 25-year-old Parks decided on a career in photography. He moved to Chicago, where he received support from the South Side Community Art Center. The center gave him a darkroom, and helped him to meet artists who taught and inspired him. Eventually, the center director, David Ross, gave him a one-man show.

This show led to new opportunities for Parks. He won a Rosenwald Fund grant, which was given to provide financial support for artists and writers so that they could continue to produce their work. The one-man show also led to a job with the Farm Security Administration, where Parks worked on photographic projects under the direction of Roy Stryker. With World War II imminent, Parks moved on to work as a photographer in the Office of Wartime Information's overseas division.

When the war was over in 1945, Parks went back to work with Stryker on a seven-person team that made documentaries for Standard Oil of New Jersey. In 1949, he got a job with *Life* magazine as a staff photographer.

At that time, *Life* was one of the most widely read magazines in the country. Most of its pages were given to photographs, showing rather than telling about the major stories of the day. Parks covered several major events for *Life,* including a story on a Harlem gang leader, segregation in the South, and crime in the United States. He was also sent to Brazil to do a picture story on a Brazilian boy named Flavio who was living in poverty. In addition to the *Life* story, Parks wrote and directed a documentary film about Flavio.

Parks was assigned to the European staff of *Life* and went to work in Paris. He lived there for more than a year with his wife, two sons, and daughter. Parks's work for *Life* took him on assignments around the world.

Parks found time to develop his interest in music as well. In 1953, his First Concerto for Piano and Orchestra was performed; in 1955, his three piano sonatas were played in concert.

But Parks is best known for his photography and his writing. His written works include a book on photography, the 1963 novel *The Learning Tree,* and the 1966 autobiography *A Choice of Weapons* (St. Paul, Minn.: Minnesota Historical Society, 1986). In 1968, he published *Photos and Poems,* and directed the film based on his novel, a movie he also called *The Learning Tree.* In 1997 the exhibition "Half Past Autumn: The Art of Gordon Parks," a retrospective showcasing Parks's entire multifaceted career, began a four-year tour throughout the United States.

Further Reading: *Glimpses Toward Infinity,* by Gordon Parks, Boston: Bulfinch Press, 1996; *Arias in Silence,* by Gordon Parks, Boston: Bulfinch Press, 1994; *Half Past Autumn: A Retrospective,* by Gordon Parks, Philip Brookman, Corcoran Gallery of Art, Boston: Bulfinch Press, 1997; *Voices in the Mirror: An Autobiography,* by Gordon Parks, New York: Doubleday, 1990; *To Smile in Autumn,* by Gordon Parks, New York: Norton, 1979; *Gordon Parks: Black Photographer and Filmmaker,* by Terry Harnan, Champaign, Ill.: Garrard Pub. Co., 1972.

—R. K.

❖ PARKS, ROSA (Rose Louise McCauley)

(1913–), *civil rights leader*

Rosa Parks began the modern Civil Rights movement when she refused to give up her seat to a white man on a crowded bus in Montgomery, Alabama. Parks's action sparked the Montgomery bus boycotts, which brought Dr. Martin Luther KING, JR., to prominence, and led to a series of other civil rights actions.

Rosa Parks was born Rosa Louise (or Lee) McCauley on February 4, 1913, in Tuskegee, Alabama. She was the daughter of a carpenter and a schoolteacher. She grew up with her mother and brother on her grandparents' Alabama farm. At age 11, she went to the Montgomery Industrial School for Girls, a private school founded by liberal northerners.

In 1932, Rosa married Raymond Parks, a barber who was active in the Civil Rights movement, particularly with black voter registration. Rosa Parks attended Alabama

Rosa Parks *(National Archives)*

State College for a while, then went to work for various civil rights groups, including the Montgomery Voters League and the National Association for the Advancement of Colored People (NAACP) Youth Council.

Parks's activity led to her election in 1943 as NAACP secretary in Montgomery. Throughout the 1940s and 1950s, she worked with that group on behalf of black targets of violence.

Parks's civil rights work was voluntary and not for profit, so she took up sewing, worked as a housekeeper, and sometimes sold life insurance. Like many others, she depended on city buses to get to work. In Montgomery, the first 10 seats of every bus were reserved for white passengers, and black people could not sit in them even if there were no whites on the bus. If the white sections were full, black people sitting in the back of the bus were required to give up their seats to white people.

That was what happened to Parks on December 1, 1955, along with three other black passengers. Four black people were asked to move—so that one white man could sit down.

Adding insult to injury, Parks recognized the bus driver as James F. Blake, who had followed a common practice: He required black passengers to pay their fares up front, get off, and get on again in the back. Sometimes bus drivers would drive away after black passengers had paid, but before they could get on. Parks recalled that, in 1943, Blake had thrown her off the bus for getting on in front.

When Blake asked Parks and the others to move, they all refused at first. Eventually the other three got up, but Parks still refused. She was arrested, taken to jail, and fined $14. Three people came to pay her bail. Clifford and Virginia Durr, white civil rights activists, and E. D. Nixon, former NAACP local president, leader of the Brotherhood of Sleeping Car Porters, and president of the Progressive Democratic Association of Montgomery. Nixon began to discuss with Parks the possibility of using her case as a test to break segregation. Her mother and husband feared for her safety, but Parks decided to go ahead. The Women's Political Council (WPC), a local black group, became most involved in planning the boycott.

The WPC gave out leaflets all over town, especially targeting black church congregations. On December 2, the congregations decided to support the boycott with or without their ministers' support. The ministers formed the Interdenominational Ministerial Alliance (IMA), which met at the Dexter Avenue Baptist Church, the congregation of Martin Luther King, Jr. The ministers wrote their own leaflet and called for a meeting on December 5.

Most white people stayed away from the buses on December 5, and almost all black people did too. By sending out extra white police to ride the buses, the city of Montgomery probably frightened away even more black passengers, who tended to fear the police.

At the December meeting, the IMA became the Montgomery Improvement Association, and Martin Luther King, Jr., was elected to head it. This was the beginning of King's leadership in the Civil Rights movement.

The city council eventually worked with the White Citizens Council, a strong pro-segregationist group. As black people formed car pools and found alternate ways of getting to work, police harassed car-pool drivers. Black people walking to work were harassed by white people.

Many boycotters, including Parks, lost their jobs. King's house was bombed, and he was fined. The NAACP in Alabama was prevented by the court from pursuing most of its activities and suppressed to such an extent that its work was curtailed for the next eight years.

Still, the boycott continued. Originally, it demanded only more courtesy from drivers, the employment of black bus drivers on routes through black neighborhoods, and permission for black people to keep the seats in the back, without having to give them up to whites. By February, the forces of the boycott had increased their demands to total integration of the city buses.

The boycott went on as the case was heard in court. In June, federal judges ruled that segregation was unconstitutional, but Montgomery officials appealed to the Supreme Court. The court upheld the ruling, but Montgomery still did not obey the order. Finally, federal marshals moved into Montgomery. On December 20, 1956, over a year after the boycott started, the buses were finally integrated.

Parks continued to be harassed, as was her husband, who suffered a nervous breakdown. Finally, the couple, along with Parks's mother, moved to Detroit and joined Parks's brother.

Parks could not find work in Detroit, and both she and her husband suffered from severe health problems. To get by, Parks took in sewing, and her husband found a caretaker's job. They were homeless for a while and lived at the Progressive Civil League. In spite of all these difficulties, Parks continued to raise money for the NAACP and traveled around the country on its behalf.

In 1965, Parks began work in the office of Congressman John Conyers, Jr., a civil rights leader in Congress.

Parks's husband died in 1977. A few years later, her mother and her brother died as well. She has suffered from heart problems, but continues to be active, working with the NAACP and other civil rights groups. She has been given numerous awards and honors in recognition of her work.

Further Reading: *Quiet Strength: The Faith, the Hope, and the Heart of a Woman Who Changed a Nation,* by Rosa Parks and Gregory J. Reed, Grand Rapids, Mich.: Zondervan Publishing House, 1995; *The Montgomery Bus Boycott and the Women Who Started It,* by Jo Ann Robinson, Knoxville, Tenn.: University of Tennessee Press, 1988; *Parting the Waters: America in the King Years 1954–1963,* by Taylor Branch, New York: Simon & Schuster, 1988; *When and Where I Enter: The Impact of Black Women on Race and Sex in America,* by Paula Giddings, New York: Morrow, 1984; *Rosa Parks: My Story,* New York: Dial Press, 1992; *Rosa Parks,* by Kai Friese, Englewood Cliffs, N.J.: Silver Burdette Press, 1990; *Don't Ride the Bus on Monday,* by Louise Meriwether, Englewood Cliffs, N.J.: Prentice-Hall, 1973.

—*R. K.*

❖ PAUL, THOMAS, SR.

(1773–1831), *pioneer Baptist organizer*

Thomas Paul began the movement for independent Baptist churches in the United States. In Paul's time,

black church members were segregated within the white churches. Paul helped to organize separate black churches where black members had full rights. One of the churches he organized was New York City's Abyssinian Baptist Church, which is still a major political and social force in the black community today.

Although slavery was still in force in 1773, Thomas Paul was born free, the son of a Revolutionary War soldier. Paul was strongly drawn to the Baptist church, as were three of his six brothers, who also became ministers.

Paul began preaching in 1801 and was ordained in 1805. In that same year, he married Catherine Waterhouse, with whom he later had three children.

After his ordination, Paul moved to Boston, where black people were just beginning to form their own African Meeting House, although much of the money for the church building came from white businesspeople.

According to the custom of the time, people were allowed to buy their own pews—but in this church, only "Africans and people of color" were allowed to buy. The African Meeting House was the first building in Boston to be built entirely by African Americans. Yet when Paul first preached there in 1806, racial customs giving white people precedence were so strong that Paul reserved the first floor for white people and the upper galleries for blacks.

In 1807, Boston's other black minister, Prince Hall, died, leaving Paul as the only black man of the church. This gave him a powerful leadership position in the city, particularly because his church was the focal point for the black community. The African School, which had had to meet in private homes before, now occupied the first floor of the church.

In the Boston of that era, it was common to note "colored" after black people's names in the city directory. Until 1821, Paul was one of the few black people who was not designated in that way—a sign that he was accepted by the white community. However, after 1821, he was also identified as "colored" in the directory, which suggests that racial designation was still important to white Bostonians and that racial barriers still existed.

Paul's fame and prestige reached as far as New York. Some Baptists from that city invited Paul to help them organize their own church. He founded the Abyssinian Baptist Church in 1809, then returned to Boston.

In 1823, Paul went to preach in Haiti, where he hoped to act as a missionary. The Catholic population was not very receptive to Paul, especially because he could not speak French. Paul soon returned to Boston, where he worked to abolish slavery and improve the black community.

As a minister, Paul was an influential leader, and he took part in many important actions. In 1827, he went to a meeting called by David WALKER in order to support John RUSSWURM's new newspaper, *Freedom's Journal.* Paul became a strong promoter for the paper.

Paul also supported white abolitionist William Lloyd Garrison. When Garrison founded the first abolitionist society in New England, the group met at Paul's church.

In 1829, Paul resigned from his ministry, and after a long and painful illness, he died in 1831. The church he had helped to build became a Jewish synagogue from 1904 to 1972 and later the Museum of Afro-American History.

—*R. K.*

❖ PAYNE, DANIEL ALEXANDER

(1811–1893), *first African-American college president; leader of the African Methodist Episcopal Church*

Daniel Alexander Payne purchased Ohio's Wilberforce University from the white church group that had founded it. As its president, he turned Wilberforce into one of the major black universities in the United States. Payne was America's first black college president, as well as the first black president of a black university (until then, America's black schools had been headed by whites).

Payne was also a bishop in the African Methodist Episcopal (A.M.E.) Church. He was active in developing educational standards for that church's ministry and promoting education for church members. After the Civil War, he was a key figure in developing higher education for African Americans.

Daniel Alexander Payne was born in 1811 in Charleston, South Carolina, to free parents of mixed black, white, and Indian ancestry. His parents died when he was not yet 10 years old and he went to live with a great-aunt. He received some formal education and some tutoring in French, Latin, and Greek.

In 1828, when he was not yet 18 years old, Payne founded his first school. During the day he taught children; at night he taught adult slaves.

In 1829, David WALKER had published his *Appeal,* in which he advocated that black people should rise up to end slavery by any means necessary. In 1831, Nat TURNER led his famous slave revolt. This so frightened slave owners that many states made it illegal for slaves to become literate. In December 1834, the South Carolina legislature decided that any teacher of slaves should be fined and whipped. In 1835, Payne left South Carolina, saying he would never return until slavery was ended.

When Payne went north, he decided to study for the ministry. From 1835 to 1837, he attended a seminary and worked in a variety of jobs, such as waiting on tables and shining shoes. Although eye problems ended his studies, he was licensed to preach in 1837 and was ordained in 1839.

Payne was offered the chance to become a traveling spokesperson for the American Anti-Slavery Society, but he felt the job would be inappropriate for a minister. Instead, in 1840, he opened a school in Philadelphia.

Payne had been involved with many different denominations, but in 1841, he settled with the African Methodist Episcopal Church. Unlike the other churches he had joined, this one was run by black people, and so offered him more scope for his leadership. Black people were more likely than the prejudiced white church leaders had been to treat his ideas with respect.

Soon Payne was helping to organize churches around the country, founding a school for ministers, and developing other church groups. He did this at a time when many white people were actively opposed to the education of black ministers. They feared that if black ministers were educated, they would become more likely to incite rebellion.

In 1847, Payne married Julia A. Ferris, but she died within the year. In 1852, Payne was ordained a bishop. With the power of this new position, he continued to travel throughout the country, even into slave territory. His focus was always on improving education, whether through setting up schools, starting literary and historical societies, or organizing mothers to teach their children at home.

Payne continually stressed that education was the key to black power—greater than gold. He argued that although money was highly valued in U.S. society, mere possession of money did not guarantee that a black person would be respected. "In a country like this, where gold is an *idol* to be worshipped, who fears a 'rich negro'?"

In 1853, Payne was married a second time, to Eliza J. Clark. He found it difficult to provide for his family but continued to be dedicated to educational church work. He also worked with Radical Republicans to convince President Lincoln to end slavery.

In 1863, Payne raised enough money from donations to buy Wilberforce University and he began to set it up as a black institution. He served as Wilberforce's president through 1876 and continued to be actively involved in its development thereafter. Under his leadership, the school developed into a major black educational center. It was Payne who was responsible for offering W. E. B. DUBOIS a position there.

In 1893, Payne died at Wilberforce, but he was buried in Baltimore.

Further Reading: *Men of Mark: Eminent, Progressive, and Rising,* by John W. Simmons, New York: Arno Press, 1968 reprint of 1887 ed.; *The Lonesome Road,* by Saunders Redding, New York: Anchor Press/Doubleday, 1973.

—*R. K.*

❖ PERKINS, MARION
(1908–1961), *sculptor*

Marion Perkins is known for his powerful sculpture, which uses black folk and religious figures to create haunting images of sorrow and endurance. His work was awarded the Art Institute of Chicago sculpture-purchase prize of 1951. His work has been exhibited throughout the United States and Europe, and is in the permanent collection of the Chicago Art Institute.

Marion Perkins was born in Arkansas, the only child of a farming family. In 1916, the Perkinses moved to Chicago, where Marion attended Wendell Phillips High School for three years. Before he could get his diploma, he left school to support himself, and worked at a variety of jobs, selling newspapers and washing dishes.

During the depression, the federal government established the Works Progress Administration (WPA), to administer a program for combating unemployment by commissioning various public works. The WPA also disbursed funds for artists and art classes. Perkins was hoping to be a playwright at the time, and enrolled in a writing class. But when he got the chance to study under noted sculptor Si Gordon, he realized that what he most wanted was to be a sculptor too.

After the WPA was ended, Perkins worked at the Southside Community Art Center, which was then directed by Peter Pollack. Pollack later became publicity director for the Chicago Art Institute, which enabled him to recommend Perkins's work for an Art Institute prize. This helped to gain Perkins national recognition.

Nevertheless, for many years Perkins had to work as a freight handler, since he could not make a living from his sculpture. Perkins was married and had three children to support.

Eventually, Perkins went to teach at Jackson State Teachers College—but found that the school did not have enough money or materials for proper art education. Perkins then returned to Chicago to raise funds and find art materials for the Jackson State students.

Financial support for Jackson State was later carried on by the Marion Perkins Memorial Foundation, which was started by Perkins's friends after the artist's death in 1961.

Perkins's work mainly consists of simple, haunting figures. "Man of Sorrows," his image of a black Christ, won a Chicago Art Institute award, as did "John Henry," a huge sculpture of the famous black folk figure. Much of his other work draws on African imagery and themes. Sculpture such as "Man Looking Upward," a depiction of a human reaction to the atomic bomb falling on Hiroshima, makes use of social issues and themes.

Perkins often had to scavenge for his sculptural materials. He might roam the city or go out at night, finding marble or stone from demolished buildings to use for his sculptures. Family members described him as being driven by a powerful, unseen force to continue with his art.

Further Reading: *Marion Perkins: A Retrospective,* by Margaret Burroughs, Washington, D.C.: Evans-Tibbs, 1982.

—*R. K.*

❖ POITIER, SIDNEY
(1924–), *actor, director*

Sidney Poitier was the first black person to win an Academy Award for Best Actor, a prize he received in 1963 for his work in *Lilies of the Field.* Poitier won fame on both stage and screen, particularly for his roles in both the Broadway and film version of Lorraine HANSBERRY's *A Raisin in the Sun,* the first play written by an African-American woman to be staged on Broadway.

Poitier was known for the dignity and passion he brought to his roles. He was one of the first black actors to appear in movies as a heroic leading man. Although some of today's critics consider the characters he portrayed as improbably faultless, at the time, the brave, kind, and competent characters he portrayed were breakthrough images for black people in the movies. Even today, Poitier remains one of the most important black actors ever to have worked in Hollywood. He has been a Kennedy Center honoree and a recipient of the American Film Institute Lifetime Achievement Award. In 1997 he was made the Bahamas' Ambassador to Japan.

Sidney Poitier was born to a Bahamian couple in Miami. He grew up in the West Indies, but returned to Miami when he was 16. He drifted on to New York and earned his living at odd jobs such as dishwashing.

Poitier's first experience in the theater was a severe rejection. He answered an ad in the paper for actors and showed up at the American Negro Theater in Harlem. The director asked Poitier if he was really an actor, gave him a script, and sent him up to read. Poitier gave a frozen performance and was told, "You're no actor. And you can't be one." Poitier left—but he had made up his mind to become an actor.

Poitier spent four years in the U.S. Army and worked for six months to overcome his strong West Indian accent. Then he returned to the American Negro Theater—and was accepted. He joined a group of such key black actors as Harry BELAFONTE, Ossie DAVIS, Ruby DEE, Earle Hyman, and Lloyd Richards. In 1959, Richards directed Poitier in *A Raisin in the Sun* on Broadway—and in the 1980s, he directed works by playwright August WILSON.

In 1946, Poitier landed a small role in an all-black Broadway production of *Lysistrata.* He said later that he was so nervous that he fumbled his way through the part, making the audience laugh. But critics praised his comic abilities. He worked in the 1948 tour of *Anna Lucasta,* then got a key role in Joseph Mankiewicz's film *No Way Out.*

This first movie part turned out to be typical of the parts Poitier would play: A young doctor, unjustly accused by white people, is imbued with such compassion that he saves the white man who is trying to kill him.

Throughout the 1950s, Poitier starred in many dramatic films, including *Cry, the Beloved Country* and *Blackboard Jungle.* The 1957 film *Edge of the City,* and *The Defiant Ones* in 1958, made Poitier a star. Both movies focus on the close friendship between Poitier and a white actor, setting precedents for the white-black "buddy" films of the 1970s and 1980s.

Poitier's next major role was in the groundbreaking *Raisin in the Sun.* The character Walter Younger was quite different from any of his previous roles. A poor chauffeur is frustrated almost to the point of violence by his dead-end job and his inability to provide a better life for his family. Though considered by many critics to be deserving of an Oscar nomination for his performance Poitier won an Oscar instead for *Lilies of the Field,* in which he plays a free-wheeling, footloose handyman who ends up helping a group of white nuns build a chapel. Many critics saw this role as a continuation of the all too typical Hollywood image of the compliant black servant.

Critics also noted that Poitier was being given a new stereotype—that of an impossibly noble, sexless "Negro" who is rarely allowed to contemplate romance, conflict, or dreams of his own, but who is seen primarily in relation to white people. In the 1965 film *A Patch of Blue,* he befriends a young, blind white girl. Although he is allowed a brief romance with a black woman, the focus of the film is on his relationship with the girl, to whom he doesn't want to reveal his race.

In the 1967 film *To Sir With Love,* he teaches a group of poor white students in London. In *Guess Who's Coming to Dinner,* of the same year, he's engaged to a wealthy white woman, but the relationship is presented in the most asexual of terms, and the focus of the film is not on his feelings for her but on her white family's reaction to his being black.

Black audiences began to criticize Poitier for not relating more deeply to the black characters he played on screen, and they criticized the implicit politics of the movies in which he played. Poitier found himself in a difficult position. As an actor, he had little control over the work he did, and his black and white audiences had very different perspectives and demands. He attempted to get more creative control over his films, but was not successful, either financially or artistically.

In the 1970s, Poitier turned from acting to directing. With such films as *Uptown Saturday Night* and *Stir Crazy,* he featured a new generation of black comic actors who did well at the box office. Although politics took a back seat in these films, black audiences enjoyed the humor and charisma of such stars as Richard Pryor and Denise Nicholas.

In the 1980s, Poitier's films did not have the dramatic range or the political substance of his earlier work. He was also more likely to be the director rather than an actor, and generally, his impact was not as great. He directed mainly comic films, with such stars as Bill COSBY.

But in the 1990s, Poitier's roles were more in keeping with his stature. For example, he portrayed South African leader Nelson Mandela in the 1997 made-for-TV movie *Mandela and DeKlerk.*

Further Reading: *This Life,* by Sidney Poitier, New York: Knopf, 1980; *The Films of Sidney Poitier,* by Alvin H. Marill, Secaucus, N.J.: Citadel Press, 1978; *The Evolution of Character Portrayals in the Films of Sidney Poitier,* ed. by Garth S. Gourett, New York: Garland Pub., 1993; *Sidney Poitier,* by Carol Bregman, New York: Chelsea House, 1988.

—R. K.

❖ POWELL, ADAM CLAYTON, JR.
(1908–1972), *U.S. representative, minister, civil rights leader*

Adam Clayton Powell, Jr., is best known for being the first black congressman from the East, serving as representative from the Harlem district, from 1945 to 1970.

In 1960, Powell took the chair of the influential House Committee on Education and Labor, a position that made him the most powerful black representative up to that time. Under his leadership, the federal commitment to education went from $450 million to $10 billion, and he helped to expedite the first federal aid to colleges and universities. He was also instrumental in the establishment of the National Endowment for the Humanities, and he legislated bills to fund teacher education and libraries.

In 1963, Lyndon Johnson called Powell "one of the most powerful men in America."

Adam Clayton Powell, Jr., was born in New Haven, Connecticut. He was the son of Adam Clayton Powell, Sr., a minister and author.

Powell grew up in New York City, attended Colgate University in upstate New York, and went on to get an M.A. from Columbia University in 1932—an unusual educational accomplishment for a black person in the midst of the Great Depression.

In 1931, while still attending school, Powell began to assist his father, who was then minister of the Abyssinian Baptist Church, a powerful Harlem institution. Powell decided to become a minister himself and obtained a doctor of divinity from Shaw University in Raleigh, North Carolina. In 1937, he took over for his father at the Abyssinian Baptist Church, preaching to the largest African-American Protestant congregation in the United States.

Traditionally, the ministers of the African-American community have been civil rights leaders as well, and Powell was no exception. He was influenced by the Buying Power movement that had begun in Chicago and helped to organize a similar movement in Harlem.

The Buying Power movement was an effort by the black community to force white employers to hire more black employees. Its focus was on white-owned businesses that depended on black customers. Its tactics were picket lines, boycotts, and mass protests.

In New York, Powell led a movement to increase black employment at the telephone, power, and bus companies; at dime stores and department stores; at beverage companies; and at the New York World's Fair. As a result, some 10,000 new jobs were brought to Harlem. White commentators of the time were surprised that so many middle- and upper-class black people joined the picket lines.

As a result of this leadership, Powell was elected to the New York City Council in 1941. In 1942, he began to publish a weekly newspaper, the *People's Voice*.

Powell's political activity had given him a firm base in Harlem. In 1945 he was able to become the first black member of Congress from the East. He used his position in Congress to push through the Kennedy and Johnson administrations' major legislation for fighting poverty and aiding education.

Adam Clayton Powell, Jr. *(Library of Congress)*

Powell was married three times: first, to the star of the Cotton Club cabaret, Isabel Washington; then to famed jazz pianist Hazel Scott; and finally to Yvette Flores Diago. He and Diago became the parents of a son, Adam Clayton Powell III.

In 1960, Powell encountered difficulties with a woman named Esther James, who sued Powell for calling her a "bag woman"—a person who helps to supply money for illegal activities. By 1966, the case had gone through 10 courts and 80 judges, and Powell still refused to pay the libel judgment, which he believed was unfair.

In November 1966, Powell was elected to his 12th term in Congress—so his constituents evidently were not convinced by the accusations and criticism directed at Powell or saw it as politically motivated and racially biased. Congress, however, was unwilling to accept Powell's response. His fellow representatives were upset, both about the court case and about Powell's alleged misuse of public funds. As a result, Powell was expelled from the House. At the time, some members of Congress were quoted as saying that, in part, their concern was that Powell did not seem sorry enough for what he had done.

Civil rights leaders claimed that if Powell had been white, he might have been censured but never expelled. They pointed to the case of Connecticut Senator Christopher Dodd, also accused of misuse of funds, who was censured but allowed to keep his seat. Apparently Harlem voters agreed, for they reelected Powell the following month, and he continued to serve until he was defeated by Charles Rangel in 1970.

After losing the 1970 election, Powell retired to Bimini, an island in the Bahamas. Two years later, he died of cancer in Miami.

Further Reading: *King of the Cats: The Life and Times of Adam Clayton Powell, Jr.,* by Wil Haygood, New York: Houghton Mifflin Co., 1994; *Adam Clayton Powell,* by Robert E. Jakoubek, New York: Chelsea House, 1988; *Adam Clayton Powell: Portrait of a Marching Black,* by James Haskins, New York: Dial Press, 1971; *Adam by Adam,* by Adam Clayton Powell, New York: Secaucus, N.J.: Citadel Press, 1994; *Marching Blacks,* by Adam Clayton Powell, New York: Dial Press, 1971.

—R. K.

Colin Powell (*Department of Defense*)

❖ POWELL, COLIN LUTHER

(1937–   ), *military leader, government official*

As the first African American to serve as the chairman of the Joint Chiefs of Staff, Colin Powell rose from humble beginnings to the highest echelons of the U.S. government. His leadership during the 1991 Persian Gulf War made him a national hero and a potential candidate for the presidency.

The son of hardworking Jamaican immigrants, Powell was born on April 5, 1937, in Harlem and grew up in a blue-collar neighborhood in the South Bronx. After graduating from Morris High School in 1954, he enrolled in the City College of New York, where he joined the Reserve Officers Training Corps (ROTC). Powell found that he enjoyed military discipline and also discovered that he had a rare gift for leadership. By his senior year, he rose to cadet colonel, the highest rank in the ROTC. When Powell received his degree in 1958, he immediately joined the U.S. Army as a second lieutenant.

In 1962, Powell was assigned to Vietnam as a military adviser and took command of a South Vietnamese infantry battalion. While leading his men on patrol the following year, he suffered a serious foot wound caused by a booby trap. Powell returned to Vietnam for a second tour of duty in 1968 and was injured again in a helicopter crash. Powell's service in Vietnam earned him a number of decorations, including the Bronze Star, the Soldiers Medal, and the Purple Heart.

Posted back to the United States, Powell began to alternate between active-duty commands and political service in Washington. After earning an M.B.A. degree from Georgetown University in 1971, he was promoted to the rank of major and served a year as a White House Fellow. The civilian officials he worked with in the White House were deeply impressed with Powell's character and abilities, and two in particular—Caspar Weinberger and Frank Carlucci—were later to play key roles in furthering his career. Powell returned to active duty in 1973 as a battalion commander of U.S. infantry forces stationed in Korea. Promoted to colonel, he attended the elite National War College in 1975 and then became a brigade commander with the 101st Airborne Division.

In 1977, Powell was promoted to the rank of brigadier general and appointed senior military assistant to the secretary of defense. After completing that assignment, he served as assistant division commander of the Fourth

Infantry Division. Powell's career took a major leap forward in 1983, when he was appointed military assistant to Secretary of Defense Caspar Weinberger. He then worked with National Security Adviser Frank Carlucci to reorganize the National Security Council. When Carlucci left the government in 1987, Powell was eager to return to military duty, but President Ronald Reagan persuaded him to step in as the new national security adviser. When the Reagan administration came to an end in January 1989, Powell happily donned his uniform again, taking over the U.S. Forces Command at Fort McPherson, Georgia. Several months later, the new president, George Bush, nominated Powell to be chairman of the Joint Chiefs of Staff, choosing him over several officers with more seniority.

Now a four-star general, Powell proved highly effective as the nation's number-one soldier. He developed what became known as the Powell Doctrine, urging that the United States use military force only to achieve clear and realistic political goals. Powell put this principle into practice in 1991, when he played a major role in planning and carrying out U.S. military operations in the Persian Gulf. Taking part in numerous news conferences and briefings, Powell inspired enormous confidence in the American public. When Operation Desert Storm succeeded in driving Iraqi forces from Kuwait, Powell emerged a national hero.

After Powell retired from the army in 1993, he settled down in an affluent Virginia suburb with his wife, Alma; wrote his autobiography; traveled the lecture circuit; and served on the boards of numerous charitable organizations. Powell stepped onto the national stage once again in 2000 when President-elect George W. Bush nominated him for the high-ranking cabinet position of secretary of state. Powell had been a strong and very visible supporter of Bush, son of the previous President Bush, during the campaign. Powell was confirmed secretary of state by the U.S. Senate in January 2001. After the attacks of September 11, 2001, on the World Trade Center and Pentagon, Powell's role became even more critical.

Further Reading: *My American Journey: An Autobiography,* by Colin Powell with Joseph E. Persico, New York: Random House, 1995; *In His Own Words: Colin Powell,* by Colin L. Powell, edited by Lisa Shaw, New York: Berkeley Publishing Group, 1995; *Colin Powell,* by Ronald L. Soble, New York: NAL Dutton, 1995; *Colin Powell: A Man of Quality,* by Libby Hughes, Parsippany, N.J.: Silver Burdett Press, 1996; *Colin Powell: Soldier & Patriot,* by Anne E. Schraff, Springfield, N.J.: Enslow Publishers, 1997.

—P. K.

❖ PRICE, LEONTYNE ("Mary")
(1927–), *opera singer*

Leontyne Price had a number of accomplishments as a performer, but she is best known for two: her performance on Broadway in the role of Bess in *Porgy and Bess* and her work with the Metropolitan Opera in the 1960s. Critics have called Price's soprano voice one of the great operatic voices of our time. She has made many recordings of songs as well as operas, and has given concerts throughout the world. She has been honored for her achievements by the Kennedy Center.

Price was born in Laurel, Mississippi, but went to school in the Midwest, receiving her B.A. from Central State College in Ohio in 1948. She went on to study music at the highly regarded Juilliard School of Music in New York. Price studied both at Juilliard and privately, with Florence Page Kimball, until 1952.

The young singer found work very quickly after her studies were completed. She first appeared in New York in 1952, in a Broadway revival of *Four Saints in Three Acts,* a choral work by the contemporary American composer Virgil Thomson. She went on to play Bess in

Leontyne Price *(Library of Congress)*

George Gershwin's *Porgy and Bess*—first in the touring company, then on Broadway.

Price won great acclaim for her work in *Porgy and Bess.* The popular opera also turned out to be significant for her personal life, as it was there that she met William Warfield, who played Porgy. Price and Warfield eventually married, but after five years, they divorced.

After *Porgy and Bess,* Price went on to develop a concert career. She sang throughout the United States and Europe, winning exceptional notices for her 1954 Town Hall concert in New York.

In 1955, Price performed in grand opera for the first time, singing the role of Floria in a network-television performance of Giacomo Puccini's *Tosca.* This led to further concerts and television appearances for Price.

Price had still not sung opera on stage. Finally in 1957, she sang with the San Francisco Opera in François Poulenc's *Dialogues des Carmelites.* Price continued to sing opera with the San Francisco company, as well as the Lyric Opera of Chicago and many European opera companies.

In 1961, Price returned to New York to make her operatic debut there. She sang the role of Leonora in Giuseppe Verdi's opera *Il Trovatore* at the Metropolitan Opera House. Critics raved about Price, and she continued to sing at the Met in roles such as Aida in the Verdi opera of that name, Donna Anna and Donna Elvira in Mozart's *Don Giovanni,* Tatiana in Tchaikovsky's *Eugene Onegin;* Elvira in Verdi's *Ernani,* Minnie in Puccini's *The Girl of the Golden West,* and Cleopatra in Samuel Barber's *Antony and Cleopatra.*

The role of Cleopatra was associated with a special honor for Price. In it, she opened the 1966 Metropolitan Opera season, which was all the more special as that was the year that the new Metropolitan Opera House in Lincoln Center was opened.

Further Reading: *Leontyne Price: Opera Superstar,* by Richard Steins, New York: Blackbirch, Marketing, 1994; *Leontyne Price: Opera Superstar,* by Sylvia Williams, Chicago, Ill.: Children's Press, 1984; *Leontyne Price: Highlights of a Prima Donna,* by Hugh Lee Lyon, New York: Vantage Press, 1973; *Aida,* by Leontyne Price, San Diego, Calif.: Harcourt, Brace, Jovanovich, 1990.

—*R. K.*

❖ PROSSER, GABRIEL

(c. 1775–1800), *leader of a slave revolt*

Gabriel Prosser led a slave revolt that included thousands of slaves—estimates range from 1,000 to 50,000.

Although the revolt was unsuccessful, it demonstrated to both black and white Americans that slaves would not passively accept their condition and were willing to risk their lives for freedom.

Little is known about Prosser's early life. He and his brothers, Martin and Solomon, were slaves on Thomas Prosser's plantation outside of Richmond, Virginia. Prosser had learned to read and write from the master's wife and thereafter studied the Old Testament. He modeled himself after Samson, and believed that God had chosen him to help free his people.

Along with his brothers and his wife, Nanny, Prosser secretly organized more than 1,000 slaves and supervised their manufacture of weapons and bullets. Their plan was to attack Richmond, the capital of Virginia. Prosser planned a three-pronged attack, dividing his forces into three groups, each of which had its own leaders.

The plan was to take the arsenal and the powder house, which would have given the rebels access to more weapons. They also planned to seal off bridges around the city in order to isolate it. The rebels planned to kill as many white people as possible, sparing only French people, Methodists, and Quakers—none of whom were perceived as slave owners.

If Richmond were taken, Prosser planned quick attacks on other cities, with the eventual goal of being named king of Virginia. If the plan failed, the rebels were supposed to go into the mountains and fight as guerrillas.

If the surprise attack had come off as planned, Prosser's uprising might have succeeded, for the city itself could have raised only about 400 or 500 men and 30 guns. The well-armed thousand or more slaves could certainly have triumphed over such a force.

However, the day before the uprising was to take place, two slaves informed the authorities. Virginia's governor responded as if to war, immediately sending troops to Richmond to lie in wait for the attack. In addition, a heavy storm caused streams to rise and wash out the roads around the Prosser plantation. Dispirited, the slaves disbanded; only a few were caught.

Prosser went into hiding, taking refuge on a ship that had run aground near Richmond. When the ship docked at Norfolk, however, he was captured, tried, and later hanged, along with 40 other captured slaves.

Further Reading: *American Negro Slave Revolts,* by Herbert Aptheker, New York: International Publishers, 1983 ed.

—*R. K.*

✤ QUEEN LATIFAH (Dana Owens)
(1970–), *musician, actor, entrepreneur*

The first woman to become a major rap star, Queen Latifah brought a new point of view to a field that had been dominated by male artists and male attitudes. She then branched out into acting and started her own production company, bringing a positive message and an inspiring example to young African Americans.

Queen Latifah was born Dana Owens in Newark, New Jersey, on March 18, 1970. Her parents separated when she was five years old, and she and her brother were raised by her mother. Rita Owens worked two jobs to provide her children with the things they needed, and her accomplishments had a powerful influence on her daughter. When she was eight years old, one of Dana's cousins nicknamed her Latifah, which means "delicate and sensitive" in Arabic.

After attending St. Anne's Roman Catholic School in Newark, Latifah went on to Irvington High School. Tall and athletic, she played forward on the school's basketball team, which won two championships. She also performed with an all-female rap group called Ladies Fresh, adopting the stage name Queen Latifah. "I feel like all black people came from a long line of kings and queens that they've never really had the opportunity to know about," she later explained. "This is my way of giving a tribute to them."

After graduating from high school in 1988, Latifah began to study broadcasting at Manhattan Community College. During this time she recorded a demo entitled "Princess of the Posse." The demo found its way to Tommy Boy Records, and the company signed Latifah immediately. Her first album, *All Hail the Queen,* was released in 1989. Containing songs that included "Wrath of My Madness," "Ladies First," and "Come into My House," *All Hail the Queen* sold 400,000 copies and earned a Grammy Award nomination. The video for "Ladies First" included images of outstanding African-American women, such as Madame C. J. WALKER and Sojourner TRUTH, and presented news footage of the struggle to end apartheid in South Africa.

In 1990, Latifah was named Best Female Rapper in *Rolling Stone* magazine's readers' poll. She released a second album, *Nature of a Sista,* the following year and then left Tommy Boy to sign a contract with Motown. At the same time, she formed her own company, Flavor Unit Management, in Los Angeles. Latifah's first album for Motown, *Black Reign,* appeared in 1993. Combining jazz and reggae elements with rap, *Black Reign* was a major hit, selling 500,000 copies. This made her the first female solo rapper with a gold record, but its success came at a difficult time in Latifah's life. Earlier in the year, her brother had been killed in a motorcycle accident at the age of 23. "That screwed me up for real," she later recalled. "I thought I was crazy. I felt out of touch with

Queen Latifah *(Reuters/David Mcnew/Archive Photos)*

other people on the planet; I was in some zone, and everyone else was here."

Despite her enduring grief, Latifah continued to build her career. She expanded Flavor Unit to include a record label and formed a partnership with Epic Records, issuing albums that featured Naughty by Nature, Heavy D, Bigga Sistas, and other artists. Latifah also branched out into acting, appearing in several films and TV shows. From 1993 to 1998, she portrayed the magazine publisher Khadijah James on the popular sitcom *Living Single.* Her film appearances have included *Jungle Fever* (1991), *My Life* (1993), *Set It Off* (1996), *Sphere* (1998), and *Living Out Loud* (1998).

Among the awards Latifah has gathered are a 1994 Grammy as Best Female Rap Soloist and the 1995 Soul Train Entertainer of the Year Award. She released her

fourth CD, *Order in the Court,* in June 1998. Her success has opened the way for a host of other female rappers, including Yo-Yo, MC Lyte, and Salt-N-Pepa, who regard Latifah as a role model. Though often called a feminist, she aims for universal relevance: "I'm just a proud black woman," Latifah told an interviewer after the release of *All Hail the Queen.* "I don't need to be labeled. . . . I speak to sisters and brothers; that's just how it is."

Further Reading: "Queen Latifah," in *Current Biography 1997 Yearbook,* New York: H. W. Wilson, 1998; "Queen Latifah," by Holly Sorensen, *Us,* March 1998; "The Lady Won't Be Restricted," *Interview,* November 1996; "The Queen Turns 25," by Deborah Gregory, *Essence,* May 1995.

—P. K.

❖ RAINEY, GERTRUDE PRIDGETT ("Ma")
(1886–1939), entertainer known as Mother of the Blues

In the first three decades of the 20th century, a new kind of music was emerging—the blues. It combined the African-American rural traditions of spirituals and work songs with some of the new rhythms being developed by musicians in honky-tonks, bars, and brothels. The music conveyed the sorrows of having no work and no money, or of losing the person you love. One of the musicians who helped shape the blues was the singer known as Ma Rainey.

Ma Rainey was born Gertrude Pridgett on April 26, 1886, in Columbus, Georgia. She was one of three children of Thomas and Ella (Allen) Pridgett. When she was 14, she sang in a talent show at the local opera house.

Four years later, the young Gertrude Pridgett married William "Pa" Rainey, a performer who was traveling through Columbus. She took the name "Ma" Rainey and traveled with her new husband, performing with various minstrel shows.

The Rainey act involved comedy, singing, and dancing. From 1914 to 1916, they called themselves "Rainey and Rainey, the Assassinators of the Blues." Eventually, however, the marriage broke up, and Ma Rainey toured on her own. She usually performed with minstrel shows in the rural South.

She was a large woman who liked to dress in bright, flashy clothes with glittering jewelry. Her mouth was full of gold teeth, which sparkled in the spotlight. Some people found her unattractive—until she began to sing. Then they would be caught up in her powerful voice.

Much of Ma Rainey's enduring fame stems from her early recordings, which permit us to hear what the early blues sounded like. Her first record was made in December 1923, when Rainey was already 37 years old. Over the next five years, she made 90 records, preserving the raw blues sound of the southern fieldworkers.

Ma Rainey wasn't the first person to record the blues, but it was Rainey, along with Bessie SMITH, who was the first to record the distinctive rural southern blues style—the blues of the sharecroppers and fieldworkers. She usually sang lyrics lamenting the loss of a love, as in such famous numbers as "Gone Daddy Blues" and "Trust No Man."

African-American audiences loved her earthy sound, and black people all over the United States bought her records, made with such stars as Louis ARMSTRONG, Fletcher Henderson, Thomas Dorsey, and Coleman Hawkins.

Ma Rainey kept singing until 1935, although record companies weren't interested in her after 1928. After the death of her mother and sister, Rainey returned to live in her home town of Columbus. She spent her last few years managing two theaters that she owned in Rome, Georgia. She died on December 22, 1939.

Further Reading: *Blues Legacies and Black Feminism: Gertrude "Ma" Rainey, Bessie Smith, and Billie Holiday,* by Angela Y. Davis, New York: Pantheon, 1998; *Ma Rainey and the Classic Blues Singers,* by Derrick Stewart-Baxter, New York: Stein & Day, 1970.

—*R. K.*

❖ RANDOLPH, ASA PHILIP
(1889–1979), *labor leader, civil rights leader*

A. Philip Randolph was a prominent leader in the labor, civil rights, and socialist movements. Although his political views changed throughout his life, he remained a highly visible figure with outspoken opinions on the major issues of the day.

Randolph is best known for organizing the Brotherhood of Sleeping Car Porters in 1925, a union that finally won a contract after 10 years of struggle with the Pullman Palace Car Company. His union activity led him, in 1960, to form the Negro American Labor Council, an organization of black trade unionists, of which Randolph served as president until 1966.

He was also active in the civil rights movement. In 1963, he was one of the organizers of the historic March on Washington, at which Martin Luther KING, JR., gave his famous "I Have a Dream" speech. In later years, Randolph founded and served as president of the A. Philip Randolph Institute in New York, working to promote education and training in the skilled trades (such as plumbing, carpentry, machine-tooling, etc.) for African Americans.

Randolph was born in 1889, the son of a Methodist minister in Crescent City, Florida. After his graduation from high school, he traveled north to New York City, where he attended the City College of New York. The young Randolph worked his way through school with a number of odd jobs. Job opportunities for black people

A. Philip Randolph (*Library of Congress*)

were limited, which is evident from Randolph's early job history as a porter, railroad waiter, and elevator operator.

Randolph's college years in New York brought him into contact with the socialist movement, and he soon became active in it. In 1917, he cofounded a major socialist weekly newspaper, *The Messenger.* During this period, he also taught at the Rand School of Social Science, a well-known socialist-oriented college in New York City. With other socialists, he opposed World War I, and often spoke out against it in his political speeches. In 1918, he was jailed for expressing such antiwar statements.

Much socialist activity of this period was oriented toward gaining elective offices, so in 1921, Randolph ran on a socialist platform as a candidate for New York's secretary of state. Although he lost, it was nevertheless of historic significance for a black person to run for statewide office.

Randolph was a gifted speaker and organizer. In addition to his electoral work and teaching, he traveled throughout the United States, making speeches about socialism and contemporary problems.

Then, in 1925, Randolph began his work as a union organizer. He helped to organize the black men working as attendants on the luxurious Pullman railway cars and founded the Brotherhood of Sleeping Car Porters. Many racially biased white trade-union leaders claimed that black people could not form trade unions. Because of the climate of discrimination and segregation, they did not believe that black people were capable of doing the arduous organizing work necessary to win contracts—especially when union organizing could be dangerous. Union workers and organizers were often fired, harassed, threatened, or even physically attacked. Nevertheless, Randolph and the porters doggedly persisted for 10 years, until they finally won their contract and unionized the trains.

In addition to his labor activities, Randolph was a national leader in promoting civil rights. In 1936, he acted as president at the founding convention of the National Negro Congress, which was attended by more than 800 people from more than 500 groups, including the National Association for the Advancement of Colored People. The congress focused on establishing local councils in as many cities as possible, to push for civil rights legislation through protest meetings and other direct actions. Randolph eventually resigned from the organization, which was broken up in 1940 by charges that communists were involved.

Meanwhile, Randolph's labor victories were the basis of further gains for black workers. Randolph pushed President Franklin D. Roosevelt to form a Fair

Employment Practices Committee, in order to fight discrimination in war-production industries and government employment. Roosevelt was reluctant to take this position, but Randolph claimed that he could mobilize 100,000 people to march on Washington.

The prospect of public pressure on the White House during wartime was upsetting to many, even to white people who had come out strongly against discrimination. But Randolph insisted that something had to be done, and done immediately, if the march was to be prevented.

Finally, Roosevelt gave in. In June 1941, he issued the first presidential executive order on race relations since the Emancipation Proclamation. It banned discrimination in war industries having government contracts and apprenticeship programs. Soon afterward, Roosevelt formed the Fair Employment Practices Committee.

Although this helped to improve conditions for black people during World War II, the end of the war was marked by attacks on black veterans, as well as setbacks to the New Deal policies that had helped to provide social services to black people. Civil rights gains seemed to be stalled in the Congress. President Harry S Truman appointed a Civil Rights Committee to look into the matter, but its recommendations were ignored. Randolph repeated his earlier tactic, threatening to lead a civil-disobedience movement against Truman's proposal for a peacetime draft, if civil rights gains were not protected.

Once again, Randolph was successful. In 1948, President Truman installed a new review board to combat discrimination in federal employment. He also formed a President's Committee on Equal Treatment and Opportunity in the armed forces.

Randolph worked for civil rights in other ways. In 1942, for example, New York City mayor Fiorello H. La Guardia appointed him to the New York Housing Authority, where he opposed discrimination in housing.

His union leadership was further recognized when Randolph was appointed to the American Federation of Labor-Congress of Industrial Organizations executive council in 1955. That was the first year of the merger of the two major union organizations, the AFL and the CIO. Two years later, in 1957, Randolph became vice president of the Brotherhood of Sleeping Car Porters.

He was quite active in the AFL-CIO, speaking out against the conservative leadership of its president, George Meany. Randolph believed that Meany and other conservatives in the labor movement were not active enough in their support of civil rights.

Randolph continued to be active in civil rights work outside the labor movement as well. In 1958, with baseball star Jackie ROBINSON and singer Harry BELAFONTE, Randolph led 10,000 students in the Youth March for Integrated Schools in Washington, D.C.

After his work in the 1963 March on Washington, his politics began to change. He became less interested in socialism and more interested in reform within the system. Instead of writing for socialist journals, he published in *Opportunity,* which was published by the National Urban League, a black reform group. Instead of working for the Socialist Party, he worked with New York's Liberal Party, which at the time was closely tied to the conservative AFL-CIO.

Many of Randolph's earlier admirers were disappointed by his modification of his political views, but he continued to function as a prominent figure in labor, civil rights, and New York politics. His death in 1979 ended the career of a historic and powerful opponent of racial discrimination.

Further Reading: *A. Philip Randolph: A Biographical Portrait,* by Jervis Anderson, Berkeley: University of California Press, 1987; *A. Philip Randolph,* by Sally Hanley, New York: Chelsea House, 1989; *The Meaning of Our Numbers,* by Jervis Anderson, New York: Harcourt, Brace, Jovanovich, 1972; *A. Philip Randolph: Pioneer of the Civil Rights Movement,* by Paula A. Pfeffer, Baton Rouge, La.: Louisiana State University Press, 1990.

—*R. K.*

❖ RAPIER, JAMES THOMAS
(1837–1883), *congressional representative, labor leader*

James Rapier served in Congress during the period of Reconstruction, the years following the Civil War when, for the first time in U.S. history, most black men were able to vote and take part in government.

Many conservatives claimed that the black officials elected during Reconstruction were corrupt or incompetent. Ironically, almost all of them, like James Thomas Rapier, were better educated than President Lincoln had been. Rapier was a congressional representative from Alabama and supported legislation to improve the schools, reduce violence, improve the economy of the city of Montgomery, and promote civil rights.

Before he was elected to Congress, Rapier had also been active in organizing the black labor movement. After he left Congress, Rapier held many government positions and stayed active in Republican politics.

James T. Rapier was born on November 13, 1837, in Florence, Alabama, the son of a free black couple, John

and Susan Rapier. However, when only five years of age, he was sent to live with his slave relatives in Nashville, Tennessee, where he attended school. In 1856, he was sent to live with his uncle in Canada, where he continued his education. It is believed that he attended both the University of Glasgow, in Scotland, and Franklin College, in Nashville, Tennessee.

In 1863, Rapier settled in Tennessee, where, in 1865, he began working to establish black people's right to vote. When this campaign was not successful, Rapier went back to Alabama, where he became one of the most successful planters in the area.

After the Civil War ended, the era of Reconstruction began. Many laws were passed making it possible for black people to participate in politics, and the ruling Republican Party sent federal troops into the South to guarantee black people's safety in this enterprise. Under these revolutionary circumstances, Rapier returned to politics and was elected a delegate to Alabama's first Republican state convention, where he chaired the committee to develop the party's platform.

While African Americans were gaining political rights, some white people were organizing to deny them. In 1866, the Ku Klux Klan, a white terrorist organization, was formed to keep black people from becoming politically active. In 1868, the Klan drove Rapier off his plantation in Florence, Alabama. He was forced to hide in Montgomery, Alabama, for nearly a year.

Rapier began to attend the national black labor conventions, which were organized by Isaac MYERS. Held between 1869 and 1872, these conventions were the beginning efforts of black workers to form a national labor organization, to win higher wages and better working conditions, and put an end to discrimination on the job.

In 1870, Rapier was elected a vice president of the National Negro Labor Union. He organized a chapter of this group in Alabama and served as its president for a while. The national organization fell apart, however, because it could not yet sustain itself against the opposition of white employers and landowners. Large numbers of black people would not be unionized until multiracial industrial unions were formed in the 1930s.

Rapier tried various strategies to enter politics and, in 1872, was elected to Congress on the Republican ticket. Alabama conservatives were not happy with his victory, however. They began a campaign to unseat him, which included race riots, miscounting ballots, and intimidating black voters. Rapier decided to withdraw from the 1874 election. He ran again in 1876, but by that time his district's constituency had been changed, and he lost.

Reconstruction ended in 1877, when the newly elected Republican president Rutherford B. Hayes pulled federal troops out of the South. This meant that conservatives and the Ku Klux Klan had free rein, and they used it to pass laws and create a climate of intimidation that once again prevented most black people from voting.

Rapier and other African-American politicians remained active, but Rapier did not believe that black people had much future in the South. He chaired the emigration committee at the Southern States Negro Convention of 1879, and from this position he encouraged black people to leave the South. He himself bought land in Kansas. Before he could leave, however, he became sick with tuberculosis and died on May 31, 1883. He was 45.

Further Reading: *America's Black Congressmen,* by Maurine Christopher, New York: T. Y. Crowell, 1971; *James Rapier and Reconstruction,* by Loren Schweninger, Chicago, Ill.: University of Chicago, 1972.

—R. K.

❖ RILLIEUX, NORBERT
(1806–1894), *inventor*

Norbert Rillieux invented a vacuum pan that revolutionized the sugar-refining industry of his day. His ideas later became an essential part of the chemical industry as a whole and were used in producing soap, glue, and gelatin and in recycling paper and other products.

Rillieux's invention helped to revitalize Louisiana's economy after the Civil War. In 1934, sugar companies from around the world dedicated a plaque to him in the Louisiana State Museum. U.S. Department of Agriculture chemist Charles Brown summed up this inventor's importance by saying that "Rillieux's invention is the greatest in the history of American chemical engineering."

Norbert Rillieux was born on March 17, 1806, in New Orleans to a white father, Vincent, and Constance Vivant, of mixed ancestry. His mother had been a slave, although she may have been freed by the time Rillieux was born. His father, an engineer and inventor, adopted Rillieux and gave him his name—a highly unusual act at the time of slavery.

As a result, he was raised with all the advantages of a rich French planter's son, including a Paris education. At 24, he graduated from a course in engineering at Paris's École Centrale, where he became the youngest teacher the school had ever had. He published many papers on steam technology in French engineering journals.

At the time that Rillieux began to study sugar refining, the process was slow and uncertain. It involved cooking cane juice in open kettles until the juice finally cooked down into crystals. Rillieux developed a method for heating the juice in enclosed vacuum pans, which meant that far less heat and time were needed.

In 1840, he returned to New Orleans to try out his invention. By the end of 1846, he had patented it. Thousands of plantations in Louisiana and the West Indies immediately used the new invention. Sugar production went up, and prices went down. Sugar quickly became a common household product.

The greater demand for sugar also led to a greater demand for field slaves to work on sugar plantations. Meanwhile, white southerners who had moved to Louisiana were also changing that state's attitudes about race, which formerly had been more liberal than other parts of the South. When Rillieux came back from Paris, he found striking differences. Some hotels were now segregated, and black veterans of the Battle of New Orleans could no longer participate in the annual parade as they previously had.

Nevertheless, he chose to stay in New Orleans, where he began to work on a sewage-disposal system. Although he came up with a workable plan, it was rejected. The city officials were afraid that abolitionists would gain too much ground if they could publicly disclose that a black person had designed a major city project. Later, a plan almost identical to Rillieux's was adopted.

In 1854, segregationists gained new ground. They passed a law requiring all black people to carry passes—pieces of paper that documented who they were, so the police could identify them. Rillieux decided to leave New Orleans and return to Paris.

In Paris, he soon became head of the École Centrale, and continued to publish articles on engineering. He also became interested in the study of Egypt, and helped to decode hieroglyphics (Egypt's pictographic written language).

At age 88, Rillieux applied for a French patent for another method of refining, but the French would not acknowledge that he had actually invented something original and turned him down. Reportedly, on October 8, 1894, Rillieux died at the age of 88 of a "broken heart"—partially due to this defeat. Rillieux was survived by his wife, Emily Cuckow Rillieux.

Further Reading: *The Hidden Contributions: Black Scientists and Inventors in America,* by Aaron E. Klein, Garden City, N.Y.: Doubleday, 1971; *Black Pioneers of Science and Invention,* by Louis Haber, San Diego, Calif.: Harcourt, Brace, Jovanovich, 1978 ed.; *Reaching for Freedom: Paul Cuffe, Norbert Rillieux, Ira Aldridge, James McCune Smith,* by David Harbison, New York: Scholastic Book Services, 1972.

—R. K.

❖ ROBESON, ESLANDA CARDOZO GOODE
(1896–1965), *civil rights and Pan-African activist, chemist, anthropologist, author, wife and business manager of Paul* ROBESON

Eslanda Robeson has been known primarily for her role as wife and business manager of Paul Robeson, joining him in his political as well as cultural activities. Yet she also produced work in her own right, as a scientist, anthropologist, civil rights activist, and Pan-Africanist.

Eslanda Robeson is the author of *African Journey* (Westport, Conn.: Greenwood Press, 1972 ed.), a 1945 account of a trip she and her son had taken in 1936, with the secretary of the American Negro YMCA, Max Yergan, and Ugandan prince Akikiki Nyabongo. She worked with the Council on African Affairs, which she represented as an observer to the 1945 United Nations founding conference.

Throughout her life she wrote and spoke on political issues supporting African independence and criticizing U.S. foreign and domestic policy. In the 1950s, she refused to sign an affidavit swearing that she was not a communist. She accused the Senate subcommittee that had summoned her of racial bias, saying, "You're white and I'm a Negro, and this is a very white committee." In 1953, in an open letter to President Eisenhower, published in the Communist Party newspaper, the *Daily Worker,* she criticized the U.S. policy that made friends of former enemies such as the Germans and Japanese, while making enemies of former allies such as the Soviets and the Chinese.

Eslanda Robeson was the daughter of John Goode, a clerk in the War Department in Chicago, and Eslanda (Cardozo) Goode. Her father died when she was six, and her mother moved the family to New York City. She earned a B.S. in chemistry from Columbia University in 1923, and is said to have been the first black analytical chemist at Columbia Medical Center in New York.

In 1920, she urged Paul Robeson to take a role in a YMCA theatrical production, and the following year, they were married. Paul Robeson was then working with the Provincetown Players, and Eslanda became his manager. Except for a few years' separation after 1932, she remained his manager for the rest of her life.

Eslanda Robeson continued her studies and her writing. She produced two books and studied anthropology in London and Leningrad. In 1945, she received a Ph.D. in anthropology from the Hartford Seminary Foundation in Hartford, Connecticut.

She also accompanied her husband on his travels abroad and campaigned with him for presidential Progressive Party candidate Henry Wallace. In 1952, Paul Robeson was denied his passport because he would not swear that he was not a communist; his world-tour concert fees were cut off, and the family had to sell their home, after their annual income had dropped from $104,000 to about $6,000. From 1958 to 1963, they lived in the Soviet Union in self-imposed exile.

Eslanda continued to attend Pan-African Congresses, and remained active in support of the newly emerging African nations. She also worked actively for protection of U.S. civil rights, particularly in protests against the assassination of Harry and Harriet Moore—NAACP activists who were killed by a bomb in their home in Miami, Florida, on Christmas night, 1951. After an illness of several months, Eslanda Robeson died on December 13, 1965, in New York City.

Further Reading: *Freedomways,* Fourth Quarter, 1966; *The Worker,* December 19, 1965, p. 3; *Paul Robeson, Negro,* by Eslanda Robeson, New York: Harper, 1930; *What Do the People of Africa Want?,* by Eslanda Robeson, New York: Council on African Affairs, 1945.

—R. K.

❖ ROBESON, PAUL
(1898–1976), *singer, actor, athlete, political leader*

Paul Robeson is best known for his career in entertainment as an actor and singer, but this multitalented man had brilliant achievements in many fields. He was an All-American football player, a Phi Beta Kappa student at Rutgers, and a graduate of Columbia University's law school. He spoke nine languages, including Chinese and Russian. He also cared passionately about civil rights and social justice throughout the world. His achievements would have been remarkable for any person, at any time. Considering the climate of racial discrimination in which he lived, they were even more remarkable.

Paul Robeson's father, William Drew Robeson, was born a slave, but he ran away during the Civil War to fight for the Union. Robeson's mother, Maria Louisa (Bustill) Robeson, came from a family of free African Americans who had long been activists. Robeson's father became a minister; his mother died in 1903, when Robeson was only five.

Robeson graduated from Somerville High School in New Jersey, and then entered Rutgers University, also in New Jersey. In his time, it was still unusual for black people to attend college, especially colleges that were not attended exclusively by black people. Robeson was one of the few African-American students at his school, graduating in 1919.

He first won prominence as an athlete, receiving a dozen varsity letters in various sports. In football he was twice named All-American.

In 1920, Eslanda Goode made an important suggestion to Robeson. She encouraged him to take part in a YMCA production of *Simon the Cyrenian.* This began Robeson's interest in theater—and in Eslanda. In 1921, the two were married, and Eslanda eventually became Robeson's business manager, in addition to pursuing her own literary-activist career. (See Eslanda Cardozo Goode ROBESON.)

Although Robeson received a law degree in 1923, he was discouraged by the lack of opportunities for black lawyers. In the 1920s, people who were not black were unlikely to hire or consult black attorneys. Meanwhile, though, he had won success in the theater, and his work came to the attention of the famous playwright Eugene O'Neill.

O'Neill had seen Robeson in the YMCA production and tried to give him the lead in his play *The Emperor Jones.* Although the producers did not cast Robeson, he went on to work with O'Neill's Provincetown Players. Eventually, he did play that lead, as well as key roles in *Porgy and Bess* and *Show Boat,* in which he sang as well as acted.

In April 1925, Robeson gave his first major concert at the Greenwich Village Theater. Although Robeson had never taken a singing lesson, his powerful voice won him immediate praise. In 1926, he sang at New York's Town Hall, and then toured Boston, Philadelphia, Baltimore, and major cities in Europe. In London, in 1930, he played the lead in Shakespeare's play *Othello.*

Robeson continued to work in both theater and in concert. He appeared in O'Neill's *The Hairy Ape* and in *Stevedore,* an important play by Paul Peters and George Sklar, which depicted African-American awareness of the larger economic issues of the 1930s.

Robeson repeated his London triumph by playing *Othello* in New York, first in 1934, then in 1943. Critics praised the latter performance, especially, which costarred Uta Hagen and José Ferrer.

Meanwhile, social issues were attracting him. He started to consider the political ideas of socialism after a luncheon he attended in 1928, where he met British playwright and social thinker George Bernard Shaw. In 1934, while on tour in Germany, he was spat upon by Nazi gangs. Robeson was concerned about Nazi acts against Jews in Europe as well as racial discrimination against black people in the United States.

At the same time, he was being warmly welcomed by the Soviet Union. He became very impressed with what he saw as the Soviet commitment to the equality of all, and admired Soviet efforts to end racial discrimination in their country, which included people of more than 100 different nationalities.

In 1937, Robeson sailed for Spain to sing for the soldiers from all countries who had come to fight against the fascist takeover of that country in the Spanish Civil War. He became even more involved with political and social issues, giving concerts and speeches in favor of those whom he saw as working for freedom, justice, and equality.

He had filmed 11 movies by this time, but finally decided that he would stop, as he found the roles for black men too degrading. He did continue his concert and recording career, eventually making more than 300 records. By the end of World War II, his income from singing was more than $100,000 a year.

Then the U.S. political climate changed. Congress established committees to hunt for evidence of "communism." Because of his social activism, Robeson came under suspicion. Although he announced publicly in 1946 that he was not a member of the Communist Party, he refused to acknowledge this to the House Un-American Activities Committee when it called on him to testify in 1947. Robeson claimed that it was a violation of the Constitution for a government body to ask a private citizen questions about his or her political activity.

As a result, his passport was taken away from him. People who tried to engage him as a singer were harassed. Hoodlums actually beat up some of the people who went to his concert at Peekskill, New York, in 1949. Even black churches that had Robeson sing for free were harassed and pressured by the F.B.I.

Under these circumstances, Robeson could not get work, and his income fell to $6,000 a year. His name was actually removed from the listings of the All-America football teams. Yet Robeson said, ". . . I will speak out . . . And if you silence my voice by making me a nonperson, there will be another voice and another voice . . ."

Paul Robeson went on to give many well-attended private concerts during the years when he was unable to travel. In 1958, in particular, he gave many performances, including sold-out events at Carnegie Hall. In 1959, he resumed his theatrical career with a seven-month run in *Othello.* In 1998, he was awarded a posthumous Grammy.

Unfortunately, Robeson later suffered from a long illness that kept him isolated in Philadelphia for many years, until his death on January 3, 1976. He continues to remain a symbol of black accomplishment and integrity in the face of persecution.

Further Reading: *Here I Stand,* by Paul Robeson and Sterling Stuckey, Boston: Beacon Press, 1988; *Paul Robeson: Actor, Singer, Political Activist,* by David K. Wright, Springfield, N.J.: Enslow Publishers, 1998; *Paul Robeson: Artist and Citizen,* ed. by Jeffrey C. Stewart, New Brunswick, N.J.: Rutgers University Press, 1998; *Paul Robeson: Citizen of the World,* by Shirley Graham, Lawrenceville, N.J.: Africa World Press, 1998; *Paul Robeson Speaks,* ed. by Philip S. Foner, Secaucus, N.J.: Citadel Press, 1982; *The Whole World in His Hands; A Pictorial Biography of Paul Robeson,* by Susan Robeson, Secaucus, N.J.: Citadel Press, 1998; *Paul Robeson,* by Martin Bauml Duberman, New York: Knopf, 1988; *Paul Robeson, All-American,* by Dorothy Butler Gilliam, Washington, D.C.: New Republic Books, 1976.

—*R. K.*

❖ ROBINSON, JACK ROOSEVELT ("Jackie")
(1919–1972), *baseball player*

Jack Roosevelt Robinson—known as "Jackie"—became a national folk hero in 1947, when he joined the Brooklyn Dodgers baseball team as the first African American to play baseball in the major leagues. His spectacular sports record includes his election to the Baseball Hall of Fame in 1962. After he left baseball, he became a prominent spokesperson and fund-raiser for the Civil Rights movement.

Jackie Robinson was born in the small town of Cairo, Georgia, in 1919, by which time baseball had long been established as a popular American sport. He went to school in California. First, he entered Pasadena Junior College in 1937 and later he transferred to the University of California at Los Angeles (UCLA).

Jackie Robinson (*Sporting News/Archive Photos*)

As early as college, Robinson was an outstanding sports figure—playing football and basketball, and competing in track-and-field sports, as well as his primary sport, baseball. Robinson would play many positions, but his preference was second base.

After Robinson graduated in 1941, he went into the army. Then he played professional baseball with the Kansas City Monarchs, a team in the Negro National League.

Until the 1950s, professional baseball in America was rigidly segregated by color. White players joined teams in the National or American Leagues; black players played in various Negro leagues.

By 1947, there was considerable pressure from black Americans to integrate professional baseball. Many believed that the first black player on a white team would be a prominent star of one of the Negro leagues, such as Satchel PAIGE, the famous black pitcher. Instead, the Dodgers decided to pick a relatively new player, one who would join the team as a rookie, rather than as an established star. They also wanted a player who could handle the enormous pressure and public attention that would come with being the first and only black player in a white system. Jackie Robinson was the choice.

Robinson was praised for his record and his ability to handle the spotlight in his new position. However, some in the black community criticized him, finding him too conservative on political issues. In 1949, for example, during an intense period of the cold war, singer-activist Paul ROBESON said publicly that black people would never fight in a war against the Soviet Union. Three months later, Jackie Robinson publicly disagreed. The Robeson-Robinson disagreement reflected two trends within black activism—one confrontational, the other more interested in working within the system.

Meanwhile, Robinson continued to amass an impressive set of baseball statistics. In 1956, when he retired, his career batting average was .311. He had contributed substantially to his team's victories—the Dodgers had won the pennant six times and the World Series once.

Robinson's accomplishments were recognized throughout his career. In 1947, he was named Rookie of the Year. In 1949, he led the National League in stolen bases, and was named Most Valuable Player in the league.

After his retirement from baseball, Robinson entered a new arena of competition—business. He was vice president of the restaurant and coffee company Chock Full O'Nuts from 1956 to 1964, a period when he also continued to speak out for civil rights. In 1958, along with singer Harry BELAFONTE and labor leader A. Philip RANDOLPH, he led 10,000 high school students in the Youth March for Integrated Schools in Washington, D.C.

Robinson's business activities included an interim period as cochair of Harlem's Freedom National Bank. He was also an aide to New York governor Nelson Rockefeller.

Jackie Robinson died in Stamford, Connecticut, in 1972. Two years later, a junior high school in East Harlem was named in his memory.

Further Reading: *I Never Had It Made,* by Jackie Robinson, New York: Putnam, 1972; *Breakthrough to the Big League,* by Jackie Robinson, New York: Harper & Row, 1965; *Baseball Has Done It,* by Jackie Robinson, Philadelphia: Lippincott, 1964; *Baseball's Great Experiment: Jackie Robinson and His Legacy,* by Jules Tygiel, New York: Oxford University Press, 1997; *Great Time Coming: The Life of Jackie Robinson, from Baseball to Birmingham,* by David Falkner, New York: Simon & Schuster, 1995;

Jackie Robinson: A Biography, Arnold Rampersad, New York: Knopf, 1997; *Jackie Robinson; An Intimate Portrait,* by Rachel Robinson, New York: Harry N. Abrams, 1998; *Stealing Home: An Intimate Family Portrait by the Daughter of Jackie Robinson,* by Sharon Robinson, New York: HarperCollins, 1996; *The Jackie Robinson Story,* by Arthur William Mann, New York: Grosset & Dunlap, 1956; *Rickey & Robinson,* by Harvey Frommer, New York: Collier Macmillan, 1982; *Baseball's Great Experiment,* by Jules Tygiel, New York: Oxford University Press, Vintage Books, 1984; *Jackie Robinson and the Story of All-Black Baseball,* by Jim O'Connor, New York: Random House, 1989.

—R. K.

✤ RUDOLPH, WILMA (Glodean)
(1940–1994), *athlete*

Wilma Rudolph was best known for her superb athletic accomplishments. She won three gold medals in the 1960 Olympics and was nicknamed the "black gazelle" by an admiring press. She received the Sullivan Award for top U.S. amateur athlete; was inducted into the Black Sports Hall of Fame, the U.S. Track and Field Hall of Fame, the U.S. Olympic Hall of Fame, and the National Women's Hall of Fame. In 1993, she became the first to receive the President's National Sports Award. In 1997, Tennessee made Rudolph's birthday, June 23, Wilma Rudolph Day.

Wilma Rudolph was born in 1940 into a poor family in St. Bethlehem, Tennessee. Children from a previous marriage of one of the parents made for a total of 22 children in the household.

In addition to her early poverty, Rudolph had to deal with physical difficulties. Bouts with scarlet fever and polio at the age of four left Rudolph frail and partially crippled. Doctors prescribed a series of exercises, which she managed with the help of her family. The determined child was able to walk by the time she was eight, and was later able to discard her leg brace.

This difficult childhood would not have foretold a brilliant career as an athlete, but Rudolph enjoyed sports. Six feet tall, she was especially good at basketball and track. At age 16, she entered the 1956 Olympics and was an outstanding athlete even then. Her performance on the track team helped the U.S. to win a bronze medal in the relay event.

With her eyes on the future, Rudolph began her studies at Tennessee State University. She returned to the Olympics, where, in 1960, she entered the 100-meter race, the 200-meter race, and the relay—and won gold medals in each.

Olympic gold medals were not Rudolph's only athletic honors. She was the third woman ever to win the Sullivan Memorial Trophy, given for athletic achievement. She was also invited to race in the Millrose Games in New York's Madison Square Garden. This last invitation was an unusual honor, in that those games were generally restricted to men.

Rudolph married William Ward, with whom she had four children. She went on to teach, coach, and become director of the Wilma Rudolph Foundation (for youth) in Indianapolis. In 1994, at age 54, she died of a brain tumor.

Further Reading: *Wilma Rudolph: Champion Athlete,* by Tom Biracree, Los Angeles: Holloway House Publishing Corp., 1991; *Wilma Rudolph (Olympic Gold),* by Wayne Coffey, Woodbridge, Conn.: Blackbirch Press, 1993; *Wilma Rudolph: Run for Glory,* by L. Jacobs, St. Paul, Minn.: EMC Corp., 1975; *Wilma Rudolph: Champion Athlete* by Victoria Sherrow, Broomall, Penn.: Chelsea House, 1995.

—*R. K.*

❖ RUSSWURM, JOHN BROWN
(1799–1851), *editor of the first black American newspaper,* Freedom's Journal; *Liberian government official*

John Brown Russwurm was one of the first African-American college graduates. He was active in the antislavery movement and was editor and cofounder of the country's first black newspaper, *Freedom's Journal.* At the end of his life, Russwurm decided that black people had a better future in Africa than in the United States. He went to the colony of Liberia, where, between 1834 and 1836, he was one of the first black colonial agents for the American Colonization Society.

John Brown Russwurm was born a slave in Jamaica in 1799. He was the son of a slave mother and a merchant father, John Russwurm. He was sent to Quebec in 1807, where he received a good formal education. In 1812, his father settled in Portland, Maine, which was then a part of Massachusetts. There, he married Susan Blanchard, who insisted that Russwurm give his son his name and take him into the family. When his father died in 1815, young John Brown Russwurm stayed with his adoptive mother.

In 1826, Russwurm became one of the first African Americans in the United States to graduate from college. His degree was from Bowdoin College in Brunswick, Maine.

After graduating, Russwurm went to New York, where the press was extremely pro-slavery and antiblack. In 1827, Russwurm worked with black Presbyterian minister Samuel Cornish to found *Freedom's Journal,* the country's first black newspaper. This journal became an important center of abolitionist opinion. David WALKER first published his famous "Appeal" in the paper, in which he stressed the connections among black people in the United States, Africa, and the West Indies, and called upon African Americans to rise up and demand their freedom.

During this time, many white people were advocating "colonization"—the emigration of black people to Africa. Most abolitionists, black and white, were strongly opposed to this idea. They believed that if free black people went to Africa, slavery would be firmly entrenched in the United States, since there would be no one left to press for an end to slavery.

Russwurm took a minority opinion within the Abolitionist movement, publishing an article in 1829 supporting colonization. This position was so unpopular with the black and abolitionist communities that he had to resign as editor of *Freedom's Journal.* He then sailed for Liberia, the African nation founded by African Americans, and lived out the rest of his days there.

Russwurm became the first black to hold the office of governor in an African state, which was regarded as a kind of test as to whether black people could actually rule themselves. Russwurm came to be known as a competent official. He held many positions: editor of the *Liberian Herald,* superintendent of education, and governor of the Maryland-in-Liberia colony, which later became part of Liberia.

During his time in Liberia, Russwurm continued to encourage black Americans to move to Africa. When he died on June 9, 1851, he left a wife, Sarah McGill Russwurm, and four surviving children. The Liberians built him a monument in Harper, Cape Palmas, where he was buried, and they named Russwurm Island in his honor.

Further Reading: *John Brown Russwurm, The Story of Freedom's Journal,* by Mary Sagarin, New York: Lothrop, Lee & Shepard, 1970.

—*R. K.*

❖ SALEM, PETER
(1750–1816), American Revolutionary War soldier

Although there was much controversy over whether black Americans should be allowed to serve in the American Revolutionary Army, Peter Salem was one of the black people who enlisted early and fought long. According to a widely accepted belief, he fired the shot that killed British major John Pitcairn at the Battle of Bunker Hill on June 17, 1775.

While the evidence for his killing Pitcairn is not absolutely certain, it is known that Salem fought at Bunker Hill, Saratoga, and Stony Point. For a time, African Americans were barred from the American army, but when they were once again permitted to serve, Salem reenlisted and fought until the end of the war.

Peter Salem was born in 1750, in Framingham, Massachusetts. He was the slave of Jeremiah Belknap, who came from Salem, from which Peter took his last name.

When Belknap sold Salem to Major Lawson Buckminster, black participation in the army was still controversial. African Americans had been barred from the military in Massachusetts since 1656, for fear that they might use their arms in slave insurrections. Because soldiers for the French and Indian Wars were in short supply, however, some black people were allowed to serve. This precedent made it easier for them to serve in the Revolutionary War.

In May 1775, the Committee on Safety refused to allow slaves into the army, but it did permit free black people to enlist. Even so, some slaves were enlisted to fight and some slaves who fought were freed. One of these was Peter Salem, who fought as a Minuteman at Concord in April 1775. A few days later, he enlisted in Captain Thomas Drury's company of the Fifth Massachusetts Regiment, with whom he fought at Bunker Hill.

In July of 1775, General George Washington issued orders that no more African Americans were to be recruited, although those who were already serving could complete their terms. Then, in November of 1775, Washington issued more stringent orders, barring all black people from armed service. However, when Washington learned that Virginia governor Lord Dunmore had offered to free all black people who fought under the British flag, he changed his mind. On December 30, 1775, Washington ordered officers to enlist free blacks. In January 1776, Salem reenlisted.

After the war was over, Salem wove cane for a living near Leicester, Massachusetts, where he had built himself a cabin. On August 16, 1816, he died in poverty in Framingham. Many years later, in 1882, the townspeople there erected a monument to the memory of Peter Salem.

Further Reading: *The Black Presence in the Era of the American Revolution 1770–1800,* by Sidney Kaplan,

Amherst, Mass.: University of Massachusetts Press, 1973, pp. 18–19, Plate 1 following p. 84; *The Negro in the American Revolution,* by Benjamin Quarles, Chapel Hill, N.C.: University of North Carolina Press, 1961; *From Slavery to Freedom,* by John Hope Franklin, New York: Knopf, 1988, 6th ed.

—*R. K.*

❖ SCARBOROUGH, WILLIAM SANDERS
(1852–1926), *scholar, university president*

William Scarborough became president of Wilberforce University in Ohio, one of the major black institutions of the 19th and early 20th centuries. Scarborough was also a classical scholar, whose textbook *First Lessons in Greek* was used throughout the United States. Scarborough was the third African American to be elected to the American Philological Association (an association of scholars studying language and literature).

William Scarborough was born on February 16, 1852, in Macon, Georgia, then a small southern town. His father, Jeremiah, was supposed to have been the great-grandson of an African chief, with some Anglo-Saxon ancestry as well. Jeremiah, a former slave, had been freed by his master in 1846. Scarborough's mother, Frances Gwynn Scarborough, was a slave of Spanish, black, and Indian ancestry.

Children of female slaves were also slaves, but Scarborough's mother was a slave in name only, as she was able to live with her husband and family. And, despite state restrictions, the couple learned to read and write. The young Scarborough studied with a local free black family and a white neighbor. Later he learned carpentry and shoemaking.

Scarborough was emancipated during the Civil War and was able to continue his education. In 1869, he entered Atlanta University; later he attended Oberlin College in Ohio. While studying, he also taught.

In 1875, he graduated and returned to the South. He had planned to teach high school there, but the school that hired him was burned down. It was a casualty of the conflicts over Reconstruction, in which black people tried to protect the political gains they had made after the Civil War while some white people fought to impede those gains.

Scarborough ran another southern school for a while, but was frustrated by the increasingly repressive atmosphere in the South. He returned to Oberlin for his M.A. degree and later became a professor of Latin and Greek at Wilberforce University, also in Ohio.

In 1881, Scarborough married Sarah Bierce, a white woman who later joined him on the Wilberforce faculty from 1877 to 1914. The couple was happy together, although Scarborough lost his job in 1892 because his classes were no longer in demand. He taught at Payne Seminary in South Carolina, but was rehired at Wilberforce in 1897, and was also made vice president.

In 1908, Scarborough was made president of the university. He had a hard time raising funds, but managed to secure the amount needed for a new women's dorm and essential services.

While serving as university president, he continued to write on linguistics (the study of language) and philology (historical linguistics). In 1886, for example, he published a translation of Aristophanes' classical Greek play *The Birds,* as well as the textbook *First Lessons in Greek.* In addition to Greek and Latin, Scarborough knew Slavonic languages, Sanskrit, and Hebrew. A Wilberforce historian called him "the greatest scholar to be connected with the institution in half a century."

Scarborough also wrote about civil rights and lobbied for improved conditions for black people. He pushed the Ohio legislature to pass an 1887 law integrating Ohio's public schools. For many years, he helped to focus attention on civil rights issues within the Ohio Republican Party. He was also a leader in the African Methodist Episcopal Church, the institution that supported Wilberforce.

In 1897, Scarborough published a key paper on black folklore and dialect. In 1903, he published *The Educated Negro and His Mission* (New York: Arno Press, 1969 reprint of 1903 ed.).

Finally, in 1920, Scarborough resigned from the presidency of Wilberforce. In 1921, despite opposition from white government workers, he was appointed to a Department of Agriculture position, which he held until the end of 1924 and the death of President Warren G. Harding, who had appointed him.

Scarborough returned to Ohio, where he died at home in 1926.

—*R. K.*

❖ SCHOMBURG, ARTHUR ALFONSO
(1874–1938), *historian, book collector*

Arthur Schomburg is best known for founding the collection that bears his name, the Schomburg Center for Research in Black Culture, located in the Harlem branch of the New York Public Library. The Schomburg Center is the most extensive library of black American culture to be found in the United States and probably in the world. Schomburg's other achievements include cofounding the Negro Society for Historical Research in 1911, and heading the American Negro Academy in 1922.

Arthur Schomburg was born on January 24, 1874, in San Juan, Puerto Rico, the son of Carlos and Mary (Joseph) Schomburg. He attended San Juan's Institute of Instruction in order to become a teacher. At St. Thomas College in the Virgin Islands, he studied black literature, an unusual subject at the end of the 19th century.

He came to the United States in 1891. There he taught and wrote, winning prominence in the organizations of black scholars that he cofounded and headed throughout the 1910s and 1920s. Schomburg was a key figure in the Harlem Renaissance, the black cultural movement of the 1920s in New York City, which saw a flowering of black art, literature, and music. He was one of the contributors to Alain LOCKE's book, *The New Negro,* published in 1925, which tried to define new currents of black thought and new prospects for the future.

Schomburg also had an active personal life. He was married three times and had eight children.

Along with teaching and publishing newspaper articles, Schomburg continued to collect materials on black Americans. Eventually, he owned 5,000 books, 3,000 manuscripts, 2,000 etchings, and several thousand pamphlets. In 1926, the Carnegie Corporation bought Schomburg's collection and donated it to the New York Public Library.

Schomburg continued to take an active interest in the collection, even though it was no longer his. In 1932, he became its curator—holding that position until he died in 1938. In 1940, the collection was named in his honor. In 1972 it became one of the Research Libraries of the New York Public Library and became the Schomburg Center for Research in Black Culture.

Further Reading: *Racial Integrity: A Plea for the Establishment of a Chair of Negro History in Our Schools and Colleges,* Baltimore, Md.: Black Classic Press, 1979 reprint of 1913 ed.

—*R. K.*

❖ SCOTT, DRED

(1795?–1858), *fugitive slave and activist*

Dred Scott became well known through his involvement in the *Scott vs. Sanford* case. That case led to a Supreme Court decision that held that a slave continued to be owned by his or her master, even if he or she was in terri-

Dred Scott (*Library of Congress*)

tory where slavery wasn't legal. Slaves were thus regarded as the personal property of their owners.

Of pure African ancestry, Scott was born a slave in rural Virginia around 1795. When he was 16, Scott was known as Sam, and was owned by Captain Peter Blow and John Moore. Sam's owners later took him to Alabama and then to St. Louis. In 1833, two years after Peter Blow died, his son, Charles Blow, sold Sam to John Emerson, an army surgeon.

Apparently, Sam had a tendency to gamble, which Emerson did not approve of. Emerson whipped his slave, who ran away, but was then caught and sent back.

The next year, in 1834, Emerson was transferred to Illinois, a state in which slavery was not legal. Nevertheless, military employees believed that state laws did not apply to them, and many had slaves. Thus, when Emerson was transferred to the Wisconsin Territory in 1836, he took his slave Sam with him, although the Missouri Compromise had made slavery illegal there.

Sam had married once, but his wife had been sold. In 1836, he married a woman named Harriet, who was also a slave. During this period, he was given the nickname "Great Scott" by soldiers in the barracks, a name changed to "Dred" by newspaper reporters who misheard the name.

Scott and Harriet continued to live with Emerson, and in 1839, they had Eliza, their first daughter. They soon had another daughter, Lizzie.

In 1843, Emerson died, leaving his property to his wife. Slaves were not mentioned in his will, but Scott was still considered to be Mrs. Emerson's property. In 1846, he tried to buy his own and his family's freedom, but was met with her refusal. Apparently Mrs. Emerson's father was strongly pro-slavery, which probably influenced her decision.

The Scotts were approached by lawyers who frequently took slave cases. The lawyers' case was based on the fact that the Scotts had been taken into a free territory and a free state, where slavery was supposed to be illegal.

The case continued through several different courts. At first, the Scotts won, in the 1850 trial under Judge Alexander Hamilton. In the same year, Mrs. Emerson remarried, to an opponent of slavery, and handed the case over to her brother, John Sanford. The case dragged on until 1852, when the court decision was reversed and the Scotts were sent back into slavery.

In 1853, Scott brought a new suit, this time against Sanford. Eventually, the case was heard before Chief Justice Roger B. Taney of the Supreme Court. In 1857, the Court ruled that Scott was not free, although he had been taken into free portions of the United States. The court based its ruling on the fact that Scott had no right to bring suit at all—as a Missouri slave, he had no legal standing to bring suit against a citizen.

After losing his case, Scott and his wife were given to Taylor Blow. Scott later worked for Mr. and Mrs. Theron Barnum, serving as a porter in their St. Louis Hotel. Historians say that Scott never fully understood the case that centered on him. The long effort to win his freedom had exhausted him and finally led to his death of tuberculosis on September 17, 1858.

Many historians believe that the Dred Scott case helped to bring about the Civil War because it dramatized the position that no compromise was possible between slave and free states.

Many of Dred Scott's descendants went on to enjoy prosperous lives. Dred Scott Madison became a police officer; John A. Madison became a lawyer who practiced in the very same court where his ancestor had been denied the right to bring suit.

Further Reading: *Extracts from the Dred Scott Decision,* New York: P. P. Simmons Co., 1915; *Dred Scott Decision: Excerpts,* U.S. Supreme Court Sound Recording, New York: Enrichment Materials, 1969.

—*R. K.*

❖ SHABAZZ, HAJJ BAHIYAH BETTY
(Betty Sanders)
(1936–1997), educator, civil rights leader

Though she first came to prominence as the widow of the murdered black nationalist Malcolm X, Betty Shabazz moved on to create a powerful legacy in her own right. As a nurse and teacher, she worked tirelessly to benefit the disadvantaged, setting a memorable example of caring and service.

Shabazz was born Betty Sanders in Detroit, Michigan, on May 28, 1936. She grew up in a comfortable home and attended the Methodist church throughout her youth. After high school she enrolled in Alabama's historic Tuskegee University, but she left before completing her degree in order to study nursing in New York. There Sanders came into contact with the Nation of Islam. Led by Elijah MUHAMMAD, the group adopted the Muslim religion and called for the creation

Betty Shabazz *(Bjorg/Archive Photos)*

of a separate black nation. While attending the group's Mosque No. 7 in Harlem, the 20-year-old Sanders met the dynamic minister Malcolm X, Elijah Muhammad's second in command, who was 10 years her senior. In 1958, Malcolm and Sanders were married.

By 1964, Malcolm had become internationally famous, admired in the black community for his fearless attacks on racism and widely feared by whites as a dangerous radical. After breaking with Elijah Muhammad in 1964, Malcolm went on a pilgrimage to Mecca, Saudi Arabia, and began to call himself El-Hajj Malik El-Shabazz; the new name signified rebirth and was also adopted by his wife. The following year, however, Malcolm was assassinated by gunmen probably allied with the Nation of Islam. Now 28 years old, Betty Shabazz already had four daughters, and she was carrying twins—with little money on hand and an incomplete education, she was facing a bleak future.

Despite the odds against her, Shabazz showed the courage and determination that had marked her husband's career. She enrolled in Jersey City State College, becoming a certified school nurse and later obtaining a B.A. in public health education. While working as a nurse and raising her family, she continued to study whenever she could. Her efforts paid off in 1975, when she was awarded a Ph.D. in education administration from the University of Massachusetts at Amherst.

In 1976, Shabazz began her long association with Medgar Evers College in New York City. Appointed an assistant professor, she also served as director of communications and director of institutional advancement. She also lectured before many different groups, proposing measures to improve the education and health of disadvantaged children and advocating Malcolm X's cherished goal of self-determination for African Americans. Among the organizations receiving her active support were the African-American Foundation, the Women's Service League, and the Day Care Council of Westchester County.

On June 1, 1997, tragedy struck once again when Shabazz was critically injured in a fire that swept through her apartment in Yonkers, New York. Authorities determined that the fire had been set by Shabazz's 12-year-old grandson, Malcolm. Malcolm had been living wih his grandmother while his mother, Qubilah, battled substance abuse problems, and he apparently set the fire in the hope of being sent back home. After more than three weeks in intensive care, Shabazz died on June 23. (Malcolm entered a guilty plea and was sentenced to 18 months in a Massachusetts psychiatric facility.) Those who knew and worked with Shabazz expressed their grief

and sense of loss. But she had also touched the lives of countless people in the community whom she had never actually met in person. "A great woman is gone," a Harlem mother told a reporter from the *New York Times.* "I prayed for her recovery every day. She worked for kids of color and she'll be missed by all of us."

Further Reading: "Hajj Bahiyah Betty Shabazz," in *Notable Black American Women,* edited by Jesse Carney Smith, Detroit: Gale, 1992; "Dr. Betty Shabazz," by Joy D. Cain, *Essence,* February 15, 1985.

—*P. K.*

❖ SHAKUR, TUPAC AMARU
(1971–1996), *musician, actor*

Though his career was violently cut short when he was only 25, Tupac Shakur ranks as one of the major rappers of the 1990s. Known to his fans as 2Pac, he produced four major albums that rank among the leading examples of gangsta rap and West Coast hardcore rap.

Born in New York City on June 16, 1971, Tupac Shakur was the son of Billy Garland and Afeni Shakur. His parents were never married, and Tupac—named after an Inca leader who fought against the Spanish invaders of Peru during the 16th century—was raised by his mother. Afeni Shakur was a member of the Black Panther Party, and her political activities made it hard for her to live a settled life. Tupac and his younger sister, Sekyiwa, often found themselves moving from place to place in Harlem and the Bronx, sometimes staying in shelters or the homes of relatives. When Tupac was 12, his mother enrolled him in a Harlem theater group; he discovered that acting allowed him to express the things he had kept bottled up during the unsettled years of his childhood.

During the mid-1980s, the Shakurs moved to Baltimore, and Tupac began to attend the Baltimore School of the Arts, where he avidly honed his acting skills and began writing rap material. A year later, however, the family moved to California. Tupac dropped out of school and began to live the life of a street hustler, selling drugs and engaging in other illegal activities.

In the early 1990s, Shakur met Shock-G (Greg Jacobs), the leader of the Oakland-based group Digital Underground. He began touring with D.U. as a dancer and roadie and resumed writing raps. In 1990, he made his first record appearance on D.U.'s album *This Is an E.P. Release,* and the following year he was featured on *Sons of the P.* In 1992, Shakur was ready to perform as a

Tupac Shakur *(Joel Levinson/Saga/Archive Photos)*

soloist. He signed with Interscope Records and released his first album, *2Pacalypse Now.* He also returned to his first love, acting—his appearance in Ernest Dickerson's film *Juice* (1992) led to a starring role in John Singleton's *Poetic Justice* (1993). The opening of *Poetic Justice* coincided with the release of Shakur's second album, *Strictly 4 My N.I.G.G.A.Z.,* which went platinum and yielded two Top-10 R&B singles.

Though Shakur was now a full-fledged star, his determination to embody the "gangsta" lifestyle brought him into conflict with the law and with violent street elements. In 1992, he was arrested in connection with a shootout that claimed the life of a six-year-old bystander. No charges were brought against Shakur in that incident, but the following year he was convicted of assaulting the director on the set of a movie he was filming, and he eventually served 15 days in jail. In 1994, Shakur was convicted of sexual assault and sentenced to four and a half years in prison. The day after the verdict, he was shot outside a New York recording studio, apparently the victim of a mugging.

After recovering from his wounds in February 1995, Shakur began serving his prison sentence. His new album, *Me Against the World,* appeared in March and immediately went to number one on the charts. Shakur's success prompted Suge Knight, the head of Death Row Records, to arrange his parole after posting a $1.4 million bond. Shakur was released after eight months, at which time he began working on a new album for Death Row. *All Eyez on Me,* released in 1996, was the first double album of original material in the history of rap and sold more than 4 million copies. Shakur also began making films again, completing work on *Bullet and Gridlock'd* during the summer. However, he was still living a tumultuous life and was involved in a public feud with the East Coast rapper Notorious B.I.G.

On September 13, 1996, Shakur was riding along the Las Vegas Strip in Knight's car when unknown assailants opened fire on the two men. Shakur was hit four times and died of his wounds six days later. Summing up Shakur's brief but spectacular career, Kevin Powell wrote in *Rolling Stone* magazine: "To me, Shakur was the most important solo artist in the history of rap . . . because he, more than any other rapper, personified and articulated what it was to be a young black man in America."

Further Reading: "The Short Life and Violent Death of Tupac Shakur: Bury Me Like a G," by Kevin Powell, *Rolling Stone,* October 31, 1996; "Conversations with Tupac," by Veronica Chambers, *Esquire,* December 1996.

—*P. K.*

✦ SIMMONS, WILLIAM J.
(1849–1890), *biographer, educator*

William Simmons was the author of a major biographical dictionary of black American men, *Men of Mark: Eminent, Progressive, and Rising* (New York: Arno Press, 1968 reprint of 1887 ed.). This book, which he published in 1887, took issue with the growing trend among white academics to regard black people and culture as basically inferior. The book was also a valuable source of information used by later scholars of black history.

William Simmons was born on June 26, 1849, the child of Edward and Esther Simmons, who were slaves living in Charleston, South Carolina. When Simmons was very young, his mother ran away to the North, taking him and her two other children. The family lived as fugitives for several years, running from city to city. They finally settled in a small New Jersey town, where an uncle helped to support the family and educate the children.

When Simmons was 12, he apprenticed with a white dentist, but he was not allowed to enter dental school because he was black. So, at age 15, he enrolled in the Union Army, and was at Appomattox when Confederate general Robert E. Lee surrendered to Union general Ulysses S. Grant, thereby ending the Civil War.

After the war, Simmons worked briefly as a dental assistant, but then decided to become a minister.

This decision inspired him to continue his education, and he eventually got an M.A. from Howard University in Washington, D.C., in 1881. While studying, Simmons taught and served as principal of Hillsdale Public School in Washington, D.C. He married Josephine Silence, with whom he later had seven children.

Simmons worked at a variety of jobs during his marriage, primarily as a teacher and minister. In 1880, he and his family finally settled in Louisville, Kentucky, where he became president of Normal and Theological Institution, a Baptist school. Under Simmons's leadership, this school, which had been in decline, became the State University of Kentucky at Louisville.

In 1882, Simmons became the editor of the magazine *American Baptist.* He organized the American National Baptist Convention and became its first president.

As an editor and college president, Simmons had two platforms from which to promote his views. Like Booker T. WASHINGTON and many others, he believed that young black people should get practical vocational training. To that end, he founded an industrial school in Cane Spring, Kentucky, just before his death on October 30, 1890. Unlike Washington, however, Simmons also believed in academic training.

Simmons favored political independence for black people, although he often supported Republican candidates. He worked actively for civil rights and for improving conditions in the South.

Simmons's *Men of Mark,* published in 1887, helped to create an awareness among white and black people that African-American history included outstanding black leaders who had accomplished a great deal. Simmons hoped it would inspire young black people to become better educated. He planned to write a similar book about women, but died of heart failure at age 41, before he could complete the project. The leading black journal, *New York Age,* wrote that Simmons's death was "a calamity to the race."

—R. K.

❖ SIMPSON, ORENTHAL JAMES ("O. J.")
(1947–), *football player, actor, broadcaster*

Ranked among the all-time greats in football history, O. J. Simpson was the first NFL running back to gain more than 2,000 yards in a single season. After retiring in 1979, Simpson enjoyed great success in films, television, and advertising before finding himself at the center of a dramatic and controversial murder trial.

Born in San Francisco, California, on July 9, 1947, Simpson was one of two children; he and his sister, Ercale, were raised by their mother, a hospital worker. Growing up in the economically depressed Potero Hills section, Simpson was involved with street gangs for several years, but he was saved from serious trouble by his love for sports. He excelled in track at Everett Junior High School and went on to become an all-city fullback at Galileo High School. In 1965, Simpson enrolled in the City College of San Francisco, where he scored 26 touchdowns in two years. He then transferred to the University of Southern California (USC) and soon became a national sports celebrity.

During his first season at USC, Simpson ran for 1,543 yards and scored 13 touchdowns. He did even better in 1968, gaining 1,709 yards, scoring 22 touchdowns, and leading USC to the Rose Bowl. His exploits won him the coveted Heisman Trophy as the nation's best collegiate player, and he was named Man of the Year by *Sport* magazine. Many experts rated him the best college running back of all time. Simpson also excelled on the USC track team, anchoring the 4 x 100 relay squad and running the 100-yard dash in 9.4, just two-tenths of a second off the world record at the time.

O. J. Simpson (*Popperfoto/Archive Photos*)

In 1969, Simpson made his professional debut with the Buffalo Bills. At that time the Bills were a lackluster team, and Simpson struggled through his first three seasons. However, the Bills' management gradually built an offensive line capable of opening holes for Simpson, and he began to show his brilliance in 1972, rushing for 1,251 yards. The following year he had a legendary season, shredding opposing defenses for 2,003 yards. Simpson surpassed 1,000 yards for the next four seasons in a row and was then traded to the San Francisco 49ers. After playing two seasons in his hometown, Simpson retired in 1979 with a total of 11,236 yards rushing and 61 touchdowns. He was elected to the Football Hall of Fame in 1984, his first year of eligibility.

Handsome, personable, and physically imposing, Simpson had begun acting in Hollywood films during the early 1970s, and he was offered a steady succession of roles after his retirement. His film credits included *The Towering Inferno* (1974), *The Cassandra Crossing* (1977), *The Naked Gun* series (1988–94), and *No Place to Hide* (1993). Simpson was a familiar figure on television, appearing in *Roots* (1977), *Goldie and the Boxer* (1979), and *High Five* (1982). He maintained his connection with sports as a commentator and analyst, including three years in the booth on ABC-TV's popular *Monday Night Football*. In addition, Simpson appeared in numerous TV commercials, notably a celebrated series of ads for Hertz rental cars that showed him dashing through a crowded airport.

Simpson's success story took a shocking turn in June 1994, when his exwife, Nicole Brown Simpson, and her friend Ronald Goldman were brutally murdered in Los Angeles. Simpson was charged with the crime, and his televised trial, which went on for eight months in 1995, was watched by 150 million viewers. On October 3, 1995, the jury found Simpson not guilty after his attorneys argued that racist officers in the Los Angeles Police Department had conspired to frame him. However, Simpson was then sued by the Goldman and Brown families, and in February 1997 a civil jury found him liable for the deaths and ordered him to pay $25 million in damages. Simpson presented his side of the issue in a 1995 book, *I Want to Tell You.*

Further Reading: *The O. J. Simpson Story: Born to Run,* by Larry Fox, New York: Dodd, Mead, 1974; *O. J. Simpson's Most Memorable Games,* by Jim Baker, New York: Putnam, 1978; *American Tragedy: The Uncensored Story of the Simpson Defense,* by Lawrence Schiller and James Willwerth, New York: Random House, 1996; *I Want to Tell You,* by O. J. Simpson, Boston: Little, Brown, 1995.

—*P. K.*

✤ SINGLETON, BENJAMIN ("Pap")
(1809–1892), *activist*

During the years after the Civil War, "Pap" Singleton led hundreds of African Americans out of the South and into Kansas, to a region known as "Singleton's Colony." Singleton's efforts were part of the so-called Great Exodus of 1879, when thousands of black people left the South after Reconstruction had ended. Because it was no longer possible to exercise their political rights in the South, African Americans went to Kansas, Missouri, Indiana, and Illinois, in search of freedom and equality.

Pap Singleton was born in 1809 in Nashville, Tennessee, where several times he was sold to slave owners and several times he escaped. Eventually, he fled to Canada, then settled in Detroit, where he ran a boardinghouse. Frequently, other runaway slaves stayed at his lodgings.

After the Civil War, he returned to Tennessee to work as a cabinetmaker. However, he was much more interested in helping his people, which he attempted to do in many different ways and with missionary zeal. At first, in the late 1860s, Singleton and others tried to help black people to buy up Tennessee farmland. This effort failed when white owners would not sell at reasonable prices.

Then Singleton began to encourage blacks in Tennessee to move to Kansas. He and Columbus Johnson had found a location for a black settlement there. Later they formed a company that helped hundreds of black people to migrate from Tennessee to Kansas between 1877 and 1879.

Black people wanted to leave the South after 1877, because that was the year that Reconstruction officially ended. The federal troops that had once guaranteed black voting rights and personal safety were pulled out of the South, giving free rein to the Ku Klux Klan and other terrorist groups. These groups were determined to keep African Americans from voting or running for office, and to preserve legal segregation and other forms of discrimination.

Many black people responded by trying to leave the South—so many that 1879 became the year of the "Great Exodus." This movement was centered in Louisiana but spread to neighboring states. Some 50,000 blacks managed to leave the South—but thousands more were forced back by white people patrolling rivers and roads.

Singleton and his colleagues finally founded two colonies in Kansas. These were soon filled with "Exodusters," as those who left were called. The migration was so dramatic that in 1880, Singleton was called before Congress to testify. Although he was not entirely accurate when he claimed that he had inspired the entire movement (others had also supported migration), he was called the Father of the Exodus.

The Great Exodus had no one leader. However, it is true that Singleton printed up many posters encouraging people to come to his colony. African Americans who left the South for other places than Singleton's colonies may well have been inspired by Singleton's work. However, many states experienced no exodus at all—such as Alabama, the Carolinas, Georgia, and Virginia. These states had also been exposed to Singleton's materials, but apparently to no effect.

In 1881, Singleton began a new effort, organizing a party called the United Colored Links in a black area of Topeka, Kansas. The area was called "Tennessee Town" because so many Tennessee natives lived there. The Links was supposed to be affiliated with the white workers' Greenback Party, to work together for fundamental social change in the United States. The main purpose of the Links was to help African Americans acquire their own factories and industries, but there was not enough wealth in the black community to achieve this goal.

Singleton did not cease his efforts. In 1883, he founded another organization, the Chief League, to encourage black people to emigrate to the island of Cyprus (now part of Greece and Turkey). This project never met with much enthusiasm among African Americans, and the group fell apart. In 1855, Singleton tried again, founding the Trans-Atlantic Society, which was supposed to help black people to move back to their "fatherland," Africa.

By 1887, this organization had also fallen apart. Singleton was in poor health and declined until his death in 1892 in St. Louis. His ideas and vision would be given new life when appropriated by Marcus GARVEY and others in the 1920s.

Further Reading: *Anyplace But Here,* by Arna Bontemps and Jack Conroy, New York: Hill & Wang, 1966; *Exodusters: Black Migration to Kansas Following Reconstruction,* by Nell Irvin Painter, Lawrence, Kan.: University Press of Kansas, 1986.

—*R. K.*

❖ SMALLS, ROBERT
(1839–1915), *Civil War hero, congressional representative*

Robert Smalls was the heroic instigator of a daring maneuver during the Civil War. As a slave on the Confederate ship *Planter* in 1862, he managed to steal the ship and sail it into Union waters, where he surrendered it to Northern forces. After the war was over, Smalls was elected to Congress, where he served several terms. Many black politicians came to power during the postwar Reconstruction era, when federal troops stationed in the South guaranteed black civil rights. However, federal troops were withdrawn in 1877, giving free rein to such white terrorist groups as the Ku Klux Klan, as well as to laws that made it extremely difficult for black people to vote. Under these circumstances, most black representatives lost their electorate or simply chose not to run, but Smalls continued to serve long after most other African-American politicians had been driven out of politics, due in large part to the considerable support he enjoyed from his political base in the coastal Sea Islands of South Carolina.

Robert Smalls was born on April 5, 1839, as a slave in Beaufort, South Carolina. He was the son of a slave mother, Lydia, and a wealthy Jewish father, Moses Goldsmith. Despite the fact that his father was free, Smalls and his mother were owned by John and Henry

Robert Smalls (*Library of Congress*)

McKee, who allowed Smalls to hire out on various jobs and keep part of the money he earned.

In 1856, Smalls married the slave Hannah Jones, with whom he had two surviving children.

Smalls had become a skilled navigator, familiar with the coastal waters of South Carolina. In 1862, he and eight other slaves were working on the Confederate steamer *Planter.* One day, Smalls, his family, and the slave crew stole the ship and sailed it up to the Union blockade, where he surrendered.

His daring exploit demonstrated that black people were both committed to the Union cause and capable of brave and skillful deeds that could help the North win the war. Smalls's daring feat convinced the secretary of war to recruit 5,000 African-American volunteers for the Union Army in South Carolina. Smalls continued to pilot the ship he had seized, completing both transport duty (carrying soldiers) and gunboat duty (carrying guns in naval battles).

While his ship was being repaired, Smalls learned to read and write. He continued to serve until 1866, when his ship was taken out of service. He then returned to Beaufort, where he continued to study as well as to acquire property. He also served in the state militia, where by 1877, he had become a brigadier general.

The years following the Civil War marked the first time in U.S. history that African Americans were able to exercise political power. Smalls was elected to South Carolina's new Constitutional Convention of 1868, where he helped to design the state's system of free education, that is, public schools that could be attended without cost. He first served in the state house (1868–70) and then the state senate (1870–74).

The 44th U.S. Congress, in session from 1875 to 1877, had a record number of black members: one senator and six representatives. One of the representatives was Smalls, who had a broad base of support.

Smalls's accomplishments in Congress were mixed. While he helped to develop naval facilities in South Carolina, he did not succeed in getting the legislature to pass an amendment to a bill countering discrimination in army recruitment.

When federal troops were withdrawn from the South in 1877, the country's political climate changed again. The number of black people in Congress declined to only four, one of whom was Smalls.

Smalls continued to push for civil rights legislation, such as a bill to integrate all eating places in the District of Columbia. Such legislation was always defeated, however. Smalls, too, was defeated in 1886, partly because of a split between light-skinned and dark-skinned black people.

Smalls later won notoriety for his objection to an attempt to make interracial marriages illegal in South Carolina. He proposed an amendment to the proposed bill: Any white man found living with a black woman would be barred from public office and would have to recognize any children from the union as legitimate heirs of his property. His purpose was to expose the large numbers of white men who had black mistresses whom they did not marry and who had mixed-race children whom they did not acknowledge as heirs or adequately provide for. The law against intermarriage was passed, without his amendment. Later, at the state Constitutional Convention of 1895, Smalls tried to prevent efforts to take the vote away from black people, but failed.

From 1889 to 1912, Smalls served as customs collector in Beaufort, South Carolina—a minor political appointment, but one that few black people received at that time. In 1913, he helped to prevent the lynching of two black prisoners by telling the sheriff that armed black citizens were ready to burn white homes if the lynchings were not stopped.

The last three years of Smalls's life were marred by poor health and he died at home in 1915. Smalls's first wife, Hannah Jones, had died in 1883. He married Annie Wigg in 1890 and had one son with her before she died in 1895.

Further Reading: *Captain of the Planter,* by Dorothy Sterling, Garden City, N.Y.: Doubleday, 1958; New York: Pocket Books, 1972 ed.; *From Slavery to Public Service: Robert Smalls,* by Okon Edet Uya, New York: Oxford University Press, 1971; *America's Black Congressmen,* by Maurine Christopher, New York: Crowell, 1971.

—*R. K.*

❖ SMITH, BESSIE
(1894–1937), *blues singer*

Like Ma RAINEY, Bessie Smith was one of the founding mothers of the blues. Blues was a form of music that evolved from African-American spirituals and work songs and was the source of jazz. Smith was one of the major blues singers of her time, selling up to 100,000 copies of her records per week. She was a major influence on later singers, such as Mahalia Jackson and Billie HOLIDAY, as well as on musicians of her own time, such as Louis ARMSTRONG, and was a symbol of black pride and resistance to unequal treatment.

Bessie Smith was born into a poor family in Chattanooga, Tennessee, to William and Laura Smith. By the time she was nine, both of her parents were dead and she was being raised by Viola, the eldest of the seven Smith children. Smith began to sing then, for spare change, on the streets of Chattanooga.

Bessie Smith (*Library of Congress*)

In 1912, Smith joined a traveling show that happened to include Ma and Pa Rainey, who were the leading blues singers of the time. For many years, Smith continued to tour the South, both with and without the Raineys, playing mainly to African-American audiences. At this time, the blues was still the music of bars, honky-tonks, and brothels and not considered a "respectable" form of music.

In 1920, Smith married Earl Love, but he died soon after their wedding. In 1923, she married John Gee, a night guard in Philadelphia. Smith and Gee adopted a child, but the marriage was a difficult one. Smith drank heavily and was frequently on the road, while Gee was made extremely jealous by her unconventional way of life. They often fought in public and finally separated in 1930.

Meanwhile, Smith had begun her recording career in 1923. Columbia Records depended on Smith to keep from going bankrupt. The first record she recorded for Columbia sold 780,000 copies in six months. Her records also made Smith the highest-paid black performer in the United States, and she become known as the Empress of the Blues. Although southern audiences were still segregated by race, Smith sang for white as well as black people, traveling through the South in her own custom-built railroad car.

As a young woman, Smith was slender, but as she become more indulgent, her weight exceeded 200 pounds. She helped to create the image of the earthy, sexy, maternal blues singer—a powerful alternative image to that of demure innocence and immaculate glamour cultivated by most white singers of the time.

Some people remember Smith as rough, unreasonable, and difficult, while others recall a kind woman who once cancelled a show to take care of her business manager's sick child. Smith certainly had a difficult life on the road, drinking heavily throughout her career to escape its pressures.

Smith also had a talent for acting, and can be seen in the 1929 film *St. Louis Blues.* If the blues style had remained popular, she might have done more acting, but Smith's popularity declined as dance music played by white orchestras became the commercial success of the post-depression era. She made her last record in 1933, although she continued to perform.

Smith died in a car accident near Clarksdale, Mississippi. For many years, a rumor circulated that her life could have been saved but for a white hospital that refused to accept her. In fact, a doctor did provide emergency treatment and got an ambulance to take her to a black hospital. Nevertheless, she died, apparently of internal injuries.

For many years, Smith lay in an unmarked grave in Philadelphia, although 7,000 people had attended her funeral. Finally, a campaign was mounted to buy a headstone to mark the resting place of the Empress of the Blues.

Further Reading: *Jazz Singing: America's Great Voices from Bessie Smith to Bebop and Beyond,* by Will Friedwald, New York: Da Capo Press, 1996; *Blues Legacies and Black Feminism: Gertrude "Ma" Rainey, Bessie Smith, and Billie Holiday,* by Angela Y. Davis, New York: Pantheon, 1998; *Bessie,* by Chris Albertson, New York: Stein & Day, 1994 ed.; *Early Jazz: Its Roots and Musical Development,* by Gunther Schuller, New York: Oxford University Press, 1986 revision of 1968 ed.

—*R. K.*

❖ SMITH, FERDINAND CHRISTOPHER
(1894–1961), *union leader*

Ferdinand Smith was one of the most powerful black labor leaders of the 1930s and 1940s. He helped to organize the National Maritime Union (NMU), which represented sailors, defining the NMU as a union that "will not tolerate segregation or discrimination of any sort."

Ferdinand Smith was born in 1894, in Jamaica, which was then part of the British West Indies. In 1918, he began going to sea and made his first visit to the United States. By 1920, he had begun U.S. citizenship proceedings and had also joined the International Seamen's Union.

At that time, conditions for sailors were very bad. They lived in crowded, filthy cabins on their ships, eating poor and rotten food, and living under the constant threat of being fired or blacklisted if they spoke up or tried to improve their circumstances in any way. Pay was low, and they might be unemployed for six months or more a year. The International Seamen's Union was very weak, and unwilling to challenge the shipowners.

The NMU was founded as part of a larger union movement in the United States. Unions were becoming much more militant, and some were also becoming more democratic. Instead of organizing only the most skilled workers into craft unions, and excluding most black people and immigrants, these new unions wanted to organize all workers into so-called industrial, or industry-wide, unions.

The NMU was part of this movement. Thus, its stand against racial discrimination was part of its overall effort to organize black workers as well as white ones.

By the time Smith joined the NMU, he had more than 19 years' experience as a sailor. He was soon elected steward—that is, a representative of a group of union members. In 1936, he was elected chief steward. In the same year he was put on the strategy committee of the NMU for the 1936–37 seamen's strike.

In 1938, Smith became an NMU vice president, having been elected by the multiracial union membership. For the first time in history, large numbers of black and white Americans were joining the same organization and electing both black and white leaders. (Although black and white Americans had worked together in the antislavery movement, far more white people were involved in the union movement. Furthermore, there were far more black leaders elected by white members in the union movement than there had been in the antislavery movement.)

In 1939, when the NMU convention abolished the position of vice president, Smith was elected national secretary, a post to which he was reelected in 1940, 1942, and 1944. He also held high-ranking offices in New York statewide union groups, as well as a seat on the board of the National Congress of Industrial Organizations (CIO), the nationwide association of industrial unions. (Later the CIO merged with the American Federation of Labor (AFL) to form today's AFL-CIO.) Smith sat on the CIO board until 1947.

He worked with NMU president Joseph Curran, and together they made the NMU one of the most radical unions of its time. Smith and Curran were both supported by the Communist Party, which had many members within the NMU. Under Smith and Curran, the NMU became a national leader in pushing for racial equality and social justice. For example, the NMU recruited a multiracial crew for the new Liberty ship *Booker T. Washington,* which in 1942 was put under the command of a black captain. (The Liberty ship was a type of supply ship used in World War II.)

In 1943, rumors that a black soldier had been killed by police in Harlem nearly set off a race riot. In fact, the soldier had been beaten but not killed—and Smith played a leading role in preventing an outbreak of violence. He worked in many other cities to promote racial harmony, speaking at meetings and working with community leaders while also continuing to crusade for civil rights.

Under Smith and Curran's leadership, black and white sailors in the NMU used the same hiring halls while waiting for jobs—even in the South, where black and white people were still rigidly segregated. On board ship, they ate at the same tables and slept in the same cabins. The NMU standard contract outlawed discrimi-

nation, and, according to Smith, some 124 shipping companies had accepted it. Smith and Curran had created one of the best integrated labor unions of their time, and had succeeded in changing the quality of life on the job for black and white seamen.

Smith was on many key boards and councils, such as the Board of Trustees of Sydenham Hospital, an integrated hospital in New York's Harlem, and the boards of directors of the Council of Pan-American Democracy, the Council on African Affairs, and the left-wing paper the *People's Voice*. He also wrote many columns in the national black press. Until 1945, he held great influence both within the labor movement and within the black community.

Then, in 1945, it was revealed that Smith had never managed to complete citizenship proceedings. Therefore, technically, he was not eligible to hold an NMU office. At the same time, Joseph Curran was becoming more conservative, frightened by the federal government's increasing pressure against communism in the labor movement. Smith remained true to their earlier ideas, so he and Curran began to quarrel more and more frequently, breaking decisively at the 1947 NMU convention.

Smith was one of the targets of the postwar hostility to the Communist Party and the people who had been involved with it. In 1948, the U.S. Justice Department began a campaign to deport aliens who had been involved in communist activity. Smith was arrested and sent to Jamaica, where he lived until his death in 1961.

—R. K.

❖ SMYTHE, JOHN H.
(1844–1908), *minister to Liberia*

John H. Smythe was one of the first ministers to go to Liberia during the era after Reconstruction, the post–Civil War period in which many black people were able to hold political office for the first time. Liberia was the African colony founded by black Americans. Smythe served in Liberia on behalf of many governments, including those of Belgium, Germany, Sweden, and Norway. His reports on that country were useful to several governments and to many scholars.

Smythe also achieved recognition as an artist. He was the first African American to be made a member of the Philadelphia Academy of Fine Arts.

John H. Smythe grew up in Philadelphia, where he attended the Quaker Institute for Colored Youth. He taught for a while, then went on to Howard University

Law School in Washington, D.C., which had only recently been established.

While studying at Howard, Smythe worked with the Freedmen's Bureau, a government agency set up to help freed slaves. Smythe also worked as an internal revenue agent for the Internal Revenue Service, the federal tax-collection agency. He later worked for the Freedmen's Bank in Washington, D.C.

In 1878, President Rutherford B. Hayes appointed Smythe minister to Liberia, an appointment that was renewed in 1882 by President Chester A. Arthur. After his service abroad, Smythe returned to Washington, where he practiced law.

Further Reading: *The Negro Vanguard,* by Richard Bardolph, New York: Rinehart, 1961.

—*R. K.*

❖ SPAULDING, CHARLES CLINTON
(1874–1952), *businessperson*

C. C. Spaulding helped to build the North Carolina Mutual Life Insurance Company and served as the firm's president for almost 30 years. With Spaulding at its head, the company became the largest black business in the United States, surviving even the 1929 stock market crash and the Great Depression of the 1930s. The company began with an investment of $350; by the time Spaulding died, its resources totaled more than $43 million.

Spaulding was active in many business activities, including the National Negro Business League and the National Negro Insurance Association. He also supported the development of black colleges.

C. C. Spaulding was born on August 1, 1874, to Benjamin McIver Spaulding and Margaret (Moore) Spaulding, North Carolina farmers. Spaulding worked on his father's farm until he was 20, when he moved to Durham, North Carolina, and began to attend school, graduating from Whitted School with a high school equivalency degree in 1898.

Spaulding immediately showed his flair for business by running a local cooperative store for African Americans. (A cooperative store is one that is owned by several people, each of whom helps to pay the store's expenses in exchange for benefiting from the store's low prices.)

In 1899, Spaulding got into the insurance business, beginning as a part-time agent, but soon becoming a member of the board of directors as well as a three-person management team. This three-person team— Spaulding, John Merrick, and Dr. Aaron Moore—

effectively ran the firm for many years, leading it to the top of its field.

Meanwhile, in 1900, Spaulding married Fannie Jones, a clerk in the company, and together they had four children. Spaulding was widowed in 1919, and the following year he married Charlotte Garner.

In his early years with the company, he had been sales agent, clerk, janitor, and manager. He supervised its expansion into other activities, such as sponsoring newspapers, drugstores, banks, and a real estate company. By 1915, the company had expanded its insurance operation into 12 states and the District of Columbia.

Spaulding took over as president in 1923, building his firm into the largest black-owned business in the United States. He was skilled at advertising, making sure that barbershops, stores, offices, fraternal lodges, and other places where people spent time had items with his company name on them: matchbooks, calendars, fans, pens, and paperweights. He advertised heavily in the black press as well. Often, the company employed schoolteachers as sales agents, which lent the company an air of respectability and security.

Spaulding believed in self-improvement and in the possibility of blacks progressing through owning their own businesses. Certainly Spaulding used his own position and financial success to support other black institutions. Often, when black colleges faced financial ruin, Spaulding bailed them out. He was a trustee of such key institutions as Howard University in Washington, D.C., Shaw University in North Carolina, and North Carolina College.

In 1952, on his 78th birthday, Spaulding died in his home, of bronchial pneumonia. His importance to his community was evidenced by the large crowd of mourners who attended his funeral.

Further Reading: *The North Carolina Mutual Story, A Symbol of Progress, 1898–1970,* by William J. Kennedy, Jr., Durham, N.C.: North Carolina Mutual Life Insurance, 1970; *Black Business in New South, A Social History of North Carolina Mutual Life Insurance Company,* by Walter Weare, Urbana, Ill.: University of Illinois Press, 1973.

—*R. K.*

❖ STILL, WILLIAM
(1821–1902), *leader of the Underground Railroad*

William Still worked for the Pennsylvania Society for the Abolition of Slavery for 14 years. During that time, he coordinated a "station" on the Underground Railroad—a network of whites and blacks in the North that helped thousands of slaves escape to freedom. Still's own estimate was that he alone helped some 649 slaves escape, in addition to the many other slaves who were assisted.

Still promoted improved treatment for African Americans in many other ways. He began a campaign to end discrimination on Philadelphia railroad cars; he helped to start an association for collecting data on living conditions for black people; and he published many works exposing problems faced by black Americans.

William Still was born in 1821 to former slaves, Levin and Sidney Steel, who were living in rural New Jersey. Levin had been living as a slave in Maryland, but had managed to buy his own freedom and leave. Still's mother, Sidney, had escaped—having been forced to leave two young children behind. So that his mother, a runaway slave, would not be detected, the family changed its name to Still, and Sidney changed her first name to Charity.

Young William was deeply affected by his family's experience. He was the youngest of 18 children and had to work on his father's farm and as a woodcutter. Finally, at age 20, he left Maryland for Philadelphia, where he arrived with only five dollars in his pocket. There he tried to expand his limited education while working as a handyman.

In 1847, he married Letitia George, with whom he later had four children. That year was a turning point in another way, for in 1847, Still began to work as a janitor and clerk for the Pennsylvania Society for the Abolition of Slavery.

At that time, the society was as yet a very small group of white people. The organization needed better ties to the black community, especially because they wanted to offer practical help to escaped slaves. Still began to keep runaways in his own house, giving fugitives a place to rest on their way to Canada.

Ironically, one of these runaway slaves was Peter Still, William's older brother—one of the children whom his mother had left behind. Still realized that he should keep careful records of everyone he helped, so that someday their families could get word concerning them.

In 1850, Congress passed the Fugitive Slave Act, which made it illegal to help any slave escape to freedom. The Philadelphia abolitionists responded by organizing a committee whose specific purpose was to help runaway slaves. Still was named chair of that committee.

Still also gave refuge to the wife of abolitionist John Brown, allowing her to stay in his home for a while after Brown's unsuccessful revolt at Harper's Ferry.

Brown was hanged for treason for leading this antislavery uprising, and his followers faced various harsh punishments. Many of those who had worked with Brown got help from Still.

In 1855, Still went to Canada to visit with escaped slaves in hiding there. He wanted to investigate rumors that Canada was not a safe place for black people—rumors possibly circulated by people who supported slavery and wanted black Americans to believe that they had no alternative. Still's reports gave a better impression of Canadian conditions, thereby making it easier for black Americans to consider settling there.

Still actively worked for black equality in other ways as well. In 1859, he wrote a letter to the press complaining about discrimination on Philadelphia railroads. This began a citywide campaign to end the discrimination, which was finally outlawed in 1867. In 1861, Still also helped to found an association to gather and disseminate information about the living conditions black people could expect to find in different parts of the country.

Meanwhile, Still began to buy land, and during the Civil War he opened a stove business. Later he went into the coal trade and also did some trading with the army.

After the Civil War, Still began to write about issues of importance to African Americans. In 1867, he wrote *A Brief Narrative of the Struggle for the Rights of the Colored People of Philadelphia in the City Railway Cars* (Wilmington, Del.: Scholarly Resources, Inc., 1970 ed.), about his successful antidiscrimination campaign. In 1872, he wrote *The Underground Railroad* (New York: Arno Press, 1968 ed.), about his experiences with runaway slaves. Unlike many white abolitionists, who focused on their own heroism, he focused on the commitment and bravery of the slaves who were willing to risk death by escaping.

Still continued to be involved in Philadelphia politics. In 1874, he supported a reform candidate for mayor. He helped to start various schools and community groups, and assisted many charities for the black community.

In 1902, William Still died of a heart condition caused by Bright's disease. His book is still valued as the only day-to-day record of work on the Underground Railroad.

Further Reading: *One Day, Levin . . . He Be Free, William Still and the Underground Railroad,* by Lurey Khan, New York: E. P. Dutton, 1972.

—R. K.

❖ TANNER, HENRY OSSAWA
(1859–1937), *artist*

Henry O. Tanner was the first black American artist to win international recognition. Tanner was known for his genre paintings (studies of people's daily life), landscapes, and religious studies. He won several prizes at the Paris Salon, one of the leading art exhibitions of its day. His work was bought by such leading American museums as New York's Metropolitan Museum of Art, the Chicago Art Institute, and the Pennsylvania Academy of Fine Arts.

Tanner was honored by the French government, which made him a member of the Legion of Honor, an award reserved for those responsible for outstanding achievement in their field. He received prizes at other international expositions, and was the first black member of America's National Academy of Design.

Henry O. Tanner was born on June 21, 1859, in Pittsburgh, Pennsylvania. His father, Benjamin Tucker Tanner, was a deacon who was descended from several generations of free black people. His mother, Sarah Elizabeth (Miller) Tanner, was the granddaughter of a black and a white plantation owner.

Tanner grew up in and around Washington, D.C., where his father was a minister and an organizer of schools for freed slaves. In 1866, the Tanners moved to Philadelphia. There, at the age of 13, young Henry Tanner saw an artist at work, and was so excited that he ran home and tried to paint his own version of the landscape from memory.

At first, his parents were skeptical about his ambitions, but when they realized that his interest in art was genuine, they gave him their support. From 1876 to 1880, he worked alone, teaching himself his craft by painting portraits and landscapes, and drawing animals at the Philadelphia Zoo.

In 1880, he enrolled at the major American art school of the time, the Pennsylvania Academy of the Fine Arts. There he studied with the prominent American painter Thomas Eakins. Tanner admired Eakins but was interested in a different artistic style than that of his teacher. He also felt that there would be less racial prejudice in Europe, so he decided to leave the art academy and earn the money to go abroad.

Although Tanner's work was shown at the Academy of Fine Arts and at New York's National Academy of Design, he was unable to earn much from his art. For a time, he worked as an illustrator and photographer, but again, this was not an easy way to earn money. For a while, Tanner taught art at Clark University in Atlanta, Georgia, but still he longed to go to Europe.

Some of his friends—Bishop Joseph Crane Hartzell and his wife—arranged to exhibit Tanner's work in Cincinnati. No paintings were sold to viewers at this exhibition, but the Hartzells bought them all, which finally enabled Tanner to leave for Europe in 1891.

Tanner spent five years at the Académie Julien in Paris, working under the tutelage of Benjamin Constant and Jean-Paul Laurens. The style he learned was known as "academic"; that is, it was realistic, depended on a good knowledge of anatomy, and often referred to classical subjects from myths, history, and the Bible.

During this period, he briefly returned home to Philadelphia but felt that racial prejudice there was too widespread to allow him to remain. Also at this time, in 1893, Tanner painted *The Banjo Lesson,* a study of black life in the realistic genre style of the time. This painting is one of his best-known works. Many critics regret that Tanner did not remain in the United States, for he painted few similar works, choosing, instead, European subjects for his later art.

In 1899, Tanner married the white singer Jessie Macauley Olssen, who lived with him in Paris, and with whom he had a child, Jesse Ossawa. This son later went to Cambridge University in England and to the London School of Mines.

For a time, the Tanners lived at an artists' community founded by wealthy art collector Atherton Curtis in upstate New York, but eventually they settled permanently in Paris.

Throughout the 1890s and early 1900s, Tanner continued to work, to sell his paintings, and to win prizes for his art. He was an active part of the American group of artists in Paris and often sold work to the French government. In 1905, he was the first African-American artist to exhibit at the Carnegie Institute in Pittsburgh, Pennsylvania.

Tanner developed his unique style between 1900 and 1914, moving from realistic detail to simpler forms and rich colors, using his famous "Tanner blues." To emphasize such colors, he began to favor moonlit scenes.

Although many Americans left France when World War I began in 1914, Tanner remained. He worked with the American Red Cross for a time and sketched and painted in the war zone.

After the war, Tanner felt more isolated in Paris. Many American artists had not come back, and more abstract art styles were becoming popular. His wife died in 1925, and soon after, his only son began to suffer a breakdown in health that lasted for many years. Tanner's own health began to suffer with age. Nevertheless, he remained in France, and continued to paint until his death on May 25, 1937.

Further Reading: *Henry Ossawa Tanner, American Artist,* by Marcia M. Matthews, Chicago, Ill.: University of Chicago Press, 1969.

—*R. K.*

❖ TERRELL, MARY CHURCH
(1863–1954), *leader in civil and women's rights*

Mary Church Terrell participated in some of the key movements for equality of her time. She helped to found the National Association of Colored Women and the National Association for the Advancement of Colored People (NAACP), the major civil rights group. She worked for women's right to vote and for women's representation in political office. In 1953, at 89, she took part in a campaign to desegregate the restaurants of Washington, D.C.

Mary Church Terrell was born in 1863 in the year that the Emancipation Proclamation ended slavery in the Confederacy, and died in 1954, the year that the Supreme Court declared segregation to be unconstitutional. Her father, Robert R. Church, Sr., was a former slave who became prosperous through real estate investments in Memphis, Tennessee, in the late 1870s.

Since the schools in the South were segregated, Terrell was sent to Ohio, to Antioch College's "Model School," an early version of a kindergarten. In 1884, she received her B.A. from Oberlin College in Ohio. Then, from 1885 to 1887, she taught at Wilberforce University in Ohio, followed by a stint teaching Latin at a prep school for African Americans in Washington, D.C. Terrell then completed her education in 1888, receiving a master's degree from Oberlin College in Ohio, after which she spent two years touring Europe.

Although Terrell was probably the first black woman offered the position of registrar at a white college—Oberlin—she turned down the offer. In those days, women often had to choose between careers and marriage, and Terrell chose instead to marry Robert Herberton Terrell, who later became a municipal court judge.

In 1895, Mary Church Terrell was appointed to the Washington, D.C., Board of Education, holding the post until 1901, and again from 1906 until 1911.

Meanwhile, she was active in fighting for women's rights, particularly those of black women. She helped to organize the Colored Women's League, then presided over that group's merger with other black women's groups to form the National Association of Colored Women. This organization, formed in 1896, elected Terrell its first president, and later, honorary president for life.

Terrell also worked with the leaders of the white women's movement, including Susan B. Anthony, Jane Addams, and Carrie Chapman Catt. Terrell was a member of the National American Woman Suffrage Association, and campaigned for the right of women to vote—which was finally granted in 1920. She was an important voice in this group, speaking of the special needs of black women, such as the racism that they faced in addition to sexism. Terrell also spoke on the general issue of women's suffrage (the right to vote).

International women's groups also respected Terrell, who spoke as part of the American delegation at the International Congress of Women, held in 1904, in Berlin, Germany. She was the only American to speak in French and German as well as English.

Later, Terrell joined the Women's International League for Peace and Freedom (WILPF), under the leadership of social work pioneer Jane Addams. In 1919, she spoke on behalf of the United States at WILPF's conference in Zurich, Switzerland.

At the end of the 19th and the beginning of the 20th century, there were two main views concerning black people and their future development and participation in American society. One view was espoused by Booker T. WASHINGTON, who advocated industrial and vocational training for black people and a gradual approach to integration. The other was articulated by W. E. B. DUBOIS, who encouraged black people to pursue higher education and become intellectual and cultural leaders of their people, while advocating persistent, militant struggle.

Terrell was torn between these two views. She worked with Washington to keep DuBois from becoming assistant superintendent of Washington, D.C.'s schools, but she also criticized Washington for making too many compromises with civil rights demands in order to placate white supremacists. When she helped DuBois found the NAACP in 1909 and 1910, she drew further away from Washington. She also served as vice president of the Washington, D.C., branch of the NAACP for many years, which brought her closer to DuBois.

After women won the vote in 1920, Terrell was active in the Republican Party. Like many other African Americans, she still regarded it as "Lincoln's party." In the 1930s, she often organized black women for various Republican campaigns.

Throughout her life, she fought to end segregation. In 1949, she succeeded in a three-year campaign to integrate the American Association of University Women when she was finally accepted to membership. Also in 1949, she served as chair of the national committee to free Rosa Lee Ingram and her two sons—a Georgia sharecropping family unjustly imprisoned for a murder that was clearly committed in self-defense.

Finally, in 1949, Terrell became chair of the Coordinating Committee for the Enforcement of the District of Columbia Anti-Discrimination Laws. During the years of Reconstruction, Washington, D.C., had

Mary Church Terrell (*Library of Congress*)

passed laws requiring restaurants to serve anyone who was "respectable" and "well-behaved," regardless of race. At 86 years of age, Terrell tested an old law against discrimination by trying to be served in several segregated restaurants and also led a fight through the press, boycotts, and picketing to enforce integration. The elderly woman cut a regal figure as she walked the picket line with her cane.

Throughout her life, Terrell lectured and wrote about civil rights, women's rights, and black history. In 1940, she wrote an autobiography, *A Colored Woman in a White World* (New York: Arno Press, 1980 ed.).

Terrell died on July 24, 1954, at the age of ninety.

Further Reading: *Mary Church Terrell—Respectable Person,* by Gladys B. Shepperd, Baltimore, Md.: Human Relations Press, 1959; *Mary Church Terrell: Leader for Equality,* by Patricia McKissach and Fredrick McKissack, Springfield, N.J.: Enslow, 1991.

—*R. K.*

✤ THOMAS, CLARENCE
(1948–), *Supreme Court Justice*

Though his 1991 appointment to the U.S. Supreme Court sparked a national controversy, Clarence Thomas's remarkable success story can serve as an inspiration to all Americans.

Born on June 23, 1948, in the small town of Pin Point, Georgia, Thomas grew up in desperate poverty. His father left home when he was two years old, leaving his mother, Leola, to raise three children on the meager wages she earned at a local seafood-processing plant. Shortly after Thomas began school, his mother moved him and his siblings to nearby Savannah, where she found work as a cleaning woman. (His sister, Emma Mae, however, was soon sent back to Pin Point to live with an aunt.) The Thomases lived in a single room in a run-down tenement, sharing a kitchen and bathroom with three other families. When Leola Thomas remarried, she thought it best to have her father, Myers Anderson, take care of the two boys.

The move to his grandfather's house in Savannah was a turning point in Thomas's life. Myers Anderson had worked hard to build up a small but successful oil-delivery business; he and his wife, Tina, were able to provide a secure and comfortable home for their grandsons. At the same time, Anderson was a no-nonsense man who believed in discipline and achievement. He enrolled the boys in St. Benedict's, a Catholic school, and demanded top-notch grades. Myers's favorite saying was, "Old Man Can't is dead—I helped bury him." Clarence blossomed under the these conditions: Throughout elementary school and high school, he was an outstanding student and a stellar athlete. In 1967, he entered the College of the Holy Cross in Worcester, Massachusetts, one of 25 African-American students. Majoring in English, Thomas graduated in 1971 and went on to Yale Law School.

Clarence Thomas (CNP/Archive Photos)

After receiving his law degree in 1974, Thomas joined the staff of the Missouri attorney general, John C. Danforth. When Danforth was elected to the U.S. Senate in 1976, Thomas spent two years working in private industry and then rejoined Danforth in Washington as a legislative aide. During this time Thomas made a favorable impression on leading conservative Republicans. When Ronald Reagan became president in 1981, Thomas was offered a post as assistant secretary for civil rights in the Department of Education. The following year he was appointed chairman of the Equal Opportunity Employment Commission (EEOC). Though Thomas opposed large-scale affirmative action programs, he vigorously pursued individual claims of discrimination and was rated an effective administrator. In 1983, he concluded a landmark $42.5 million settlement—the largest in history up to that point—with General Motors. Under the agreement, the company agreed to compensate employees who had suffered discrimination, to set up training programs for minorities, and to support black colleges and other organizations. In 1989, Thomas was rewarded for his work at the EEOC with an appointment to the U.S. Court of Appeals for the District of Columbia.

In 1991, President George Bush nominated Thomas to fill the Supreme Court seat vacated by the retirement of Thurgood MARSHALL. "As a child," Thomas reflected, "I could not dream that I would ever see the Supreme Court, not to mention be nominated to it." But the path to confirmation was not going to be smooth. Because of Thomas's conservative views, the nomination was attacked by virtually every liberal and civil rights organization. On the other hand, many former colleagues and employees praised Thomas as a man of talent and integrity. The controversy became even more dramatic when Anita Hill, a law professor who had worked with Thomas at the EEOC, accused him of sexual harassment. (At the time in question, Thomas's first marriage had recently ended in divorce; he remarried in 1987.) The Senate confirmation hearings in October drew a nationwide TV audience, as Hill repeated her charges and Thomas heatedly denied them. In the end, Thomas was confirmed by the Senate and took his place on the Supreme Court. As an associate justice, Thomas has been allied with the Court's conservative faction; overall, he has concentrated on his job and has kept a low public profile. In his office, he keeps a bust of his grandfather, who remains his inspiration.

Further Information: *Clarence Thomas,* by Norman Macht, New York: Chelsea House, 1995; Justices of the Supreme Court web site, http://supct.law.cornell.edu/supct/justices/

fullcourt.html (provides the texts of all the opinions written by Justice Thomas during his tenure on the Court); *The Complete Transcripts of the Clarence Thomas-Anita Hill Hearings,* edited by Nina Totenberg and Anita Miller, Chicago: Academy, 1994.

—*P. K.*

✤ THURMAN, HOWARD
(1900–1981), *theologian*

Howard Thurman's religious thinking and writing helped to provide a framework for the nonviolent theories of Martin Luther KING, JR., and the Civil Rights movement. In 1953, *Life* magazine called him one of the 12 great preachers of the 20th century. In 1958, the Chicago Bible Society bestowed the Gutenberg Award on him for his achievement in communicating the gospel.

Thurman was awarded numerous honorary degrees from colleges and universities. He received awards for his teaching, religious writing, and community service from many organizations, including the San Francisco Council of Churches, *Ebony* magazine, and the National Association for the Advancement of Colored People (NAACP).

Howard Thurman was born on November 18, 1900, in Daytona Beach, Florida, where he was raised by his grandmother, a former slave. He attended Morehouse College in Atlanta, Georgia, where he graduated in 1923. He was ordained as a Baptist minister in 1925 and received a theological degree in 1926, from Colgate-Rochester Theological Seminary in New York.

After serving as pastor of the Baptist church in Oberlin, Ohio, from 1926 to 1928, the Reverend Dr. Howard Thurman taught religious studies, first at Morehouse, then at Howard University in Washington, D.C., where he remained until 1944.

Meanwhile, in 1932, he married writer and social historian Sue E. Bailey, with whom he later had two children. He also began to write on theological subjects, publishing *The Greatest of These* (Oakland, Calif.: Mills College/Eucalyptus Press, 1944 ed.) in 1941.

Thurman's religion had a mystical orientation. He had traveled through India, Ceylon (now Sri Lanka), and Burma in the 1930s and had met the great Mohandas Gandhi, the pacifist leader of the Indian independence movement. These experiences had shaped his ideas of Christianity, which he wanted to "live for the weak as well as the strong—for all peoples whatever their color, whatever their caste," according to a newspaper article about him.

His contact with Gandhi had also inspired him to think about nonviolence. It was through Thurman and his writings that Martin Luther King, Jr., first came to study Gandhi.

In 1944, Thurman went to San Francisco, where he cofounded the interracial Church for the Fellowship of All Peoples. He went on to publish numerous books, articles, and collections of his sermons. Two of his most recent publications are *With Head and Heart: The Autobiography of Howard Thurman* (New York: Harcourt, Brace, Jovanovich, 1980) and *For the Inward Journey: The Writings of Howard Thurman,* selected by Anne Spencer Thurman, (San Diego, Calif.: Harcourt, Brace, Jovanovich, 1984).

Thurman was an inspired speaker and was invited to address schools and churches, and radio and television audiences around the world. Thurman also recorded some of his key sermons and meditations. He died on April 10, 1981.

Further Reading: *Howard Thurman: Portrait of a Practical Dreamer,* by Elizabeth Yates, New York: John Day Co., 1964.

—*R. K.*

✤ TOLTON, AUGUSTINE
(1854–1897), *priest*

Augustine Tolton was one of the first black priests in the United States. He served as pastor at St. Joseph's Catholic Church for Negroes in Quincy, Illinois, and later presided over the opening of St. Monica's Church for Negro Catholics in Chicago.

Augustine Tolton was born on April 11, 1854, on a plantation in northeastern Missouri. His parents were Catholic slaves from different plantations who together had four children. In 1861, when Fort Sumter fell and the Civil War was beginning, the Toltons decided to escape to freedom.

Tolton's father, Peter Tolton, ran off to join the Union Army, and died during the war. His mother, Martha Jane Chisley, escaped with her four children, one of whom was still an infant. She was stopped by some Missouri citizens who saw she was a runaway slave, but federal soldiers rescued her and she settled near Quincy, Illinois.

There, Tolton's mother, Augustine's older brother, and Augustine himself went to work at the Harris tobacco factory. When factory work was not in season, Tolton went to school. The local priest decided to accept Augustine and his brother into the parish school, although many townspeople strongly objected to black and white children attending school together.

In 1875, Tolton's mother moved the family into northeastern Missouri, where she had been hired as housekeeper to a priest. Although Augustine was tutored by the priest, the family was apprehensive and stayed in Missouri for less than a year. (Although slavery was illegal, black people in Missouri were still being kidnapped and sold as slaves.)

When they returned to Quincy, Augustine took up his studies with teachers at the local Catholic high school, while working all day in a factory. Eventually, Tolton decided that he, too, would become a priest. With the help of the local Franciscan order, arrangements were made for Tolton to go to Rome and study at the College of the Propagation of the Faith, which he attended from 1880 to 1885.

When he was ordained, the church was not sure whether to send him to foreign missions or back to the United States, where he would have been the only black priest in the country. According to Tolton, one of the cardinals said, "America has been called the most enlightened nation; we will see if it deserves that honor."

In 1886, Tolton returned to America, where he seems to have been well accepted as a priest. He began his work at St. Joseph's Catholic Church for Negroes, a poor parish in Quincy. Tolton frequently lectured around the country, and in 1889, he spoke at the First Catholic Colored Congress in Washington, D.C.

In 1889, a wealthy woman, Anne O'Neill, gave $10,000 to establish St. Monica's Church for Negro Catholics, located in Chicago. Father Tolton took up his work anew there, where he remained until July 9, 1897—when he suddenly died, apparently from heat stroke, at age 43.

Further Reading: *From Slave to Priest,* by Sister Caroline Hemesath, Chicago, Ill.: Franciscan Herald Press, 1973; *God's Men of Color,* by Albert S. Foley (see Chapter IV, "Good Father Gus," pp. 32–41), New York: Farrar, Straus & Young, 1970 revision of 1955 ed.

—R. K.

❖ TOOMER, NATHAN JEAN
(1894–1967), *poet, playwright, fiction writer*

Jean Toomer wrote one of the most important works of fiction in the history of African-American literature. His book *Cane* (New York: Norton, 1988 reprint of 1923 ed.) was a groundbreaking collection of sketches and stories portraying rural black people of the South. Toomer's work was the first to portray these people in a poetic way, showing that black Americans could be the subject of serious literature. His work inspired many of the writers of the Harlem Renaissance (a black literary and artistic movement of the 1920s), including Langston HUGHES, Countée CULLEN and Zora Neale HURSTON.

Jean Toomer was born in Washington, D.C., in 1894. Shortly after his birth, Toomer's father deserted his mother, who went to live with her father, Pinckney Benton Stewart Pinchback. Toomer's grandfather had been a renowned black leader during Reconstruction, the post–Civil War era that brought new political power to African Americans. Toomer later recalled the angry arguments between his mother and his grandfather, which finally led Nina Toomer to move to New York in 1904.

She soon remarried, and the family joined her there. However, Grandfather Pinchback insisted that young Jean be called Eugene Pinchback, so that there would be no memory of his father. Toomer later assumed his father's name again.

In 1909, Nina Toomer died, and the Pinchbacks returned once again to Washington, where Toomer attended public school. He later studied agriculture at the University of Wisconsin and the Massachusetts College of Agriculture; attended a physical training college in Chicago; and took various odd jobs in the Midwest and New Jersey: car salesman, physical education teacher, ship fitter. Finally, in 1921, he settled down for a while as temporary superintendent of a black industrial school in rural Georgia.

Toomer's Georgia experience was of great importance to him, because it provided much of the material for *Cane,* which he published in 1923. Before that, he had been publishing prose sketches and poetry in various small literary magazines—and would continue to do so throughout the 1920s.

After *Cane* was published, Toomer went to France, where he studied at the Gurdjieff Institute in Fontainebleau. Gurdjieff was a mystical philosopher of the time, who greatly influenced Toomer. In the 1930s, Toomer summed up his own philosophy when he wrote, "We do not have states of being, we have states of dreaming." This inward focus was reflected in his work, which became more personal and abstract.

In 1931, Toomer married white novelist Margery Latimer, but she died the following year in childbirth. In 1934, Toomer married another white woman, Margery Content, the daughter of a wealthy Wall Street broker.

After his second marriage, Toomer became even more withdrawn. He and his wife lived within the Quaker community of Bucks County, Pennsylvania, and Toomer wrote very little.

Although Toomer had been a major influence on black writers, he himself had mixed feelings about his own racial status, and often objected to being called a "black writer." Toward the end of his life, he said, "I would consider it libelous for anyone to refer to me as a colored man . . . I have not lived as one, nor do I really know whether there is any colored blood in me or not."

In fact, Toomer was extremely light-skinned, and was aware that he had French, Dutch, Welsh, Jewish, German, and Indian ancestry, as well as African. On another occasion, he wrote, "I am of no particular race. I am of the human race, a man at large in the human world, preparing a new world." Although some see Toomer as flatly rejecting his African-American background, others see him as a man asking profound questions about his identity and about the nature of one's culture.

In fact, Toomer did allow his work to be published in *The Negro Caravan* (New York: Arno Press, 1970 ed.), a 1941 anthology of African-American literature, and the central focus of *Cane* is on the experience of being black in America.

After this groundbreaking work, however, Toomer's concerns changed, and so did his questions about race and culture. In his last essay, "The Flavor of Man," published in 1949, he wrote: "A man's roots must go down into what is deeper than himself, his crown touch what is higher, his heart open to the beyond, and the whole move forward. Then he will be connected with the great heart and power of life."

Further Reading: *In a Minor Chord: Three Afro-American Writers in Their Search for Identity,* by Darwin Turner, Carbondale, Ill.: Southern Illinois University Press, 1971; *From the Dark Tower, Afro-American Writers 1900 to 1960,* by Arthur P. Davis, Washington, D.C.: Howard University Press, 1974 (pp. 44–51); *The Wayward and the Seeking: A Collection of Writings by Jean Toomer,* edited by Darwin T. Turner, Washington, D.C.: Howard University Press, 1980.

—R. K.

❖ TROTTER, JAMES MONROE
(1842–1892), army officer, writer and musicologist

James Monroe Trotter won prominence as the author of *Music and Some Highly Musical People* (Chicago: Afro-

Am Press, 1969 ed.), published in 1878. He also served as the District of Columbia recorder of deeds, a top political post in Washington previously held by Frederick DOUGLASS. This job involved recording all real-estate transactions in the area. Trotter held the job during a real-estate boom in Washington, and, since his salary was based on a percentage of these sales, he did well financially.

James Monroe Trotter was born on February 7, 1842, in rural Mississippi. His father was a white slave owner, Richard S. Trotter; his mother was Letitia, Trotter's slave. Letitia had three children with Trotter, who then married and sent her away to the free city of Cincinnati in 1854.

Trotter attended a Cincinnati school for freed slaves, worked as a hotel bellboy, and served as cabin boy on a riverboat. Although he had some other schooling, he was mainly self-educated. Nevertheless, when the Civil War began, he was working as a schoolteacher.

In 1863, Trotter went to Boston to join the 54th Massachusetts Regiment, the Union Army's first black regiment (later depicted in the 1990 movie *Glory*). Although most of the officers were white, he became one of the four black commissioned officers, achieving the rank of second lieutenant. When not fighting, he was teaching his fellow soldiers to read and write. He also organized a regimental band.

Trotter grew concerned with the fact that black soldiers were being given the pay of laborers rather than the higher pay of white soldiers, and he organized a movement among his regiment to protest the injustice. For more than a year, the regiment refused to accept any pay at all. At one point, the Massachusetts legislature said that they would reimburse the regiment with the money that the federal government had refused to pay. Trotter insisted that the principle mattered more than the money, and encouraged his men to hold out. Finally, the federal government gave in and granted the African-American soldiers equal pay.

In 1865, Trotter was released from service in Boston, where he received an appointment to the post office. In 1868, he married Virginia Isaacs, whom he had known for several years. The marriage was a happy one, and produced three children.

In 1878, he published *Music and Some Highly Musical People.* Although the book asserts Trotter's pride in black accomplishments, it also discloses his belief that white culture was on a higher level. On the other hand, he criticized "the hateful, terrible spirit of *color-*

prejudice," and praised the blind pianist Thomas Greene Bethune ("Blind Tom"), a slave who had learned to become a highly skilled classical pianist. Trotter called slave spirituals "our only distinctively *American* music."

In 1882, a white man was promoted over Trotter at the post office. In protest, he resigned. Although, like most black people, he had been part of "Lincoln's" Republican Party, he now switched his support to the Democrats. As a prominent black Democrat, he was able to win the appointment as recorder of deeds under President Grover Cleveland in 1887.

In 1889, the Republicans took over the federal government and Trotter returned to Boston. He began a real-estate business there, which he ran until his death from tuberculosis on February 26, 1892.

Further Reading: *The Guardian of Boston: James Monroe Trotter,* by Stephen R. Fox, New York: Atheneum, 1970.

—*R. K.*

❖ TRUTH, SOJOURNER
(1797–1883), *abolitionist, women's rights activist*

Sojourner Truth was one of the great antislavery orators of her time—and the first African-American woman to speak publicly against slavery. She traveled throughout several states, speaking to thousands of people and spreading the antislavery message.

After slavery ended, Truth continued to speak out—this time, for women's rights, and for black women to be included in the women's movement of the time. One of her most famous remarks came in response to a speaker who doubted whether women could handle the responsibility of political freedom and the right to vote. Truth listed the many types of hard work she had done during and after slavery, and then asked, "And ain't I a woman?"

When a heckler in one of her audiences, referring to her height and strength and deep voice, expressed doubt that she *was* a woman, she ripped open her blouse to the waist, declaring that it was to his shame and not hers that she should have to answer the question.

Sojourner Truth was born around 1797 to James and Elizabeth, slaves of a wealthy Dutch-speaking farmer in upstate New York. Her given name is variously known as Belle, Isabelle, or Isabella. Even as a child, Belle believed that she and God had conversations, a conviction that intensified after she was separated from her mother at any early age.

Belle had many difficult experiences under four different slave owners. With Thomas, a fellow slave, she had five children, one of whom was sold and sent to Alabama, even though this was against New York State law. Her son Peter later became emotionally disturbed as a result of numerous beatings administered by an insane master.

In 1826, her master James Dumont broke his promise to free her a year before the New York law ending slavery was to take effect. "Belle" ran away and found protection with a Quaker couple, Isaac and Maria Van Wagenen.

Finally, in 1827, Belle was legally free. She turned to other Quaker friends and went to court to get her son Peter returned from Alabama.

In 1829, she was both a domestic servant and an evangelist (a zealous preacher of the Christian gospel) in New York. She then came under the influence of Matthias, a self-styled religious leader who claimed to be founding a new "Kingdom" at Ossining, in upstate New York. When this community fell apart in 1834, Belle lost all the savings and worldly possessions that she had donated to the group. She returned to New York City once more to work as a servant.

Then, in 1843, Belle had a profound religious experience. She heard a voice telling her to travel through America, testifying against the sins that had been committed against her people. She took the name "Sojourner," which means wanderer, and said that when she asked God for a second name, it was "Truth."

At age 46, Sojourner Truth began her travels, going to the Northampton Association of Education and Industry, a utopian colony in Northampton, Massachusetts. In Northampton, Truth became an abolitionist. She worked with such famous abolitionists as William Lloyd Garrison, Wendell Phillips, and Frederick DOUGLASS.

In 1850, Truth discovered the women's rights movement as well. She began a long friendship and association with the suffragists (those working for legislation to give women the right to vote) Lucretia Mott and Elizabeth Cady Stanton.

During the 1850s, Truth spoke against slavery throughout the western states. She found a home in Battle Creek, Michigan, and was joined there by her three daughters and grandchildren. When the Civil War began, they helped to raise supplies for the black regiments fighting for freedom. In 1864, Truth went to Washington, D.C., where she worked with freed slaves and nursed wounded black soldiers.

After the Civil War ended, Truth was distressed by the huge number of black refugees and former slaves who had left their old plantations but had nowhere to go. In

Sojourner Truth (*Library of Congress*)

1870, she began to agitate for a "Negro State" in the West. Although this idea never gained enough backing to become a reality, some believe that her work contributed to the "Exodus" of 1877—when thousands of black families left Louisiana and neighboring states and went to Kansas, in a movement directly inspired and led by Benjamin "Pap" SINGLETON.

All her life, Truth continued to speak out for what she believed in. Her death on November 26, 1883, at home in Battle Creek, convoked the largest funerary procession ever seen there. Today, her life and resounding name have become an inspiration for the civil rights and women's rights movements.

Further Reading: *Journey Toward Freedom: The Story of Sojourner Truth,* by Jacqueline Bernard, New York: Feminist Press, 1990 revision of 1967 ed.; *Sojourner Truth,* by Peter Krass, New York: Chelsea House, 1988; *Sojourner Truth,* by Victoria Ortiz, Philadelphia, Pa.: Lippincott, 1974; *Sojourner Truth: Fearless Crusader,* by Helen Stone Peterson, Champaign, Ill.: Garrard Publishing Company, 1972; *Narrative of Sojourner Truth,* by Olive Gilbert, New York: Oxford University Press, 1991.

—R. K.

❖ TUBMAN, HARRIET

(1821?–1913), *runaway slave, abolitionist, nurse, spy, social reformer*

Harriet Tubman, is known as the "Moses" of her people–for just as Moses led the Israelites out of slavery in ancient Egypt, Tubman led some 300 African Americans out of slavery in the South. A runaway slave herself, Tubman went back to the South time and again to help other southern slaves go north to freedom. During the Civil War, Tubman worked closely with the Union Army. After the war, she helped to establish schools for the newly freed African Americans, and campaigned for women's rights.

Harriet Tubman was born into slavery at some time around 1821, the daughter of Harriet and Benjamin Ross, on the eastern shore of Maryland. She was named Araminta by her master, but she defied him and took her mother's first name as her own. When she was a child, Harriet received a serious head injury, and for the rest of her life she suffered from sleeping spells that would periodically overcome her.

Since slaves were not allowed to attend school, Harriet received no formal education and was put to work in the field, where she was known for her unusual strength, in spite of being a small woman. In 1844, her mother forced her to marry John Tubman, a free black man, but Harriet remained a slave.

Then, in 1849, her master died, raising fears on the plantation that his slaves would be sold into the Deep South, where conditions for slaves were far worse. She and her brothers decided to escape to the North. Her brothers eventually gave up the idea of escaping and returned to the plantation—but Harriet Tubman didn't return. She reached Philadelphia, where she was able to live as a free woman.

Her journey north had been aided by an organization called the Underground Railroad—a network of people who helped slaves escape to freedom. It was called "underground" because it had to operate in secret. At that time, slavery was legal in the South, so those who helped slaves become free were actually breaking the law by stealing the "property" of slave owners.

Freedom for herself was not enough for Harriet Tubman. Two years later, she returned to help her husband escape to freedom, although he had married another woman. She made approximately 19 trips into the South and brought some 300 slaves back to freedom in the North.

Between her trips, Tubman supported herself and helped those she rescued by working as a laundress, cook, or seamstress.

Tubman knew the way north by following the North Star in the "Big Dipper" constellation. In black folksongs of the time, it was called "the Drinking Gourd," with Harriet Tubman herself referred to as "Moses" or "the Old Man."

Sometimes her "passengers" grew fearful. If they were caught, they faced beatings, torture, and even murder. If they had intentions to return, however, Tubman would point her shotgun at them, saying, "Live North or die here."

The abolitionists—people who wished to abolish slavery—considered Harriet Tubman a hero, but those who favored slavery considered her a serious enemy. She was attacked and beaten in 1860 when she led a group that retrieved a runaway slave from the police in Troy, New York, and helped the man escape to Canada. Her enemies offered a $40,000 reward for her arrest, dead or alive—but Tubman would not be stopped. She rescued her aged parents from slavery in 1857 and settled them on land she had bought for them in Auburn, New York.

In 1858, Tubman met the abolitionist John Brown, and the two became friends. Brown had devised a plan

Harriet Tubman (*Library of Congress*)

for a general revolt against slavery by seizing the government store of arms at Harper's Ferry, Virginia. Tubman supported Brown's plan, and he admired her leadership so much that he called her "General Tubman." When Brown was defeated and eventually hanged for treason, Tubman was deeply grieved for the man she called the "Savior of our people."

When the Civil War broke out, she welcomed it as a new opportunity to fight against slavery and worked for the Union Army as cook, nurse, scout, and spy. After the war, she married Nelson Davis, a black veteran. She helped to put together a short book about her life—*Scenes in the Life of Harriet Tubman*—worked in the temperance (antidrinking) and women's movements, and endured more harsh resistance in the attempt to establish new schools for freed slaves in North Carolina.

The federal government showed little gratitude for her wartime services. After 30 years of deliberation, and with the recommendation of Secretary of State William Seward, Congress finally awarded her the tiny sum of $20 a month. However, when she died of pneumonia in March 1913, she received full military honors at her funeral and was commemorated by the U.S. government in 1978 with a postage stamp.

Further Reading: *Harriet Tubman,* by Terry Bisson, New York: Chelsea House, 1990; *Harriet Tubman,* by Francene Sabin, Mahwah, N.J.: Troll Associates, 1985; *A Woman Called Moses,* by Marcy Heidish, Boston, Mass.: Houghton Mifflin, 1976; *Rebel Slave,* by Nancy Kelton, Milwaukee, Wis.: Raintree, 1977.

—*R. K.*

❖ TURNER, HENRY McNEAL
(1834–1915), *army chaplain, bishop, college president, colonizationist*

Henry McNeal Turner was a leading figure in the African Methodist Episcopal (AME) Church. During the Civil War, he was the first black chaplain for black troops. He later became president of Morris Brown College in Atlanta, Georgia.

Turner is perhaps best known for his work advocating colonization. He was one of the leading African-American figures to encourage black Americans to emigrate to Africa, since he believed they had no real future in the United States. Although many other black leaders opposed this position, it had great, politically symbolic significance, in implicitly reminding the American public that black Americans not only had an African heritage but were demanding full political equality.

Henry McNeal Turner was born in 1834 to free parents near Abbeville, South Carolina. Turner's maternal grandfather was thought to have been the son of an African king, which sparked Turner's interest in Africa from an early age.

His father died while Turner was still young; as a child, he worked in the cotton fields and as an apprentice blacksmith. Although state laws forbade black people from learning to read, Turner learned with the help of white people. He later went to work in a law firm, where he learned to write and do arithmetic.

In 1851, Turner joined the Methodist Episcopal (ME) Church, and in 1853, he was licensed to preach. He traveled throughout the South, preaching, until he settled in St. Louis in 1857. Then, in 1858, Turner broke with the ME Church and joined the black AME. He continued his studies, living and working in Baltimore and Washington, D.C., over the next five years.

In 1863, President Lincoln heard about Turner's work in recruiting black people into the army. Lincoln appointed the minister to be an army chaplain—probably as the first African American to hold that position.

Throughout the war, Turner worked first as a chaplain, then as the founder of a number of black churches. He saw the churches as a key political base for black people, a place where they could organize for political and civil rights as well as religious causes.

When the Civil War ended, Reconstruction began. This was the era of political reorganization in the South that allowed black people to participate in the political process for the first time. Turner was elected to the Georgia Constitutional Convention of 1867.

Some of his positions were controversial. He helped to pass laws preventing the confiscation or sale of property whose owners were unable to pay their taxes—legislation of potential benefit to white as well as black landowners. He also voted to pardon Confederate leader Jefferson Davis and to institute an educational requirement for voting—which worked against less-educated black voters.

However, Turner was feared by some white politicians, and he was brought to trial on many groundless charges. Even though acquitted, he had to resign from his jobs as postmaster and customs inspector.

At the same time, white supremacists and black activists in Georgia were at odds as to whether black people should really be allowed access to political power. In 1868, the state legislature declared that none of its black members were eligible to hold their seats. Turner helped to rally a protest against this move.

Meanwhile, Congress passed the Fifteenth Amendment, which declared that every citizen should be able to vote, regardless of race, color, or "previous condition of servitude." Georgia refused to ratify this amendment, so Congress sent federal troops into the state. Finally, Georgia gave in. In 1870, the state legislature ratified the Fifteenth Amendment and allowed black members to take back their seats.

After his one term from 1868 to 1870, Turner left the legislature and focused on AME activities. From 1880 to 1892, he served as bishop of the church. He wrote a book on religion, founded several church newspapers and magazines, and served as president of Morris Brown College.

At the same time, he strongly advocated black emigration to the new African colony of Liberia. In 1876, he was elected vice president of the American Colonization Society, which lent organizational support to the back-to-Africa movement.

Turner believed that God had arranged for the existence of slavery so that black people would be brought to America, converted to Christianity, learn necessary skills, and then return to "save" Africa. He also believed that the federal government should help black people and Africa by paying for the time black people had spent as slaves. The AME Church, according to Turner, would help to unify Africa through its participation in the movement.

He journeyed to Africa four times between 1891 and 1898. He lectured around the world on colonization and wrote many articles about it. In this, he was opposed by Frederick DOUGLASS and other black leaders, who believed that African Americans should fight for their freedom in the United States.

Turner married four times, and although he had many children, only two survived him. He was known as a strong-willed man and a passionate speaker.

Henry McNeal Turner had made a vow that he would not die in the United States. Consequently, he died in Windsor, Ontario, on May 18, 1915, but was buried in Atlanta. In 1973, he was chosen as one of three black people whose portrait was to hang in the Georgia State Capitol.

Further Reading: *The Bishops of the A.M.E. Church,* by Robert R. Wright, Jr., Nashville, Tenn.: Harry Berlin Publishers, 1963; *Black Exodus, Black Nationalist and Back-to-Africa Movements 1890–1910,* by Edwin Redkey, New Haven, Conn.: Yale University Press, *Respect Black: The Writings and Speeches of Henry McNeal Turner,* edited by Edwin Redkey, New York: Arno Press, 1971.

—*R. K.*

❖ TURNER, NAT
(1800–1831), *antislavery leader*

In 1831, Nat Turner led a slave uprising that ultimately involved some 60 to 80 slaves and led to the deaths of some 57 to 65 white people. Although this rebellion was put down and Turner was executed, the action sparked many other plots and uprisings throughout all of America's slave states. Turner's rebellion did not succeed in ending slavery, but it did succeed in provoking resistance and inspiring a great deal of antislavery debate.

Nat Turner was born on October 2, 1800, to slave parents owned by Benjamin Turner in rural Virginia. Turner's father ran away when Turner was still a child. Historians believe that his father became one of the many fugitive slaves who lived in hiding in the marshy area known as the Great Dismal Swamp of Virginia and North Carolina.

Turner was himself a runaway in 1821, but for some reason, he returned after a month. Although other slaves criticized him, he said he returned for religious reasons, believing that he still owed service to his master.

The young Turner became a field slave, working in cotton and tobacco fields. He also became a preacher, whose influence even reached white people. In 1825, a white overseer allowed the enslaved Turner to baptize him, and thereafter changed his ways, thus creating a legend about Turner's extraordinary power.

He lived and had children with a woman whom he considered his wife, although as a slave he was not allowed to marry.

In 1828, Turner said he had a vision and heard voices telling him to struggle against slavery. Two years later, he was moved to the home of Joseph Travis, the new husband of his owner. In February 1831, there was a solar eclipse, which was a portentous sign to many people of that era. To Turner, it meant that the time had come to rebel against slavery. He began to plan an uprising for July 4, choosing that date in order to connect the American Revolution's demand for political freedom with black Americans' desire for the same thing.

Turner became ill, and the July 4 uprising was put off. In August, however, there was another "sign"—the sun had an odd, bluish green color—which inspired Turner and five followers to have another meeting, on August 21. They decided to begin the uprising after midnight that night.

The uprising, known as the Southampton Insurrection, began as a campaign of terror against all slave owners. Turner said that no one should be spared, no

Nat Turner (*Library of Congress*)

matter how young or old. He believed that only by killing all slave-owning families in their path would the slaves have any chance of freedom. However, at least one white family was spared—a household of poor whites who owned no slaves. Turner decided these people were but little better off than slaves themselves.

At least 57 people were killed in the rebellion, including infants and children, women and men. As the rebellion began, it continued to grow, until some 60 to 80 slaves were involved. When the authorities realized what was happening, a total of 3,000 armed men were sent into the area, including federal forces, state patrols, and volunteers.

The rebel slaves had been poorly armed from the start, and they were exhausted from 40 straight hours of fighting. If Turner and his men had made it to the county seat, they might have seized arms and ammunition that would have given them a chance to succeed. Instead, the rebellion was put down, and Turner went into hiding in a cave. While Turner was in hiding, his wife was tortured and beaten, but she did not reveal his whereabouts.

At the end of October, Turner was captured; he was tried and executed on November 11, 1831. Contemporary accounts say that he remained brave and defiant. When he was asked whether his coming execution had made him regret what he had done, he replied, "Was not Christ crucified?"

It is believed that Turner's wife and children were sold into slavery in the Deep South after his execution. Some 200 black people in the area of the uprising were also killed.

Many other events had recently happened to unsettle slave owners: Denmark VESEY's 1822 plot; David WALKER's famous *Appeal* of 1829, in which he called on black people to rise up and take arms against slavery; the founding of *The Liberator,* William Lloyd Garrison's antislavery paper. As a result, restrictions on slaves became more stringent, in order to prevent such revolts as Nat Turner's.

For as long as 18 months after Turner's execution, hundreds of slaves throughout the South were arrested and charged with other antislavery plots, and dozens were executed. Although Turner's rebellion had not suc-ceeded, it stimulated increased resistance to slavery in the United States.

Turner was brought into contemporary prominence with William Styron's best-selling historical novel *The Confessions of Nat Turner* (New York: Random House), published in 1967 and winner of a Pulitzer Prize for fiction. However, many historians objected strongly to the book, believing that it falsely portrayed Turner as a madman and villain instead of an important slave leader. *Ten Black Writers Respond* (Boston: Beacon Press), edited by John Henrik Clarke, was published in 1968 to offer a different view of Nat Turner.

Further Reading: *Nat Turner's Slave Rebellion,* by Herbert Aptheker, New York: Humanities Press, 1966; *Afro-American History: The Modern Era,* by Herbert Aptheker, New York: Citadel Press, 1971 (pp. 80–95, on Styron's book and its controversy); *The Fires of Jubilee: Nat Turner's Fierce Rebellion,* by Stephen B. Oates, New York: Harper & Row, 1975.

—R. K.

❖ VANN, ROBERT LEE
(1879–1940), *editor of the* Pittsburgh Courier

Robert Vann helped to start one of the most influential black newspapers in the United States, the *Pittsburgh Courier* (Pittsburgh Courier Publishing Co., 1910–1950). In addition, he practiced law as a criminal defense attorney, which eventually led him to a career in politics.

Vann served as assistant city solicitor of Pittsburgh, a delegate to the National Republican Convention, and publicity director for Calvin Coolidge's presidential campaign. He was on a committee to revise Pennsylvania's state constitution. When he switched from the Republican to the Democratic Party, he was appointed special assistant to the U.S. attorney general by President Franklin D. Roosevelt.

Robert Vann was born on August 27, 1879, in rural North Carolina. He was the son of Lucy Peoples and an unknown father. Lucy was the child of ex-slaves who ran a general store. She was a cook for the Vann family and gave her son their name.

Vann graduated in 1901 at the head of his class in Waters Training School, a Baptist College in Winton, North Carolina. He then went to Wayland Academy in Richmond, Virginia, from 1901 to 1903. There, he was influenced by John Mitchell, editor of the black newspaper the *Richmond Planet,* which took militant political stands for voting rights and against segregation.

In 1903, Vann went to school at Western University of Pennsylvania in Pittsburgh, working summers and contributing to the school paper while attending classes. In his senior year, he became the paper's first African-American editor. He went on to Wesleyan's law school and was admitted to the bar in December 1909. A few months later, he married Jessie E. Matthews.

Vann's real interest was in establishing a law practice, but in the meantime, he needed more money. A month after his marriage, he became a lawyer for the *Pittsburgh Courier.* A few months later, he began to edit the paper, a position he held until his death.

The *Courier* soon became famous for its crusades against segregation and for its insistence on black issues being recognized in the white press. The *Courier* was also supported by the numerous black people migrating to Pittsburgh from the South during World War I.

In 1918, Vann became the first black assistant city solicitor (lawyer)—until that time, the highest position held by a black person in local city government.

Vann was strongly in favor of civil rights, but his approach to this goal was sometimes conservative in attitude. Unlike many other black leaders of the time, Vann supported black participation in World War I. He also supported Booker T. WASHINGTON's theories of black self-improvement, which assumed that black people would achieve equality by starting their own businesses and learning marketable job skills rather than by confronting the established white culture to demand voting rights and an end to segregation. However, Vann did not have enough money to promote his views beyond the *Courier*. A magazine that he founded soon failed, and he lost other businesses during the depression.

His positions were inconsistent in other ways. From 1919 to 1922, he opposed strikes by unions trying to win the 12-hour workday at a time when workdays for many were far longer than that. However, in 1925, he supported A. Philip RANDOLPH's attempt to organize the Brotherhood of Sleeping Car Porters. Then, three years later, he demanded that Randolph resign from union leadership because of his socialist past.

The *Courier* continued to grow, even though some of Vann's crusades did not take hold. In the 1930s, for example, he criticized the popular radio series *Amos 'n' Andy*, which he and many other black leaders felt was racist and demeaning to black people. However, some black leaders enjoyed the show and did not support Vann's position. It remained popular for many years.

Vann also supported Marcus GARVEY, the black nationalist leader who wanted black Americans to found their own colony in Africa. His position, like the movement itself, provoked controversy in the black community. So did Vann's position on the "Scottsboro boys"—the young black men who had been falsely accused of raping two white women in Alabama. Vann criticized the Communist Party's participation in the defense of the young men, stating that its own controversial public image could actually hurt the defendants' case.

Despite the controversies, the *Courier* continued to grow in influence. And Vann took strong positions on many events of the era that had great significance for blacks. He supported Ethiopia after the Italian invasion of 1935; he supported the careers of prize-fighter Joe LOUIS and Olympics champion Jesse OWENS; and he reported in detail on Hitler's contempt for black people at the 1936 Olympics in Berlin. All of these aspects of his journalism were popular with readers.

During World War II, Vann supported better treatment of African Americans in the armed forces and worked to establish black fighting divisions. (At that time, it was still controversial as to whether to allow black troops into combat.)

Vann had been a Republican for many years, following the tradition of black people who supported "Lincoln's party." In 1932, however, he switched his support to the Democrat Franklin Roosevelt, who he believed would support the social programs that black people needed. Roosevelt appointed him special assistant

to the U.S. attorney general, but Vann soon realized that this was just a token position.

Nevertheless, he remained with the Democrats for a few more years, working with them to enact an equal-rights law in Pennsylvania. Then, in 1940, he supported the Republican candidate Wendell Willkie for president, having become disenchanted with the Democrats.

Vann died of abdominal cancer on October 24, 1940, after suffering from the disease for several years. His legacy endured as public schools and scholarships were named in his honor.

Further Reading: *Robert L. Vann of the Pittsburgh Courier: Politics and Black Journalism,* by Andrew Buni, Pittsburgh, Pa.: University of Pittsburgh Press, 1974.

—R. K.

❖ VARICK, JAMES
(1750–1827), *founder and first bishop of the African Methodist Episcopal Zion (AME Zion) Church*

James Varick founded one of the major black churches of the United States. Varick was a firm believer in African Americans establishing their own churches, rather than remaining part of white church institutions. After Richard ALLEN and Absalom Jones founded the African Methodist Episcopal Church, Varick began the second national black church in the United States.

James Varick was born in upstate New York, near Newburgh, the son of a slave woman and a member of the Varick family that owned her. His mother was later set free, and he lived with his family in New York City, where he may have gone to the Free School for Negroes.

By the time the Revolutionary War had ended, Varick was operating his own shoemaker's shop. In 1790, he married Aurelia Jones, with whom he had four surviving children.

From the age of 16, Varick had been a member of the John Street Methodist Episcopal Church. Although that congregation was white, Varick was licensed to preach there. (Being licensed to preach didn't mean Varick was a minister; it simply gave him the right to speak in church.) But discrimination was so strong that black people had to sit in the back of the church. So in 1796, Varick and about 30 others left the church, forming the first black congregation in New York City.

In 1800, Varick and his congregation dedicated a new church building, which they called "Zion." In 1801, he incorporated the new church organization as the African Methodist Episcopal Church in New York. Richard Allen had earlier founded an organization with the same name, so Varick's group later added the word "Zion"—meaning a city of God.

In 1806, Varick became one of three black deacons ordained in New York. All the while, he continued to work as a shoemaker, a tobacco-cutter, and a teacher at the school he ran in the Zion Church and in his own home. Then, in 1822, Varick was elected first bishop of the AME Zion Church. In 1824, he was reelected.

Varick was active in black community affairs, through the African Society for Mutual Relief and an African Masonic lodge. He helped to lead the New York African Bible Society and worked to establish another branch of his church in Connecticut.

The church work was not Varick's only concern. He was also active in civil rights struggles. In 1821, he and some other black businesspeople and ministers petitioned the New York State Constitutional Convention for the right to vote. In 1827, he and Alexander CRUMMELL, John RUSSWURM, Richard Allen, and others founded the first African-American newspaper, *Freedom's Journal.*

Varick was a member of the opposition to the colonization movement. In his time, many white people believed that blacks should return to Africa. Although some black Americans in the 20th century would one day agree with this radical position, during the 19th century, most did not. Varick, Richard Allen, and others were active organizers against this movement, which they saw as a way to deprive black people of their rights as Americans.

Zion Church was an important base for Varick's political activities. The *Journal* was published there; meetings were held there; and the church became a center for black community and political life. In 1827, when New York State finally freed all slaves within its borders, African Americans in New York celebrated their gratitude at the church.

Varick died at his home two weeks later, on July 22, 1827. Although he was buried in upstate New York, his ashes were later transferred to Mother Zion Church in Harlem.

Further Reading: *The African Methodist Episcopal Zion Church: Reality of the Black Church,* by William Walls, Charlotte, N.C.: AME Zion Press, 1974.

—R. K.

❖ VESEY, DENMARK
(1767–1822), *antislavery leader*

Denmark Vesey led one of the largest and most elaborate slave revolts in U.S. history. Some 9,000 people throughout the region of Charleston, South Carolina, were involved. Vesey's activities and the risks he took are all the more remarkable because he himself was free.

Vesey was betrayed by one of the slaves he had trusted, preventing the revolt from taking place, but the extent of its plans and organization remained an ominous warning to slave owners throughout the South.

It's not certain where Vesey was born; Africa and the West Indies have been suggested. In 1781, he was a slave in St. Thomas, Danish West Indies, and in that year was shipped to Captain Joseph Vesey, a slave trader in St.-Dominigue, the French West Indian colony that today is Haiti.

Captain Vesey sold Denmark to work in the sugar fields, but the slave was returned to him. Denmark apparently had epilepsy and could not work as required. Some scholars believe that Denmark only pretended to have epilepsy, to avoid the brutal labor in the cane fields.

Denmark then became Captain Vesey's personal slave on his slave-trading trips to Africa and the West Indies. When Captain Vesey gave up the slave trade in 1783, he and Denmark settled in Charleston, South Carolina. However, St.-Dominigue was still important to Denmark. In 1791, Toussaint l'Ouverture led a great slave revolt, resulting in St.-Dominigue's eventually being governed wholly by black people. Haitian slave owners had to leave the country. Many came to Charleston to get help from Captain Vesey. Thus Denmark learned a great deal about the revolt, from which he drew both ideas and inspiration.

In 1799, Denmark Vesey had a remarkable piece of luck: He won $1,500 in a lottery. He was able to use $600 of it to buy his freedom, although he was unable to purchase the freedom of his wife or children. As a free man, Denmark began his own carpentry business. He prospered but remained unable to buy his family's freedom.

Vesey soon became a powerful leader of the African-American community in Charleston. Although he had an opportunity to emigrate to Africa, he didn't. According to a witness, "He wanted to stay and see what he could do for his fellow creatures." Vesey became a minister in the African Methodist Church and preached fiery sermons to the congregation. Privately, he talked continually to local slaves about the need to win their freedom. He told them about the great revolt in what was now Haiti, quoted the Bible to them, and reported on congressional debates and senators' speeches—anything to convince them of the need for liberation from the slave system.

By 1821, Vesey had worked out a complicated organizational network. Slaves were grouped into units that reported to a leader. Each leader might know the whole plan, but the individual slaves did not; if any one person was caught, the plan as a whole might still be safe.

Vesey's leaders were primarily artisans—skilled workers who were highly regarded by the others. Peter Poyas, a ship's carpenter, was second in command.

Poyas had a real gift for organizing people and for choosing reliable leaders to whom he could delegate responsibility. Poyas continually stressed the need to avoid "house slaves"—the slaves who worked in owners' homes, rather than in the fields. Poyas believed that house slaves would feel more personal attachment to their masters and would be unwilling to kill them, as the revolt required. He also feared that a house slave might tell his or her master about the plot.

Besides Poyas, Denmark relied on Ned and Rolla Bennett, who were slaves of the governor; Gullah Jack, who was believed to have magical powers; and Blind Phillip, who was supposed to be able to see ghosts. (Many slaves who would not listen to more rational arguments were convinced by the alleged magic powers of these men.) In addition, a sympathetic white barber made wigs and mustaches out of white people's hair, so that light-skinned black people could disguise themselves and move freely about.

Denmark and his followers raised money to buy weapons. They worked out a detailed plan that included some 9,000 slaves. At midnight on the second Sunday in July 1821, the slave army would begin its military action. It would block bridges, seize arsenals, and attack the guardhouse (where soldiers lived), in order to take over completely. Then the slaves would kill the owners and their families. The July date was chosen because plantation workers could be seen in town on Sunday with less suspicion, and many white people would be on vacation.

However, the plan began to unravel. Against the orders of Poyas and Vesey, someone tried to involve a house slave in the revolt, and the house slave told his master. The authorities were suspicious, yet had no hard evidence about the planned uprising.

Vesey and his lieutenants did not back down. The lieutenants who had been named by the house slave went to the city officials and indignantly protested that their honor had been attacked. They insisted that they were innocent and demanded that they be cleared of suspicion. The authorities were completely bewildered—surely guilty slaves would not act in such a way.

Meanwhile, Vesey moved up the date of the revolt to a day in June. Even under these dangerous circumstances, he continued to hold meetings and to organize. His plan still might have worked.

Then another house slave, who had more information, revealed the rest of the plot's details to his master.

The governor created a new regiment specifically to defend Charleston at every conceivable weak point. Vesey tried to signal his troops to attack, but his messenger was turned back by some soldiers on patrol.

Vesey realized that all he could do was try to protect those he had recruited. Everyone was sent home, and all records were destroyed. When the Bennetts and Poyas were arrested, Vesey went into hiding. The slaves were put on trial, with no black people allowed within two blocks of the courthouse.

The rebel slaves were tortured, threatened, and abused. Finally, someone—not Poyas or the Bennetts—broke down and gave information that helped the police find Vesey. When Vesey went on trial, he continued to be brave and defiant. The judge commented, "You were a free man; were comparatively wealthy; and enjoyed every comfort . . . You had, therefore, much to risk, and little to gain."

On July 2, 1822, Vesey and five others were hanged in public. Gullah Jack had tried to free them, but more arrests weakened his forces and he was eventually arrested as well. Federal troops were sent to Charleston as slaves continued to be tried and executed. The informers, on the other hand, were set free and given money for life.

The repercussions from the revolt went on. That winter, the South Carolina Assembly passed the Negro Seamen Act, which made it illegal for free black people to come into South Carolina ports. Although the Supreme Court found this unconstitutional, it continued to be enforced. Some of the people who had worked against Vesey also became key leaders in South Carolina's efforts to secede from the Union.

Although Vesey's revolt itself did not succeed, it was a source of fear and apprehension for slave owners everywhere—and a source of inspiration for all existing slaves. John Brown is said to have been inspired in his own revolt by Vesey's work. During the Civil War, Frederick DOUGLASS brought a new slogan to the first black regiment: "Remember Denmark Vesey of Charleston."

Further Reading: *The Trial Record of Denmark Vesey,* Introduction by John O. Killens, Boston, Mass.: Beacon Press, 1970; *Great Gettin' Up Morning* (a fictionalized biography), by John O. Killens, Garden City, N.Y.: Doubleday, 1972; *Insurrection in South Carolina, The Turbulent World of Denmark Vesey,* by John Lofton, Yellow Springs, Ohio: Antioch University Press, 1964; *American Negro Slave Revolts,* Herbert Aptheker, New York: International Publishers, 1983 reprint of 1943 ed.

—R. K.

❖ WALKER, ALICE MALSENIOR
(1944–   ), *writer, poet*

Alice Walker's novels have been widely admired and praised by critics and the public alike. Her third novel, *The Color Purple* (San Diego, Calif.: Harcourt, Brace, Jovanovich), published in 1982, won a Pulitzer Prize, an American Book Award, and a National Book Critics Circle Award nomination. Walker also won a National Book Award nomination for her 1973 book of poetry, *Revolutionary Petunias and Other Poems* (San Diego, Calif.: Harcourt, Brace, Jovanovich, 1986). In 1986, she won an O. Henry Award for her short story "Kindred Spirits."

Alice Walker was born on February 9, 1944, in Eatonton, Georgia, to Willie Lee and Minnie Tallulah (Grant) Walker. She attended Spellman College in Atlanta, Georgia, from 1961 to 1963, then earned her B.A. from Sarah Lawrence College in New York in 1965. She had written poetry as a young person and began writing fiction at Sarah Lawrence.

In her early years, Walker was deeply involved in the Civil Rights movement, as a voter-registration worker in Georgia and a Head Start worker in Mississippi (Head Start was a government-assistance program for black schoolchildren). She also worked for the welfare department in New York City. She then began her career as a writer and a teacher of literature and writing. She was a writer-in-residence and a teacher of black studies at Jackson State College in Jackson, Mississippi, 1968–69, and Tougaloo College in Tougaloo, Mississippi, 1970–71. In 1968, she published *Once: Poems* (San Diego, Calif.: Harcourt, Brace, Jovanovich), her first volume of poetry, which was reprinted in 1988.

In 1970, Walker also published her first novel, *The Third Life of Grange Copeland*, (New York: Pocket Books, 1993), a portrait of a southern black man who lives through the days of intense segregation and racial hatred to see the dawning of a new era with the coming of the Civil Rights movement. Many critics believe *Grange Copeland* is a remarkable study of how black men are led by racism to mistreat black women, with the book holding out the hope of redemption for black people of both sexes.

In 1967, Walker married Melvyn Leventhal, a white civil rights lawyer. Walker gave birth to their daughter three days after finishing her first novel in 1970.

In the early 1970s, Walker taught at Wellesley College in Massachusetts and at the University of Massachusetts. She published *Five Poems,* 1972; *Revolutionary Petunias and Other Poems,* 1973; and *In Love and Trouble: Stories of Black Women* (San Diego, Calif.: Harcourt, Brace, Jovanovich, 1985), a collection of short stories.

In 1976, Walker and Leventhal divorced. She continued to win many awards and fellowships for her writing and in 1976, she published *Meridian* (New York: Pocket

Books, 1996), a work that many critics consider to be the best novel ever written about the Civil Rights movement. *Meridian* also explores the painful relations among blacks and whites, male and female, holding out the hope of some kind of unity after long years of struggle.

Walker continued to write and to teach. In 1979, she published another book of poetry, *Goodnight, Willie Lee, I'll See You in the Morning* (San Diego, Calif.: Harcourt, Brace, Jovanovich). In 1981, she brought out more short fiction, collected in *You Can't Keep a Good Woman Down* (San Diego, Calif.: Harcourt, Brace, Jovanovich). In 1982, she taught at the University of California at Berkeley, and Brandeis University in Massachusetts.

Then, in 1982, Walker published her most celebrated book, *The Color Purple* (New York: Washington Square Press, 1998). This novel, related through letters, is the story of Celie and Nettie, sisters separated at a young age. With Celie living in the Deep South of the 1920s and 1930s, and Nettie living with a missionary's family in Africa, Walker was able to weave a rich tapestry of African and African-American life, once again focusing on relations among men and women, black and white.

In 1984, she published more poetry, *Horses Make a Landscape Look More Beautiful* (San Diego, Calif.: Harcourt, Brace, Jovanovich). She has also written several books of essays: *In Search of Our Mothers' Gardens: Womanist Prose* (San Diego, Calif.: Harcourt, Brace, Jovanovich), 1983 and *Living by the Word: Selected Writings, 1973–1987* (San Diego: Calif.: Harcourt, Brace, Jovanovich, 1988). Walker is the author of a children's novel, *To Hell With Dying* (San Diego, Calif.: Harcourt, Brace, Jovanovich, 1988), and a children's biography of Langston HUGHES, *Langston Hughes, American Poet* (New York: Crowell, 1974). She is also the editor of a collection of Zora Neale HURSTON's writings, *I Love Myself When I Am Laughing . . . and Then Again When I Am Looking Mean and Impressive: A Zora Neale Hurston Reader* (Old Westbury, N.Y.: Feminist Press, 1979).

Walker acted as consultant to the film version of *The Color Purple,* directed by Steven Spielberg. The film received several Academy Award nominations.

The original novel had generated a controversy over Walker's portrayal of black men; the movie was equally controversial. Many critics objected to Walker's image of black men, particularly since Celie is raped by a man she believes to be her father when she is still a child and then is cruelly dominated by another man whom her supposed father forces her to marry. Other critics believed that Walker had finally exposed an important truth about male-female relations. Women readers in particu-

lar wrote to her about their own experience of incest and abuse and thanked the author for telling stories they recognized as their own.

Another controversial feature of *The Color Purple* is Celie's lesbian relationship with Shug, a black blues singer. Again, many critics objected to her sexual politics, while many others praised Walker for dealing with and putting value into a woman-to-woman relationship.

Walker stands by her work. She has written that she appreciates the controversies, since they have helped to broaden people's understanding of her subject matter, as well as how literary criticism works.

In 1996, Walker published *The Same River Twice: Honoring the Difficult: A Meditation of Life, Spirit, Art, and the Making of the Film "The Color Purple" Ten Years Later* (Chicago: Wheeler Pub.), in which she discusses the effect of the enormous fame she received as a result of writing *The Color Purple,* as well as her experience of having Spielberg make her movie. Later, she published *Banned* (Chicago: Aunt Lute Books, 1996), which contains two short stories and the opening of *The Color Purple,* as well as a discussion of various efforts to censor Walker's work.

In 1984, Walker founded Wild Trees Press, which she directed for several years. She is currently a member of the board of trustees of Sarah Lawrence College. Her fourth novel, *The Temple of My Familiar* (New York: Washington Square Press, 1997) was published in 1989.

Walker's next novel was *Possessing the Secret of Joy* (New York: Pocket Books, 1993), a novel about the practice of female genital mutilation, set in Africa. This, too, was a controversial book, with some welcoming Walker's exposure of these practices and others criticizing what they called her culture-bound view of Africa. Partly in response to the criticism, Walker collaborated with Pratibha Parmar and editor Vicki Austin-Smith to produce *Warrior Marks: Female Genital Mutilation and the Sexual Blinding of Women* (New York: Harvest Books, 1996), based on a film by Parmar about the two authors' investigation of this issue.

Walker continues to be an activist as well as a writer. *Anything We Love Can Be Saved: A Writer's Activism* (New York: Random House, 1997), chronicles what she calls her "cultural, political, spiritual" activism—her efforts to "save the world," or at least to make it a better place. One example of such activism was her 1996 letter to President Bill Clinton, urging him to develop better relations with Cuba's president Fidel Castro and protesting Clinton's action to tighten the blockade that kept medicine and other goods from reaching Cuba.

Further Reading: *Her Blue Body, Everything We Know: Earthling Poems, 1965–1990 Complete,* by Alice Walker, New York: Harvest Books 1993; *Alice Walker* (Twayne's United States Authors Series), by Donna Haisty Winchell, New York: Twayne Pub., 1992; *Alice Walker: Critical Perspectives: Past and Present,* by Henry L. Gates, K.A. Appiah, and Alice Walker, New York: Amistad Press, 1993; *Everyday Use,* ed. by Barbara T. Christian, with work by Alice Walker et al., New Brunswick, N.J.: Rutgers University Press, 1994; *Alice Malsenior Walker: An Annotated Bibliography, 1968–1986,* by Louis H. Pratt, Westport, Conn.: Meckler Publishing Corp., 1990; *Alice Walker: An Annotated Bibliography, 1968–1986,* by Erma Davis Banks and Keith Byerman, New York: Garland Pub., 1989; *Alice Walker and Zora Neale Hurston: The Common Bond,* ed. by Lillie P. Howard, Westport, Conn.: Greenwood Publishing Group, 1993; *Making American Tradition: Visions and Revisions from Ben Franklin to Alice Walker,* by Cushing Strout, New Brunswick, N.J.: Rutgers University Press, 1990; *The Voices of African American Women: The Use of Narrative and Authorial Voice in the Works of Harriet Jacobs, Zora Neale Hurston, and Alice Walker,* by Yvonne Johnson, New York: Peter Lang Publishing, 1998.

—R. K.

❖ WALKER, MADAME C. J. (Sarah Breedlove)
(1867–1919), *entrepreneur, millionaire*

Madame C. J. Walker was one of the first black American millionaires. Her story sounds like a typical rags-to-riches legend. She was the orphaned daughter of poor farmers, then a widowed washerwoman supporting a daughter. After remarrying, she invented a product that black women could use to straighten their hair, and almost overnight she became a rich woman. When she died, she owned her own factory, as well as a luxurious villa and a New York townhouse.

Madame Walker began life in 1867 as Sarah Breedlove, the daughter of poor farmers in northeast Louisiana. Owen and Minerva Breedlove died when Sarah was quite young, so the child went to live with her married sister. At age 14, Sarah married a man named McWilliams, with whom she had a daughter. By the time Sarah was 20, her husband had died.

In 1887, Sarah Breedlove McWilliams moved to St. Louis, Missouri, where she worked for many years as a laundress. Then, in 1905, the turning point in her life, she began to work on a formula that black women could use to straighten their hair. Until then, hair could only be straightened by ironing it. Breedlove-McWilliams invented a hair relaxer that could be used with a straightening comb.

Breedlove-McWilliams invented other cosmetics, such as a cream that "improved" the complexion. In 1906, she moved her business to Denver, Colorado, where she married the journalist Charles Walker and initiated more aggressive marketing of her products. She sold her goods door-to-door, demonstrating how they worked. She also trained others to sell for her, much as successful cosmetics companies operate today.

By 1908, Madame Walker was ready to open a new office, in Pittsburgh, that was run by her daughter. In 1910, she consolidated her offices in Indianapolis, where she also opened a manufacturing plant.

Walker's business success owed a great deal to her use of advertising, especially in black papers. She employed some 3,000 people, mostly women, to manufacture and sell her products—all her women workers using her products to straighten their hair. As a result, other black women went into business with their own hair-straightening products, and straightened hair remained in fashion for many years to come. The famous entertainer Josephine Baker adopted Walker's style, and a French company also began to make a hair-straightener.

Walker eventually built a house and a beauty parlor in Harlem, as well as a country house, Villa Lewaror, in Irvington-on-Hudson, designed by African-American architect Vertner Tandy. She furnished that house with a gold-plated piano, antique furniture, Persian rugs, and other luxuries.

In addition, she gave money to the NAACP (the National Association for the Advancement of Colored People), homes for the aged, the Colored YMCA, poor people in Indianapolis, scholarship funds for young women attending Tuskegee Institute in Alabama, and the Palmer Memorial Institute of Sedalia, North Carolina. She organized her sales agents to do community service, and gave prizes for those who did so. After her death in 1919, her will stipulated that certain sums be set aside to establish a school in West Africa, as well as to support various schools and charities in the United States.

—R. K.

❖ WALKER, DAVID
(1785–1830), *antislavery writer*

David Walker wrote one of the most militant antislavery tracts that had ever been published. In 1829, he wrote a pamphlet called *Walker's Appeal* (New York: Hill &

Wang, 1965 reprint), in which he urged black people all over the world to rise up and free themselves. "Kill or be killed," he wrote. ". . . Had you not rather be killed than to be slave to a tyrant, who takes the life of your mother, wife, and dear little children? . . . Believe this, that it is not more harm for you to kill a man, who is trying to kill you, than it is for you to take a drink of water when thirsty."

Walker's Appeal was read all over the United States. Although both black and white antislavery leaders rejected the violence he advocated, people continued to read the work, which went into three editions by 1830.

David Walker was born in 1785 to a free mother, which meant that he himself was free. His father, however, was a slave in Wilmington, North Carolina. Walker decided that he had to leave the South, where slavery so profoundly affected the lives of all black people.

He went to live in Boston, where he taught himself to read and write, and he started a business buying and selling old clothes. He is supposed to have been a good businessperson, but he never became rich; instead of working on expanding his business, he devoted a great deal of his time to reading about slavery and world history and was overly generous in his financial transactions.

Walker did not come to his radical position on slavery immediately. Late in 1828, he published an article in *Freedom's Journal* that encouraged his audience to seek freedom—but without violating the U.S. Constitution.

The next year, he published his *Appeal,* whose full title is *David Walker's Appeal in four articles together with a Preamble, to the Coloured Citizens of the World, but in particular and very expressly, to those of The United States of America.* In this work, Walker stressed the connections among black people in the United States, Africa, and the West Indies. He believed that black people could not be free until they were free worldwide.

When the *Appeal* was published, legislatures all over the South met secretly to pass laws against circulation of the document. They did everything possible to suppress these ideas. Still, people continued to read and circulate the work. Partly as a result of this pamphlet, the Georgia state legislature made it a crime to teach slaves to read or write, as well as a capital crime (punishable by death) to circulate literature advocating the overthrow of slavery. Georgia also made it illegal for black sailors to come ashore in Georgia ports.

Other southern legislatures passed similar laws. In Virginia, for example, black ministers were prevented from preaching to their own people, because of fears that they would read the *Appeal* as a sermon.

In 1828, Walker had married a fugitive slave, Eliza, whose last name was kept secret to protect her newly won freedom. She and his friends urged Walker to go to Canada, where he would be safe from the attacks of the slave owners. Already, a group of Georgia men had offered a reward of $1,000 for Walker dead and $10,000 for him alive. When he did die in 1830, many believed he had been poisoned.

Walker and Eliza had one child, Edwin G. Walker, who was born after Walker died. Later, in 1866, Edwin Walker became the first African American to be elected to the Massachusetts legislature. In 1848, the black abolitionist Henry Highland GARNET wrote a book praising David Walker and his appeal.

Further Reading: *The Ideological Origins of Black Nationalism* (which contains the full text of the *Appeal*), by Sterling Stuckey, Boston, Mass.: Beacon Press, 1972; *One Continual Cry,* by Herbert Aptheker, 1965; *A Documentary History of the Negro People in the United States,* by Herbert Aptheker, New York: Citadel Press, 1962 revision of 1951 ed.; *The Negro Vanguard,* by Richard Bardolph, New York: Rinehart, 1961.

—R. K.

❖ WALKER, GEORGE
(1873–1911), *entertainer*

George Walker was one of the great entertainers of his time. Besides being a member (with his partner Bert WILLIAMS) of the comedy team Williams and Walker, he was also a great producer and promoter. He put together a company of black performers whose shows helped to create black theater in America. Walker fought with white producers to secure unprecedentedly large budgets for his shows. He tried to involve African themes in his work, and often succeeded. In many ways, Walker helped to create not only black theater but musical theater itself—a transition from a series of disjointed skits and songs into a fully worked-out story, with plot, characters, and musical numbers all related to a central theme.

Born in 1873, George Walker was the son of a police officer in Lawrence, Kansas. He entered show business at an early age, joining a traveling medicine show. At that time, people selling "medicine" would travel throughout the country, with featured singers, dancers, and comics in order to attract a crowd to whom the medicine could be sold.

Walker traveled with the show to San Francisco. Although he liked performing, he disliked the stereotypical roles he was required to perform. He looked for work in the theater but had trouble finding it.

Then, at age 20, he met Bert Williams, who one day would become America's first black superstar. The two met on a city sidewalk, and, out of that meeting, a great partnership was born. Although their act failed at first, they soon worked out a new formula for success.

Their success seems somewhat ironic from a modern perspective. Williams and Walker billed themselves as "Two Real Coons," identifying themselves as the genuine article, not the white minstrels in blackface that audiences were used to viewing. This did give the two men a chance to develop the authentic humor of black people, but they still had to conform to the stereotypes that white people had promoted.

The team's first big hit came in 1896, with a show at Koster and Bial's Music Hall, New York City's most important vaudeville theater. The team ended their show with a high-stepping dance called the cakewalk. The dance caught on, especially among white socialites and Williams and Walker continued their show for another 39 weeks.

Gradually, the two men began to work in musical shows. Instead of vaudeville's series of disjointed skits and songs, their shows had plots and characters. Then they formed their own company, performing such works as *Sons of Ham,* in 1900; *In Dahomey,* in 1902; *In Abyssinia,* in 1908; and *Bandana Land,* in 1911. As the titles make clear, these shows had black and African themes—a breakthrough for their time.

The shows also featured a new type of black humor. Walker usually played a type of razzle-dazzle con man, whom audiences recognized as seizing one of the few opportunities open to an ambitious black person. Williams was usually the downtrodden simpleton of whom Walker tried to take advantage. Yet this character, as presented by Williams, was not just an innocent—he used his innate intelligence to outwit the con man. Although there were many stereotypes and caricatures in the team's work, Walker and Williams found a way to convey some genuine aspects of black culture that delighted both black and white audiences.

Walker was the real producer of the team. He planned the shows, made the deals with white backers, and generally took care of all the complicated arrangements. He pushed for big budgets for his shows, which were always denied at first. Williams might be ready to concede, but Walker never gave in. Somehow, he always managed to get more than the producers had expected to give—and his shows always made a profit for them, as well.

Walker had married the performer Aida Overton (called by *Variety* "easily the foremost Afro-American stage artist") in 1899, but apparently continued to be a ladies man who lived a fast life. He appeared on stage for the last time in 1911, before succumbing to a slow and painful death from syphilis. Although his partner Bert Williams went on to a triumphant theatrical career of his own, he couldn't keep the theater company going without Walker.

Further Reading: *Toms, Coons, Mulattoes, Mammies and Bucks, An Interpretive History of Blacks in Films,* by Donald Bogle, New York: Viking Press, 1973; *Black Manhattan,* by James Weldon Johnson, New York: Arno Press, 1968 reprint of 1940 ed.

—*R. K.*

❖ WALKER, MAGGIE LENA
(1867–1934), *banker, civil rights activist, newspaper founder, community leader*

The first female bank president in the United States, Maggie Lena Walker founded the St. Luke Penny Savings Bank in Richmond, Virginia, in 1903. Committed to civil rights since her childhood, she used the bank's funds to provide numerous benefits for the African-American community.

Walker was born in Richmond on July 15, 1867. Her parents, William and Elizabeth Mitchell, worked in the mansion of a wealthy white woman. When Walker was quite small, her family moved to a small house in downtown Richmond. Not long afterward, James Mitchell, who was working as headwaiter in a hotel, was found dead in the James River, apparently a murder

Maggie Lena Walker (front row, third from left) *(Courtesy of the National Park Service)*

victim. Elizabeth Mitchell had to support her two children by taking in laundry. Maggie helped out by doing the ironing and taking the bundles of washing back and forth to her mother's customers, and during these hard years she learned the value of hard work and self-reliance. "I was not born with a silver spoon in my mouth, but with a laundry basket practically on my head," she later recalled.

While attending Richmond's segregated schools, Walker was an exceptional student, and following her graduation in 1883 she worked as a teacher for three years. She continued to study in her free time, taking classes in accounting and business management. Walker was also a devoted churchgoer, having been a member of the Old First Baptist Church since she was a small girl. Her religious faith underpinned her belief that African Americans, and especially black women, could overcome racism and achieve great things. While attending a church meeting she met Armstead Walker, whom she married in 1886.

When she was only 14, Walker had joined the Independent Order of St. Luke (IOSL), a black mutual aid society formed after the Civil War to help deserving individuals with medical bills and funeral expenses. After her marriage, Walker stopped teaching and devoted much of her free time to the IOSL. In 1890, when Walker became the IOSL's grand secretary, the society's funds totaled only $31.61, and there were numerous unpaid bills on hand. Walker got to work, seeking ways to raise funds and increase the society's membership.

One of Walker's most important moves was to found a newspaper, *The St. Luke Herald,* in 1902. The *Herald* forged a link between the IOSL and the community at large, taking a strong stand against segregation and racial oppression. The following year, Walker persuaded the IOSL leadership to establish a bank, the St. Luke Penny Savings Bank. Her idea was to encourage African Americans to deposit their pennies and nickels, building up enough capital for the bank to finance the purchase of homes. Walker paid special attention to children, handling out small cardboard boxes that they could use to save their pennies in. Walker's efforts paid off handsomely; by 1920 the bank had financed 645 black-owned homes, and by 1924 the IOSL's total assets had risen to $3.5 million. Walker's management was so effective that the St. Luke Penny Savings Bank survived the Great Depression and still exists today, having merged with another bank to become the Consolidated Bank and Trust Company.

In 1905, Walker and her family—she now had two sons—moved into an impressive red-brick house at $110^1/_2$ East Leigh Street, in Richmond's Jackson Ward district. (The house is now a National Historic Site.) In addition to Walker's beloved mother, the household came to include her daughters-in-law and grandchildren. Walker loved to entertain, and her home became a center of social and business activity for Richmond's black community. She was involved in numerous organizations, including the National Association for the Advancement of Colored People, the Colored Women's Clubs, and the National Urban League. She helped set up a community house in Richmond, a visiting nurse service, and a sanitorium for tuberculosis patients.

When Walker died in December 1934, her funeral was one of the largest that Richmond had ever seen. Recounting her achievements in a long obituary, the *Richmond News Leader* called her "the greatest of all Negro leaders of Richmond" and praised "her outstanding achievements as Christian mother, fraternalist, banker, philanthropist, and minister of interracial good will."

Further Reading: "Maggie L. Walker," in *Notable Black American Women,* edited by Jesse Carney Smith, Detroit: Gale, 1992; "Maggie Lena Walker Historic Site," in *The African-American Experience* (American Historic Places), by Ray Spangenburg and Diane K. Moser, New York: Facts On File, 1997.

—P. K.

❖ WALKER, MARGARET ABIGAIL
(Margaret Walker Alexander)
(1915–), writer, poet

Margaret Walker is the author of *Jubilee* (New York: Demco Media, 1991), one of the first modern novels to tell about slavery from the slaves' point of view. *Jubilee* was carefully researched, and was based on the life of Walker's great-grandmother, a slave who lived through the Civil War and the early years of Reconstruction. *Jubilee* won a Houghton-Mifflin literary fellowship when it was published in 1966.

Walker has also written several books of poetry. Her first collection, *For My People* (New York: Arno Press, 1968 ed.), won the prestigious Yale Younger Poets competition when it was published in 1942.

Margaret Walker was born on July 7, 1915, in Birmingham, Alabama. She graduated from Northwestern University in Chicago in 1935 and she received her M.A. in English literature from the University of Iowa in 1940. Three years later, she married Firnist Alexander, with whom she later had four children.

Walker has worked at a variety of jobs, including social worker, reporter, and magazine editor. In 1941, she began to teach in college and has done so ever since. Her association with Jackson State College in Mississippi began in 1949.

Walker's first book, *For My People* (North Stratford, N.H.: Ayer Co. Publishers, 1968), was a critical success when she published it in 1942. For many years afterward, however, Walker published nothing more, although she continued to win various academic and artistic honors. In 1944, she received a Rosenwald fellowship, and in 1954, she was given a Ford Foundation fellowship to study English at Yale. In 1962, she finally published again with *Come Down from Yonder Mountain* (Toronto: Longmans), a novel.

Soon after that, Walker returned to school, getting her Ph.D. in English literature from the University of Iowa in 1965. In 1968, she became director of the Institute for the Study of the History, Life and Culture of Black Peoples at Jackson State.

In addition to *Jubilee*, in 1966, she brought out three more books of poetry: *Ballad of the Free* (Detroit: Broadside Press, 1966), *Prophets for a New Day* (Detroit: Broadside Press, 1970), and *October Journey* (Detroit: Broadside Press, 1973). She also began to win various fellowships and scholarships, including a Fulbright in 1971 and a National Endowment for the Arts grant in 1972, both in recognition of her writing.

Walker has received numerous honorary degrees and much acclaim. *Jubilee* saw renewed interest after the publication of Alex HALEY's *Roots*, which also involved a black family during slavery. (In fact, Walker sued Haley for plagiarism, claiming that he had taken much of his material from *Jubilee*. The two authors were finally able to come to an agreement, and an out-of-court settlement was reached in Walker's favor.)

In 1982, Walker published *The Daemonic Genius of Richard Wright* (New York: Warner Books, 1988 reprint of 1982 ed.)

Further Reading: *Margaret Walker's "For My People"; A Tribute,* by Roland L. Freeman, Jackson: University of Mississippi, 1992; *On Being Female, Black, and Free: Essays by Margaret Walker, 1932–1992,* ed. by Maryemma Graham, Knoxville: University of Tennessee Press, 1997; *This Is My Century: New and Collected Poems,* by Margaret Walker, Athens: University of Georgia Press, 1989; *How I*

Wrote "Jubilee" and Other Essays on Life and Literature, by Margaret Walker, New York: Feminist Press, 1990; *A Poetic Equation: Conversations Between Margaret Walker and Nikki Giovanni,* Washington, D.C.: Howard University Press, 1983.

—*R. K.*

❖ WASHINGTON, BOOKER TALIAFERRO
(1856–1915), *educator, political leader, adviser*

Booker T. Washington was probably the most influential black leader of his time. He wielded an enormous amount of power among both black and white people. He advised presidents on race relations; helped to decide black political appointments throughout the nation and white political appointments in the South; and was supported by the major part of the black press of his day.

Yet Washington was also an enormously controversial figure. He believed that black people should concentrate their energies on improving themselves through industrial education—learning a trade—so that they could become employed and self-supporting. This, he argued, was more important than trying to win political power through electing black officials, and more useful than trying to win social equality through integrating restaurants, trains, schools, and other public places.

Many influential black leaders strongly disagreed with Washington, most notably, W. E. B. DUBOIS, James Monroe TROTTER, Henry McNeal TURNER and Charles Waddell CHESNUTT. Those writers believed that black people must aspire to both political power and social equality—to elect their own officials, develop highly educated black professionals, and work to fully integrate American society.

Washington's most visible achievement was the establishment of Tuskegee Institute (now Tuskegee University), the industrial school in Alabama that was supposed to be a model for black self-improvement through education. Under his leadership, Tuskegee, which began as a collection of temporary shelters and shanties, grew to more than 60 permanent buildings endowed with nearly $3 million. The school was built through the efforts of the students, and through the donations of wealthy white northerners, who agreed with Washington's theories of black self-improvement.

Booker T. Washington was born Booker Taliaferro, on April 5, 1856, the child of an unknown white man and Jane, the slave cook of a small planter in rural

Booker T. Washington (front row, center) *(Library of Congress)*

Virginia. After Booker was born, his mother married a slave, Washington Ferguson. Later, when Booker enrolled in school, he used "Washington" as his surname.

His childhood was spent as a slave on the Virginia farm where he was born. In 1865, when slavery had ended, his mother took the children to Malden, West Virginia, where her husband had found work in the salt mines. Washington was then only nine. For the next three years, he packed salt for a meager wage, and worked in a coal mine.

In 1871, Washington went to work as a houseboy for the local mine owner. He had been trying in the meantime to educate himself, and could now attend school while working. Thus, in 1872, at 16, he was able to enter Hampton Normal and Agricultural Institute in Virginia. He had to walk most of the way from his home in West Virginia to the school in Hampton, Virginia. Once there, he worked as a janitor for room and board. Fortunately, the school principal, Samuel Chapman Armstrong, found a patron to pay his tuition.

Washington, graduated with honors in 1875, and returned to West Virginia to teach. In 1878, he continued his education at Wayland Seminary in Richmond, Virginia. In contrast to the practical teaching at Hampton, Wayland's curriculum was all academic. The two experiences convinced Washington that practical skills were more important, and in 1879, he went back to Hampton to teach American Indians.

In 1881, Washington's great opportunity came. The Alabama legislature wanted to establish a school at Tuskegee to train black teachers. Armstrong, the Hampton principal, was invited to recommend a white teacher—but he named Washington. Washington accepted, only to find that the school had no money, no land, and no buildings. Only $2,000 was available to pay teachers' salaries.

Somehow, Washington managed to put together an institution. He recruited local black students, gained the support of local white residents, and found a shack that was lent to him by a black church for his first building. Eventually by borrowing money and involving students in construction, he was able to buy a local plantation and build dorms, classrooms, a dining hall, and a chapel. These buildings were built with bricks from a kiln the students themselves had made, and they continued to sell bricks to raise money.

Little by little, Washington built Tuskegee, focusing always on practical skills, such as carpentry and farming for boys, and homemaking tasks for girls. (In those days, few people questioned such a division of labor.) He also taught students personal hygiene and manners, and stressed "building good character."

In 1882, Washington married Fannie N. Smith, who died two years later after bearing a child. In 1885, he married again—Olivia A. Davidson, the assistant principal of Tuskegee. She too died young, in 1889, after having two children. Finally, in 1893, Washington married a third time, to Margaret Murray, who had become a principal at Tuskegee in 1889. She later directed all the girls' programs at Tuskegee and initiated programs for local women.

Tuskegee's influence was growing. The school held annual Tuskegee Negro Conferences beginning in 1892, inviting thousands of black people to come and learn new farming methods. Graduates of Tuskegee went on to found similar schools around the South.

Washington's influence was also growing. His fundraising efforts brought him into contact with many northern millionaires. He helped to establish the Anna T. Jeanes Fund and the Phelps-Stokes Fund—philanthropic foundations that provided channels for the wealthy to assist black education.

Washington's political influence gained ground in 1895, when he was invited to speak to a multiracial audience at the International Exposition in Atlanta. In this speech, he apologized for black people having started at the "top"—electing black political officials under Reconstruction—instead of at the "bottom"—through educating themselves. He stressed that black people should not actively seek social equality, but rather educate themselves and rely on the kindness and fairness of white southerners.

The white people in the audience received this message with thunderous cheers. According to a white reporter, however, at the end of the speech, "most of the Negroes in the audience were crying, perhaps without knowing just why."

After this speech, Washington's political power grew even greater, and he was much in demand as a speaker around the country. His fame grew further in 1901 with the publication of *Up from Slavery* (New York: Doubleday, 1998), his autobiography. When Theodore Roosevelt was elected president in the same year, Washington became an influential adviser, although he eventually lost this political inroad when Democrat Woodrow Wilson took office in 1913. Wilson was known for his lack of sympathy for civil rights, and his Democratic Party was the stronghold of southerners who had opposed political equality for black Americans since well before the Civil War.

Modern historians speak of the many contradictions in Washington's career. He told southern black people that Jim Crow laws (laws enforcing rigid segregation) did not matter; yet, he broke those laws by riding first class in the white Pullman cars of southern railroads. He hoped to prevent lynchings and to get some kind of economic justice for black people through compromise and accommodation, but during the years of his influence, racial violence and black poverty increased.

Washington died on November 14, 1915, from arteriosclerosis, at the relatively young age of 59. He had become ill while in New York City but managed to return home to Tuskegee to die. Nearly 8,000 people attended his funeral. Later, he became the first African American to be commemorated on a postage stamp.

Washington's legacy is a mixed one. He is remembered as the target of a great deal of criticism for his efforts to accommodate and pacify white supremacists by urging black Americans to avoid political action and militant organizing. But he founded a major black institution that continues to exist today, achieving a level of tremendous power and influence in both black and white communities, and he provided inspiration and leadership for later generations of black Americans.

Further Reading: *The Story of My Life and Work,* by Booker T. Washington, Westport, Conn.: Greenwood Press, 1909; *My Larger Education,* by Booker T. Washington, Miami, Fla.: Mnemosyne Publishers Inc., 1969 reprint of 1911 ed.; *A New Negro for a New Century,* by Booker T. Washington, North Stratford, N.H.: Ayer Co. Pub., 1969; *Booker T. Washington,* Bass, New York: Twayne Pub., 1996; *Booker T. Washington and the Negro's Place in American Life,* by Samuel R. Spencer, Jr., Boston, Mass.: Little, Brown, 1955; *Booker T. Washington: The Making of a Black Leader,* by Louis R. Harlan, New York: Oxford University Press, 1972; *Negro Thought in America, 1880–1915: Racial Ideologies in the Age of Booker T. Washington,* by August Meier, Ann Arbor, Mich.: University of Michigan Press, 1988 revision of 1963 ed.; *Booker T. Washington and his Critics,* edited by Hugh Hawkins, Boston, Mass.: Heath, 1962; *Booker T. Washington,* edited by Emma Lou Thornbrough, 1969.

—R. K.

❖ WATERS, ETHEL
(1900–1977), *singer, actress*

Ethel Waters had a long and varied career as a nightclub singer, performer on Broadway, jitterbug queen in Hollywood films, and dramatic actress in such films as *Pinky* (1950) and *Member of the Wedding* (a 1950 Broadway play that was made into a movie in 1952). Waters was nominated for an Academy Award as Best Supporting Actress for her performance in *Pinky.*

In addition to her work on stage and screen, Waters achieved success on television, starring in the series *Beulah* in 1950 and appearing in various dramatic roles on television specials in the 1960s and 1970s. She also performed on television with evangelist Billy Graham, whose revival team she joined in the 1960s.

Ethel Waters was born at the beginning of the 20th century to poor, unmarried parents in Chester,

Pennsylvania. She grew up in a red-light district and as a child, she ran errands for the prostitutes and pimps who worked there. She married at 13, but the marriage lasted only two years.

She worked briefly as a chambermaid and laundress. Then she began to sing in vaudeville and nightclubs in Baltimore, Maryland, and then in New York. Her early stage name was "Sweet Mama Stringbean," and she was a sexy, rowdy singer. Waters toured with a number of shows, and with Fletcher Henderson's Black Swan Troubadours. In 1925, she replaced Florence Mills in a revue at the Plantation Club and established herself in New York, signing a 10-year contract with Columbia Records.

In 1927, Waters appeared in her first Broadway musical, *Africana,* one of many black revues of the late 1920s and 1930s. Waters would go on to star in many Broadway productions, including *Blackbirds,* in 1930; *Rhapsody in Black,* in 1931 and 1932; *As Thousands Cheer,* in 1933; *At Home Abroad,* in 1935; *Tales of Manhattan,* in 1942; and *Cabin in the Sky,* in 1943.

As Waters gained more confidence and success, she polished her singing style. Throughout the 1920s and 1930s, she introduced a number of hit songs, including "Dinah," "Stormy Weather" and "Am I Blue?"

Until then, Waters was known primarily as a singer and dancer. Then, in 1939, she gave a powerful dramatic performance in the play *Mamba's Daughters.* Previously, many critics assumed that black women could not handle serious dramatic parts, but Waters's work in *Mamba's Daughters* exploded that prejudice. Although she worked for years after that in musical comedy, she was able to attain another dramatic role in 1950, in Carson McCullers's play *A Member of the Wedding.*

Waters was an ambitious performer, determined to succeed in Hollywood as well as on Broadway. In 1929, she was still singing risqué songs in the film *On With the Show.* But in the 1930s, she tried out a more sophisticated style in some short-subject films.

By 1942, Waters was no longer the slender young woman who had sung suggestive songs in nightclubs. Instead, her role as Jeanette MacDonald's maid in *Cairo* shows her drawing closer to the "mammy" stereotype to which most black actresses were restricted at the time. Her increasing weight contributed to this image. Nevertheless, in *Stage Door Canteen* and *Cabin in the Sky,* both released in 1943, she has a much more serious and energetic presence.

By the 1950s, Waters's work was primarily in television series and specials. Although she did some theatrical work in the 1960s, her personal and professional focus was on singing with the Reverend Billy Graham's religious-revival tours. Her death in 1977 concluded a long bout with cancer.

Further Reading: *His Eye Is on the Sparrow* (Waters's autobiography), by Ethel Waters, Westport, Conn.: Greenwood Press, 1978 reprint of 1951 ed.; *To Me It's Wonderful,* by Ethel Waters, Westport, Conn.: Greenwood Press, 1972.

—R. K.

❖ WEAVER, ROBERT CLIFTON
(1907–1997), *economist, government official, educator*

Robert Weaver had a long and distinguished career, but he is noted for the high-level government posts he held in the 1950s and 1960s. His appointment as secretary of housing and urban development, an office he held from 1966 to 1968, made Weaver the first African American to serve in the cabinet, and the first person to hold that cabinet post, newly created by President Lyndon B. Johnson.

Previously, Weaver had served as New York state rent commissioner and as vice chair of New York City's housing and redevelopment board. He had also worked as an aide or adviser to various federal officials in the administration of President Franklin D. Roosevelt. After leaving his cabinet post, Weaver became the president of Bernard M. Baruch College of the City University of New York.

Robert Weaver was born on December 29, 1907. He earned a B.A. in 1931 and an M.A. and doctorate from Harvard in 1934.

The year before he was granted his Ph.D. in economics, Weaver began his government career, when Secretary of the Interior Harold Ickes hired Weaver as an aide. Weaver continued to serve as an adviser to a number of government agencies under Roosevelt. Usually, his work involved minority problems.

Weaver soon became part of the "black cabinet," a group of African-American intellectuals in the Roosevelt administration. This so-called black cabinet welcomed Weaver as a leader in the work to abolish discrimination in government hiring.

After World War II, the administration came under the more conservative leadership of President Harry S Truman, and Weaver decided to leave government service. He lectured at Northwestern University in Chicago in 1947 and 1948. From academia, Weaver entered the private sector. At first he directed the John Hay Whitney Foundation's opportunity fellowships program. At times,

he was also on the selection committees of other fellowship programs.

Meanwhile, Weaver wrote a number of works on race relations and urban problems. In 1946, he published *Negro Labor: A National Problem* (Port Washington, N.C.: Kennikat Press, 1969 ed.) and, in 1948, *The Negro Ghetto* (New York: Russell & Russell, 1967 ed.).

Then in 1955, a Democratic administration was elected to the leadership of New York State, and Weaver was appointed to the office of New York state rent commissioner. Weaver went from state to city office in 1960, when he was made vice chair of New York City's housing and redevelopment board, an agency that oversees the housing needs of the city.

The mid-1960s saw a rise in national concern about black people and the inner cities. Weaver contributed to the national debate with his books *The Urban Complex* (Garden City, N.Y.: Doubleday), published in 1964, and *Dilemmas of Urban America* (Cambridge, Mass.: Harvard University Press), which came out in 1965. These undoubtedly helped to bring him the national prominence that won him a seat in the cabinet.

Weaver served in President Johnson's cabinet from 1966 to 1968, and was president of Baruch College in 1969. In 1970, he became Distinguished Professor of Urban Affairs at Hunter College of the City University of New York—a position he held until 1978, when he became the director of urban programs for Hunter College's Brookdale Center on Aging. Weaver died in 1997.

Further Reading: *Negro Labor: A National Problem,* by Robert Clifton Weaver, Port Washington, N.C.: Kennikat Press, 1969; *The Negro Ghetto,* by Robert Clifton Weaver, New York: Russell & Russell, 1967.

—R. K.

❖ WELLS-BARNETT, IDA BELL
(1862–1931), *antilynching campaigner, journalist, lecturer, civil rights leader*

In the long and active career of Wells-Barnett, best known as Ida B. Wells, she is most closely associated with her campaign against lynching, which had become a major threat to African Americans after the end of Reconstruction. Wells headed the Anti-Lynching League and was a member of the Committee of Forty, formed in 1909, which led to the founding of the National Association for the Advancement of Colored People (NAACP) in 1910. She served for a time on the

Ida Wells-Barnett (*Library of Congress*)

NAACP's executive committee, then became an active promoter of women's suffrage. She was one of the most widely syndicated black columnists in the United States, publishing articles on race issues in black newspapers nationwide.

She also worked successfully with Jane Addams, the social activist and reformer, to prevent the establishment of separate schools for black children in Chicago. Segregationists wanted to educate blacks and whites separately, whereas most African Americans and progressive whites believed that integration would result in better social and educational services for black people. Wells also served as a director of Chicago's Cook County League of Women's Clubs.

Ida B. Wells was born on July 6, 1862, to slave parents, Lizzie Bell and James Wells, who continued to work for their former master after emancipation. Wells attended Rust University, a high school and industrial school for freed slaves, established in her home town of Holly Springs, Mississippi. At age 14, her parents having died, Wells began to teach in a rural school for $25 a month.

The young woman taught in and around Memphis, Tennessee, from 1884 to 1891. Then, because of her militant resistance to segregation, the Memphis School Board dismissed her. In 1887, she had refused to accept a seat in a Jim Crow streetcar and had carried an unsuccessful suit to the Tennessee Supreme Court; under the pen name Iola, she had also criticized the inadequate schools for African Americans.

In 1892, she became half-owner of the *Memphis Free Speech,* in which she denounced the lynching of three of her friends. Although these men were accused of raping three white women, Wells knew their real crime had been competing with white storekeepers. She urged a boycott of the streetcars; she also encouraged the emigration of black Memphis residents to the West. The incident sparked her interest in lynchings, which she began to investigate and report. On May 27, 1882, while she was on a trip to Philadelphia and New York, a mob destroyed the offices of her newspaper.

Wells continued her antilynching crusade, working with T. Thomas FORTUNE, the major black journalist who founded and edited the *New York Age,* and contacting Catherine Impey, of the English Anti-Caste Society. Her major antilynching work, *A Red Record,* was published in 1895, disclosing the statistical record of three years of lynchings, while calling on churches and religious women's organizations to join her crusade.

Her civil rights activities were not limited to the antilynching cause. In 1893, she edited a pamphlet protesting the virtual exclusion of black people from the World's Columbian Exposition in Chicago. In that year, she also organized a black women's club, which led to the formation of many other such clubs. One of her club activities was to found the Negro Fellowship League, a social center that helped black men to find work, and provided reading rooms and a dormitory.

On June 27, 1895, Wells married Ferdinand Lee Barnett, a lawyer and editor of the *Chicago Conservator.* Barnett became one of his wife's most active supporters. From 1913 to 1916, she served as a probation officer for the Chicago court, aided by her husband. After the East St. Louis race riot of 1918, she went there to help secure legal aid for black victims.

Wells-Barnett worked with W. E. B. DUBOIS, joining his opposition to Booker T. WASHINGTON's accommodationist policies, which held that black Americans should focus on self-improvement rather than make demands for political and civil rights. In 1898, she was elected secretary of the National Afro-American Council, a forerunner of the NAACP, where she served until Washington gained control of the group in 1902. She also worked with DuBois in his Niagara movement, which he organized to encourage black Americans to make more militant civil rights demands. Wells-Barnett was one of two women to sign "The Call" on February 12, 1909, which called for a meeting "To Discuss Means for Securing Political and Civil Equality for the Negro." She then worked with the NAACP, serving on its Executive Committee until 1912.

The first black women's suffrage organization, the Alpha Suffrage Club of Chicago, was founded by Wells-Barnett, who also marched in the famous 1913 women's suffrage parade in Washington. Her work for suffrage, and with women's clubs, as well as on other civil rights causes, continued until her death from uremia on March 25, 1931. Later, Mrs. Alfreda Duster, one of her four children, published Wells-Barnett's autobiography, *Crusade for Justice* (Chicago, Ill.: University of Chicago Press, 1991). Wells-Barnett's life was celebrated in the PBS documentary *A Passion for Justice.*

Further Reading: *Selected Works of Ida B. Wells-Barnett,* ed. by Harris Trudier and Henry Louis Gates, New York: Oxford University Press, 1991; *NAACP, A History of the National Association for the Advancement of Colored People,* Vol. I, *1909–1920,* by Charles Flint Kellogg, Baltimore, Md.: Johns Hopkins University Press, 1967; *Notable American Women,* Vol. 3, pp. 565–567, article by Eleanor Flexner, Boston, Mass.: Harvard University Press, 1971.

—*R. K.*

❖ WEST, CORNEL
(1953–   ), *educator, philosopher, author*

One of the leading commentators on African-American issues in the United States, Cornel West has ranged widely over the intellectual landscape, writing on religion, philosophy, politics, and race. As a professor at Princeton and Harvard Universities, he has helped create a national dialogue on the most important issues facing contemporary society.

West was born on June 2, 1953, in Tulsa, Oklahoma, the younger of two sons. His father was a civilian employee of the U.S. Air Force, and the family moved several times, eventually settling in Sacramento, California. In delicate health during his childhood, West drew a great deal of strength from the local Baptist church, and he also spent a good deal of time at the local office of the Black Panther Party, where he learned about Black Power and absorbed ideas about political revolution.

At the age of 17, West entered Harvard University, where he quickly stood out as a brilliant and dedicated student. Majoring in Near Eastern languages and literature, he graduated magna cum laude a year early, in 1973, and went on to graduate study at Princeton University, where he earned an M.A. (1975) and Ph.D. (1980). West began his teaching career at the Yale Divinity School and then moved on to a series of faculty posts at Barnard College, Williams College, Haverford College, and the University of Paris. In 1977 he accepted a teaching post at the Union Theological Seminary in New York, where he remained until 1984.

West began his career as a writer in 1982 with the publication of *Prophesy Deliverance!: An Afro-American Revolutionary Christianity.* The book was an example of West's unique style, combining ideas from different spheres—such as African-American religious doctrine, Karl Marx's revolutionary socialism, and traditional Western philosophy—into a new whole. *Prophesy Deliverance!* got favorable reviews in academic journals, and in 1984, West returned to Princeton as professor of religion and director of the university's Afro-American studies department.

During his years at Princeton, West produced several more books, including *Prophetic Fragments* (1988), *The American Evasion of Philosophy* (1989), *The Ethical Dimensions of Marxist Thought* (1991), and (with bell hooks) *Breaking Bread: Insurgent Black Intellectual Life* (1991). All these publications showed the wide sweep of West's interests and imagination, but he was still little known to the public at large. That changed in 1993, with the appearance of *Race Matters,* a collection of essays examining relations between blacks and Jews, the 1992 Los Angeles riots, the failure of black leadership, the nomination of Clarence THOMAS to the Supreme Court, and other hotly debated issues. Surveying the contemporary scene with a critical eye, West concluded that "the fundamental crisis in black America is twofold: too much poverty and too little self-love." He called for black leaders to follow the example of Martin Luther KING, JR., and look beyond racial categories to a broadly based moral vision of justice and humanity. "Let us hope and pray," he wrote, "that the vast intelligence, imagination, humor, and courage of Americans will not fail us. Either we learn a new language of empathy and compassion, or the fire this time will consume us all."

Though not all reviewers were persuaded by West's arguments in *Race Matters,* all were impressed by his intellectual power and moral passion. He emerged as a major spokesperson for African-American concerns and a sought-after commentator on racial issues, frequently appearing on television programs such as the *MacNeil/Lehrer NewsHour* and *Firing Line.* In 1995, Henry Louis

GATES, Jr., convinced West to leave Princeton and join the faculty at Harvard, where he was appointed professor of Afro-American studies and of the philosophy of religion. In addition to his teaching and writing, West has played an active role in a number of organizations, including the American Academy of Religion, the American Philosophical Association, and the Afro-American Commission of Democratic Socialists of America.

Further Reading: *Race Matters,* by Cornel West, Boston: Beacon, 1993; *Keeping Faith: Philosophy and Race in America,* by Cornel West, New York: Routledge, 1993; *Prophesy Deliverance!: An Afro-American Revolutionary Christianity,* by Cornel West, Philadelphia: Westminster, 1982; *The Future of the Race,* by Henry Louis Gates, Jr., and Cornel West, New York: Knopf, 1996; "Princeton's Public Intellectual," by Robert S. Boynton, *New York Times Magazine,* September 15, 1991.

—*P. K.*

❖ WHEATLEY, PHILLIS
(1753–1784), *poet*

Although Phillis Wheatley grew up as a slave, she won widespread fame as a poet. At a time when many white people in the United States considered Africans and black Americans to be uneducable, Wheatley's accomplishments helped to challenge this misconception. Her work was celebrated in both the United States and England, and continues to be studied today.

It is likely that Wheatley was born on the west coast of Africa in 1753. She was captured and put on a slave ship when she was still very young. John Wheatley and his wife Susannah purchased her off the ship in 1761. Since the little girl was still losing her first teeth, the Wheatleys guessed her age to be seven or eight.

Phillis had been bought to be a lady's maid, but she was young and somewhat frail, and the Wheatleys asked much less of her than maid's work. They and their 18-year-old twin children treated her differently from their other slaves. The slaves lived in a carriage house, but Phillis was given her own room in the Wheatley house. She ate with the family, except when company was present.

Perhaps the most unusual part of Phillis's treatment was her being taught to read and write. John Wheatley wrote that when he took her from the ship, she spoke no English at all, but 16 months later she not only could speak but easily read the most difficult passages of the Bible.

Phillis Wheatley   *(Library of Congress)*

The young girl was drawn to writing, and to learning. She became proficient in Latin and read English writers eagerly. Her first poem, written at age 17 in 1770, is written in the style of the British poet Alexander Pope.

This first poem was to make Phillis quite famous; it was titled "On the Death of the Reverend George Whitefield," a popular preacher. Many people mourned his death and welcomed Phillis Wheatley's poem, which had been widely distributed.

Phillis seemed to be very much influenced by the Wheatley family, whose concerns were rather narrow. They were monarchists and so was Phillis. They were against slavery but believed that black people were better off as Christian slaves in America than they were in "benighted, heathen Africa." Phillis agreed with that, too. Generally, she and the Wheatleys took little interest in the larger problems of politics or social issues, and focused their concerns on family and friends.

Wheatley kept on writing her poetry, mostly about these personal concerns. In 1773, when she had suffered a period of debilitating illness, the Wheatleys set her free and sent her on a voyage to England with their son, thinking the sea air would be beneficial to her.

This visit was a great success, for the British knew of her poetry and admired her. She met such luminaries as Brook Watson, lord mayor of London; William Legge, the earl of Dartmouth; and the countess of Huntington. She attended parties and social functions and was honored in various ways. Her book, *Poems on Various Subjects, Religious and Moral* (New York: Arno Press, 1976 ed.), was published in London later that year. In October, she returned home.

There is little information about Wheatley's life between 1774 and 1778. It is understood that she had inherited some money from her ex-master and was able to move into her own home. She soon married John Peters, who appears to have been a spendthrift who squandered her money. Peters does not seem to have appreciated either Wheatley or her talent, and during the six years she lived with him, she published only two poems.

In the last months of Wheatley's life, her husband was away. With her inheritance gone, she was supporting herself by working in a boardinghouse in Boston. Of her three children, two had died, and one was an infant. She and her child died within a few hours of each other on December 5, 1784, when Wheatley was only 31 years old.

Further Reading: *Poems,* by Phillis Wheatley, Chapel Hill, N.C.: University of North Carolina Press, 1966; *Phillis Wheatley,* by William Henry Robinson, Boston, G. K. Hall, 1981; *Critical Essays on Phillis Wheatley,* Boston, G. K. Hall, 1982.

—*R. K.*

❖ WHIPPER, IONIA ROLLIN
(c. 1872–1953), *doctor, social reformer*

Ionia Whipper became one of the few African-American women doctors to practice in the United States. Beyond her community service as a physician, she organized several groups to help young black women, including the Lend-a-Hand Club, to help unwed mothers, and the Tuesday Evening Club, for girls who were likely to become juvenile delinquents.

Whipper came from a family of reformers. Her paternal grandfather was William Whipper, a "conductor" on the Underground Railroad, a network of antislavery activists who assisted runaway slaves. Her father, William Whipper, Jr., had been a delegate to South Carolina's constitutional conventions during Reconstruction. Her mother, Frances A. Rollin Whipper, and her mother's sisters were all political activists in Charleston, South Carolina. When Ionia Whipper was born in 1872, in Beaufort, South Carolina, she was born into a tradition of service to the community.

Whipper graduated from Howard University Medical School in Washington, D.C., in 1903. Her specialty was obstetrics—the care of women during pregnancy and after childbirth. While Whipper was in the midst of completing her medical training, her mother died. The young woman had to interrupt her work as a doctor, since there was no longer assistance from her mother. She taught school for some years to support herself, and borrowed money to pay for her education. Finally, in 1911, she was ready to go into private practice.

Whipper settled in Washington, D.C., where she delivered babies at Freedmen's Hospital, a health facility for African Americans. She noticed many unmarried young women were having babies there—women who had nowhere to go and no one to help them.

She took many of these women into her own home, but soon realized that this personal service was inadequate. In 1931, during the first years of the depression, she organized the Lend-a-Hand Club, which was a fundraising organization for the purpose of building a permanent home for unmarried mothers. Meanwhile, Whipper's Tuesday Evening Club offered help to young women whose family or personal problems were pushing them toward juvenile delinquency.

It wasn't easy to raise money during the depression, but by 1941, Whipper was able to establish the Ionia R. Whipper Home for Unwed Mothers. For many years, this was the only resource of its kind for black women in Washington, D.C. No other places were available to black women in Washington until the 1960s, when formerly white facilities were desegregated.

Segregation in Washington, D.C., was very strongly entrenched, and the Whipper Home could not get funded by the local United Way (a funding group that provides money to many charities). Local black people and groups in Washington had to support the home themselves. Whipper had to be doctor, teacher, and social worker at the home—whose budget was so small that it could not accommodate the necessary staff.

Whipper died in Harlem, on April 23, 1953, after a long illness. The month after her death, the Whipper Home was closed, so that public housing could be built in the same location. The board of directors managed to purchase the home, with the purpose of reopening it, but first they had to raise money to renovate the building. Finally, in 1955, the new home was reopened, under the name Ionia Whipper Rehabilitation Home for Unwed Mothers.

—*R. K.*

❖ WHIPPLE, PRINCE

(?–?), Revolutionary War soldier

Prince Whipple is remembered for two significant accomplishments. He served honorably during the American Revolutionary War and he was one of 19 slaves who won their freedom with a special petition to the New Hampshire government.

Prince Whipple was born in Amabou, Africa, where he lived until he was 10 years old (his African name is unknown). Whipple's older brother had lived in America briefly, so Whipple's parents sent him and a cousin to America for education.

This was an unwise decision in colonial days. The captain of the ship carrying Whipple and his cousin sold the boys into slavery in Baltimore. Eventually, he was bought by General William Whipple and went to live in Portsmouth, New Hampshire.

According to traditional accounts of Prince Whipple's life, he was with General George Washington on the famous crossing of the Delaware River. An 1819 painting of Washington before this crossing indeed shows the general with a young black soldier. An 1851 painting of the event also shows a young black man in Washington's boat. The historian William C. Nell believes these pictures portray Prince Whipple, who was General William Whipple's bodyguard. Since General Whipple was Washington's aide, it is logical to assume that Prince Whipple would have taken part in the famous crossing.

Whipple was one of 19 African Americans of Portsmouth to petition the New Hampshire government for their freedom in 1779. They argued that since God gave them freedom, and since freedom is an inherent right of every person, they should be allowed to go free. Whipple was eventually freed because of his service in the Revolutionary War, as were other soldier-slaves.

Prince Whipple later married and had children. He died at the age of 32, in Portsmouth.

Further Reading: *The Black Presence in the Era of the American Revolution, 1770–1800,* by Sidney Kaplan, Greenwich, Conn.: New York Graphic Society, 1973.

—*R. K.*

❖ WHITE, CLARENCE CAMERON

(1879–1960), composer

Clarence Cameron White had a long career as a classical violinist and educator, but he is best known for his opera *Ouanga,* about Jean Jacques Dessalines, the first emperor of Haiti. The *South Bend Tribune,* praising the opera's debut in South Bend, Indiana, wrote that the music "often sweeps to majestic terrifying heights. [White's] score is a gem of orchestration." The opera was later performed in Philadelphia and was favorably reviewed by the *New York Times, Musical Courier, Musical America, Philadelphia Bulletin,* and *Amsterdam News.* It was also performed in New York City at the Metropolitan Opera House and Carnegie Hall.

Among White's other compositions are works for string quartet, some of which were performed in Paris; orchestral works; works for voice and for chorus; and arrangements of popular songs.

White won many awards and honors during his lifetime, including the 1954 "Tranquil Music" Benjamin Award for his orchestral work *Elegy.* He held honorary degrees from Atlanta University in Georgia and Wilberforce University in Ohio. His music has been performed by such famous musicians as Fritz Kreisler and Jascha Heifetz.

Clarence Cameron White was born in 1879 to James W. White and Jennie (Scott) White in Clarksville, Tennessee. James White, of black and white ancestry, was a doctor and school principal who died before Clarence was two years old. Clarence then went to live in the home of the parents of his mother, who was of mixed white and Indian ancestry.

The Scott family lived in Oberlin, Ohio, home of Oberlin Conservatory. Clarence White's mother had studied violin there, and his childhood years were undoubtedly affected by this musical atmosphere. Clarence was a soloist in church choirs and, at age eight, he began to study the violin.

After her husband died, White's mother had moved to Chattanooga, Tennessee, to teach in the public school system. There she met and married William H. Conner, who assumed the role of father to young Clarence.

When Conner took a government job in Washington, D.C., in 1890, and moved his family there, it gave White the opportunity to study with Will Marion Cook, a prestigious music teacher. At 14, White was a violin soloist in church and was already composing music. His eight-year-old piano accompanist, Beatrice Warrick, would later be his wife.

In 1896, Clarence returned to Oberlin Conservatory, where he was the only black student for four years. After he graduated in 1901, with a major in violin, he played in Boston, New York, and New Haven. In New York, he met the poet Paul Laurence DUNBAR and the educator Booker T. WASHINGTON, who invited him to play at Tuskegee Institute in Alabama.

In 1903, he began to teach at the new Washington, D.C., Conservatory of Music. He later taught in the public schools. In 1905, he married Beatrice Warrick, with whom he later had two children.

White's interest in composition continued to grow, particularly after 1906, when he studied with Afro-British composer Samuel Coleridge-Taylor in London. He also continued with his performing career, playing first violin with the String Players Club of Croydon, England, and giving concerts with Coleridge-Taylor in Europe and the United States from 1908 through 1911.

In 1910, White settled in Boston, Massachusetts, where he established a studio, taught in the public schools, and conducted the Victoria Concert Orchestra.

In 1924, he became director of music at West Virginia State College. There he became interested in Haitian music and culture, and began to work with Professor John F. Matheus on his opera, *Ouanga*, based on the life of the emperor Dessalines.

White and Matheus went to Haiti in 1930 and 1931 to study voodoo, so they could incorporate this aspect of Haitian culture into their opera. They gradually developed the story of a Christian emperor's fight against the forces of voodoo, which had captured the woman he loved. They included many historical incidents in their work, such as the emperor's assassination.

The opera was finished in 1932 and performed in concert that year in Chicago. In 1949, it was fully staged in South Bend, Indiana; in 1950, it was performed in Philadelphia at the Academy of Music, by the Negro Dra-Mu Opera Company; and in 1956, it was performed by the National Negro Opera Company in New York.

Composer Arthur Farewell praised *Ouanga,* writing, "Too much cannot be said of the beauty and masterfulness of the orchestration."

During 1930 and 1931, White was also studying composition in Paris, where his work was performed at the École Normale de Musique. From 1931 to 1935, he was director of music at Hampton Institute in Virginia, where he conducted the choir. He went on to organize community music programs for the National Recreation Association from 1937 to 1941.

During these later years, White's wife died; their two sons had already died at an early age. White remarried in 1943, to Pura Belpré, a specialist in Puerto Rican folk culture, and he went to live with her in New York City, where he continued to compose until he died on June 30, 1960. White also wrote many studies of black contributions to American music.

Though White's music may not have been the most innovative of its time, it had a strong sense of folk tradi-

tions and dwelt on the lyrical, with beautiful, expressive melodies.

—R. K.

❖ WHITE, WALTER FRANCIS
(1893–1955), *chief executive of the NAACP*

Walter White led the National Association for the Advancement of Colored People (NAACP), helping it to become the largest and most influential civil rights organization in the United States for many years. Under White's leadership, the organization's center of power shifted from the board of directors, which was dominated by whites, to the organization's officers, who in White's time were black.

Although White was criticized by some black leaders for focusing too much on middle-class concerns and not enough on efforts (such as unionization) to help working-class African Americans, everyone agreed that the NAACP's achievements were considerable under his leadership. He and his organization worked to fight against lynching, to increase black electoral participation, and to desegregate the public schools, culminating in the

Walter White *(Library of Congress)*

NAACP's 1954 victory in *Brown vs. Board of Education*, in which the Supreme Court ruled that separate schools were unequal by definition and must be integrated.

Walter White was born in 1893, in Atlanta, Georgia. His father George, a mail carrier, was light-skinned and might have been able to pass for white. He later died in a Georgia hospital, waiting for medical care, because doctors were unsure of whether or not he was "a Negro," and therefore unsure whether they should treat him.

When White was 13, he saw the Atlanta race riot of 1906, which had resulted from a year-long period of racial tension in response to black citizens' agitation for racial, social, and political equality. During the riot, a mob of some 3,000 white men attacked black people throughout Atlanta, and White saw a white mob almost invade his home. He later said that that was the night when "I discovered what it meant to be a Negro."

White himself was light-skinned, blond-haired, and blue-eyed. He might have passed for white, but chose instead to become a leader in Atlanta's black community after graduating from Atlanta University in 1916. He soon became involved in a campaign against the increasing racial discrimination of the city's Board of Education. Although public high schools were available to white children, the board decided to stop black schooling after the sixth grade. In response, Atlanta citizens formed a branch of the NAACP—the upcoming, increasingly militant civil-rights organization that had been formed by W.E.B. DUBOIS and others. White became the Atlanta branch secretary, and the campaign was successful in turning back the Board of Education's decision.

In the course of the fight, White met James Weldon JOHNSON, the NAACP field secretary. Johnson got White a job as assistant secretary, for which he moved to New York in 1918.

At this time, the NAACP was a small organization whose top position—secretary—was held by a white social worker. Originally, White was supposed to help the secretary with routine office work, but instead, he became involved in developing NAACP branches, and in negotiating with government officials on civil rights matters. White also fought against lynchings and dedicated himself to eradication of the murderous practice, often using his ability to pass for white to ferret out inside information on upcoming violence. In one case, he was almost lynched himself when his disguise was discovered.

In 1920, the NAACP made a major shift by appointing its first black secretary, James Weldon Johnson. Until then, the organization, founded by both black and white people, had been primarily under the leadership of whites. With Johnson's appointment, the power of blacks in the organization increased.

Under Johnson's leadership, White's talent for administration became apparent. By the 1920s, the NAACP's focus had turned to the courts, and White became administrator for the group's legal committee. He worked closely with committee chair Arthur B. Spingarn, a white lawyer.

Meanwhile, like Johnson, White was also interested in writing. He won a Guggenheim fellowship, given to distinguished writers and artists, to work on his fiction. White wrote three books: *Rope and Faggot* (1920), a non-fiction work on lynching (a faggot is a flaming wooden stick, used to burn people who were lynched); *The Fire in the Flint* (1924), a novel about lynching; and *Flight* (1926), a novel about passing for white.

In 1929, Johnson was on sick leave, suffering from overwork. White became acting secretary and led the campaign against confirming Judge John J. Parker for the Supreme Court. Parker had come out publicly in favor of keeping African Americans from voting. With the NAACP's strategy depending on winning Supreme Court battles, Parker's installation would have been disastrous. White helped to mobilize a letter-writing campaign and used all the influence his group had to convince senators to vote against Parker's confirmation. The American Federation of Labor (AFL), the major trade union group of the time, also opposed Parker, because of his antiunion record.

Parker was finally defeated. Historians today credit the AFL, but the NAACP's contribution was also important. White followed up this victory by targeting the pro-Parker senators for defeat in their upcoming elections. At least two were voted down, largely because of the black voters whom the NAACP had mobilized.

When Johnson left his position in 1931, White became the new NAACP head. He faced a difficult time—the Great Depression—which decreased the organization's income and put black Americans under severe economic stress.

He turned to rich white people to build the group's assets. He also cut staff salaries. This provoked a challenge from the staff, led by W.E.B. DuBois, editor of the NAACP journal, the *Crisis*. Eventually, most of the staff relented, and White gained further control of the group—except for DuBois, who remained independent.

White and DuBois continued to clash. DuBois, who had helped to found the NAACP, had always maintained an independent position, and at this time he advocated "nondiscriminatory segregation," that is, that black people should separate to form their own organizations, rather than try to win entry into white groups. The official NAACP position was that black people should strive for their constitutional rights in American society. As a result of this fight, DuBois resigned in 1934, and Roy Wilkins took over his position.

Critics of White included the young Howard University professor Ralphe BUNCHE (later undersecretary general of the United Nations), who believed that the NAACP should focus on trade-union activity. The new union efforts, under the Congress of Industrial Organizations (CIO), were organizing black and white workers into the same groups, which Bunche and others believed offered new possibilities for equality and integration. The NAACP continued to keep its agenda focused on winning legal battles in the courts, although by 1941, White was working with the union of the United Automobile Workers (UAW).

Under White's leadership, fights continued over who would really control the organization. The main clashes came between the white people who had helped to found the group, the black officers, and the young black intellectuals who wanted to change the group's direction. Ultimately, the black officers of the group emerged as the dominant center of power. Meanwhile, White continued to be active in efforts to found the United Nations. He wrote for many publications and published a book on political affairs, *A Rising Wind* (Westport, Conn.: Negro University Press, 1971 ed.), in 1945.

With White in command, the NAACP continued to grow through World War II and after, reaching perhaps its greatest victory in 1954, when the Supreme Court ruled that segregated schools were unconstitutional. Yet White was also criticized for having too much power and being too much of a celebrity. He divorced his wife of more than 27 years, Gladys (Powell) White, with whom he had had two children, to marry a white woman, Poppy Cannon. This led to further criticism from white people who did not believe in intermarriage and from black people who thought it reflected badly on the organization. In spite of various conflicts, however, White continued to lead the organization until his death of a heart attack in 1955.

Further Reading: *A Man Called White,* by Walter White, New York: Arno Press, 1969; *E. J. Spingarn and the Rise of the NAACP,* by B. Joyce Ross, New York: Atheneum, 1972.

—*R. K.*

✦ WILLIAMS, BERT
(1873–1922), *entertainer*

Bert Williams was one of the most successful black entertainers who ever lived. Contemporary accounts claimed that he made more money than the president of the United States. In 1910, Williams was the first black star of an otherwise all-white Broadway production, the Ziegfeld Follies. Civil rights leader Booker T. WASHINGTON once said, "Bert Williams has done more for the race than I have. He has smiled his way into people's hearts. I have been obliged to fight."

Yet Williams was also a target of prejudice and segregation, and his own work was marked by many racial contradictions. His career shows both the heights that a talented black entertainer could achieve in William's time and the restrictions that black performers still faced.

Williams was born Egbert Austin Williams in 1873 in Nassau (in the West Indies) and grew up speaking English with the British accent of that region. His grandfather was a Danish consul who married a Spanish and African woman. Their son, Williams's father, married an African woman, with whom he lived on a plantation, making papier-maché for a living.

When his father became sick, the family moved to California. There Williams had his first contact with American racial prejudice. The family also suffered economic hardship, which prevented Williams from studying engineering at Stanford University in California. Instead, he became an entertainer in cafés and honky-tonks.

In 1895, Williams had a significant meeting, with George Nash WALKER. The comedy team of Williams and Walker soon became famous, and remained so for 16 years. Walker played a fast-talking con man while Williams played the bumbling stooge who was always being duped. Because his own features were rather Caucasian, and because of the prejudices of the time, Williams went on stage in blackface and spoke in an exaggerated dialect quite different from his own educated speech.

During this time, Williams married Lottie Thompson, another performer. Along with Walker, his own wife, and Walker's wife Aida, plus some other talented actors, Williams formed a company that specialized in black folk humor and became vastly popular with both black and white audiences.

In 1907, Walker became ill and had to leave the company. Williams discovered then that he could perform solo. He went on to work in vaudeville—an entertainment form similar to our variety shows. Williams did pantomimes, comic songs, and other humorous routines.

An outgrowth of vaudeville was the Ziegfeld Follies, a splashy, glamorous New York show that included many of the most successful vaudeville acts, plus the "Ziegfeld girls"—beautifully dressed women who paraded onstage throughout various musical numbers. Williams scored a first for a black performer in 1910, when producer Florenz Ziegfeld signed him to star in that year's Follies.

His appearance with the Follies broke new ground for black performers. Although such entertainers had been used in shows before, they had never received the star billing given to white actors. Likewise, although there were many black singers and comics in vaudeville, they rarely played the most prestigious vaudeville theaters, and never made the high salaries that white stars received. Williams, however, was well promoted and well paid.

Williams continued to appear in the Follies for the next 10 years. He played with some major white stars, including Eddie Cantor, who also put on blackface for a father-son routine. Although some modern critics consider his blackface demeaning, Williams himself said that, like many actors, he felt freer when he was in disguise.

The racial codes of the time were of great concern to Williams. Reportedly, he put it on his Ziegfeld contract that he would never appear on stage with a white female star, apparently fearing this would alienate white audiences. Williams also refused to tour the South. Even at the height of his career, in the North, he was barred from the best hotels—or, if he were somehow allowed to stay, he was kept out of hotel restaurants and forced to take the freight elevator and to eat in his room.

When Williams was not performing, he lived quietly with his wife, working on his book collection and pursuing other private activities. Offstage, he was often moody and depressed. The great comic W. C. Fields, who also played for Florenz Ziegfeld, once described Williams as "the funniest man I ever saw; the saddest man I ever knew." His mix of humor and sadness, his projected pathos, gave his stage work its special power. His signature song was "Nobody," which typified this mix. Modern critics have conjectured that some of his sadness may have stemmed from his awareness that he was playing caricatures and stereotypes of black people and from his frustration with what white audiences would accept.

Williams finished his career with two shows of his own, *Broadway Brevities,* in 1920, and *Under the Bamboo Tree,* in 1922. While performing in *Bamboo Tree,* he collapsed in a Detroit theater. He later developed pneumonia and died before reaching the age of 50.

Further Reading: *Nobody: The Story of Bert Williams,* by Ann Charters, New York: Macmillan, 1970; *Toms, Coons, Mulattoes, Mammies and Bucks, An Interpretive History of Blacks in American Films,* by Donald Bogle, New York: Macmillan, 1973.

—R. K.

❖ WILLIAMS, DANIEL HALE ("Dr. Dan")
(1856–1931), *heart surgeon*

Dr. Daniel Hale Williams performed the world's first successful heart operation on July 9, 1893. Until then, no doctor had actually opened a person's chest and operated directly to repair damage to the heart. Williams performed this unprecedented operation at the struggling, underfunded Provident Hospital in Chicago.

Another of his accomplishments was the founding of Provident Hospital itself, in 1891. Up to that point, African-American doctors in Chicago were not allowed to use hospital facilities, which were segregated and therefore restricted to white doctors. Even if a black doctor was a trained surgeon, he or she would have to operate on a kitchen table or a couch. For the first time, Provident Hospital offered a place where all doctors, black and white, could use the facilities.

Williams also contributed greatly to the development of Freedmen's Hospital, in Washington, D.C., where he began to work in 1894. Williams developed Freedmen's from a primitive, pre–Civil War facility into

Daniel Hale Williams *(Library of Congress)*

an institution that was up-to-date and well-functioning. He also founded the first nursing school for black people in Washington.

His accomplishments were recognized by the white medical establishment as well. He was the only black doctor among the 100 charter members of the American College of Surgeons.

Daniel Hale Williams was born in 1856 in Hollidaysburg, Pennsylvania, to Daniel Williams, Jr., a barber, and Sarah (Price) Williams, a housewife. After their father died, Williams and his sister moved to Wisconsin, while their mother moved to Illinois. Williams was more or less on his own from the age of 12. Although he managed to finish high school, he also worked at a number of jobs, including apprentice shoemaker, roustabout (deckhand) on a lake steamer, and barber.

Finally in 1878, he apprenticed himself to a white doctor, who helped him get into Chicago Medical College. In 1883, Williams graduated and began his practice in an interracial Chicago neighborhood.

He maintained an interest in public health and was keenly aware of the difficulties caused by the lack of proper hospital facilities for black doctors. In 1891, he opened the first Chicago hospital that was available to all races, but stressed internships for black doctors and training for black nurses. When Williams founded Provident Hospital, he was not yet 35 years old.

Because of his concern for his patients, Williams got the nickname "Dr. Dan," which expressed their affection and sense of him as a relative rather than a distant medical practitioner. Although he was busy with his practice and his administration of the hospital, he also managed to present papers and keep up with developments in his field.

Then, in 1893, he initiated a new development of his own: the heart operation on James Cornish, a young man who, during a street fight, had suffered a knife wound in an artery quite close to the heart. Although Williams had none of today's X rays, blood transfusions, or infection-preventing drugs, he still managed to open Cornish's chest and operate on the pericardium—the membrane around the heart.

The next year, Williams went to Freedmen's Hospital in Washington, D.C., the major health facility serving the city's black community, where he worked as chief surgeon. While at Freedmen's, Williams organized the hospital into departments, hired an ambulance (horse-drawn), reorganized the nurses' training program, and greatly reduced the hospital's death rate.

In 1898, he resigned from Freedmen's. Because the institution was federally funded, Williams found the

bureaucratic regulations and internal politics to be quite restrictive. After marrying schoolteacher Alice Johnson, Williams returned to Chicago, his practice, and Provident Hospital.

Williams continued to do research into medical issues, particularly concerning the health of black people. He was also active in public health work, visiting 20 states and helping to establish some 40 hospitals that served mainly black patients. He helped to found the National Medical Association, as well as the interracial Medico-Chirurgical (Surgical) Society for doctors and surgeons.

Sometimes his honors brought him troubles. In 1913, he was appointed attending surgeon at a white hospital, which created jealousy and divisions among the Provident staff. Tired of such politics, William resigned. In 1925, he invited another doctor into his practice, but three years later, the doctor left. By then, Williams was 72 years old. Although he had remained married to Alice, he continued to have strong personal conflicts with her.

In 1924, his wife died. Two years later, he had a stroke and went into semiretirement. He died at home, on August 4, 1931, in Idlewild, Michigan. He left much of his estate to the Washington, D.C., YWCA, Howard and Meharry Medical Schools in Washington, D.C., and the NAACP. He was commemorated with a plaque at Provident Hospital.

Further Reading: *Daniel Hale Williams: Negro Surgeon,* by Helen Buckler, New York: Pitmann Publishing, 1968; *Daniel Hale Williams: Open Heart Doctor,* by Lewis H. Fenderson, New York: McGraw-Hill, 1971.

—R. K.

✤ WILLIAMS, GEORGE WASHINGTON
(1849–1891), *first major African-American historian*

George W. Williams was the author of the first major work of African-American history, the two-volume *History of the Negro Race in America from 1619 to 1880* (New York: Bergman, 1968 ed.). He also wrote *History of Negro Troops in the War of Rebellion* (New York: Bergman, 1968 ed.).

Williams's varied career included service in the Union Army during the Civil War, 14 months as pastor of an influential black congregation in Boston, a term as state legislator in Ohio, and an appointment as minister to Haiti—although the incoming U.S. administration did not allow him to serve. In 1889, in a poll taken by the *Indianapolis Freeman,* black Americans voted Williams one of the 10 greatest black people in history.

George Washington Williams was born on October 16, 1849, in Bedford Springs, Pennsylvania, the child of Thomas and Ellen (Rouse) Williams. Thomas Williams was a laborer who kept moving throughout Pennsylvania. As a child, George had no formal education and was put in an orphanage, where he was taught to be a barber.

In 1863, when black people were allowed to enlist in the Union Army, Williams joined up, though he was only 14 at the time. When his age was discovered, he was discharged, but after much pleading on his part, they took him back.

In 1868, Williams left the Army because of a wound to his lung. After some time at Howard University in Washington, D.C., and Wayland Seminary in Richmond, Virginia, he graduated from Massachusetts's Newton Theological Institution in 1874, with the intention of becoming a minister. In 1874, he married Sarah A. Sterrett, with whom he later had a son.

Williams held a number of jobs over the next few years, including service as pastor to various congregations; editor of a magazine; postal worker; and state legislator in Ohio. Throughout his changing career, he continued to maintain his interest in history, and in 1876, he began the work that was to be his greatest achievement: the first major study of African-American history, which was published in 1882.

His book the two-volume *History of the Negro Race in America from 1619 to 1880,* received many positive reviews in highly respected magazines. His second book, *History of the Negro Troops in the War of Rebellion,* published in 1887, received even more critical praise. Both books were not only the first of their kind but stood on their own merit as significant works that made important contributions to history.

In 1885, Williams appeared to be headed for yet another honor when he was appointed minister to Haiti by President William Henry Harrison, the outgoing Republican leader. However, the incoming Democratic administration would not let him serve. Williams fought this decision for years, but was unsuccessful.

Meanwhile, Williams had been studying law for several years, and had been admitted to the Ohio bar in 1881. In 1883, he moved to Boston, where he began a law practice. Then the publisher S. S. McClure commissioned him to write about the Belgian Congo, where he went in 1890. He published several strong and controversial critiques of Belgium, the occupying colonial power.

In 1891, Williams went to England, where he planned to work further on exposés of the Belgians in the Congo. But he became sick with tuberculosis and pleurisy. Although friends took him to Blackpool, a seaside resort, they were unable to save him, and he died there on August 26, 1891.

Further Reading: *History of the Negro Race in America from 1619 to 1880,* by George Washington Williams, New York: Bergman Publishers, 1968; *History of Negro Troops in the War of Rebellion,* by George Washington Williams, New York: Bergman Publishers, 1968.

—R. K.

❖ WILLIAMS, PAUL REVERE
(1894–1980), *architect*

Paul Williams rose to prominence as an architect in Southern California during the 1920s and 1930s. Over the course of his career, he designed more than 400 homes and some 2,600 other buildings. Many of the homes he designed were for movie stars.

Williams was born in 1894, in Los Angeles. As a California resident, he had access to an excellent university system and he managed to work his way through the University of California at Los Angeles (UCLA).

Williams taught art before resuming his education, at the Beaux-Arts Institute of Design.

Eventually, he became an architect, receiving his certification in 1915. He had expressed the desire to move in this direction while attending Polytechnic High School, but his teachers had tried to dissuade him. At this time, architecture was an unusual profession for African Americans to pursue. Nevertheless, by 1923, Williams had opened his own office and begun a successful career.

Williams received many awards and honors throughout his life. In 1953, the National Association for the Advancement of Colored People (NAACP) awarded him the Spingarn Medal, for outstanding achievement. Williams was also granted honorary degrees from Hampton Institute, in Virginia; Atlanta University, in Georgia; Lincoln University, in Nebraska; and Howard University, in Washington, D.C.

His projects included Los Angeles college fraternity and sorority houses, the residence of movie star Lon Chaney, and other "showcase" homes of the rich and/or famous. He also designed more notable structures, such as the Music Corporation of America building in New York, to name but one.

—R. K.

❖ WILSON, AUGUST
(1945–), *Pulitzer Prize–winning playwright*

August Wilson has won the Pulitzer Price twice, for his plays *Fences* and *The Piano Lesson.* Few playwrights have two such awards to their credit—not to mention the host of other awards and honors Wilson has won for his writing. A number of other plays by Wilson have appeared in New York (on Broadway and off), where he is one of the few black playwrights to be consistently produced.

August Wilson grew up in a Pittsburgh ghetto known as "the Hill." He was so frustrated with the racist treatment he experienced at school that he dropped out after the ninth grade.

Although he no longer attended school, Wilson did not stop studying. He read at the local library, discovering for himself the black writers of the Harlem Renaissance of the 1920s. He also read contemporary black writers.

At first, Wilson thought he wanted to be a poet, but could never quite find his own voice in that form. Then, in 1968, he responded to the Civil Rights movement— the campaign by black Americans in the 1950s and 1960s to win full political and social equality through protest marches, sit-ins, and political action—by helping to found a theater called Black Horizon on the Hill. The theater's goal was to raise black people's consciousness of themselves and their culture. Wilson began to write plays for this theater, where he learned and practiced his craft.

In 1978, after 10 years of working on a community level, Wilson was invited by African-American director Claude Purdy to write a play for his new black theater in St. Paul, Minnesota. He began to draw on the unique qualities of the black speech of his native Pittsburgh— the poetic images and turns of phrase that he realized were part of everyday speech—and his work took off in a new direction.

Wilson's first two plays received little recognition. But his third, *Ma Rainey's Black Bottom* (New York: New American Library, 1988), was accepted at the National Playwrights Conference in 1982. There, he met Lloyd Richards, the black director who has since directed all of his plays on Broadway. Their collaboration began with *Ma Rainey,* which Richards directed at the highly respected Yale Repertory Theater of Yale University and then took to Broadway.

After *Ma Rainey,* Wilson wrote *Fences* (New York: New American Library, 1995), *Joe Turner's Come and Gone* (New York: New American Library, 1992), *The Piano Lesson* (New York: Dutton, 1990), *Two Trains Running* (New York: Plume, 1993), and *Seven Guitars* (New York: Plume, 1997). He has several other plays currently in development.

So far, each of Wilson's major productions has taken place in a different decade. Wilson has said that his goal as a playwright is to tell the story of the black experience throughout the 20th century.

Further Reading: *August Wilson and the African-American Odyssey,* by Kim Pereira, Champaign: University of Illinois Press, 1995; *May All Your Fences Have Gates: Essays on the Drama of August Wilson,* ed. by Alan Nadel, Iowa City: University of Iowa Press, 1994; *August Wilson: A Research and Production Sourcebook,* by Yvonne Shafer, Westport, Conn.: Greenwood Publishing Group, 1998; *The Dramatic Vision of August Wilson,* by Sandra G. Shannon, Washington, D.C.: Howard University Press, 1996; *I Ain't Sorry for Nothin I Done: August Wilson's Process of Playwriting,* by Joan Herrington, New York: Limelight Editions, 1998.

—*R. K.*

❖ WILSON, JAMES FINLEY
(1881–1952), *fraternal leader*

J. Finley Wilson served for close to 30 years as the grand exalted ruler of the Improved Benevolent Protective Order of the Elks of the World (I.B.P.O.E. of W.), which, under his leadership, became the largest of the black fraternal organizations. Groups like the I.B.P.O.E. have been important mainstays of the black community, offering scholarships to black youth, support for black professionals, and a sense of prestige to its members.

Wilson was born on August 28, 1881, near Nashville, Tennessee, to the Reverend James L. and Nancy (Wiley) Wilson, the grandchild of emancipated slaves. He left home at 13, wandering west toward Denver. He worked with Buffalo Bill, a famous cowboy who had a traveling circus, and was part of Coxey's Army (a group of unemployed workers that marched and demonstrated for better treatment). Eventually, he returned to complete Pearl High School in Nashville, Tennessee, and briefly attended Fisk University there.

As a young man, Wilson continued to travel— through the West, Alaska, Utah, and eventually New York City—working as a miner, a cowboy and, finally, a newspaper editor. During his travels, he joined the Elks, and he was elected to their highest post, grand exalted ruler.

When he first joined the Elks, they were a fairly small group based mainly in Ohio and Kentucky. (Of course, the all-white original Elks group was much larger.) Under Wilson's leadership, however, the group grew quickly, adding more than 15,000 members in his first year and establishing 85 new lodges.

In 1925, the Elks began a scholarship program; two years later, they founded their Oratorical Contest. These programs gave a sense of pride to black youth and gave many the means to attend college. Under Wilson, the Elks also started the first systematic survey of black health. During World War II, the Elks raised funds for war work.

At the time of his death, the Elks had grown to more than half a million members, with some 900 lodges. The organization had become larger than some similar white groups, such as the Odd Fellows.

Wilson made the Elks an attractive group, sponsoring many gala parades, purchasing a huge building for the organization's headquarters in Washington, and generally drawing many professional black people into its ranks. Although many upper-class black people looked down upon the group, others realized that lawyers, doctors, or other professionals who joined were given new business from fellow lodge members.

The power and size of the Elks led Wilson to seek political power as well. He tried to work within the Republican Party, but never actually achieved a position of political importance and power.

During World War II, Wilson hoped that black soldiers fighting in active combat would nurture a climate of support for civil rights at home. He supported both black participation in the war effort and measures such as the ending of the poll tax (by which people had to pay in order to vote) and improved education.

Wilson had married Leah Belle Farrar in 1924, and continued to live with her until his death from diabetes, on February 18, 1952.

—R. K.

❖ WILSON, WILLIAM JULIUS
(1935–), *sociologist, educator, writer*

One of the leading sociologists in the United States, William Julius Wilson has probed deeply into the problems of contemporary society. His writings, incorporating 25 years of firsthand research on Chicago's South Side, have examined the effects of racism, unemployment, substandard housing, and poor education on the residents of inner-city communities.

Born in Derry Township, Pennsylvania, on December 20, 1935, Wilson was one of six children. His father, a coal miner, died when Wilson was 12 years old, and after that his family struggled constantly to make ends meet. Wilson spent his summers in New York City with an aunt, Janice Wardlaw, who was a psychiatric social worker. Wardlaw introduced her nephew to the city's cultural resources and encouraged him to study hard. When he was admitted to Wilberforce University in Ohio, she helped him with tuition and expenses.

During his undergraduate years at Wilberforce, Wilson decided to become a sociologist, due in part to his study of the great African-American scholar W. E. B. DUBOIS. After receiving his B.A. in 1958 he served two years in the U.S. Army and obtained a master's degree in sociology from Bowling Green University in 1961. Wilson then enrolled in the Ph.D. program at Washington State University. In 1965, a year before he received his doctorate, Wilson began his teaching career as an associate professor at the University of Massachusetts. In 1970, the university named him Teacher of the Year.

With his reputation as a teacher and scholar growing rapidly, Wilson was invited to join the University of Chicago's prestigious sociology department in 1971 as an associate professor. Two years later, he published his first book, *Power, Racism, and Privilege,* a comparative study of race relations in the United States and South Africa. In 1975, Wilson was appointed a full professor, and in 1978 he became the chairman of the department.

The publication of Wilson's second book, *The Declining Significance of Race,* in 1978, drew widespread attention in and out of the academic world. In the book, Wilson focused on the growing divide between middle-class African Americans and those African Americans trapped in inner-city poverty. Noting that the plight of the urban poor was worsening as jobs and income moved to the suburbs, Wilson argued that class—defined in part by negative patterns of behavior—was becoming more important than racism in isolating the black poor from other social groups. Wilson's book won an award from the American Sociological Association, but a number of commentators—including the Association of Black Sociologists—were highly critical of his approach. They accused Wilson of siding with conservatives who believed that the poor were to blame for their own problems. The debate took on added importance after 1980, when the conservative Reagan administration began cutting back on aid to disadvantaged communities.

Wilson broke sharply with the conservatives' approach in his next book, *The Truly Disadvantaged*

(1987), calling for increased social spending on the part of government. He also launched an ambitious project called the Urban Poverty and Family Life Study, which undertook an in-depth survey of inner-city problems, incorporating interviews with 2,500 Chicagoans. At this time, Wilson's work was aided by a prestigious "genius award" from the MacArthur Foundation, and in 1990, he became Lucy Flower University Professor of Sociology and Public Policy at Chicago. He was also elected to the American Academy of Arts and Sciences.

When Bill Clinton entered the White House in 1993, he and his aides eagerly sought Wilson's views on public policy, though they did not always follow his advice. In 1996, Wilson published *When Work Disappears,* incorporating many of the findings from his massive study of poverty in Chicago. Removing any doubts about Wilson's position on the role of government in fighting poverty, the book called for a massive New Deal–type effort to reverse the decline of urban neighborhoods. In the same year, Wilson left Chicago for Harvard University, where he became Malcolm Wiener Professor of Social Policy at the John F. Kennedy School of Government and a member of the board of directors of the W. E. B. DuBois Institute of Afro-American Research.

Further Reading: *Power, Racism, and Privilege,* by William Julius Wilson, New York: Macmillan, 1973; *The Declining Significance of Race,* by William Julius Wilson, Chicago: University of Chicago Press, 1978; *The Truly Disadvantaged,* by William Julius Wilson, Chicago: University of Chicago Press, 1987; *When Work Disappears,* by William Julius Wilson, New York: Knopf, 1996, "Dr. Wilson's Neighborhood," by David Remnick, *New Yorker,* April 29–May 6, 1996.

—P. K.

❖ WINFREY, OPRAH GAIL

(1954–), *talk-show host, actress, producer*

"All my life I have always known I was born to greatness," Oprah Winfrey once remarked. Combining drive, intelligence, and a dynamic personality, she has become one of the most influential figures on the American scene.

Born on January 29, 1954, in Kosciusko, Mississippi, to unwed teenage parents, Winfrey endured a childhood that included extreme poverty, sexual abuse, and the birth of a stillborn child when she was only 14. Winfrey's life finally turned around in 1968 when she went to live with her father in Nashville, Tennessee, and began to make the most of her talents. Bright and outgoing, Winfrey blossomed at Nashville's East High School, taking part in

Oprah Winfrey (*George Dabrowsky/Archive Photos*)

school plays and other activities. In 1971 she entered Tennessee State University to study speech and performing arts.

Winfrey had already begun working part time as a radio announcer during her senior year at high school. She continued to pursue this line of work while in college and soon began earning substantial amounts of money. By 1976, only a few credits short of her degree, Winfrey decided to pursue her media career in earnest; she left Nashville and took a new job with WJZ-TV in Baltimore. After a brief stint as a news reporter, a job for which she felt ill-suited, Winfrey hit her stride as the cohost of a morning show entitled *People Are Talking.* The success of the show led to still greater opportunities. In 1984, Winfrey moved to Chicago and became the host of a half-hour talk show, *A.M. Chicago.* Forced to compete with a nationally popular program hosted by Phil Donahue, Winfrey was up against heavy odds. But viewers responded to her intelligence, openness, and energy; she inspired them to believe that they could overcome the obstacles in their path, just as she had. Within a year, *A.M. Chicago* was the top morning program in the city. The station expanded its time slot to an hour and renamed it *The Oprah Winfrey Show.*

Long interested in acting, Winfrey broadened her horizons in 1985 when she played the role of Sofia in Steven Spielberg's film *The Color Purple.* Winfrey's performance earned her an Academy Award nomination for Best Supporting Actress and made her known to a nationwide audience. Her recognition increased even more when *The Oprah Winfrey Show* went into national syndication in 1986, placing Winfrey in every major TV market.

Winfrey earned $30 million from the syndication deal, and she used that money to start her own company, Harpo Productions (*Harpo* is *Oprah* spelled backwards). Winfrey spent $20 million to buy and renovate a huge production facility in downtown Chicago. She then bought all the rights to her show from Capital Cities/ABC; as a result, Winfrey receives all the revenues from each new syndication deal.

With a vast audience tuned in to her show every weekday, Winfrey's influence on popular tastes became truly phenomenal. If she recommended a diet, an exercise program, or a book, millions of people followed her lead. But by 1994, after eight years of unparalleled success, Winfrey began to talk about leaving television and seeking new challenges. Ultimately, she decided to stay on and revitalize her show. To set herself apart from the numerous Oprah Winfrey imitators filling the airwaves, she moved away from lurid topics and concentrated on weightier subjects, including child abuse and drugs. Viewers embraced the new format, and in 1995 Winfrey signed a new syndication contract running through 2000, with the provision that she could quit whenever she desired. At the same time, she branched out into producing films and TV specials.

In 1997, *Forbes* magazine ranked Winfrey as the highest-paid entertainer in the United States, estimating her 1995–96 income at $171 million. Winfrey has always been eager to share her success; she has been a major supporter of her alma mater, Tennessee State University, and the Family for Better Lives Foundation, which she created. When not hard at work in Chicago, Winfrey relaxes on her Indiana country estate and her Colorado ranch.

Further Reading: *The Oprah Winfrey Story: Speaking Her Mind: An Authorized Biography,* by Geraldine Woods, Minneapolis: Dillon, 1991; *The Uncommon Wisdom of Oprah Winfrey: A Portrait in Her Own Words,* by Oprah

Winfrey, edited by Bill Adler, Secaucus, N.J.: Birch Lane, 1997; *Oprah Winfrey: Queen of Daytime TV,* by Ann Weil, Parsippany, N.J.: Silver Burdett Press, 1998; *Oprah,* by Oprah Winfrey, New York: David McKay Company, Inc., 1997.

—P. K.

❖ WOODS, ELDRICK ("Tiger")
(1975–), *golf champion*

The first African American (and the first Asian American) to win a major golf tournament (the 1997 Masters), Tiger Woods has electrified the sports world. He has been hailed as a role model capable of opening golf to members of minority groups, who often felt excluded from the sport in the past.

Born on December 30, 1975, in Cypress, California, Tiger Woods is the son of Earl Woods, a former Green Beret in the U.S. Army, and Kultida Woods, a native of Thailand. Earl Woods had become an avid golfer after retiring from the military, and he was convinced that golf would help his son grow up with sound values and a sense of achievement. Young Tiger (nicknamed after one of his father's friends, a Vietnamese soldier) first swung a golf club when he was only six months old. By the age of three, he was good enough to shoot a 48 for nine holes. By the time he reached high school, Woods was being hailed by sportswriters as a future star.

After winning the USGA Junior Championship in 1991, 1992, and 1993, Woods enrolled at Stanford University. He began to dominate the amateur ranks, winning an unprecedented three successive U.S. Amateur titles (1994, 1995, and 1996) as well as the 1996 NCAA championship. With nothing left to achieve as an amateur, Woods left Stanford in the summer of 1996 to join the PGA Tour, vowing that he would eventually complete the requirements for his degree.

Under the pressure of intense media attention, Woods made his professional debut at the Greater Milwaukee Open in August 1996. Slender and lithe at 6'2" and 160 pounds, he astounded seasoned professionals with his booming tee shots and his all-around feel for the game. Playing in eight tournaments on the 1996 tour, Woods finished in the Top 10 on five occasions and won both the Las Vegas Invitational and the Walt Disney World Classic. His play earned him the PGA Rookie of the Year Award, and *Sports Illustrated* named Woods as Sportsman of the Year. In addition to his outstanding

Tiger Woods *(Reuters/Gary Hershorn/Archive Photos)*

play, Woods was widely admired for his maturity, friendly demeanor, and willingness to serve as a role model. In recognition of his growing stature as a public figure, Woods signed lucrative endorsement contracts with a number of companies, including Nike, Titleist, and American Express.

In 1997, Woods came out of the gate quickly, winning the first event on the PGA Tour, the Mercedes Championship. His greatest moment came in April, when he won the prestigious Masters Tournament in Augusta, Georgia. His total score of 270—18 under par—and his 12-stroke margin of victory were both records for the tournament. At 21, Woods was the youngest Masters champion of all time and the youngest golfer to win a major tournament since World War II. He won three more PGA Tour events during the year, ending as the first player in history to earn more than $2 million in prize money. Woods's spectacular success earned him the PGA Player of the Year Award, and the

Associated Press also named him the Male Athlete of the Year for 1997.

Woods is very conscious of his role in sports history. He has often paid tribute to older African-American golfers such as Charlie Sifford and Lee Elder, who battled discrimination to compete in the professional ranks. Honoring his Asian heritage, he makes a point of playing tournaments in Thailand and Japan every winter. In addition to his athletic activities and endorsements, Woods is also active in charitable work. The Tiger Woods Foundation, founded by Earl Woods, provides minority youngsters with the opportunity to take part in golf and other activities.

Further Information: *Tiger Woods: The Making of a Champion,* by the editors of *Sports Illustrated,* New York: Simon & Schuster, 1996; *Training a Tiger: A Father's Account of How to Raise a Winner in Both Golf and Life,* by Earl Woods and Pete McDaniel, New York:

HarperCollins, 1997; *Tiger Woods: An American Master,* by Nicholas Edwards and Greg Quinn, New York: Scholastic, 1997; *Tiger: A Biography of Tiger Woods,* by John Strege, New York: Broadway, 1997; iGolf web site: http://www.igolf.com/tiger/news.html#Feature (contains dozens of feature articles and news stories about Tiger Woods, as well as career statistics).

—*P. K.*

❖ WOODS, GRANVILLE T.
(1856–1910), *inventor*

Granville Woods was a prolific inventor who invented many communications systems used by railroads to prevent accidents. He also invented various types of electrical railways, brakes, and other means of controlling railroad cars. Altogether, he had more than 60 patents to his credit. In 1974, half a century after his death, Ohio governor John J. Gilligan called Woods the "Black Edison" and issued a proclamation in his honor.

Woods was a native of Columbus, Ohio, born on April 23, 1856, the son of Tailer and Martha Woods. His childhood prepared him for his lifelong career—at age 10, he began to work in a machine shop during the day, while going to school at night.

It was important that he help support his family, so at 16, he went to work in Missouri as a railway fireman (the person who stokes the engine with coal) and engineer. This experience gave Woods his early training in the practical side of railways, the field in which he was to develop so many key inventions.

He continued to work on railways, in steel mills, and in a machine shop, while studying engineering at night. From 1878 to 1884, he worked on steamships and railroad, saving his money, until in 1884, at age 28, he and his brother Lyates opened their own machine shop in Cincinnati.

In 1884, Woods received his first patent, for a modified boiler furnace that saved on fuel. His second patent, issued later that year, was for a transmitter that sent messages by electricity. It was a great improvement over the telephones then in use, and was picked up by the American Bell Telephone Company of Boston.

He patented some 35 inventions between 1884 and 1907, largely in electrical and mechanical applications. Some of his patents were for improved telephone systems, used by trains to communicate with each other and with railway stations. This greatly increased railway safety, as accidents or potential dangers could be reported and tracks kept clear.

Woods further improved railway safety by inventing an electromagnetic brake, which used magnets, powered by electricity, to stop the trains.

In 1890, Woods moved to New York City. Without the responsibilities of his machine shop, he was able to spend more time on his inventions, most of which concerned electrical and railway devices. Westinghouse, General Electric, and other major companies picked up his inventions for manufacture and development.

Woods seems never to have married. The end of his life was not happy; he died in almost complete poverty. Part of his financial troubles were caused by the massive expenses of an 1892 court case. Woods believed that a company had stolen his inventions, and said so. The company sued him for libel. Woods paid huge legal fees in his own defense and was briefly jailed when he was unable to post his bail.

In 1910, Woods suffered a stroke and was taken to Harlem Hospital, where he died two days later, on January 30, 1910. In the late 1960s and early 1970s, he was honored in various ways, including the Ohio governor's proclamation and the naming of a Brooklyn public school.

Further Reading: *The Black Book,* by M. A. Harris, New York: Random House, 1974; *Black Inventors,* by Nathan Aaseng, New York: Facts On File, 1997.

—*R. K.*

❖ WOODSON, CARTER GODWIN
(1875–1950), *historian*

Carter Woodson is known as the Father of Black History. Although many great African-American scholars had written about black history before Woodson, no one had as yet treated the subject so systematically.

In addition to his own pioneering works, Woodson helped to create many organizations to develop the field of African-American studies. In 1915, he organized the Association for the Study of Negro Life and History, which over the years has published many important historical works by Woodson and others. In 1916, Woodson founded the *Journal of Negro History,* which historian Arthur M. Schlesinger, Sr., said was one of the "best . . . periodicals of the country." In 1926, Woodson started the idea of Black History Week (then called "Negro History Week"). In 1937, the Association that Woodson had founded started another publication, *The Negro History Bulletin,* which helped scholars and researchers keep up with each other's work.

Carter G. Woodson was born on December 19, 1875, in rural Virginia, to former slaves James and Anne

Eliza (Riddle) Woodson. Although there was a school in the area, he was unable to attend—his family depended on his income from working in the local coal mines. Until he was 17, Woodson's education was limited to his studies on his own. Later, he was able to attend high school, but only on a part-time schedule. Yet, while working in the mines, and despite all the obstacles, Woodson completed high school in a year and a half, graduating in 1896. He then entered Berea College in Kentucky, from which he graduated in 1903.

Woodson continued with his work and studies. From 1900 to 1903, he first taught high school, then became a principal. In 1908, he received a degree from the University of Chicago in Illinois—earned by combining summer school, correspondence courses, and regular school attendance. He spent 1903 to 1906 supervising schools in the Philippines (a recent U.S. colony, taken from Spain in the Spanish-American War). He also spent a year studying and traveling through Asia, North Africa, and Europe, and included a session at the University of Paris.

Only a few months after getting his B.A., Woodson received an M.A. from Chicago as well. And, in 1912, he earned his Ph.D. from Harvard—with more teaching and service as a principal along the way.

While working in Washington, D.C., public schools, Woodson founded the *Journal of Negro History,* which he edited until his death. With several other scholars, he established the Association for the Study of Negro Life and History, which he also directed until his death.

The Association's focus was on historical research as well as promotion of the teaching of history. Besides publishing books and collecting historical documents, the Association encouraged schools, churches, and community groups to educate black people about themselves and their own history. In 1919, Woodson moved into higher academic circles, serving for a year as dean of the School of Liberal Arts and head of the graduate faculty at Howard University in Washington, D.C. The following year, he became dean of West Virginia Collegiate Institute (later West Virginia State College), where he stayed until 1922.

Meanwhile, in 1921, he organized a major black-owned publishing company, the Associated Publishers, as part of the Association for the Study of Negro Life and History. After reorganizing the curriculum at West Virginia Collegiate, he retired to devote his life to research, writing, and the promotion of black history.

Despite Woodson's accomplishments, white organizations were occasionally condescending. In 1928, for example, his grant from the Social Science Research

Council carried a provision that three white historians would have to supervise his spending of the money.

Woodson's focus on black history was unusual, as similar and related school courses were not yet available. He did visit Egypt in 1907, which may have sparked an interest in the African roots of the black American experience.

Meanwhile, in the United States, other black scholars were paying attention anew to black history. In 1896, at Atlanta University in Georgia, a series of studies on "Negro Problems" had begun; in 1897, the American Negro Academy and the American Negro Historical Society were founded—research groups whose objective was scholarship about the conditions and history of black Americans. Similar groups were established in the 1910s, supporting the growth of interest and research work in black history.

In 1926, Woodson began Negro History Week, which included the birthdays of Abraham Lincoln and Frederick DOUGLASS. Woodson promoted this event heavily, sending material to the press, schools, and community groups; speaking with mayors and at large meetings in various cities; and preparing exhibits, pamphlets, and lectures.

Woodson wrote for scholarly audiences and junior high, high school, and college students. His major books include *The History of the Negro Church* (Washington, D.C.: Associated Publishers, 1921) and *The African Background Outlined* (New York: New American Library, 1969 reprint of 1936 ed.); for junior and senior high-school students, *Negro Makers of History* (Washington, D.C.: Associated Publishers, 1968 ed.), *African Myths* (New York: Golden Press, 1972 ed.), *The Miseducation of the Negro* (Trenton, N.J.: Africa World Press, 1972 ed.), and *African Heroes and Heroines* (Washington, D.C.: Associated Publishers, 1969 reprint of 1939 ed.).

Woodson was something of a loner, known as a demanding but fair teacher and a disciplined man totally dedicated to his work. He lived alone in Washington, D.C., devoted to his research and study. On April 3, 1950, he died of a heart attack at his home.

—*R. K.*

❖ WRIGHT, RICHARD
(1908–1960), *author*

Richard Wright was a major black writer whose work continues to be read as a scathing depiction of black life in a segregated, racist society. His novel *Native Son* (New York: Harper Perennial, 1989 reprint of 1940

Richard Wright *(Library of Congress)*

ed.) was a huge success when it was published in 1940, becoming a Book-of-the-Month Club selection, and making Wright a famous man. His autobiography, *Black Boy* (New York: Harper Perennial, 1990 reprint of 1943 ed.), outsold *Native Son,* and was translated into several languages.

Although none of his other works matched these successes, Wright's fame continued to grow. At the time of his death in 1960, he was internationally known as the greatest African-American novelist of his time.

Richard Wright was born on September 4, 1908, to farmhand Nathan Wright, and to teacher and housemaid Ella (Wilson) Wright, in a small rural cabin near Natchez, Mississippi. When Wright was five, his father left the family. His mother took the children to Memphis, then into Arkansas, until she suffered a series of strokes.

With Ella Wright paralyzed and unable to work, Richard and his brother had to depend on her family,

although Richard also spent some time in an orphanage. Eventually, he went to live with his grandparents in Jackson, Mississippi. His grandmother was deeply committed to Seventh-Day Adventism, a Christian fundamentalist religion, which he later wrote about in his books. Since her religion was so different from the Baptist culture around them, Wright grew up isolated from community life.

The 1910s and 1920s were a difficult time for southern black people, and lynchings or other types of racial violence were a constant threat. So, after finishing the ninth grade, Wright left for Memphis, where he stayed from 1925 to 1927, working in an optical company and studying on his own. In 1927, he made his personal exodus to the North, bringing his family to Chicago, where he worked as a dishwasher, porter, insurance sales agent, and substitute postal clerk.

In 1929, the Great Depression hit—the unemployment rate soared to almost one third of the nation's work force. In the ongoing climate of segregation and prejudice, the rate of unemployment among African Americans rose even higher than the national level, and Wright was unable to find work.

All over the country, dissatisfaction with existing conditions led people to an interest in left-wing politics, and especially in the Communist Party. The communists attacked economic and racial inequality and advocated a system where all social resources would be held in common and all would enjoy equal rights. The party was militantly active, leading many skirmishes to block the eviction of poor tenants, protesting racial discrimination, agitating for welfare assistance and social services, and assisting workers in organizing unions to press for better working conditions.

Wright was attracted to this high level of political energy and commitment, and he joined the Communist Party in 1933. For the first time, he found people who discerned his ability to write and encouraged him. The party literary group was the John Reed Club, which Wright also joined. He soon began to publish poems in left-wing magazines, such as *Left Front, The Anvil, International Literature,* and *New Masses.*

During the 1930s, the Federal Theater Project and the Federal Writers Project were established. These federally funded programs paid writers to work on various projects, which also freed them to pursue their own writing. Through these programs, Wright began to write short stories. He also headed a writers club, which included novelist Margaret WALKER.

In 1937, Wright was an ambitious young writer, and he decided to move to New York. There he was again supported by the Communist Party, which hired him to report on Harlem activities for the party newspaper, the *Daily Worker.*

By 1937, Wright had already written a novel, *Lawd Today* (Boston, Mass.: Northeastern University Press, 1989 ed.), but it was not published until after his death. His short stories, however, were collected as *Uncle Tom's Children* (New York: Harper Parennial, 1989 reprint of 1938 ed.), which was published to great acclaim. The book focused on the racial conflicts of the rural South.

Uncle Tom's success, plus the 1938 *Story Magazine* prize for one of his short stories, enabled Wright to leave his newspaper job and concentrate on a new novel, *Native Son,* which was published in 1940. This work concerned a young black man in a northern ghetto. Unlike the main characters in *Uncle Tom's Children,* who eventually managed to behave in a heroic way, the main character in *Native Son* has many problems. As Wright portrays him, Bigger Thomas has the potential of being heroic, but he is a violent, dangerous man as well. The pressures of racism and capitalism hurt Bigger, bringing out the bad and good in him.

Left-wing reviewers of the time were critical of *Native Son* because of its negative portrayal of Bigger. More conservative critics had the opposite reaction. They did not like Wright's depiction of racism and its oppressive features. They also criticized Wright's involvement with the Communist Party.

However, many readers loved *Native Son,* and Wright became quite financially secure and nationally famous as a result. His life became more stable, especially with his second marriage, to Ellen Poplar, in 1941 (he had married Dhinah Meadman in 1939). Wright and Poplar eventually had two daughters.

Wright's fame and newfound security permitted him to continue with other literary projects. He collaborated on the stage adaptation of his novel and wrote a black folk history called *Twelve Million Black Voices* (New York: Harper Perennial, 1989 ed.) and a novella, *The Man Who Lived Underground* (New York: Lion Library, 1956).

In 1943, Wright published the early part of his autobiography, *Black Boy,* beginning with his childhood and ending with his move to Chicago, Illinois. The acclaim he received from this book surpassed that of *Native Son. Black Boy* is considered an American classic. It also raised Wright to the level of a cultural symbol for both black and white audiences.

By 1942, Wright had left the Communist Party. In his opinion, it was more concerned with general social issues than with the specifics of attaining black equality. However, he still carried the reputation of being a "Red,"

and was often criticized for it. Throughout the early 1940s, Wright had traveled to Mexico, Canada, and France, but for political reasons, he had difficulty in securing a passport. In 1944, he published *I Tried to Be a Communist,* the last part of his autobiography, which explained how he had quit the party. Once again, he was criticized both by left-wing critics and by the government.

Wright sailed for France in 1946, where he became friends with the existentialists Jean-Paul Sartre and Simone de Beauvoir. The existentialists were a group of writers and philosophers who believed the only thing possible to know is our actual existence—that any ideas of God or religious order in the world are myths that we create in trying to give life meaning. According to existentialists, we should accept that life only has the meaning we give it by our daily actions, and we should try to act well for the sake of giving meaning to our existence, not to please God or to follow moral rules.

This philosophy appealed to Wright, as did the Europeans' acceptance of his race. Wright did go back to New York in 1947, but was frustrated with several incidents of racism in his Greenwich Village neighborhood. He decided to return to France, where he lived for the rest of his life.

Wright continued with his writing. He had become an international celebrity and was well known to many other writers and artists. In 1953, he wrote *The Outsider* (New York: Harper Perennial, 1989), which reflected his new interest in existentialism. In that year, he also published *Savage Holiday* (New York: Avon Publications, 1954), which was affected by his circle's interest in psychological themes.

Wright traveled to Latin America and Africa as well as European countries. He wrote *Black Power* (Westport, Conn.: Greenwood Press, 1974), narrating his trip to the Gold Coast of Africa; *The Color Curtain* (Cleveland, Ohio: World, 1974), a report on an African conference that excluded white Westerners; and *White Man, Listen* (Westport, Conn.: Greenwood Press, 1978 reprint of 1957 ed.), a collection of lectures on race issues. He also authored a section of *The God That Failed* (Chicago, Ill.: Regnery Gateway, 1983 reprint of 1949 ed.), a book by several intellectuals who had become disillusioned with communism.

Poetry caught his interest, and he experimented with the Japanese haiku form. He continued his fiction, as well, writing *The Long Dream* (New York: Harper Perennial, 1987 reprint of 1958 ed.), the first book in a planned trilogy about a young black man who travels from the South to Paris, to Africa, and back to the United States. *Eight Men* (New York: Thunder's Mouth

Press, 1989 reprint of 1960 ed.) is a late collection of his short stories, heavily influenced by existentialism. He also wrote two plays for German radio that were funnier and more satirical than most of his other work.

The exiled Wright died of a heart attack in Paris on November 28, 1960; he was 52. His health had been weakened by amoebic dysentery, a disease he had contracted in Africa. He suffered further deterioration from tensions caused by the many attacks on him during the 1950s by those who were critical of his changing political views. Since the 1950s were a time when communists were persecuted in the United States, many of Wright's former colleagues were angry with him for joining in the attack—which they saw as his effort to preserve his own position.

Wright's work continues to be read and studied today and receives more critical attention now than when he was alive.

Further Reading: *Richard Wright: Daemonic Genius: A Portrait of the Man, a Critical Look at His Work,* by Margaret Walker, New York: Amistad Press, 1993; *The Unfinished Quest of Richard Wright, a Critical Biography,* by Michel Fabre, New York: William Morrow, 1973; *The Example of Richard Wright,* by Dan McCall, New York: Harcourt, Brace & World, 1969; *Richard Wright's Native Son,* edited by Richard Abcarian, Belmont, Calif.: Wadsworth, 1970; *Twentieth Century Interpretations of Native Son,* edited by Houston A. Baker, Jr., Englewood Cliffs, N.J.: Prentice-Hall, 1972; *The Art of Richard Wright,* by Edward Margolies, Carbondale, Ill.: Southern Illinois Press, 1968; *The Emergence of Richard Wright,* by Kenneth Kinnamon, Urbana, Ill.: University of Illinois Press, 1990 reprint of 1933 ed.; *Richard Wright: Impressions and Perspectives,* edited by David Ray and Robert Farnsworth, Ann Arbor, Mich.: University of Michigan Press, 1973.

—R. K.

❖ X, MALCOLM (Malcolm Little; Al Hajj Malik al-Shabazz)
(1925–1965), *civil rights leader*

Malcolm X was one of the most influential black leaders of his time. Although he was assassinated before his goals could be fully realized, his thinking and his writing continue to exert a strong influence on black politics today.

Malcolm X's thinking underwent much change over his lifetime. At one time, he was a member of the Nation of Islam, the "Black Muslim" religion founded by Elijah MUHAMMAD, which held that white Christians are inherently evil and black people must separate themselves from them. At the time of his murder, he had come to believe that black and white people could work together, and stressed the importance of the unity of black people around the world.

Malcolm X was born Malcolm Little on May 19, 1925, the son of Earl and Louise Little, in Omaha, Nebraska. Earl Little had been a preacher and a follower of Marcus GARVEY, an early black nationalist, who believed there were no lasting solutions to racial problems for black Americans within the United States. Garvey advocated both black self-help in the United States—such as black-owned businesses—and the ultimate goal of African Americans returning to their ancestral Africa.

By 1931, Earl Little had moved his family to Lansing, Michigan, where he was killed by white people. Young Malcolm was only six years old at the time. Louise Little, a Grenada native, moved Malcolm and her other seven children to Detroit, but the strain of supporting her large family after her husband's murder proved to be too much. She was committed to a mental institution, and Malcolm was sent to a foster home.

For the next nine years, Malcolm was shuttled between foster homes, state institutions, and boardinghouses. In 1940, he was placed in a school in Mason City, Iowa, where he just managed to finish the eighth grade. He had been involved with delinquency and crime, although he had also shown better than average promise as a student. After finishing the eighth grade, however, he dropped out and went to Boston.

There, he lived with his sister and worked as a shoeshine boy, waiter, soda jerk, and at other such odd jobs. Three years later, he moved to New York, where he settled in Harlem.

This period in Harlem was for Malcolm a time of criminal involvement: He participated in the numbers racket, bootlegging (illegally bringing in liquor), selling drugs, and prostitution. He also developed a drug addiction. He became known as "Big Red," "Detroit Red," and "Red," because of his hair color. In 1946, before he had yet turned 21, he had been sentenced to 10 years in prison for burglary.

Malcolm X (*Library of Congress*)

In the state prison of Charlestown, Massachusetts, he was introduced to the political and religious thinking that would change his life. From 1946 to 1952, Malcolm served his prison term and studied the teachings of Elijah Muhammad, who had founded the Nation of Islam and the Black Muslim religion.

Malcolm began to write to Elijah Muhammad, whose version of Islam held that white Christians were evil by their very nature. It followed that black people had to separate themselves from this evil as far as possible, in order to preserve the purity and goodness of their culture and their better natures.

After prison, Malcolm went to work with the Black Muslims. In 1953, he had become a minister of the faith.

He began as assistant minister of the Muslim's mosque in Detroit, Michigan. He was so effective that Elijah Muhammad sent him to Philadelphia, where he established a new mosque. He also founded a newspaper, *Muhammad Speaks*.

Malcolm had now dropped the name Little—which, like other Black Muslims, he considered a "slave name" given by a white master. To signify the loss of his original name, he took the last name X.

Malcolm X was a dynamic leader, and he rose quickly in the ranks of the Black Muslims. In 1954, he was transferred to Harlem, to head its mosque. By the end of 1956, it was one of the most successful mosques in the movement. He continued to promote the ideas of black self-defense, nonparticipation in white society, and the fundamentally negative influence of white culture. In 1958, he married Betty Sanders (see Betty SHABAZZ).

As Malcolm X's power and influence grew, he became a threat to Elijah Muhammad, the leader of the movement. He also became more independent. In 1963, when President Kennedy was assassinated, Malcolm X commented that this was a case of "chickens coming home to roost"—meaning that it was the logical outcome of the violence of an immoral white society. This comment was widely publicized and shocked many people who were grieved by Kennedy's death. It led Elijah Muhammad to suspend Malcolm X from the movement.

Malcolm X responded by starting two groups of his own: the Muslim Mosque Inc. and the Organization of Afro-American Unity. Both were nationalist groups, unwilling to work with white people. However, the Organization of Afro-American Unity was dedicated to working with other civil rights groups, including those that were not nationalist.

He made a pilgrimage to Mecca, in Saudi Arabia, the city holy to Muslims. This was a profound religious experience for Malcolm, as well as a turning point in his political thinking. He changed his name to Al Hajj Malik al-Shabazz, and adopted the view that not all white people were evil. It was possible, he believed, to work with some whites and with all black people around the world to create freedom and equality for all people.

These views were not popular with other black nationalists, and for some time, Malcolm X had reason to fear for his life. On February 21, 1965, he was assassinated at the Audubon Ballroom in Harlem, New York City.

Malcolm X's many views continue to be read and studied, and he remains as a symbol of black pride and black power. In 1965, after he had died, *The Autobiography of Malcolm X* (New York: Ballantine Books, 1992) was published, a book he had written with Alex HALEY (later, the author of *Roots*). Many other works were published after his death: *Malcolm X Speaks* (New York: Grove Press, 1990); *The Speeches of Malcolm X at Harvard* (New York: William Morrow, 1968); *Malcolm X: The Last Speeches* (New York: Pathfinder Press, 1989) *By Any Means Necessary: Speeches, Interviews, and a Letter by Malcolm X* (New York: Pathfinder Press, 1970); *The End of White Supremacy* (New York: Merlin House, 1971); and *Malcolm X on Afro-American History* (New York: Pathfinder Press, 1990).

Further Reading: *One Day When I Was Lost: A Scenario Based on Alex Haley's "The Autobiography of Malcolm X"* [Screenplay], by James Baldwin, New York: Dell Publishing Co., 1992; *From Civil Rights to Black Liberation: Malcolm X and the Organization of Afro-American Unity;* by William W. Sales, Boston: South End Press, 1994; *Making Malcolm: The Myth and Meaning of Malcolm X,* by Michael Eric Dyson, New York: Oxford University Press, 1996; *Malcolm X (The Importance of),* by Roger Barr, San Diego, Calif.: Lucent Books, 1994; *Malcolm X: As They Knew Him,* by David Gallen, New York: Del Rey, 1996; *Malcolm X: Make It Plain,* by William Strickland, New York: Viking Press, 1994; *Malcolm X: The Assassination,* by Michael Friedly, New York: Ballantine Books, 1995; *Malcolm X: The FBI File,* ed. by David Gallen, New York: Ballantine Books, 1995; *Malcolm X: The Man and His Times,* by John Henrik Clarke, Lawrenceville, N.J.: Africa World Press, 1990; *On the Side of My People: A Religious Life of Malcolm X,* by Louis A. DeCaro, New York: New York University Press, 1995; *The Victims of Democracy: Malcolm X and the Black Revolution,* by Eugene Victor Wolfenstein, New York: Guilford Press, 1993; *Malcolm: A Life of the Man Who Changed Black America,* by Bruce Perry, New York: Station Hill Press, 1991.

—*R. K.*

❖ YOUNG, ANDREW

(1932–   ), civil rights leader, congressional representative, ambassador to the United Nations, mayor of Atlanta

Andrew Young began his political career working with Martin Luther KING, JR., in the Civil Rights movement of the early 1960s. He helped to draft the Civil Rights Act of 1964 and the Voting Rights Act of 1965. He eventually became executive director and vice president of the Southern Christian Leadership Conference (SCLC), the civil rights organization of ministers and other leaders that King had helped to found.

From 1972 through 1977, Young served as the first black congressman from the South since the days of Reconstruction. In 1977, President Jimmy Carter appointed him United States ambassador to the United Nations, a post he held until 1979. In 1982, Young was elected mayor of Atlanta, where he served successfully for eight years.

Andrew Young was born on March 12, 1932, to Dr. Andrew Young, a dentist, and Daisy (Fuller) Young, a teacher. The Youngs were the only black family in their neighborhood, but they were better off economically than their neighbors and, as a child, Andrew was known as "the rich kid." Nevertheless, under the system of segregation at the time, Young was bused to an all-black school. Inasmuch as Young's mother had taught him to read at an early age, he started school at the third grade,

and graduated from Gilbert Academy, a private high school in New Orleans, when he was only 15.

Young began his college career at Dillard University in New Orleans but resumed it at Howard University in Washington, D.C., where he graduated in 1951 with a pre-med degree—at the age of 19.

He first planned to become a doctor, but he was growing increasingly concerned with social problems. Instead, he decided on the ministry and earned his divinity degree in 1955 at Hartford Theological Seminary, in Connecticut. While in school, he helped to organize the Charter Oak Community Church, an interracial project in Hartford.

Young was ordained as a Congregational minister and served as a pastor in Marion, Alabama, where he met his wife, Jean Childs. The Youngs eventually had three daughters.

Young became the pastor of churches in rural Georgia until 1957, when he went to New York as associate director of the Department of Youth Work of the National Council of Churches. This position gave him the opportunity to work with young people, but he found himself working almost exclusively with white youth.

In 1961, Young decided to return to his native South, where working with Martin Luther King, Jr., offered a real opportunity to overcome segregation and improve conditions for southern black people. He helped to train fieldworkers to register black people to vote—a dangerous job in those days, when segregationists used violence to prevent African Americans from gaining political power.

As Young continued to work in the South, he grew closer to King and the SCLC. With other key leaders, he risked his life and safety to fight segregation and discrimination. He helped to lead the famous Birmingham demonstrations of 1963, in which Sheriff Eugene "Bull" Connor attacked peaceful protestors repeatedly with police dogs and fire hoses. When the Birmingham demonstrations were successful, Young, King, and other leaders knew they had helped to overcome segregation in the South.

In 1964, King promoted Young to the position of executive director of the SCLC. Young became known as a good mediator, working with two opposing sides to come up with solutions. Young also helped to draft the key civil rights legislation of the mid-1960s. When King went to Chicago to work with northern black people, Young joined him, and he was at his side when King was assassinated on April 4, 1968.

After King's death, his successor, Ralph ABERNATHY, promoted Young to executive vice president of the SCLC. He continued his civil rights activity in this capacity until 1970, when he ran for Congress. Although he won the Democratic nomination, he lost to the Republican incumbent, Fletcher Thompson.

In 1972, Atlanta was redistricted (the congressional districts were given new boundaries), creating a district that had a higher percentage of African Americans. Coincidentally, Thompson decided to run for a higher office. Young decided to try for the congressional seat once more—and he won. He was reelected in 1974 and 1976.

Young's first election reinforced his philosophy that black and white people had to work together. Although black people made up less than half of his district, he won some 60 percent of the vote. During his campaign, he said. "The political and economic facts of life are that we have to stand together or we will not survive. There is no black economy and white economy. There is no real black and white education problem . . . You will deal with it for everybody or for nobody."

On another occasion, Young noted, ". . . We must . . . deracialize our problems. Blacks and whites face the same problems. What the black folks suffer today, whites will tomorrow."

In Congress, Young concentrated his interests on constituent services—helping to solve the problems of people who lived in his district. He also opposed the bombing of Indochina, as well as the entire Vietnam War, and he fought to extend the Voting Rights Act of 1965. Unlike the rest of the Congressional Black Caucus, however, Young voted to confirm Gerald Ford as vice president, despite Ford's poor record on Civil rights.

In 1977, Young was appointed ambassador to the United Nations, a position he held until 1979. He played an important role in U.S. relations with Africa and other emerging regions.

In 1982, Young became mayor of Atlanta. He was regarded as a successful mayor by both black and white residents, serving for eight years.

Further Reading: *A Way Out of No Way: The Spiritual Memoirs of Andrew Young,* by Andrew Young, Nashville, Tenn.: Thomas Nelson, 1966: *The History of the Civil Rights Movement,* by Andrew Young, New York: Silver Burdett Press, 1990: *Flawed Triumphs: Andy Young at the United Nations,* by Bartlett C. Jones, New York: University Press of America, 1996; *Andrew Young, Man With a Mission,* by James Haskins, New York: Lothrop, Lee and Shepard, 1979; *Andrew Young: Biography of a Realist,* by Eddie Stone, Los Angeles, Calif.: Hollaway House Publishing Company, 1980; *Andrew Young: Champion of the Poor,* by Paul Westman, Minneapolis, Minn.: Dillon Press, 1983.

—R. K.

❖ YOUNG, CHARLES
(1864–1922), army officer

Charles Young was the ninth African American to begin West Point, the third to graduate, and the last at the Military Academy for nearly 50 years—until Benjamin O. DAVIS, JR. graduated in 1936. Young was eventually promoted to lieutenant colonel in the U.S. Army, largely due to his heroics in the Mexican skirmishes. He had fought in the Spanish-American War and in the Philippines (a Spanish colony that the United States seized during the war); he served under General Pershing in Mexico; and he commanded various military groups at home and abroad. He was the first black American military attaché, serving in Haiti and the Dominican Republic. He also served in Liberia, the African colony founded by black Americans, where he took over Benjamin O. DAVIS, SR.'s reorganization of the Liberian Frontier Force and Constabulary.

He is also known for the controversy surrounding his retirement from the army. When the United States entered World War I, he and the black community expected that he would be promoted to full colonel and sent to command troops in France. Instead, he was forced to retire, apparently because of medical findings of poor health. Young and many supporters claimed that these findings were racially motivated, although later evidence suggests that the army's findings were correct.

Charles Young was the son of former slaves who lived in a log cabin in Kentucky when their child was born on March 12, 1864. It is believed that Young's father had been a Union Army private. When Young was nine, the family went to Ripley, Ohio, where Young attended high school and prepared for West Point.

Entrance to West Point, the prestigious U.S. military academy, is quite selective. A student must be appointed by an official who believes that he or she is qualified to become a U.S. military officer. Young was one of a few black men appointed during the Reconstruction era, when some opportunities for black people were temporarily available. Charles Young graduated from West Point as a second lieutenant in 1889.

In 1894, Young was appointed to be a professor of tactics and military science at Wilberforce University of Ohio. When the Spanish-American War broke out, Young was promoted to the rank of first lieutenant, and he requested active service. He commanded black units in the United States, and, in 1901, was sent to conduct jungle warfare in the Philippines.

In 1903, he supervised the Sequoia and General Grant National Parks in California, while drilling troops stationed there. He was then stationed in San Francisco, where he married Ada Mills in 1904.

That was also the year that Young was sent to Haiti as military attaché. There he helped to survey remote areas of Haiti and the Dominican Republic, revising maps and noting military fortifications. His work was useful to the U.S. Marines when they occupied Haiti in 1915.

His first son was born at the end of 1906. The following year, he was sent back to the United States, where he worked with the intelligence division of the war staff in Washington, D.C. He spent the next few years in both the United States and the Philippines, until he was sent to Liberia for two years.

After returning to the United States, Young received the NAACP's Spingarn Award (given for outstanding achievement by a African American) for his work in Liberia. He was ordered to Mexico from 1916 to 1917, on a punitive expedition, in response to the Mexican Revolution to demonstrate U.S. military power. When he returned from Mexico, where he had commanded a cavalry squadron, he began a school for black soldiers, to prepare them for combat in future wars.

By this time, Young had been promoted first to major and then to lieutenant colonel. But he was never promoted to full colonel. When World War I broke out, army doctors claimed that Young had high blood pressure and later revealed that he also had Bright's disease, or chronic nephritis, an illness of the kidneys, which was to cause his death within five years. At the time African Americans believed that the medical findings were simply an excuse to avoid promoting a black man to such a commanding position. Later evidence suggests that the army findings were accurate.

In any case, Young never accepted the army's findings. He rode a horse from Ohio to Washington to prove that he was physically fit, but the army insisted that he retire. Then he was promoted to full colonel on the retired list, which meant that he had the advanced rank but would probably not be called to active duty.

Young was actually called to active duty during the last five days of World War I—a delay that he bitterly resented. The next year, 1919, he was again sent to advise the Liberian government. On January 8, 1922, while on an inspection visit to Nigeria, Young died of nephritis. Although he was first buried in Lagos, Nigeria, his remains were later returned to the United States and eventually buried with great honor in Arlington Cemetery. At a 1923 service honoring Young, then Assistant Secretary of the Navy Franklin D. Roosevelt (later President Roosevelt) said, "[Young] overcame prejudices which would have discouraged many of lesser man."

Further Reading: *The Early Life of Colonel Charles Young: 1864–1880,* by Robert Ewell Greene, Washington, D.C.: Howard University, 1973.

—R. K.

RECOMMENDED SOURCES ON AFRICAN-AMERICAN STUDIES

Note: General titles are listed here. For information on specific people see Further Reading and Information lists after entries.

Aaseng, Nathan. *Black Inventors*. New York: Facts On File, 1997.

Abraham, Roger D. (editor). *Afro-American Folk Tales: Stories from Black Traditions in the New World*. New York: Pantheon Books, 1984.

Adamcyzk, Alice I. *Black Dance: An Annotated Bibliography*. New York: Garland Publishing Inc., 1989.

Allen, Norm R. *African American Humanism: An Anthology*. New York: Prometheus Books, 1991.

Andrews, William L. (editor). *African American Autobiography: A Collection of Critical Essays* (New Century Views Series). New York: Prentice Hall, 1994.

———. *African American Literature: Voices in a Tradition*. New York: Henry Holt & Co., 1992.

——— and William Pickens (editors). *Bursting Bonds: The Heir of Slaves: The Autobiography of a 'New Negro' (Blacks in the Diaspora)*. Bloomington, Ind.: Indiana University Press, 1991.

———. *Classic American Autobiographies: Mary Rowlandson/Benjamin Franklin/Frederick Douglass/Mark Twain/Zitkala-Sa*. New York: Mentor, 1992.

———. *Classic Fiction of the Harlem Renaissance*. New York: Oxford University Press, 1994.

———. *From Fugitive Slave to Free Man: The Auto-biographies of William Wells Brown*. New York: Mentor, 1992.

———. *Journeys in New Worlds: Early American Women's Narratives*. Madison, Wis.: University of Wisconsin Press, 1991.

———. *Literature of the American South: a Norton Anthology*. New York: W. W. Norton, 1997.

———. *The Oxford Companion to African American Literature*. New York: Oxford University Press, 1997.

———. *Looking Up at Dawn: The Emergence of Blues Culture*. Philadelphia, Pa.: Temple University Press, 1987.

———. *Sisters of the Spirit: Three Black Women's Autobiographies of the Nineteenth Century*. Bloomington, Ind.: Indiana University Press, 1988.

———. *Six Women's Slave Narratives* (Schomburg Library of Nineteenth-Century Black Women Writers). New York: Oxford University Press, 1995.

———. *Three Classic African American Novels*. New York: New American Library, 1990.

———. *To Tell a Free Story: The First Century of Afro American Autobiography 1760–1865*. Champaign, Ill.: University of Illinois Press, 1989.

Aptheker, Herbert. *A Documentary History of the Negro People in the United States* (5 volumes). Secaucus, N.J.: Citadel Press, 1995.

———. *Negro Slave Revolts in the United States*. 1943. New York: International Publishers, 1993.

Baugh, John. *Black Street Speech: Its History, Structure and Survival*. Austin, Tex.: University of Texas Press, 1983.

Bates, Timothy, and William D. Bradford. *Financing Black Economic Development*. New York: E.P. Dutton, 1990.

Beardon, Romare. *A History of African American Artists: From 1792 to the Present.* New York: Pantheon, 1993.

Beckham, Barry (editor). *The Black Student's Guide to Colleges.* New York: E.P. Dutton, 1990.

Bennett, Jr., Lerone. *Before the Mayflower: A History of Black America.* Chicago: Johnson Publishing Co., 1982.

Berlin, Ira, et. al. (editors). *Freedom: A Documentary History of Emancipation 1861–1867: Selected from the Holdings of the National Archives of the United States.* New York: Cambridge University Press, 1989.

Berry, Mary Frances, and John W. Blassingame. *Long Memory: The Black Experience in America.* New York: Oxford University Press, 1987.

Blackburn, Robin. *The Overthrow of Colonial Slavery 1776–1848.* New York: Verso, 1989.

Blockson, Charles L. *The Underground Railroad.* New York: Berkeley Books, 1994.

Bogle, Donald. *Blacks in American Films and Television: An Illustrated Encyclopedia.* New York: Viking Press, 1983.

———. *Black Arts Annual, 1989/90* (Garland Reference Library of the Humanities, 1411). New York: Garland Publishing, 1992.

Branch, Taylor. *Parting the Waters: America in the King Years 1954–63.* New York: Simon & Schuster, 1988.

———. *Pillar of Fire: America in the King Years 1963–1965.* New York: Simon & Schuster, 1998.

Brodie, James Michael. *Created Equal: The Lives and Ideas of Black American Innovators.* New York: Morrow, 1993.

Bullard, Sara. *Free at Last: A History of the Civil Rights Movements and Those Who Died in the Struggle.* New York: Oxford University Press, 1993.

Caldwell, Hansonia. *African American Music—A Chronology: 1619–1995.* New York: Ikoro Communications, 1996.

Cham, Mbye B., and Claire Andrade-Watkins (editors). *Black Frames: Critical Perspectives on Independent Black Cinema.* Cambridge, Mass.: MIT Press, 1988.

Chesnutt, Charles W. *The Collected Stories of Charles W. Chesnutt.* New York: Mentor, 1992.

Creel, Margaret Washington. *A Peculiar People: Slave Religion and Community Culture Among the Gullahs.* New York: New York University Press, 1986.

Dabbs, Henry E. *Black Brass: Black Generals and Admirals in the Armed Forces of the United States.* Freehold, N.J.: Afro-American Heritage House Publishers, 1983.

Davis, Arthur P., and J. Saunders Redding. *Cavalcade: Negro American Writing from 1760 to the Present.* Westport, Conn.: Greenwood Press, 1983.

Davis, Charles T., and Henry Louis Gates, Jr. (editors). *The Slave's Narrative.* New York: Oxford University Press, 1987.

Davis, Lenwood G., and Belinda S. Daniels (compilers). *Black Athletes in the United States: A Bibliography of Books, Articles, Autobiographies, and Biographies on Black Professional Athletes in the United States, 1800–1981.* Westport, Conn.: Greenwood Press, 1983.

———. *Blacks in the American Armed Forces, 1776–1983: A Bibliography.* Westport, Conn.: Greenwood Press, 1984.

———. *Black-Jewish Relations in the United States, 1752–1984: A Selected Bibliography.* Westport, Conn.: Greenwood Press, 1985.

Douglass, Frederick. *Narrative of the Life of Frederick Douglass, an American Slave, Written by Himself: Authoritative Text, Contexts, Criticism.* New York: W.W. Norton, 1997.

Driskell, David, David Levering Lewis, Deborah Willis Ryan, and Mary Schmidt Campbell. *Harlem Renaissance: Art of Black America.* New York/Harry N. Abrams, Inc., 1994.

Egerton, John. *Speak Now Against the Day: The Generation Before the Civil Rights Movement in the South.* New York: Alfred A. Knopf, 1994.

Emery, Lynne F. *Black Dance in the United States from 1619 to Today,* 2nd ed. Pennington, N.J.: Princeton Book Company, 1991.

Estell, Kenneth. *African American: Portrait of a People.* New York: Visible Ink Press, 1994.

Evans, Mari (editor). *Black Women Writers 1950–1980: A Critical Evaluation.* New York: Anchor Press/Doubleday, 1984.

Farmer, James. *Lay Bare the Heart: An Autobiography of the Civil Rights Movement.* New York: Arbor House, 1988.

Foner, Philip S. *Organized Labor and the Black Worker, 1619–1981.* New York: International Publishers, 1984.

Fox, Ted. *Show Time at the Apollo.* New York: Holt, Rinehart and Winston, 1990.

Gates, Henry Louis (editor). *The Schomburg Library of Nineteenth Century Black Women Writers* (30 volumes of fiction, poetry, autobiography, biography, essays, and journalism). New York: Oxford University Press, 1988.

Gubert, Betty Kaplan. *Early Black Bibliographies 1863–1918.* New York: Garland Publishing, 1986.

Harding, Vincent. *There Is a River: The Black Struggle for Freedom in America.* New York: Harcourt, Brace, Jovanovich, 1989.

Haskins, James. *Black Theater in America.* New York: T.Y. Crowell, 1989.

Hay, Samuel A. *African American Theater: A Historical and Critical Analysis.* New York: Cambridge University Press, 1994.

Hedgepath, Chester. *Twentieth Century African American Writers and Artists.* Chicago: American Library Association Editions, 1991.

Hill, Erroll. *Shakespeare in Sable: A History of Black Shakespearian Actors.* Amherst, Mass.: University of Massachusetts Press, 1989.

Hines, Darlene Clark, and Kathleen Thompson (editors). *Facts On File Encyclopedia of Black Women in America* (11 volumes). New York: Facts On File, 1997.

Hoobler, Dorothy, and Thomas Hoobler. *The African American Family Album.* New York: Oxford University Press, 1995.

Hughes, Langston, Milton Meltzer, and C. Eric Lincoln. *A Pictorial History of Black America.* New York: Crown Publishers, 1983.

Igoe, Lynn Moody, with James Igoe. *250 years of Afro-American Art: an Annotated Bibliography.* New York: R.R. Bowker, 1987.

Jacobs, Harriet A. *Incidents in the Life of a Slave Girl, Written by Herself.* Edited by Jean Fagan Yellin. Cambridge, Mass.: Harvard University Press, 1987.

Johnson, Michael P., and James L. Roark. *Black Masters: A Free Family of Color in the Old South.* New York: W.W. Norton, 1989.

Jones, Hettie. *Big Star Fallin': Five Women in Black Music.* New York: Puffin, 1997.

Jones, Howard. *Mutiny on the Amistad: The Saga of a Slave Revolt and Its Impact on American Abolition, Law and Diplomacy.* New York: Oxford University Press, 1986.

Kaplan, Sidney. *The Black Soldier of the Civil War in Literature and Art.* The Chancellor's Lecture Series 1979–1980. Amherst, Mass.: University of Massachusetts Press, 1981.

Katz, William Loren. *Black People Who Made the Old West.* New York: Crowell, 1977.

———. *The Black West.* Seattle, Wash.: Open Hand, 1987.

———. *Breaking the Chains.* New York: Macmillan, Atheneum, 1990.

———. *Eyewitness.* New York: Simon & Schuster, Touchstone, 1995.

———. *The Invisible Empire.* Seattle, Wash.: Open Hand, 1986.

Kellner, Bruce (editor). *The Harlem Renaissance: A Historical Dictionary for the Era.* Westport, Conn.: Greenwood Press, 1987.

Krouse, Ann Woulk. *Who's Who Among Black Americans.* Lake Forest, Ill.: Educational Communications Inc., 1986.

Lewis, David Levering. *When Harlem Was in Vogue.* New York: Oxford University Press, 1981.

Lewis, Samella. *African American Art and Artists.* Berkeley, Calif.: University of California Press, 1994.

Library of Congress. *The African American Mosaic: A Library of Congress Resource Guide for the Study of Black History and Culture.* Washington, D.C., 1997.

Lincoln, C. Eric. *The Black Muslims in America.* Grand Rapids, Mich.: Trenton, N.J.: Africa World Press, 1994.

Logan, Rayford W., and Michael R. Winston (editors). *Dictionary of American Negro Biography.* New York: W.W. Norton, 1982.

McAdam, Doug. *Freedom Summer.* New York: Oxford University Press, 1988.

McPherson, James. *The Abolitionist Legacy: From Reconstruction to the NAACP.* Princeton, N.J.: Princeton University Press, 1995.

———. *For Cause and Comrades: Why Men Fought in the Civil War.* New York: Oxford University Press, 1997.

Newman, Richard. *Black Access: A Bibliography of Afro-American Bibliographies.* Westport, Conn.: Greenwood Press, 1988.

Olson, James S. *Slave Life in America: A Historiography and Selected Bibliography.* Lanham, Md.: University Press of America, 1983.

Pasteur, Alfred B., and Ivory L. Toldson. *Roots of Soul: The Psychology of Black Expressiveness.* New York: Anchor Press/Doubleday, 1989.

Peterson, Robert. *Only the Ball Was White.* New York: McGraw-Hill, 1989.

Pleasant, Henry. *The Great American Popular Singers: Their Lives, Careers and Art.* New York: John Wiley and Sons, 1983.

Quarles, Benjamin. *Black Abolitionists.* New York: Da Capo Press, Plenum, 1991.

———. *Black Mosaic: Essays in Afro-American History and Historiography.* Amherst, Mass.: University of Massachusetts Press, 1988.

———. *The Negro in the Making of America.* New York: Macmillan, Collier Books, 1987.

Rabinowitz, Howard N. (editor). *Southern Black Leaders of the Reconstruction Era.* Champaign, Ill.: University of Illinois Press, 1986.

Reagon, Bernice Johnson (editor). *We'll Understand It Better By and By: Pioneering African American Gospel Composers.* Washington, D.C.: Smithsonian Institution Press, 1993.

Reef, Catherine. *Black Explorers.* New York: Facts On File, 1996.

Reynold, Gary A., and Beryl J. Wright. *Against the Odds: African American Artists and the Harmon Foundation.* Newark, N.J.: Newark Museum Associates, 1990.

Ribowsky, Mark. *A Complete History of the Negro Leagues 1884–1955.* New York: Carol, Birch Lane Press, 1995.

Robinson, Joyntle Theresa, and Maya Angelou (editors). *Bearing Witness: Contemporary Works by African American Women Artists.* New York: Rizzoli International Publications, 1996.

Rogosin, Donn. *Invisible Men: Live in Baseball's Negro Leagues.* New York: Athenaeum, 1986.

Rust, Jr., Art, and Edna Rust. *Art Rust's Illustrated History of the Black Athlete.* New York: Doubleday and Co., 1988.

Savage, Beth. *African American Historic Places.* Washington, D.C.: Preservation Press, 1994.

Sewell, George A., and Margaret L. Dwight. *Mississippi Black History Makers.* Jackson, Miss.: University Press of Mississippi, 1985.

Shaw, Arnold. *Black Popular Music in America from the Spirituals, Minstrels and Ragtime to Soul, Disco and Hip Hop.* New York: Schirmer Books, 1986.

Southern, Eileen. *The Music of Black Americans: A History.* New York: W.W. Norton & Company, 1997.

Spangenburg, Ray and Diane K. Moser. *The African-American Experience.* New York: Facts On File, 1997.

Starling, Marion Wilson. *The Slave Narrative: Its Place in American History.* Boston: G.K. Hall, 1986.

Sterling, Dorothy (editor). *We Are Your Sisters: Black Women in the Nineteenth Century.* New York: W.W. Norton, 1984.

Steward, Jeffrey C. *1001 Things Everyone Should Know About African American History.* New York: Doubleday, 1997.

Terry, Wallace. *Bloods: An Oral History of the Vietnam War by Black Veterans.* New York: Random House, 1984.

Thomas, Arthur E. *Like It Is: Arthur Thomas Interviews Leaders on Black America.* New York: Elsevier-Dutton, 1985.

Walton, Hanes. *African American Power and Politics: The Political Context Variable (Power, Conflict and Democracy).* New York: Columbia University Press, 1997.

Warren, Gwendolyn Sims. *Ev'ry Time I Feel the Spirit: 101 Best-Loved Psalms, Gospel Hymns, and Spiritual Songs of the African American Church.* New York: Henry Holt & Co., 1998.

Williams, Juan. *Eyes on the Prize: America's Civil Rights Years, 1954–1965.* New York: Viking Press, 1986.

Willis-Thomas, Deborah. *An Illustrated Bio-Bibliography of Black Photographers, 1940–1988.* New York: Garland Publishing, 1989.

Wilson, Jr., Fallin. *The African American Church in Birmingham, Alabama, 1815–1963: A Shelter in the Storm.* New York: Garland Publishing, 1997.

Wilson, Joseph (compiler and editor). *Black Labor in America, 1865–1983: A Selected Bibliography.* Westport. Conn.: Greenwood Press, 1985.

Wright, Richard. *12 Million Black Voices.* New York: Thunder's Mouth Press, 1988.

Yount, Lisa. *Black Scientists.* New York: Facts On File, 1991.

ENTRIES BY AREA OF ACTIVITY

Note: Individuals known for more than one activity are listed multiple times.

Abolitionists

Delany, Martin Robinson 56
Douglass, Frederick 58
Forten, James, Sr. 81
Garnet, Henry Highland 85
Truth, Sojourner 232
Tubman, Harriet 234

Activists

Ali, Muhammad (Cassius Marcellus Clay) 5
Baraka, Imanu Amiri (LeRoi Jones) 19
Davis, Angela Yvonne 51
Delany, Martin Robinson 56
DuBois, William Edward Burghardt 62
Garvey, Marcus Mosiah 86
Hale, Clara McBride ("Mother") 99
King, Martin Luther, Sr. 144
Newton, Huey Percy 177
Robeson, Eslanda Cardozo Goode 204
Scott, Dred 211
Singleton, Benjamin ("Pap") 217
Truth, Sojourner 232
Walker, Maggie Lena 249
Wells-Barnett, Ida Bell 255

Actors/Actresses

Aldridge, Ira Frederick 4
Belafonte, Harold George, Jr. ("Harry") 25
Childress, Alice 40
Cosby, William Henry, Jr. ("Bill") 44
Davis, Ossie 54
Dee, Ruby 55
Freeman, Morgan 83
Gilpin, Charles Sidney 91
Goldberg, Whoopi (Caryn Johnson) 93
Horne, Lena Mary Calhoun 110
Jones, James Earl 130
Lee, Canada (Lionel Cornelius Canegata) 149
McDaniel, Hattie 160
Poitier, Sidney 191
Queen Latifah (Dana Owens) 197
Robeson, Paul 204
Shakur, Tupac Amaru 213
Simpson, Orenthal James ("O. J.") 216
Waters, Ethel 254
Winfrey, Oprah Gail 269

Artists

Alston, Charles H. 7
Bannister, Edward Mitchell 18
Barthé, Richmond 21
Bearden, Fred Romare Howard 23
Hunt, Richard Howard 114

ENTRIES BY YEAR OF BIRTH

CHRONOLOGY

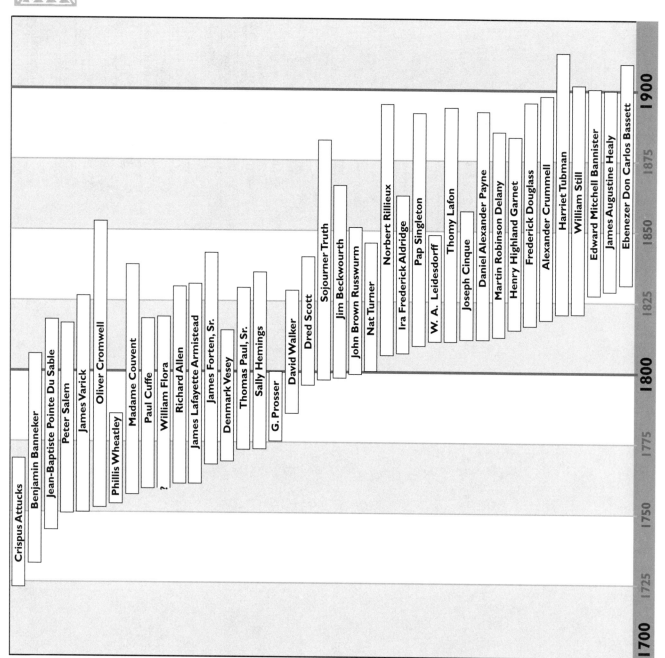

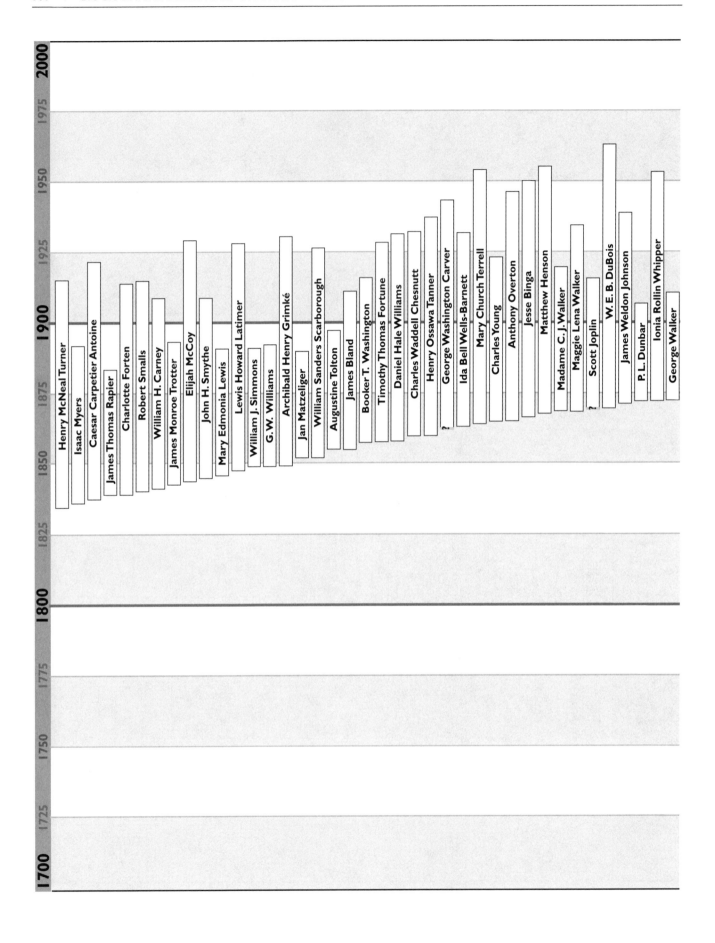

Chronology timeline (1700–2000):

- Bert Williams
- William Christopher Handy
- Arthur Alfonso Schomburg
- Charles Clinton Spaulding
- Carter Godwin Woodson
- Mary McLeod Bethune
- Garrett A. Morgan
- Benjamin Oliver Davis, Sr.
- Charles Sidney Gilpin
- Robert Lee Vann
- Clarence Cameron White
- James Finley Wilson
- Ernest Everett Just
- Eubie Blake
- Oscar Micheaux
- Leadbelly
- Jessie Redmon Fauset
- Ulysses Grant Dailey
- Ma Rainey
- Alain Leroy Locke
- Marcus Garvey
- Roland Hayes
- Claude Albert Barnett
- A. Philip Randolph
- Claude McKay
- Zora Neale Hurston
- Madame Lillian Evanti
- Bessie Coleman
- Theodore K. Lawless
- Arthur George Gaston
- Walter Francis White
- Charles Spurgeon Johnson
- Nella Larsen
- Bessie Smith
- Ferdinand Christopher Smith
- Nathan Jean Toomer
- Paul Revere Williams
- Charles Hamilton Houston
- Hattie McDaniel

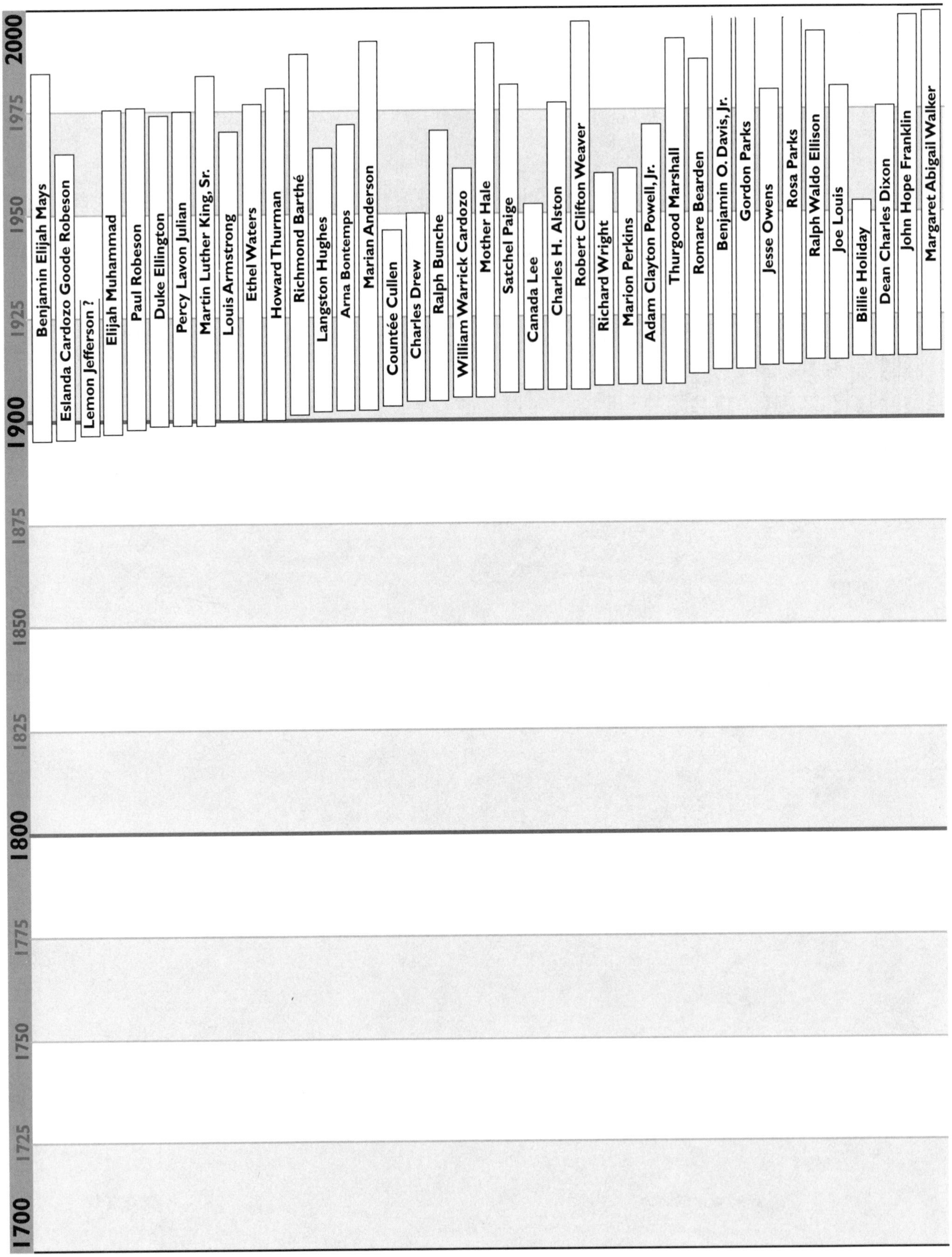
2000
1975
1950
1925
1900
1875
1850
1825
1800
1775
1750
1725
1700
Benjamin Elijah Mays
Eslanda Cardozo Goode Robeson
Lemon Jefferson ?
Elijah Muhammad
Paul Robeson
Duke Ellington
Percy Lavon Julian
Martin Luther King, Sr.
Louis Armstrong
Ethel Waters
Howard Thurman
Richmond Barthé
Langston Hughes
Arna Bontemps
Marian Anderson
Countée Cullen
Charles Drew
Ralph Bunche
William Warrick Cardozo
Mother Hale
Satchel Paige
Canada Lee
Charles H. Alston
Robert Clifton Weaver
Richard Wright
Marion Perkins
Adam Clayton Powell, Jr.
Thurgood Marshall
Romare Bearden
Benjamin O. Davis, Jr.
Gordon Parks
Jesse Owens
Rosa Parks
Ralph Waldo Ellison
Joe Louis
Billie Holiday
Dean Charles Dixon
John Hope Franklin
Margaret Abigail Walker

	1700	1725	1750	1775	1800	1825	1850	1875	1900	1925	1950	1975	2000
Gwendolyn Brooks													
Ossie Davis													
Lena Horne													
Jacob Lawrence													
John Harold Johnson													
Jackie Robinson													
Edward William Brooke													
Katherine Dunham													
Charlie Parker													
Alice Childress													
Alex Haley													
Constance Baker Motley													
Geraldine Hamilton McCullough													
Ruby Dee													
Mari Evans													
James Baldwin													
Sidney Poitier													
Medgar Evers													
Malcolm X													
Ralph Abernathy, Sr.													
Harry Belafonte													
Althea Gibson													
Maya Angelou													
Martin Luther King, Jr.													
Berry Gordy, Jr.													
Leontyne Price													
Lorraine Hansberry													
Odetta													
Alvin Ailey, Jr.													
James Earl Jones													
Toni Morrison													
Andrew Young													
Joycelyn Elders													
Hank Aaron													
Imamu Amiri Baraka													
Richard Howard Hunt													
Vernon Jordan													
William Julius Wilson													
Wilt Chamberlain													

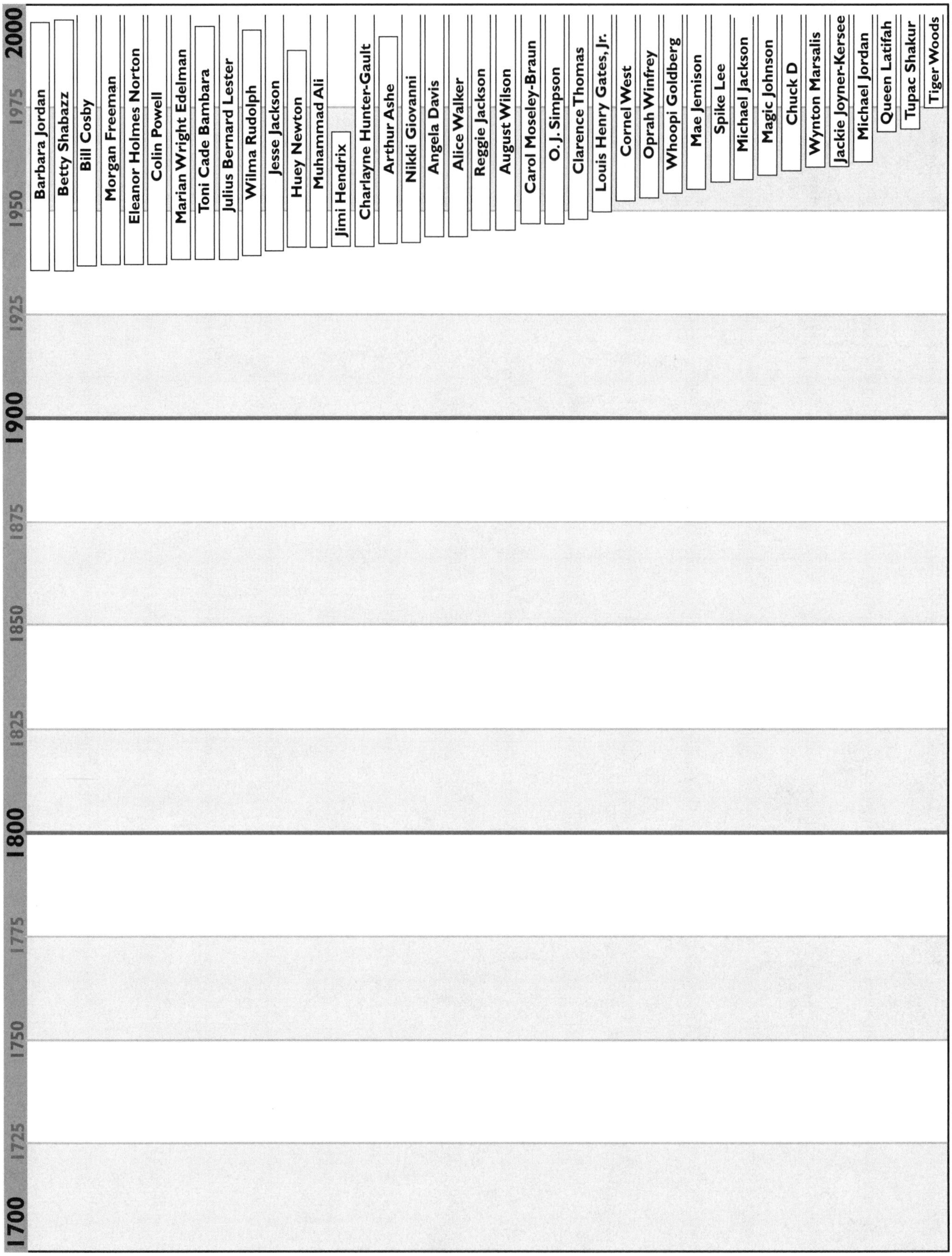

2000	1975	1950	1925	1900	1875	1850	1825	1800	1775	1750	1725	1700

Barbara Jordan
Betty Shabazz
Bill Cosby
Morgan Freeman
Eleanor Holmes Norton
Colin Powell
Marian Wright Edelman
Toni Cade Bambara
Julius Bernard Lester
Wilma Rudolph
Jesse Jackson
Huey Newton
Muhammad Ali
Jimi Hendrix
Charlayne Hunter-Gault
Arthur Ashe
Nikki Giovanni
Angela Davis
Alice Walker
Reggie Jackson
August Wilson
Carol Moseley-Braun
O. J. Simpson
Clarence Thomas
Louis Henry Gates, Jr.
Cornel West
Oprah Winfrey
Whoopi Goldberg
Mae Jemison
Spike Lee
Michael Jackson
Magic Johnson
Chuck D
Wynton Marsalis
Jackie Joyner-Kersee
Michael Jordan
Queen Latifah
Tupac Shakur
Tiger Woods

INDEX

Page numbers in **boldface** indicate subjects of articles. Those in *italics* indicate illustrations.